BASIC FINANCIAL MANAGEMENT

John D. Martin
Texas A & M University

J. William Petty
Texas Tech University

Arthur J. Keown
Virginia Polytechnic Institute
and State University

David F. Scott, Jr.
Virginia Polytechnic Institute
and State University

PRENTICE-HALL, Inc., Englewood Cliffs, New Jersey 07632

BASIC
FINANCIAL
MANAGEMENT

Library of Congress Cataloging in Publication Data

Main entry under title:
Basic financial management.

   Includes bibliographies and index.
   1. Business enterprises—Finance.   2. Corporations—
Finance.   I. Martin, John D.
HG4026.B318   658.1'5   78-11223
ISBN 0-13-060541-7

Editorial/production supervision by Ann Marie McCarthy
Interior and cover design by Lee Cohen
Manufacturing buyer: Trudy Pisciotti

BASIC FINANCIAL MANAGEMENT
John D. Martin / J. William Petty / Arthur J. Keown / David F. Scott, Jr.

Printed in the United States of America

10 9 8 7 6 5 4 3

PRENTICE-HALL INTERNATIONAL, INC., *London*
PRENTICE-HALL OF AUSTRALIA PTY. LIMITED, *Sydney*
PRENTICE-HALL OF CANADA, LTD., *Toronto*
PRENTICE-HALL OF INDIA PRIVATE LIMITED, *New Delhi*
PRENTICE-HALL OF JAPAN, INC., *Tokyo*
PRENTICE-HALL OF SOUTHEAST ASIA PTE. LTD., *Singapore*
WHITEHALL BOOKS LIMITED, *Wellington, New Zealand*

TO OUR FAMILIES

Contents

BASIC TOOLS OF FINANCIAL ANALYSIS, PLANNING, AND CONTROL

WORKING-CAPITAL MANAGEMENT

Preface

Financial management during the twentieth century has undergone significant change. The perspective and activities of financial managers have historically been a function of the economic and business activity at that particular time. For example, during the early 1900s the giant oil, steel, and automobile corporations were being formed. Consequently, the financial literature emphasized consolidations, mergers, and public regulation of such large corporate entities. When the economy expanded during the 1920s, the acquisition of new funds in the capital markets became of interest. Then as the depression era was encountered in the 1930s, a significant amount of time was devoted to the study of business failure and reorganization. During the 1940s and the early 1950s the past interests persisted, with the finance discipline continuing to be descriptive in nature. However, a greater emphasis was placed on liquidity management, financial planning, and cash budgeting. Since the middle 1950s and continuing to the present, the finance discipline has experienced major shifts both in perspective and content. The perspective is no longer limited to the viewpoint of an external financial analyst. Instead we have become far more concerned with the internal financial management of a business. Moreover, the scope is not restricted to acquiring capital. While continuing to draw upon the past, the literature has exploded in terms of its coverage of the firm's investment and dividend policy decisions. The approach taken to problems has become far more analytical. Also, through a greater understanding of the theoretical issues and the greatly expanded empirical evidence, the financial theory of the firm has been carefully developed. However, increased complexity has accompanied the advances in the finance literature; often this places comprehension of the literature completely beyond the threshold of learning for the introductory student in finance.

In the foregoing context, numerous financial management textbooks have been written in an effort to reduce the gap between the cutting edge of current finance literature and the needs and capabilities of both students and managers. As a result, the finance instructor has had an almost limitless number of textbooks from which to select. Different approaches are readily available to suit most pedagogical preferences.

Recognizing the diversity available to the finance instructor, the personnel at Prentice-Hall, Inc., became involved in an extensive effort to determine if any general commonalities exist among financial management instructors in terms of their desires regarding the approach taken by a text. The results, which came from questionnaires and personal interviews of faculty members from across the nation, suggested that a common thread exists in terms of the instructors' desires. *Basic Financial Management* has been carefully developed to comply with these needs and preferences.

Basic Financial Management provides the reader with an overview of financial management. The text is intended for use in an introductory course in financial management taught in a one-semester or one- or two-quarter course. The orientation is managerial with an emphasis on the identification and solution of the financial problems confronting the business enterprise. In the preparation of the manuscript, three primary standards were used. First, we made a strong effort to offer a *completeness* of the respective topics. Second, we have placed *readability* as a high priority throughout the text. We have taken extra precaution to use a clear and concise writing style, especially in the treatment of concepts requiring the use of mathematics. Third, complete, *step-by-step examples* are frequently used to increase clarity and to crystalize the critical issues in the student's mind. Finally, we have relied heavily upon the Prentice-Hall research and personal experience in developing a logical chapter organization that provides a continuity in the presentation of the subject matter. In summary, the pedagogical approach taken, particularly for the more difficult topics, progresses from an intuitive presentation of the problem to the introduction and illustration of the appropriate decision-making framework.

A complete and balanced instructional package has been developed to complement *Basic Financial Management*. Realizing that a textbook in and of itself is incomplete in attaining the requisite educational goals for the

Accompanying Materials

student, additional materials are available. First, two case books have been developed. *Cases in Finance* by David F. Scott, Jr., John D. Martin, J. William Petty, and Arthur J. Keown provides a broad spectrum of short cases both in terms of complexity and topics. *Cases in Basic Financial Management* by John D. Martin, J. William Petty, Arthur J. Keown, and David F. Scott, Jr., is designed to parallel the topics covered in *Basic Financial Management*, providing the instructor with cases rather than problems that illustrate the use of financial tools and concepts in a real world setting. The more complex cases found in *Cases in Finance* are omitted. Second, the *Study Guide* serves as an excellent supplement to the *Basic* text by providing a detailed sentence outline, self-test questions, and solved problem sets for each chapter. In addition, self-teaching supplements for mathematics of finance and capital budgeting are included. Third, approximately seventy-five transparency masters that are useful in presenting the key issues of the text are available to adopters. Finally, in addition to the *Instructor's Manual*, a *Supplemental Question-Problem Test File* by John M. Pinkerton has been prepared for adopters. This test bank consists of ten true-false, ten multiple choice, and six to ten solved problems for each chapter of the text.

Acknowledgments

We gratefully acknowledge the assistance, support, and encouragement of those individuals who have contributed to the successful completion of *Basic Financial Management*. Specifically, we wish to recognize the very helpful insights provided by colleagues at our respective universities. We thank John Pinkerton for his support in preparing the supplementary test file. Also, for their careful review of the text, we are indebted to Donald L. Stevens, University of Tennessee, Knoxville; Charles R. Idol, Idaho State University, Pocatello; Gary L. Trennepohl, Arizona State University, Tempe; Terry S. Maness, Baylor University, Waco, TX; Samuel C. Hadaway, University of Alabama, University, AL; Russell P. Boisjoly, University of Maryland, College Park; David W. Cole, Ohio State University, Columbus; Dwight C. Anderson, Arizona State University, Tempe; Sam G. Berry, Virginia Commonwealth University, Richmond; Hadi Alwan, Northern Illinois University, DeKalb; and James A. Millar, University of Arkansas, Fayetteville. Finally, we should thank the Prentice-Hall staff, including David Hildebrand, Ernest Hursh, Ann Marie McCarthy, Lee Cohen, Mike Melody, and Karen Thompson. Their support throughout the writing, production, and marketing of the text was quite valuable.

Even with the very fine efforts of all involved in preparing *Basic Financial Management*, some errors inevitably will exist. Unfortunately, for these we, the authors, must accept final responsibility.

BASIC FINANCIAL MANAGEMENT

THE SCOPE AND ENVIRONMENT OF FINANCIAL MANAGEMENT

The Role of Financial Management

*F*inancial management during this century has undergone dramatic changes. Whereas the financial manager was once limited to some book-keeping, cash management, and the acquisition of funds, he now has a major voice in all aspects of both the raising and allocation of financial capital. This book will introduce you to specific problems and areas that concern the financial manager. First we explain the environment surrounding the problem, then propose a solution methodology. We shall also stress the interrelationships among the financial manager's various concerns and decisions. To develop a proper perspective on the role of the financial manager and the financial decision-making process, we will first look at the development of financial thought.

At the turn of the century, financial thought focused upon the legal environment within which the firm operated. The topics receiving most attention were mergers, formation of new companies, investment banking, public regulation, and the process of raising funds in the capital markets. The economic and business activity of the time determined what was of primary importance in the finance field. During the early 1900s financial and economic news emphasized consolidations, mergers, and public regulation of the new business giants. This was the era when the great oil, auto,

and steel firms were being formed and Teddy Roosevelt was making his
name as a corporate trust buster.

In the 1920s the economy began to expand, and raising new funds in
the capital markets became more important. As a result, the emphasis in
finance shifted from mergers and regulation to methods and procedures
for acquiring funds. Arthur Stone Dewing devoted about a third of his
landmark financial text, *The Financial Policy of Corporations* (1920), to the
description of methods and procedures for acquiring funds. The remainder of the book dealt primarily with consolidations, mergers, and a legalis-
tic look at corporate bankruptcy.

Business failures during the Depression helped change the focus in
finance during the thirties. While finance continued to be taught as a descriptive discipline, increased emphasis was placed on bankruptcy, liquidity
management, and avoidance of financial problems. The political changes
that dominated the thirties also influenced the field of finance, bringing
increased government regulation and control of both business and the
securities market, and increased requirements to disclose large volumes of
corporate financial data. These data allowed analysts to more effectively
assess potential corporate performance, stirring new interest in financial
analysis.

During the 1940s and early 1950s financial theory continued to be
taught as a descriptive discipline. The major financial texts of the day
continued to emphasize methods and instruments for fund raising, corporate bankruptcy and reorganization, and mergers and consolidations. Increased emphasis was given, however, to liquidity management, financial
planning, and cash budgeting.[1]

During the mid-1950s the field of finance underwent drastic changes.
First, the point of view shifted from that of an outsider assessing the condition and performance of a firm to that of an insider charged with the
management and control of the firm's financial operations. The work of
Joel Dean promoted the area of capital budgeting as a major topic in
finance. This led to an increased interest in related topics, most notably
firm valuation. Interest in these topics grew and in turn spurred interest in
security analysis, portfolio theory, and capital structure theory. In effect
the field of finance evolved from a descriptive discipline dealing primarily
with mergers, regulation, and the raising of capital funds to a more encompassing one dealing with all aspects of acquiring and efficiently utilizing
those funds.

Development of the field of finance continues at a lively pace. Economic activity, primarily increased inflationary worries, and new theoretical developments in all areas of finance are constantly reshaping financial
thought.

Before discussing the financial decision-making process, we will exam-

---

[1]Among the major financial texts of this period were Arthur S. Dewing's *The Financial Policy of
Corporations*, which went through five revisions between 1920 and 1953, and Charles W.
Gerstenberg's *Financial Organization and Management of Business*, first published in 1939.

ine the appropriate goal of the firm; we can then better understand the role and significance of financial decision making.

In our work we will designate the goal of the firm to be maximization of shareholder wealth, by which we mean maximization of the total market value of the firm's common stock. As we will see, this is an extremely inclusive goal, in that it is affected by all financial decisions. To better understand it we will first examine the frequently suggested goal of profit maximization, focusing on its deficiencies and drawbacks. Then we will shift our attention to the goal of shareholder wealth maximization, examining how it differs from profit maximization and why it is the appropriate goal for the firm.

While profit maximization is frequently used as the goal of the firm in microeconomics courses, it is not adequate for finance. The goal of profit maximization does stress the efficient use of capital resources. It assumes away, however, many of the complexities of the real world that we will try to address in our decisions. In being too simplistic, the goal of profit maximization is insufficient. Two of the major criticisms of this goal are that it does not adequately deal with uncertainty and with time.

UNCERTAINTY OF RETURNS

In beginning microeconomics courses uncertainty or risk is simply ignored. Projects and investment alternatives are compared by examining their expected values or weighted average profits. Whether or not one project is riskier than another does not enter these calculations. In reality, projects do differ with respect to risk characteristics, and to assume away these differences can result in incorrect decisions. To better understand the implications of ignoring risk, let us look at two mutually exclusive investment alternatives (that is, only one can be accepted). The first project involves the use of existing plant to produce plastic combs, a product with an extremely stable demand. The second project uses existing plant to produce electric vibrating combs. This latter product may catch on and do well, but could also bomb. The possible outcomes (optimistic prediction, pessimistic prediction, and expected outcome) are given in Table 1-1.

Table 1-1 POSSIBLE PROJECT OUTCOMES

	PROFIT	
	Plastic Comb	Electric Comb
Optimistic prediction	$10,000	$20,000
Expected outcome	$10,000	$10,000
Pessimistic prediction	$10,000	$0

No variability is associated with the possible outcomes for the plastic comb project. If things go well, poorly, or as expected the outcome will still be $10,000. With the electric comb, however, the range of possible outcomes goes from $20,000 if things go well, to $10,000 if they go as expected, to zero if they go poorly. If we just look at the expected outcomes, the two projects appear equivalent. They are not. The returns associated with the electric comb involve a much greater degree of uncertainty or risk.

Since the goal of profit maximization ignores uncertainty and considers these projects equivalent in terms of desirability, we must reject it. Later in this text we will closely examine the evaluation of risky projects. At that time we will find that investors are decidedly risk averse. To ignore this fact could lead to incorrect investment decisions.

TIMING OF RETURNS

The second major objection to the goal of profit maximization is that it ignores the timing of the project's returns. To illustrate, let us reexamine our plastic comb versus electric comb investment decision. This time let us ignore risk and say that each of these projects is going to return a profit of $10,000 for one year; however, it will be one year before the electric comb can go into production, while the plastic comb can begin production immediately. The timing of the profits from these projects is illustrated in Table 1-2.

In this case the total profits from each project are the same, but the timing of the returns differs. As we will see later, money has a definite time value. Thus, the plastic comb project is the better of the two. After one year the $10,000 profit from the plastic combs could be invested in a savings account earning 5 percent interest. At the end of the second year it would have grown to $10,500. Since investment opportunities are available for money in hand, we are not indifferent to the timing of the returns. Given equivalent flows, we want those flows sooner rather than later. Thus, ignoring the timing of the returns, as profit maximization does, can result in incorrect investment decisions.

Ignoring the timing and uncertainty associated with returns, then, makes the profit-maximization goal ineffective as a decision criterion. While it may be used in microeconomics courses, its inapplicability to real-world complexities renders it useless for our purposes. For this reason we

Table 1-2   TIMING OF PROFITS

	PROFIT	
	Plastic Comb	Electric Comb
Year 1	$10,000	$0
Year 2	$0	$10,000

will turn to a more robust goal for the firm, maximization of shareholder wealth.

In formulating our goal of maximization of shareholder wealth we are doing nothing more than modifying the goal of profit maximization to deal with the complexities of the operating environment. We have chosen maximization of shareholder wealth—that is, maximization of the market value of the firm's common stock—because the effects of all financial decisions are thereby included. The shareholders react to poor investment or dividend decisions by causing the total value of the firm's stock to fall and react to good decisions by pushing the price of the stock upward. In this way all financial decisions are evaluated, and all financial decisions affect shareholder wealth.

Obviously there are some serious practical problems in directly employing this goal and evaluating the reaction to various financial decisions by examining changes in the firm's stock value. Many things affect stock prices. To attempt to pull out a reaction to a particular financial decision would simply be impossible. Fortunately, that is not necessary. In order to employ this goal, we need not consider every stock price change to be a market interpretation of the worth of our decisions. Other factors, such as economic expectations, also affect the stock's price movements. What we do focus on is the effect that our decision *should* have on the stock price if everything were held constant. The market price of the firm's stock reflects the value of the firm as seen by its owners. It takes into account uncertainty or risk, time, and any other factors that are important to the owners. Thus, the shareholder-wealth-maximization framework allows for a decision environment that includes the complexities and complications of the real world.

Much of our future discussion will center upon evaluation of risk-return tradeoffs available to the financial manager. We will, in fact, find that almost all financial decisions involve some sort of risk-return tradeoff. The more risk the firm is willing to assume, the higher the expected return from the given course of action. For example, in the area of working-capital management, the less inventory held on hand, the higher the expected return (since less of the firm's assets are involved in non-income-producing functions), but also the greater the risk of running out of inventory. As we will see, similar examples will turn up in the areas of financial structure and management of long-term assets.

Allowing the financial manager to assess the various risk-return tradeoffs available and incorporating this into the maximization-of-shareholder-wealth framework, we can show the financial decision-making process graphically as in Figure 1.1. Given the risk-return tradeoffs available to the financial manager, the various financial decisions are made

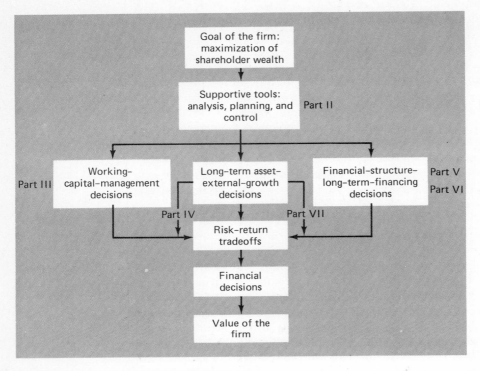

FIGURE 1.1 *Financial Decision-Making Process*

assuming a firm goal of maximization of shareholder wealth. These decisions are then evaluated by the owners of the firm, and their correctness is reflected in changes in the firm's share price.

This text is divided into seven parts, each dealing with one major area of financial concern:

OVERVIEW OF THE TEXT

Part I: The Scope and Environment of Financial Management
   II: Basic Tools of Financial Analysis, Planning, and Control
  III: Working-Capital Management
  IV: Management of Long-Term Assets
   V: The Cost of Capital and Financial Structure
  VI: Long-Term Financing
 VII: External Growth and Contraction

Figure 1.1 relates these sections to the financial decision-making process, indicating where each decision is discussed in the text. We describe these sections briefly below.

Part I begins by discussing the history and role of financial management and develops the goal of the firm to be used in financial decision making. Chapter 2 develops the legal and tax environment in which these decisions are to be made. Since this environment sets the ground rules, it is necessary to understand it before decision principles can be formulated.

Part I: The Scope and Environment of Financial Management

Part II introduces the basic financial tools the financial manager uses in maintaining control over the firm and its operations. These tools enable him to locate potential problem areas, to move accurately, and to plan for the future. Also introduced are the preparation of financial statements and ratio analysis, which allow the financial manager to achieve greater control over ongoing operations. The mathematics of finance and the concept of time value of money also are examined. An understanding of these topics allows us to make benefits and costs that occur in different time periods comparable. We introduce these financial tools at this early stage because they are used as input to all financial decisions.

Part II: Basic Tools of Financial Analysis, Planning, and Control

The third part of the book deals with working-capital management—that is, the management of current assets. Methods are discussed for determining the appropriate investment in cash, marketable securities, inventory, and accounts receivable. The risks associated with these investments, and the control of these risks, also are discussed.

Part III: Working-Capital Management

The capital-budgeting decision, involving the financial evaluation of investment proposals in fixed assets, is discussed in Part IV. First, we look at methods for evaluating new projects under certainty. Then the assumption of certainty is lifted, and methods are introduced to incorporate risk into the analysis.

Part IV: Management of Long-Term Assets

This part discusses how a firm is valued, and what costs are associated with alternative ways for raising new funds. The firm's capital structure is examined along with the impact of leverage on returns to the enterprise. This part closes with a discussion of the determination of the dividend-retained earnings decision.

Part V: The Cost of Capital and Financial Structure

Part VI describes and analyzes the various sources of long-term funding available to the firm, examining in detail the pros and cons of these sources in addition to their particular characteristics.

Part VI: Long-Term Financing

The final part of the book deals with mergers, business failures, and reorganizations, describing the legal environment in addition to the relevant financial decisions.

Part VII: External Growth and Contraction

This chapter has outlined the framework for the remainder of the book. It first traced the development of financial thought from the turn of the century to the present. During this period the field of finance reacted and changed with the prevailing economic environment. Business failures and the Depression of the thirties created concern and interest in working-capital management and bankruptcy. More recently, increased inflation and new theoretical developments have continued to reshape financial thought. Given this historical framework, the goal of the firm was examined, and the commonly accepted goal of profit maximization was declared inappropriate because it does not deal adequately with uncertainty and time. The goal of maximization of shareholder wealth was then suggested and accepted as the proper goal for the firm because it adequately deals with all the complexities of reality.

Finally the financial decision-making framework was examined and the format of the book was related to this process. The seven parts of the book were analyzed and briefly previewed.

SUMMARY

STUDY QUESTIONS

1-1. How has financial thought developed over the past century? What factors have affected it?

1-2. What are some of the problems involved in the use of profit maximization as the goal of the firm? How does the goal of shareholder wealth maximization deal with those problems?

1-3. Compare and contrast the goals of profit maximization and maximization of shareholder wealth.

1-4. Firms often involve themselves in projects that do not result directly in profits; for example, IBM and Mobil Oil frequently support public television broadcasts. Do these projects contradict the goal of maximization of shareholder wealth? Why or why not?

1-5. What is the relationship between financial decision making and risk and return? Would all financial managers view risk-return tradeoffs similarly?

SELECTED REFERENCES

ANTHONY, ROBERT N., "The Trouble with Profit Maximization," *Harvard Business Review,* 38 (November–December 1960), 126–34.

BRANCH, BEN, "Corporate Objectives and Market Performance," *Financial Management,* 2 (Summer 1973), 24–29.

DONALDSON, GORDON, "Financial Goals: Management vs. Stockholders," *Harvard Business Review,* 41 (May–June 1963), 116–29.

FINDLAY, M. CHAPMAN, III, and G. A. WHITMORE, "Beyond Shareholder Wealth Maximization," *Financial Management,* 3 (Winter 1974), 25–35.

LEWELLEN, WILBUR G., "Management and Ownership in the Large Firm," *Journal of Finance,* 24 (May 1969), 299–322.

SIMKOWITZ, MICHAEL A., and CHARLES P. JONES, "A Note on the Simultaneous Nature of Finance Methodology," *Journal of Finance,* 27 (March 1972) 103.

SOLOMON, EZRA, *The Theory of Financial Management,* Chaps. 1 and 2. New York: Columbia University Press, 1963.

——————, "What Should We Teach in a Course in Business Finance?" *Journal of Finance,* 21 (May 1966), 411–15.

WESTON, J. FRED, "New Themes in Finance," *Journal of Finance,* 29 (March 1974), 237–43.

——————, *The Scope and Methodology of Finance.* Englewood Cliffs, N.J.: Prentice-Hall, Inc., 1966.

Legal Forms of Organization and the Tax Environment

*T*he financial manager must understand the **legal environment** in which the business functions. Otherwise, management decisions may be ineffective, if not entirely self-defeating. Two areas of primary concern are the legal forms of business organization and the tax legislation affecting the firm's financial decisions. Accordingly, this chapter will (1) identify and evaluate the different legal forms of organization, and (2) provide an overview of the federal income tax system. Certainly, the financial executive should not attempt to be entirely self-reliant in these matters; he should seek legal counsel. However, an overview of the key issues should be helpful.

The legal forms of business organization are quite diverse and numerous. However, there are three basic categories: the sole proprietorship, the partnership, and the corporation. We shall first examine the definition of and the procedures for establishing each of these forms, then identify the relevant factors for evaluating which form is best for a particular company.

LEGAL FORMS OF BUSINESS ORGANIZATION

The **sole proprietorship** is a business owned by a single individual. The owner maintains title to the assets and is personally responsible, without limitation, for the liabilities incurred. The proprietor is entitled to the profits from the business but must also absorb any losses. This form of business is initiated by the mere act of beginning business operations. Typi-

Sole Proprietorship

cally, no legal requirement must be met in starting the operation, particularly if the proprietor is conducting the business in his own name. Even if an assumed name is used, usually only a small registration fee is required. The sole proprietorship has no time limit on its existence and is concluded as easily as it was orginated. Termination occurs when the owner discontinues the business or by his death. Briefly stated, the sole proprietorship is the absence of any *legal* business structure.

The primary difference between a **partnership** and a sole proprietorship is that the partnership has more than one owner. Hence, a partnership is an association of two or more individuals coming together as co-owners for the purpose of operating a business for profits. Partnerships fall into two types: (1) general partnership, and (2) limited partnership.

GENERAL PARTNERSHIP

In a **general partnership** all partners are fully liable for the indebtedness incurred by the partnership. Also, if a partner acts in a manner even having the appearance of conducting the firm's business, the remaining partners may be jointly liable for these actions. The relationship between partners is dictated entirely by the partnership agreement, which may be an oral commitment or a formal document. Generally the partners should draft a written agreement that explicitly sets forth the basic relationships within the firm. At a minimum, the agreement should include the nature and amount of capital to be invested by each partner, the authority of the individual partners, the means for determining how profits and losses are to be shared, the duration of the partnership, the procedures for admitting a new partner, and the method for reformulating the partnership in the event of a partner's death or withdrawal from the partnership. The inclusion of important terms in the agreement is essential to minimize later misunderstandings. In addition, if a dispute arises and court action becomes necessary to resolve the problem, the court may be required to act in a manner conflicting with the partners' original intent. For example, if no agreement is evident, the law stipulates that each partner is to share in the profits and losses equally.

LIMITED PARTNERSHIP

In addition to the general partnership, in which all partners are jointly liable without limitation, many states provide for a **limited partnership.** The statutes within these states permit one or more of the partners to have limited liability, restricted to the amount of capital invested in the partnership. Several conditions must be met to qualify as a limited partner. First, at least one general partner must remain in the association, for whom the privilege of limited liability does not apply. Second, the names of the limited partners may not appear in the name of the firm. Third, the limited partners may not participate in the management of the business. If one of these restrictions is violated, all partners forfeit their right to limited liability. In essence, the intent of the statutes creating the limited partnership is to provide limited liability for a person whose interest in the partnership is purely as an investor. Hence, the individual may not assume a management function within the organization.

The nature of a **corporation** has been a significant factor in the economic development of the United States. As early as 1819, Chief Justice John Marshall set forth the legal definition of a corporation as "an artificial being, invisible, intangible, and existing only in the contemplation of law."[1] This entity *legally* functions separate and apart from its owners. As such, the corporation can individually sue, and be sued, purchase, sell, or own property, and is subject to criminal punishment for crimes. However, despite this legal separation, the corporation is comprised of owners who dictate its direction and policies. The owners elect a board of directors, who in turn select individuals to serve as the corporate officers, including the president, the vice-president, the secretary, and the treasurer. Ownership is reflected by common stock certificates, designating the number of shares owned by its holder. The number of shares owned relative to the total number of shares outstanding determines the stockholder's proportionate ownership in the business. Since the shares are transferable, ownership in a corporation may be changed by a shareholder's simply remitting the shares to the new owner. The investor's liability is confined to the amount of the investment in the company, thereby preventing creditors from confiscating the stockholders' personal assets in settlement of unresolved claims. Finally, the life of a corporation is not dependent upon the status of the investors. The death or withdrawal of an investor does not affect the continuity of the corporation.

The foregoing presentation of the legal forms of operation is relatively straightforward. However, the actual choice among these legal entities when beginning a new business may be a difficult one. Not only must a number of different factors be considered, but the variables used in making the decision may be in conflict. One consideration might suggest that a partnership is the best route, while another might indicate that a corporation is needed. An overview of the important criteria is provided in Table 2-1. At the bottom of the table an indication is given, if possible, as to the form of business that is generally favored. Exceptions to these conclusions definitely could be found.

ORGANIZATION REQUIREMENTS AND COSTS

In every instance, the sole proprietorship is the "cheapest" organization to organize. Generally, no legal requirement must be satisfied; the owner simply begins operating. (Exceptions do exist, depending upon the nature of the product or service.) The general partnership may possibly be

---

[1]*The Trustees of Dartmouth College* v. *Woodward*, 4 Wheaton 636 (1819).

as inexpensive to create as the proprietorship, in that no legal criterion must be met. However, if a partnership is to be functional in the long term, a written agreement is usually advisable. The importance of this contract cannot be overemphasized. This document, if properly prepared, may serve to avoid personal misunderstandings and may even minimize several disadvantages usually associated with the partnership form of organization. The limited partnership is more expensive, owing to statutory requirements. The partners must provide a certification of the general partners and the limited partners and indicate the rights and responsibilities of each. Also, a written agreement is compulsory. The corporation is typically the most expensive form of business. As indicated earlier, compliance with numerous statutory provisions is required. The legal costs and the time entailed in creating a corporation exceed those for the other legal types of organization. In short, the organizational requirements increase as the formality of the organization increases. However, this consideration is of minimum importance, and to forego a choice because of its initial cost may prove to be expensive in the long term.

LIABILITY OF THE OWNERS

The sole proprietorship and the general partnership have an inherent disadvantage: the feature of unlimited liability. For these organizations, no distinction is made between business assets and personal assets. The creditors lending money to the business can require the owners to sell personal assets if the firm is financially unable to repay its loans. The limited partnership alleviates this problem for the limited partner. However, care must be taken by a limited partner to retain this protection. Failure to give *due notice* or to refrain from actively participating in management may result in the loss of this privilege. The corporation has a definite advantage in terms of limited liability, with the creditors being able to look only to the corporate assets in resolving claims. However, this advantage for the corporation may not always be realized. If a firm is small, its president may be required to guarantee the loan personally. Also, if the corporate form is being used to defraud creditors, the courts may "pierce the corporation veil" and hold the owners personally liable. Nevertheless, the limitation of liability is usually an important concern in the selection of the legal organization.

CONTINUITY OF THE BUSINESS

The continuity of the business is largely a function of the legal form of organization. The sole proprietorship is immediately dissolved upon the owner's death. Likewise, the general partnership is terminated upon the death or withdrawal of a partner. This weakness can be minimized in the partnership through the written agreement, by specifying what is to occur if a partner dies or desires to withdraw. Failure to incorporate such a provision into the agreement may result in a forced liquidation of the firm, possibly at an inopportune time. Finally, the corporation offers the greatest

Table 2-1   SELECTION OF LEGAL FORM OF ORGANIZATION

FORM OF ORGANIZATION	ORGANIZATIONAL REQUIREMENTS AND COSTS	LIABILITY OF THE OWNERS	CONTINUITY OF THE BUSINESS
Sole proprietorship	Minimum requirements: Generally no registration or filing fee.	Unlimited liability.	Dissolved upon proprietor's death.
General partnership	Minimum requirements: Generally no registration or filing fee. Partnership agreement not legally required but is strongly suggested.	Unlimited liability.	Unless partnership agreement specifies differently, dissolved upon withdrawal or death of partner.
Limited partnership	Moderate requirements: Written agreement often required, including identification of general and limited partners.	General partners: Unlimited liability. _____ Limited partners: Liability limited to investment in company.	General partners: Same as general partnership. _____ Limited partners: Withdrawal or death does not affect continuity of business.
Corporation	Most expensive and greatest requirements: Filing fees; compliance with state regulations for corporations.	Liability limited to investment in company.	Continuity of business unaffected by shareholder withdrawal or death.
Form of organization normally favored	Proprietorship or general partnership.	Limited partnership or corporation.	Corporation.

Table 2-1 *(cont.)*

TRANSFERABILITY OF OWNERSHIP	MANAGEMENT CONTROL AND REGULATIONS	ATTRACTIVENESS FOR RAISING CAPITAL	INCOME TAXES
May transfer ownership in company name and assets.	Absolute management freedom, negligible formal requirements.	Limited to proprietor's personal capital.	Income from the business is taxed as personal income to the proprietor.
Requires the consent of all partners.	Majority vote of partners required for control; negligible formal requirements.	Limited to partners' ability and desire to contribute capital.	Income from the business is taxed as personal income to the partners.
General partners: Same as general partnership. Limited partners: May sell interest in the company.	General partners: Same as general partnership. Limited partners: Not permitted any involvement in management.	General partners: Same as general partnership. Limited partners: Limited liability provides a stronger inducement in raising capital.	Same as general partnership.
Easily transferred by transferring shares of stock.	Shareholders have final control, but usually board of directors controls company policies.	Usually the most attractive form for raising capital.	The corporation is taxed on its income and the stockholder is taxed when dividends are paid.
Depends upon the circumstances.	Control: Depends upon the circumstances. Regulation: Proprietorship and general partnership.	Corporation.	Depends upon circumstances.

degree of continuity. The status of the investor simply does not affect the corporation's existence. Hence, the corporate form of conducting business has a distinct advantage in its perpetual nature.

TRANSFERABILITY OF OWNERSHIP

Transferability of ownership is intrinsically neither good or bad; its desirability depends largely upon the owners' preferences. In certain businesses the owners may want the option to evaluate any prospective new investors. In other circumstances, unrestricted transferability may be preferred. The sole proprietor has complete freedom to sell any interest in the business. At the other extreme, the members of a general partnership may not sell or assign their interest without the prior consent of the remaining partners. However, this limitation may be removed by providing otherwise in the partnership agreement. The limited partnership has a twofold nature: the assignment of interest by general partners requires the prior consent of the other partners, while the limited partners have unrestricted transferability. The corporation affords the investors complete flexibility in transferring their interest.

MANAGEMENT CONTROL AND REGULATIONS

The sole proprietor has absolute control of the firm and is not restrained by government regulation. With the few exceptions relating to assumed or fictitious names and special licensing, the sole proprietorship may operate in any state without complying with registration and qualification requirements. The general partnership is likewise not impeded by any significant government regulations. However, since control within this legal form of business is normally based upon the majority vote, an increase in the number of partners reduces each partner's voice in management. The limited partnership is characterized by a restricted separation of ownership from control, which is nonexistent in the sole proprietorship and the general partnership. As to government regulation, the limited partnership requires detailed registration to inform the public of the authority of the individual partners. Within the corporation, the control factor has two dimensions: (a) the **formal control** vested in the stockholders having the majority of the voting common shares, and (b) the **functional control** exercised by the corporate officers in conducting the daily operations. For the small corporation, these two controls usually rest in the same individuals. However, as the size of the corporation increases, these two facets of control become distinctly separate. Finally, the corporation is encumbered with substantial government regulations and formalities in terms of registrations as well as continued compliance with statutory requirements.

ATTRACTIVENESS FOR RAISING CAPITAL

As a result of the limited liability, the ease of transferring ownership through the sale of common shares, and the flexibility in dividing the shares, the corporation is the supreme business entity in attracting new capital. In contrast, the unlimited liability of the sole proprietorship and the general partnership is a deterrent in raising equity capital. Between these extremes, the limited partnership does provide limited liability for the limited partners, which has a tendency to attract wealthy investors. However, the impracticality of having a large number of partners and the restricted marketability of an interest in a partnership prevent this form of organization from effectively competing with the corporation.

INCOME TAXES

Income taxation frequently has a major impact upon the owner's selection of the legal form of business. In the remainder of this chapter we shall examine the basic tax implications for the financial manager. However, a brief comment at this point would appear appropriate.

The sole proprietorship and the partnership organization are not taxed as separate entities, but rather the owners report the business profits on their personal tax return. Thus, the earnings from the company are taxable to the owner, regardless of whether these profits have been distributed to the investors. This feature may place the owner in a cash squeeze if taxes are due but the income has been retained within the company. On the other hand, the corporation is taxed as a separate and distinct entity. This same income is again taxed when distributed to the shareholder in the form of dividends. Determination of the best form of legal entity with respect to taxes should be based upon the objective of maximizing the after-tax profits to the owners.[2] This decision depends partly upon the tax rates of the individual relative to those of the corporation. Also, whether or not the profits are to be retained in the business or paid as dividends to the common stockholders has a direct bearing on the issue.

FEDERAL INCOME TAXATION

Objectives of Income Taxation

Originally, the sole objective of the federal government in taxing income was to generate financing for government expenditures. Although this purpose continues to be important, additional *social* objectives and *economic* objectives have been specified. For instance, the Tax Reform Act of 1969 entitles a company to possible reductions in taxes if (1) pollution control facilities are installed, or (2) on-the-job training and job care are provided to employees. Other socially oriented stipulations in the tax laws include exemptions for dependents, old age, and blindness, and a reduction in taxes if the income is associated with retirement. As to the economic objective, the government employs a number of procedures in attempting to stabilize the economy. In recessionary periods the taxes may be reduced, giving the public more discretionary income in the hope that it will be spent so as to increase the demand for products and thereby generate new jobs. Also, tax incentives may be offered to businesses for making

[2]The firm's objective is to maximize the shareholders' wealth. However, since no risk is involved in selecting the form of business, maximizing profits will also maximize wealth.

investments that will stimulate the economy. For example, companies making investments in certain types of equipment may be permitted to reduce their taxes by a percentage of the amount of funds invested (Investment Tax Credit). This benefit was initially included in the tax laws in 1962 as an incentive for businesses to expand their operations. Since that time this feature has been repealed and reincorporated into the legislation on several occasions, depending upon the administration's thoughts regarding the prevailing economic conditions.

In summary, three objectives may be given for the taxation of revenues: (1) the provision of revenues for government expenditures, (2) the achievement of socially desirable goals, and (3) economic stabilization.

Having gained these insights, let us look at the tax legislation in greater detail. We must first identify what constitutes being a "taxpayer." In this regard, three basic types of **taxable entities** exist: individuals, corporations, and fiduciaries. Individuals are considered to include company employees, self-employed persons owning their own businesses, and members of a partnership. Income is reported by these individuals in their personal tax returns. Thus, a partnership does not pay income taxes as a separate entity. The corporation, as a separate legal entity, does report its income and remits a tax payment related to these profits. The owners (stockholders) of the corporation need not report these earnings in their personal tax return, except when all or a part of the profits are distributed in the form of dividends. Finally, fiduciaries, such as estates and trusts, do file a tax return and pay taxes on the income generated by the estate or trust.

We shall now (1) examine the tax provisions applicable to the individual taxpayer, (2) briefly comment on the partnership's tax status, and (3) specify the treatment of corporate taxes. (A fiduciary relationship is typically not relevant in the managerial setting, so no further comment is made regarding this tax entity.) Tax legislation can quickly change, and we should be aware that certain details discussed here may cease to be applicable.

MEASURING TAXABLE INCOME

The measurement process in determining taxable income for the individual is as shown in Figure 2-1. "Gross income" is defined as any wealth that flows to the taxpayer, but not including the principal part of an investment. More specifically, gross income includes compensation for personal and professional services, business income, dividends, interest, rent, gains from the sale or exchange of property, and any profit or income derived from other sources. In other words, practically any form of income, unless specifically exempted from taxes, is to be included in gross income. Exclusions from taxable income include gifts, inheritances, life insurance proceeds resulting from death, disability benefits, interest re-

Income Taxes for Individuals

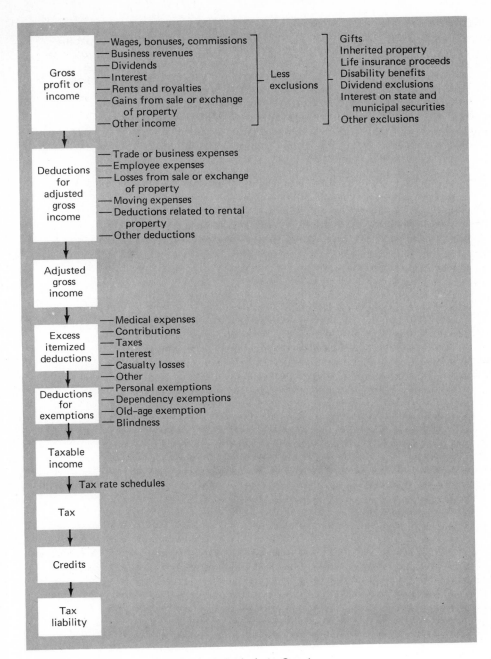

FIGURE 2-1 *Income Taxation for the Individual: An Overview*

(Source: Adapted from Federal Tax Course, 1977, Englewood Cliffs, N.J.: Prentice-Hall, Inc., 1976.)

ceived from state and local government indebtedness, and the first $100 in dividend income.[3]

INDIVIDUAL TAX DEDUCTIONS

In calculating the **adjusted gross income,** ordinary and necessary expenses incurred in carrying on a trade or business may be deducted. Also, employee expenses for travel, transportation, and other job-related activities may be used in reducing the adjusted gross income. Finally, certain expenses that relate neither to a "business" nor to employee activities may serve as a deduction. These "nonbusiness" expenses include ordinary and necessary payments in (1) producing or collecting income, (2) managing or conserving property held for production of income, or (3) collecting a tax refund. For example, these costs would include expenses associated with rental property or personal investments.

After determining the adjusted gross income, the taxpayer then subtracts any tax-deductible personal expenses. These personal deductions may include *medical expenses, contributions* to qualified charitable organizations, *interest,* certain types of *taxes,* and casualty or theft *losses* exceeding any insurance reimbursements. However, only expenses that exceed $3200 for a married couple filing a joint tax return or $2200 for a single person may be used for tax deductions.

Personal Exemptions. Certain exemptions may be taken by the individual taxpayer—for example, a **personal exemption** in the amount of $750. If a joint return is submitted, an exemption is permissible for the spouse and for each dependent. A family of four may be eligible for $3000 in personal exemptions ($750 × 4 exemptions).

Example. To demonstrate the process for computing the taxable income for an individual, assume the following information: T. J. Griggs is president of Bank of the Southwest. In this capacity he receives $50,000 in annual salary plus a year-end bonus amounting to 10 percent of his salary. He has investment income consisting of $2000 in dividends and $3000 in interest. The interest income includes $1000 in bonds issued by the local municipal water district. Also, Griggs serves as a member of the board of directors for a regional trucking firm, receiving $100 per month in director's fees. As a part of his profession, he subscribes to several banking journals and economic forecasting services, which cost $1000 per year. In addition, he subscribes to an investment service for managing his personal

---

[3]If a tax return is filed jointly by a husband and wife (joint return), the $100 dividend exclusion is applicable to each spouse. However, the securities must be owned separately. Hence, if the wife has stock paying $150 in dividends and the husband's investments pay $40 in dividends, only $140 may be excluded from income. An exception to this ruling exists if the securities are "community property." In this situation, one-half of the dividend is assumed to be received by each spouse.

investments, totaling $1100 annually. For itemized deductions, he contributed $1000 during the year to a university; taxes and interest on his residence were $800 and $2200, respectively. Griggs is married and has two small children. Computation of his taxable income is shown in Table 2-2. In these calculations we have assumed that the stock is owned separately by Griggs, resulting in only a $100 dividend exclusion.

PERSONAL TAX RATE STRUCTURE

The taxes to be paid by the individual are determined by applying the tax rates reflected in Table 2-3 to taxable income. The rate depends upon whether the individual is single or married and filing a joint return with his (her) spouse. These rates are subject to change from year to year.

As an example of the tax computation, recall that T. J. Griggs had taxable income totaling $54,200 (Table 2-2). Assuming that he is filing a joint return, his tax would be computed from the line in Table 2-3 that is extracted on p. 24.

Table 2-2 T. J. GRIGGS'S TAXABLE INCOME

Salary		$50,000
Year-end bonus		5,000
Dividends		2,000
Interest		3,000
Director's fees		1,200
Total income		$61,200
Income exclusions:		
Interest on municipal bonds	$1,000	
Dividend exclusion	100	$1,100
Gross income		$60,100
Deductions for adjusted gross income:		
Employee expenses		$ 1,000
Investment expenses		1,100
Adjusted gross income		$58,000
Itemized deductions:		
Contributions	$1,000	
Taxes	800	
Interest	2,200	
Gross itemized deductions	$4,000	
Nondeductible amount	3,200	
Excess itemized deductions		$ 800
Personal exemptions		
($750 × 4)		3,000
Total excess itemized deductions		
and personal exemptions		$ 3,800
Taxable income		$54,200

Table 2-3 1977 TAX RATE SCHEDULES

SINGLE TAXPAYER

If Taxable Income Is:		Tax	Of the Amount
Over	But Not Over	Equals	Over
$ 0	$ 2,200	$ 0 + 0%	$ 0
$ 2,200	$ 2,700	+ 14%	$ 2,200
$ 2,700	$ 3,200	$ 70 + 15%	$ 2,700
$ 3,200	$ 3,700	$ 145 + 16%	$ 3,200
$ 3,700	$ 4,200	$ 225 + 17%	$ 3,700
$ 4,200	$ 6,200	$ 310 + 19%	$ 4,200
$ 6,200	$ 8,200	$ 690 + 21%	$ 6,200
$ 8,200	$ 10,200	$ 1,110 + 24%	$ 8,200
$ 10,200	$ 12,200	$ 1,590 + 25%	$ 10,200
$ 12,200	$ 14,200	$ 2,090 + 27%	$ 12,200
$ 14,200	$ 16,200	$ 2,630 + 29%	$ 14,200
$ 16,200	$ 18,200	$ 3,210 + 31%	$ 16,200
$ 18,200	$ 20,200	$ 3,830 + 34%	$ 18,200
$ 20,200	$ 22,200	$ 4,510 + 36%	$ 20,200
$ 22,200	$ 24,200	$ 5,230 + 38%	$ 22,200
$ 24,200	$ 28,200	$ 5,990 + 40%	$ 24,200
$ 28,200	$ 34,200	$ 7,590 + 45%	$ 28,200
$ 34,200	$ 40,200	$10,290 + 50%	$ 34,200
$ 40,200	$ 46,200	$13,290 + 55%	$ 40,200
$ 46,200	$ 52,200	$16,590 + 60%	$ 46,200
$ 52,200	$ 62,200	$20,190 + 62%	$ 52,200
$ 62,200	$ 72,200	$26,390 + 64%	$ 62,200
$ 72,200	$ 82,200	$32,790 + 66%	$ 72,200
$ 82,200	$ 92,200	$39,390 + 68%	$ 82,200
$ 92,200	$102,200	$46,190 + 69%	$ 92,200
$102,200	. . .	$53,090 + 70%	$102,200

(Source: Adapted from 1977 Federal Income Tax Forms.)

If Taxable Income Is:		Tax Equals	Of the Amount
Over	But Not Over		Over
$47,200	$55,200	$14,060 + 50%	$47,200

Table 2-3 *(cont.)*

MARRIED TAXPAYERS FILING JOINT RETURNS

If Taxable Income Is:		Tax	Of the Amount
Over	But Not Over	Equals	Over
$ 0	$ 2,200	$ 0 + 0%	$ 0
$ 3,200	$ 4,200	14%	$ 3,200
$ 4,200	$ 5,200	$ 140 + 15%	$ 4,200
$ 5,200	$ 6,200	$ 290 + 16%	$ 5,200
$ 6,200	$ 7,200	$ 450 + 17%	$ 6,200
$ 7,200	$ 11,200	$ 620 + 19%	$ 7,200
$ 11,200	$ 15,200	$ 1,380 + 22%	$ 11,200
$ 15,200	$ 19,200	$ 2,260 + 25%	$ 15,200
$ 19,200	$ 23,200	$ 3,260 + 28%	$ 19,200
$ 23,200	$ 27,200	$ 4,380 + 32%	$ 23,200
$ 27,200	$ 31,200	$ 5,660 + 36%	$ 27,200
$ 31,200	$ 35,200	$ 7,100 + 39%	$ 31,200
$ 35,200	$ 39,200	$ 8,660 + 42%	$ 35,200
$ 39,200	$ 43,200	$ 10,340 + 45%	$ 39,200
$ 43,200	$ 47,200	$ 12,140 + 48%	$ 43,200
$ 47,200	$ 55,200	$ 14,060 + 50%	$ 47,200
$ 55,200	$ 67,200	$ 18,060 + 53%	$ 55,200
$ 67,200	$ 79,200	$ 24,420 + 55%	$ 67,200
$ 79,200	$ 91,200	$ 31,020 + 58%	$ 79,200
$ 91,200	$103,200	$ 37,980 + 60%	$ 91,200
$103,200	$123,200	$ 45,180 + 62%	$103,200
$123,200	$143,200	$ 57,580 + 64%	$123,200
$143,200	$163,200	$ 70,380 + 66%	$143,200
$163,200	$183,200	$ 83,580 + 68%	$163,200
$183,200	$203,200	$ 97,180 + 69%	$183,200
$203,200	. . .	$110,980 + 70%	$203,200

Thus Griggs would owe $17,560 in federal income taxes: $14,060 + [50% ($54,200 − $47,200)]. In this instance the "marginal tax rate," the rate at which the next dollar of income is to be taxed, is 50%. The "average tax rate" is 32.49% (that is, $17,560 ÷ $54,200) and represents the average amount of tax per dollar of income to be paid for a particular income level.

INDIVIDUAL CAPITAL GAINS AND LOSSES

The previous material has made no distinction between "ordinary income" and "gains and losses from the sale of capital assets." However, different tax treatment may be given to these two categories.

A capital gain or loss is defined by the Revenue Code as a gain or loss resulting from the sale or exchange of a capital asset. Capital asset includes any property except assets held primarily for sale in the ordinary course of business or depreciable and real property used in conducting a business. The asset need not be owned as a part of a trade or business. Capital gains and losses are divided into short-term and long-term, with a short-term gain or loss resulting from the sale of an asset held for nine months or less. In 1978 this holding period was increased to 12 months. Thus, the long-term gain or loss applies to a capital asset held for more than 9 months if sold during 1977 and more than 12 months for any exchange occurring in 1978 or thereafter.

In figuring the tax effect of capital gains and losses, several possible situations may result:

1. If the taxpayer only has short-term capital gains, they are treated as ordinary income, such as salaries or interest income.

2. For long-term gains, only one-half of the gains are taxed, with the maximum effective tax rate not to exceed 25 percent. For example, assume a capital asset has been held for 18 months, at which time it is sold for $1500. If the tax-payer's "cost" in the asset is $1000, a $500 long-term gain occurs. However, only 50 percent of the gain, or $250, is subject to taxes. If the taxpayer is in a 40 percent tax bracket, the taxes on the gain would be $100 ($250 × 40%). However, for a taxpayer who is in a 60 percent tax bracket, the tax would be $125, which represents the 25 percent maximum tax rate on long-term capital gains, or 25 percent of the total $500 gain.

3. Net short-term capital losses are deductible for tax purposes, but only by the *lesser of* (1) the actual loss, (2) the amount of ordinary income, or (3) $3000. To illustrate, if the loss is $4000 and other taxable income amounts to $10,000, only $3000 in losses may be applied against the $10,000 ordinary income, for a taxable income of $7000. However, the remaining $1000 loss may be carried forward into future taxable years indefinitely until completely deducted.

4. For net long-term capital losses, only 50 percent of the loss may be recognized in reducing taxable income. For instance, assuming a long-term loss of $1000, only $500 may be used against ordinary income. The limitations as to the maximum amount of the writeoff and the carryforward privileges are the same as those imposed for short-term losses.

In summary, a short-term gain or loss is essentially treated as ordinary income or expense. However, limitations are imposed on the total amount of loss that may be used in offsetting ordinary income. For long-term capital gains or losses, only 50 percent of the gain or loss is to be recognized in computing taxable income.

As indicated earlier, the partnership itself is exempt from paying any tax, but the law does stipulate that a partnership must report its earnings and indicate the part of the profits attributable to each partner. This report is made by completing a partnership tax return. Every transaction of the partnership that has a tax consequence is to be reported and allocated among the partners as specified by the partnership agreement. The individual partners then include this income within their personal tax returns. In this manner, if any tax is due as a result of business conducted by the partnership, this tax is paid immediately by the individual partners whether or not a distribution of this income is actually made to them. In brief, the partnership is considered to be merely a conduit for each partner's income.

For the most part, the taxable income for a corporation is determined in the same manner as for the individual. In essence, the gross income from all sources, except for exclusions, less deductible expenses equals the corporation's taxable income. However, differences do exist between the individual and the corporation in determining the tax liability. For instance, personal exemptions and nonbusiness expenses are not permissible deductions for the corporation.

We will study special deductions for the corporations, the corporate tax rate schedule, capital gains treatment, net operating losses, depreciation, and investment tax credit. Furthermore, additional taxes may be imposed upon the corporation for the "excessive accumulation" of profits within the business. Finally, we will examine briefly the tax provision allowing a corporation to be taxed as a partnership.

SPECIAL DEDUCTIONS

The term **special deduction** is not to be confused with deductions relating to expenses incurred in the normal course of business. Actually, the special deduction is at times more closely related to the income exclusions for the individual. These special deductions may apply to dividends, income received from certain foreign companies, and charitable contributions.

Dividend Deduction. A corporation may normally deduct 85 percent of any dividends received from another corporation. For instance, if Corporation A owns common stock in Corporation B and receives dividends of $1000 in a given year, only $150 will be subject to tax, with the remaining $850 (85% of $1000) being tax exempt. If the corporation receiving the dividend income is in a 48 percent tax bracket, only $72 in taxes (48% of $150) will result. Also, a corporation receiving a dividend may deduct the *entire* amount if both corporations are members of the same "affiliated group," where affiliation is expressed in terms of owning, either directly or indirectly, 80 percent of the firm paying the dividend. Finally, if the corporation issuing the dividend is a foreign corporation and satisfies certain restrictions, a 100 percent dividend deduction is permissible.

Income from Foreign Corporations. A United States corporation that conducts business entirely within the western hemisphere, termed a **Western Hemisphere Trade Corporation,** may possibly be permitted a special deduction. If 95 percent of the firm's income is from sources external to the United States and at least 90 percent of the gross income resulted from the active conduct of a trade or business, a special deduction of 29.167 percent of the corporate income may be taken. However, this tax benefit was scheduled to be phased out by the end of 1979.

Charitable Contributions. Contributions by a corporation to charitable institutions may be claimed as a special deduction. The contribution is not to exceed 5 percent of the taxable income prior to the deduction of the contribution. Contributions exceeding this limitation are not deductible; however, these "excessive donations" may be carried forward into the five succeeding years and used as a deduction if the limit is not being exceeded in these subsequent periods. This 5 percent restriction does not apply to a contribution that is in fact a business expense.

CORPORATE RATE STRUCTURE

The corporate tax rate structure is relatively simple. In 1965 the rates were established at 22 percent on the first $25,000 taxable income and 48 percent for any earnings exceeding the $25,000. In 1975 a temporary tax cut for corporations was initiated, taxes being 20 percent for the initial $25,000 in taxable profits, 22 percent for income greater than $25,000 but not exceeding $50,000, and 48 percent for any additional earnings. For example, if a corporation has $125,000 in taxable earnings, the tax is determined as follows:

EARNINGS	×	MARGINAL TAX RATE	=	TAXES
$25,000	×	20%		$ 5,000
25,000	×	22%		5,500
75,000	×	48%		36,000
$125,000				$46,500

Average tax rate = $46,500 ÷ $125,000 = 37.2%

Thus, the first $50,000 in income is taxed at a relatively low rate, with earnings in excess of $50,000 requiring the corporation to pay almost $.50

per $1 of profits in federal income taxes. As a consequence, we would expect the management of a corporation having taxable income in excess of $50,000 to divide the company into two or more smaller corporations, thereby taking greater advantage of the lower tax rates. To prevent such a stratagem, the tax legislation was revised in 1969 to eliminate the benefit of multiple corporations. Currently, if a group of corporations having common ownership file separate tax returns, only one of the companies is permitted to use the low rates.

CAPITAL GAINS AND LOSSES

The recognition of capital gains and losses is essentially the same for corporations and individuals. For the corporation, however, a capital gains deduction (50 percent of the net long-term gain) is *not* permitted. Also, while the corporation offsets capital losses against capital gains in the same manner as shown for individuals, the corporate entity may not deduct any capital losses against ordinary income.

The actual computation of corporate taxes when capital gains and losses are involved requires two approaches. First, the excess of net long-term capital gains over net short-term capital losses is added to ordinary income, and all income is taxed at the ordinary income tax rates. Alternatively, the tax is measured by calculating the taxes related only to the corporation's ordinary income. To this amount, a capital gains tax rate of 30 percent is applied to the net excess long-term capital gains. The alternative providing the lower taxes may be selected.

Example. Assume that the Pipes Corporation had ordinary income in 1978 of $80,000. In addition, the capital gains and losses shown in Table 2-4 were incurred. To determine the firm's tax liability, the two alternate tax computations are made in Table 2-5. The second alternative provides lower taxes and should be selected.

If capital losses do exceed capital gains in a given year, the corporation may apply these losses against capital gains in other years. When this situation occurs for the individual, the loss may only be carried forward,

Table 2-4 PIPES CORPORATION CAPITAL GAINS AND LOSSES

Short-term capital gains	$ 5,000	
Short-term capital losses	8,000	
Net short-term losses		$3,000
Long-term capital gains	$12,000	
Long-term capital losses	4,000	
Net long-term capital gains		8,000
Excess of net long-term capital gain over net short-term capital losses		$5,000

Table 2-5 COMPUTATION OF TAXES FOR PIPES CORPORATION

Alternative 1:

Ordinary income			$80,000
Capital gains			5,000
Taxable income			$85,000
Taxes:	20% × $25,000 =		$ 5,000
	22% × 25,000 =		5,500
	48% × 35,000 =		16,800
Total taxes			$27,300

Alternative 2:

Ordinary income			$80,000
Taxes on ordinary income:			
	20% × $25,000 =		$ 5,000
	22% × 25,000 =		5,500
	48% × 30,000 =		14,400
			$24,900
Taxes on capital gains,			
30% × $5,000			1,500
Total taxes			$26,400

but no time limitation exists. For the corporation, the loss may be carried back for three years and, if any loss still remains, it may be used to offset capital gains in the ensuing five years. When carried into another year, all capital losses are treated as short-term and are grouped with the short-term losses in offsetting any capital gains.

NET OPERATING DEDUCTION

A corporation could conceivably have a high income in one year and a substantial loss the following year. If provisions were not made for such circumstances, a taxpayer might be subject to a large tax in the first year and no tax in the latter year, so that the corporation would pay taxes, even though the earnings during the two-year period might average out to zero. For example, assume a corporation earned $100,000 in 1978 but had a $100,000 tax loss in 1979. Though no tax would be owed in 1979, the taxes in 1978 would be $34,500, even though, on average, no profit existed. For this reason the tax laws provide for a **net operating loss carryback and carryforward,** which permits the taxpayer first to apply the loss against the profits in the three prior years (carryback). If the loss has not been completely absorbed by the profits in these three years, the loss may be carried forward to each of the seven following years (carryforward). At that time, any loss still remaining may no longer be used as a tax deduction. To illustrate, a 1978 operating loss may be used to recover, in whole or in part, the taxes paid during 1975, 1976, and 1977. If any part of the loss still remains, this amount may be used to reduce taxable income, if any, during the seven-year period of 1979 through 1985.

Example. As an example of the net operating loss carryback and carryforward, assume D. Francis, Inc., a trucking operation, has had the profits and losses reported in Table 2-6. In 1978 and 1980 the corporation incurred operating losses, which may be applied to reduce taxable income and taxes in other years. The tax payments and tax refunds for each year are calculated in Table 2-7. In examining the table, we note that taxes were paid for the original three years of 1975, 1976, and 1977. As a consequence of the $152,000 loss in 1978, the taxes initially paid in 1975 and 1976 ($11,460 plus $22,980) are to be returned to D. Francis, Inc., plus a $11,520 refund from the 1977 taxes. The $11,520 refund from 1977 is determined by recomputing the 1977 taxes based upon a $76,000 income rather than the original $100,000 reported in 1977. The $24,000 reduction in taxable income represents the unused carryback from the 1978 loss. The remaining calculations are determined in a similar fashion.

DEPRECIATION

If an asset is purchased that has a limited life beyond one year but its usefulness gradually declines over time, the taxpayer is *not* permitted to show the cost of the asset as a tax deduction in the year it is acquired. However, if the property is used in a business or profession or in the production of income, a part of the original cost may be written off as a tax deduction in each year of the asset's anticipated economic life. Examples of assets that may be depreciated include machinery and buildings.

The methods acceptable for tax purposes for computing the annual depreciation expense include (1) straight-line, (2) declining balance, (3) sum-of-the-years' digits, and (4) other "consistent methods." The actual computational procedures for these methods are given in Appendix 3A. However, we should note that the declining balance and the sum-of-the-years' digits are "accelerated depreciation techniques," allowing the owner of the asset to take greater amounts of depreciation during the early years of the asset's life. In this way, some of the taxes are deferred until later years. Also affecting the amount of depreciation in a given year is the length of time used as the asset's economic life. Naturally, by shortening the life, the taxpayer may take greater amounts of depreciation in the earlier years, which again shifts taxes to later years. However, the Internal Reve-

Table 2-6 D. FRANCIS, INC., TAXABLE INCOME

1975	$ 52,000	1979	$100,000
1976	76,000	1980	(194,000)
1977	100,000	1981	12,000
1978	(152,000)	1982	94,000

Table 2-7 D. FRANCIS, INC., NET OPERATING LOSS COMPUTATIONS

YEAR	TAXABLE INCOME BEFORE CARRYBACK ADD CARRYFORWARD	TAX PAYMENT	CARRYBACK	CARRYFORWARD	TAX REFUNDS
1975	$ 52,000	$11,460	$52,000 from 1978		
1976	76,000	22,980	76,000 from 1978		
1977	100,000	34,500	24,000 from 1978		
			76,000 from 1980		
1978	(152,000)	-0-			$45,960[a]
1979	100,000	34,500	100,000 from 1980		
1980	(194,000)[b]	-0-			57,480[c]
1981	12,000	-0-		$12,000 from 1980	
1982	94,000	28,740[d]		6,000 from 1980	

[a]1978 refund = $11,460 (1975 taxes) + $22,980 (1976 taxes) + $11,520 (correction of 1977 taxes from $100,000 to $76,000) = $45,960.

[b]$176,000 of the $194,000 loss is carried back to 1977 and 1979. The remaining $18,000 is to be carried forward.

[c]1980 refund = $22,980 ($76,000 taxable income in 1977) + $34,500 (1979 taxes) = $57,480.

[d]1982 payment = taxes on $88,000 taxable income ($94,000 income for 1982 less a $6000 carryforward from 1980).

nue Service has established guidelines for ascertaining a reasonable length of time for depreciation purposes.

Another tax implication relating to depreciable assets is the exclusion of these assets from the **capital asset category.** Thus, the sale of a depreciable asset normally does not result in a capital gain or a capital loss. For this purpose, the gain from the sale of the asset is computed as the selling price less the asset's **book value.** For instance, assume machinery was purchased in 1975 at an original cost of $25,000, and sold in 1977 for $20,000. Further assume that the equipment had an expected five-year life, with no anticipated salvage value, and that the annual depreciation charge was $5000. The book value of the asset at the time of sale, which is the taxpayer's basis, would be $15,000 (original cost less total depreciation taken to date). Hence, the gain from the sale of the asset is $5000 ($20,000 less $15,000). The gain from the sale is considered as ordinary income, thereby not receiving the preferential capital gains treatment. Only if the asset were sold for more than its original cost would any capital gain result. Altering the example, suppose that the machinery were sold for $28,000 rather than $20,000. In this case the total gain would be $13,000 ($28,000 selling price less $15,000 book value). The gain would be broken into $3000 capital gain and $10,000 ordinary income. Stated differently, the gain from a depreciable asset is ordinary income to the extent of the accumulated depreciation. Any gain beyond this amount is considered to be a capital gain.

INVESTMENT TAX CREDIT

The Revenue Act of 1962 initiated the **investment tax credit** to stimulate increased business investment in machinery and equipment. The Tax Reform Act of 1976 extended this provision with a tax credit amounting to 10 percent of qualified investments. Qualified investments include (1) machinery and equipment, and (2) depreciable real property used in manufacturing, or in the furnishing of utility services, except for buildings. For example, trucks, production equipment, office equipment, and gas pipelines would be eligible.

The investment tax credit is limited to the first $25,000 of the taxes plus one-half of the remaining taxes. For instance, if a corporation has a tax liability of $100,000 prior to the credit, the maximum credit that can be used to offset the taxes is $25,000 plus one-half of $75,000, or $62,500. If any unused credit remains, the taxpayer may possibly apply it against taxes in other years. A restriction also exists in terms of the useful life of the asset, with the entire dollar investment qualifying if the useful life is seven years or more; two-thirds of the investment if the life is between five and six years; one-third of the investment if the asset life is between three and four years; and no tax credit if the useful life is less than three years. Therefore, for a taxpayer acquiring $50,000 in equipment having a useful life of ten years and expending $24,000 for a qualified asset with a five-year life, the investment credit would be $6600 [10% of $50,000 + 10% of $\frac{2}{3}$ ($24,000)].

ACCUMULATED EARNINGS TAX

The earnings generated by a corporation are potentially subject to "double taxation," first at the corporate level and then at the stockholder level (assuming a noncorporate shareholder) as the firm's profits are distributed in the form of dividends. If the shareholders had no immediate need for the dividend income, the corporation could retain its profits and even employ the funds for the personal benefit of the company's owners. For example, the management could retain the corporate profits but make a personal loan to the stockholders. Also, if the profits are accumulated within the firm, the price of the common stock should increase. The investor could eventually sell the stock at the increased value, with the gain being taxed at the preferential long-term capital gains rate rather than at the higher ordinary income rates.

To prevent such stratagems, a penalty surtax in addition to the regular income tax is assessed at the corporate level on any accumulation of earnings by a corporation for the purpose of avoiding taxes on its shareholders. The tax does not apply to the retention of profits for *reasonable business needs*. Nor must the money be reinvested immediately as long as there is evidence that future needs require the current accumulation of earnings. Although it is difficult to state exactly when the accumulation of profits is thought to be *reasonable,* several examples would include (1) providing for the replacement of plant and equipment, (2) retiring debt created in connection with the corporation's business, (3) providing for working-capital requirements, and (4) financing the acquisition of a new business. In contrast, the use of accumulated earnings for the following reasons would probably be considered as *unreasonable:* (1) loans to shareholders or to their relatives and friends who have no valid relationship to the business, (2) expenditures of corporate monies for the personal benefit of the common stockholders, (3) investment in securities that are unrelated to the business activities of the corporation, and (4) accumulation of earnings in anticipation of *unrealistic* contingencies. In providing that the earnings retention is reasonable and not for the purpose of avoiding taxes, the taxpayer normally bears the burden of proof.

In determining the penalty, the computation is based upon the **accumulated taxable income** and not upon the total retained earnings shown in the balance sheet. In its simplest form, accumulated taxable income is equal to the firm's taxable income less dividends paid and accrued during the year, and less an **accumulated earnings credit.** The accumulated earnings credit equals the greater of (1) the profits for the year retained for reasonable business needs, and (2) $150,000 less the retained earnings shown in the balance sheet. Stated differently, the first $150,000 accumulated earnings during a firm's life is not subject to the penalty tax.

Example. Assume a corporation had $225,000 in taxable income in 1978 and paid dividends during the year of $25,000. Its retained earnings, as shown in the balance sheet at the end of 1977, were $70,000. As computed in Table 2-8, the *accumulated taxable income* is $120,000. Notice that the automatic accumulated earnings credit of $150,000 is now com-

Table 2-8 ACCUMULATED TAXABLE INCOME

Taxable income		$225,000
Less:		
Dividends paid	$25,000	
Accumulated earnings credit is the greater of:		
1. Actual business needs	(Assume none)	
2. Unused cumulative retained earnings		
Maximum cumulative credit	$150,000	
Retained earnings at the end of the prior year	70,000	
Unused accumulated earnings credit	$80,000	
Total credits		105,000
Accumulated taxable income		$120,000

pletely exhausted. If any credit is to be realized in future years, management must be able to justify its retention policy in terms of the firm's reasonable business needs.

Based upon the accumulated taxable income, the actual tax may now be calculated. The rate of the penalty is $27\frac{1}{2}$ percent on the first $100,000 and $38\frac{1}{2}$ percent on any amount exceeding the $100,000. In this example, the accumulated earnings tax would be $35,200, computed as follows:

$$\$100,000 \times 27\tfrac{1}{2}\% = \$27,500$$
$$\$\ 20,000 \times 38\tfrac{1}{2}\% = \underline{\ \ \ 7,700}$$
$$\underline{\$35,200}$$

SUBCHAPTER S CORPORATION

The tax considerations in deciding between the sole proprietorship or partnership and the corporation are important. As already suggested, the owners attempt to select the form of business organization that maximizes their *after-tax* returns. To minimize the tax influence upon the decision, Congress established the **Subchapter S Corporation,** which enables a corporation to be taxed as a partnership. This provision eliminates the "double taxation" effect of the corporation. The Subchapter S Corporation files a tax return for information purposes only and pays no taxes. The profits from the business are taxed at the stockholder level, whether or not the earnings are distributed to the owners. However, to qualify as a Subchapter S Corporation, the following requirements must be met:

1. The firm must be a domestic corporation, with no more than 80 percent of its gross sales coming from outside the United States.
2. There may be no more than 10 shareholders at the beginning of the corporation's life. However, after five years of existence, there may be as many as 15 stockholders.
3. All shareholders must be individuals as opposed to corporations, partnerships, or trusts.
4. The corporation cannot be a member of an affiliated group eligible to file a consolidated tax return with another corporation. Eligibility for two firms filing a consolidated return normally requires that 80 percent of the stock of one company is owned by the other corporation.
5. No more than 20 percent of the gross revenues is to be from interest, dividends, rents, royalties, and capital gains.

Thus, only small to moderate-sized firms typically can satisfy the Subchapter S Corporation requirements. However, if the qualifications can be met, the company may potentially receive the benefits of being a corporation while being taxed as a partnership.

Taxes play an important role in financial decision making. Hardly a decision is made by the financial manager without consideration of the impact of taxes. In general, the tax consequences in each of the functional areas of the financial executive are important. As we examine these functions later in the text, we shall recognize the tax-related influences. In fact, a complete understanding of these tax consequences is not feasible until the underlying financial principles have been presented. However, while the tax legislation is still fresh in the reader's mind, a brief integration of taxes into the three primary functional areas of the financial manager should be helpful.

TAXES AND CAPITAL INVESTMENT DECISIONS

As will be explained in more depth later, income taxes are a significant element in evaluating the firm's investment decisions. When the company is analyzing the possible acquisition of a plant or equipment, the returns from the investment should be measured on an after-tax basis. Otherwise, the company will be omitting an important variable. For example, suppose management is considering the purchase of production equipment costing $1000. If the $1000 is spent, the financing of the expenditure must come from *after-tax dollars*. Stated differently, the firm may keep this $1000 without having to be concerned about any tax consequences. However, if the capital is expended on a capital project (plant or equipment), a portion of the cash inflows to be received from the investment will be taxed. Ignoring the time value of money, assume the project, if accepted, is expected to generate $1200 in *cash inflows before taxes,* which at first might appear to be satisfactory. However, this $1200 is *before-tax dollars,* which simply means that the firm has not paid the taxes that will be owed as a result of receiving these funds. If the company eventually has to pay $300 in taxes, only $900 will be received in *after-tax cash flows,* which is the amount directly comparable with the $1000 investment cost. Clearly the project is undesirable, but the taxes had to be included in the analysis before this fact could be determined.

In computation of the taxes resulting from an investment decision, two related issues affect the timing and the amount of cash flow after taxes. First, the depreciation method will have an impact upon the timing of taxes. Although the *total amount* of taxes is not altered, the use of accelerated depreciation, as opposed to straight-line depreciation, does result in lower taxable profits in the earlier years of the project's life and larger profits in later years. In this manner, less taxes are paid in the initial years with counterbalancing higher taxes in later years. If the time value of money is recognized, this shift in taxes to later time periods is beneficial by increasing the cash flows to the firm in earlier years.

A second factor that may have a tax impact is the estimated **salvage value** of a capital expenditure. The greater the anticipated salvage value, the less the amount of annual depreciation charges. As a result, the taxable operating profits in each year would increase; however, a larger cash inflow should occur in the terminal year of the investment life. Also, if the asset is sold exactly for the originally estimated salvage value, no tax consequence arises. To illustrate, presume that a capital investment costs $10,000 and management assigns an economic life of five years and a projected $2000 salvage value. If in five years the asset is depreciated to a book value of $2000 and sold at that time for $2000, no gain or loss occurs and no tax liability occurs. However, if the project is sold in five years for $3000, the $1000 gain will be taxed as ordinary income. Conversely, if the asset is actually salvaged only at $1000, a loss of $1000 is reported for tax purposes, which will be considered to be an operating loss rather than a capital loss.

TAXES AND THE FIRM'S CAPITAL STRUCTURE

The second major policy variable for the financial manager is to determine the appropriate mix between debt and equity financing. Extensive controversy on this issue has continued for well over two decades. However, regardless of the different views maintained, the tax laws are observed to give debt financing a definite cost advantage over preferred stock and common stock. As already noted, *interest payments are a tax-deductible expense, while dividend payments both to preferred stockholders and to common stockholders may not be used as deductions in computing a corporation's taxable profits.*

TAXES AND CORPORATE DIVIDEND POLICIES

The importance of taxes with respect to the firm's dividend policy is recognized primarily at the common stockholder level rather than at the corporate level. However, since the financial manager's objective is to maximize the common stockholder's wealth, the impact of taxes upon the shareholder is important. Remember that the corporate earnings are taxed, whether or not the earnings are paid out in dividends or retained to be reinvested. Yet, if the dividends are paid, the investor will be required to record this income as ordinary income and be taxed accordingly. On the other hand, if the profits are retained and reinvested, the price of the company's stock should increase. The stock may then be sold, with the shareholder being taxed at the lower capital gains rate. Hence, this differential tax treatment for the firm's common investors might influence their preference between capital gains and dividends. In turn, this preference may affect the corporation's dividend policy.

Financial management should be aware of the external influences affecting the company. An important part of this overall environment is the legal atmosphere existing for the firm. This chapter has examined two key elements: the legal forms of business organization and the tax structure.

Legal Forms of Organization

The sole proprietorship is a business operation owned and managed by a single individual. The initiation of this form of business is extremely simple and generally does not involve any substantial organizational costs. The proprietor has complete control of the firm but must be willing to assume full responsibility for the outcome.

The general partnership, which is simply a coming together of two or more individuals, is quite similar to the sole proprietorship. The limited partnership has been created by states to permit all but one of the partners to have limited liability if agreeable to all partners.

The corporation has served to increase the flow of capital from the investment public to the business community. Although larger organizational costs and regulations are imposed upon this legal entity, the corporation is more conducive to raising large amounts of capital. Limited liability, continuity of life, and ease of transfer in ownership, which increases the marketability of the investment, have contributed greatly in attracting large numbers of investors into the business. The formal control of the corporation is vested in the parties having the greatest number of shares. However, the day-to-day operations are determined by the corporate officers, who theoretically serve in behalf of the common stockholders.

Taxes

Several forms of taxation exist; however, the primary tax concern in a business relates to income taxation. The objective of income taxes from a national perspective is threefold: (1) to provide a revenue source for the government, (2) to achieve socially desirable goals, and (3) to facilitate economic stability. In implementing the tax structure three taxable entities exist: the individual, including partnerships, the corporation, and the fiduciary. Since the fiduciary has little relationship to the business setting, no information on this entity has been given here.

INDIVIDUAL TAXPAYER

In measuring taxable income for the individual, all gross income less certain exclusions must be recognized. From this amount, the taxpayer calculates adjusted gross income by deducting certain expenses, such as those incurred in a business or profession, employee-related expenses, and losses from the sale of property. From adjusted gross income, deductions may be taken for particular personal expenses—primarily for medical expenses, contributions to qualified charitable organizations, taxes, interest, and casualty and theft losses. Also, special tax treatment is given to capital gains and losses, with long-term capital gains receiving a tax advantage.

CORPORATE TAXPAYER

For the most part, the taxable income for the corporation is determined in the same manner as for individuals. However, the personal deductions allowed the individual do not exist for the corporate entity. Also special deductions are permitted for the corporation, including income exclusions of (1) 85 percent of the dividends received from another corporation, and (2) certain income received from foreign countries. Contributions, not to exceed 5 percent of the taxable income, may also be taken. A corporation's long-term capital gains and losses are subject to a different maximum tax rate than for the individual, that being 30 percent. If the Internal Revenue Service considers the corporation to be retaining unreasonable amounts of earnings within the business, an accumulated earnings tax may be imposed. To minimize the tax influence in selecting the form of legal organization, a corporation may choose to be a Subchapter S Corporation and be taxed as a partnership, provided certain qualifications can be satisfied.

Tax consequences have a direct bearing upon the decisions of the financial manager. The relationships result from the taxability of investment income and from the difference in tax treatment for interest expense and dividend payments. Also, shareholders' tax status may influence their preference between capital gains and dividends, which may influence the corporate dividend policy.

Taxes and Financial Decision Making

STUDY QUESTIONS

2-1. Define (a) sole proprietorship, (b) partnership, and (c) corporation.

2-2. Identify the primary characteristics of each form of legal organization.

2-3. Distinguish between the articles of incorporation, the charter, and the corporate bylaws.

2-4. Using the following criteria, specify the legal form of business that is favored: (a) organizational requirements and costs, (b) liability of the owners, (c) continuity of business, (d) transferability of ownership, (e) management control and regulations, (f) capability to raise capital, and (g) income taxes.

2-5. Explain the concept of *adjusted gross income* for the individual.

2-6. Define a capital gain and a capital loss. Distinguish between the tax treatment for capital gains and ordinary income.

2-7. Does a partnership pay taxes on its income? Explain.

2-8. When a corporation receives a dividend from another corporation, how is it taxed?

2-9. Define a Western Hemisphere Trade Corporation. What are the tax consequences of this arrangement?

2-10. A corporation is taxed at a relatively low tax rate for the first $50,000 in income. After the initial $50,000, the tax rate is 48 percent. What prevents a corporation from dividing itself into numerous small corporations to take advantage of the initial low tax rates?

2-11. Distinguish between the capital gain and loss treatment for an individual taxpayer and for a corporate taxpayer.

2-12. What is the purpose of the *net operating deduction?*

2-13. What is the rationale for an *accumulated earnings tax?*

2-14. What is the purpose of the Subchapter S Corporation? In general, what type of firm would qualify as a Subchapter S Corporation?

2-1. Mike Phillips is employed as a financial analyst by the Buy Hi–Sell Lo Investment Corporation. He is married and has two children. His salary this past year was $24,000. In addition, he and his wife owned investments jointly which provided $1400 in dividends and $1800 in interest. The Phillipses had church contributions of $2500. Interest expense on a personal loan during the year amounted to $750. Compute Phillips' taxable income and the tax liability for the year.

2-2. Earl "Boo" Arnold is a professional football player. He receives a salary of $60,000 plus a season bonus of $10,000. In addition, during the off season he works in the promotion department for E. H. Hamilton, Inc., for which he receives $20,000. He recently sold 100 shares of stock for $10,000; he purchased the stock for $8000 two years ago. During the year he contributed $5000 to charitable institutions. He also incurred $2000 in travel expenses related to his work. Recognizing that Arnold is single, compute his taxable income and the tax liability.

2-3. The A. V. Cooper Corporation had sales of $2 million this past year. Its cost of goods sold was $1.2 million and the operating expenses were $400,000. Interest expenses on outstanding debts were $100,000, and the company paid $50,000 in preferred stock dividends. The corporation received $10,000 in preferred stock dividends and interest income of $12,000. The firm sold stock for $40,000 that had been owned for two years; the original cost of the stock was $30,000. Determine the corporation's taxable income and its tax liability.

2-4. Guinn, Inc., has a chain of fast-food restaurants. The firm has been operating for eight years, during which the profits have fluctuated significantly. The taxable income for the past eight years is shown below. Compute the tax payments and refunds for each year.

| 1972 | $(50,000) | 1974 | 150,000 |
| 1973 | 25,000 | 1975 | (225,000) |

| 1976 | $ 50,000 | 1978 | 200,000 |
| 1977 | 150,000 | 1979 | (50,000) |

2-5. The Shelby Standlee Corporation is a regional International Harvester dealer. The firm sells new and used trucks and is actively involved in the parts business. During the most recent year the company generated sales of $3 million. The combined cost of goods sold and the operating expenses were $2.1 million. Also, $400,000 in interest expense was paid during the year. The firm received $6000 during the year in dividend income from 1000 shares of common stock that had been purchased three years previously. However, the stock was sold toward the end of the year for $100 per share; its initial cost was $80 per share. The company also sold land that had been recently purchased and had been held for only six months. The selling price was $50,000; the cost was $45,000. Calculate the corporation's tax liability.

2-6. Sales for L. B. Menielle, Inc., during the past year amount to $5 million. The firm provides parts and supplies for oil field service companies. Gross profits for the year were $3 million. Operating expenses totaled $1 million. The interest and dividend income from securities owned were $20,000 and $25,000, respectively. The firm's interest expense was $100,000. The firm sold securities on two occasions during the year, receiving a gain of $40,000 on the first sale but losing $50,000 on the second. The stock sold first had been owned for four years; the stock sold second had been purchased six months prior to the sale. Compute the corporation's tax liability.

2-7. The taxable income for J. Bryant, Inc., for the past seven years is given below. From the information provided, determine the firm's tax payments and tax refunds in each year.

1973	$25,000	1977	$(125,000)
1974	(75,000)	1978	(20,000)
1975	100,000	1979	80,000
1976	50,000		

2-8. The C. Hunt Association made six investments that qualify for investment tax credit. Their amounts and depreciable lives are provided below. Calculate the tax credit the firm should receive for making these investments.

INVESTMENT	COST	DEPRECIABLE LIFE
A	$100,000	3 years
B	200,000	3 years
C	50,000	6 years
D	125,000	3 years
E	25,000	12 years
F	100,000	4 years

2-9. C. Mullican, Inc., reported taxable profits in 1978 of $250,000. From these profits $40,000 in dividends were paid to the common stockholders. At the beginning of the year the firm had $120,000 in retained earnings. Management anticipates that required investments for the forthcoming year should approximate $60,000. What accumulated earnings tax might the federal government be expected to impose?

SELECTED REFERENCES

BITTKER, BORIS I., and JAMES S. EUSTICE, *Federal Income Taxation of Corporations and Shareholders*. Boston: Warren Gorham and Lamont, 1971.

CORLEY, R. N., and R. L. BLACK, JR., *The Legal Environment of Business*, 2nd ed., Chap. 7. New York: McGraw Hill, 1968.

DAVIES, ROBERT M., and MELVIN H. LAWRENCE, *Choosing a Form of Business Organization*. Durham N. C.: Duke University Law School, 1963.

HOLZMAN, R. S., *Tax Basis for Managerial Decision*. New York: Holt, Rinehart and Winston, 1968.

NATIONAL INDUSTRIAL CONFERENCE BOARD, *Organizing and Managing the Corporate Finance Functions*, Studies in Business Policy, No. 129, New York, 1969.

1978 Federal Tax Course. New York: Commerce Clearing House, 1977.

1978 Federal Tax Course. Englewood Cliffs, N. J.: Prentice-Hall, Inc., 1977.

SOMMERFELD, R. M., *Federal Taxes and Management Decisions*. Homewood, Ill.: Richard D. Irwin, Inc., 1976.

SMITH, DAN THROOP, *Tax Factors in Business Decisions*. Englewood Cliffs, N. J.: Prentice-Hall, Inc., 1968.

Tax Reform Act of 1976—Law and Explantion. Chicago: Commerce Clearing House, Inc., 1976.

BASIC TOOLS OF FINANCIAL ANALYSIS, PLANNING, AND CONTROL

Financial Analysis

*F*inancial analysis involves the assessment of a firm's past, present, and anticipated future financial condition. The objective is to identify any *weaknesses* in the firm's *financial health* that could lead to future problems and to determine any *strengths* that the firm might capitalize upon. For example, an internal financial analysis might be aimed at assessing the firm's liquidity or measuring its past performance. Alternatively, financial analysis may come from outside the firm in an effort to determine the firm's creditworthiness or investment potential. Regardless of the origins of the analysis, the tools used are basically the same.

Financial ratios comprise the principal tool of financial analysis, since they can be used to answer a variety of questions regarding a firm's financial well-being. For example, a commercial bank loan officer considering an application for a six-month loan might want to know whether the applicant firm is solvent or liquid, a potential investor in the firm's common stock might wish to know how profitable the firm has been, and an internal financial analyst might want to know whether the firm can reasonably afford to borrow all or part of the funds needed to finance a planned expansion. Answers to these and related questions can be obtained through the use of financial ratios.

We begin our discussion of financial analysis with an overview of the firm's basic financial statements. These include the balance sheet, income statement, and statement of changes in financial condition (source and use of funds statement). The next step is to survey a set of key financial ratios that can be used to assess the firm's financial condition.

Three **financial statements** are generally used to depict the financial status of a firm. These statements provide the raw material for the financial analyst, and they must be fully understood before any meaningful analysis can be undertaken.[1]

The **balance sheet** represents a statement of the financial position of the firm on a given date, including its asset holdings, liabilities, and owner-supplied capital. Assets represent the resources owned by the firm, whereas liabilities and owner's equity indicate how those resources were financed. Table 3-1 gives an example balance sheet for Jimco, Inc., as of December 31, 1978. Jimco had $30,802,000 in assets, which it financed with $10,809,000 in current (short-term) liabilities, $10,647,000 in noncurrent (long-term) liabilities, and $9,346,000 in owner-supplied funds.

LIMITATIONS OF THE BALANCE SHEET

Although a firm's balance sheet might be prepared within guidelines of generally accepted accounting practice,[2] the analyst must be aware of certain limitations of the statement. Some of the more obvious are listed below:

1. The balance sheet does not reflect current value, because accountants have adopted historical cost as the basis for valuing and reporting assets and liabilities.[3]
2. Estimates must be used to determine the level of several accounts. Examples include accounts receivable estimated in terms of collectibility; inventories

[1]Two appendices have been added to this chapter for those desiring a brief accounting review. Appendix 3-A is a review of the fundamental accounting practices underlying financial statement preparation, and Appendix 3-B is a glossary of accounting terminology.

[2]The sources of accounting principles are many; however, the main contributors certainly have been The Opinions of the Accounting Principles Board (APB), which was created by the American Institute of Certified Public Accountants (AICPA), and since 1973 the Financial Accounting Standards of the Financial Accounting Standards Board (FASB).

[3]There has been some interest among those in the accounting profession to adjust the cost basis of the firm's assets through the use of an index of the general price level. One such index is the "Gross National Product Implicit Price Deflator" issued quarterly by the Office of Business Economics of the Department of Commerce. However, the general policy statement provided by "Opinion 6" of the Accounting Principles Board of the Institute of Certified Public Accountants recommends that accounting statements be prepared and maintained on a cost basis. On March 23, 1976 the Securities and Exchange Commission issued A.S.R. 190 which requires the disclosure of replacement cost information for certain very large firms. This represents a first step away from strict adherence to the historical cost principle.

Table 3-1

JIMCO, INC.
Balance Sheet
December 31, 1978
(Thousands of Dollars)

Assets

Current assets	
Cash	$ 1,378
Marketable securities—at cost	276
(market value, $320)	
Accounts receivable	9,921
Inventories	12,217
Prepaid expenses	247
Total current assets	$24,039
Noncurrent assets (Tangible assets)	
Investments	1,720
Plant and equipment	12,261
Less: Accumulated depreciation	7,638
Net plant and equipment	$ 4,623
Other assets (Intangible assets)	
Patents[a]	420
Total Assets	$30,802

Liabilities and Owner's Equity

Current liabilities	
Accounts payable	$ 3,418
Notes payable, 9%, due March 1, 1979	3,788
Accrued salaries, wages, and other expenses	3,110
Current portion of long-term debt	493
Total current liabilities	$10,809
Noncurrent liabilities	
Deferred income taxes	1,447
First mortgage bonds, 7%, due January 1, 1992	6,300
Debentures, 8½%, due June 30, 1988	2,900
Total noncurrent liabilities	$10,647
Owner's equity	
Common stock (par value $1.00)	$ 100
Additional paid-in capital	2,000
Retained earnings	7,246
Total owner's equity	$ 9,346
Total liabilities and owner's equity	$30,802

[a]Patent acquired on December 15, 1977, for $420,000.

based on salability; and noncurrent tangible and intangible assets based on useful life.[4]

3. The depreciation of long-term assets is accepted practice; however, appreciation or enhancement in asset values is generally ignored.[5] This is particularly crucial to firms holding large investments in appreciable assets such as land, timberlands, and mining properties.

4. Many items that have financial value are omitted from the balance sheet because they involve extreme problems of objective evaluation. The most obvious example consists of the human resources of the firm.[6]

The analyst can do little in most cases to alleviate these shortcomings; however, he should at least be aware of their existence so that he can temper his analysis accordingly.

The **income statement** represents an attempt to measure the net results of the firm's operations over a specified interval such as one quarter or one year. The income statement (sometimes referred to as a **profit and loss statement**) is compiled on an *accrual* rather than a *cash basis*. This means that an attempt is made to match the firm's revenues from the period's operations with the expenses incurred in generating those revenues. Thus, the reported revenues and expenses need not represent actual cash flows for the period, so that the computed net earnings for the period do not equal the actual cash provided by the firm's operations. A condensed income statement for the year ended December 31, 1978, is provided in Table 3-2 for Jimco, Inc.

NET INCOME AND CASH FLOW

There are two basic reasons why the firm's net income does not equal net cash flow for the period. First, revenues and expenses are included in the income statement even though no cash flow might have occurred. For example, sales revenues consist of credit as well as cash sales. Furthermore, cash collections from prior period credit sales are not reflected in the current period's sales revenues. In addition, the expenses for the period rep-

[4]In "Opinion 20" the Accounting Principles Board states that preparing financial statements requires estimating the effects of future events. Examples of items for which estimates are necessary include uncollectible receivables, inventory obsolescence, service lives and salvage values of depreciable assets, warranty costs, periods benefited by a defined cost, and recoverable mineral reserves. Since future events cannot be perceived with certainty, estimating requires the exercise of judgment. The implication here is that no reference guidelines can be constructed regarding these estimates; thus subjectivity enters in determining the affected accounts.

[5]The Internal Revenue Service has set forth asset depreciation range (useful life) guidelines to be used under the Asset Depreciation Range (ADR) election in computing depreciation for tax purposes. Furthermore, these guidelines are often used to compute depreciation for financial statement purposes. See Section 167(m)(1) of the Internal Revenue Code.

[6]The subject of human resource accounting has received increased attention in recent years. For an overview of the subject see Edwin H. Caplan and Stephen Landeckich, *Human Resource Accounting: Past, Present and Future* (National Association of Accountants, 1974) and Eric Flamholtz, *Human Resource Accounting* (Dickinson Publishing Company, Inc., 1974).

Table 3-2

JIMCO, INC.
Statement of Income
for the Year Ended December 31, 1978
(Thousands of Dollars)

Net sales	$51,224
Cost of goods sold	38,162
Gross profit	$13,062
Operating expenses	
Selling expenses	3,100
General and administrative expense^a	5,351
Net operating income	$ 4,611
Interest expense	1,237
Net income before taxes	$ 3,374
Federal income taxes	1,606
Net income (earnings available to common stockholders)	$ 1,768
Common dividends	150
Change in retained earnings	$ 1,618
Number of shares outstanding	100,000
Earnings per share	$17.68
Dividends per share	$1.50

^aDepreciation expense for the period was $498,000 and is included in the $5,351,000 of general administrative expense.

resent all those expenditures made in the process of generating the period's revenues. Thus, wages, salaries, utilities, and other expenses may not be paid during the period in which they are *recognized* in the income statement. Second, certain expenses included within the income statement are not cash expenses at all. For example, depreciation expense does not involve a cash outflow to the firm, yet it is deducted from revenues for the period in computing net income. Other examples of noncash expenses include the amortization of goodwill, patent rights, and bond discounts.

The **statement of changes in financial position** (often referred to as a **source and use of funds statement**) provides an accounting for the resources provided during a specific period and the uses to which they were put. Specifically, the source and use statement provides the basis for answering such questions as:

Statement of Changes in Financial Position

1. Where did the profits go?
2. Why were the dividends not larger?
3. Why was money borrowed during the period?
4. How was the expansion in plant and equipment financed?
5. How was the retirement of debt accomplished?
6. What became of the proceeds of the bond issue?

Because of the very useful information found in the source and use statement it has become a standard tool of financial analysis, as well as one of the firm's three basic financial statements.[7]

No single format is universally adopted for the source and use of funds statement. The statement form used here is as follows:

> Cash: Beginning balance
> Plus: Sources of cash for the period
> Minus: Uses of cash for the period
> Cash: Ending cash balance

Thus, the source and use statement *explains* the changes that took place in the firm's cash balance over the period of interest. Note that funds are defined as cash, such that the two terms can be used interchangeably.

SOURCES OF FUNDS

The firm can obtain funds from one of four principal sources: (1) by its operations (commonly referred to as funds provided by operations); (2) by borrowing (by means of either a short-term note payable or long-term debt in the form of a bond issue); (3) by the sale of assets, and (4) by issuing common or preferred stock. The firm's sources of funds (with the exception of funds provided by operations) are identified by observing changes in the firm's balance sheet between the beginning and ending of the period for which the statement is being prepared. For example, a decrease in accounts receivable over the period would signal that the firm collected more dollars from its credit accounts than it created through new credit sales; hence this was a source of funds. In general a decrease in an asset balance denotes a source of funds. Furthermore, an increase in a liability account signals that net additional borrowing took place during the period, thus providing a source of funds to the firm. An increase in the common and preferred stock accounts also indicates sources of funds to the firm. Finally, funds provided by operations are found by summing net income for the period and any noncash expenses (such as depreciation and amortizations of goodwill or bond discount). Noncash expenses are deducted from the firm's revenues, since they are tax deductible. However, since no cash changes hands for these noncash expenses, they must be added back to net income to measure the firm's funds provided by operations.

USES OF FUNDS

A firm uses funds to purchase assets, repay loans, repurchase outstanding shares of its common and preferred stock, and pay cash dividends to preferred and common stockholders. Thus, uses of funds are just the opposite of the sources discussed earlier.

---

[7]Opinion 19 of the Accounting Principles Board indicates that the source and use statement should accompany the income statement and balance sheet as a basic financial statement. It also specifies that the statement be entitled The Statement of Changes in Financial Position.

Jimco's comparative balance sheets for 1977 and 1978 are given in Table 3-3. These statements, along with Jimco's 1978 income statement (Table 3-2), provide all the information needed to prepare the firm's statement of sources and uses of funds for the year ended December 31, 1978.

The column entitled *changes* in Table 3-3 conveniently provides the basis for determining Jimco's sources and uses of funds. Cash decreased by $134,000 during the year. This change in cash is *explained* by the statement of sources and uses of funds. Thus it can be ignored for the time being. Marketable securities did not change; thus no source or use of funds was provided. The accounts receivable balance increased by $981,000, indicating that more credit sales were made during the period than were collected. Hence, the firm *used* funds to invest in accounts receivable. Likewise, inventories and prepaid expenses increased by $566,000 and $86,000, respectively, indicating uses of funds. In addition, Jimco increased plant and equipment by $1,052,000, which constitutes still another use of funds.[8] Note that the increase in accumulated depreciation of $498,000 equals depreciation expense for the period. Since depreciation expense is included in the source and use statement in conjunction with our analysis of the firm's income statement, we will defer considering this item until later.

Looking at the changes in the firm's liabilities, accounts payable decreased by $793,000. Thus, the firm paid off more accounts payable than it created during the year. This constitutes a use of funds. Notes payable increased by $2,931,000, signaling a source of funds from short-term borrowing. The accrued salaries, wages, and other expense accounts decreased during the period, which indicates a use of funds. Deferred income taxes, first mortgage bonds, and debenture bonds all decreased for the period, such that uses of $28,000, $300,000, and $193,000, respectively, were recognized.

The common stock accounts (common stock at par and paid-in-capital) did not change for the period, indicating no new stock was issued and none was repurchased. Jimco's retained earnings increased by $1,618,000. This represents the net income for 1978 of $1,768,000 less common stock dividends of $150,000. Since net income is included as a source of funds as a part of funds provided by operations and dividends are accounted for as a use of funds, the change in the retained earnings

---

[8]The use of funds attributed to the purchase of plant and equipment can also be obtained from an analysis of the change in the net plant and equipment account. For Jimco, Inc., this can be accomplished as follows:

Net plant and equipment (1978)	$4623
Plus: Depreciation expense for the period	498
	5121
Less: Net plant and equipment (1977)	(4069)
Net purchase (sale) of plant and equipment	$1052

Table 3-3

JIMCO, INC.
Comparative Balance Sheets
December 31, 1977 and 1978
(Thousands of Dollars)

Assets	1977	1978	CHANGES
Current assets			
Cash	$ 1,512	$ 1,378	$ (134)
Marketable securities	276	276	—
Accounts receivable	8,940	9,921	981
Inventories	11,651	12,217	566
Prepaid expenses	161	247	86
Total current assets	$22,540	$24,039	$1,499
Noncurrent assets			
Investments	1,720	1,720	—
Plant and equipment	11,209	12,261	1,052
Less: Accumulated depreciation	7,140	7,638	498
Net plant and equipment	$ 4,069	$ 4,623	$ 554
Other assets			
Patents	—	420	420
Total assets	$28,329	$30,802	$2,473

Liabilities and Owner's Equity	1977	1978	CHANGES
Current liabilities			
Accounts payable	$ 4,211	$ 3,418	$ (793)
Notes payable	857	3,788	2,931
Accrued salaries, wages, and other expenses	3,872	3,110	(762)
Current portion of long-term debt	493	493	—
Total current liabilities	9,433	10,809	1,376
Noncurrent liabilities			
Deferred income taxes	1,475	1,447	(28)
First mortgage bonds	6,600	6,300	(300)
Debenture bonds	3,093	2,900	(193)
Total noncurrent liabilities	$11,168	$10,647	$ (521)
Owner's equity			
Common stock (par value $1.00)	100	100	—
Additional paid-in capital	2,000	2,000	—
Retained earnings	5,628	7,246	1,618
Total owner's equity	$ 7,728	$ 9,346	$1,618
Total liabilities and owner's equity	$28,329	$30,802	$2,473

account is not used directly in preparing the source and use of funds statement.

Table 3-4 contains Jimco's statement of sources and uses of funds for the year ended December 31, 1978. Note that Jimco's sources of funds were from operations (44%) and notes payable (56%). The firm's principal uses of funds related to the purchase of plant and equipment (20%); increases in its investment in accounts receivable (18%) and inventories (11%); and reductions in accounts payable (15%) and accrued expenses (14%). *Thus, the source and use of funds statement provides the analyst with a useful tool for determining where the firm obtained cash during a prior period and how that cash was spent.*

FINANCIAL RATIOS

Financial ratios give the analyst a way of making meaningful comparisons of a firm's financial data at different points in time and with other firms. For example, the inventories for a firm with $10,000,000 in annual sales would be expected to be larger than those for a comparable firm with sales of only $5,000,000. However, the ratio of sales to inventory might well

Table 3-4

JIMCO, INC.
Statement of Sources and Uses of Funds
for the Year Ended December 31, 1978
(Thousands of Dollars)

Cash balance (December 31, 1977)		$1512	
Sources of funds			
Funds provided by operations:			
Net income	$1768		
Depreciation	498	2266	44%
Increase in notes payable		2931	56%
Total funds provided		$5197	100%
Uses of funds			
Common stock dividends		150	3%
Purchase of plant and equipment		1052	20%
Increase in accounts receivable		981	18%
Increase in inventories		566	11%
Increase in prepaid expenses		86	2%
Purchase of patent rights		420	8%
Decrease in accounts payable		793	15%
Decrease in accrued salaries, wages, and other expenses		762	14%
Decrease in deferred income taxes		28	—[a]
Decrease in mortgage bonds		300	5%
Decrease in debenture bonds		193	4%
Total uses of funds		$5331	100%
Cash balance (December 31, 1978)		$1378	

[a]Less than 1 percent of total uses of funds for the period.

be similar for the two firms. *Thus, financial ratios represent an attempt to standardize financial information so as to facilitate meaningful comparisons.*

Specifically, financial ratios provide the basis for answering some very important questions concerning the financial *well-being* of the firm. Examples include the following:

1. *How liquid is the firm?* Liquidity refers to the firm's ability to meet maturing obligations and to convert assts into cash. This factor is particularly important to the firm's creditors.
2. *Is management generating sufficient profits from the firm's assets?* Since the primary purpose for purchasing an asset is to produce profits, the analyst often seeks an indication of the adequacy of the profits being realized. If the level of profits appears insufficient in relation to the investment, an investigation into the reasons for the inferior returns is in order.
3. *How does the firm's management finance its investments?* These decisions have direct impact upon the returns provided to the common stockholders.
4. *Are the common stockholders receiving sufficient returns on their investment?* The objective of the financial manager is to maximize the value of the firm's common stock, and the level of returns being received by the investors relative to their investment is a key factor in determining that value.

The mathematical skills required in ratio analysis are quite low. However, using and interpreting financial ratios to answer questions such as those stated above requires a great deal of skill and a thorough understanding of the tools of financial analysis. The balance of this chapter will be devoted to a discussion of financial ratios and their use in financial analysis.

Using Financial Ratios

Financial ratios provide useful tools for analysis when compared against a standard or norm. Two such norms are commonly used. The first consists of similar ratios for the same firm from previous financial statements. An analysis based upon comparisons of this type is commonly referred to as a **trend analysis.** A second norm comes from the ratios of other firms that are considered comparable in their general characteristics to the subject firm—generally this involves the use of published industry average ratios.

There are two widely used sources of industry average ratios. Dun and Bradstreet publishes annually a set of 14 key ratios for each of 125 lines of business. Robert Morris Associates, the national association of bank loan and credit officers, publishes a set of 16 key ratios for over 300 lines of business. Table 3-5 gives an example of the Robert Morris standard ratios for the farm machinery and equipment manufacturing industry.

The ratio norms in Table 3-5 are classified by firm size so as to provide the basis for more meaningful comparisons. Thus, a firm with total assets of less than $1 million would not be compared with firms having a much larger asset base. Note also that **common size financial statements** are reported as well as the 16 key ratios. The common size balance sheet simply represents each asset, liability, and owner's equity account as a percent of total assets, whereas each entry in the income statement is stated as a percent of sales. Thus, ratios have been effectively related to each of the 17 entries in the balance sheet and six entries in the income statement. Furthermore, three levels are reported for each of the 16 key ratios. These refer to the first, second, and third quartiles. Thus, the analyst is given some idea as to how much variation exists within the industry in regard to each ratio.

For ease of presentation we shall discuss financial ratios in terms of three basic categories, each representing an important aspect of the firm's financial condition. The categories consist of liquidity, leverage, and profitability ratios. Each category is discussed through the use of an example set of financial ratios computed using the 1978 financial statements of Jimco, Inc. Jimco's balance sheet and income statement were presented in Tables 3-1 and 3-2, respectively.

Categories of Financial Ratios

Jimco, Inc., is involved in the manufacture and sale of light-duty garden tractors and implements. The firm has been in business for more than 20 years and is considered by its competitors to be well managed.

Liquidity ratios provide the basis for answering the question *Is the firm liquid?* In other words, does the firm have sufficient cash and near cash assets to pay its bills on time? Within this category of ratios two subcategories of financial ratios prove useful: measures of overall liquidity and measures of liquidity in specific assets.

Liquidity Ratios

OVERALL MEASURES OF LIQUIDITY

Current Ratio.   The **current ratio** is computed as follows:

$$\text{current ratio} = \frac{\text{current assets}}{\text{current liabilities}} \tag{3-1}$$

$$= \frac{\$24,039,000}{\$10,809,000}$$

$$= 2.22 \text{ times}$$

Thus, for 1978 Jimco's current assets were 2.22 times larger than its current liabilities. Although no firm plans to liquidate a major portion of its current assets to meet its maturing current liabilities, this ratio does indicate the margin of safety (the liquidity) of the firm.

Using the 1977 industry norms provided in Table 3-5, Jimco's current ratio is below the median industry ratio of 2.8. Note that Jimco has between $10 million and $50 million in total assets; thus the third-column figures are appropriate. However, Jimco's 2.22 current ratio falls well within range of the first and third quartile of 1.8 to 3.3 observed for its industry. Thus,

Table 3-5 ROBERT MORRIS AND ASSOCIATES INDUSTRY AVERAGE RATIOS, 1977

MANUFACTURERS		FARM MACHINERY & EQUIPMENT			
Asset Size Number of Statements[c]	0–250M[a] 3	250M–1MM[b] 22	1–10MM 67	10–50MM 19	ALL 111
Assets	%	%	%	%	%
Cash and equivalents		3.9	6.7	6.3	6.4
Accounts and notes receivable—trade (net)		19.1	20.2	23.7	22.4
Inventory		52.4	47.9	43.4	45.1
All other current		1.7	1.5	3.2	2.6
Total current		77.1	76.3	76.6	76.5
Fixed assets (net)		20.7	19.5	16.7	17.7
Intangibles (net)		.1	.9	2.2	1.7
All other noncurrent		2.1	3.3	4.5	4.1
Total		100.0	100.0	100.0	100.0
Liabilities					
Notes payable—short term		16.9	16.3	8.0	10.9
Current maturity—LTD		3.1	2.3	1.7	1.9
Accounts and notes payable—trade		13.3	10.3	11.8	11.3
Accrued expenses		8.2	6.0	5.4	5.7
All other current		2.2	5.5	8.0	7.0
Total current		43.6	40.4	34.9	36.9
Long-term debt		14.5	12.3	16.8	15.3
All other noncurrent		2.0	1.6	2.5	2.2
Net worth		39.9	45.7	45.8	45.7
Total liabilities and net worth		100.0	100.0	100.0	100.0
Income data					
Net sales		100.0	100.0	100.0	100.0
Cost of sales		73.2	73.1	73.3	73.2
Gross profit		26.8	26.9	26.7	26.8
Operating expenses		20.1	17.3	17.0	17.2
Operating profit		6.7	9.6	9.6	9.6
All other expenses (net)		1.0	1.9	2.0	2.0
Profit before taxes		5.7	7.7	7.6	7.6
Ratios[d]					
Current		2.3 1.9 1.4	2.4 1.8 1.4	3.3 2.8 1.8	2.8 1.9 1.4
Quick		.8 .6 .4	.9 .6 .4	1.6 1.1 .6	1.1 .6 .4
Sales/receivables[e]	17 33 48	20.9 11.0 7.6	23 15.9 39 9.3 60 6.1	43 8.4 53 6.9 70 5.2	23 15.7 39 9.3 58 6.3
Cost of sales/inventory[f]	96 126 183	3.8 2.9 2.0	99 3.7 135 2.7 192 1.9	118 3.1 152 2.4 192 1.9	96 3.8 130 2.8 192 1.9
Sales/working capital		4.2 6.0 11.0	3.5 5.1 9.4	2.8 3.5 3.7	3.5 4.8 9.5

Table 3-5   (cont.)

MANUFACTURERS	FARM MACHINERY & EQUIPMENT			
Asset Size Number of Statements[c]	0–250M[a] 3	250M–1MM[b] 22	1–10MM 67	10–50MM 19	ALL 111
EBIT/interest		7.5 4.5 1.8	7.6 3.8 1.6	5.5 3.5 2.3	6.8 3.8 1.8
Cash flow/current maturity of long term debt		9.6 3.0 1.5	13.3 4.3 1.4	12.3 5.5 2.4	12.2 4.3 1.7
Fixed assets/tangible net worth		.3 .5 .9	.3 .5 .9	.3 .3 .5	.3 .4 .8
Total debt/tangible net worth		1.0 1.6 2.2	.7 1.3 2.7	.6 1.3 1.9	.7 1.4 2.3
Profit before taxes/tangible net worth (%)		54.1 26.8 6.1	50.1 26.4 8.0	38.6 23.3 13.9	47.6 25.9 8.3
Profit before taxes/total assets (%)		17.1 11.5 2.3	20.3 10.3 2.8	15.0 10.5 4.7	20.0 10.3 2.9
Sales/net fixed assets		26.8 12.4 7.1	15.6 8.8 6.2	11.2 7.8 6.4	16.4 8.9 6.7
Sales/total assets		2.7 2.1 1.7	2.2 1.7 1.4	1.8 1.5 1.1	2.2 1.8 1.4
Depreciation, depletion, amortization/ sales (%)		1.0 1.4 2.0	1.1 1.7 2.3	1.1 1.9 2.2	1.1 1.7 2.2
Lease and rental expense/sales (%)		.5 1.0 1.5	.2 .4 1.1		.2 .6 1.2
Officers' compensation/sales (%)		2.5 3.8 7.2	.8 1.4 2.6		1.2 2.1 3.9
Net sales ($) Total assets ($)	1536M 426M	27582M 12777M	412504M 231868M	617972M 443265M	1059594M 688336M

[a]M = $ thousand.

[b]MM = $ million.

[c]When there are fewer than ten financial statements for a particular size category, the composite data are not shown in that category because such a small sample is usually not representative and could be misleading.

[d]Three ratio values are reported. The middle value is the median and represents the ratio falling halfway between the strongest ratio and the weakest ratio. The figure that falls halfway between the median and the strongest ratio is the upper quartile and the figure that falls halfway between the median and the weakest ratio is the lower quartile.

[e]The cols. in bold type are "day's receivables" or average collection period.

[f]The cols. in bold type are "day's inventory" or the average number of days that a dollar is held in inventory.

although Jimco's current ratio is below the median ratio for the industry, it does not appear to be substantially *out of line* with respect to many of the firms in its industry.

Acid Test or Quick Ratio. Since inventories are generally the least liquid of the firm's current assets, it may be desirable to remove them from the numerator of the current ratio, thus obtaining a more refined liquidity measure. For Jimco the **acid test ratio** is computed below:

$$\text{acid test ratio} = \frac{\text{current assets} - \text{inventories}}{\text{current liabilities}} \tag{3-2}$$

$$= \frac{\$11,822,000}{\$10,809,000}$$

$$= 1.09 \text{ times}$$

Again Jimco's acid test ratio is only slightly below the median ratio for its industry of 1.1. On the basis of its current and acid test ratios Jimco offers no visible evidence of a serious liquidity problem.

The next group of ratios provides the basis for assessing the liquidity of the firm's receivables and inventories.

MEASURES OF LIQUIDITY IN SPECIFIC ASSETS

In general, the liquidity of an asset is indicated in how quickly it can be converted into cash; this factor is expressed by a subcategory of liquidity ratios.

Average Collection Period. The **average collection period ratio** serves as the basis for determining how rapidly the firm's credit accounts are being collected. We can also think of this ratio in terms of *the number of daily credit sales contained in accounts receivable.* That is, the average collection period is equal to the accounts receivable balance divided by the firm's average daily credit sales. Computing the ratio for Jimco we find

$$\text{average collection period} = \frac{\text{accounts receivable}}{\text{annual credit sales}/360} \tag{3-3}$$

$$= \frac{\$9,921,000}{\$(51,224,000/360)} = 69.7 \text{ days}$$

Therefore, on average, Jimco collects its credit sales every 69.7 days.

The **accounts receivable turnover ratio** is often used in the place of the average collection period ratio. For Jimco this ratio would equal

$$\text{accounts receivable turnover} = \frac{\text{credit sales}}{\text{accounts receivable}} \qquad (3\text{-}4)$$

$$= \frac{\$51{,}224{,}000}{\$9{,}921{,}000} = 5.16 \text{ times}$$

Thus, Jimco is turning its accounts receivable over at a rate of 5.16 times per year. This easily translates into an average collection period of 69.7 days. That is, if Jimco's receivables turnover is 5.16 times in a 360-day year, then its average collection period must be 360/5.16 = 69.7 days.

The industry norm for the receivables turnover ratio is 6.9 times, which translates into an average collection period of 360/6.9 = 53 days. In terms of both standards Jimco does not compare favorably with the industry norm. In fact, Jimco's average collection period is roughly equal to the highest quartile (lowest in terms of receivable turnover) in the industry. This *could* indicate the presence of some slow-paying accounts, which calls for analysis in greater depth.[9] Before performing such an analysis it is necessary to know whether Jimco's credit terms are longer than those of other firms in the industry. For example, if Jimco allows its customers terms calling for payment in 75 days when 60 days is the norm for the industry, then the longer average collection period is to be expected.

Inventory Turnover. The liquidity of the firm's inventories is reflected in the number of times that its inventories are turned over (replaced) during the year. The **inventory turnover ratio** is defined as follows:

$$\text{inventory turnover} = \frac{\text{cost of goods sold}}{\text{inventories}} \qquad (3\text{-}5)$$

$$= \frac{\$38{,}162{,}000}{\$12{,}217{,}000}$$

$$= 3.12 \text{ times}$$

Thus, Jimco turns over its inventories 3.12 times per year.[10] Where quarterly or monthly information is available, an average inventory figure

---

[9]Although it will not be discussed here, one tool for further assessing the liquidity of a firm's receivables is an **aging of accounts receivable schedule.** Such a schedule identifies the number and dollar value of accounts outstanding for various periods. For example, accounts that are less than 10 days old, 11 to 20 days, and so forth might be examined. Still another way to construct the schedule would involve analyzing the length of time to eventual collection of accounts over a past period. For example, how many accounts were outstanding less than 10 days when collected, between 10 and 20 days, and so forth.

[10]Some analysts prefer the use of sales in the numerator of the inventory turnover ratio. However, cost of goods sold is used here, since inventories are stated at cost, and to use sales in the numerator would add a potential source of distortion to the ratio when comparisons are made across firms that have different "markups" on their cost of goods sold.

should be used in order to eliminate the influence of any seasonality in inventory levels from the ratio.

Jimco's inventory turnover compares very favorably with the industry norm of 2.4 times; in fact, it may even be a little too high, as it exceeds the third quartile of 3.10. Too high an inventory turnover could signal the possibility of being out of necessary materials and thus lost sales.

This concludes the discussion of liquidity ratios. Jimco compared favorably in all cases but one, the average collection period.

Leverage ratios provide the basis for answering two questions: *How has the firm financed its assets?* and *Can the firm afford the level of fixed charges associated with its use of non-owner-supplied funds?* The first answer is sought through the use of balance sheet leverage ratios, the second by using income statement based ratios or simply *coverage ratios*.

Leverage Ratios

It will be useful at this point to define **leverage.** As related to financial ratios the term will be used to mean financial leverage.[11] Financial leverage results when a firm obtains financing for its investments from sources other than the firm's owners. For a corporation this means funds from any source other than the common stockholders. Thus **financial leverage** will be defined here as resulting from the firm's use of debt financing, financial leases, and preferred stock. These sources of financing share a common characteristic: they all require a fixed cash payment or return for their use. That is, debt requires contractually set interest and principal payments, leases require fixed rental payments, and preferred stock usually requires a fixed cash dividend. This attribute provides the basis for the *leverage* in financial leverage. If the firm earns a return higher than that which is required by the suppliers of leverage funds, then the excess goes to the common stockholders. However, should the return earned fall below the required return, then the common stockholders must make up the difference out of the returns on their invested funds. This, in a nutshell, is the concept of financial leverage.

BALANCE SHEET LEVERAGE RATIOS

These ratios provide the basis for answering the question, *Where did the firm obtain the financing for its investments?* The caption **balance sheet leverage ratios** is used to indicate that these ratios are computed using information from the balance sheet alone.

Debt Ratio. The **debt ratio** measures the extent to which the total assets of the firm have been financed using borrowed funds. For Jimco the ratio is computed as follows:

[11]The concept of leverage is discussed more fully in Chapter 15.

$$\text{debt ratio} = \frac{\text{total liabilities}}{\text{total assets}} \quad \text{or}$$

$$\frac{\text{current liabilities} + \text{noncurrent liabilities}}{\text{total assets}} \qquad (3\text{-}6)$$

$$= \frac{\$(10,809,000 + 10,647,000)}{\$30,802,000}$$

$$= .697 \text{ or } 69.7\%$$

Thus, Jimco has financed approximately 70% of its assets with borrowed funds. This compares with only 54.2% for the industry. Note that this ratio is found by using the common size balance sheet in Table 3-5. Simply sum the percent of total assets financed by current liabilities, long-term debt, and all other noncurrent liabilities. Jimco has relied on the use of non-owner financing to a far greater extent than the average firm in its industry.

Long-Term Debt to Total Capitalization. The **long-term debt to total capitalization ratio** indicates the extent to which the firm has used long-term debt in its permanent financing. **Total capitalization** represents the sum of all the permanent sources of financing used by the firm, including long-term debt, preferred stock, and common equity. For Jimco the ratio is computed as follows:

$$\begin{array}{l}\text{long-term debt} \\ \text{to total capitalization}\end{array} = \frac{\begin{array}{c}\text{noncurrent liabilities or} \\ \text{long-term debt}\end{array}}{\begin{array}{c}\text{long-term debt} + \text{preferred stock} + \\ \text{common equity}\end{array}} \qquad (3\text{-}7)$$

$$= \frac{\$10,647,000}{\$(10,647,000 + 9,346,000)}$$

$$= .533 \text{ or } 53.3\%$$

Therefore, Jimco has obtained a little more than half of its permanent financing from debt sources.

Once again referring to the common size balance sheet in Table 3-5 for an industry norm, note that current liabilities account for 34.9 percent of total assets; thus permanent financing is equal to $(1 - .349)$ or 65.1 percent of total assets. Furthermore, long-term debt accounts for 16.8 percent of total assets; thus it accounts for $16.8/65.1 = 25.8$ percent of the firm's total capitalization. It is evident that Jimco utilizes far more long-term debt in its total capitalization than is characteristic of its industry.

One final point should be made concerning the balance sheet leverage ratios. This point concerns the importance of lease financing as a source of financial leverage. Since most firms do not include the value of long-term financial lease agreements in the assets and liabilities of the balance sheet, it is not possible to assess their impact on the firm's balance sheet leverage ratios.[12] Annual lease payments generally are contained in footnotes to the firm's financial statements; thus, their effect on the firm's coverage ratios, which are discussed next, can be assessed.

COVERAGE RATIOS

Coverage ratios are used to measure the firm's ability to cover the finance charges associated with its use of financial leverage. Thus, they provide the basis for answering the question, "Has the firm used too much financial leverage?"

Times Interest Earned Ratio. The **times interest earned ratio** measures the firm's ability to meet its interest payments out of its annual operating earnings. Jimco's ratio is computed as follows:

$$\text{times interest earned} = \frac{\text{net operating income or}}{\text{earnings before interest and taxes (EBIT)}} \quad (3\text{-}8)$$
$$\phantom{\text{times interest earned}} = \frac{\$4,611,000}{\$1,237,000}$$
$$\phantom{\text{times interest earned}} = 3.73 \text{ times}$$

This ratio is slightly less than the industry norm of 3.8 times, which is somewhat surprising in light of Jimco's higher-than-average use of financial leverage. However, it appears that Jimco's earnings are such that it can reasonably *afford* the higher use of financial leverage.

The times interest earned ratio, although very useful, has a number of potential weaknesses. First, net operating income (EBIT) does not reflect the total amount of earnings available to meet interest and other finance-related charges. Specifically, net operating income understates the amount of income available to meet finance charges by an amount equal to the firm's depreciation expense for the period.[13] Also, when rental expense is considered to be one of the firm's fixed finance charges, it too must be

[12]The Financial Accounting Standards Board issued Statement No. 13 in late 1976 which established that a lease that transfers substantially all of the benefits and risks incident to the ownership of property should be accounted for as an acquisition of an asset and the incurrence of an obligation by the lessee. As a result, many firms will be forced to include the value of their lease agreements directly in the balance sheet rather than treat them as operating leases which are reported in footnotes to the balance sheet.

[13]Net operating income plus depreciation expense provides an estimate as to the cash flow available to cover the firm's finance charges from its operations. As stated earlier, a number of sources of cash are not related to the firm's operating earnings, such as the sale of assets or issuance of debt or equity. However, these sources are temporary in that they cannot be continually called upon to provide the basis for meeting the firm's annual finance charges. Thus operating earnings (EBIT) provides a more meaningful basis for computing a firm's coverage ratios.

added to net operating income to determine the level of operating earnings available to cover finance charges. Note that rent expense is considered an operating expense in the preparation of the income statement. Therefore, it is subtracted from revenues in the process of computing net operating earnings or EBIT.

The second basic objection to the times interest earned ratio relates to the fact that the denominator of the ratio includes interest expense as the sole finance charge which must be covered. In practice the firm must meet lease payments, principal payments, and preferred dividends to completely satisfy the claims on it from its use of financial leverage. The next ratio described attempts to rectify each of these weaknesses in the times interest earned ratio.

Cash Flow Overall Coverage Ratio. For Jimco the **cash flow overall coverage ratio** is computed as follows:

↙ Omit

$$\text{cash flow overall coverage ratio} = \frac{\text{net operating income} + \text{lease expense} + \text{depreciation}}{\text{interest} + \text{lease expense} + \text{preferred dividends}/(1 - \text{marginal tax rate}) + \text{principal payments}/(1 - \text{marginal tax rate})}$$

$$= \frac{\$(4,611,000 + 498,000)}{\$(1,237,000 + 493,000/(1 - .48))} \qquad (3\text{-}9)$$

$$= \frac{\$5,109,000}{\$2,185,077} = 2.34 \text{ times}$$

The current portion of the firm's long-term debt ($493,000) is used as the firm's principal payment for the period. Furthermore, principal payments (and preferred dividends) are not tax deductible and must be adjusted to a before-tax basis by dividing by one minus the firm's marginal tax rate. Jimco's marginal tax rate is 48%, since the firm earns taxable income in excess of $50,000. Thus, Jimco's operating earnings were 3.73 times its interest expense, whereas the firm's operating cash flows were only 2.34 times its total finance charges.

One further refinement may be desirable in the cash flow overall coverage ratio. This relates to the coverage of any common dividends the firm wishes to pay. For example, should Jimco desire to pay dividends to the common stockholders totaling $150,000, then the firm must earn $150,000/(1 - .48) = $288,462 on a before-tax basis. Adding this figure for common dividends to the firm's existing finance charges reduces the coverage ratio to 2.07 times. This latter version of the coverage ratio will prove particularly useful when the firm is analyzing alternative sources of long-term financing and wishes to maintain a stable dividend payment to its common stockholders.

Summarizing the results of Jimco's leverage ratios we have made two basic observations: First, Jimco has utilized more nonowner financing than is characteristic of its industry. Second, Jimco's earnings are such that it can apparently afford the higher use of financial leverage.

The ratios discussed here help us answer some very important questions regarding the effectiveness of the firm's management in producing profits from the resources entrusted to them. Specifically, **profitability ratios** can be used to answer such questions as, *How much of each sales dollar was management able to convert into profits?* and *Did the common stockholders receive an adequate return on their investment?* For discussion purposes we shall divide profitability ratios into two groups: profitability in relation to sales and profitability in relation to investment.

PROFITABILITY IN RELATION TO SALES

Ratios of **profitability in relation to sales** can be used to assess the ability of the firm's management to control the various expenses involved in generating sales. The profit ratios discussed here are commonly referred to as **profit margins** and include the gross profit margin, operating profit margin, and net profit margin.

Gross Profit Margin. The **gross profit margin** is calculated as follows:

$$\text{gross profit margin} = \frac{\text{gross profit}}{\text{net sales}} \tag{3-10}$$

$$= \frac{\$13,062,000}{\$51,224,000}$$

$$= .255 \text{ or } 25.5\%$$

Thus, Jimco's gross profit constitutes 25.5% of firm sales. This margin reflects the firm's markup on its cost of goods sold as well as the ability of management to minimize the firm's cost of goods sold in relation to sales (and the method for determining that cost).

The common size income statement found in Table 3-5 provides an industry norm of 26.7 percent. Thus, Jimco's gross profit margin does not appear to be out of line. Note that the gross profit margin reflects both the level of Jimco's cost of goods sold and the size of the firm's markup on those costs, or its pricing policy.

Operating Profit Margin. Moving down the income statement, the next profit figure encountered is net operating income (or earnings before interest and taxes—EBIT). This profit figure serves as the basis for com-

puting the **operating profit margin.** For Jimco this profit margin is found
as follows:

$$\text{operating profit margin} = \frac{\text{net operating income}}{\text{sales}} \qquad (3\text{-}11)$$

$$= \frac{\$\ 4,611,000}{\$51,224,000}$$

$$= .09 \text{ or } 9\%$$

The operating profit margin reflects the firm's operating expenses as well as its cost of goods sold. Therefore, this ratio serves as an overall measure of operating effectiveness.

Again the industry norm is obtained from the common size income statement in Table 3-5. Jimco's operating profit margin is slightly below the industry norm of 9.6 percent. However, at least part of this difference relates to the fact that the gross profit margin (25.5 percent) was less than its industry norm (26.7 percent).

Net Profit Margin. The final profit margin considered involves the net after-tax profits of the firm as a percent of sales. For Jimco the **net profit margin** is computed as follows:

$$\text{net profit margin} = \frac{\text{net income}}{\text{sales}} = \frac{\$\ 1,768,000}{\$51,224,000} = .035 \text{ or } 3.5\% \qquad (3\text{-}12)$$

Therefore, $.035 of each sales dollar is converted into profits after taxes. Note that this profit margin reflects the firm's cost of goods sold, operating expenses, finance charges (interest expense), and taxes. For the industry, profits before taxes are 7.6 percent of sales. Assuming that firms on the average pay approximately 48 percent of their taxable earnings in taxes, this produces a net profit margin of $.076(1 - .48) = .0395$ or 3.95 percent. Hence, Jimco's net profit margin is slightly below par for its industry. In the next category of profitability ratios we investigate this lower-than-average net profit margin to find out whether it results in a below-average return on the firm's total investment and, more importantly, to find out the return on the investment of the common stockholders.

PROFITABILITY IN RELATION
TO INVESTMENT

This category of profitability ratios attempts to measure firm profits in relation to the invested funds used to generate those profits. Thus, these ratios are very useful in assessing the overall effectiveness of the firm's management.

Operating Income Return on Investment.   The **operating income return on investment** reflects the rate of return on the firm's total investment before interest and taxes. For Jimco this return measure is computed as follows:

$$\text{operating income return on investment} = \frac{\text{net operating income}}{\text{total tangible assets}} \quad (3\text{-}13)$$

$$= \frac{\$\ 4{,}611{,}000}{\$(30{,}802{,}000 - 420{,}000)}$$

$$= .152 \text{ or } 15.2\%$$

Thus, Jimco's management produced a 15.2% return on its total tangible assets before interest and taxes. Intangible assets are subtracted from total assets in an effort to measure the firm's rate of return on total *invested* capital.[14] It is this 15.2% rate of return that should be compared to the cost of borrowed funds to determine whether leverage is *favorable* or *unfavorable*. If the firm is borrowing at a cost less than 15.2%, then leverage is favorable and will result in higher after-tax earnings to the firm's stockholders.[15]

This rate of return is particularly useful when assessing the operating effectiveness of the firm's management. The operating return on investment does not reflect the influence of the firm's use of financial leverage; thus it provides a measure of management's effectiveness in making operating decisions as opposed to financing decisions. The reason is that neither the numerator (operating income) nor the denominator (total tangible assets) is affected by the way in which the firm has financed its assets.

An industry norm for this ratio is not readily available in Table 3-5. However, we can calculate one, using the information given there. Sales divided by total assets equals 1.5, and operating profit is 9.6 percent of sales for the industry. Using the following relationship,

$$\frac{\text{operating income}}{\text{sales}} \times \frac{\text{sales}}{\text{total assets}} = \frac{\text{operating income}}{\text{total assets}} \quad (3\text{-}14)$$

$$.096 \quad\times\quad 1.5 \quad=\quad .144 \text{ or } 14.4\%$$

---

[14]The lack of physical qualities of intangible assets makes evidence of their existence elusive, their value often difficult to estimate, and their useful lives indeterminable. The Accounting Principles Board gives this subject attention in Opinion 17.

[15]The concept of leverage is fully developed in Chapter 15. Very simply, when a firm borrows money that requires a fixed return, then the return to the common shareholders will be enhanced only if the return the firm earns on these borrowed funds exceeds their cost. For the firm as a whole the operating income rate of return measures the before-tax-and-interest rate of return on the firm's investment. This rate must exceed the cost of borrowed funds for the firm as a whole to experience *favorable* financial leverage. The favorableness of financial leverage is determined by the effect of its use on earnings per share to the firm's common stockholders.

we derive an industry norm of 14.4 percent. Thus, Jimco's operating rate of return compares favorably with the industry norm.

In deriving the industry norm we have identified a very useful relationship between operating profit margin and the ratio of sales divided by total tangible assets (which we will refer to as **total tangible asset turnover).** That is, a firm's rate of return on investment is a function of (1) how much profit it *squeezes* out of each dollar of sales, and (2) how much it has invested in assets to produce those sales. Thus, Jimco's lower-than-average operating profit margin was offset by a higher-than-average turnover of its total investment in tangible assets.

Jimco's total tangible asset turnover ratio can be computed as follows:

$$\text{total tangible asset turnover} = \frac{\text{sales}}{\text{total tangible assets}} \qquad (3\text{-}15)$$

$$= \frac{\$51,224,000}{\$(30,802,000 - 420,000)}$$

$$= 1.69 \text{ times}$$

Note again that total *tangible* assets are used as the denominator in this ratio. Total tangible assets are found by subtracting patents and all other intangible assets from total assets. This adjustment to total assets eliminates the influence of those assets whose values are highly subjective.

Jimco's total asset turnover ratio compares very favorably with the industry norm of 1.5. This ratio indicates that Jimco's management has efficiently utilized its resources in generating sales as compared with other firms in its industry.

Return on Total Assets or Return on Investment. The **return on total assets** or **return on investment** ratio relates after-tax net income to the firm's total investment in assets. For Jimco this ratio is found as follows:

$$\text{return on total assets} = \frac{\text{net income}}{\text{total tangible assets}} \qquad (3\text{-}16)$$

$$= \frac{\$ 1,768,000}{\$30,382,000}$$

$$= .058 \text{ or } 5.8\%$$

Again total tangible assets are used in an attempt to measure total investment. An industry norm can be obtained from Table 3-5 in a manner similar to that used with the operating rate of return. That is,

$$\text{return on total assets} = \frac{\text{net income}}{\text{sales}} \times \frac{\text{sales}}{\text{total tangible assets}} \qquad (3\text{-}17)$$

Earlier the net income to sales ratio for the industry was estimated to be 3.95 percent. Using the industry's sales to total assets ratio of 1.5 produces an industry norm for return on total assets of $.0395 \times 1.5 = .0593$ or 5.93 percent. Thus, Jimco provides a satisfactory return on its total investment.

Return on Common Equity. The **return on common equity ratio** measures the rate of return earned on the common stockholder's investment. Jimco earned the following rate of return for its common stockholders:

$$\text{return on common equity} = \frac{\text{net income available to common}}{\text{tangible common equity}} \qquad (3\text{-}18)$$

$$= \frac{\$1,768,000}{\$9,346,000 - 420,000}$$

$$= .198 \text{ or } 19.8\%$$

Net income available to common equity is simply net income less any preferred dividends the firm might have to pay. This earnings figure is sometimes referred to as **net common stock earnings** (NCSE). **Tangible common equity** is simply the common equity of the firm less intangible assets, such that the denominator of the ratio represents the investment of the common stockholders in the firm.

Table 3-5 does not contain an industry norm for this ratio. However, the following relation can be used to derive an industry norm from the return on total assets ratio and the debt ratio:

$$\text{return on common equity} = \frac{\text{return on total assets}}{(1 - \text{debt ratio})} \qquad (3\text{-}19)$$

Recall that the debt ratio is simply total liabilities divided by total assets. The industry norm for the return on common equity ratio is found as follows:

$$\frac{.058}{(1 - .542)} = .127 \text{ or } 12.7\%$$

Thus, Jimco's 19.8 percent return compares very favorably with that of the industry. This higher than average return reflects both the firm's efficient use of its investment in assets to generate sales (indicated by the turnover of total tangible assets ratio) and its above average use of financial leverage (as reflected in its debt ratio).

This concludes the discussion of profitability ratios. In summary, Jimco was observed to have slightly below-average profits in relation to its sales; however, this factor was more than offset by the firm's very efficient use of its assets to generate sales (as evidenced by the high total tangible asset turnover ratio) and the fact that Jimco utilized more leverage than the norm for its industry.

We noted earlier that a firm's financial ratios can be compared to two types of standards. We have discussed industry norms as the basis for comparison; we now demonstrate the use of trend comparisons. Figure 3-1 displays graphs of Jimco's current ratio, acid test ratio, debt ratio, and return on total asset ratio for the past five years.

Surveying the trend in Jimco's liquidity ratios indicates that a gradual deterioration has been taking place. This deterioration in liquidity does not, at least for the present, represent a problem, as Jimco's current and acid test ratios compared very favorably with their respective industry norms. However, any continuation in the trend could pose a problem for Jimco and should be monitored closely.

Jimco's debt ratio appears to have declined slightly over the past five years with moderate interim fluctuations. However, no material change in the ratio appears to have occurred over the period. In light of Jimco's current use of leverage, any further increases in this ratio may be unwarranted.

Finally, the return on total assets ratio for the past five years depicts the relatively volatile nature of Jimco's business, with returns of 8 and 10 percent for 1976 and 1977, respectively, and lower returns for the remaining three years. However, based upon Jimco's return on total assets ratio for 1978 and that of the industry, it would appear that Jimco has done as well as other firms in its industry.

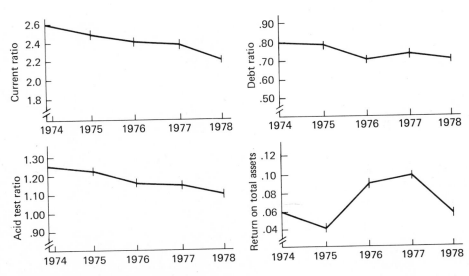

FIGURE 3-1 *Trend Analysis Illustration*

Table 3-6 summarizes Jimco's financial ratios, as well as the corresponding industry norms. Each ratio is evaluated in relation to the appropriate norm. Briefly, the results of those comparisons were as follows:

1. Jimco's liquidity position is very closely in line with the industry.
2. Jimco has made extensive use of financial leverage. In fact, the firm has financed almost 70 percent of its assets with nonowner funds.
3. The firm can apparently *afford* its higher use of financial leverage, as is indicated by its coverage ratios.
4. Jimco's profit margins are slightly below the respective norms; however, the firm has been able to convert these profit margins into better-than-average rates of return on investment. This resulted from the higher-than-average sales per dollar invested in assets.
5. Finally, Jimco has benefited from the favorable use of financial leverage. The firm earned a very favorable 19.8 percent return on the investment of its common stockholders compared with only 12.7 percent for the industry.

The return on total assets ratio provides the basis for the **DuPont system of financial analysis.** The system's value lies in its capacity to *tie together* or *sum up* the overall financial performance of the firm and relate it to many of the crucial areas of financial condition discussed earlier. Figure 3-2 applies the DuPont system to Jimco, Inc., based on its 1978 financial statements. The detailed breakdown of the return on total assets ratio allows the analyst to pinpoint the source of any deviation from either prior years' ratios or those of other firms with which Jimco might be compared.

The return on total tangible assets ratio is decomposed into the following components:

$$\text{return on total tangible assets} = \frac{\text{net income}}{\text{sales}} \times \frac{\text{sales}}{\text{total tangible assets}} \quad (3\text{-}21)$$

$$= \frac{\$\ 1,768,000}{\$51,224,000} \times \frac{\$51,224,000}{\$30,382,000}$$

$$= .035 \times 1.69 = .058 \text{ or } 5.8\%$$

Should the 5.8% return be lower than anticipated, the analyst could easily determine if the low return was a result of expenses that were out of line in relation to sales (net profit margin) or sales that were too low in relation to the firm's total investment (total tangible asset turnover). To test the former proposition the analyst could utilize the gross profit margin (indicating the relationship between cost of goods sold and sales), operating profit margin (reflecting operating expenses as well as cost of goods sold), and net profit margin (indicating taxes, interest expense, operating expenses, and cost of

Table 3-6 SUMMARY OF RATIOS FOR JIMCO, INC.

RATIO	FORMULA	CALCULATION	INDUSTRY AVERAGE	EVALUATION
Liquidity				
1. Current ratio	Current assets/current liabilities	$24,039,000/10,809,000 = 2.22 times	2.80 times	Satisfactory
2. Acid test ratio	(Current assets − inventories)/current liabilities	$11,822,000/10,809,000 = 1.09 times	1.10 times	Satisfactory
3. Average collection period	Average accounts receivable/(annual credit sales/360)	$9,921,000/(51,224,000/360) = 69.7 days	53 days	Poor
4. Inventory turnover	Cost of goods sold/ending inventory	$38,162,000/12,217,000 = 3.12 times	2.40 times	Satisfactory
Leverage				
5. Debt ratio	Total liabilities/total assets	$21,456,000/30,802,000 = 69.7%	54.2%	Poor
6. Long-Term debt to total capitalization	Long-term debt/total capitalization	$10,647,000/19,993,000 = 53.3%	25.8%	Poor
7. Times interest earned	Net operating income/annual interest expense	$4,611,000/1,237,000 = 3.73 times	3.8 times	Satisfactory
8. Cash flow overall coverage ratio	(NOI + lease expense + depreciation)/[interest + lease expense + principal payments/(1 − tax rate)]	$5,109,000/2,185,077 = 2.34 times	N.A.[a]	—
Profitability				
9. Gross profit margin	Gross profit/sales	$13,062,000/51,224,000 = 25.5%	26.7%	Satisfactory
10. Operating profit margin	Net operating income/sales	$4,611,000/51,224,000 = 9.0%	9.6%	Satisfactory
11. Net profit margin	Net income/sales	$1,768,000/51,224,000 = 3.5%	3.95%	Poor
12. Total tangible asset turnover	Sales/total tangible assets	$54,224,000/30,382,000 = 1.78 times	1.50 times	Good
13. Operating income return on investment	Net operating income/total tangible assets	$4,611,000/30,382,000 = 15.2%	14.4%	Satisfactory
14. Return on total assets	Net income/total tangible assets	$1,768,000/30,382,000 = 5.8%	5.93%	Satisfactory
15. Return on common equity	Net income available to common/tangible common equity	$1,768,000/8,926,000 = 19.8%	12.7%	Good

[a]Norm was not available.

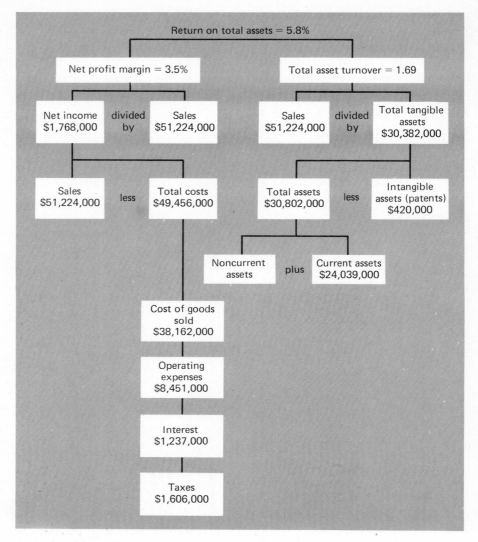

FIGURE 3-2 *Applying the DuPont System of Financial Analysis to Jimco, Inc.*

goods sold). If the problem lies in the firm's total tangible asset turnover, then the fixed asset turnover might be used to determine whether fixed or current asset investments (or both) are out of line in regard to sales. Should current assets be involved, then the average collection period can be used to assess whether the firm's investment in accounts receivable is too high, and the inventory turnover ratio can be used to determine the appropriateness of the firm's investment in inventories. Each of these comparisons can be made using industry norms or trend comparisons, as we discussed earlier.

The analyst who works with financial ratios must be aware of the potential limitations involved in their use. The following list includes some of the more important *pitfalls* that may be encountered in computing and interpreting financial ratios:

1. It is sometimes difficult to identify the industry category to which a firm belongs when the firm engages in multiple lines of business.

2. Published industry averages are only approximations and provide the user with *general guidelines* rather than scientifically determined averages of the ratios of all or even a representative sample of the firms within the industry. Note, for example, the cautionary statement contained in Figure 3-3 which was prepared by Robert Morris Associates in conjunction with their published industry ratios (as contained in Table 3-5).

3. Accounting practices differ widely among firms and can lead to differences in computed ratios. For example, the use of last-in, first-out (LIFO) in inventory valuation can, in a period of rising prices, lower the firm's inventory account and increase its inventory turnover ratio vis-a-vis that of a firm which utilizes first-in, first-out (FIFO). Still another source of differences in accounting practices among firms relates to the choice of a method of depreciating its fixed assets.

4. Financial ratios can be too high or too low. For example, a current ratio which exceeds the industry norm may signal the presence of excess liquidity which results in a lowering of overall profits in relation to the firm's investment in assets. On the other hand, a current ratio which falls below the norm indicates the possibility that the firm has inadequate liquidity and may at some future time not be able to pay its bills on time.

5. An industry average may not provide a desirable target ratio or norm. At best an industry average provides a guide to the financial position of the average firm in the industry. We might note here that the industry norms provided in Table 3-5 contain both the average ratio and the upper and lower quartiles for the firms used in preparing the average. Thus, the greater the difference in the upper and lower quartiles the less meaningful is the industry average in terms of its ability to represent that ratio for the industry.

6. Many firms experience seasonality in their operations. Thus, balance sheet entries and their corresponding ratios will vary with the time of year when the statements are prepared. To avoid this problem an average account balance should be used (for several months or quarters during the year) rather than the year-end total. For example, an average of month-end inventory balances might be used to compute a firm's inventory turnover ratio when the firm is subject to a significant seasonality in its sales (and correspondingly in its investment in inventories).

Given their limitations, financial ratios provide the analyst with a very useful tool for assessing a firm's financial condition. The analyst should, how-

Interpretation of Statement Studies Figures

RMA recommends that *Statement Studies* data be regarded only as general guidelines and not as absolute industry norms. There are several reasons why the data may not be fully representative of a given industry:

(1) The financial statements used in the *Statement Studies* are not selected by any random or statistically reliable method. RMA member banks voluntarily submit the raw data they have available each year, with these being the only constraints: (a) The fiscal year-ends of the companies reported may not be from April 1 through June 29, and (b) their total assets must be less than $50 million.

(2) Many companies have varied product lines; however, the *Statement Studies* categorize them by their primary product Standard Industrial Classification (SIC) number only.

(3) Some of our industry samples are rather small in relation to the total number of firms in a given industry. A relatively small sample can increase the chances that some of our composites do not fully represent an industry.

(4) There is the chance that an extreme statement can be present in a sample, causing a disproportionate influence on the industry composite. This is particularly true in a relatively small sample.

(5) Companies within the same industry may differ in their method of operations which in turn can directly influence their financial statements. Since they are included in our sample, too, these statements can significantly affect our composite calculations.

(6) Other considerations that can result in variations among different companies engaged in the same general line of business are different labor markets; geographical location; different accounting methods; quality of products handled; sources and methods of financing; and terms of sale.

For these reasons, RMA does not recommend the Statement Studies *figures be considered as absolute norms for a given industry. Rather the figures should be used only as general guidelines and in addition to the other methods of financial analysis. RMA makes no claim as to the representativeness of the figures printed in this book.*

FIGURE 3-3   *Cautionary Statement on Use of Industry Norms*

(© 1977 by The Robert Morris Associates, 1432 Philadelphia National Bank Building, Philadelphia, PA 19107.)

ever, be aware of these potential weaknesses when performing a ratio analysis.

SUMMARY

This chapter has presented a general overview of the basic financial statements of the firm and the use of ratio analysis.

Basic Financial Statements

Three basic financial statements are commonly used to describe the financial condition and performance of the firm: the balance sheet, the income statement, and the statement of changes in financial condition (source and use of funds statement). The balance sheet provides a picture of the firm's assets, liabilities, and owners' equity on a particular date, whereas the income statement reflects the net revenues from the firm's operations over a given period. The statement of changes in financial condition combines information from both the balance sheet and income statement to describe sources and uses of funds for a given period in the firm's history.

Financial Ratios

Financial ratios are of three main kinds: (1) liquidity, (2) leverage, and (3) profitability ratios. The financial statements of Jimco, Inc., were used to demonstrate the computation of a sample listing of ratios from each category. The set of possible ratio calculations is limited only by the analyst's imagination, and those discussed here represent only one possible listing that can be used in performing a financial analysis.

Use of Financial Ratios

Two methods were demonstrated for analyzing financial ratios. The first involved trend analysis for the firm over time; the second involved making ratio comparisons with industry norms. An example set of industry norms from Robert Morris and Associates were presented and used in the analysis of Jimco, Inc.

STUDY QUESTIONS

3-1. The basic financial statements of an organization consist of the balance sheet, income statement, and statement of changes in financial position. Describe the nature of each and explain how their functions differ.

3-2. Why is it that the preferred stockholders' equity section of the balance changes only when new shares are sold, whereas the common equity section changes from year to year regardless of whether new shares are bought or sold?

3-3. Why is it that net sales for a period do not necessarily represent cash inflow for the period?

3-4. An asset is purchased for $55,000 that has an expected useful life of seven years and an anticipated salvage value of $6000. Compute the depreciation expense for the first 12 months under each of the following methods (refer to Appendix 3-A if you need help):

(a) Straight-line.

(b) Sum-of-the-years' digits.

(c) Double-declining balance.

3-5. Discuss two reasons why net income for a particular period does not reflect a firm's cash flow during that period.

3-6. The three basic groups of financial ratios are liquidity, leverage, and profitability ratios. Discuss the nature of each group and list two example ratios that you would use to measure that aspect of a firm's financial condition.

3-7. Discuss briefly the two sources of standards or norms used in performing ratio analyses.

3-8. Where can the analyst obtain industry norms? What limitations does the use of industry average ratios suffer from? Discuss briefly.

3-1. On February 3, 1979, Mr. Jerry Simmons, chief financial officer for M & G Industries, contacted the firm's bank regarding a loan. The loan was to be used to repay notes payable and to finance current assets. Mr. Simmons wanted to repay the loan plus interest in one year. Upon receiving the loan request, the bank asked that the firm supply it with complete financial statements for the past two years. These statements are presented below:

STUDY PROBLEMS

M & G INDUSTRIES
Balance Sheets
at the End of Calendar Year

	1977	1978
Cash	$ 9,000	$ 500
Accounts receivable	12,500	16,000
Inventories	29,000	45,500
Total current assets	$50,500	$62,000
Land	20,000	26,000
Buildings and equipment	70,000	100,000
Less: Allowance for depreciation	28,000	38,000
Total fixed assets	$62,000	$88,000
	$112,500	$150,000
Accounts payable	$ 10,500	$ 22,000
Bank notes	17,000	47,000
Total current liabilities	$27,500	$69,000
Long-term debt	28,750	22,950
Common stock	31,500	31,500
Retained earnings	24,750	26,550
	$112,500	$150,000

M & G INDUSTRIES
Income Statements
for Years Ending December 31

	1977	1978
Sales	$125,000	$160,000
Cost of goods sold	75,000	96,000
Gross profit	$ 50,000	$ 64,000
Operating expense:		
Fixed cash operating expense	21,000	21,000
Variable operating expense	12,500	16,000
Depreciation	4,500	10,000
Total operating expense	38,000	47,000
Earnings before interest and taxes	$ 12,000	$ 17,000
Interest	3,000	6,100
Earnings before taxes	$ 9,000	$ 10,900
Taxes	4,500	5,450
Net income	$ 4,500	$ 5,450

(a) Based upon the preceding statements, complete the table below:

M & G INDUSTRIES
Ratio Analysis

	INDUSTRY AVERAGES	ACTUAL 1977	ACTUAL 1978
Current ratio	1.80		
Acid test ratio	.70		
Average collection period[a]	37 days		
Inventory turnover[a]	2.50		
Debt to total assets	58%		
Long-term debt to total capitalization	33%		
Times interest earned	3.8×		
Gross profit margin	38%		
Net profit margin	3.5%		
Return on total assets	4.0%		
Return on common equity	9.5%		

[a]Based on a 360-day year and on end-of-year figures.

(b) Analyze Mr. Simmons's loan request. Would you grant the loan? Explain.

3-2. (a) Prepare a statement of sources and uses of funds for M & G Industries for 1978, using information given in Study Problem 3-1. (b) How does this funds statement supplement your ratio analysis from Study Problem 3-1? Explain.

3-3. Pamplin, Inc., has recently applied for a loan from the Second National Bank to be used to expand the firm's inventory of soil pipe used in construction and agriculture. This expansion is predicated on expanded sales predicted for the coming year. Pamplin's financial statements for the two most recent years are as follows:

PAMPLIN, INC.
Balance Sheet at 12/31/77 and 12/31/78
(000's)

Assets

	12/31/77	12/31/78
Cash	$ 200	$ 150
Accounts receivable	450	425
Inventory	550	625
Current assets	1200	1200
Plant and equipment	2200	2600
Less: Accumulated depreciation	1000	1200
Net plant and equipment	1200	1400
Total assets	$2400	$2600

Liabilities and Owners' Equity

	12/31/77	12/31/78
Accounts payable	$ 200	$ 150
Notes payable—current (9%)	0	150
Current liabilities	200	300
Bonds	600	600
Owners' equity		
Common stock	300	300
Paid-in capital	600	600
Retained earnings	700	800
Total owners' equity	1600	1700
Total liabilities and owners' equity	$2400	$2600

PAMPLIN, INC.
Income Statement
Year Ended 12/31/77 and 12/31/78

	1977	1978
Sales	$1200	$1450
Cost of goods sold	700	850
Gross profit	$ 500	$ 600
Operating expenses	30	40
Depreciation	220	200
Net operating income	$ 250	$ 360
Interest expense	50	60

PAMPLIN, INC. *(cont.)*

	1977	1978
Net income before taxes	$ 200	$ 300
Taxes (40%)	80	120
Net income	$ 120	$ 180

(a) Compute the following ratios for Pamplin, Inc., from the financial statements provided above:

	1977	1978	INDUSTRY NORM
Current ratio			5.0
Acid-test (quick) ratio			3.0
Inventory turnover			2.2
Average collection period			90 days
Debt ratio			.33
Times interest earned			7.0
Net profit margin			.12
Return on total assets			.09

(b) Based on your answer in (a) above, what are Pamplin's financial strengths and weaknesses?

(c) Would you make the loan? Why or why not?

3-4. Prepare a statement of changes in financial position for Pamplin, Inc., for 1978 (Problem 3-3).

3-5. (a) Prepare a statement of sources and uses of funds for the Waterhouse Co. in the year 1978. (b) What were the firm's primary sources and uses of funds?

	1977	1978
Cash	$ 75,000	$ 82,500
Receivables	102,000	90,000
Inventory	168,000	165,000
Prepaid expenses	12,000	13,500
Fixed assets	325,500	468,000
Accumulated depreciation	94,500	129,000
Patents	61,500	52,500
	$649,500	$742,500
Accounts payable	$124,500	$112,500
Taxes payable	97,500	105,000
Mortgage payable	150,000	—
Preferred stock	—	225,000
Additional paid-in capital—preferred	—	6,000
Common stock	225,000	225,000
Retained earnings	52,500	69,000
	$649,500	$742,500

Additional information

1. The only entry in the accumulated depreciation account is the depreciation expense for the period.
2. The only entries in the retained earnings account are for dividends paid in the amount of $18,000 and for the net income for the year.
3. The income statement for 1978 is as follows:

Sales	$187,500
Cost of sales	141,000
Gross profit	46,500
Operating expenses	12,000
Net income	$ 34,500

3-6. Prepare a balance sheet and income statement at December 31, 1978, for the Sharpe Mfg. Co. from the scrambled list of items below.

Accounts receivable	120,000
Machinery and equipment	700,000
Accumulated depreciation	236,000
Notes payable—current	100,000
Net sales	800,000
Inventory	110,000
Accounts payable	90,000
Long-term debt	160,000
Cost of goods sold	500,000
Operating expenses	280,000
Common stock	320,000
Cash	96,000
Retained earnings—prior year	?
Retained earnings—current year	?

3-7. The consolidated balance sheets of the TMU Processing Company are presented below for June 1, 1979 and May 31, 1980 (millions of dollars).

	JUNE 1, 1979	MAY 31, 1980	CHANGE SOURCE	USE
Cash	$10	$ 8	_____	_____
Accounts receivable	12	22	_____	_____
Inventories	8	14	_____	_____
Current assets	$30	$ 44	_____	_____
Gross fixed assets	100	110	_____	_____
Less: Accumulated depreciation	40	50	_____	_____
Net fixed assets	$60	$ 60	_____	_____
Total assets	$90	$104	_____	_____
Accounts payable	$12	$ 9	_____	_____
Notes payable	7	7	_____	_____
Long-term debt	11	24	_____	_____

	JUNE 1, 1979	MAY 31, 1980	CHANGE SOURCE	USE
Common stock	20	20	_____	_____
Retained earnings	40	44	_____	_____
Total liabilities and owner's equity	$90	$104	_____	_____

TMU earned $14 million after taxes during the year ended May 31, 1980 and paid common dividends of $10 million.

    a. Fill in the changes in TMU's balance sheet for 1980.

    b. Prepare a Source and Use Funds Statement for TMU Processing Co.

    c. Summarize your findings.

3-8. **Case problem.** The L. M. Myers Company is one of the three largest grain exporters in the United States. The firm also engages in soybean processing and several other related activities. During fiscal 1976–77 Myers derived 72.1% of its sales from its exporting activities, 14.8% from agriproducts, and the remainder from chemical and consumer products. Myers's nonexport sales are derived almost completely from soybean processing activities, including the production and sale of a number of food ingredients. One of the most promising soybean derivatives produced by the company is a newly developed meat substitute called "Prosoy." At present Prosoy is marketed almost strictly as a ground beef substitute; however, plans are under way to market the product in a number of other forms resembling familiar cuts of meat, such as bacon and even roasts. The success that the company has enjoyed with Prosoy in its initial three years of production promises to make the firm's soybean processing business an even more important segment of the firm's overall sales. Other soybean-related products produced by the firm include a number of derivatives used in animal and poultry feeds. Myers's export business primarily involves corn, wheat, and some soybeans. The principal investment made by the firm related to its exporting operations involves a chain of grain elevators at strategic locations along the Mississippi River. These elevators are used to store grain and load it onto ships, which deliver it all over the world.

    For the fiscal year just ended Myers experienced an overall sales growth of 10%. This increase represented a mere 5% increase in export-related activities and a whopping 20% increase in sales related to soybean processing. This and other factors have led the company to make a commitment to expand its processing capacity by $20 million during the next three years. The firm plans to finance the expansion through an $11 million bond issue and through the retention of earnings.

    Owing to the seasonal nature of its export business, Myers has had to borrow heavily during the harvest months to finance seasonal inventory buildups and then repay the loans as sales are made throughout the year. In the past the company has arranged with a group of banks for a line of credit (discussed in Chapter 10) sufficient to meet its credit needs; however, in recent years this arrangement has become increasingly more cumbersome as the firm's total needs for funds have grown. This and cost considerations have led Myers's financial vice-president, Mr. James Graham, to consider the possibility of raising all or at least a part of the firm's credit needs through a commercial paper issue (discussed in Chapter 10). Mr. Graham is somewhat concerned about his firm's creditworthiness in light of the industry norms generally used by banks and other creditors. His concern relates to the fact that Myers has never issued commercial paper and the belief that only the most creditworthy of borrowers can successfully use the commercial paper market to raise funds.

Questions:

(a) Using the financial statements for Myers presented below, complete the calculation of the financial ratios contained in Exhibit 1.

(b) Based upon your calculated ratios and the associated industry norms, what is your financial analysis of Myers?

L. M. MYERS, INC.
Balance Sheets
for Years Ended December 31
($000)

Assets

	1977	1976
Cash	$ 12,844	$ 11,451
Accounts receivable	52,599	64,199
Marketable securities	33,995	—
Inventories	75,366	69,814
Deferred income taxes	2,750	2,948
Prepaid expenses	1,794	1,089
Total current assets	$178,348	$149,501
Investments and advances	12,012	11,681
Other assets	3,735	14,509
Net property and equipment	153,856	118,810
Total assets	$348,951	$294,501

Liabilities and Stockholders' Equity

	1977	1976
Accounts payable	$ 35,099	$ 34,327
Notes payable	20,907	14,544
Accrued income and other taxes	40,112	28,526
Other accrued expenses	22,299	19,854
Total current liabilities	118,417	97,251
Long-term debt	67,006	75,817
Cumulative preferred stock	565	582
Common stock	26,812	26,596
Capital surplus	2,606	2,030

Liabilities and Stockholders' Equity *(cont.)*

	1977	1976
Retained earnings	133,559	92,683
Less common stock held in treasury	(14)	(458)
Total stockholders' equity	163,528	121,433
Total liabilities and stockholders' equity	$348,951	$294,501

L. M. MYERS, INC.
Income Statements
for the Years Ended December 31
($000)

	1977	1976
Sales (net)	$777,104	$706,457
Less: Cost of goods sold	662,093	637,224
Gross profit	$115,011	$ 69,238
Operating expenses:		
Selling and administrative expenses	17,804	17,612
Labor expense	15,263	9,418
Depreciation	7,428	6,976
Miscellaneous operating expenses	2,011	1,887
Total	$ 42,506	$ 35,893
Net operating income	$ 72,505	$ 33,340
Interest income	2,012	512
	74,517	33,852
Less: Interest expense	8,408	9,127
Earnings before taxes	$ 66,109	$ 24,725
Less: Taxes payable	25,232	5,440
Net income	$ 40,877	$ 19,285
Less: Preferred dividends	56	58
Net earnings available to common	$ 40,821	$ 19,227

Exhibit 1 FINANCIAL RATIOS FOR L. M. MYERS, INC.

RATIO	1977	1976	INDUSTRY NORM[a]
Liquidity			
Acid test ratio			1.00×
Current ratio			1.61×
Receivables turnover[b]			12.00×
Average collection period[b]			30.00 days
Inventory turnover[b]			10.1×
Leverage			
Debt ratio			49.1%

Exhibit 1 (cont.)

RATIO	1977	1976	INDUSTRY NORM[a]
Long-term debt to total capitalization			31.0%
Times interest earned			5.87×
Cash flow overall coverage ratio			7.42×
Profitability			
Gross profit margin			11.7%
Operating income margin			7.6%
Operating income rate of return			14.75%
Return on total assets			8.45%
Return on common equity			21.39%

[a]These industry norms pertain to Myers's grain export operations, which comprised over 70% of the firm's sales for 1977. Also, the industry averages are applicable to both 1976 and 1977.

[b]Compute using end-of-year figures and assuming all sales are credit sales.

SELECTED REFERENCES

ALTMAN, EDWARD I., "Financial Ratios, Discriminant Analysis and the Prediction of Corporate Bankruptcy," *Journal of Finance,* 23 (September 1968), 598–609.

BEAVER, WILLIAM H., "Financial Ratios as Predictors of Failure," *Empirical Research in Accounting: Selected Studies in Journal of Accounting Research* (1966), 71–111.

BENISHAY, HASKELL, "Economic Information in Financial Ratio Analysis," *Accounting and Business Research,* 2 (Spring 1971), 174–79.

HELFERT, ERICH A., *Techniques of Financial Analysis,* 4th ed., Chap. 2. Homewood, Ill.: Richard D. Irwin, 1977.

LEV, BARUCH, *Financial Statement Analysis: A New Approach.* Englewood Cliffs, N.J.: Prentice-Hall, Inc., 1974.

MURRAY, ROGER F., "The Penn Central Debacle: Lessons for Financial Analysis," *Journal of Finance,* 26 (May 1971), 327–32.

O'CONNOR, MELVIN C., "On the Usefulness of Financial Ratios to Investors in Common Stock," *Accounting Review,* 48 (April 1973), 339–52.

SORTER, GEORGE H., and GEORGE BENSTON, "Appraising the Defensive Position of a Firm: The Internal Measure," *Accounting Review,* 35 (October 1960), 663–40.

REVIEW OF SELECTED ACCOUNTING PRINCIPLES AND PRACTICES

APPENDIX 3A

Successful financial analysis requires a thorough understanding of the basic principles which underlie the preparation of financial statements. Our objective in this appendix is to review fundamental principles of financial accounting. A complete treatment is, of course, outside the purview of this text. In addition, we discuss the valuation of fixed assets and inventories, since both these account balances are materially affected by the underlying method used.

Historical Cost Principle

The **historical cost principle** provides the basis for determining the book values of the firm's balance sheet accounts. The principle advantage of historical cost is its objectivity. Its primary disadvantage relates to the fact that the asset balances do not correspond to market values or replacement costs. Furthermore, since asset book values are not equal to market values, the book value of owner's equity does not equal its market value. Thus, in analyzing the firm's financial statements the analyst must keep in mind that asset balances reflect historical costs of the related assets and not current market values.

Revenue Realization (Recognition) Principle

When a firm's income statement is prepared, the accountant must decide what revenues should be allocated to the period covered by the statement. As simple as this may sound, it can present the analyst with some very serious difficulties. In principle, revenue is recognized during the period in which (1) the earning process is virtually complete and (2) an exchange transaction has occurred. In most cases these conditions are satisfied at the point of sale. However, in practice several methods other than determination of the amount of sales for the period can be used to measure revenue. These include

1. *Percentage of completion.* Here recognition of revenue is allowed in certain long-term contracts (construction) before the contract is completed. Revenue is recognized in each period equal to the product of the contract price and the ratio, period costs/total estimated project costs.
2. *End of production.* In some instances revenue is recognized before an actual sale (but after production has ended). This is the case where the price is certain as well as the amount, as in revenues involving agricultural commodities where governmental price floors are in effect.
3. *Receipt of cash.* The cash basis is used for revenue recognition when, as a result of the uncertainty of collection, it is impossible to establish the revenue figure at the time of sale. This is common where installment sales are made and payments cover long periods.

The diversity of methods used and the complexity of the problem of determining when revenues are realized can lead the financial analyst to erroneous conclusions. For example, during the 1960s a great number of franchising operations were established for a variety of businesses, such as McDonald's, Kentucky Fried Chicken, and Shakey's Pizza. In nearly all cases, as soon as the franchisor found an individual franchisee and received a down payment, the entire franchise price was treated as realized income. Consequently, to avoid any dip in income that would damage their growth in earnings, many franchisors signed up franchisees at an increasingly faster rate each year. This was necessary because the initial franchise fees were treated as revenue immediately—even though in many situations those fees were payable over a period of years and in some instances, as in the case of franchises that never got started, were refundable or uncollectible.

To compute net income for a given year's operations accountants must identify all revenue and expense items that belong within the year. The **accrual basis of accounting** attempts to allocate revenue and expense properly among the years that an enterprise is in operation. This method utilizes the **revenue realization principle** such that revenue is recognized in the period in which it is earned, and uses the **matching principle** to determine the amount of expenses necessary during the period for the revenue to be generated. These expenses are thus *matched* against revenue for the period. The basic principle, therefore, involves matching expenses with the revenues, or *"Let the expense follow the revenue."* Thus, the wage expense is not recognized when it is paid nor necessarily when the work is performed, but when the work performed actually contributes to revenues.

An example of the potential difficulties posed for the analyst in implementation of the matching principle can be found in the depreciation policies followed by different firms for like assets. For example, Delta Air Lines depreciates its planes over 10 years, United Air Lines over as long as 16 years. Thus, other things being the same, Delta would report higher expenses and lower profits from its operations than would United. Depreciation methods are discussed later in this appendix.

This principle simply requires that accounting entities account for transactions according to the same methods from period to period. Companies can and do switch from one method of accounting to another; however, changes are restricted to situations in which it can be demonstrated that any newly adopted principle is preferable to the old. Further, the nature and effect of the accounting change as well as the justification for it must be disclosed in the financial statements for the period in which the change is made. Such disclosures are made in "footnotes" to the financial statements, which offer supplemental and explanatory information.

Since many events and circumstances that relate to the financial position of a firm may not be reflected in the body of the financial statement, this principle requires that there must be full disclosure in the financial statements of all relevant facts such that an informed reader can appropriately evaluate the statements. Common methods of disclosure include (1) parenthetical disclosure, and (2) footnote disclosure. Particularly difficult problem areas include accounting for leases, investment credits, pension fund liabilities, franchising, options, and mergers. Further, it may be necessary to report (in a footnote) events subsequent to the date of the financial statements in order to provide full disclosure.

The idea here is that data should be objectively determined and verifiable such that another accountant faced with the same situation would have arrived at the same conclusions. The purpose is to provide more credibility to financial statements.

This concludes our very brief overview of accounting principles. Perhaps most important to the analyst are the historical cost, revenue realization, and matching principles. We should also note that deviations from these general principles can and do occur. Notable exceptions arise where the item being analyzed is considered *immaterial* or insignificant, where accepted industry practice deviates from the guiding principle, or where governmental reporting requirements disagree in some way with the basic principle involved.

Depreciation expense represents an allocation of the cost of a fixed asset over its useful life. The objective is to match such costs with the revenues that result from their utilization in the enterprise. Furthermore, depreciation expense is used to reduce the balance-sheet book value of the firm's fixed assets. Thus, the method used to determine depreciation expense also serves as the basis for determining the book value of fixed assets. We will consider three commonly used methods for computing depreciation: straight-line, sum-of-the-years' digits, and double-declining balance.[1] Of the three, **straight-line** (SL) is the simplest to understand and to use. Consider the following example: a firm purchases a fixed asset for $12,000 that has a five-year expected useful life and a $2000 anticipated salvage value at the end of that period. Straight-line depreciation on the asset would be $2000 per year, since the asset's $10,000 depreciable book value ($12,000 purchase price less the $2000 salvage value) would be spread evenly over the five years of its expected useful life ($10,000 ÷ 5 = $2000).

*DEPRECIATION
OF FIXED ASSETS*

The **sum-of-the-years' digits method** (SYD) is referred to as **an accelerated depreciation method,** since it provides for a more rapid rate of expensing the asset cost than does the straight-line depreciation method. Returning to our example involving the $12,000 asset, we can compute the annual depreciation expense for each of the five years (see Table 3A-1). Note that the SYD factor for the first year is simply the ratio of the number of years over which the asset is to be depreciated, divided by the sum of those years—that is, the sum of the numbers one through five.[2] The

[1]The Internal Revenue Service allows the use of straight-line, double-declining balance, sum-of-the-years' digits, or other *consistent methods* for computing depreciation expense for purposes of determining taxable income. The straight-line method may be used for any depreciable property. The other methods are applicable only to new tangible property having a useful life of three or more years.

[2]The SYD factor can be computed using the following equation:

$$\text{SYD Factor} = N \left[\frac{N + 1}{2} \right]$$

where N is the depreciable life of the asset.

Table 3A-1 SUM-OF-THE-YEARS' DIGITS METHOD FOR COMPUTING DEPRECIATION

YEAR	DEPRECIABLE BOOK VALUE		SYD FACTOR		DEPRECIATION EXPENSE
1	10,000.00	×	5/15	=	$3,333.33
2	10,000.00	×	4/15	=	2,666.67
3	10,000.00	×	3/15	=	2,000.00
4	10,000.00	×	2/15	=	1,333.33
5	10,000.00	×	1/15	=	666.67

second-year SYD depreciation factor is the ratio of the useful life minus one, divided once again by the sum of the years' digits; the third-year factor involves subtracting two from the useful life to get the numerator of the ratio, and so forth for the remaining years.

Still another commonly used method of accelerated depreciation is the **double-declining balance method** (DDB). This depreciation method involves depreciating the undepreciated value of the asset at twice the rate of the straight-line method. This method is demonstrated in Table 3A-2.[3] In terms of the preceding example, the straight-line rate is simply $2000 ÷ $10,000 or .2. Thus, the double-declining rate is 2 × .2 or .4.

Under the DDB method the asset is not fully depreciated. The Internal Revenue Code allows the firm to switch over from DDB to straight-line any time prior to the end of the useful life of the asset. The optimal time to make the switch is in that year where straight-line depreciation exceeds that of the DDB method. Note in Table 3A-2 that the switch occurs in year four such that the remaining book value at the end of year five equals $2000 or the asset's salvage value.

With regard to all three methods for computing depreciation it should be noted that the two accelerated methods offer the very real advantage of deferring the payment of taxes, which reduces their present value.[4] This can be demonstrated by a very simple example based on the straight-line and sum-of-the-years' digits examples presented earlier.

Let us assume that the firm expects to have operating income before depreciation of $4000 for each of the next five years, and let us further assume that the firm faces a 50% tax rate. Table 3A-3 contains the funds provided by operations for each of the next five years and for both the straight-line and SYD depreciation methods.

It is obvious from Table 3A-3 that for the five-year period the total amount of taxes paid, after-tax income, and funds provided by operations[5]

---

[3]The remaining book value would be written off as depreciation expense in year five.

[4]We discuss the present-value concept in Chapter 5. Very simply, the present value of a future cash flow is that amount of cash which will grow at some rate i to equal the future cash flow at the end of N years, e.g., where $i = 10\%$, $N = 1$, and the future value is $110. The corresponding present value is $100.

[5]Funds provided by operations, it will be recalled, equals the sum of the period's after-tax net income and depreciation expense.

Table 3A-2 COMPUTATION OF DOUBLE-DECLINING BALANCE DEPRECIATION EXPENSE

YEAR	BOOK VALUE OF ASSET (FIRST OF YEAR)[a]	DEPRECIATION RATE	DEPRECIATION EXPENSE	ACCUMULATED DEPRECIATION	BOOK VALUE (END OF YEAR)
1	$12,000.00	.40	$4,800.00	$4,800.00	$7,200.00
2	7,200.00	.40	$2,880.00	7,680.00	4,320.00
3	4,320.00	.40	1,728.00	9,408.00	2,592.00
4	2,592.00	—	296.00[b]	10,000.00	2,296.00
5	2,296.00	—	296.00	10,000.00	2,000.00

[a]Under this method the salvage value is not subtracted from the asset's cost to determine the base used in calculating depreciation expense.

[b]Depreciation expense for years four and five is limited to a total of $592.00, as the asset's salvage value is $2,000.00. Thus, switching to straight-line depreciation in year four produces a depreciation expense of $592.00/2 = $296.00 for each of the two remaining years in the useful life of the asset.

Table 3A-3 FUNDS PROVIDED BY OPERATIONS USING STRAIGHT-LINE VERSUS SUM-OF-THE-YEARS DIGITS DEPRECIATION

STRAIGHT-LINE METHOD

Year	Operating Income[a]	Depreciation, Straight-Line	Taxable Income	Income Taxes	Net After-Tax Income	Funds from Operations[b]
1	$4,000.00	$2,000.00	$2,000.00	$1,000.00	$1,000.00	$3,000.00
2	4,000.00	2,000.00	2,000.00	1,000.00	1,000.00	3,000.00
3	4,000.00	2,000.00	2,000.00	1,000.00	1,000.00	3,000.00
4	4,000.00	2,000.00	2,000.00	1,000.00	1,000.00	3,000.00
5	4,000.00	2,000.00	2,000.00	1,000.00	1,000.00	3,000.00
Totals	$20,000.00	$10,000.00	$10,000.00	$5,000.00	$5,000.00	$15,000.00

SUM-OF-THE-YEARS METHOD

Year	Operating Income	Depreciation, SYD	Taxable Income	Income Taxes	Net After-Tax Income	Funds from Operations
1	$4,000.00	$3,333.33	$ 666.67	$ 333.33	$ 333.33	$3,666.66
2	4,000.00	2,666.67	1,333.33	666.67	666.66	3,333.33
3	4,000.00	2,000.00	2,000.00	1,000.00	1,000.00	3,000.00
4	4,000.00	1,333.33	2,666.67	1,333.34	1,333.33	2,666.66
5	4,000.00	666.67	3,333.33	1,666.67	1,666.66	2,333.33
Totals	$20,000.00	$10,000.00	$10,000.00	$5,000.01	$4,999.99	$14,999.99

[a]Operating income is used here to mean that amount of revenue from operations after the deduction of all selling, general, and administrative expenses other than depreciation.

[b]Funds from operations equal the sum of net after-tax profit and depreciation expense. Depreciation expense is added back to net profits, since it does not constitute a cash expense.

for the five-year period are the same regardless of which depreciation method is used. The respective totals from Table 3A-3 are $5000 in taxes, $5000 in after-tax income, and $15,000 in funds from operations. There is, however, one very important difference, which relates to the timing of tax payments and the consequent effect on funds or cash flow from operations. Note that the SYD method results in lower taxes being paid in years one and two, so that the figure for funds provided by operations is higher in those years. The reverse is true in years four and five. Since cash flows in years one and two are worth more to the firm than like cash flows in years four and five (in terms of their present value), the time pattern of cash flows produced by the SYD method is preferred.

The number of years over which a fixed asset can be depreciated (for purposes of computing taxable income) is prescribed by the Internal Revenue Code. Specific guidelines are provided in the class life Asset Depreciation Range (ADR) system. The ADR system is based upon broad industry classes of assets. For example, depreciable assets used in mining can be depreciated over a period as short as 8 years or as long as 12 years with an asset guideline period of 10 years.[6]

ACCOUNTING FOR INVENTORIES AND COST OF GOODS SOLD

Several methods can be used to determine a firm's cost of goods sold. Each relates to the basis used in valuing the firm's inventory, since the firm's purchases that are *not* passed through the income statement as cost of goods sold remain in the firm's inventory account. We will discuss two very common methods for determining the cost of goods sold and consequently the value of the inventory account. The first involves assigning to the period's cost of goods sold the prices paid for the oldest items of inventory held by the firm at the beginning of the period. This is commonly referred to as the **first-in, first-out** or FIFO method. The second assigns the cost of the most recently purchased inventory items to the period's cost of goods sold. This is called the **last-in, first-out** or LIFO method. The method selected can have a material effect on the firm's computed net earnings during a period where the prices of its purchases consistently rose or fell. For example, in a period when prices have been rising, the use of the FIFO method results in a lower cost of goods sold, a larger gross profit, a higher tax liability, a higher inventory amount, and a higher net earnings figure than LIFO; LIFO (which costs the firm's sale items using the most recent prices paid by the firm) will result in a lower inventory amount, a higher cost of goods sold figure, and, consequently, lower gross profits, lower taxes, and lower net earnings. The opposite results would follow should prices have fallen during the period.

What importance should be attached to the choice of methods for determining cost of goods sold? Under either method the cash flows that result from sales will be the same, for the actual cost of the items sold *does*

---

[6]*1977 U.S. Master Tax Guide*, p. 414.

not vary with the method chosen for computing cost of goods sold. However, a very real cash flow effect can result in terms of the amount of taxes that the firm must pay. During a period of rising prices LIFO results in lower taxes being paid than FIFO, while during a period of falling prices the opposite is true.[7] Further, it should be noted that the reported inventory amounts may vary considerably with the application of one method as compared to the other—but the physical quantity and composition of the goods is not affected.

[7]The Internal Revenue Service does not allow frequent changes in inventory policy. Once a policy has been adopted, it may not be changed without the Commissioner's consent. Furthermore, changing the inventory costing method solely for the purpose of reducing taxes is not accepted by the Internal Revenue Service. Instead, the taxpayer must show that the new method more closely matches revenues with cost of goods sold. See Regulation 1.471-2 of the Internal Revenue Code for a more detailed discussion.

GLOSSARY OF ACCOUNTING TERMS

APPENDIX 3B

accelerated depreciation. A term encompassing any method for computing depreciation expense wherein the charges decrease with time. Examples of accelerated methods include sum-of-the-years' digits and double-declining balance as contrasted with straight-line.

accrual basis of accounting. The method of recognizing revenues when the earning process is virtually complete and when an exchange transaction has occurred, and recognizing expenses as they are incurred in generating those revenues. Thus, revenues and expenses recognized under the accrual basis of accounting are independent of the time when cash is received or expenditures are made. This contrasts with the cash basis of accounting.

accumulated depreciation. The sum of depreciation charges on an asset since its acquisition. This total is deducted from gross fixed assets to compute net fixed assets. This balance sheet entry is sometimes referred to as the reserve for depreciation, accrued depreciation, or the allowance for depreciation.

administrative expense. An expense category used to report expenses incurred by the firm but not reflected in specific activities such as manufacturing or selling.

amortizing. The procedure followed in allocating the cost of long-lived assets to the periods in which their benefits are derived. For fixed assets the amortization is called depreciation expense, whereas for wasting assets (natural resources), it is called depletion expense.

authorized capital stock. This specifies the total number of shares of stock the firm can issue and is specified in the articles of incorporation.

bad debt expense. An adjustment to income and accounts receivable reflecting the value of uncollectible accounts.

balance sheet. A statement of financial position on a particular date. The balance sheet equation is as follows: Total Assets = Total Liabilities + Owners' Equity.

bond. Long-term debt instrument carried on the balance sheet at its face amount or par value (usually $1000 per bond), which is payable at maturity. The coupon rate on the bond is the percent of the bond's face value payable in interest each year. Bonds usually pay interest semiannually.

book value. The net amount of an asset shown in the accounts of a firm. When referring to an entire firm, it relates the excess of total assets over total liabilities (also referred to as owners' equity and net worth).

capital. Sometimes, the total assets of a firm; at other times, the owners' equity alone.

capitalization. Stockholders' equity plus the par value of outstanding bonds.

capital stock. All shares of outstanding common and preferred stock.

cash flow. The excess (deficiency) of cash receipts over cash disbursements for a given period.

common stock. The stock interest of the residual owners of the firm. These owners have claim to earnings and asset values remaining after the claims of all creditors and preferred stockholders are satisfied.

cost of goods sold. The total cost allocated to the production of a completed product for the period.

current assets. Assets that are normally converted into cash within the operating cycle of the firm (normally a period of one year or less). Such items as cash, accounts receivable, marketable securities, prepaid expenses, and inventories are frequently found among a firm's current assets.

current liabilities. Liabilities or debts of the firm that must be paid within the firm's normal operating cycle (usually one year or less), such as accounts and notes payable, income taxes payable, and wages and salaries payable.

depreciable life. The period over which an asset is depreciated. See footnote 4 on p. 48.

depreciation expense. Amortization of plant, property, and equipment cost during an accounting period.

dividend. A distribution of earnings to the owners of a corporation either in the form of cash (cash dividend) or shares of stock (stock dividend).

double-declining balance depreciation. A method for computing declining balance depreciation expense in which the constant percentage is equal to $2/N$, where N represents the depreciable life of the asset. See Appendix 3A for an example of double-declining balance depreciation.

earnings. A synonym for net income or net profit after taxes.

earnings after taxes (EAT). Other terms often used synonymously are net income and net profit.

earnings before interest and taxes (EBIT). A commonly used synonym for net operating income. Note that where other income exists, EBIT equals net operating income plus other income.

earnings before taxes (EBT). Often used to identify income before taxes or taxable income.

earnings per share. Net income after taxes available to the common stockholders (after preferred dividends) divided by the number of outstanding common shares.

equity financing. The raising of funds through the sale of common or preferred stock.

extraordinary item. A revenue or expense that is both unusual in nature and infrequent in occurrence. Such items and their tax effects are separated from ordinary income in the income statement.

FIFO. A method for determining the inventory cost assigned to cost of goods sold wherein the cost of the oldest items in inventory are charged to the period's cost of goods sold (first in, first out). Ending inventories therefore will reflect the prices paid for the most recent purchases. See also the discussion in Appendix 3A.

fixed assets. These assets share the characteristic that they are not converted into cash within a single operating cycle of the firm; they include buildings, equipment, and land.

goodwill. Included as an asset entry in the balance sheet to reflect the excess over fair market value paid for the assets of an acquired firm.

gross profit. The excess of net sales over cost of goods sold.

income statement. The statement of profit or loss for the period comprised of net revenues less expenses for the period. (See *accrual basis of accounting*.)

income tax. An annual expense incurred by the firm based upon income and paid to a governmental entity.

intangible asset. An asset that lacks physical substance, such as goodwill or a patent.

inventory. The balance in an asset account such as raw materials, work in process, or finished goods. (See LIFO and FIFO.)

LIFO. A method for determining the inventory cost assigned to cost of goods sold whereby the cost of the most recent purchases of inventory is assigned to the period's cost of goods sold (last-in, first-out). Ending inventories thus contain the cost of the oldest items of inventory.

lease. A contract requiring payments by the user (lessee) to its owner (lessor) for the use of an asset. In accordance with FASB Statement 13 most financial lease agreements entered into after January 1, 1977, must be included in the assets and liabilities of the lessee's balance sheet. The right of the lessee to use the asset is represented by an asset called a leasehold.

liability. An obligation to pay a specified amount to a creditor in return for some current benefit.

liquid assets. Those assets of the firm which can be easily converted into cash with little or no loss in value. Generally included are cash, marketable securities, and sometimes accounts receivable.

long-term debt. All liabilities of the firm that are not due and payable within one year. Examples include installment notes, equipment loans, and bonds payable.

marketable securities. The securities (bonds and stocks) of other firms and governments held by a firm.

net income. See *earnings after taxes (EAT)*.

net sales. Gross sales less returns, allowances, and cash discounts taken by customers.

owners' equity. Total assets minus total liabilities, sometimes referred to as net worth.

paid-in capital. The excess of total capital paid in over the stock's par or stated value. For example, if a share of stock with a $1 par value is sold by a firm for $10, the common stock account will be increased by $1 and paid-in capital will rise by $9.

par value. The face value of a security.

patent. The rights to the benefits of one's invention granted to the inventor by the government. These rights are extended for a maximum of 17 years.

preferred stock. The capital stock of the owners of the firm whose claim on assets and income is secondary to that of bondholders but preferred as to that of the common stockholders.

profit and loss statement. Another name for the income statement.

retained earnings. The sum of a firm's net income over its life less all dividends paid.

revenue. See *net sales*.

sinking fund. Assets and their earnings set aside to retire long-term debt obligations of the firm. Payments into sinking funds are made after taxes and are usually described in the bond indenture (contract between the borrowing firm and the bondholders).

stock dividend. A dividend that results in a transfer of retained earnings to the capital stock and paid-in capital accounts. This contrasts with a cash dividend. (See *dividend*.)

Financial Forecasting, Planning, and Budgeting

*T*his chapter has two primary objectives: First, it will develop an appreciation for the role of forecasting in the firm's financial planning process. Basically, forecasts of future sales revenues and their associated expenses give the firm the information needed to project its future needs for financing. Second, the chapter will provide an overview of the firm's budgetary stystem, including the cash budget and the pro forma or planned income statement and balance sheet. Pro forma financial statements give the financial manager a useful tool for analyzing the effects of the firm's forecasts and planned activities on its financial performance as well as its needs for financing. In addition, pro forma statements can be used as a benchmark or standard to compare against actual operating results. Used in this way, pro forma statements are an instrument for controlling or monitoring the firm's progress throughout the planning period.

FINANCIAL FORECASTING

The need for forecasting in financial management arises where the future financing needs of the firm are being estimated. The basic steps involved in predicting those financing needs include the following: *Step 1:* Project the firm's sales revenues and expenses over the planning period. *Step 2:* Estimate the levels of investment in current and fixed assets that are necessary to support the projected sales. *Step 3:* Determine the firm's financing needs throughout the planning period. Steps 1 and 2 are discussed under the general heading of financial forecasting, while step 3 is discussed in conjunction with financial planning and budgeting later in the chapter.

The entire firm's operations can be visualized through the use of a **cash flow cycle diagram.** The diagram, as shown in Figure 4-1, depicts the firm's operations as a large pump that pushes cash through various reservoirs such as inventories and accounts receivable and dispenses cash for taxes, interest and principal payments on debt, and cash dividends to the shareholders. The problem in financial forecasting, then, is one of predicting cash inflows and outflows and the corresponding financial needs of the firm. These needs are related to the size of the various reservoirs that hold cash. These reservoirs represent the various assets in which the firm must make investments in order to produce the expected level of sales.

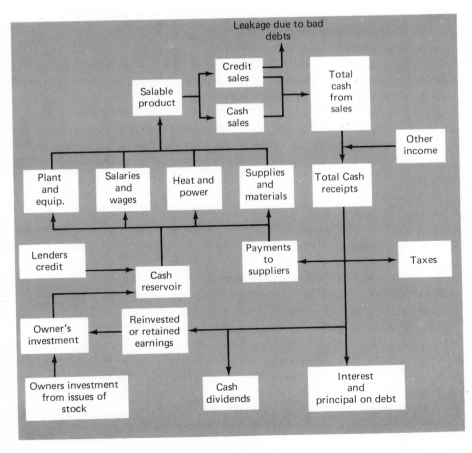

FIGURE 4-1   *Cash Flow Diagram*

TRACING THROUGH
THE CASH FLOW CYCLE

Since the firm's cash flow cycle is a continuous process, we will find it useful for illustrative purposes to consider the first cycle of a new firm. The process begins with the firm's cash reservoir, which consists initially of the owner's investment and of funds borrowed from lenders. This cash is used to acquire plant and equipment, as well as supplies and materials. It is also used to pay wages and salaries, to pay for utilities such as heat and power, and to replace materials, plant, and equipment used in making the firm's product. These expenditures make up the cost of goods sold for the firm's salable product. Sales are then made either for cash or on credit (with some leakage for bad debt losses). To this cash flow stream are added cash inflows resulting from the sale of assets such as equipment, land, or securities. In the final phase of the cycle cash is dispersed to pay obligations to suppliers for materials purchased on credit, income taxes to the government, interest and principal to the firm's creditors, and finally cash dividends to the firm's owners.

FORECASTING CASH FLOWS

The problem of financial forecasting, to summarize, consists of predicting future sales, which in turn provides the basis for predicting the level of investment required in inventories, receivables, plant, and equipment. Through the use of the cash budget the information from these projections is combined to provide an estimate of the firm's future financing needs.

The key ingredient in the firm's planning process is the **sales forecast.** This projection will generally be derived using information from a number of sources. At a minimum, the sales forecast for the coming year would reflect (1) any past trend in sales that is expected to carry through into the new year, and (2) the influence of any events that might materially affect that trend.[1] An example of the latter would be the initiation of a major advertising campaign or a change in the firm's pricing policy.

Sales Forecast

Traditional financial forecasting takes the sales forecast as a given and makes forecasts of its impact on the firm's various expenses, assets, and liabilities. There are two commonly used methods for making these projections: (1) the percent of sales method, and (2) regression analysis.

*Forecasting
Financial
Variables*

[1] A discussion of forecast methodology is outside the scope of this book. The interested reader is referred to John C. Chambers, Satinder K. Mullick, and Donald D. Smith, *An Executive's Guide to Forecasting* (New York: John Wiley & Sons, Inc., 1974); Roger K. Chisholm and Gilbert R. Whitaker, Jr., *Forecasting Methods* (Homewood, Ill.: Richard D. Irwin, Inc., 1971); and Carl A. Dauten, *Business Cycles and Forecasting* (Cincinnati, Ohio: Southwestern Publishing Company, 1974).

PERCENT OF SALES METHOD

The **percent of sales method** involves estimating the level of an expense, asset, or liability for a future period as a percent of the sales forecast. The percentage used can come from the most recent financial statement item as a percent of current sales, from an average computed over several years, from the judgment of the analyst, or from some combination of these sources.

For illustrative purposes we shall forecast 1979 inventories for the J. B. Chamblis Company (JBCC). Table 4-1 gives JBCC's sales and inventories for 1977 and 1978, respectively. In 1977 inventories comprised 6.6 percent of sales and in 1978 they made up roughly 6.2 percent. Thus, for predictive purposes the analyst might use 6 to 7 percent of the 1979 forecasted sales to predict 1979 inventories.

This rather simplistic forecast method assumes that no other information is available that would indicate a change in the observed relationship between sales and inventories. For example, if the firm plans to restrict any buildup in inventories during the coming year (even though sales might be rising), then the historical percentages will overestimate the actual level of investment in inventories. Assuming that JBCC's inventory as a percentage of sales will be stable and that 1979 sales are predicted to be $23 million, then JBCC would predict inventories to be between 6 and 7 percent of that amount or $1,380,000 to $1,610,000, respectively.

SCATTER DIAGRAM OMIT
AND REGRESSION METHODS

Historical sales and inventories for JBCC covering the past 10 years are given in Table 4-2. Figure 4-2 is a visual representation of the relationship between JBCC's inventories and sales.

Scatter Diagram Method.   Figure 4-2, called a **scatter diagram,** can be used to determine the relationship between sales and inventories. To estimate this relationship we simply fit a line through the scatter of points. The line is visually fitted such that the scatter of points about the line is minimized. To predict JBCC's inventories for 1979, first locate the estimate of 1979 sales on the horizontal axis. Next, draw a vertical line from the sales estimate up to the fitted line and then horizontally over to the inventory

Table 4-1 INVENTORY AND SALES DATA FOR THE J. B. CHAMBLIS COMPANY

YEAR	INVENTORY	SALES	INVENTORIES AS A PERCENT OF SALES
1977	$1,414,102	$21,418,202	6.6%
1978	1,397,248	22,703,229	6.2%

Table 4-2 HISTORICAL INVENTORY AND SALES INFORMATION FOR JBCC (THOUSANDS OF DOLLARS)

YEAR	INVENTORY	SALES
1969	$1,155	$19,278
1970	1,277	19,751
1971	1,188	19,753
1972	1,097	19,948
1973	1,279	20,748
1974	1,275	21,250
1975	1,314	20,022
1976	1,225	20,761
1977	1,414	21,418
1978	1,397	22,703

axis. Thus, for a sales estimate of $23 million we project an inventory level of $1,490,000 using the inventory-sales relationship in Figure 4-2.

Simple Regression Method. **Least squares regression** represents a procedure for mechanically *fitting* a line through a scatter diagram such as Figure 4-2. The sum of the squared deviations of the observed sales-inventory points from the fitted line is minimized, thus the name *least squares*. These deviations are identified in Figure 4-3 with dashed lines. If the regression line were to perfectly fit the observed sales-inventory data, then all data points would lie on the regression line, *BB′*.

The resulting regression equation for JBCC's inventory-sales relationship is

$$\text{estimated inventory } (t) = -\$210{,}224 + .0716 \text{ sales } (t) \qquad (4\text{-}1)$$

where sales (t) is the level of sales for period t and estimated inventory (t) is the corresponding inventory forecast. Both $-\$210{,}244$ and $.0716$ are *coefficients* of the predictive equation and are determined in accordance with the least squares method.

To estimate 1979 inventories we simply substitute the 1979 sales estimate for sales into equation (4-1). Using a sales projection of $23 million, we obtain an estimate of 1979 inventories as follows:

$$\text{estimated inventory } (1979) = -\$210{,}224 + .0716(\$23{,}000{,}000)$$

$$= \$1{,}436{,}576$$

Inventories for 1979 are estimated to be $1,436,576; however, estimated sales may not be the sole or even the most important determinant of JBCC's inventories.

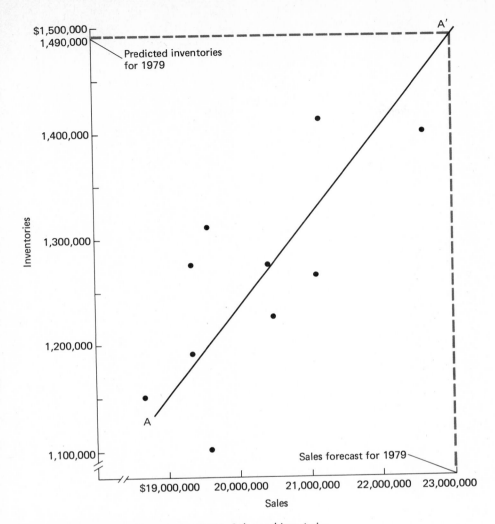

FIGURE 4-2   *Scatter Diagram for JBCC's Sales and Inventories*

Multiple Regression Analysis.   JBCC's inventory level could well be related to the lead time required to obtain shipments. In addition, other factors such as strikes, availability of raw materials, favorable buying opportunities, and simple errors in judgment could affect JBCC's investment in inventories. Thus, a predictive equation employing two or more predictor variables may be useful. For example, consider the following two-variable regression equation:

$$\text{estimated inventories } (t) = a + b \cdot \text{sales } (t) + c \cdot \text{lead time } (t) \qquad (4\text{-}2)$$

99

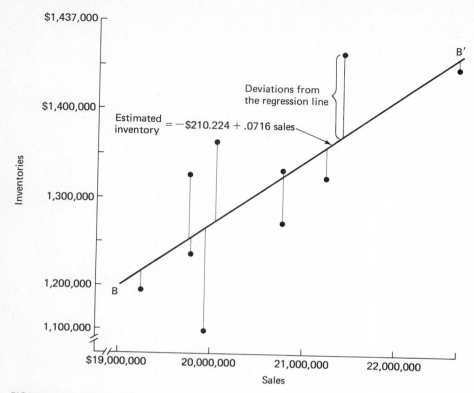

FIGURE 4-3 *Simple Regression Line for JBCC's Sales and Inventories*

where *sales* (*t*) is the level of sales for period *t* and *lead time* (*t*) represents the average lead time (in days) between the order date and actual receipt of materials for period *t*. The *a, b,* and *c* terms are the coefficients of the multiple regression equation, which are again estimated using the method of least squares.[2]

Table 4-3 gives historical sales, lead time, and inventory data for JBCC spanning the last ten years of its operations. These data serve as the basis for estimating the *a, b,* and *c* coefficients of equation (4-2). The resulting multiple regression equation for JBCC's inventories is

$$\text{estimated inventories } (t) = \$179{,}634 + .0574 \text{ sales } (t) + 9{,}923.1 \text{ lead time } (t) \tag{4-3}$$

We can use equation (4-3) to predict JBCC's 1979 inventory level by substituting for estimated 1979 sales ($23,000,000) and the estimated lead time (30 days). The resulting inventory estimate is

[2]An excellent reference for multiple regression analysis is found in Chapters 4 through 8 of N. R. Draper and H. Smith, *Applied Regression Analysis* (New York: John Wiley & Sons, 1966).

$$\text{estimated inventories (1979)} = \$179,684 + .0574(\$23,000,000) + 9923.1(30 \text{ days})$$

$$= \$1,438,209$$

The resulting estimate of JBCC's 1979 inventories is $1,438,209. The multiple regression estimate offers the advantage of considering more information than the simple sales-inventory regression equation. Whether it will prove more accurate depends upon how accurately average lead time can be projected for 1979 and upon the stability of the relationships between lead time, sales, and inventories.

Table 4-3 INVENTORY, SALES, AND LEAD TIME DATA FOR JBCC, 1969–1978

YEAR	INVENTORY	SALES	AVERAGE LEAD TIME (DAYS)
1969	$1,155,000	$19,248,000	21
1970	1,277,000	19,751,000	32
1971	1,188,000	19,753,000	24
1972	1,097,000	19,948,000	17
1973	1,279,000	20,748,000	23
1974	1,275,000	21,250,000	24
1975	1,314,000	20,022,000	35
1976	1,225,000	20,761,000	22
1977	1,414,000	21,418,000	38
1978	1,397,000	22,703,000	27

SUMMARY
OF THE INVENTORY FORECASTS

Table 4-4 gives the different forecasts for JBCC's 1979 inventories. Ultimately, one will prove to be the most accurate. Based upon all five estimates, the 1979 inventory level is projected to fall within the range of 6 to 7 percent of sales. Note that for a very small range of values for firm sales, the simplistic percent of sales method provides inventory projections very close to those of the more sophisticated regression methods. However,

Table 4-4 INVENTORY FORECASTS FOR JBCC

FORECAST METHOD	INVENTORIES (1979)
Percent of sales:	
6%	$1,380,000
7%	1,610,000
Scatter diagram, Figure 4-2	1,490,000
Simple regression, equation (4-1)	1,436,576
Multiple regression, equation (4-3)	1,438,209

when the sales level used in computing the percent of sales differs substantially from the projected sales level, the percent of sales estimates can be grossly in error.[3]

This concludes a very brief overview of financial forecasting. The subject is far too broad to cover here in its entirety. Rather, we have given a basic introduction to the use of several forecast models in financial planning, emphasizing the importance of the resulting forecasts to the ultimate success of the firm's planning efforts.

FINANCIAL PLANNING AND BUDGETING

Budget Functions

Financial forecasts are put to use in constructing financial plans. These plans culminate in the preparation of a cash budget and a set of pro forma statements for a future period in the firm's operations.

A **budget** is simply a forecast of future events. For example, students preparing for final exams make use of time budgets, which help them allocate their limited preparation time among their courses. Students also must budget their financial resources among competing uses such as books, tuition, food, rent, clothes, and "extracurricular activities."

Budgets perform three basic functions for the user. First, they indicate the firm's needs for future financing. Second, they provide the basis for taking corrective action in the event that budgeted figures do not match the actual or realized figures. Third, budgets provide the basis for performance evaluation. Plans are carried out by people, and budgets provide benchmarks that can be used to evaluate the performance of those responsible for carrying out those plans and, in turn, controlling their actions.

In the pages that follow, we shall develop an example budgetary system for a retailing firm. The primary emphasis will be on the cash budget and pro forma financial statements, which provide the necessary information for estimating the firm's future financing requirements.

---

[3]To understand the underlying reason for the errors resulting from the use of the percent of sales method, we have to define the method in equation form. That is, a percent of sales forecast for inventories can be defined as follows:

$$\text{estimated inventories } (t) = \frac{\text{inventories}}{\text{sales}} \times \text{estimated sales } (t)$$

Comparing this formulation to the simple regression model in equation (4-1) we see that the percent of sales equation assumes an intercept of zero and a slope equal to the ratio of inventories to sales. This model is appropriate only where inventories vary as a constant proportion of sales for all levels of sales. Given that most firms maintain some safety stock of inventories that does not vary with sales and that inventories usually decrease as a percent of sales as sales rise, the percent of sales method provides only an approximation to the true model relating inventories and sales. However, where the level of sales used in calculating the percent of sales is very near the projected level of sales, the percent of sales forecast may provide reasonably accurate forecasts.

Although our interest in financial planning focuses on the cash budget, a number of other budgets provide the basis for its preparation. This system of budgets allows planning for each source of cash flow, both inflow and outflow, that will affect the firm throughout the planning period. In general, a business will utilize four types of budgets: physical budgets, cost budgets, profit budgets, and cash budgets. Figure 4-4 presents an overview of the budgetary system.

Physical budgets include budgets for unit sales, personnel or manpower, unit production, inventories, and actual physical facilities. These budgets are used as the basis for generating cost and profit budgets. **Cost budgets** are prepared for every major expense category of the firm. For example, a manufacturing firm would prepare cost budgets for manufacturing or production cost, selling cost, administrative cost, financing cost, and research and development cost. These cost budgets along with the sales budget provide the basis for preparing a **profit budget.** Finally, converting

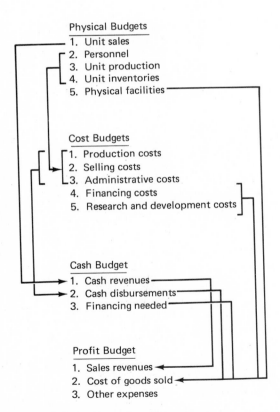

FIGURE 4-4   *The Budget System*

all the budget information to a cash basis provides the information required to prepare the cash budget.

THE CASH BUDGET

The **cash budget** represents a detailed plan of future cash flows and is composed of four elements: cash receipts, cash disbursements, net change in cash for the period, and new financing needed.

Example. To demonstrate the construction and use of the cash budget consider Salco, Inc., a regional distributor of household furniture. Salco's sales are highly seasonal, peaking in the months of March through May. Roughly 30 percent of Salco's sales are collected one month after the sale, 50 percent two months after the sale, and the remainder during the third month.

Salco attempts to pace its purchases with expected sales. Purchases generally equal 75 percent of sales and are made two months in advance of anticipated sales. Payments are made in the month following purchases. For example, June sales are estimated at $100,000, thus April purchases are .75 × $100,000 = $75,000. Correspondingly, payments for purchases in May equal $75,000. Wages, salaries, rent, and other cash expenses are recorded in Table 4-5, which gives Salco's cash budget for the six-month period ended in June 1979. Additional expenditures are recorded in the cash budget related to the purchase of equipment in the amount of $14,000 during February and the repayment of a $12,000 loan in May.

Salco presently has a cash balance of $20,000 and wants to maintain a minimum balance of $10,000. Additional borrowing necessary to maintain that minimum balance is estimated in the final section of Table 4-5. Note that even though sales peak in May, Salco's cash inflows from those sales do not actually become positive until June. This, of course, results from the particular pattern of payments and collections that Salco experiences.

The *financing needed* line on Salco's cash budget indicates that the firm will need to borrow $36,350 in February, $65,510 in March, $85,610 in April, and $95,110 in May; only in June will the firm be able to reduce its borrowing.

FIXED VERSUS VARIABLE BUDGETS

The cash budget given in Table 4-5 for Salco, Inc., is an example of a **fixed budget**. Cash flow estimates are made for a single set of monthly sales estimates. Thus, the estimates of expenses and new financing needed are meaningful only for the level of sales from which they were computed. To avoid this limitation, several budgets corresponding to different sets of sales estimates can be prepared. Such a flexible budget fulfills two of management's basic needs: It gives added information regarding the range of the firm's possible financing needs, and it

Table 4-5 SALCO FURNITURE COMPANY, INC. Cash Budget for the Six Months Ended June 30, 1979

WORKSHEET	OCT.	NOV.	DEC.	JAN.	FEB.	MAR.	APR.	MAY	JUNE	JULY	AUG.
Sales	$55,000	62,000	50,000	60,000	75,000	88,000	100,000	110,000	100,000	80,000	75,000
Collections:											
First month (30%)				15,000	18,000	22,500	26,400	30,000	33,000		
Second month (50%)				31,000	25,000	30,000	37,500	44,000	50,000		
Third month (20%)				11,000	12,400	10,000	12,000	15,000	17,600		
Total				$57,000	55,400	62,500	75,900	89,000	100,600		
Purchases			$56,250	66,000	75,000	82,500	75,000	60,000	56,250		
Payments (one-month lag)				56,250	66,000	75,000	82,500	75,000	60,000		
Cash receipts:											
Collections				$57,000	55,400	62,500	75,900	89,000	100,600		
Cash disbursements:											
Purchases				$56,250	66,000	75,000	82,500	75,000	60,000		
Wages and salaries				3,000	10,000	7,000	8,000	6,000	4,000		
Rent				4,000	4,000	4,000	4,000	4,000	4,000		
Other expenses				1,000	500	1,200	1,500	1,500	1,200		
Taxes					14,000	4,460			5,200		
Purchase of equipment								12,000			
Loan repayment											
Total				$64,250	94,500	91,660	96,000	98,500	74,400		
Net monthly change:				$ (7,250)	(39,100)	(29,160)	(20,100)	(9,500)	26,200		
Beginning cash balance				$20,000	12,750	10,000	10,000	10,000	10,000		
Ending balance—no borrowing				12,750	(26,350)	(19,160)	(10,100)	500	36,200		
Financing needed				—	36,350	29,160	20,100	9,500	(26,200)		
Ending cash balance				12,750	10,000	10,000	10,000	10,000	10,000		
Cumulative borrowing				—	36,350	65,510	85,610	95,110	68,910		

provides a standard against which to measure the performance of subordinates who are responsible for the various cost and revenue items contained in the budget.[4]

This second function deserves some additional comment. The obvious problem that arises relates to the fact that costs vary with the actual level of sales experienced by the firm. Thus, if the budget is to be used as a standard for performance evaluation or control, it must be constructed so as to match realized sales and production figures. This can involve much more than simply "adjusting cost figures up or down in proportion to the deviation of actual from planned sales." That is, costs may not vary in strict proportion to sales, just as inventory levels may not vary as a constant percent of sales. Thus, preparation of a flexible budget involves reestimating all the cash expenses that would be incurred at each of several possible sales levels. This estimation process might utilize a variant of the percent of sales method or the regression method discussed earlier.[5]

BUDGET PERIOD

There are no strict rules for determining the length of the budget period. However, as a general rule it should be long enough to show the effect of management policies, yet short enough so that estimates can be made with reasonable accuracy. Applying this rule of thumb to the Salco example in Table 4-5 indicates that the six-month budget period is probably too short, in that it is not known whether the planned operations of the firm will be successful over the coming fiscal year. That is, for most of the first six-month period the firm is operating with a cash flow deficit. If this does not reverse in the latter six months of the year, then a reevaluation of the firm's plans and policies is clearly in order.

Longer-range budgets are also prepared in the form of the capital expenditure budget. This budget details the firm's plans for acquiring plant and equipment over a 5-year, 10-year or even longer period. Furthermore, firms very often develop comprehensive long-range plans extending up to 10 years into the future. These plans are generally not as comprehensive as the annual cash budget but they do consider such major components as sales, capital expenditures, new product development, capital funds acquisition, and employment needs (manpower planning).

---

[4]For a discussion of the development of flexible budgets the interested reader is referred to D. F. Scott, Jr., and L. J. Moore, "Simulating Cash Budgets," *Journal of Systems Management,* November 1973, pp. 28–33, and J. L. Pappas and G. P. Huber, "Probabilistic Short-Term Financial Planning," *Financial Management,* Summer 1975, pp. 13–20.

[5]A general overview of financial planning models is found in T. H. Naylor, "Elements of a Planning and Modeling System," *Conference Proceedings of the National Computer Conference,* 45 (Montvale, N. J.: AFIPS Press, 1976), pp. 1017–1026.

The final stage in the budgeting process involves construction of a set of **pro forma financial statements** depicting the end result of the planning period's operations. Salco, Inc., is used to demonstrate the construction of the pro forma income statement and balance sheet. To do this, we need Salco's cash budget and its beginning balance sheet, which depicts the firm's financial condition of the firm at the start of the planning period (see Table 4-6).

THE PRO FORMA INCOME STATEMENT

The **pro forma income statement** represents a statement of planned profit or loss for a future period. For Salco a six-month pro forma income statement is constructed from the information contained in the cash budget found in Table 4-5. The final statement is presented in Table 4-7.

Net sales, found by summing the six monthly sales projections from Table 4-5, total $533,000. Cost of goods sold is computed as 75 percent of sales or $399,750. This figure could also have been found by summing purchases for November through April which represent items sold from January through June. Recall that purchases are made two months in advance, such that items sold in January were purchased in November.

Depreciation expense cannot be obtained from the cash budget, since it does not constitute a cash flow. Thus, this expense must be determined from the depreciation schedules of Salco's plant and equipment. On its existing fixed assets Salco has an annual depreciation expense of $17,200. In addition, the $14,000 piece of equipment purchased at the end of Feb-

Table 4-6	SALCO FURNITURE CO., INC.
	Balance Sheet
	December 31, 1978

Assets

Cash	$ 20,000
Accounts receivable	104,400
Inventories	101,250
Net plant and equipment	180,000
Total assets	$405,650

Liabilities and Owners' Equity

Accounts payable	$ 56,250
Notes payable (due in May 1979)	12,000
Taxes payable	4,460
Long-term debt	150,000
Common stock ($1 par value)	20,000
Paid-in capital	50,000
Retained earnings	112,940
Total liabilities and owners' equity	$405,650

Table 4-7

SALCO FURNITURE CO., INC.
Pro Forma Income Statement
for the Six-Month Period Ended June 30, 1979

Sales	$533,000
Cost of goods sold	399,750
Gross profit	$133,250
Depreciation expense	8,830
Wages and salaries	38,000
Rent	24,000
Other expenses	6,900
Net operating income	$ 55,520
Interest expense	8,100
Earnings before taxes	$ 47,420
Income taxes payable	9,932
Net income	$ 37,488

ruary will be depreciated over a 15-year life toward a 3650 salvage value. Using straight-line depreciation and depreciating the asset for four months of the budget period, we find this amounts to roughly $230. Thus, total depreciation expense for the period is $8830.

Wages and salaries, rent, and other expenses are found by summing the relevant cash flow items from the cash budget for the months of January through June. This assumes, of course, that all of these expenses are paid at the end of each month in which they are earned, rent is not paid in advance, and all other expenses are paid on a monthly basis. Wages and salaries total $38,000, rent expense equals $24,000, and other expenses are expected to be $6900.

Subtracting the above operating expenses from gross profit leaves a net operating income of $55,520. Interest expense of $8100 is then deducted from net operating income to obtain earnings before taxes of $47,420. Federal income taxes payable are found using the corporate income tax schedule discussed in Chapter 2—that is, 20 percent of the first $25,000 in taxable income, 22 percent of the next $25,000, and 48 percent of all income in excess of $50,000. For Salco this equals a tax expense for the period of $9932. Finally, subtracting the estimated taxes from earnings before taxes indicates net income for the period of $37,488.

NET CASH FLOW VERSUS NET INCOME

The difference in the cash and accrual bases of accounting for corporate income is vividly demonstrated in the cash budget and pro forma income statements for the period. On a cash flow basis the firm has a substantial net negative cash flow, while on an accrual basis the firm earned $37,488. The difference, of course, relates to when revenues and expenses are accounted for or *recognized* in the two statements.

We can construct the **pro forma balance sheet** for Salco by using information from the cash budget (Table 4-5), the December 31, 1978, balance sheet (Table 4-6), and the pro forma income statement (Table 4-7). Salco's pro forma balance sheet for June 30, 1979, is presented in Table 4-8. Estimates of the individual statement entries are provided below.

Ending cash from the cash budget, $10,000, becomes the cash entry in Salco's pro forma balance sheet. The accounts receivable balance is found as follows:

Accounts receivable (12/31/78)	$104,400
+ Credit sales	533,000
− Collections	(440,400)
Accounts receivable (6/30/79)	$197,000

The beginning balance for accounts receivable is taken from the December 31, 1978, balance sheet (Table 4-6), and credit sales and collections are

Table 4-8

SALCO FURNITURE CO., INC.
Pro Forma Balance Sheet
June 30, 1979

Assets

Cash	$ 10,000
Accounts receivable	197,000
Inventories	116,250
Net plant and equipment	185,170
Total assets	$508,420

Liabilities and Owners' Equity

Accounts payable	$ 56,250
Notes payable[a]	68,910
Accrued interest	8,100
Taxes payable	4,732
Long-term debt	150,000
Common stock	20,000
Paid-in capital	50,000
Retained earnings	150,428
Total liabilities and owners' equity	$508,420

[a]Cumulative borrowing for the period was assumed to take the form of notes payable.

obtained by summing across the relevant cash budget monthly totals. Inventories are determined in a similar manner:

Inventories (12/31/78)	$101,250
+ Purchases	414,750
− Cost of goods sold	(399,750)
Inventories (6/30/79)	$116,250

Purchases were found by summing relevant monthly figures from the cash
budget for all six months of the budget period; and cost of goods sold was
taken from the pro forma income statement in Table 4-7. The net plant
and equipment figure is found as follows:

Net plant and equipment (12/31/78)	$180,000
+ Purchases of plant and equipment	14,000
− Depreciation expense	(8,830)
Net plant and equipment (6/30/79)	$185,170

Purchases of plant and equipment are reflected in the cash budget, and
depreciation expense is taken from the pro forma income statement. The
only changes that took place during the period involved the $14,000 pur-
chase and depreciation expense of $8830, leaving a net balance of
$185,170. Total assets for Salco are therefore expected to be $534,670.

The liability accounts are estimated using the same basic methodology
used in finding asset balances. Accounts payable is found as follows:

Accounts payable (12/31/78)	$ 56,250
+ Purchases	414,750
− Payments	(414,750)
Accounts payable (6/30/79)	$ 56,250

Again purchases and payments were taken from the cash budget for each
of the six months of the budget period. Notes payable are found as follows:

Notes payable (12/31/78)	$ 12,000
+ Borrowing (6/30/78)	68,910
− Repayments	(12,000)
Notes payable (6/30/79)	$ 68,910

Here it is assumed that the total new financing needed during the period
($68,910) would be raised through notes payable. Salco's use of short-term

financing may or may not be desirable, as we shall see in Chapter 6 in discussing working-capital management. An accrued interest expense item of $8100 is created as a result of interest expense in that amount that was incurred (see Salco's income statement in Table 4-7) but not paid (see the cash budget in Table 4-5). Next, compute taxes payable as follows:

Taxes payable (12/31/78)	$ 4,460
+ Tax liability for the period	9,932
− Tax payments made during the period	(9,660)
Taxes payable (6/30/79)	$ 4,732

Long-term debt, common stock, and paid-in capital remain unchanged for the period, as no new stock or long-term debt was issued nor was any repurchased or retired. Finally, the retained earnings balance is found as follows:

Retained earnings (12/31/78)	$112,940
+ Net income for the period	37,448
− Cash dividends	0
Retained earnings (6/30/79)	$150,428

Since no common dividends were paid (none were considered in the cash budget—Table 4-5), the new retained earnings figure is $150,428.

Salco's management may now wish to perform a financial analysis using the newly prepared pro forma statements. Such an analysis would provide the basis for evaluating the firm's planned financial performance over the next six months. It would entail use of a set of ratios such as those discussed in Chapter 3, which could be compared to prior-year figures and industry averages. If this analysis identified any weaknesses, the firm could take steps to correct them before they became reality.

FINANCIAL CONTROL

The pro forma statements just prepared can be used to *monitor* or control the firm's financial performance. One approach would involve preparing pro forma statements for each month during the planning period. Actual operating results for each month's operations could then be compared with the projected or pro forma figures. This type of analysis would provide an *early warning system* to detect financial problems as they develop. In particular, by comparing actual monthly (or even weekly) operating results with projected revenue and expense items (from pro forma income statements), the financial manager can maintain a very close watch on the firm's overall profitability and take an active role in determining the firm's overall performance for the planning period.

FINANCIAL PLANNING AND BUDGETING: CLOSING COMMENTS

112
BASIC TOOLS OF
FINANCIAL ANALYSIS,
PLANNING, AND
CONTROL

Two aspects of pro forma statements should be emphasized. First, these figures represent single point estimates of each of the items in the entire system of budgets and the resulting pro forma statements. Although these may be the *best estimates* as to what the future will hold for Salco, at least two additional sets of estimates may be desired, corresponding to the very worst set of circumstances that the firm might face and the very best. These extremes provide the necessary input for formulating contingency financing plans, should a deviation from the expected figures occur. Second, notes payable was used as a *plug* figure for additional financing needed. The actual source of financing selected will depend on a number of factors, including (1) the length of the period for which the financing will be needed, (2) the cost of alternative sources of funds, and (3) the risk preferences of the firm's management. These factors will be further investigated in Chapter 10, when we discuss short-term financing, and in Chapter 16, which deals with the firm's financing mix.

SUMMARY

This chapter has developed the role of forecasting within the context of the firm's financial planning efforts. Specifically, we have seen that forecasts of the firm's sales revenues and related expenses provide the basis for projecting the firm's future financing needs. Methods for forecasting financial variables include the percent of sales method, the scatter diagram method, and the regression method.

Forecasts of firm sales and expenses were used to develop the cash budget for the planning period, which was then used to estimate the firm's future financing needs. In this chapter all *needed financing* was supplied through short-term notes. However, in Chapters 6 and 16 we will look more closely at sources of financing. Chapter 6 deals with the choice between current or short-term financing versus long-term financing, Chapter 16 with the choice among long-term sources (bonds, preferred stock, and common stock).

Finally, pro forma financial statements were discussed. These statements provide the user with the basis for (1) evaluating the results of the firm's financial plans and (2) controlling the firm's operations during the planning period.

STUDY QUESTIONS

1. Discuss the shortcomings of the percent of sales method of financial forecasting.
2. Explain how a fixed cash budget differs from a variable or flexible cash budget.
3. What two basic needs does a flexible (variable) cash budget serve?
4. What would be the probable effect on a firm's cash position of the following events?

(a) Rapidly rising sales.

(b) A delay in the payment of payables.

(c) A more liberal credit policy on sales (to the firm's customers).

(d) Holding larger inventories.

5. How long should the budget period be? Why would a firm not set a rule that all budgets be for a 12-month period?

6. A cash budget is usually thought of as a means of planning for future financing needs. Why would a cash budget also be important for a firm that had excess cash on hand?

7. Explain why a cash budget would be of particular importance to a firm that experienced seasonal fluctuations in its sales.

8. Is there a difference between estimated net profit after taxes for a period and the estimated net addition to the cash balance? Explain.

STUDY PROBLEMS

4-1. The following represents the balance sheet of Odom Manufacturing Company at December 31, 1977:

ODOM MANUFACTURING CO.
Balance Sheet
December 31, 1977

Cash	$ 250,000	Accounts payable	$ 850,000
Accounts receivable	760,000	Notes payable	550,000
Inventory	860,000	Current Liabilities	$1,400,000
Current Assets	$1,870,000	Long-term debt	800,000
Property, plant, and		Common stock	600,000
equipment	1,730,000	Retained earnings	800,000
		Total liabilities and	
Total assets	$3,600,000	stockholders' equity	$3,600,000

The Treasurer of the Odom Manufacturing wishes to borrow $500,000, the funds from which would be applied in the following manner:

(1) $100,000 to reduce accounts payable.

(2) $ 75,000 to retire current notes payable.

(3) $175,000 to expand existing plant facilities.

(4) $ 80,000 to increase inventories.

(5) $ 70,000 to increase cash on hand.

Repayment would be in 20 equal annual installments, beginning one year from date of the loan.

(a) Assuming that the loan is obtained, prepare a pro forma balance sheet for Odom Manufacturing that reflects the use of the loan proceeds.

(b) Did the firm's liquidity improve after the loan was obtained and the proceeds were dispensed in the above manner? Why or why not?

4-2. The Sharpe Corporation's projected sales for the first eight months of 1979 are as follows:

January	$ 90,000	May	$300,000
February	120,000	June	270,000
March	135,000	July	225,000
April	240,000	August	150,000

Of Sharpe's sales, 10 percent is for cash, another 60 percent is collected in the month following sale, and 30 percent is collected in the second month following sale. November and December sales for 1978 were $220,000 and $175,000, respectively.

Sharpe purchases its raw materials two months in advance of its sales for 60 percent of their final sales price. The supplier is paid one month after it makes delivery (the month of purchase).

In addition, Sharpe pays $10,000 per month for rent and $20,000 each month for other expenditures. Tax prepayments of $22,500 are made each quarter, beginning in March.

The company's cash balance at December 31, 1977, was $22,000; a minimum balance of $15,000 must be maintained at all times. Assume that any short-term financing needed to maintain the minimum cash balance would be paid off in the month following the month of financing if sufficient funds are available. Interest on short-term loans (12%) is paid monthly.

(a) Prepare a cash budget for Sharpe covering the first seven months of 1979.

(b) Sharpe has $200,000 in notes payable due in July that must be repaid or renegotiated for an extension. Will the firm have ample cash to repay the notes?

4-3. The Bell Retailing Company has been engaged in the process of forecasting its financing needs over the next quarter and has made the following forecasts of planned cash receipts and disbursements:

(1) Historical and predicted sales:

HISTORICAL		PREDICTED	
April	$ 80,000	July	$130,000
May	100,000	August	130,000
June	120,000	September	120,000
		October	100,000

(2) The firm incurs and pays a monthly rent expense of $3000.

(3) Wages and salaries for the coming months are estimated as follows:

July	$18,000
August	18,000
September	16,000

with payments coinciding with the month in which the expense is incurred.

(4) Of the firm's sales, 40 percent is collected in the month of sale, 30 percent one month after sale, and the remaining 30 percent two months after sale.

(5) Merchandise is purchased one month before the sales month and is paid for in the month it is sold. Purchases equal 80 percent of sales.

(6) Tax prepayments are made on the calendar quarter, with a prepayment of $1000 in July based on earnings for the quarter ended June 30, 1979.

(7) Utilities for the firm average 2 percent of sales and are paid in the month following their incurrence.

(8) Depreciation expense is $12,000 annually.

(9) Interest on a $40,000 bank note (due in November) is payable at an 8 percent annual rate in September for the three-month period just ended.

(10) The firm follows a policy of paying no cash dividends.

Based on the above, supply the following items:

(a) Prepare a monthly cash budget for the three-month period ended September 30, 1979.

(b) If the firm's beginning cash balance for the budget period is $5000 and this is its minimum desired balance, determine when and how much the firm will need to borrow during the budget period. The firm has an $80,000 line of credit with its bank with interest (12 percent annual) paid monthly (for example, for a loan taken out at the end of December, interest would be paid at the end of January and every month thereafter so long as the loan was outstanding).

(c) Prepare a pro forma income statement for Bell covering the three-month period ended September 30, 1979. Use a 22 percent tax rate and round your estimate to the nearest $10.

(d) Given the following balance sheet dated June 30, 1979, and your pro forma income statement from part (c), prepare a pro forma balance sheet for September 30, 1979.

BELL MANUFACTURING CO.
Balance Sheet
June 30, 1979

Cash	$ 5,000	Accounts payable	$104,000
Accounts receivable	102,000	Bank notes (8%)	40,000
Inventories	114,000	Accrued taxes	1,000

Current assets	221,000	Current	145,000
Net fixed assets	120,000	Common stock ($1 par)	100,000
		Paid-in capital	28,400
		Retained earnings	67,600
		Total liabilities	
Total assets	$341,000	and capital	$341,000

4-4. A new firm, or one contemplating entering a new industry, may use industry average ratios as a guide to what its financial position should look like. The following data represent the ratios for the widget manufacturing industry for 1976:

Common equity ratio	50%
Sales to common equity	4 times
Long-term debt/total assets	16.67%
Current ratio	1.5
Quick ratio	.75
Average collection period	40 days

(a) Complete the accompanying pro forma balance sheet for Wheiler's Widget World (round to the nearest thousand) assuming Wheiler's 1976 sales are $1.2 million.

WHEILER'S WIDGET WORLD
Pro Forma Balance Sheet
December 31, 1976

Cash	$_____	Current debt	$_____
Accounts receivable	_____	Long-term debt	_____
Inventory	_____	Total debt	_____
Total current assets	_____	Common equity	_____
Fixed assets	_____	Total liabilities	
Total assets	_____	and common equity	_____

(b) What does the use of the financial ratio composites accomplish in this instance?

4-5. The Jason Marshall Manufacturing Company (JMMC) is beginning its planning for next year. Jim Jamison, the firm's comptroller, is attempting to get a rough estimate of the firm's total needs for financing during the planning period. Jim has compiled income statement and balance sheet data for the last five years, which he hopes will enable him to project the firm's pro

forma income statement and balance sheet. The historical fianancial statements for JMMC are found below:

JMMC
Balance Sheets
for 1974 through 1978

	1974	1975	1976	1977	1978
Current assets	$2,000	$3,000	$3,000	$4,000	$5,000
Net plant and equipment	2,000	2,000	3,000	4,000	4,000
Total assets	$4,000	$5,000	$6,000	$8,000	$9,000
Current liabilities	$1,000	$1,120	$1,270	$1,270	$1,400
Long-term debt	1,000	1,400	1,400	1,500	1,500
Common stock	1,000	1,000	1,000	2,000	2,000
Retained earnings	1,000	1,480	2,330	3,230	4,100
Total liabilities and owners' equity	$4,000	$5,000	$6,000	$8,000	$9,000

JMMC
Income Statements
for the Years Ended December 31, 1974 through 1978

	1974	1975	1976	1977	1978
Net sales	$ 4,000	$ 6,000	$ 8,000	$10,000	$12,000
Cost of goods sold	(2,000)	(3,000)	(4,000)	(5,000)	(6,000)
Gross profit	2,000	3,000	4,000	5,000	6,000
Selling expenses	(400)	(500)	(560)	(600)	(610)
General administrative expenses	(1,300)	(1,400)	(1,400)	(1,450)	(1,500)
Operating income	300	1,100	2,040	2,950	3,890
Interest expense	(100)	(140)	(140)	(150)	(150)
Net income before taxes	200	960	1,900	2,800	3,740
Taxes	(100)	(480)	(950)	(1,400)	(1,870)
Net income	$ 100	$ 480	$ 950	$ 1,400	$ 1,870
Cash dividends	$ 0	$ 0	$ 100	$ 500	$ 1,000

Sales for 1979 have been estimated at $16,000. Furthermore, the
firm plans to replace worn-out equipment during 1979 such that net plant
and equipment should not change materially. The firm plans to pay $1500
in cash dividends in 1979.

Jim believes that current assets and current liabilities are very responsive to the level of firm sales. In addition, cost of goods sold and both
selling and administrative expenses tend to follow sales very closely. Net

plant and equipment, long-term debt, and common stock are not expected to be very responsive to sales. Interest expense varies closely with long-term debt, which is not expected to change in 1979.

(a) Develop a pro forma balance sheet and income statement for 1979, using the percent of sales method and basing your percentages on the 1978 balance sheet and income statement figures. Use "additional financing needed" as a plug figure in the balance sheet.

(b) Develop a pro forma balance sheet and income statement for JMMC, using scatter diagrams to predict current assets, current liabilities, cost of goods sold, and selling and administrative expenses. Again use "additional financing needed" to balance the pro forma balance sheet.

(c) Which of the above estimates of "additional financing needed" do you prefer? Why do they differ? Explain.

4-6. The Ace Traffic Company sells its merchandise on credit terms of 2/10, net 30 (2 percent discount if payment is made within 10 days or the net amount is due in 30 days). Only a part of the firm's customers take the trade discount such that the firm's average collection period is 20 days.

(a) Based upon estimated sales of $400,000, project Ace's accounts receivable balance for the coming year.

(b) If Ace changes its cash discount terms to 1/10, net 30, it expects its average collection period will rise to 28 days. Estimate Ace's accounts receivable balance based on the new credit terms and expected sales of $400,000

4-7. Which of the following accounts would most likely vary directly with the level of firm sales? Discuss each briefly.

	YES	NO
Cash	——	——
Marketable securities	——	——
Accounts payable	——	——
Notes payable	——	——
Plant and equipment	——	——
Inventories	——	——

4-8. The balance sheet of the Thompson Trucking Company (TTC) is found below:

THOMPSON TRUCKING COMPANY
Balance Sheet
January 31, 1979
(Millions of Dollars)

Current assets	$10	Accounts payable	$ 5

Net fixed assets	15	Notes payable	0
Total	$25	Bonds payable	10
		Common equity	10
		Total	$25

TTC had sales for the year ended 1/31/79 of $50 million. The firm follows a policy of paying all net earnings out to its common stockholders in cash dividends. Thus, TTC generates no funds from its earnings that can be used to expand its operations (assume that depreciation expense is just equal to the cost of replacing worn out assets).

(a) If TTC anticipates sales of $80 million during the coming year, develop a pro forma balance sheet for the firm for 1/31/80. Assume that current assets vary as a percent of sales, net fixed assets remain unchanged, accounts payable vary as a percent of sales, and use notes payable as a plug figure.

(b) How much "new" financing will TTC need next year?

(c) What limitations does the percent of sales forecast method suffer from? Discuss briefly.

SELECTED REFERENCES

CARLETON, W. T., "An Analytical Model for Long-Range Financial Planning," *Journal of Finance,* 25 (May 1970), 291–315.

————— C. L. DICK, and D. H. DOWNES, "Financial Policy Models: Theory and Practice," *Journal of Financial and Quantitative Analysis,* 8 (December 1973), 691–710.

CHAMBERS, JOHN C., SATINDER K. MULLICK, and DONALD D. SMITH, "How to Choose the Right Forecasting Technique," *Harvard Business Review,* 49 (July–August 1971), 45–74.

PAPPAS, J. L., and G. P. HUBER, "Probabilistic Short-Term Financial Planning," *Financial Management,* 2 (Autumn 1973).

PARKER, G. G. C., and E. L. SEGURA, "How to Get a Better Forecast," *Harvard Business Review,* 49 (March–April 1971), 99–109.

WESTON, J. FRED, "Forecasting Financial Requirements," *Accounting Review,* 33 (July 1958), 427–40.

Mathematics of Finance

In coming chapters we will concern ourselves with evaluating the desirability of investment proposals. In doing this we will recognize that there is a time value associated with money; that is, a dollar today is worth more than a dollar received a year from now. Intuitively this idea is easy to understand. We are all familiar with the concept of interest, and this concept illustrates what economists call an opportunity cost of passing up the earning potential of a dollar today. This opportunity cost is the time value of money.

In evaluating and comparing investment proposals, we will want to examine the dollar values accruing from accepting these proposals. To do this we must first make all dollar values comparable, and since a dollar received today is worth more than a dollar received in the future, we must move all dollar flows either back to the present or out to a common future date. For this reason an understanding of the mathematics of interest is essential to an understanding of advanced financial management.

COMPOUND INTEREST

Most of us encounter the concept of compound interest at an early age. Anyone who has ever had a savings account at a commercial bank or savings and loan association or purchased a U. S. Government savings bond has received compound interest. **Compound interest** occurs when interest paid on the investment during the first period is added to the principal and, during the second period, interest is earned on this new sum.

As an example, suppose we place $100 in a savings account that pays 6 percent interest, compounded annually. How will our savings grow? At the end of the first year we have earned 6 percent or $6 on our initial deposit of $100, giving us a total of $106 in our savings account. The mathematical formula illustrating this phenomenon is

$$FV_1 = P(1 + i) \qquad (5\text{-}1)$$

where FV_1 = the future value of the investment at the end of one year,
    i = the annual compound interest rate,
    P = the principal or original amount invested at the beginning of the first year.

In our example

$$FV_1 = P(1 + i) \qquad (5\text{-}1)$$

$$= \$100(1 + .06)$$

$$= \$100(1.06)$$

$$= \$106$$

Carrying these calculations one period further, we find that we now earn the 6 percent interest on a principal of $106, which means we earn $6.36 in interest during the second year. Why do we earn more interest during the second year than we did during the first? Simply because we now earn interest on the sum of the original principal and the interest we earned in the first year. In effect we are now earning interest on interest; this is the concept of compound interest. Examining the mathematical formula illustrating the earning of interest in the second year, we find:

$$FV_2 = FV_1(1 + i) \qquad (5\text{-}2)$$

which, for our example, gives

$$FV_2 = \$106(1.06)$$

$$= \$112.36$$

Looking back at equation (5-1), we can see that FV_1, or $106, is actually equal to $P(1 + i)$, or $100(1 + .06)$. If we substitute these values into equation (5-2), we get

$$FV_2 = P(1 + i)(1 + i) \qquad (5\text{-}3)$$

$$= P(1 + i)^2$$

Carrying this forward into the third year, we find that we enter the year with $112.36 and we earn 6 percent or $6.74 in interest, giving us a total of $119.10 in our savings account. Expressing this mathematically,

$$FV_3 = FV_2(1 + i) \tag{5-4}$$
$$= \$112.36(1.06)$$
$$= \$119.10$$

If we substitute the value in equation (5-3) for FV_2 into equation (5-4), we find that

$$FV_3 = P(1 + i)(1 + i)(1 + i) \tag{5-5}$$
$$= P(1 + i)^3$$

By now a pattern is beginning to be evident. We can generalize this formula to illustrate the value of our investment if it is compounded annually at a rate of i for n years to be

$$FV_n = P(1 + i)^n \tag{5-6}$$

where FV_n = the future value of the investment at the end of n years,
n = the number of years during which the compounding occurs,
i = the annual compound interest rate,
P = the principal or original amount invested at the beginning of the first year.

Table 5-1 illustrates how this investment of $100 would continue to grow for the first 10 years at a compound interest rate of 6 percent. It is easy to see that the amount of interest earned annually increases each year. Again, the reason is that each year interest is received upon the sum of the original investment and any interest earned in the past.

When we examine graphically the relationship between the number of years an initial investment is compounded for and its future value, as shown in Figure 5-1, we see that we can increase the future value of an investment by either increasing the number of years we let it compound or

Table 5-1 ILLUSTRATION OF COMPOUND INTEREST CALCULATIONS

YEAR	BEGINNING VALUE	INTEREST EARNED	ENDING VALUE
1	$100.00	$ 6.00	$106.00
2	106.00	6.36	112.36
3	112.36	6.74	119.10
4	119.10	7.15	126.25
5	126.25	7.57	133.82
6	133.82	8.03	141.85
7	141.85	8.51	150.36
8	150.36	9.02	159.38
9	159.38	9.57	168.95
10	168.95	10.13	179.08

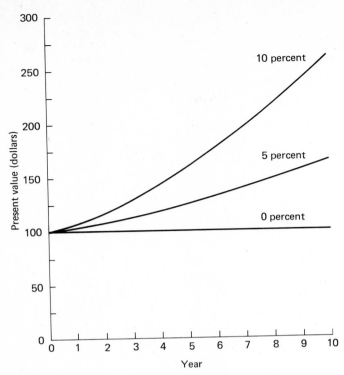

FIGURE 5-1 *Future value of $100 initially deposited and compounded at 0, 5, and 10 percent*

compounding it at a higher interest rate. We can also see this by examining equation (5-6), as an increase in either i or n while P is held constant will result in an increase in FV_n.

Example. If we place $1000 in a savings account paying 5 percent interest compounded annually, how much will our account accrue to in 10 years? Substituting $P = \$1000$, $i = 5$ percent, and $n = 10$ years into equation (5-6), we get

$$FV_n = P(1 + i)^n \qquad (5\text{-}6)$$

$$= \$1000(1 + .05)^{10}$$

$$= \$1000(1.62889)$$

$$= \$1628.89$$

Thus at the end of 10 years we will have $1628.89 in our savings account.

As the determination of future value can be quite time-consuming when an investment is held for a number of years, tables have been compiled for values of $(1 + i)^n$. An abbreviated compound interest table ap-

123

pears in Table 5-2. (A more comprehensive version of this table appears in Appendix A in the back of this book.) Note that the compounding factors given in these tables represent the value of $1 compounded at rate i at the *end* of the nth year. Thus, to calculate the future value of an initial investment we need only determine the table value and multiply this times the initial investment.

   Example.   If we invest $500 in the bank where it will earn 8 percent compounded annually, how much will it be worth at the end of seven years? Looking in Table 5-2 in the row $n = 7$ and column $i = 8\%$, we find a value of 1.714. Substituting this in equation (5-6), we find

$$FV_n = P(1 + i)^n \tag{5-6}$$
$$= \$500(1.714)$$
$$= \$857$$

Thus, we will have $857 at the end of seven years.

   In the future we will find several uses for equation (5-6); not only will we find the future value of an investment, but we can also solve for P, i, or n. In any case we will be given three of the four variables and will have to solve for the fourth.

   Example.   How many years will it take for an initial investment of $300 to grow to $774 if it is invested at 9 percent compounded annually? In this problem we know the initial investment, $P = \$300$, the future value, $FV_n = \$774$, the compound growth rate, $i = 9$ percent, and we are solving

Table 5-2   COMPOUND SUM OF $1

N	1%	2%	3%	4%	5%	6%	7%	8%	9%	10%
1	1.010	1.020	1.030	1.040	1.050	1.060	1.070	1.080	1.090	1.100
2	1.020	1.040	1.061	1.082	1.102	1.124	1.145	1.166	1.188	1.210
3	1.030	1.061	1.093	1.125	1.158	1.191	1.225	1.260	1.295	1.331
4	1.041	1.082	1.126	1.170	1.216	1.262	1.311	1.360	1.412	1.464
5	1.051	1.104	1.159	1.217	1.276	1.338	1.403	1.469	1.539	1.611
6	1.062	1.126	1.194	1.265	1.340	1.419	1.501	1.587	1.677	1.772
7	1.072	1.149	1.230	1.316	1.407	1.504	1.606	1.714	1.828	1.949
8	1.083	1.172	1.267	1.369	1.477	1.594	1.718	1.851	1.993	2.144
9	1.094	1.195	1.305	1.423	1.551	1.689	1.838	1.999	2.172	2.358
10	1.105	1.219	1.344	1.480	1.629	1.791	1.967	2.159	2.367	2.594
11	1.116	1.243	1.384	1.539	1.710	1.898	2.105	2.332	2.580	2.853
12	1.127	1.268	1.426	1.601	1.796	2.012	2.252	2.518	2.813	3.138
13	1.138	1.294	1.469	1.665	1.886	2.133	2.410	2.720	3.066	3.452
14	1.149	1.319	1.513	1.732	1.980	2.261	2.579	2.937	3.342	3.797
15	1.161	1.346	1.558	1.801	2.079	2.397	2.759	3.172	3.642	4.177

for the number of years it must compound for, $n = ?$ Substituting the known values in equation (5-6), we find

$$FV_n = P(1 + i)^n \qquad (5\text{-}6)$$

$$\$774 = \$300(1 + .09)^n$$

$$2.58 = (1 + .09)^n$$

Thus we are looking for a table value of 2.58, and we know it must be in the 9% column. Looking down the 9% column for the value closest to 2.58, we find that it occurs in the $n = 11$ row. Thus, it will take 11 years for an initial investment of $300 to grow to $774 if it is invested at 9 percent compounded annually.

Example. At what rate must $100 be compounded annually for it to grow to $179.10 in 10 years? In this case we know the initial investment, $P = \$100$, the future value of this investment at the end of n years, $FV_n = \$179.10$, and the number of years that the initial investment will compound for, $n = 10$ years. Substituting into equation (5-6), we get

$$FV_n = P(1 + i)^n \qquad (5\text{-}6)$$

$$\$179.10 = \$100(1 + i)^{10}$$

$$1.791 = (1 + i)^{10}$$

We know we are looking in the $n = 10$ row for a table value of 1.791, and we find this in the $i = 6\%$ column. Thus, if we want our initial investment of $100 to accrue to $179.10 in 10 years, we must invest it at 6 percent.

Until now we have assumed the compounding period was always annual; however, it need not be, as we can see by examining savings and loan associations and commercial banks that compound on a quarterly, daily, and in some cases continuous basis. Fortunately, this adjustment of the compounding period poses us no major problem. If we invest our money for five years at 8 percent interest compounded semiannually, we are really investing our money for 10 six-month periods during which we receive 4 percent interest each period. If it is compounded quarterly, we receive 2% interest per period for 20 three-month periods. This process can easily be generalized, giving us the following formula for finding the future value of an investment where interest is compounded in nonannual periods:

COMPOUND INTEREST WITH NONANNUAL PERIODS

$$FV_n = P\left(1 + \frac{i}{m}\right)^{mn} \qquad (5\text{-}7)$$

where $FV_n =$ future value of the investment at the end of n years,
$\qquad n =$ number of years during which the compounding occurs,

i = annual compound interest rate,

P = principal or original amount invested at the beginning of the first year,

m = the number of times compounding occurs during the year.

In the case of continuous compounding, the value of m in equation (5-7) is allowed to approach infinity. As this happens, the value of $[1 + (i/m)]^{mn}$ approaches e^{in}, with e being defined as follows and having a value of approximately 2.71828:

$$e = \lim_{m \to \infty} \left(1 + \frac{i}{m}\right)^m \qquad (5\text{-}8)$$

where ∞ indicates infinity. Thus the future value of an investment compounded continuously for n years can be determined from the following formula,

$$FV_n = P \cdot e^{in} \qquad (5\text{-}9)$$

where FV_n = the future value of the investment at the end of n years,

e = 2.71828,

n = the number of years during which the compounding occurs,

i = the annual compound interest rate,

P = the principal or original amount invested at the beginning of the first year.

While continuous compounding appears quite complicated, it is used frequently and is a valuable theoretical concept. Continuous compounding takes on this importance because it allows interest to be earned on interest more frequently than any other compounding period. We can easily see the value of intrayear compounding by examining Table 5-3. Since interest is earned on interest more frequently as the length of the compounding period declines, there is an inverse relationship between the effective annual interest rate and the length of the compounding period.

Example. If we place $100 in a savings account that yields 12 percent compounded quarterly, what will our investment grow to at the end of five years? Substituting $n = 5$, $m = 4$, $i = 12$ percent, and $P = \$100$ into equation (5-7), we find

$$FV_5 = \$100 \left(1 + \frac{.12}{4}\right)^{5 \cdot 4}$$
$$= \$100(1 + .03)^{20}$$
$$= \$100(1.806)$$
$$= \$180.60$$

Thus, we will have $180.60 at the end of five years.

Table 5-3 THE VALUE OF $100 COMPOUNDED AT VARIOUS INTERVALS

FOR ONE YEAR AT i PERCENT

$i =$	2%	5%	10%	15%
Compounded annually	$102.00	$105.00	$110.00	$115.00
Compounded semiannually	102.01	105.06	110.25	115.56
Compounded quarterly	102.02	105.09	110.38	115.87
Compounded monthly	102.02	105.12	110.47	116.08
Compounded weekly (52)	102.02	105.12	110.51	116.16
Compounded daily (365)	102.02	105.13	110.52	116.18
Compounded continuously	102.02	105.13	110.52	116.18

FOR 10 YEARS AT i PERCENT

$i =$	2%	5%	10%	15%
Compounded annually	$121.90	$162.89	$259.37	$404.56
Compounded semiannually	122.02	163.86	265.33	424.79
Compounded quarterly	122.08	164.36	268.51	436.04
Compounded monthly	122.12	164.70	270.70	444.02
Compounded weekly (52)	122.14	164.83	271.57	447.20
Compounded daily (365)	122.14	164.87	271.79	448.03
Compounded continuously	122.14	164.87	271.83	448.17

Example. How much money will we have at the end of 20 years if we deposit $1000 in a savings account yielding 10 percent interest continuously compounded? Substituting $n = 20$, $i = 10$ percent, and $P = \$1000$ into equation (5-9) yields

$$FV_{10} = \$1000 \cdot (2.71828)^{.10 \cdot 20}$$

$$= \$1000(2.71828)^2$$

$$= \$1000(7.38905)$$

$$= \$7389.05$$

Thus, we would have $7389.05 at the end of 20 years.

PRESENT VALUE

Up until this point we have been moving money forward in time—that is, knowing how much we have at one point in time and trying to determine how much it will grow to in a certain number of years when compounded at a specific rate. We are now going to look at the reverse question: what is the value in today's dollars of a sum of money to be received in the future? In this case we are moving money back in time, back to the present. We will be determining the **present value** of a lump sum, which in simple terms is the current value of a future payment. What we will be doing is, in fact, nothing other than inverse compounding. The differences in these techniques come about merely from the investor's point of view. In compounding we talked about the compound rate or interest rate and the initial investment; in determining the present value we will talk about the "opportunity cost" of money or the discount rate and present value. Other than that, the technique and the terminology remain the same, and the mathematics are simply reversed. In equation (5-6) we were attempting to determine the future value of an initial investment. We now want to determine the initial investment or present value. By dividing both sides of equation (5-6) by $(1 + i)^n$, we get

$$P = FV_n \left[\frac{1}{(1 + i)^n} \right]$$ (5-10)

where FV_n = the future value of the investment at the end of n years,
 n = the number of years until the payment will be received,
 i = the opportunity rate or discount rate,
 P = the present value of the future sum of money.

As the mathematical procedure for determining the present value is exactly the inverse of determining the future value, we also find that the relationships among n, i, and P are just opposite of those we observed with the future value. The present value of a future sum of money is inversely related to both the number of years until the payment will be received and the opportunity rate. Graphically, this relationship can be seen in Figure 5-2.

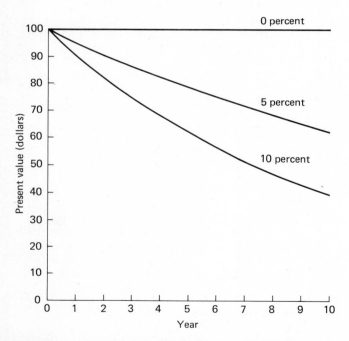

FIGURE 5-2 *Present value of $100 to be received at a future date and discounted back to the present at 0, 5, and 10 percent*

While equation (5-10), the present-value equation, will be used extensively in evaluating new investment proposals, it should be stressed that
equation (5-10) is actually the same as equation (5-6), where it is solved for
P.

> *Example.* What is the present value of $500 to be received 10 years
from today if our opportunity rate is 6 percent? Substituting FV_{10} = $500, n
= 10, and i = 6 percent into equation (5-10), we find

$$P = \$500 \left[\frac{1}{(1 + .06)^{10}} \right]$$

$$= \$500 \left(\frac{1}{1.791} \right)$$

$$= \$500(.558)$$

$$= \$279$$

Thus, the present value of the $500 to be received in 10 years is $279.

To aid in the computation of present values, tables have been compiled for values of $[1/(1 + i)^n]$; they appear in Appendix B in the back of
this book. An abbreviated version of Appendix B appears in Table 5-4. A
close examination shows that the values in Table 5-4 are merely the in-
verses of those in Appendix A. This, of course, is as it should be, as the
values in Appendix A are $(1 + i)^n$ and those in Appendix B are $[1/(1 + i)^n]$.
Now, to determine the present value of a sum of money to be received at
some future date, we need only determine the appropriate table value and
multiply it by the future value.

Table 5-4 PRESENT VALUE OF $1

n	1%	2%	3%	4%	5%	6%	7%	8%	9%	10%
1	.990	.980	.971	.962	.952	.943	.935	.926	.917	.909
2	.980	.961	.943	.925	.907	.890	.873	.857	.842	.826
3	.971	.942	.915	.889	.864	.840	.816	.794	.772	.751
4	.961	.924	.888	.855	.823	.792	.763	.735	.708	.683
5	.951	.906	.863	.822	.784	.747	.713	.681	.650	.621
6	.942	.888	.837	.790	.746	.705	.666	.630	.596	.564
7	.933	.871	.813	.760	.711	.665	.623	.583	.547	.513
8	.923	.853	.789	.731	.677	.627	.582	.540	.502	.467
9	.914	.837	.766	.703	.645	.592	.544	.500	.460	.424
10	.905	.820	.744	.676	.614	.558	.508	.463	.422	.386
11	.896	.804	.722	.650	.585	.527	.475	.429	.388	.350
12	.887	.789	.701	.625	.557	.497	.444	.397	.356	.319
13	.879	.773	.681	.601	.530	.469	.415	.368	.326	.290
14	.870	.758	.661	.577	.505	.442	.388	.340	.299	.263
15	.861	.743	.642	.555	.481	.417	.362	.315	.275	.239

Example. What is the present value of $1500 to be received at the end of 10 years if our opportunity cost is 8 percent? By looking in the $n = 10$ row and $i = 8\%$ column of Table 5-4, we find the value of $[1/(1 + .08)^{10}]$ is .463. Substituting this value into equation (5-10), we find

$$P = \$1500(.463)$$

$$= \$694.50$$

Thus, the present value of this $1500 payment is $694.50.

Before moving on, it should be again stressed that we only have one present-value–future-value equation; that is, equations (5-6) and (5-10) are, in fact, identical. We have introduced them as separate equations to simplify our calculations; in one case we are determining the value in future dollars and in the other case the value in today's dollars. In either case the reason is the same: in order to compare values on alternative investments and to recognize that the value of a dollar received today is not the same as that of a dollar received at some future date, we must measure the dollar values in dollars of the same time period. Since all present values are comparable, as they are all measured in dollars of the same time period, we can add and subtract the present value of inflows and outflows to determine the present value of an investment.

Example. What is the present value of an investment that yields $500 to be received in five years and $1000 to be received in 10 years if our opportunity rate is 4 percent? Substituting the values of $n = 5$, $i = 4$ percent, and $FV_5 = \$500$ and $n = 10$, $i = 4$ percent, and $FV_{10} = \$1000$ into equation (5-10) and adding these values together, we find

$$P = \$500 \left[\frac{1}{(1 + .04)^5}\right] + \$1000 \left[\frac{1}{(1 + .04)^{10}}\right]$$

$$= \$500(.822) + \$1000(.676)$$

$$= \$411 + \$676$$

$$= \$1087$$

Again, present values are comparable because they are measured in the same time period's dollars.

An **annuity** is a series of equal dollar payments for a specified number of years. Because annuities occur frequently in finance—for example, as bond interest payments—we will treat them specially. While the processes of compounding and determining the present value of an annuity can be dealt with by using the methods we have just described, they can be quite time-consuming, especially for larger annuities. Thus we have modified these formulas and developed tables to deal directly with annuities.

ANNUITIES

A **compound annuity** involves depositing or investing an equal sum of money at the end of each year for a certain number of years and allowing it to grow. Perhaps the money is being saved to provide for a child's future education, or for a new car, or a vacation home. In such cases we wish to know how much our savings will have grown to by some point in time.

Actually, we can find the answer by using equation (5-6), our compounding equation, and compounding each of the individual deposits to the future. For example, if to provide for a college education we are going to deposit $500 at the end of each year for the next five years in a bank where it will earn 6 percent interest, how much will we have at the end of five years? Compounding each of these values using equation (5-6), we find that we will have $2818.50 at the end of five years.

$$FV_5 = \$500(1 + .06)^4 + \$500(1 + .06)^3 + \$500(1 + .06)^2 + \$500(1 + .06)^1$$
$$+ \$500$$

$$= \$500(1.262) + \$500(1.191) + \$500(1.124) + \$500(1.060) + \$500$$

$$= \$631.00 + \$595.50 + \$562.00 + \$530.00 + \$500.00$$

$$= \$2818.50$$

From examining the mathematics involved and the graph of the movement of money through time in Table 5-5, we can see that this procedure can be generalized to

$$FV_n = A\left[\sum_{t=0}^{n-1} (1 + i)^t \right] \tag{5-11}$$

where FV_n = the future value of the annuity at the end of the nth year,
A = the annuity value deposited at the end of each year,
i = the annual compound interest rate,
n = the number of years for which the annuity will last.

Table 5-5   ILLUSTRATION OF A FIVE-YEAR $500 ANNUITY COMPOUNDED AT 6%

YEAR	0	1	2	3	4	5
Dollar deposits at end of year		500	500	500	500	500
						↓
						$ 500.00
						530.00
						562.00
						595.50
						631.00
						$2818.50
Future value of the annuity						

Because compounding an annuity is so time-consuming, tables are provided in Appendix C for $\left[\sum_{t=0}^{n-1}(1+i)^t\right]$ for various combinations of n and i; an abbreviated version is shown in Table 5-6. Reexamining the previous example, in which we determined the value of $500 deposited at the end of each of the next five years in the bank at 6 percent after five years, we would look in the $n = 5$ year row and $i = 6\%$ column and find a table value of 5.637. Substituting this value into equation (5-11), we get

$$FV_5 = \$500(5.637)$$

$$= \$2818.50$$

—the same answer we obtained earlier.

Rather than asking how much we will accumulate if we deposit an equal sum in a savings account each year, a more common question is how much we must deposit each year in order to accumulate a certain amount of savings. This problem frequently occurs with respect to saving for large expenditures and pension funding obligations.

For example, we may know that we need $10,000 for our son's education in eight years; how much must we deposit at the end of each year in the bank at 6 percent interest in order to have the college money ready? In this case we know the values of n, i, and FV_n in equation (5-11); what we do not know is the value of A. Substituting these example values in equation (5-11), we find

Table 5-6 SUM OF AN ANNUITY OF $1 FOR n YEARS

n	1%	2%	3%	4%	5%	6%	7%	8%	9%	10%
1	1.000	1.000	1.000	1.000	1.000	1.000	1.000	1.000	1.000	1.000
2	2.010	2.020	2.030	2.040	2.050	2.060	2.070	2.080	2.090	2.100
3	3.030	3.060	3.091	3.122	3.152	3.184	3.215	3.246	3.278	3.310
4	4.060	4.122	4.184	4.246	4.310	4.375	4.440	4.506	4.573	4.641
5	5.101	5.204	5.309	5.416	5.526	5.637	5.751	5.867	5.985	6.105
6	6.152	6.308	6.468	6.633	6.802	6.975	7.153	7.336	7.523	7.716
7	7.214	7.434	7.662	7.898	8.142	8.394	8.654	8.923	9.200	9.487
8	8.286	8.583	8.892	9.214	9.549	9.897	10.260	10.637	11.028	11.436
9	9.368	9.755	10.159	10.583	11.027	11.491	11.978	12.488	13.021	13.579
10	10.462	10.950	11.464	12.006	12.578	13.181	13.816	14.487	15.193	15.937
11	11.567	12.169	12.808	13.486	14.207	14.972	15.784	16.645	17.560	18.531
12	12.682	13.412	14.192	15.026	15.917	16.870	17.888	18.977	20.141	21.384
13	13.809	14.680	15.618	16.627	17.713	18.882	20.141	21.495	22.953	24.523
14	14.947	15.974	17.086	18.292	19.598	21.015	22.550	24.215	26.019	27.975
15	16.097	17.293	18.599	20.023	21.578	23.276	25.129	27.152	29.361	31.772

$$\$10,000 = A\left[\sum_{t=0}^{8-1}(1+.06)^t\right]$$

$$\$10,000 = A(9.897)$$

$$\frac{\$10,000}{\$9.897} = A$$

$$A = \$1010.41$$

Thus, we must deposit \$1010.41 in the bank at the end of each year for eight years at 6 percent interest in order to accumulate \$10,000 at the end of eight years.

Example. How much must we deposit in an 8 percent savings account at the end of each year in order to accumulate \$5000 at the end of 10 years? Substituting the values $FV_{10} = \$5000$, $n = 10$, and $i = 8$ percent into equation (5-11), we find

$$\$5000 = A\left[\sum_{t=0}^{10-1}(1+.08)^t\right]$$

$$\$5000 = A(14.487)$$

$$\frac{\$5000}{14.487} = A$$

$$A = \$345.14$$

Thus, we must deposit \$345.14 per year for 10 years at 8 percent in order to accumulate \$5000.

Present Value of an Annuity

Pension funds, insurance obligations, and interest received from bonds all involve annuities. To compare them, we would like to know the present value of each. While we can find this by using the present-value table in Appendix B, this can be quite time-consuming, particularly when the annuity lasts for several years. For example, if we wish to know what \$500 received at the end of the next five years is worth to us given the appropriate discount rate or opportunity rate of 6 percent, we can simply substitute the appropriate values into equation (5-10), such that

$$P = \$500\left[\frac{1}{(1+.06)}\right] + 500\left[\frac{1}{(1+.06)^2}\right] + 500\left[\frac{1}{(1+.06)^3}\right]$$

$$+ 500\left[\frac{1}{(1+.06)^4}\right] + 500\left[\frac{1}{(1+.06)^5}\right]$$

$$= \$500(.943) + \$500(.890) + \$500(.840) + \$500(.792) + \$500(.747)$$

$$= \$2106.00$$

Thus, the present value of this annuity is $2106.00. From examining the mathematics involved and the graph of the movement of these funds through time in Table 5-7, we see that this procedure can be generalized to

$$P = A \left[\sum_{t=1}^{n} \frac{1}{(1 + i)^t} \right] \qquad (5\text{-}12)$$

where A = the annuity received at the end of each year,
$\quad i$ = the annual interest or discount rate,
$\quad P$ = the present value of the future annuity,
$\quad n$ = the number of years for which the annuity will last.

To simplify the process of determining the present value of an annuity, tables are provided in Appendix D for $\left[\sum_{t=1}^{n} 1/(1 + i)^t \right]$ for various combinations of n and i; an abbreviated version is given in Table 5-8. Solving the previous example to find the present value of $500 received at the end of each of the next five years discounted back to the present at 6 percent, we look in the $n = 5$ year row and $i = 6\%$ column and find a table value for $\left[\sum_{t=1}^{5} 1/(1.06)^t \right]$ or 4.212. Substituting the appropriate values into equation (5-12), we find

$$P = \$500(4.212)$$

$$= \$2106$$

This, of course, is the same answer we calculated when we individually discounted each cash flow back to the present. The reason is that we really only have *one* table; the Table 5-8 value for an n-year annuity for any

Table 5-7 ILLUSTRATION OF A FIVE-YEAR $500 ANNUITY DISCOUNTED BACK TO THE PRESENT AT 6 PERCENT

YEAR	0	1	2	3	4	5
Dollars received at the end of year		500	500	500	500	500
	$ 471.50					
	445.00					
	420.00					
	396.00					
	373.50					
Present value of the annuity	$2106.00					

Table 5-8 PRESENT VALUE OF AN ANNUITY OF $1

n	1%	2%	3%	4%	5%	6%	7%	8%	9%	10%
1	0.990	0.980	0.971	0.962	0.952	0.943	0.935	0.926	0.917	0.909
2	1.970	1.942	1.913	1.886	1.859	1.833	1.808	1.783	1.759	1.736
3	2.941	2.884	2.829	2.775	2.723	2.673	2.624	2.577	2.531	2.487
4	3.902	3.808	3.717	3.630	3.546	3.465	3.387	3.312	3.240	3.170
5	4.853	4.713	4.580	4.452	4.329	4.212	4.100	3.993	3.890	3.791
6	5.795	5.601	5.417	5.242	5.076	4.917	4.767	4.623	4.486	4.355
7	6.728	6.472	6.230	6.002	5.786	5.582	5.389	5.206	5.033	4.868
8	7.652	7.326	7.020	6.733	6.463	6.210	5.971	5.747	5.535	5.335
9	8.566	8.162	7.786	7.435	7.108	6.802	6.515	6.247	5.995	5.759
10	9.471	8.983	8.530	8.111	7.722	7.360	7.024	6.710	6.418	6.145
11	10.368	9.787	9.253	8.760	8.306	7.887	7.499	7.139	6.805	6.495
12	11.255	10.575	9.954	9.385	8.863	8.384	7.943	7.536	7.161	6.814
13	12.134	11.348	10.635	9.986	9.394	8.853	8.358	7.904	7.487	7.103
14	13.004	12.106	11.296	10.563	9.899	9.295	8.746	8.244	7.786	7.367
15	13.865	12.849	11.938	11.118	10.380	9.712	9.108	8.560	8.061	7.606

discount rate i is merely the sum of the first n values in Table 5-4. We can see this by comparing the value in the present-value-of-an-annuity table (Table 5-8) for $i = 8\%$ and $n = 6$ years, which is 4.623, to the sum of the values in the $i = 8\%$ column and $n = 1, \ldots, 6$ rows of the present-value table (Table 5-4), which is equal to 4.623, as shown in Table 5-9.

Example. What is the present value of a 10-year $1000 annuity discounted back to the present at 5 percent? Substituting $n = 10$ years, $i = 5$ percent, and $A = \$1000$ into equation (5-12), we find

$$P = \$1000\left[\sum_{t=1}^{10} \frac{1}{(1 + .05)^t}\right]$$

Table 5-9 PRESENT VALUE OF A SIX-YEAR ANNUITY DISCOUNTED AT 8 PERCENT

One dollar received at the end of year	1	2	3	4	5	6
Present value						
.926 ←						
.857 ←						
.794 ←						
.735 ←						
.681 ←						
.630 ←						
4.623	Present value of the annuity					

Determining the value for $\left[\sum_{t=1}^{10} 1/(1 + .05)^t\right]$ from Table 5-8, row $n = 10$,

column $i = 5\%$, and substituting it in, we get

$$P = \$1000(7.722)$$

$$= \$7722$$

Thus, the present value of this annuity is $7722.

As with our other compounding and present-value tables, given any three of the four unknowns in equation (5-12) we can solve for the fourth. In the case of the present-value-of-an-annuity table we may be interested in solving for A, if we know i, n, and P. The financial interpretation of this action would be: how much can be withdrawn, perhaps as a pension or to make loan payments, from an account, that earns i percent compounded annually for each of the next n years if we wish to have nothing left at the end of n years? For example, if we have $5000 in an account earning 8 percent interest, how large an annuity can we draw out each year if we want nothing left at the end of five years? In this case the present value, P, of the annuity is $5000, $n = 5$ years, $i = 8$ percent, and P is unknown. Substituting this into equation (5-12), we find

$$\$5000 = A(3.993)$$

$$\$1252.19 = A$$

Thus, this account will fall to zero at the end of five years if we withdraw $1252.19 at the end of each year.

While some projects will involve single dollar flows and some annuities, many projects will involve uneven cash flows over several years. This situation will become quite common in Chapter 11 when we examine investments in fixed assets. There we will not only be comparing the present value of cash flows between projects, but we will also be comparing cash inflows and outflows within a particular project, trying to determine that project's present value. However, this will not be difficult, because the present value of any cash flow is measured in today's dollars and thus can be compared, through addition for inflows and subtraction for outflows, to the present value of any other cash flow that also is measured in today's dollars. For example, if we wished to find the present value of the following cash flows:

Present Value of an Uneven Stream

YEAR	CASH FLOW
1	$500
2	200
3	−400
4	500

YEAR	CASH FLOW (cont.)
5	500
6	500
7	500
8	500
9	500
10	500

given a 6 percent discount rate, we would merely discount the flows back to the present and total them by adding in the positive flows and subtracting the negative ones. However, this problem is complicated by the annuity of $500 that runs from years four through ten. To accommodate this factor, we can first discount the annuity back to the beginning of period four (or end of period three) by using the present-value-of-an-annuity table and get its present value at that point in time. We then use the present-value-of-a-single-flow table (Table 5-4) and discount the present value of this annuity at the end of period three back to the present. In effect we discount twice, first back to the end of period three then back to the present. This is shown graphically in Table 5-10 and numerically in Table 5-11. Thus, the present value of this uneven stream of cash flow is $2657.94.

Example. What is the present value of an investment involving $200 received at the end of years one through five, a $300 cash outflow at the end of year six, and $500 received at the end of years seven through ten given a 5 percent discount rate? Here we have two annuities, one that can be discounted directly back to the present using the present-value-of-an-annuity table and one that must be discounted twice to bring it back to the present. This second annuity must first be discounted back to the beginning of period seven or end of period six, using the present-value-of-an-

Table 5-10 ILLUSTRATION OF AN EXAMPLE OF PRESENT-VALUE CALCULATIONS INVOLVING ONE ANNUITY DISCOUNTED TO PRESENT AT 6 PERCENT

YEAR	0	1	2	3	4	5	6	7	8	9	10
Dollars received at end of year		500	200	−400	500	500	500	500	500	500	500
	$ 471.50 ←										
	178.00 ←										
	− 336.00 ←										
				$2791 ←							
	2344.44 ←										
Total present value	$2657.94										

Table 5-11 DETERMINATION OF PRESENT VALUE OF AN EXAMPLE INVOLVING ONE ANNUITY DISCOUNTED TO PRESENT AT 6 PERCENT

1. Present value of $500 received at the end of one year $= \$500(.943)$	$ 471.50
2. Present value of $200 received at the end of two years $= \$200(.890) =$	178.00
3. Present value of a $400 outflow at the end of year three $= -\$400(.840) =$	-366.00
4. (a) Value at the end of year three of a $500 annuity, years four through ten: $\$500(5.582) = \$2791.00$ (b) Present value of $2791.00 received at the end of year three $= \$2791.00(.840) =$	2344.44
5. Total present value $=$	$2657.94

annuity table; then the present value of the annuity at the end of period six must be discounted back to present, using the present-value-of-a-single-flow table. From the sum of the present value of these two annuities the present value of the $300 cash outflow at the end of year six is subtracted to give us the total present value of this investment. This is shown graphically in Table 5-12; the calculations are shown in Table 5-13. Thus, the present value of this series of cash flows is $1964.66.

A **perpetuity** is an annuity that continues forever; that is, every year from now on this investment pays the same dollar amount. An example of a perpetuity is preferred stock that yields a constant dollar dividend infinitely. Determining the present value for a perpetuity is delightfully simple, as we merely need to divide the constant flow by the discount rate[1]. For example the present value of a $100 perpetuity discounted back to the

PERPETUITIES

Table 5-12 ILLUSTRATION OF EXAMPLE OF THE PRESENT VALUE OF AN UNEVEN STREAM INVOLVING TWO ANNUITIES DISCOUNTED AT 5 PERCENT

YEAR	0	1	2	3	4	5	6	7	8	9	10
Dollars received at end of year		200	200	200	200	200	−300	500	500	500	500

$865.80 ←

−223.80 ←

$1773 ←

1322.66 ←

Total present value $1964.66

[1]See Chapter 13 for a mathematical derivation.

138

Table 5-13 DETERMINATION OF PRESENT VALUE OF AN EXAMPLE WITH UNEVEN STREAM INVOLVING TWO ANNUITIES DISCOUNTED AT 5 PERCENT

1. Present value of first annuity, years one through five = \$200(4.329) =	\$865.80
2. Present value of \$300 cash outflow = −\$300(.746) =	−223.80
3. (a) Value at end of year six of second annuity, years seven through ten = \$500(3.546) = \$1773.00 (b) Present value of \$1773.00 received at end of year 6 = \$1773.00(.746) =	1322.66
4. Total present value =	\$1964.66

present at 5 percent is \$100/.05 = \$2000. Thus the equation representing the present value of a perpetuity is

$$P = \frac{PP}{i} \qquad (5\text{-}13)$$

where P = the present value of the perpetuity,

$\quad PP$ = the constant dollar amount provided by the perpetuity,

$\quad i$ = the annual interest or discount rate.

Example. What is the present value of a \$500 perpetuity discounted back to the present at 8 percent? Substituting $PP = \$500$ and $i = .08$ into equation (5-13), we find

$$P = \frac{\$500}{.08} = \$6250$$

Thus the present value of this perpetuity is \$6250.

The existence of profitable investment alternatives and interest rates creates the time value of money. In future chapters we will find that in order to make logical financial decisions we must incorporate the time value of money into our calculations. The reason is that we will be comparing the costs and benefits of financial decisions that do not all occur during the same time period. To do this we must first make all dollar values comparable, and since money has a time value, we must move all dollar flows either back to the present or out to a common future date. All formulas presented in this chapter to move money back and forth in time actually stem from the simple compounding formula,

SUMMARY

$$FV_n = P(1 + i)^n$$

and have been formulated to deal more simply with common financial situations—for example, discounting single flows, compounding annuities, and discounting annuities.

The future or compound value (FV_n) at the end of n years of an original amount (P) invested at the beginning of the first year that is compounded at an annual interest rate of i can be determined using the following formula: **Compound Interest**

$$FV_n = P(1 + i)^n$$

As the determination of the future value of an investment can be quite time-consuming when the investment is held for a number of years, tables have been compiled for values of $(1 + i)^n$; these compilations appear in Table 5-2 and more completely in Appendix A to this book. Substituting the table value into the above equation, we find

$$FV_n = P \begin{bmatrix} \text{Table Value} \\ \text{Appendix A,} \\ n \text{ years,} \\ i \text{ percent} \end{bmatrix}$$

In the case in which nonannual compounding periods are used, the compounding equation is adjusted such that

$$FV_n = P \left(1 + \frac{i}{m}\right)^{mn}$$

where m is the number of times compounding occurs during the year.

The present value of a future sum of money can be determined from the following equation: **Present Value**

$$P = FV_n \left[\frac{1}{(1 + i)^n}\right]$$

where FV_n = the future value of the investment at the end of n years,
$\quad n$ = the number of years until payment will be received,
$\quad i$ = the opportunity or discount rate,
$\quad P$ = the present value of the future sum of money.

This is exactly the same formula we used to find the compound value of money, except here we are solving for P instead of FV_n. To aid in the computation of present values, tables have been compiled for values of $[1/(1 + i)^n]$; they appear in Appendix B in the back of this book. Thus to find the present value of a future sum of money we need only consult Table

5-4 or Appendix B and plug the appropriate value into the following equation:

$$P = FV_n \begin{bmatrix} \text{Table Value} \\ \text{Appendix B,} \\ n \text{ years,} \\ i \text{ percent} \end{bmatrix}$$

Compound Annuities

An annuity is a series of equal dollar payments for a specified number of years. A compound annuity involves depositing or investing an equal sum of money at the end of each year for a specified number of years and allowing it to grow. Mathematically, this process can be generalized to

$$FV_n = A \left[\sum_{t=0}^{n-1} (1 + i)^t \right]$$

where FV_n = the future value of the annuity at the end of the nth year,
A = the annuity value deposited at the end of each year,
i = the annual compound interest rate,
n = the number of years for which the annuity will last.

To simplify the process of compounding an annuity, an expanded version of Table 5-6 is provided in Appendix C for $\left[\sum_{t=0}^{n-1} (1 + i)^t \right]$ for various combinations of n and i. When we use this table, the calculation of a compound annuity reduces to determining the appropriate table value and plugging it into the following equation:

$$FV_n = A \begin{bmatrix} \text{Table Value} \\ \text{Appendix C,} \\ n \text{ years,} \\ i \text{ percent} \end{bmatrix}$$

Present Value of an Annuity

The present value of annuity can be determined by using the formula:

$$P = A \left[\sum_{t=1}^{n} \frac{1}{(1 + i)^t} \right]$$

where A = the annuity received at the end of each year,
i = the annual interest or discount rate,
P = the present value of the future annuity,
n = the number of years for which the annuity will last.

To simplify this process an expanded version of Table 5-8 is provided in Appendix D for $\left[\sum_{t=1}^{n} \frac{1}{(1+i)^t}\right]$. Using the table, we can determine the present value of an annuity as follows:

$$P = A \begin{bmatrix} \text{Table Value} \\ \text{Appendix D,} \\ n \text{ years,} \\ i \text{ percent} \end{bmatrix}$$

A perpetuity is an annuity that continues forever. To determine the present value of a perpetuity we merely need to divide the constant flow by the discount rate. Thus,

Perpetuities

$$P = \frac{PP}{i}$$

where P = the present value of the perpetuity,
PP = the constant dollar amount provided by the perpetuity,
i = the annual interest or discount rate.

5-1. What is the "time value of money"? Why does it exist?

5-2. The processes of discounting and compounding are obviously related. Explain this relationship.

5-3. How would an increase in the interest rate (i) or a decrease in the holding period (n) affect the future value (FV_n) of a sum of money? Explain why.

5-4. Suppose you were considering depositing your savings in three banks, all of which paid 5 percent interest; bank A compounded annually, bank B compounded semiannually, and bank C compounded continuously. Which bank would you choose. Why?

5-5. What is the relationship between the present-value table (Table 5-4) and the present-value-of-an-annuity table (Table 5-8)? What is the table factor from Table 5-8 for the present value of a 10-year annuity discounted back to present at 10 percent? Add up the table factors from Table 5-8 in the $i = 10\%$ column and rows $n = 1, \ldots, 10$. What is this value? Why do these values have the relationship they do?

5-6. What is an annuity? Give some examples of annuities. Distinguish between an annuity and a perpetuity.

5-7. What does continuous compounding mean?

STUDY QUESTIONS

5-1. What will the following investments accumulate to?
   (a) $5000 invested for 10 years at 10 percent compounded annually.
   (b) $8000 invested for seven years at 8 percent compounded annually.
   (c) $775 invested for 12 years at 12 percent compounded annually.
   (d) $21,000 invested for five years at 5 percent compounded annually.

5-2. How many years will it take for the following?
   (a) $500 to grow to $1039.50 if invested at 5 percent compounded annually.
   (b) $35 to grow to $53.87 if invested at 9 percent compounded annually.
   (c) $100 to grow to $298.60 if invested at 20 percent compounded annually.
   (d) $53 to grow to $78.76 if invested at 2 percent compounded annually.

5-3. At what annual rate would the following have to be invested?
   (a) $500 in order to grow to $1948.00 in 12 years.
   (b) $300 in order to grow to $422.10 in 7 years.
   (c) $50 in order to grow to $280.20 in 20 years.
   (d) $200 in order to grow to $497.60 in 5 years.

5-4. What is the present value of the following future amounts?
   (a) $800 to be received 10 years from now discounted back to present at 10 percent.
   (b) $300 to be received 5 years from now discounted back to present at 5 percent.
   (c) $1000 to be received 8 years from now discounted back to present at 3 percent.
   (d) $1000 to be received 8 years from now discounted back to present at 20 percent.

5-5. What is the accumulated sum of each of the following streams of payments?
   (a) $500 a year for 10 years compounded annually at 5 percent.
   (b) $100 a year for 5 years compounded annually at 10 percent.
   (c) $35 a year for 7 years compounded annually at 7 percent.
   (d) $25 a year for 3 years compounded annually at 2 percent.

5-6. What is the present value of the following annuities?
   (a) $2500 a year for 10 years discounted back to the present at 7 percent.
   (b) $70 a year for 3 years discounted back to the present at 3 percent.
   (c) $280 a year for 7 years discounted back to the present at 6 percent.
   (d) $500 a year for 10 years discounted back to the present at 10 percent.

5-7. Ted Kitchel, who recently sold his Porsche, placed $10,000 in a savings account paying annual compound interest of 6 percent.
   (a) Calculate the amount of money that will have accrued if he leaves the money in the bank for 1, 5, and 15 years.
   (b) If he moves his money into an account that pays 8 percent or one that pays 10 percent, rework part (a) using these new interest rates.

(c) What conclusions can you draw from the relationship between interest rates, time, and future sums from the calculations you have done above?

5-8. Calculate the amount of money that will be in each of the following accounts at the end of the given deposit period:

ACCOUNT	AMOUNT DEPOSITED	ANNUAL INTEREST RATE	COMPOUNDING PERIOD (COMPOUNDED EVERY __ MONTHS)	DEPOSIT PERIOD (YEARS)
Gordy Byran	$ 1,000	10%	12	10
Wayne Robinson	$ 95,000	12%	1	1
Les Henson	$ 8,000	12%	2	2
Marshall Ashford	$120,000	8%	3	2
Jeff Schneider	$ 30,000	10%	6	4
Dale Solomon	$ 15,000	12%	4	3

5-9. (a) Calculate the future sum of $5000, given that it will be held in the bank five years at an annual interest rate of 6 percent.

(b) Recalculate part (a) given that the compounding period is semiannual; and bimonthly.

(c) Recalculate parts (a) and (b) for a 12 percent annual interest rate.

(d) Recalculate part (a) given that the time horizon used changes to 12 years (annual interest rate is still 6 percent).

(e) With respect to the effect of changes in the stated interest rate and holding periods on future sums in parts (c) and (d), what conclusions do you draw when you compare these figures to answers found in parts (a) and (b)?

5-10. Gwen Kortier, a sophomore mechanical engineering student, receives a call from an insurance agent, who believes that Gwen is an older woman ready to retire from teaching. He explains to her about several annuities that she could buy that would guarantee her an annual fixed income. The annuities are as follows:

ANNUITY	PAYMENT INTO ANNUITY	AMOUNT OF MONEY RECEIVED PER YEAR	DURATION OF ANNUITY (YEARS)
A	$50,000	$8500	12
B	$60,000	$7000	25
C	$70,000	$8000	20

If Gwen could earn 11 percent on her money by placing it in a savings account, should she place it instead in any of the annuities? Which ones, if any? Why?

5-11. Sales of a new finance book were 15,000 copies this year and were expected to increase by 20 percent per year. What are expected sales during each of the next three years? Graph this sales trend and explain.

5-12. Jason Thompson of the Detroit Tigers hit 31 home runs in 1977. If his home run output grew at a rate of 17 percent per year, what would it be over the following five years?

5-13. Jim Crews just purchased a new house for $80,000. He paid $20,000 down and agreed to pay the rest over the next 25 years in 25 equal annual payments, which include principal payment plus 9 percent compound interest on the unpaid balance. What will these equal payments be equal to?

5-14. To pay for your child's education you wish to have accumulated $15,000 at the end of 15 years. To do this you plan on depositing an equal amount into the bank at the end of each year. If the bank is willing to pay 6 percent compounded annually, how much must you deposit each year in order to obtain your goal?

5-15. If you were offered $1079.50 ten years from now in return for an investment of $500 currently, what annual rate of interest would you earn if you took the offer?

5-16. What is the present value of the following?
(a) A $300 perpetuity discounted back to the present at 8 percent.
(b) A $1000 perpetuity discounted back to the present at 12 percent.
(c) A $100 perpetuity discounted back to the present at 9 percent.
(d) A $95 perpetuity discounted back to the present at 5 percent.

5-17. What is the value of $500 after five years if it is invested at 10 percent compounded continuously? (If you don't have a calculator capable of solving this problem, simply set it up.)

5-18. About how many years would it take for your investment to grow fourfold if it were invested at 16 percent compounded semiannually?

DRAPER, JEAN E., and JANE S. KLINGMAN, *Mathematical Analysis*. New York: Harper & Row, 1967.

HART, WILLIAM L., *Mathematics of Investment*, 5th ed., Lexington, Mass.: D. C. Heath and Company, 1975.

HOWELL, JAMES E., and DANIEL TEICHROEW, *Mathematical Analysis for Business Decisions*, chap. 10. Homewood, Ill.: Richard D. Irwin, 1963.

SHAO, STEPHEN P., *Mathematics for Management and Finance*, 3d ed. Cincinnati: South-Western Publishing Co., 1974.

SELECTED REFERENCES

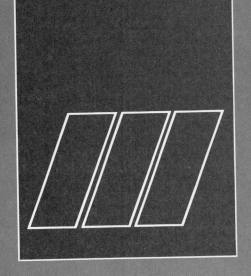

WORKING-
CAPITAL
MANAGEMENT

Introduction to Working-Capital Management

*T*raditionally, **working capital** has been defined as the firm's investment in current assets. **Current assets** are comprised of all assets that the firm expects to convert into cash within the year, including cash, marketable securities, accounts receivable, and inventories. Managing the firm's working capital, however, has come to mean more than simply managing the firm's investment in current assets. In fact, a more descriptive title for this chapter might be *Net-Working-Capital Management*, where **net working capital** refers to the difference in the firm's current assets and its current liabilities:

$$\text{net working capital} = \text{current assets} - \text{current liabilities} \qquad (6\text{-}1)$$

Thus, in managing the firm's net working capital we are concerned with *managing the firm's liquidity*. This entails considering two related problems:

1. Managing the firm's investment in current assets, and
2. Managing the firm's use of short-term or current liabilities.

This chapter provides the basic principles underlying the analysis of each of these problems. These principles are then applied in each of the remaining chapters in this section.

Chapters 7 through 9 investigate the decision-making process in managing the firm's investment in current assets, while Chapters 11 and 12 are devoted to the management of fixed asset investments. At present we need only be aware that these investment decisions are undertaken in expectation of future benefits. That is, a firm invests in inventories because of the expected benefits derived from holding an inventory. Likewise, the firm acquires fixed assets because of the future cash flows those assets are expected to generate. In this chapter our interest in the firm's investment decisions relates to their effect on the firm's net working capital or liquidity. Other things remaining the same, the greater the firm's investment in current assets the greater is its liquidity.

As a means of increasing its liquidity the firm may choose to invest additional funds in cash and/or marketable securities (discussed in Chapters 7 and 8). Such action involves a tradeoff, however, since such assets earn little or no return. The firm thus finds that it can reduce its risk of illiquidity only by reducing its overall return on invested funds and vice versa.

The *risk-return tradeoff* involved in managing the firm's liquidity is illustrated in the following example. Firms A and B are identical in every respect but one: Firm B has invested $10,000 in marketable securities. The balance sheets and net incomes of the two firms are shown in Table 6-1. Note that Firm A has a current ratio of 2.5 and earns a 10 percent return

Table 6-1 THE EFFECTS OF INVESTING IN CURRENT ASSETS ON LIQUIDITY AND PROFITABILITY

	BALANCE SHEETS (1978)	
	Firm A	Firm B
Cash	$ 1,000	1,000
Marketable securities	—	10,000
Accounts receivable	19,000	19,000
Inventories	30,000	30,000
Current assets	$ 50,000	$ 60,000
Net fixed assets	100,000	100,000
Total	$150,000	$160,000
Current liabilities	$ 20,000	$ 20,000
Long-term debt	30,000	30,000
Common equity	100,000	110,000
Total	$150,000	$160,000
Net income	$ 15,000	$ 15,300[a]
Current ratio (current assets/current liabilities)	2.5 times	3.0 times
Return on total assets (net income/total assets)	10%	9.6%

[a]During the year Firm B held $10,000 in marketable securities which earned a 6 percent return or $600 for the year. After paying taxes at a rate of 50 percent the firm netted a $300 return on this investment.

on its total assets. Firm B, with its larger investment in marketable securities, has a current ratio of 3. Since the marketable securities earn a return of only 6 percent before taxes (3 percent after taxes with a 50 percent tax rate), Firm B earns only 9.6 percent on its total investment. Thus, investing in current assets, and in particular in marketable securities, does have a favorable effect on firm liquidity, but it also has an unfavorable effect on the firm's rate of return earned on invested funds.

The second and final determinant of the firm's liquidity relates to its use of current versus long-term debt. Here, too, the firm faces a risk-return tradeoff. Other things remaining the same, the greater its reliance upon short-term debt or current liabilities in financing its asset investments, the lower will be its liquidity. On the other hand, the use of current liabilities offer some very real advantages to the user.

FLEXIBILITY

Current liabilities offer the firm a flexible source of financing. They can be used to match the timing of a firm's needs for short-term financing. If, for example, a firm needs funds for a three-month period to finance a seasonal expansion in inventories, then a three-month loan can provide substantial cost savings over a long-term loan (even if the interest rate on short-term financing should be higher). This brings us to the second advantage generally associated with the use of short-term financing.

INTEREST COST

In general, interest rates on short-term debt are lower than on long-term debt for a given borrower. This relationship is usually referred to as the **term structure of interest rates.** For a given firm the term structure might appear as follows:

LOAN MATURITY	INTEREST RATE
3 months	7.75%
6 months	8.50%
1 year	9.00%
3 years	9.25%
5 years	9.50%
10 years	9.75%
30 years	10.00%

Note that this term structure reflects the rates of interest applicable to a given borrower at a particular point in time; thus, it would not describe the rates of interest available to another borrower or even those to the same borrower at a different point in time.[1]

The use of current liabilities or short-term debt as opposed to long-term debt subjects the firm to a greater risk of illiquidity. That is, short-term debt due to its very nature must be repaid or *rolled over* more often, and so it enhances the possibility that the firm's financial condition might deteriorate to a point where the needed funds might not be available.[2]

A second disadvantage of short-term debt is the uncertainty of interest costs from year to year. For example, where a firm borrows during a six-month period each year to finance a seasonal expansion in current assets, it might incur a different rate of interest each year. This rate reflects the current rate of interest at the time of the loan, as well as the lender's perception of the firm's riskiness. If long-term debt were used, then the interest cost would be known for the entire period of the loan agreement. Remember, however, that the use of long-term debt in this situation involves borrowing for the entire year rather than for the period when the funds are needed; this increases the level of interest cost the firm experiences. Also, should the general trend in short-term rates of interest be downward, then short-term debt offers a cost saving.

Example. Consider the risk-return characteristics of Firm X and Firm Y, whose balance sheets and income statements are given in Table 6-2. Both firms had the same seasonal needs for financing throughout the past year. Thus, in December they each required $40,000 to finance a seasonal expansion in accounts receivable. In addition, during the four-month period beginning with August and extending through November both firms needed $20,000 to support a seasonal buildup in inventories. Firm X financed its seasonal financing requirements using $40,000 in long-term debt carrying an annual interest rate of 10 percent. Firm Y, on the other hand, raised its seasonal financing needs using short-term borrowing on which it paid 9 percent interest. Since Firm Y borrowed only when it needed the funds and did so at the lower rate of interest on short-term debt, its interest expense for the year was only $900, whereas Firm X incurred $4000 in annual interest expense.[3]

The end result of the two firms' financing policies is evidenced in their current ratio and return on total assets which appear at the bottom of Table 6-2. Firm X, using long-term rather than short-term debt, has a current

---

[1]The term *structure of interest rates* is discusssed more fully in Chapter 18.

[2]The dangers of such a policy are readily apparent in the experiences of firms that have been forced into bankruptcy. Penn Central, for example, had $80 million in short-term debt that it was unable to rollover when it became bankrupt.

[3]Interest expense calculations are found in the footnotes to Table 6-2.

Table 6-2 EFFECT OF CURRENT VERSUS LONG-TERM DEBT ON FIRM LIQUIDITY AND PROFITABILITY

BALANCE SHEETS (DECEMBER 31, 1978)		
	Firm X	*Firm Y*
Current assets	$ 60,000	$ 60,000
Net fixed assets	140,000	140,000
Total	$200,000	$200,000
Accounts payable	$ 20,000	$ 20,000
Notes payable	—	40,000
Current liabilities	$ 20,000	$ 60,000
Long-term debt	40,000	—
Common equity	140,000	140,000
Total	$200,000	$200,000

INCOME STATEMENTS		
Net operating income	$ 44,000	$ 44,000
Less: Interest expense	4,000[a]	900[b]
Earnings before taxes	40,000	43,100
Less: taxes (50%)	20,000	21,550
Net income	$ 20,000	$ 21,550
Current ratio	3 times	1 time
Return on total assets	10%	10.8%

[a]Firm X paid interest during the entire year on $40,000 in long-term debt at a rate of 10 percent. Its interest expense for the year was $.10 \times \$40,000 = \$4,000$.

[b]Firm Y paid interest on $40,000 for one month and on $20,000 for four months at 9 percent interest during the year. Thus, Firm Y's interest expense for the year equals $\$40,000 \times .09 \times \frac{1}{12}$ plus $\$20,000 \times .09 \times = \frac{4}{12}$ or $300 + 600 = \$900$.

ratio of 3 times whereas Firm Y's current ratio is only 1. However, owing to its lower interest expense, Firm Y was able to earn 10.8 percent on its invested funds whereas Firm X produced a 10 percent return. Thus, a firm can reduce its risk of illiquidity through the use of long-term debt at the expense of a reduction in its return on invested funds.

Managing the firm's net-working-capital position (that is, its liquidity) has been shown to involve simultaneous decisions regarding the firm's investment in current assets and its use of current liabilities. Fortunately, a guiding principle exists that can be used as a *benchmark* for the firm's working-capital policies: the **hedging principle** or **principle of self-liquidating debt**. This principle provides a *guide* to the maintenance of a

APPROPRIATE LEVEL OF WORKING CAPITAL

level of liquidity sufficient for the firm to meet its maturing obligations on time.[4]

Very simply, the **hedging principle** involves *matching* the cash flow generating characteristics of a firm's assets with the maturity of the source of financing used. For example, a seasonal expansion in inventories, according to the hedging principle, should be financed with a short-term loan or current liability. The rationale underlying the rule is straightforward. Funds are needed for a limited period of time, and when that time has passed, the cash needed to repay the loan will be generated by the sale of the extra inventory items. Obtaining the needed funds from a long-term source (longer than one year) would mean that the firm would still have the funds after the inventories (they helped finance) had been sold. In this case the firm would have "excess" liquidity, which they either hold in cash or invest in low-yielding marketable securities. This would result in an overall lowering of firm profits.

Consider a second example in which a firm purchases a new conveyor belt system, which is expected to produce cash savings to the firm by eliminating the need for two laborers and, consequently, their salaries. This amounts to an annual savings of $14,000, while the conveyor belt cost $150,000 to install and will last 20 years. If the firm chooses to finance this asset with a one-year note, then it will not be able to repay the loan from the cash flow generated by the asset. Hence, in accordance with the hedging principle, the firm should finance the asset with a source of financing which more nearly matches the expected life and cash flow generating characteristics of the asset. In this case a ten-to twenty-year loan would be more appropriate than a one-year loan.

PERMANENT AND TEMPORARY ASSETS

The notion of *maturity matching* in the hedging principle can be most easily understood when we think in terms of the distinction between **permanent** and **temporary investments in assets** as opposed to the fixed and current asset categories. A permanent investment in an asset is one that the firm expects to hold for a period longer than one year. Permanent investments are made in the firm's minimum level of current assets, as well as in its fixed assets. Temporary asset investments, on the other hand, are comprised of the firm's investments in current assets, which will be liquidated and not replaced within the current year. For example, a seasonal

[4]A value-maximizing approach to the management of the firm's liquidity would involve assessing the value of the benefits derived from increasing the firm's investment in liquid assets and weighing them against the added costs to the firm's owners resulting from investing in low-yielding assets. Unfortunately, the benefits derived from increased liquidity relate to the expected costs of bankruptcy to the firm's owners, and these costs are "unmeasurable" by existing technology. Thus, a "valuation" approach to liquidity management exists only in the theoretical realm. For a discussion of bankruptcy cost and the associated measurement problems see J. B. Warner, "Bankruptcy Costs: Some Evidence," *Journal of Finance,* May 1977, 337–49, and J. C. Van Horne, "Bankruptcy and Liquidity Costs," Research Paper No. 205, Stanford Graduate School of Business, 1976.

increase in the level of inventories is a temporary investment, as the build-up in inventories will be eliminated when it is no longer needed.

The hedging principle can be stated very succinctly: *Permanent investments in assets should be financed with permanent sources of financing and temporary investments should be financed with temporary sources of financing.* Now, what constitutes a **permanent and a temporary source of financing?** Basically, a temporary source of financing is a current liability. Thus, temporary financing consists of the various sources of short-term debt discussed in Chapter 10, including secured and unsecured bank loans, commercial paper, loans secured by accounts receivable, and loans secured by inventories. Permanent sources of financing include intermediate- and long-term debt, preferred stock, and common equity.[5]

Besides permanent and temporary sources of financing, there also exist **spontaneous** sources. Spontaneous sources consist of the trade credit and other accounts payable that arise *spontaneously* in the firm's day-to-day operations. Examples include wages and salaries payable, accrued interest, and accrued taxes. These expenses accrue throughout the period until they are paid. For example, if a firm has a wage expense of $10,000 a week and pays its employees monthly, then its employees effectively provide financing equal to $10,000 by the end of the first week following a payday, $20,000 by the end of the second week, and so forth. Since these expenses generally arise in direct conjunction with the firm's ongoing operations, they are referred to as *spontaneous*.

Still another example of a spontaneous source of financing involves the use of trade credit. As the firm acquires materials for its inventories, credit is often made available spontaneously or on *demand* by the firm's suppliers. Trade credit appears on the firm's balance sheet as accounts payable. The size of the accounts payable balance varies directly with the firm's purchases of inventory items, which, in turn, are related to the firm's anticipated sales. Thus, a part of the financing needed by the firm is spontaneously provided by its use of trade credit.

Therefore, the firm's total investment in permanent and temporary assets must be financed by the sum of its spontaneous, temporary, and permanent sources of financing.

HEDGING PRINCIPLE: GRAPHICAL ILLUSTRATION

The hedging principle is depicted in Figure 6-1. Total assets are broken down into temporary and permanent asset investment categories. The firm's permanent investment in assets is financed by the use of either permanent sources of financing (intermediate- and long-term debt, preferred stock, and common equity) or spontaneous sources (trade credit and other

---

[5]Intermediate-term debt is discussed in Chapter 19, while long-term debt, preferred stock, and common stock are covered in Chapter 20. Retained earnings or internal equity financing is presented in conjunction with dividend policy in Chapter 17.

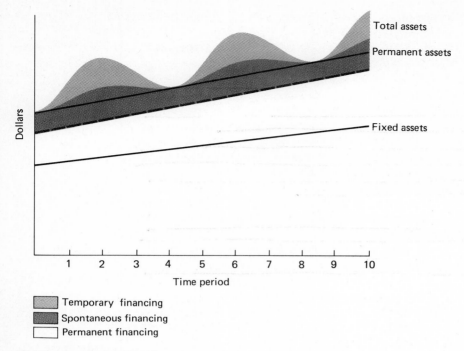

Total assets

Permanent assets

Fixed assets

Dollars

Time period

	Temporary financing
	Spontaneous financing
	Permanent financing

FIGURE 6-1 *The Hedging Principle*

accounts payable). Its temporary investment in assets is financed with temporary (short-term debt) and/or spontaneous sources of financing.

Note that the hedging principle has been modified to state: *Asset needs of the firm not financed by spontaneous sources should be financed in accordance with the rule: permanent asset investments financed with permanent sources and temporary investments financed with temporary sources.*

Since total assets must always equal the sum of spontaneous, temporary, and permanent sources of financing, the hedging approach provides the financial manager with the basis for determining the sources of financing to use at any point in time.

HEDGING PRINCIPLE: NUMERICAL ILLUSTRATION

The hedging principle can be implemented by using the five-step procedure outlined in Table 6-3. Note that each step is described both verbally and algebraically. The example provided in Table 6-4 will be analyzed using this procedure.

Step 1 involves projecting current, fixed, and total assets for the planning horizon (3 years or 12 quarters). These projections are included in columns (1), (2), and (3), respectively, of Table 6-4.[6]

---

[6]Projecting the level of these assets is an example of the type of problem encountered in financial forecasting (discussed earlier in Chapter 4).

Table 6-3 APPLYING THE HEDGING PRINCIPLE TO WORKING-CAPITAL MANAGEMENT

STEP	DESCRIPTION	EQUATION
1	Project the firm's asset needs for each quarter (month) of the planning horizon. The resulting forecast will be our estimates of the firm's total assets (TA), which can be further broken down into both current assets (CA) and fixed assets (FA).	$TA = CA + FA$
2	Distinguish between permanent asset (P) and temporary asset investments (T) for each quarter of the planning period.	$TA = P + T$
3	Project the level of spontaneous financing (SF) for each quarter.[a]	
4	Determine the level of permanent financing (PF) for each quarter of the planning horizon. This equals the difference in permanent assets (P*) and spontaneous financing (SF*) for the nearest calendar quarter where temporary assets (T) equal zero.[b]	$PF = P^* - SF^*$
5	Determine the level of short-term debt or temporary financing (TF). This equals the difference in total assets for the quarter and the sum of permanent (PF) plus spontaneous sources of financing (SF).	$TF = TA - (PF + SF)$

[a]In the example used in the text discussion, SF is estimated as a percent of current assets. Since SF usually rises with the purchase of inventories, this estimation procedure is often useful.

[b]The asterisk (*) on SF* and P* indicate those levels of SF and P corresponding to a particular calendar quarter. That is, that quarter where temporary financing equals zero.

Step 2 involves distinguishing between permanent and temporary asset investments for each quarter of the three-year planning period. This step can be accomplished by using the graph of the firm's projected asset investments contained in Figure 6-2. In order to simplify the illustration, the firm's permanent investments in assets are assumed not to grow. Thus, the level of investment in permanent assets remains constant at $100 million throughout the three-year period. These permanent assets consist of a $60 million investment in fixed assets and a $40 million investment in current assets. The level of total assets varies over the period, peaking in the first and fourth quarters of each year when the maximum investment in inventories (quarter IV) and receivables (quarter I) occurs. Temporary and permanent investments in assets are found in columns (4) and (5), respectively, of Table 6-4.

Step 3 involves projecting the level of spontaneous financing for each quarter. For illustrative purposes we assume that spontaneous financing

Table 6-4 USING THE HEDGING PRINCIPLE: AN EXAMPLE

YEAR	QUARTER	(1) FIXED ASSETS (FA)	(2) CURRENT ASSETS (CA)	(3) TOTAL ASSETS (TA)	(4) TEMPORARY ASSETS (T)	(5) PERMANENT ASSETS (P)	(6) PERMANENT FINANCING[b] (PF)	(7) SPONTANEOUS FINANCING[c] (SF)	(8) TEMPORARY OR SHORT-TERM FINANCING[d] (TF)	(9) TOTAL FINANCING
1978	I	$60[a]	$60	$120	$20	$100	$88	$18	$14	$120
	II	60	45	105	5	100	88	14	3	105
	III	60	40	100	0	100	88	12	0	100
	IV	60	50	110	10	100	88	15	7	110
1979	I	60	62	122	22	100	88	19	15	122
	II	60	48	108	8	100	88	14	6	108
	III	60	42	100	0	100	88	12	0	100
	IV	60	55	115	15	100	88	17	10	115
1980	I	60	61	121	21	100	88	18	15	121
	II	60	47	107	7	100	88	14	5	107
	III	60	40	100	0	100	88	12	0	100
	IV	60	52	112	12	100	88	16	8	112

[a]All figures in millions of dollars.

[b]Permanent financing plus the minimum level of spontaneous financing should equal the anticipated level of permanent assets. Permanent assets represent the minimum planned investment in assets that the firm expects to have in the foreseeable future. Since our example firm anticipates neither growth nor decline in its permanent assets, the level of these assets remains constant at $100 million. The majority of these permanent assets will be financed by permanent sources of financing with remainder being financed using spontaneous sources of short-term credit (see footnote [c] below). The need for permanent financing is therefore limited to the firm's $60 million in fixed assets plus 70 percent of its current assets or .70 × $40 million = $28 million. Thus, total permanent financing needs are estimated to be $60 million + 28 million = $88 million.

[c]This includes trade credit and other payables such as accrued wages and accrued taxes that arise "spontaneously" with the firm's operations. Here we assume for simplicity that these sources of spontaneous financing are equal to 30 percent of the firm's current assets.

[d]This would include one or more of the sources of short-term financing discussed in this chapter. The level of short-term debt is, in accordance with the hedging approach, equal to the difference in total assets and the sum of permanent plus spontaneous sources of financing.

for each quarter will equal 30 percent of projected current assets. Thus, for quarter I of 1978 spontaneous financing equals 30 percent of projected current assets, or .30 × $60 million = $18 million.

Step 4 may be the most involved part of the procedure. Here the firm's level of permanent financing is estimated. To do this, we can use either Figure 6-2 or Table 6-4 to find the nearest future quarter where temporary asset investments equal zero or where total assets equal the firm's permanent investment in assets. Beginning our analysis in quarter I of 1978, temporary assets are projected to equal zero in quarter III of that year. At this point, temporary financing should also equal zero in accordance with the hedging principle.[7] Thus, for quarter III of 1978 total assets should be financed by spontaneous plus permanent sources of financing. Since spontaneous financing for this quarter has been estimated to equal 30 percent of the quarter's current assets or $12 million, then permanent financing must equal $88 million. That is, permanent financing should equal total assets of $100 million less spontaneous financing of $12 million. This level of permanent financing should be used through quarter III of 1978, when the level of permanent financing would again have to be estimated. For the example presented in Table 6-4, permanant assets do not grow or decline, so that the firm's need for permanent financing is unchanged throughout the three-year planning period. Thus, permanent financing needs remain equal to $88 million for the entire 12-quarter planning period.

Step 5 involves estimating the level of temporary financing needed for

[7]The hedging principle states that temporary financing be used to finance temporary asset investments alone. Thus, where no temporary asset investments exist, the firm should be free of all temporary sources of financing.

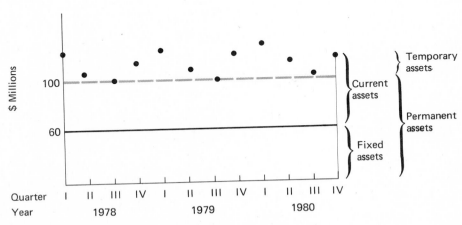

FIGURE 6-2 *Graphical Illustration of the Hedging Principle. (The dots indicate the firm's projected level of total assets for each quarter of the planning period.)*

each future quarter. This estimate is found by subtracting the sum of both permanent and spontaneous financing from total assets (which represents total financing needed for each future quarter). Thus, for quarter I of 1978 the firm's temporary financing needs will be $120 million − $88 million − $18 million = $14 million.

This completes the firm's financial *plan* for the 12-quarter planning period. The plan indicates the firm's expected use of spontaneous, short-term financing (temporary financing) and permanent financing. In Chapter 10 we address the problem of selecting the source or sources of short-term financing, while Chapters 16 and 17 deal with the problems surrounding the selection of permanent sources of financing.

Modifications to the Hedging Principle

Figures 6-3 and 6-4 depict two modifications of the strict hedging approach to working-capital management. In Figure 6-3 the firm follows a more cautious plan, whereby permanent sources of financing exceed permanent assets in trough periods (quarter III) such that excess cash is available (which must be invested in marketable securities).[8] Note that the firm actually has excess liquidity during the low ebb of its asset cycle and thus faces a lower risk of being caught short of cash than a firm that follows the pure hedging approach. However, the firm also increases its investment in relatively low yielding assets such that its return on investment is diminished (recall the example from Table 6-1).

Figure 6-4 depicts a firm that continually finances a part of its permanent asset needs with temporary or short-term funds and thus follows a more aggressive strategy in managing its working capital. It can be seen

[8]Marketable securities and cash management are discussed in Chapters 7 and 8.

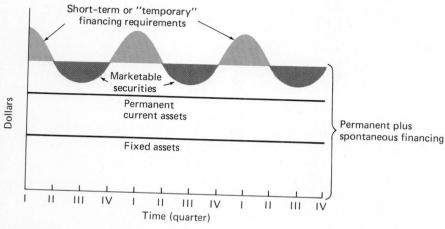

FIGURE 6-3 *Cautious Working-Capital Plan*

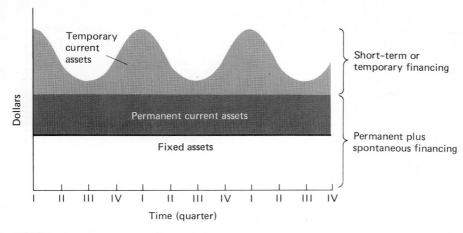

FIGURE 6-4 *Aggressive Working-Capital Plan*

that even when its investment in asset needs is lowest (in quarter III) the firm must still rely on short-term or temporary financing. Such a firm would be subject to increased risks of a cash shortfall in that it must depend on a continual *rollover* or replacement of its short-term debt with more short-term debt. The benefit derived from following such a policy relates to the possible savings resulting from the use of lower cost short-term debt (as opposed to long-term debt).

Most firms will not exclusively follow any one of the three strategies outlined here in determining their reliance on short-term credit. Instead, a firm will at times find itself overly reliant on permanent financing and thus holding excess cash, and at other times it may have to rely on short-term financing throughout an entire operating cycle. The hedging approach does, however, provide an important *benchmark* that can be used to guide decisions regarding the appropriate use of short-term credit.

SUMMARY

This chapter has overviewed the problems involved in managing the firm's working capital, defined in terms of **net working capital,** which equals current assets less current liabilities. Thus, working-capital management involves managing the firm's liquidity, which, in turn, involves managing (1) the firm's investment in current assets, and (2) its use of current liabilities. Each of these problems was shown to involve risk-return tradeoffs. Investing in current assets was found to reduce the firm's risk of illiquidity at the expense of lowering its overall rate of return on its investment in assets. Furthermore, the use of long-term sources of financing was found to enhance the firm's liquidity while reducing its rate of return on assets.

Finally, the **hedging principle** or **principle of self-liquidating debt** was provided as a benchmark for the firm's working-capital decisions. Basically, this principle involves matching the cash flow generating characteristics of an asset with the cash flow requirements of the source of funds used to finance its acquisition.

Chapters 7 through 9 discuss the problems involved in managing the firm's investment in current assets. This includes the management of cash, marketable securities, accounts receivable, and inventories. Chapter 10 discusses short-term financing. Two basic problems are encountered in attempting to manage the firm's use of short-term financing: (1) How much short-term financing should the firm use? (2) What specific sources should be selected? This chapter has addressed the first of these questions with the hedging or self-liquidating-debt principle. The answer to the second question involves analyzing the relative costs of the available sources of short-term credit, an issue addressed at length in Chapter 10.

STUDY QUESTIONS

6-1. Define and contrast the terms *working capital* and *net working capital*.

6-2. Discuss the risk-return relationship involved in the firm's asset investment decisions as it pertains to working-capital managment.

6-3. What advantages and disadvantages are generally associated with the use of short-term debt? Discuss.

6-4. Explain what is meant by the statement, "The use of current liabilities as opposed to long-term debt subjects the firm to a greater risk of illiquidity."

6-5. Define the hedging principle. How can this principle be used in the management of working capital?

6-6. Define the following terms:
(a) Permanent asset investments.
(b) Temporary asset investments.
(c) Permanent sources of financing.
(d) Temporary sources of financing.
(e) Spontaneous sources of financing.

STUDY PROBLEMS

6-1. The current balance sheet for the J. S. Smith Manufacturing Company appears as follows:

J. S. SMITH MFG. CO.
Balance Sheet
March 31, 1979
(in millions of dollars)

Current assets	$ 100	Accounts payable and	
Fixed assets	100	accrued expenses	$ 25
		Notes payable	25
Total	$ 200	Long-term debt	50

Common equity		100
Total		$ 200

Estimated current and fixed asset investments for the firm are presented below for each quarter of the next three years:

QUARTER ENDED	FIXED ASSETS ($ MILLIONS)	CURRENT ASSETS ($ MILLIONS)
6/30/79	100	105
9/30/79	100	106
12/31/79	101	108
3/31/80	101	104
6/30/80	102	105
9/30/80	102	107
12/31/80	103	109
3/31/81	103	106
6/30/81	104	107
9/30/81	104	109
12/31/81	105	110
3/31/82	105	107

The firm wants to develop a financial plan that will accommodate its total needs for funds. Further, Smith believes that a minimum issue of $2 million is required to justify the issuance of long-term debt or common stock.

(a) Develop a financing plan for Smith, using the hedging concept, where accounts payable and accrued expenses are expected to equal 25 percent of current assets and the firm expects quarterly earnings after taxes of $1 million. The firm also plans to pay cash dividends equal to the full $1 million each quarter.

(b) Modify your plan in (a) above to include compliance with the following objectives for each quarter in the planning period:
   (1) A 40–60 percent debt ratio (total liabilities/total assets).
   (2) A current ratio of 1.5 or higher.

(c) If short-term debt will cost Smith 6 percent and long-term debt 8 percent, what is the total cost of your plan in (b) above to Smith over the three-year period?

6-2. H. O. Hielregal, Inc., estimates that its current assets are about 25 percent of sales. The firm's current balance sheet is presented on p. 164.

H. O. HIELREGAL
Balance Sheet
12/31/79
(millions of dollars)

Current assets	$ 2.0	Trade credit and	
Fixed assets	2.8	accounts payable	$ .8
		Long-term debt	1.0
Total	$ 4.8	Common equity	3.0
		Total	$ 4.8

Hielregal pays out all of its net income in cash dividends to its stockholders. Trade credit and accounts payable equal 10 percent of firm sales.

(a) Based on the following five-year sales forecast, prepare five end-of-year pro forma balance sheets which indicate "additional financing needed" for each year as a balancing account. Fixed assets are expected to increase by $.2 million each year.

YEAR	PREDICTED SALES ($ MILLIONS)
1980	10
1981	11
1982	13
1983	14
1984	15

(b) Develop a financing plan for Hielregal [using your answer to (a) above] that is consistent with the following goals:
(1) A minimum current ratio of 2.0 and a maximum of 3.0.
(2) A debt to total assets ratio of 35–45 percent. You may issue new common stock to raise equity funds.

KNIGHT, W. D., "Working Capital Management—Satisficing versus Optimization," *Financial Management,* 1 (Spring 1972), 33–40.

MEHTA, DILEEP R., *Working Capital Management*. Englewood Cliffs, N.J.: Prentice-Hall, Inc., 1974.

MERVILLE, L. J., and L. A. TAVIS, "Optimal Working Capital Policies: A Chance-Constrained Programming Approach," *Journal of Financial and Quantitative Analysis,* 8 (January 1973), 47–60.

———— , "A Total Real Asset Planning System," *Journal of Financial and Quantitative Analysis,* 9 (January 1974), 107–15.

SMITH, KEITH V., *Management of Working Capital*. New York: West Publishing, 1974.

SELECTED
REFERENCES

STANCILL, JAMES McN., *The Management of Working Capital*. Scranton, Pa.: Intext, 1971.

TINSLEY, P. A., "Capital Structure, Precautionary Balances, and Valuation of the Firm: The Problem of Financial Risk," *Journal of Financial and Quantitative Analysis*, 5 (March 1970), 33–62.

VANHORNE, JAMES C., "A Risk-Return Analysis of a Firm's Working Capital Position," *Engineering Economist*, 14 (Winter 1969), 71–89.

WALKER, ERNEST W., "Towards a Theory of Working Capital," *Engineering Economist*, 9 (January–February 1964), 21–35.

Cash and Marketable Securities Management - I

7

*C*hapter 6 introduced and overviewed the concept of working-capital management. Now we will consider the various elements of the firm's working capital in some depth. This chapter and the next one center on the formulation of financial policies for management of cash and marketable securities. Taken together they explore three major areas: (1) techniques available to management for favorably influencing their cash receipts and disbursements patterns, (2) some straightforward models that can assist financial officers in deciding on how much cash to hold, and (3) sensible investment possibilities that enable the company to productively employ excess cash balances. The two latter areas are explored in Chapter 8.

First it will be helpful to distinguish among some terms. **Cash** is the currency and coin that the firm has on hand in petty cash drawers, in cash registers, or in checking accounts at the various commercial banks where its demand deposits are maintained. **Marketable securities** are those security investments that the firm can quickly convert into cash balances. Those held by most firms in the United States tend to have very short maturity periods—less than one year. No law, of course, dictates that instruments with longer terms to maturity must be avoided. Rather, the decision to keep the average maturity quite short is based upon some sound business reasoning, which will be detailed in the next chapter. Marketable securities are also referred to as **near cash** or **near-cash assets** because they can be turned into cash in a short period of time. Taken together, cash and near cash are known as **liquid assets.**

A thorough understanding of why and how a firm holds cash requires an accurate conception of how cash flows into and through the enterprise. Figure 7-1 depicts the process of cash generation and disposition in a typical manufacturing setting. The arrows designate the direction of the flow—that is, whether the cash balance is being increased or decreased.

*Cash Flow
Process*

The firm experiences irregular increases in its cash holdings from several external sources. Funds can be obtained in the financial markets from the sale of securities, such as bonds, preferred stock, and common stock, or nonmarketable debt contracts can be entered into with lenders such as commercial banks. These irregular cash inflows do not occur on a daily basis. They tend to be episodic, in that the financing arrangements that give rise to them are effected at wide intervals. The reason is that external financing contracts usually involve huge sums of money stemming from a major need identified by the company's management, and these needs do not occur every day. For example, a new product might be in the process of being launched, or a plant expansion might be required to provide added productive capacity.

In most organizations the financial officer responsible for cash management also controls the transactions that affect the firm's investment in marketable securities. As excess cash becomes temporarily available, marketable securities will be purchased. When cash is in short supply, a portion of the marketable securities portfolio will be liquidated.

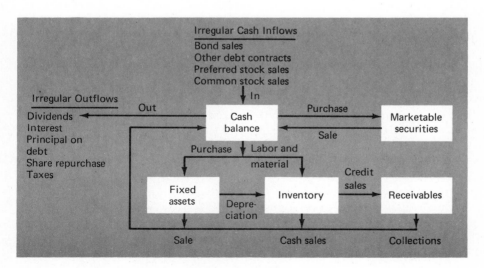

FIGURE 7-1 *The Cash Generation and Disposition Process*

Whereas the irregular cash inflows are from external sources, the other main sources of cash to the firm arise from internal operations and occur on a more regular basis. Over long periods the largest receipts will come from accounts receivable collections and to a lesser extent from direct cash sales of finished goods. Many manufacturing concerns also generate cash on a regular basis through the liquidation of scrap or obsolete inventory. In the automobile industry large and costly machines called chip crushers grind waste metal into fine scrap that brings considerable revenue to the major producers. At various times fixed assets may also be sold, thereby generating some cash inflow. This is not a large source of funds except in unusual situations where, for instance, a complete plant renovation may be taking place.

Apart from the investment of excess cash in near-cash assets, the cash balance will experience reductions for three key reasons. First, on an irregular basis withdrawals will be made to (1) pay cash dividends on preferred and common stock shares, (2) meet interest requirements on debt contracts, (3) repay the principal borrowed from creditors, (4) buy the firm's own shares in the financial markets for use in executive compensation plans or as an alternative to paying a cash dividend, and (5) pay tax bills. Again, by an "irregular basis" we mean items *not* occurring on a daily or highly frequent schedule. Second, the company's capital expenditure program will designate that fixed assets be acquired at various intervals. Third, inventories will be purchased on a rather regular basis to ensure a steady flow of finished goods off of the production line. Note that the arrow linking the investment in fixed assets with the inventory account is labeled depreciation. This indicates that a portion of the cost of fixed assets is charged against the products coming off the assembly line. This cost is subsequently recovered through the sale of the finished goods inventory, as the product selling price will be set by management to cover all of the costs of production, including depreciation.

The variety of influences we have mentioned that constantly affect the cash balance held by the firm can be synthesized in terms of the classic motives for holding cash, as identified in the literature of economic theory.

Motives for Holding Cash

In a classic economic treatise John Maynard Keynes segmented the firm's, or any economic unit's, demand for cash into three categories: (1) the transactions motive, (2) the precautionary motive, and (3) the speculative motive.[1]

TRANSACTIONS MOTIVE
Balances held for transactions purposes allow the firm to dispense with cash needs that arise in the ordinary course of doing business. Referring to Figure 7-1, transactions balances would be used to meet the irregular outflows as well as the planned acquisition of fixed assets and inventories.

[1]John Maynard Keynes, *The General Theory of Employment, Interest, and Money* (New York: Harcourt Brace Jovanovich, 1936).

The relative amount of transactions cash held will be significantly affected by the industry in which the firm operates. If revenues can be forecast to fall within a tight range of outcomes, then the ratio of cash and near cash to total assets will be less for the firm than if the prospective cash inflows might be expected to vary over a wide range. In this regard it is well known that utility concerns can forecast cash receipts quite accurately, owing to stable demand for their services arising from their quasi-monopoly status. This enables them to stagger their billings throughout the month and to time them to coincide with their planned expenditures. Inflows and outflows of cash are thereby synchronized. Thus, we would expect the cash holdings of utility firms relative to sales or assets to be less than those associated with a major retail chain that sells groceries. The grocery concern experiences a large number of transactions each day, almost all of which involve an exchange of cash.

Firms competing in the *same* industry may even experience notably different strains upon their cash balances. Transactions balances in the railroad industry are simultaneously influenced by a seasonal factor and a geographic factor. Consider first the seasonal factor. During the summer months all of the railroads that crisscross the North American continent pay out large amounts of cash for materials and labor necessary to upgrade their track beds. Old ties are replaced, new rail is laid, switches are adjusted, and signal systems are overhauled. Now, consider the geographic factor. The railroad companies that serve the northernmost routes, including Canada, will also suffer sizable cash drains throughout the winter season. The harsh weather conditions are the cause. Snow must be swept out of switches, ice is actually burned off of the rails, and derailments occur with far greater frequency than at any other time of the year. Cash balances for the railroads in the northern states and Canada will, therefore, be expected to be relatively higher during the winter season than for railroads operating in more southerly areas.

THE PRECAUTIONARY MOTIVE

Precautionary balances are a buffer stock of liquid assets. This motive for holding cash relates to the maintenance of balances to be used to satisfy possible, but as yet indefinite, needs.

In our discussion of transactions balances we saw that cash flow predictability could affect a firm's cash holdings through synchronization of receipts and disbursements. Cash flow predictability also has a material influence on the firm's demand for cash through the precautionary motive. The airline industry provides a typical illustration. Air passenger carriers are plagued with a very high degree of cash flow uncertainty. The weather, rising fuel costs, and continual strikes by operating personnel make cash forecasting a most difficult activity for any airline company. The upshot of this problem is that because of all the things that *might* happen, the minimum cash balances desired by the managements of air carriers tend to be large.

In addition to cash flow predictability the precautionary motive for holding cash is affected by the firm's access to external funds. Especially important are those cash sources that can be tapped on short notice. Good banking relationships and established lines of credit can reduce the firm's need to keep cash on hand. This unused borrowing power will obviate somewhat the need to invest in precautionary balances.

In actual business practice the precautionary motive is met to a large extent by the holding of a portfolio of *liquid assets,* not just cash. Notice in Figure 7-1 the two-way flow of funds between the company's holdings of cash and marketable securities. In large corporate organizations funds may flow either into or out of the marketable securities portfolio on a daily basis. Because some actual rate of return can be earned on the near-cash assets, compared to a zero rate of return available on cash holdings, it is logical that the precautionary motive will be met in part by investment in marketable securities.

THE SPECULATIVE MOTIVE

Cash is held for speculative purposes in order to take advantage of hoped-for, profit-making situations. Construction firms that erect private dwellings will at times accumulate cash in anticipation of a significant drop in lumber costs. If the price of building supplies does drop, the companies that built up their cash balances stand to profit by purchasing materials in large quantities. This will reduce their cost of goods sold and increase their net profit margin. Generally, the speculative motive is the least important component of a firm's preference for liquidity. The transactions and precautionary motives account for most of the reasons why a company holds cash balances.

The level of cash balances held by the company for transactions and precautionary purposes is influenced by a variety of factors. Because an appreciation of the diverse elements that play on company cash balances aids our conception of cash management, we shall briefly summarize some of these factors:

Review of Motivations for Holding Cash

1. Changing technology and plans for capital expenditures. The firm operating in a "high-technology industry" may invest heavily in liquidity in order to be in a position to acquire, use, and manufacture the newest kinds of productive equipment. At times IBM has exemplified this type of enterprise.
2. Seasonality and the cash cycle. During spring and summer the firm manufacturing toys may severely draw down its cash, invest in inventory, and speed up production. The finished goods manufactured during this period will be shipped on credit to wholesalers and retail outlets in the late summer and early fall. Not until late fall and winter will the cash balance be replenished; this will occur when receivables are collected.
3. Cash commitments as required by debt contracts. The cash balance will rise in advance of an interest or principal payment on a debt instrument and decline after the payment.

4. Financial flexibility. This factor is a function of the company's access to the credit markets. Ready borrowing power enables the firm to reduce the balances actually held for precautionary purposes.

5. The cash budget and cash flow predictability. Recall that we discussed the details of cash budget preparation in Chapter 4. If the anticipated net cash flows projected by the cash budget are unacceptably low, the firm might draw on its established lines of credit with commercial banks and, thereby, raise its actual cash balances. Should large deviations about the expected net cash flows be possible, then precautionary balances will probably be increased.

6. The risk-bearing preferences of management with respect to the chances of running out of cash. A highly conservative management team will choose to avoid the prospect of cash insolvency. Its cash balances will be relatively higher than those of a firm whose policies are set by a less risk-averse management.

7. The effectiveness of the company's cash management system. A well-designed and coordinated cash management system enables the enterprise to operate with a minimum investment in cash. Key aspects of a sound cash management system are described in the remainder of this and the next chapter.

The list above is not intended to exhaust every agent that affects the firm's cash holdings; such a list would be as long as your imagination. Rather, we have shown and emphasized that the influences upon company cash balances are diverse. As would be expected, firms react to these key influences in diverse ways. We shall explore these reactions through an overview of actual business practice related to cash and near-cash holdings.

VARIATIONS IN LIQUID ASSET HOLDINGS

Decisions that concern the amounts of liquid assets to hold rest with the financial officer responsible for cash management. A number of factors that can be expected to influence the financial officer's investment in cash and near-cash have just been reviewed. Not all of these factors affect every firm. Moreover, factors that do affect many companies will do so in differing degrees. Since the executives responsible for the ultimate cash management choices will have different risk-bearing preferences, we might expect that liquid asset holdings among major industry groupings and firms would exhibit considerable variation. Such is the case, as shown by Tables 7-1 and 7-2.

Table 7-1 indicates the liquid asset positions of some major industrial groups. Notice that as a percent of total assets (1) contract construction, (2) total services, and (3) total retail trade invest quite heavily in liquid assets. Both the retail trade and services group maintain considerable cash balances relative to their asset levels because they experience so many cash transactions on a daily basis. The contract construction group is subject to wide variations in cash flows over a period of years, because the construction industry is highly sensitive to the general state of the economy and to interest rate changes. This industry, then, holds large cash balances for precautionary purposes.

Table 7-1 LIQUID ASSET POSITIONS OF SELECTED INDUSTRY GROUPS (IN PERCENT) FOR 1971

RATIOS	ALL INDUS-TRIES	TOTAL MANUFAC-TURING	CONTRACT CONSTRUC-TION	TOTAL MINING	TOTAL RETAIL TRADE	TOTAL SERVICES	UTILITIES[b]
Cash to total assets	6.8	3.5	10.0	4.6	6.7	8.0	1.9
Cash to sales	10.3	2.9	4.9	6.2	2.5	6.8	3.9
Marketable securities to total assets[a]	7.7	1.5	0.8	1.2	0.4	1.1	1.0
Marketable securities to sales	11.7	1.2	0.4	1.5	0.2	1.0	2.0
Total liquid assets to total assets	14.5	5.0	10.8	5.8	7.1	9.1	2.9
Total liquid assets to sales	22.0	4.2	5.3	7.7	2.7	7.7	5.9

[a]Marketable securities, here, represents only federal, state, and local government obligations.
[b]Utilities include transportation, communication, electric, gas, and sanitary services.
SOURCE: Internal Revenue Service, *Statistics of Income, 1971, Corporation Income Tax Returns* (Washington, D.C.: U. S. Government Printing Office, 1976), pp. 18–24.

The utility group has a rather low investment in liquid assets relative to its asset level. The reasons were given in our discussion of the transactions motive for holding cash.

The liquid asset investment for "all industries" appears high in comparison to that of the other specific groups examined in Table 7-1. This is because the finance group is *not* listed individually in the table. The finance sector includes banks, insurance carriers, real estate companies, securities firms, and investment companies. All of these classes of firms have very high liquid asset holdings because of the very nature of their business.

Table 7-2 LIQUID ASSET POSITIONS OF SELECTED FIRMS (IN PERCENT) FOR 1975

RATIOS	ALLIS-CHALMERS	IBM	MOBIL OIL	KIRSCH	OHIO-SEALY
Cash to total assets	3.3	1.2	1.5	1.8	3.0
Cash to sales	2.2	1.3	1.0	1.4	2.1
Marketable securities to total assets	2.5	29.5	6.1	0.5	8.4
Marketable securities to sales	1.7	31.8	4.1	0.4	5.7
Total liquid assets to total assets	5.8	30.7	7.5	2.4	11.4
Total liquid assets to sales	3.9	33.0	5.1	1.8	7.8

SOURCE: *Annual Reports, 1975,* for the respective companies.

They deal primarily in financial assets, such as securities, as opposed to real assets, such as productive equipment.

Table 7-2 displays the investments in liquidity by some individual companies. All of these firms would be part of the group called "total manufacturing" in Table 7-1. A wide variety of liquidity postures is observed, reflecting disparate cash management strategies.

The very heavy investment by IBM in marketable securities stands out. The cash to total assets percentage of 1.2 for the IBM is less than that of any of the other firms listed in Table 7-2. Marketable securities for IBM, however, is 29.5 percent of assets and 31.8 percent of sales. In early 1977 the management of IBM moved dramatically to reduce the firm's heavy investment in liquidity. A tender offer was announced for 4 million of its own shares.

Both the Kirsch Company and the Ohio-Sealy Mattress Manufacturing Company operate in the home furnishings industry. However, their cash management policies were notably unalike at the end of 1975. Ohio-Sealy evidenced a much higher investment in short-term securities. It is interesting to point out, though, that by the end of Kirsch's 1976 fiscal year its liquid asset position changed materially. Cash and marketable securities as a percent of total assets rose to 10.1 percent from the previous level of 2.4 percent. This was attributable to an increase in short-term investments to $6.5 million from the 1975 level of only $.4 million.[2]

This abrupt change in the liquidity position of the Kirsch Company makes it obvious that as long as any firm operates, the movement of cash into and through the enterprise is continual. Assets are acquired, wasted, and sold every day. This dictates that we view the management of cash and near cash as a dynamic process. The flow of cash as depicted in Figure 7-1 never ceases. The cash inflows and outflows affecting the size of the firm's cash reservoir occur simultaneously. This ensures that the overall problem of cash and marketable securities management will be complex. In order to cut through this complexity it is imperative that the firm's cash management system be designed to operate within clearly defined objectives.

CASH MANAGEMENT OBJECTIVES AND DECISIONS

The Big Tradeoff

A companywide cash management program must be concerned with minimizing the firm's risk of insolvency. In this and the next chapter the term **insolvency** is used to describe the situation where the firm is unable to meet its maturing liabilities on time. In such a case the company is **technically insolvent** in that it lacks the necessary liquidity to make prompt payment on its current debt obligations. This problem could be met quite easily by carrying large cash balances to pay the bills that come due. Production, after all, would soon come to a halt should payments for raw material purchases be continually late or omitted entirely. The firm's suppliers would just cut off further shipments. In fact, the fear of irritating a key supplier by being past due on the payment of a trade payable does cause some financial managers to invest in too much liquidity.

[2]*Kirsch Company Annual Report, 1976* (Sturgis, Mich.: Kirsch Company, 1976), p. 12.

The management of the company's cash position, though, is one of those major problem areas where you are criticized if you don't, and criticized if you do. True, the production process will eventually be halted should too little cash be available to pay bills. If excessive cash balances are carried, however, the value of the enterprise in the financial marketplace will be suppressed because of the large cost of income forgone. The explicit return earned on idle cash balances is zero.

The financial manager must strike an acceptable balance between holding too much cash and too little cash. This is the focal point of the big tradeoff. A large cash investment minimizes the chances of insolvency, but penalizes company profitability. A small cash investment frees excess balances for investment in both marketable securities and longer-lived assets; this enhances company profitability and thereby the value of the firm's common shares, but increases the chances of running out of cash. This risk-versus-return tradeoff is summarized in Figure 7-2.

The risk-return tradeoff can be reduced to two prime objectives for the firm's cash management system:

The Objectives

1. Enough cash must be on hand to dispense effectively with the disbursal needs that arise in the course of doing business.
2. The firm's investment in idle cash balances must be reduced to a minimum.

Evaluation of these operational objectives, and a conscious attempt on

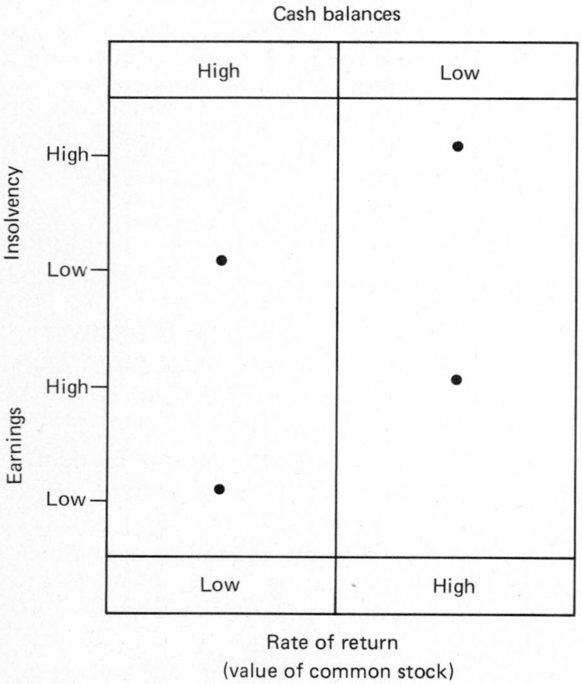

FIGURE 7-2   The Big Tradeoff

the part of management to meet them, gives rise to the need for some typical cash management decisions.

Two conditions would allow the firm to operate for extended periods with cash balances near or at a level of zero: (1) a completely accurate forecast of net cash flows over the planning horizon, and (2) perfect synchronization of cash receipts and disbursements.

Cash flow forecasting is the initial step in any effective cash management program. This is usually accomplished by the finance function's evaluation of data supplied by the marketing and production functions in the company. The device used to forecast the cash flows over the planning period is the cash budget. Cash budgeting procedures were explained in Chapter 4, so there is no need to review them here. It is emphasized, though, that the net cash flows pinpointed in the formal cash budget are mere estimates, subject to considerable variation. Thus, a totally accurate cash flow projection is only an ideal, not a reality.

Our discussion of the cash flow process depicted in Figure 7-1 showed that cash inflows and outflows are not synchronized. Some inflows and outflows are irregular; others are more continual. Some finished goods are sold directly for cash, but more likely the sales will be on account. The receivables, then, will have to be collected before a cash inflow is realized. Raw materials have to be purchased, but several suppliers are probably used, and each may have its own payment date. Further, no law of doing business fixes receivable collections to coincide with raw material payments dates. So the second criterion that would permit operation of the firm with extremely low cash balances is not met in actual practice either.

Given that the firm will, as a matter of necessity, invest in some cash balances, certain types of decisions related to the size of those balances dominate the cash management process. These include formulation of answers to the following questions:

1. What can be done to speed up cash collections and slow down or better control cash outflows?
2. How should our investment in liquid assets be split between actual cash holdings and marketable securities?
3. What should be the composition of our marketable securities portfolio?

The remainder of this chapter dwells on the first of these three questions. The others are explored in the next chapter.

The efficiency of the firm's cash management program can be enhanced by knowledge and use of various procedures aimed at (1) accelerating cash receipts and (2) improving the methods used to disburse cash. We will see that greater opportunity for corporate improvement lies with the cash receipts side of the funds flow process, but it would be unwise to ignore opportunities for favorably affecting cash disbursement practices.

COLLECTION AND DISBURSEMENT PROCEDURES

The reduction of **float** lies at the center of the many approaches employed to speed up cash receipts. Float (or total float) has four elements as follows:

1. **Mail float** is caused by the time lapse from the moment a customer mails his remittance check until the firm begins to process it.
2. **Processing float** is caused by the time required for the firm to process remittance checks before they can be deposited in the bank.
3. **Transit float** is caused by the time necessary for a deposited check to clear through the commercial banking system and become usable funds to the company. Credit is deferred for a maximum of two business days on checks that are cleared through the Federal Reserve System.
4. **Disbursing float** derives from the fact that funds are available in the company's bank account until its payment check has cleared through the banking system. Typically, funds available in the firm's banks *exceed* the balances indicated on its own books (ledgers).

We will use the term "float" to refer to the total of its four elements just described. Float reduction can yield considerable benefits in terms both of usable funds that are released for company use and of returns produced on such freed-up balances. As an example, for the year 1975 IBM reported total revenues of $14.4 billion.[4] The amount of usable funds that would be released if IBM could achieve a one-day reduction in float can be approximated by dividing annual revenues (sales) by the number of days in a year.[5] In this case one day's freed-up balances would be

$$\frac{\text{annual revenues}}{\text{days in year}} = \frac{\$14,400,000,000}{365} = \$39,452,055$$

If these released funds, which represent one day's sales, of approximately $39.5 million could be invested to return 8 percent a year, then the annual value of the one-day float reduction would be

$$(\text{sales per day}) \times (\text{assumed yield}) = \$39,452,055 \times .08 = \$3,156,164$$

It is clear that effective cash management procedures can yield impressive opportunities for profit improvement. Let us look now at specific techniques for reducing float.

THE LOCK-BOX ARRANGEMENT

The lock-box system is the most widely used commercial banking service for expediting cash gathering. Banks have offered this service since 1946. Such a system speeds up the conversion of receipts into usable funds

---

[3]The discussions on cash receipt and disbursement procedures draw heavily on materials that were generously provided by the managements of The Chase Manhattan Bank, Continental Bank, and The First National Bank of Chicago.

[4]*International Business Machines Corporation Annual Report,* 1975 (Armonk, N.Y.: IBM, 1975), p. 19.

[5]Frederick W. Searby, "Use Your Hidden Cash Resources," *Harvard Business Review,* 46 (March–April 1968), 71–80.

by reducing both mail float and processing float. For large corporations that receive checks from all parts of the country float reductions of two to four days are not unusual.

The lock-box arrangement is based upon a simple procedure. The firm's customers are instructed to mail their remittance checks not to company headquarters or regional offices but to a numbered post office box. The bank that is providing the lock-box service is authorized to open the box, collect the mail, process the checks, and then deposit the checks directly into the company's account.

Commercial banks have gone to great lengths in refining their lock-box procedures in an attempt to gain an edge over their competitors. For example, major banks have their own zip code to accelerate postal handling. Even helicopters are sometimes used to speed documents from the post office to the bank or from the bank to a local clearinghouse.

Typically a large bank will collect payments from the lock box at one- to two-hour intervals, all 365 days of the year. During peak business hours the bank may pick up mail every 30 minutes.

Once the mail is received at the bank, the checks will be examined, totaled, photocopied, and microfilmed. A deposit form is then prepared by the bank and each batch of processed checks is forwarded to the collection department for clearance. Funds deposited in this manner are usually available for company use in one business day or less.

The bank can notify the firm via some type of telecommunications system the same day deposits are made as to their amount. At the conclusion of each day all check photocopies, invoices, deposit slips, and any other documents included with the remittances are mailed to the firm.

Note that the firm that receives checks from all over the country will have to utilize several lock boxes to gain full advantage of a reduction in mail float. The firm's major bank should be able to offer as a service a detailed lock-box study, analyzing the company's receipt patterns to determine the proper number and location of lock-box receiving points.

In summary, the benefits of a lock-box arrangement are:

1. Increased working cash. The time required for converting receivables into available funds is reduced. This frees up cash for use elsewhere in the enterprise.
2. Elimination of clerical functions. The bank takes over the tasks of receiving, endorsing, totaling, and depositing checks. With less handling of receipts by employees better audit control is achieved and the chance of documents' becoming lost is reduced.
3. Early knowledge of dishonored checks. Should a customer's check be uncollectible because of lack of funds, it is returned, usually by special handling, to the firm.

These benefits are not free. Usually the bank levies a charge for each check processed through the system. The benefits derived from the acceleration of receipts must exceed the incremental costs of the lock-box system or the firm would be better off without it. Companies that find the average size of their remittances to be quite small, for instance, might avoid a lock-box plan. One major Chicago bank has pointed out for companies with less than $500,000 in average monthly sales or with customer remittance checks averaging less than $1000 the lock-box approach would probably not yield a great enough benefit to offset its costs. Later in this chapter a straightforward method for assessing the desirability of a specific cash management service, such as the lock-box arrangement, will be illustrated.

PREAUTHORIZED CHECKS (PAC'S)

Whereas the lock-box arrangement can often reduce total float by two to four days, for some firms the use of PAC's can be an even more effective way of converting receipts into working cash. A PAC resembles the ordinary check, but it does not contain or require the signature of the person on whose account it is being drawn. A PAC is created only with the individual's legal authorization.

The PAC system is advantageous when the firm regularly receives a large volume of payments of a fixed amount from the same customers. This type of cash management service has proved useful to insurance companies, savings and loan associations, consumer credit firms, leasing enterprises, and charitable and religious organizations.

The operation of a PAC system is illustrated in Figure 7-3. It involves the following sequence of events:

1. The firm's customers authorize it to draw checks on their respective demand deposit accounts.
2. Idemnification agreements are signed by the customers and forwarded to the banks where they maintain their demand deposit accounts. These agreements authorize the banks to honor the PAC's when they are presented for payment through the commercial bank clearing system.
3. The firm prepares a magnetic tape that contains all appropriate information about the regular payments.
4. At each processing cycle (monthly, weekly, semimonthly) the corporation retains a hard copy listing of all tape data for control purposes. Usually the checks that are about to be printed will be deposited in the firm's demand deposit account, so a deposit ticket will also be forwarded to the bank.
5. Upon receipt of the tape the bank will produce the PAC's, deposit them to the firm's account, forward them for clearing through the commercial banking system, and return a control report to the firm.

For firms that can take advantage of a PAC system the benefits include:

1. Highly predictable cash flows.
2. Reduced expenses. Billing and postage costs are eliminated, and the clerical processing of customer payments is significantly reduced.
3. Customer preference. Many customers prefer not to be bothered with a regular billing. With a PAC system the check is actually written for the customer and the payment made even if he is on vacation or otherwise out of town.
4. Increased working cash. Mail float and processing float can be dramatically reduced in comparison to other payment processing systems.

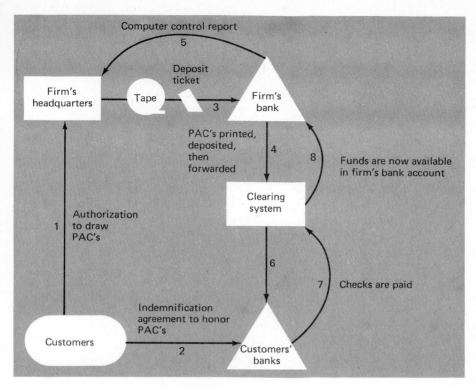

FIGURE 7-3 *Preauthorized Check System (PAC)*

DEPOSITORY TRANSFER CHECKS

Both depository transfer checks and wire transfers are used in conjunction with what is known as **concentration banking.** A concentration bank is one where the firm maintains a major disbursing account.

In an effort to accelerate collections many companies have established multiple collection centers. We have already seen that regional lock-box networks are one type of approach to strategically located collection points. Even without lock boxes firms may have numerous sales outlets throughout the country and collect cash over the counter. This requires many local bank accounts to handle daily deposits. Rather than have funds sitting in these multiple bank accounts in different geographic regions of the country, most firms will regularly transfer the surplus balances to one or more concentration banks. Centralizing the firm's pool of cash provides the following benefits:

1. Lower levels of excess cash. Desired cash balance target levels are set for each regional bank. These target levels consider both compensating balance requirements and necessary working levels of cash. Cash in excess of the target levels can be regularly transferred to concentration banks for deployment by the firm's top-level management.
2. Better control. With more cash held in fewer accounts, stricter control over

the firm's available cash is achieved. Quite simply, there are fewer problems of which to keep track. The concentration banks can prepare sophisticated reports that detail corporatewide movements of funds into and out of the central cash pool.

3. **More efficient investments in near-cash assets.** The coupling of information from the firm's cash forecast with data on available funds supplied by the concentration banks allows the firm to quickly transfer cash to the marketable securities portfolio.

Depository transfer checks provide a means for moving funds from local bank accounts to concentration accounts. The depository transfer check itself is an unsigned, nonnegotiable instrument. It is payable only to the bank of deposit (the concentration bank in our discussion) for credit to the firm's specific account. An authorization form is filed by the firm with each bank from which it might withdraw funds. This form instructs the bank to pay the depository transfer checks without any signature. The movement of cash through the use of depository transfer checks can operate with either a conventional mail system or an automated system.

When the mail system is used, a company employee deposits the day's receipts in a local bank and fills out a preprinted depository transfer check for the exact amount of the deposit. The company then mails the depository transfer check to the firm's concentration bank. While this document is traveling in the mails, the checks just deposited at the local bank are being cleared. As soon as the concentration bank receives the depository transfer check, the firm's account is credited for the designated amount. The funds credited to the concentration account are not available for the firm's use, of course, until the document has been cleared with the local depository bank for payment.

If the firm's depository banks are geographically dispersed such that the mail will take several days in reaching the concentration bank, then *no* float reduction might be achieved through this system. In an attempt to reduce the mail float associated with conventional depository transfer check systems some banks have initiated a type of special mail handling of these instruments. Continental Bank (Chicago), for example, cooperates with the U.S. Postal Service at O'Hare International Airport. Extra large, specially marked envelopes are used by firms to air mail their transfer checks to Chicago. These envelopes are intercepted at the airport, sorted into special Continental Bank pouches, and at frequent intervals are taken to the bank by special messenger for ultimate deposit of the contents. This procedure can cut as much as one full day off regular mail delivery schedules.

A recent innovation in speeding cash into concentration accounts is the **automated depository transfer check system.** In this system the mail float involved in moving the transfer document from the local bank to the concentration bank is *completely eliminated.* Here is how it works.

The local company employee makes the daily deposit as usual. He does *not,* however, manually fill out the preprinted depository transfer check; instead, he telephones the deposit information to a regional data collection center. Usually the center is operated for a fee by a firm, such as National Data Corporation. Various data collection centers will accumulate information throughout the day on the firm's regional deposits. Then, at specified cutoff times the deposit information from all local offices is transmitted to the concentration bank.

At this point the concentration bank prepares the depository transfer check and credits it to the company's account. A sample depository transfer check prepared at a concentration bank is shown in Figure 7-4. The transfer checks are placed into the commercial bank check-clearing process and presented to the firm's local bank for payment. When paid by the local bank, the funds become available in the concentration account for company use. Major banks claim that funds transferred by use of the automated depository transfer check system can become available for company use in one business day or less. This system is depicted in Figure 7-5.

WIRE TRANSFERS

The fastest way to move cash between banks is by use of **wire transfers,** which eliminate transit float. Funds moved in this manner, then, immediately become usable funds or "good funds" to the firm at the receiving bank. The following two major communication facilities are used to accommodate wire transfers:

1. Bank Wire. This is a private wire service used and supported by approxi-

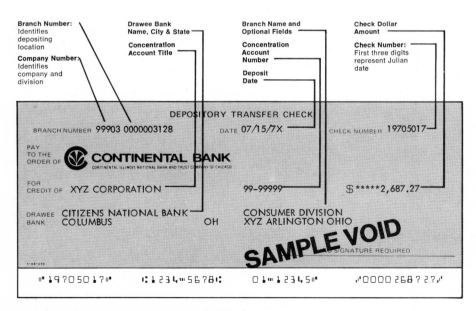

FIGURE 7-4 *Sample Depository Transfer Check*

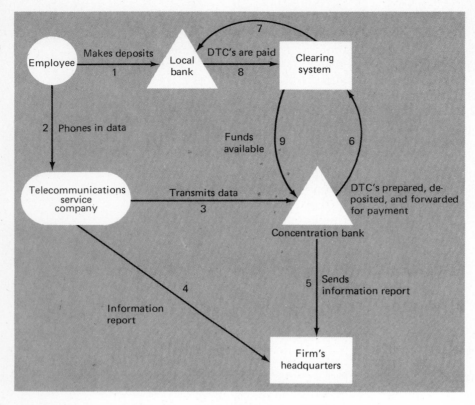

FIGURE 7-5 *Automated Depository Transfer Check System (DTC)*

mately 250 banks in the United States for transferring funds, exchanging credit information, or effecting securities transactions.

2. Federal Reserve Wire System. The Fed Wire is directly accessible to commercial banks that are members of the Federal Reserve System. A commercial bank that is not on the Bank Wire or is not a member of the Federal Reserve System can use the wire transfer concept through its correspondent bank.

Wire transfers are often initiated on a standing-order basis. By means of a written authorization from company headquarters a local depository bank might be instructed to regularly transfer funds to the firm's concentration bank. For example, available funds in excess of $100,000 might be transferred every Tuesday and Thursday to the concentration bank.

As might be expected, wire transfers are a relatively expensive method of marshalling funds through a firm's money management system. A single wire transfer costs about $4. This is about fifteen times as costly as a conventional depository transfer check. Generally, the movement of small amounts does not justify the use of wire transfers.

Significant techniques and systems for improving the firm's management of cash disbursements include (1) zero balance accounts, (2) payable-through drafts, and (3) remote disbursing. The first two offer markedly better control over companywide payments, and as a secondary benefit they *may* increase disbursement float. The last technique, remote disbursing, aims solely to increase disbursement float.

ZERO BALANCE ACCOUNTS

Large corporations that operate multiple branches, divisions, or subsidiaries often maintain numerous bank accounts (in different banks) for the purpose of making timely operating disbursements. It does make good business sense for payments for purchased parts that go into, say, an automobile transmission to be made by the Transmission and Chassis Division of the auto manufacturer rather than its central office. The Transmission and Chassis Division originates such purchase orders, receives and inspects the shipment when it arrives at the plant, authorizes payment, and writes the appropriate check. To have the central office involved in these matters would be a total waste of company time.

What tends to happen, however, is that with several divisions utilizing their own disbursal accounts, excess cash balances build up in outlying banks and rob the firm of earning assets. Zero balance accounts are used to alleviate this problem. They also provide other benefits, which will be mentioned shortly.

Zero balance accounts permit centralized control (at the headquarters level) over cash outflows while maintaining divisional disbursing authority. Under this system the firm's authorized employees, representing their various divisions, continue to write checks on their individual accounts. Note that the numerous individual disbursing accounts are now *all* located in the same concentration bank. Actually, these separate accounts contain no funds at all, thus their appropriate label, "zero balance." These accounts have all of the characteristics of regular demand deposit accounts including separate titles, numbers, and statements.

A zero balance account system works as follows. The firm's authorized agents write their payment checks as usual against their specific accounts. These checks clear through the banking system in the usual way. On a daily basis checks will be presented to the firm's concentration bank (the drawee bank) for payment. As the checks are paid by the bank, negative (debit) balances will build in the proper disbursing accounts. At the end of each day the negative balances will be restored to a zero level by means of credits to the zero balance accounts; a corresponding reduction in funds is made against the firm's concentration (master) demand deposit account. Each morning a report is electronically forwarded to corporate headquarters reflecting the balance in the master account as well as the previous day's activity in each zero balance account. Reflecting on this report, the financial officer in charge of near-cash investments is ready to initiate appropriate transactions.

Managing the cash outflow through use of a zero balance account system offers the following benefits to the firm with many operating units:

1. Centralized control over disbursements is achieved, even though payment authority continues to rest with operating units.
2. Management time spent on superficial cash management activities is reduced. Exercises such as observing the balances held in numerous bank accounts, transferring funds to those accounts short of cash, and reconciling the accounts demand less attention.
3. Excess balances held in outlying accounts can be reduced.
4. The costs of cash management can be reduced, as wire transfers to build up funds in outlying disbursement accounts are eliminated.
5. Funds may be made available for company use through an increase in disbursement float. When local bank accounts are used to pay nearby suppliers, the checks clear rapidly. The same checks, if drawn on a zero balance account located in a more distant concentration bank, will take more time to clear against the disbursing firm's account.

A schematic presentation of a zero balance account disbursing system is shown in Figure 7-6. The firm is assumed to have three operating divisions—each with its own zero balance account (ZBA).

PAYABLE-THROUGH DRAFTS

Payable-through drafts are a legal instrument that have the physical appearance of ordinary checks (see Figure 7-7), but are *not* drawn on a bank. Instead, payable-through drafts are drawn on and paid by the issuing firm. Like checks, the drafts are cleared through the banking system and are presented to the issuing firm's bank. The bank serves as a collection point and passes the drafts on to the firm. The corporate issuer usually has to return by the following business day all drafts it does not wish to cover (pay). Those documents not returned to the bank are automatically paid. The firm inspects the drafts for validity by checking signatures, amounts, and dates. Stop payment orders can be initiated by the company on any drafts considered inappropriate.

The main purpose of using a payable-through draft system is *to provide for effective control over field payments*. Central office control over payments begun by regional units is provided as the drafts are reviewed in advance of final payment. Payable-through drafts, for example, are used extensively in the insurance industry. The claims agent does not typically have check-signing authority against a corporate disbursement account. He can issue a draft, however, for quick settlement of a claim.

In the not-so-distant past a firm could increase its disbursing float by use of payable-through drafts. In most cases this is no longer true. The Federal Reserve System requires transfer of available or "good" funds upon presentation of drafts to the payable-through bank. The payable-

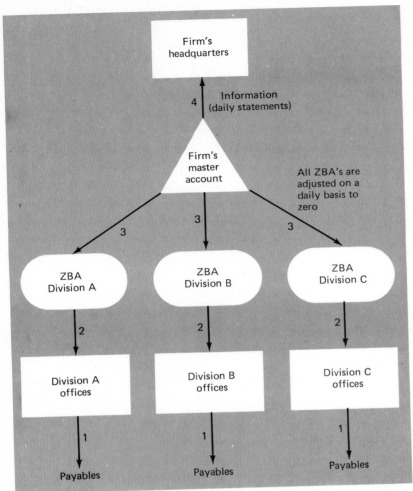

FIGURE 7-6 Zero Balance Account Cash Disbursement System (ZBA)

Northwest Marketing
2815 NORTH DRYDEN PLACE
ARLINGTON HEIGHTS, ILLINOIS 60004

2-3
710

26860

BRANCH OFFICE AT
Duluth

November 26 19 XX

PAY TO THE
ORDER OF   R. A. Magee $ 164.00

One hundred sixty-four and 00/100 ———————— DOLLARS

FOR   Commission Pd. # 4619
                        4620

PAYABLE THROUGH
CONTINENTAL BANK
CONTINENTAL ILLINOIS NATIONAL BANK AND TRUST COMPANY OF CHICAGO

NORTHWEST MARKETING

BY   K. A. Vasek

⑆0710⑈0003⑆   12⑈99077⑈   ⑇00000016400⑈

FIGURE 7-7 Sample Payable-Through Draft

through bank will cover drafts, but will be reluctant to absorb the float that would occur until the issuing firm authorized payment the next business day. Therefore, the drafts that are presented for payment will usually be charged *in total* against the corporate master demand deposit account. This is for purposes of measuring usable funds available to the firm on that day. Legal payment of the *individual drafts* will still take place after their review and approval by the firm. Figure 7-8 illustrates a payable-through draft system.

REMOTE DISBURSING

A few banks will provide the corporate customer with a cash management service specifically designed to extend disbursing float. The firm's concentration bank may have a correspondent relationship with a smaller bank located in a distant city. In that remote city the Federal Reserve System is unable to maintain frequent clearings of checks drawn on local banks. For example, a firm that is located in Dallas and maintains its master account there may open an account with a bank situated in, say, Amarillo, Texas. The firm will write the bulk of its payment checks against the account in the Amarillo bank. The checks will probably take at least one business day longer to clear, so the firm can "play the float" to its advantage.

We emphasize that a firm must use this technique of remote disbursing with extreme care. If a key supplier of raw materials located in Dallas has to wait the extra day for his funds drawn on the Amarillo account, the possibility of incurring his ill-will might outweigh the apparent gain from

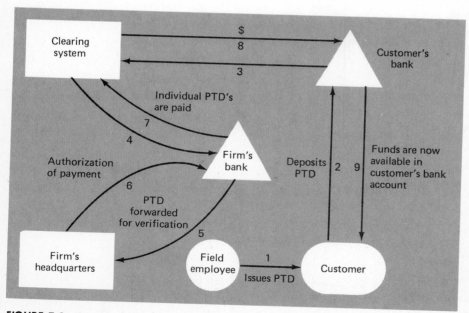

FIGURE 7-8 *Payable-Through Draft Cash Disbursement System (PTD)*

an increase in the disbursing float. The impact upon the firm's reputation of using remote disbursing should be explicitly evaluated.

A form of breakeven analysis can help the financial officer decide whether a particular collection or disbursement service will provide an economic benefit to the firm. The evaluation process involves use of a very basic relationship in microeconomics:

$$\text{added costs} = \text{added benefits} \qquad (7\text{-}1)$$

If equation (7-1) holds exactly, then the firm is no better or worse off for having adopted the given service. We will illustrate this procedure in terms of the desirability of installing an additional lock box. Equation (7-1) can be restated on a per-unit basis as follows:

$$P = (D)(S)(i) \qquad (7\text{-}2)$$

where P = increase in per-check processing cost, if the new system is adopted;

D = days saved in the collection process (float reduction);

S = average check size in dollars;

i = the daily, before-tax opportunity cost (rate of return) of carrying cash.

Assume now that check processing costs, P, will rise by $.18 a check if the lock box is used. The firm has determined that the average check size, S, that will be mailed to the lock-box location will be $900. If funds are freed by use of the lock box, they will be invested in marketable securities to yield an *annual* before-tax return of 6 percent. It is possible with these data to determine the reduction in check collection time, D, that is required to justify use of the lock box. That level of D is found to be

$$\$.18 = (D)(\$900) \left(\frac{.06}{365} \right)$$

$$1.217 \text{ days} = D$$

Thus, the lock box is economically justified if the firm can speed up its collections by *more* than 1.217 days. This same style of analysis can be adapted to analyze the other tools of cash management just discussed.

SUMMARY

Firms hold cash in order to satisfy transactions, precautionary, and speculative needs for liquidity. Because cash balances provide no direct return, the precautionary motive for investing in cash is met in part by holdings of marketable securities. In this chapter we initiated our two-chapter study of the effective management of cash and marketable securities.

The financial manager must (1) make sure that enough cash is on hand to meet the payment needs that arise in the course of doing business and (2) attempt to reduce the firm's idle cash balances to a minimum. Meeting such objectives requires that the financial officer (1) accelerate cash receipts and delay or improve control of cash disbursements, (2) arrive at a proper split between cash and marketable securities holdings, and (3) select the instruments that comprise the marketable securities portfolio. The first of these three decision areas was the focus of the present chapter; the latter two are studied in Chapter 8.

By use of (1) lock-box arrangements, (2) preauthorized checks, (3) special forms of depository transfer checks, and (4) wire transfers the firm can achieve considerable benefits in terms of float reduction. Lock-box systems and preauthorized checks serve to reduce mail and processing float. Depository transfer checks and wire transfers move funds between banks; they are often used in conjunction with concentration banking. Both the lock-box and preauthorized check systems can be employed as part of the firm's concentration banking setup to speed receipts to regional collection centers.

The firm can delay and favorably affect the control of its cash disbursements through the use of (1) zero balance accounts, (2) payable-through drafts, and (3) remote disbursing. Zero balance accounts allow the company to maintain central-office control over payments while permitting the disbursing authority to rest with the firm's several divisions. Because key disbursing accounts are located in one major concentration bank, rather than in multiple banks across the country, excess cash balances that tend to build up in the outlying banks are avoided. Payable-through drafts are legal instruments that look like checks but are drawn on and paid by the issuing firm rather than its bank. The bank serves as a collection point for the drafts. The main reason for use of such a system is to provide for effective central-office control over field-authorized payments; it is not used as a major vehicle for extending disbursing float. Remote disbursing, however, is used to increase disbursing float. Remote disbursing refers to the process of writing payment checks on banks located in cities distant from the one where the check is originated.

Before any of these collection and disbursement procedures is initiated by the firm, a careful analysis should be undertaken to see if the expected benefits outweigh the expected costs.

7-1. What is meant by the cash flow process?
7-2. Identify the principal (classical) motives for holding cash and near-cash assets. Explain the purpose of each motive.
7-3. What is concentration banking and how may it be of value to the firm?
7-4. Distinguish between depository transfer checks and automated depository transfer ctecks (ADTC).

7-5. In general what type of firm would benefit from the use of a preauthorized check system? What specific types of companies have successfully used this device to accelerate cash receipts?

7-6. What are the two major objectives of the firm's cash management system?

7-7. What three decisions dominate the cash management process?

7-8. Within the context of cash management, what are the key elements of (total) float? Briefly define each element.

STUDY PROBLEMS

7-1. Mustang Ski-Wear, Inc., is investigating the possibility of adopting a lock-box system as a cash receipts acceleration device. In a typical year this firm receives remittances totaling $12 million by check. The firm will record and process 6000 checks over this same time period. The Colorado Springs Second National Bank has informed the management of Mustang that it will expedite checks and associated documents through the lock-box system for a unit cost of $.20 per check. Mustang's financial manager has projected that cash freed by adoption of the system can be invested in a portfolio of near-cash assets that will yield an annual before-tax return of 7 percent. Mustang financial analysts use a 365-day year in their procedures.

(a) What reduction in check collection time is necessary for Mustang to be neither better nor worse off for having adopted the proposed system?

(b) How would your solution to part (a) above be affected if Mustang could invest the freed balances only at an expected annual return of 4.5 percent?

(c) What is the logical explanation for the difference in your answers to parts (a) and (b) above?

7-2. Next year P. F. Anderson Motors expects its gross revenues from sales to be $80 million. The firm's treasurer has projected that its marketable securities portfolio will earn 6.50 percent over the coming budget year. What is the value of one day's float reduction to the company? Anderson Motors uses a 365-day year in all of its financial analysis procedures.

7-3. Peggy Pierce Designs, Inc., is a vertically integrated, national manufacturer and retailer of women's clothing. Currently, the firm has no coordinated cash management system. A proposal, however, from the First Pennsylvania Bank aimed at speeding up cash collections is being examined by several of Pierce's corporate executives.

The firm currently uses a centralized billing procedure, which requires that all checks be mailed to the Philadelphia head office for processing and eventual deposit. Under this arrangement all of the customers' remittance checks take an average of five business days to reach the head office. Once in Philadelphia another two days are required to process the checks for ultimate deposit at the First Pennsylvania Bank.

The firm's daily remittances average $1 million. The average check size is $2000. Pierce Designs currently earns 6 percent annually on its marketable securities portfolio.

The cash acceleration plan proposed by officers of First Pennsylvania involves both a lock-box system and concentration banking. First Pennsylvania would be the firm's only concentration bank. Lock boxes would be established in (1) San Francisco, (2) Dallas, (3) Chicago, and (4) Philadelphia. This would reduce funds tied up by mail float to three days, and processing float will be totally eliminated. Funds would then be transferred twice each business day by means of automated depository transfer checks from local banks in San Francisco, Dallas, and Chicago to the First Pennsylvania Bank. Each depository transfer check (ADTC) costs $15. These transfers will occur all 270 business days of the year. Each check processed through the lock-box system will cost $.18.

(a) What amount of cash balances will be freed if Pierce Designs, Inc., adopts the system suggested by First Pennsylvania?

(b) What is the opportunity cost of maintaining the current banking setup?

(c) What is the projected annual cost of operating the proposed system?

(d) Should Pierce adopt the new system? Compute the net annual gain or loss associated with adopting the system.

7-4. The Alex Daniel Shoe Manufacturing Company currently pays its employees on a weekly basis. The weekly wage bill is $500,000. This means on the average the firm has accrued wages payable of ($500,000 + $0)/2 = $250,000.

Alex Daniel, Jr., works as the firm's senior financial analyst and reports directly to his father, who owns all of the firm's common stock. Alex Daniel, Jr., wants to move to a monthly wage payment system. Employees would be paid at the end of every fourth week. The younger Daniel is fully aware that the labor union representing the company's workers will not permit the monthly payment system to take effect unless the workers are given some type of fringe benefit compensation.

A plan has been worked out whereby the firm will make a contribution to the cost of life insurance coverage for each employee. This will cost the firm $35,000 annually. Alex Daniel, Jr., expects the firm to earn 7 percent annually on its marketable securities portfolio.

(a) Based on the projected information, should Daniel Shoe Manufacturing move to the monthly wage payment system?

(b) What annual rate of return on the marketable securities portfolio would enable the firm to just break even on this proposal?

7-5. The Cowboy Bottling Company will generate $12 million in credit sales next year. Collections of these credit sales will occur evenly over this period. The firm's employees work 270 days a year. Currently, the firm's processing system ties up four days' worth of remittance checks. A recent report from a financial consultant indicated procedures that will enable Cowboy Bottling to reduce processing float by two full days. If Cowboy invests the released funds to earn 6 percent, what will be the annual savings?

7-6. Montgomery Woodcraft is a large distributor of woodworking tools and accessories to hardware stores, lumber yards, and tradesmen. All of its sales are on a credit basis, net 30 days. Sales are evenly distributed over its 12 sales regions throughout the United States. There is no problem with delinquent accounts. The firm is attempting to improve its cash management procedures. Montgomery recently determined that it took an average of 3.7 days for customers' payments to reach their office from the time they were mailed, and another day for processing before payments could be deposited. Monthly sales average $5,200,000, and investment opportunities can be found to return 7 percent per year. What is the opportunity cost to the firm of the funds tied up in mailing and processing? In your calculations use a 365-day year.

7-7. To mitigate the float problem discussed above, Montgomery Woodcraft is considering the use of a lock-box system in each of its regions. By so doing, it can reduce the mail float by 1.7 days and receive the other benefits of a lock-box system. It also estimates that transit float could be reduced to half its present duration, which is at the maximum Federal Reserve System clearance time. Use of the lock-box arrangement in each of its regions will cost $134 per month. Sould Montgomery Woodcraft adopt the system? What would the net cost or savings be?

7-8. Bradford Construction Supply Company is suffering from a prolonged decline in new construction in its sales area. In an attempt to improve its cash position, the firm is considering changes in its accounts payable policy. After careful study it has determined that the only alternative available is to slow disbursements. Purchases for the coming year are expected to be $37.5 million. Sales will be $65 million, which represents about a 20 percent drop from the current year. Currently, Bradford discounts approximately 25 percent of its payments at 3 percent 10 days, net 30, and the balance of accounts are paid in 30 days. If Bradford adopts a policy of payment in 45 days or 60 days, how much can the firm gain if the annual opportunity cost of investment is 12 percent? What will be the result if this action causes Bradford Construction suppliers to increase their prices to the company by 0.5 percent to compensate for the 60-day extended term of payment? In your calculations use a 365-day year and ignore any compounding effects related to expected returns.

See the end of the next chapter. **SELECTED REFERENCES**

Cash and Marketable Securities Management – II

*I*n this chapter we continue our discussion of the management of the firm's cash position and design of its marketable securities portfolio. In Chapter 7 we dwelled upon the overall objectives of company cash management, described some actual liquid asset holdings of selected industries and firms, and overviewed a wide array of cash collection and disbursement procedures.

We now consider the problems of properly dividing the firm's liquid asset holdings between cash and near cash, and determining the ultimate mix of marketable securities in the near-cash portfolio.

Through use of the cash budgeting procedures outlined in Chapter 4, the financial manager can pinpoint time periods when funds will be in either short or excess supply. If a shortage of funds is expected, then alternative avenues of financing must be explored. On the other hand, the cash budget projections might indicate that large, positive net cash balances in excess of immediate transactions needs will be forthcoming. In this more pleasant situation the financial manager ought to decide on the proper split of the expected cash balances between actual cash holdings and marketable securities. To hold all of the expected cash balances as actual balances would needlessly penalize the firm's profitability.

LIQUID ASSETS: CASH VS. MARKETABLE SECURITIES

The ensuing discussion centers upon various methods by which the financial manager can develop useful cash balance level benchmarks.

A basic method for indicating the proper *average* amount of cash to have on hand involves use of the economic order quantity concept so familiar in discussions of inventory management (Chapter 9).[1] The objective of this analysis is to balance the lost income that the firm suffers from holding cash rather than marketable securities against the transactions costs involved in converting securities into cash. The rudiments of this decision model can be easily introduced by use of an illustration.

Suppose that the firm knows with certainty that it will need $250,000 in cash for transactions purposes over the next two months and that this much cash is currently available. This transactions demand for cash will be represented by the variable, T. Let us assume, for purposes of this illustration, that when the firm requires cash for its transactions needs it will sell marketable securities in any one of five lot sizes, ranging from $30,000 to $70,000. These cash conversion (order) sizes, C, are identified in line 1 of Table 8-1.

Line 2 shows the number of times marketable securities will be turned into cash over the next two months, if a particular order size is utilized. For example, should it be decided to liquidate securities in amounts of $40,000, then the number of cash conversions needed to meet transactions over the next two months is $250,000/$40,000 = 6.25. In general, the number of cash withdrawals from the near-cash portfolio can be represented as T/C.

Benchmark 1:
When Cash Need
Is Certain

[1] The roots of a quantitative treatment of the firm's cash balance as just another type of inventory are found in William J. Baumol, "The Transactions Demand For Cash: An Inventory Theoretic Approach," *Quarterly Journal of Economics*, 66 (November 1952), 545–56.

Table 8-1 DETERMINATION OF THE OPTIMAL CASH ORDER SIZE

1. Cash conversion size (the dollar amount of marketable securities that will be sold to replenish the cash balance)	$30,000	$40,000	$50,000	$60,000	$70,000
2. Number of cash orders per time period (the time period is two months in this example) ($250,000 ÷ line 1)	8.33	6.25	5.00	4.17	3.57
3. Average cash balance (line 1 ÷ 2)	$15,000	$20,000	$25,000	$30,000	$35,000
4. Interest income forgone (line 3 × .01)	$150.00	$200.00	$250.00	$300.00	$350.00
5. Cash conversion cost ($50 × line 2)	$416.50	$312.50	$250.00	$208.50	$178.50
6. Total cost of ordering and holding cash (line 4 + line 5)	$566.50	$512.50	$500.00	$508.50	$528.50

Next, we assume that the firm's cash payments are of constant amounts and are made continually over the two-month planning period. This implies that the firm's cash balance behaves in the sawtooth manner shown in Figure 8-1. The assertion of regularity and constancy of payments allows the firm's average cash balance over the planning period to be measured as $C/2$ (see Figure 8-1). When marketable securities are sold and cash flows into the demand deposit account, the cash balance is equal to C. As payments are made on a regular and constant basis, the cash balance is reduced to a level of zero. The average cash balance over the period is then

$$\frac{C + 0}{2} = \frac{C}{2}$$

The average cash balances corresponding to the different cash conversion sizes in our example are noted in line 3 of Table 8-1.

Line 4 measures the opportunity cost of earnings forgone based upon holding the average cash balance recorded on line 3. If the *annual* yield available on marketable securities is 6 percent, then over the *two-month period* we are analyzing, the forfeited interest rate is $.06/6 = .01$.[2] Multiplying each average cash balance, $C/2$, by the $.01$ interest rate, i, available over the two-month period produces the opportunity costs entered on line 4.

The very act of liquidating securities, unfortunately, is not costless. Transacting conversions of marketable securities into cash can involve any of the following activities, which require the time of company employees as well as direct payment by the firm for various services:

1. Assistant treasurer's time to order the trade.
2. Long-distance phone calls to effect the trade.
3. Secretarial time to type authorization letters, make copies of the letters, and forward the letters to the company treasurer.
4. Treasurer's time to read, approve, and sign the documents that authorize the trade.
5. General accountant's time to record and audit the transaction.
6. The value of fringe benefits incurred on the above times.
7. The brokerage fee on each transaction.

[2]If we were studying a *one-month* planning period, rather than the two-month period being discussed, the annual yield would have to be stated on a monthly basis or $.06/12 = .005$.

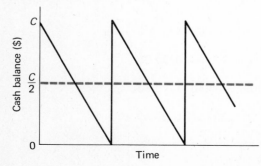

FIGURE 8-1 *Cash Balances According to the Inventory Model*

Suppose that the firm has properly studied the transaction costs, similar to those enumerated above, and finds they are of a fixed amount, *b*, per trade equal to $50. The transaction cost variable, *b*, is taken to be independent of the size of a particular securities order. Multiplying the transaction cost of $50 per trade by the number of cash orders that will take place during the planning period produces line 5. In general, the cash conversion cost (transactions cost) is equal to $b(T/C)$.

We are now down to the last line in Table 8-1. This is the sum total of the income lost by holding cash rather than marketable securities and the cash ordering costs. Line 6, then, is the total of lines 4 and 5. The inventory model seeks to *minimize* these *total costs* associated with holding cash balances. Table 8-1 tells us, if cash is ordered on five occasions in $50,000 sizes over the two-month period, the total costs of holding an average cash balance of $25,000 will be $500. This is less than the total costs associated with any other cash conversion size.

At the beginning of the two-month planning horizon, all of the $250,000 available for transactions purposes need not be held in the firm's demand deposit account. To minimize the total costs of holding cash, only $50,000 should immediately be retained to transact business. The remaining $200,000 should be invested in income-yielding securities and then turned into cash as the firm's disbursal needs dictate.

It is useful to put our discussion of the inventory model for cash management into a more general form. Summarizing the definitions developed in the illustration, we have

C = the amount per order of marketable securities to be converted into cash,
i = the interest rate per period available on investments in marketable securities,
b = the fixed cost per order of converting marketable securities into cash,
T = the total cash requirements over the planning period,
TC = the total costs associated with maintenance of a particular average cash balance.

As just pointed out, the total costs (TC) of having cash on hand can be expressed as

$$TC = i\left(\frac{C}{2}\right) + b\left(\frac{T}{C}\right) \qquad (8\text{-}1)$$

total interest income forgone	total ordering costs

If equation (8-1) is applied to the $50,000 cash conversion size column in Table 8-1, the total costs can be computed in a direct fashion as follows:

$$TC = .01 \left(\frac{\$50,000}{2}\right) + 50 \left(\frac{\$250,000}{\$50,000}\right)$$

$$= \$250 + \$250 = \$500$$

You can see that the $500 total cost is the same as was found deductively in Table 8-1.

The optimal cash conversion size, C^*, can be found by use of equation (8-2):

$$C^* = \sqrt{\frac{2bT}{i}} \qquad (8\text{-}2)$$

When the data in our example are applied to equation (8-2), the optimal cash order size is found to be

$$C^* = \sqrt{\frac{2(50)(250,000)}{.01}} = \$50,000$$

This solution to our example problem is graphically displayed in Figure 8-2. Notice that the optimal cash order size of $50,000 occurs at the minimum point of the total cost curve associated with keeping cash on hand.

INVENTORY MODEL IMPLICATIONS

The solution to equation (8-2) tells the financial manager that the optimal cash order size, C^*, varies directly with the square root of the order costs, bT, and inversely with the yield, i, available on marketable securities. Notice that as transactions requirements, T, increase, owing perhaps to an augmented sales demand, the optimal cash order size does *not* rise proportionately. This implies that economies of scale are possible in cash management. Each new project that the firm takes on, resulting in expanded revenues and transactions needs, does not require that cash balances rise by the same percentage as the transactions requirements.

How do these economies of scale come about? One way is by utilization of the banking methods we have reviewed (Chapter 7) that result in an acceleration of the firm's cash receipts. If transactions needs rise, but available cash does not rise proportionately, then cash turnover must increase to accomplish the higher transactions level. Efficient management of the firm's cash inflow, then, can produce economies of scale.

Further, the model indicates that as interest rates rise on near-cash investments, the optimal cash order size decreases, with the effect dampened by the square-root sign as equation (8-2) suggests. With higher yields to be earned on the marketable securities portfolio the financial manager will be more reluctant to make large withdrawals because of the interest income that will be lost.

Some final perspectives on the use of the economic order quantity model in cash management can be obtained by reviewing the assumptions

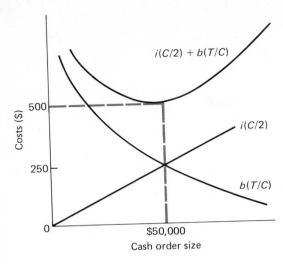

FIGURE 8-2 *Solution to the Inventory Model for Cash Management*

upon which it is derived. Among the more important of these assumptions are the following:

1. Cash payments over the planning period are (a) of a regular amount, (b) continuous, and (c) certain.
2. No unanticipated cash receipts will be received during the analysis period.
3. The interest rate to be earned on investments remains constant over the analysis period.
4. Transfers between cash and the securities portfolio may take place at any time at a cost that is fixed, regardless of the amount to be transferred.

Clearly, the strict assumptions of the inventory model will not be completely realized in actual business practice. For instance, the amount and timing of cash payments will not be known with certainty; nor are cash receipts likely to be as discontinuous or lumpy as is implied. If relaxation of the critical assumptions is not so prohibitive as to render the model useless, then a benchmark for possible managerial action is provided. The model's output is not intended to be a precise and inviolable rule. On the other hand, if the assumptions of the model cannot be reasonably approximated, the financial manager must look elsewhere for possible guides that indicate a proper split between cash and marketable securities.

It is entirely possible that the firm's cash balance pattern does *not* at all resemble that indicated in Figure 8-1. The assumptions of certain regularity and constancy of cash payments may be unduly restrictive when applied to some organizations.[3] Rather, the cash balance might behave more like the jagged line shown in Figure 8-3. In this figure it is assumed that the firm's cash balance changes in an irregular fashion from day to day. The changes are unpredictable; that is, they are *random*. Further, let us suppose the chances that a cash balance change will be either (1) positive or (2) negative are equal at .5 each.

Benchmark 2: When Cash Balances Fluctuate Randomly

[3]This discussion is based upon Merton H. Miller and Daniel Orr, "A Model of the Demand for Money by Firms," *Quarterly Journal of Economics*, 80 (August 1966), 413–35.

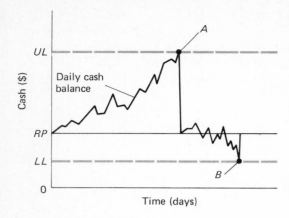

FIGURE 8-3 *Randomly Fluctuating Cash Balances*

As cash receipts exceed expenditures, the cash balance will move upward until it hits an upper control limit, *UL,* expressed in dollars. This occurs at point *A* in Figure 8-3. At such time, the financial officer will initiate an investment in marketable securities equal to *UL − RP* dollars, where *RP* is the cash return point.

If cash payments exceed receipts, the cash balance will move downward until it hits a lower control limit, *LL.* This situation is noted by point *B* in Figure 8-3. When this occurs, the financial officer will sell marketable securities equal to *RP − LL* dollars. This will restore the cash balance to the return point, *RP.*

To make this application of control theory to cash management operational, we must determine the upper control limit, *UL,* the lower control limit, *LL,* and the cash return point, *RP.* For the present case where a net cash increase is as likely to occur as a net cash decrease, use of the following variables will allow computation of the cash return point, *RP:*[4]

> b = the fixed cost per order of converting marketable securities into cash,
> i = the *daily* interest rate available on investments in marketable securities,
> σ^2 = the variance of daily changes in the firm's expected cash balances (this is a measure of volatility of cash flow changes over time).

The optimal cash return point, *RP,* can be calculated as follows:

$$RP = \sqrt[3]{\frac{3b\sigma^2}{4i}} \qquad (8\text{-}3)$$

The upper control limit, *UL,* can be computed quite simply:

$$UL = 3RP \qquad (8\text{-}4)$$

[4]Situations where the probabilities of cash increases and decreases are not equal are extremely difficult to evaluate within the framework of the Miller-Orr decision model. See Miller and Orr, "A Model of the Demand for Money by Firms," 427–29, 433–35.

We see, then, that the upper control limit is three times as large as the optimal cash return point.

Recall that in this analysis the firm's cash balances over time are assumed to be random. The average cash balance, CB^*, that will be held by the firm over the analysis period, therefore, can only be computed on an *expected* basis.[5] Under these conditions it is approximated by

$$CB^* = \frac{UL + RP}{3} \tag{8-5}$$

Of course, once the subject time period has become history, the actual average cash balance can be derived from the firm's records.

The actual value for the lower limit, LL, is set by management. In business practice a minimum is typically established below which the cash balance is not permitted to fall. Among other things, it will be affected by (1) the firm's banking arrangements, which may require compensating balances, and (2) management's risk-bearing tendencies.

To illustrate use of the model, suppose that the annual yield available on marketable securities is 9 percent. Over a 360-day year, i becomes .09/360 = .00025 per day. Assume that the fixed cost, b, of transacting a marketable securities trade is $50. Moreover, the firm has studied its past cash balance levels and has observed that the standard deviation, σ, in daily cash balance changes is equal to $800. The firm sees no reason why this variability should change in the future. It is the firm's policy to maintain $1000 in its demand deposit account (LL) at all times. Finally, the firm has established that each day's actual cash balance is random. The equations that comprise this control limit system can be applied to provide guidelines for cash management policy.

The optimal cash return point for transactions purposes becomes

$$RP = \sqrt[3]{\frac{3(50)(800)^2}{4(.00025)}} = \sqrt[3]{\frac{96,000,000}{.001}} = \$4579$$

The upper cash balance limit that will trigger a transfer of cash to marketable securities is

$$UL = 3(4579) = \$13,737$$

The expected average cash balance level that the firm will carry is approximated by equation (8-5):

$$CB^* = \frac{13,737 + 4579}{3} = \$6105$$

The cash balance control limits derived from this example are graphed in

[5]In the basic cash management inventory model suggested by Baumol, the average cash balance can be determined *exactly* in advance of the cash flows occurring, owing to the crucial assumption of *certainty* of cash payments.

Figure 8-4. Should the cash balance bump against the upper limit of
$13,737 (point *A*), then the financial officer is instructed to buy $9158 of
marketable securities. At the other extreme, if the cash balance level should
drop to the lower limit of $1000 (point *B*), then the financial officer is
instructed to sell $3579 of marketable securities to restore the cash balance
level to $4579. As long as the cash balance wanders within the *UL − LL*
range, no securities transactions take place. By acting in this manner, the
financial officer will *minimize* the sum of interest income forgone and the
costs of purchasing and selling securities.[6]

CONTROL LIMIT MODEL IMPLICATIONS

Use of equation (8-3) results in determination of the optimal cash
return point within the framework of the control limit model. Inspection of
this equation indicates to the financial officer that the optimal cash return
level, *RP*, will vary directly with the cube root of both the transfer cost
variable, *b*, and the volatility of daily cash balance changes, σ^2. Greater
transfer costs or cash balance volatility result in a greater *absolute* dollar
spread between the upper control limit and the cash return point. This
larger spread between RP and RP means that securities purchases will be
effected in larger lot sizes. It is further evident that the optimal cash return
point varies inversely with the cube root of the lost interest rate.

Similar to the basic inventory model reviewed in the previous section,
the control limit model implies that economies of scale are possible in cash
management. In addition, the optimal cash return point always lies well
below the midpoint of the range, *UL − LL*, over which the cash balance is
permitted to "walk." This means that the liquidation of marketable securities will occur (1) more frequently and (2) in smaller lot sizes than purchases
of securities. This suggests that firms with highly volatile cash balances
must be acutely concerned with the liquidity of their marketable securities
portfolio.

[6]As with the Baumol inventory model, the Miller-Orr control limit model seeks to minimize
the total cost of managing the firm's cash balance over a finite planning horizon.

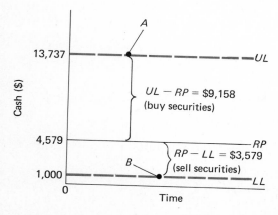

FIGURE 8-4 Control Limit Model

An important element of the commercial banking environment that affects corporate cash management deserves special mention. This is the practice of the bank's requiring, either formally or informally, that the firm maintain deposits of a given amount in its demand deposit account. Such balances are referred to as **compensating balances.**

The compensating balance requirement became typical banking practice after federal action forbade the payment of interest on demand deposits in the early 1930s.[7] In the face of prospective withdrawals the procedure allowed banks to maintain favorable levels of their basic raw material—deposits. Such balances are normally required of corporate customers in three situations: (1) where the firm has an established line of credit (loan commitment) at the bank, but it is not entirely used; (2) where the firm has a loan outstanding at the bank; and, or (3) in exchange for various other services provided by the bank to its customer.

As you would expect, compensating balance policies vary among commercial banks and, further, are influenced by general conditions in the financial markets. Still, some tendencies can be identified. In the case of the unused portion of a loan commitment, the bank might require that the firm's demand deposits average anywhere from 5 to 10 percent of the commitment. If a loan is currently outstanding with the bank, the requirement will probably be 10 to 20 percent of the unpaid balance. During periods when monetary policy is restrictive, so-called "tight money" periods, the ranges just mentioned rise by about 5 percent across the board.[8]

Instead of charging directly for certain banking services, the bank may ask the firm to "pay" for them by the compensating balance approach. These services include check-clearing, the availability of credit information, and any of the array of receipts acceleration or payment control techniques that we discussed in the previous chapter.

If the bank asks for compensation in the form of balances left on deposit rather than charging unit prices for services rendered, the requirement may be expressed as (1) an absolute amount or (2) an average amount. The latter is preferable to most firms, as it provides for some flexibility in use of the deposits. With the average balance requirement being calculated over a month, and in some instances as long as a year, the balance can be low on occasion as long as it is offset with heavy balances in other time periods.

COMPENSATING BALANCE REQUIREMENT IMPLICATIONS

In the analysis that the financial officer undertakes to determine the split between cash and near cash, explicit consideration must be given to compensating balance requirements. This information can be used in con-

---

[7]Paul S. Nadler, "Compensating Balances and the Prime at Twilight," *Harvard Business Review,* 50 (January–February 1972), 112.

[8]See Howard D. Crosse and George H. Hempel, *Management Policies For Commercial Banks,* 2d ed. (Englewood Cliffs, N.J.: Prentice-Hall, Inc., 1973), pp. 200–202; and E. W. Reed, R. V. Cotter, E. K. Gill, and R. Smith, *Commercial Banking* (Englewood Cliffs, N.J.: Prentice-Hall, Inc., 1976), pp. 153–54.

junction with the basic inventory model (benchmark 1) or the control limit model (benchmark 2).

One approach is to use either of the models, and in the calculations ignore the compensating balance requirement. This is logical in many instances. Generally, the compensating balance required by the bank is beyond the firm's control.

In using the models, then, the focus is upon the discretionary cash holdings above the required levels. Once the solution to the particular model is found, the firm's optimal average cash balance will be the *higher* of that suggested by the model or the balance requirement set by the bank.

A second approach is to introduce the size of the compensating balance into the format of the cash management model and carry out the requisite calculations. We noted previously that in the control limit model, the lower control limit (LL) could be the compensating balance requirement faced by the firm as opposed to a value of zero for LL. In the basic inventory model the compensating balance can be treated as a safety stock. In Figure 8-1, then, the cash balance would not touch the zero level and trigger a marketable securities purchase; rather it would fall to the level of the compensating balance (some amount greater than zero) and initiate the securities purchase. Under ordinary circumstances in neither model is the calculated optimal order size of marketable securities altered by consideration of compensating balances,[9] so useful information on the proper split between near cash and discretionary cash (cash held in excess of compensating balances) is still provided by these two benchmarks.

Recent trends indicate that compensating balances are slowly giving way to unit pricing of bank services. Under unit pricing the bank quotes a stated price for the service. The firm pays that rate only for the services actually used. Such a trend means that the importance of this third benchmark may diminish in the foreseeable future. At the same time, the policies suggested by application of cash management models, similar to those just presented, may well attract attention.

COMPOSITION OF MARKETABLE SECURITIES PORTFOLIO

Once the division between cash and near-cash holdings has been determined, the financial manager faces the task of selecting appropriate financial assets for inclusion in the firm's marketable securities portfolio. We deal with that problem in this section.

General Selection Criteria

An assessment of certain criteria can provide the financial manager with a useful framework for selecting a proper marketable securities mix. These considerations include evaluation of the (1) financial risk, (2) interest rate risk, (3) liquidity, (4) taxability, and (5) yields among different financial assets. The above criteria will be briefly delineated from the investor's point of view.

[9]Extraordinary circumstances could be, for example, (1) when the compensating balance *exceeds* the cash return point, *RP*, in the control limit model, or (2) when maintenance of the required balance leaves no excess liquidity for investment in securities.

Financial risk refers to the uncertainty of expected returns from a security attributable to possible changes in the financial capacity of the security issuer to make future payments to the security owner. If the chance of default on the terms of the instrument is high, (low), then the financial risk is said to be high (low). It is clear that the financial risk associated with holding commercial paper, which we will see shortly is nothing more than a corporate IOU, exceeds that of holding securities issued by the United States Treasury. In both financial practice and research, when estimates of risk-free returns are desired, the yields available on Treasury securities are consulted and the safety of other financial instruments is weighed against them. As the marketable securities portfolio is designed to provide a return on funds that would otherwise be tied up in idle cash held for transactions or precautionary purposes, the financial officer will not usually be willing to assume much financial risk in the hope of greater return within the makeup of the portfolio.

INTEREST RATE RISK

The uncertainty that envelops the expected returns from a financial instrument attributable to changes in interest rates is known as **interest rate risk.** Of particular concern to the corporate treasurer is the price volatility associated with instruments that have long, as opposed to short, terms to maturity. An illustration can help clarify this point.

Suppose that the financial officer is weighing the merits of investing temporarily available corporate cash in a new offering of U.S. Treasury obligations that will mature in either (1) three years or (2) 20 years from the date of issue. The purchase price of either the three-year notes or 20-year bonds is at their par value of $1000 per security. The maturity value of either class of security is equal to par, $1000, and the coupon rate (stated interest rate) is set at 7 percent, compounded annually.

If after one year from the date of purchase prevailing interest rates rise to 9 percent, the market prices of these currently outstanding Treasury securities will fall to bring their yields to maturity in line with what investors could obtain by buying a new issue of a given instrument. The market prices of *both* the three-year and 20-year obligations will decline. The price of the 20-year instrument will decline by a greater dollar amount, however, than that of the three-year instrument.

One year from the date of issue the price obtainable in the marketplace for the original 20-year instrument, which now has 19 years to go to maturity, can be found by computing P as follows:

$$P = \sum_{T=1}^{19} \frac{\$70}{(1 + .09)^T} + \frac{\$1000}{(1 + .09)^{19}} = \$821.01$$

In the above expression (1) T is the year in which the particular return, either interest or principal amount, is received; (2) $70 is the annual interest payment; and (3) $1000 is the contractual maturity value of the bond.

The rise in interest rates has forced the market price of the bond down to $821.01.

Now, what will happen to the price of the note that has two years remaining to maturity? In a similar manner we can compute its price, P:

$$P = \sum_{T=1}^{2} \frac{\$70}{(1 + .09)^T} + \frac{\$1000}{(1 + .09)^2} = \$964.84$$

The market price of the shorter-term note will decline to $964.84. It is evident from Table 8-2 that the market value of the shorter-term security was penalized much less by the given rise in the general level of interest rates.

If we extended the illustration, we would see that, in terms of market price, a one-year security would be affected less than a two-year security, a 90-day security less than a 182-day security, and so on. Equity securities would exhibit the largest price changes, owing to their infinite maturity periods. To hedge against the price volatility caused by interest rate risk, the firm's marketable securities portfolio will tend to be composed of instruments that mature over short periods.

LIQUIDITY

In the present context of managing the marketable securities portfolio, **liquidity** refers to the ability to transform a security into cash. Should an unforeseen event require that a significant amount of cash be immediately available, then a sizable portion of the portfolio might have to be sold. The financial manager will want the cash *quickly,* and he will not want to accept a large *price concession* in order to convert the securities. Thus, in the formulation of preferences for the inclusion of particular instruments in the portfolio, consideration will be given to (1) the time period needed to sell the security and (2) the likelihood that the security can be sold at or near its prevailing market price. The latter element, here, means that "thin" markets, where relatively few transactions take place, or where trades are accomplished only with large price changes between transactions, will be avoided.

TAXABILITY

The tax treatment of the income that a firm receives from its security investments does not affect the ultimate mix of the marketable securities

Table 8-2 MARKET PRICE EFFECT OF A RISE IN INTEREST RATES

ITEM	THREE-YEAR INSTRUMENT	TWENTY-YEAR INSTRUMENT
Original price	$1000.00	$1000.00
Price after one year	964.84	821.01
Decline in price	$ 35.16	$ 178.99

portfolio as much as do the criteria mentioned earlier. This is because the interest income from most instruments suitable for inclusion in the portfolio is taxable at the federal level. Still, the taxability of (1) interest income and (2) capital gains is seriously evaluated by some corporate treasurers, so a few observations will be made.

The interest income from only one class of securities escapes the federal income tax. That class of securities is generally referred to as **municipal obligations,** or more simply as **municipals.** Owing to the tax-exempt feature of interest income from state and local government securities, they sell at lower yields to maturity in the market than do securities that pay interest that is taxable. The after-tax yield on a municipal obligation, however, could be higher than that obtainable from a non-tax-exempt security. This would depend mainly on the purchasing firm's tax situation.

Consider Table 8-3. A firm is assumed to be analyzing whether to invest in a one-year tax-free debt issue yielding 5 percent on a $1000 outlay, or a one-year taxable issue that yields 8 percent on a $1000 outlay. The firm pays federal taxes at the rate of 48 percent. The yields quoted in the financial press and in the prospectuses that describe debt issues are *before-tax* returns. The actual *after-tax* return enjoyed by the investor depends on his tax bracket. Notice that the actual after-tax yield received by the firm is only 4.16 percent on the taxable issue versus 5.00 percent on the tax-exempt obligation. The lower portion of Table 8-3 shows that the fully taxed bond must yield 9.615 percent to make it comparable to the tax-exempt issue.

Table 8-3 COMPARISON OF AFTER-TAX YIELDS

TAX-EXEMPT DEBT ISSUE (5% COUPON)		TAXABLE DEBT ISSUE (8% COUPON)	
Interest income	$50.00	$80.00	
Income tax (.48)	0.00	38.40	
After-tax interest income	$50.00	$41.60	
After-tax yield	$\dfrac{\$50}{\$1000.00} = 5\%$	$\dfrac{\$41.60}{\$1000.00} = 4.16\%$	

Derivation of Equivalent Before-Tax Yield on a Taxable Debt Issue

$$r = \frac{r^*}{1-T} = \frac{.05}{1-.48} = 9.615\% \qquad (8\text{-}6)$$

where r = equivalent before-tax yield,
r^* = after-tax yield on tax-exempt security,
T = firm's marginal income tax rate.

Proof: Interest income	$96.15
Income tax (.48)	46.15
After-tax interest income	$50.00

Because capital gains are taxed at a lower rate than is ordinary income (such as interest), bonds selling at a discount from their face value may at times be attractive investments to tax-paying firms. Should a high level of interest rates currently exist, the market prices of debt issues that were issued in the past at low coupon rates will be depressed. This, as we said previously, brings their yield to maturity up to that obtainable on a new issue. Part of the yield to maturity on a bond selling at a discount is a capital gain, or the difference between the purchase price and the maturity value. Provided the firm held the fixed-income security for more than 12 months, the return after tax that is earned could be higher than that derived from a comparable issue carrying a higher coupon but selling at par.[10] We say *could* be higher, as the marketplace is rather efficient and recognizes well this feature of taxability; consequently, discount bonds will sell at lower yields than issues that have similar risk characteristics but larger coupons. For short periods, though, a firm *might* find a favorable yield advantage by purchasing discount bonds.

YIELDS

The final selection criterion that we mention is a significant one—the yields that are available on the different financial assets suitable for inclusion in the near-cash portfolio. By now it is probably obvious that the factors of (1) financial risk, (2) interest rate risk, (3) liquidity, and (4) taxability all influence the available yields on financial instruments. Thus, the yield criterion involves a weighing of the risks and benefits inherent to these factors. If a given risk is assumed, such as a lack of liquidity, then a higher yield may be expected on the instrument lacking the liquidity characteristic.

Figure 8-5 summarizes our framework for designing the firm's marketable securities portfolio. The four basic considerations are shown to influence the yields available on securities. The financial manager must focus on the risk-return tradeoffs that are identified through his analysis. Coming to grips with these tradeoffs will enable him to determine the proper marketable securities mix for his company.

[10]Beginning in 1978 the holding period for long-term capital gain situations increased to 12 months. See Chapter 2.

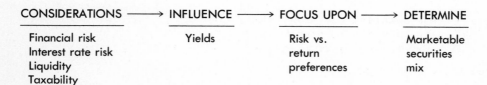

CONSIDERATIONS ⟶	INFLUENCE ⟶	FOCUS UPON ⟶	DETERMINE
Financial risk	Yields	Risk vs.	Marketable
Interest rate risk		return	securities
Liquidity		preferences	mix
Taxability			

FIGURE 8-5 *Designing the Marketable Securities Portfolio*

Let us look now at the marketable securities that are prominent in firms' near-cash portfolios.

U. S. TREASURY BILLS

U. S. Treasury bills are the best-known and most popular short-term investment outlet among firms. A Treasury bill is a direct obligation of the United States government sold on a regular basis by the U. S. Treasury. New Treasury bills are issued in denominations of $10,000, $15,000, $50,000, $100,000, $500,000, and $1,000,000. In effect, therefore, one can buy bills in multiples of $5000 above the smallest purchase price of $10,000 by combining $10,000 bills and $15,000 bills to reach the desired sum.

It is of interest to small firms and individuals to point out that prior to March, 1970, bills could be obtained in denominations of $1000 and $5000. The Treasury did away with these small-sized securities in order to (1) reduce processing costs associated with small orders, and (2) reduce the tendency of small savers to pull their funds out of commercial banks and savings and loan associations in order to invest in bills. This latter tendency was thought to strain the mortgage market to the extent that higher interest rates would result. So, while large corporations were purchasing bills yielding in excess of 9 percent during September, 1974, smaller investors earning 5 to 5.5 percent on savings accounts and time deposits could find solace in the fact that they were holding down governmental processing costs and reducing pressure in the mortgage markets.

At present bills are regularly offered with maturities of 91, 182, and 365 days. A nine-month bill has been sold from time to time, but due to its lack of popularity among investors it is not now being issued. The three-month and six-month bills are auctioned weekly by the Treasury, and the one-year bills are offered every four weeks. Bids (orders to purchase) are accepted by the various Federal Reserve Banks and their branches, which perform the role of agents for the Treasury. Each Monday, bids are received until 1:30 P.M.; after that time they are opened, tabulated, and forwarded to the Treasury for allocation (filling the purchase orders).

Treasury bills are sold on a discount basis; for that reason the investor does not receive an actual interest payment. The return is the difference between the purchase price and the face (par) value of the bill.

The bills are marketed by the Treasury only in *bearer* form. They are purchased, therefore, without the investor's name upon them. This attribute makes them easily transferable from one investor to the next. Of prime importance to the corporate treasurer is the fact that a very active secondary market exists for bills. After a bill has been acquired by the firm, should the need arise to turn it into cash, a group of securities dealers stand ready to purchase it. This highly developed secondary market for bills not only makes them extremely liquid, but it also allows the firm to buy bills with maturities of a week or even less.

As bills have the full financial backing of the United States government they are, for all practical purposes, risk-free. This negligible financial risk and high degree of liquidity makes their yields lower than those obtainable on other marketable securities. The income from Treasury bills is subject to federal income taxes but *not* to state and local government income taxes. An often neglected taxability feature of Treasury bills relates to their capital gains status. In the eyes of the Internal Revenue Service, bills are *not* capital assets. This means any financial gain on their sale prior to maturity is taxed as an *ordinary* gain. This would not be the case with other government securities, such as Treasury notes (original maturities of one to seven years) or Treasury bonds (generally with original maturities of over five years). As Treasury notes and bonds approach maturity, they can become attractive alternatives to bills in the firm's near-cash portfolio.

FEDERAL AGENCY SECURITIES

Federal agency securities are debt obligations of corporations and agencies that have been created to effect the various lending programs of the United States government. Five such government-sponsored corporations account for the majority of outstanding agency debt. These "big five" agencies are:

1. The Federal National Mortgage Association (FNMA). FNMA renders supplementary assistance to the secondary market for mortgages. During periods of tight credit FNMA provides liquidity by purchasing mortgages from private financial institutions, such as savings and loan associations. When credit is easier to obtain, FNMA sells mortgages.
2. The Federal Home Loan Banks (FHLB). The 12 regional banks in the FHLB system operate as a credit reserve system under the supervision of the Federal Home Loan Bank Board. The credit reserve system is provided for the benefit of the system's members, all of which engage in home mortgage lending.
3. The Federal Land Banks. The 12 regional banks are owned by almost 600 local Federal Land Bank Associations. Federal Land Bank loans are arranged by the local associations. Loans are made to persons who are (or become) members of the associations and who are engaged in agriculture, provide agricultural services, or own rural homes.
4. The Federal Intermediate Credit Banks. There are 12 of these banks that make loans to and purchase notes originating from loans made to farmers by other financial institutions involved in agricultural lending.
5. The Banks for Cooperatives. The 12 district Banks for Cooperatives make loans to cooperative associations, owned and controlled by farmers, that market farm products, purchase farm supplies, or provide general farm business services.

It is a mistaken notion in some circles that the "big five" federally sponsored agencies are owned by the United States government and, therefore, the securities they issue are fully guaranteed by the government. Neither assertion is true. The "big five" agencies are now entirely owned by either their member associations or the general public. In addition, it is the issuing agency that stands behind its promises to pay, not the federal government.

These agencies sell their securities in a variety of denominations. The entry barrier caused by the absolute dollar size of the smallest available Treasury bill—$10,000—is not as severe in the market for agencies. A wide range of maturities is also available. Obligations at times can be purchased with maturities as short as 30 days or as long as 15 years. The vast majority of outstanding agency debt, in excess of 80 percent, will mature in five years or less.

Agency debt usually sells on a coupon basis and pays interest to the owner on a semiannual schedule, although there are exceptions. Some issues have been sold on a discount basis, and some have paid interest only once a year.

If the likelihood is great that a marketable security will have to be liquidated before its contractual maturity date, then the financial officer must take care in his selection of agency debt. The secondary market for the debt of the "big five" agencies is well developed in the shorter maturity categories—five years or less. It is not as strong in the longer maturity categories. To move such an issue, then, the financial officer may have to sell it at a depressed price.

The income received by the investor in agency debt is subject to taxation at the federal level. Of the "big five" agencies, only the income from FNMA issues is taxed at the state and local level.

The yields available on agency obligations will always exceed those of Treasury securities of similar maturity. This yield differential is attributable to their lesser marketability and greater default risk. The financial officer might keep in mind, however, that none of these agency issues has ever gone into default.

BANKERS' ACCEPTANCES

Bankers' acceptances are one of the least understood instruments suitable for inclusion in the firm's marketable securities portfolio. Their part in United States commerce today is largely concentrated in the financing of foreign transactions. Generally, an acceptance is a draft (order to pay) drawn on a specific bank by an exporter in order to obtain payment for goods he has shipped to a customer, who maintains an account with that specific bank. An example of the sequence of events leading to the creation of a bankers' acceptance would go like this:

1. A retailer located in San Francisco wants to import a shipment of stereo equipment from Tokyo. He goes to his commercial bank, which examines his credit standing and finds it satisfactory.
2. The importer's commercial bank sends the Tokyo exporter a letter of credit (a sophisticated reference letter) which authorizes the exporter to draw a draft on the San Francisco commercial bank. In the meantime, the importer has signed a contract with his bank agreeing to pay the bank the amount of the draft plus a commission in time for the bank to honor the draft at maturity.
3. Having received the letter of credit, the exporter draws a time draft on the San Francisco bank for the amount of the sale price and releases the stereo

equipment for shipment. He retains possession of critical documents associated with the sale, such as the bill of lading, the transfer of title to the merchandise, and insurance papers.

4. The exporter will probably not want to wait several months for his funds, so he will obtain cash at once by selling (discounting) the draft with his bank in Tokyo at less than its face value. The shipping documents are turned over to the Tokyo bank.

5. The Tokyo bank will forward the draft and shipping documents to its correspondent bank in the United States. The correspondent bank will present the draft to the importer's San Francisco bank for acceptance.

6. The San Francisco bank (the drawee bank) will observe that the draft was authorized by its own letter of credit, will detach all shipping documents, and will stamp the draft "accepted." At this time, and not before, the bankers' acceptance is created. It is now a negotiable instrument, payable to the bearer.

7. The maturity period of the acceptance will be prearranged between the firm importing the stereo equipment and its San Francisco bank. When the draft is presented for acceptance, the maturity period begins, as most drafts are "sight drafts." This means, for instance, that if the maturity period is to be 90 days, the 90-day period begins *after* the drawee bank accepts the draft.

8. After accepting the draft, the San Francisco bank will notify its customer (the importer) that he can pick up the shipping documents, which will enable him to take possession of his stereo equipment. In exchange for the shipping documents the drawee bank will obtain a signed document from the importer (a trust receipt) giving the bank a security interest in the goods. The importer can take title to his goods, sell them, and pay the San Francisco bank the face value of the acceptance (plus the stipulated service fee) shortly before its maturity.

9. The United States correspondent bank, which now holds the acceptance, will be instructed by the Tokyo bank to take either of two courses of action: (1) hold the acceptance until it matures as an investment, or (2) immediately sell the acceptance in the market and credit its deposit account.

10. This latter course of action makes acceptances available to corporate treasurers for inclusion in their near-cash portfolios.

Now that we know what a bankers' acceptance is, we can proceed to discuss its characteristics. Since acceptances are used to finance the acquisition of goods by one party, the document is not "issued" in specialized denominations; its dollar size is determined by the cost of the goods being purchased. Usual sizes, however, range from $25,000 to $1 million.

The maturities on acceptances run predominantly from 30 to 180 days, although longer periods are available from time to time. The most common maturity period is 90 days.

Acceptances, like Treasury bills, are sold on a discount basis and are payable to the bearer of the paper. A secondary market for the acceptances of large banks does exist. These transactions in acceptances are handled by only seven major dealers, all located in New York City. Included in this group are such well-known firms as The First Boston Corporation and Merrill Lynch, Pierce, Fenner & Smith, Inc.

The income generated from investing in acceptances is fully taxable at the federal, state, and local levels. Owing to their greater financial risk and lesser liquidity, acceptances provide investors a yield advantage over Treasury bills and agency obligations. In fact, the acceptances of major banks are a very safe investment, making the yield advantage over Treasuries worth looking at from the firm's vantagepoint.

NEGOTIABLE CERTIFICATES OF DEPOSIT

A **negotiable certificate of deposit, CD,** is a marketable receipt for funds that have been deposited in a bank for a fixed time period. The deposited funds earn a fixed rate of interest. These are not to be confused with ordinary passbook savings accounts or nonmarketable time deposits offered by all commercial banks. CD's are offered by major money-center banks.

CD's are offered by key banks in a variety of denominations running from $25,000 to $10,000,000. The popular sizes are $100,000, $500,000, and $1,000,000.

The original maturities on CD's can range from one to 18 months. Periodic reporting surveys of commercial banks that are members of the Federal Reserve System consistently indicate that from 70 to 87 percent of outstanding CD's have maturity periods of four months or less.

CD's are offered by banks on a basis differing from Treasury bills; that is, they are not sold at a discount. Rather, when the certificate matures, the owner receives the full amount deposited plus the earned interest.

A secondary market for CD's does exist, the heart of which is found in New York City. While CD's may be issued in either registered or bearer form, the latter facilitates transactions in the secondary market and, thus, is the most common.

Even though the secondary market for CD's of large banks is well organized, it does not operate as smoothly as the after-market in Treasuries. CD's are more heterogeneous than Treasury bills. Treasury bills have similar rates, maturity periods, and denominations; more variety is found in CD's. This makes it harder to liquidate large blocks of CD's, because a more specialized investor must be found. The securities dealers who "make" the secondary market in CD's mainly trade in $1 million units. Smaller denominations can be traded but will bring a relatively lower price. The First Boston Corporation and Salomon Brothers are two of the major dealers in CD's.

The income received from an investment in CD's is subject to taxation at all governmental levels. In recent years CD yields have been above those available on bankers' acceptances.

COMMERCIAL PAPER

Commercial paper refers to short-term, unsecured promissory notes sold by large businesses in order to raise cash. These are sometimes described in the popular financial press as short-term, corporate IOU's. Because they are unsecured, the issuing side of the market is dominated by large corporations, which typically maintain sound credit ratings. The issuing (borrowing) firm can sell the paper to a dealer who will in turn sell it to the investing public; or, if the firm's reputation is solid, the paper can be sold directly to the ultimate investor.

The denominations in which commercial paper can be bought can vary over a wide range. At times paper can be obtained in sizes from $5000 to $5 million, or even more. Sometimes dealers will sell notes in multiples as small as $1000 or $5000 above the initial $5000 denomination. This depends upon the dealer. The most usual denominations are $25,000, $50,000, $100,000, $250,000, $500,000, and $1 million. Major dealers in the dealer-placed market include The First Boston Corporation; Goldman, Sachs & Co.; Merrill Lynch, Pierce, Fenner & Smith, Inc.; and Salomon Brothers.

Commercial paper can be purchased with maturities that range from three to 270 days. Notes with maturities exceeding 270 days are very rare, because they would have to be registered with the Securities and Exchange Commission—a task that firms avoid, when possible, because of its time-consuming and costly nature.

These notes are *generally* sold on a discount basis in bearer form, although paper is available at times that is interest bearing and can be made payable to the order of the investor.

The next point is of considerable interest to the financial officer responsible for management of the firm's near-cash portfolio. For practical purposes there is *no* active trading in a secondary market for commercial paper. This distinguishes commercial paper from all of the previously discussed short-term investment vehicles. On occasion, a dealer or finance company (the borrower) will redeem a note prior to its contractual maturity date, but this is not a regular procedure. Thus, when the corporation evaluates commercial paper for possible inclusion in its marketable securities portfolio, it should plan to hold it to maturity.

The return on commercial paper is fully taxable to the investor at all levels of government. Because of its lack of marketability, commercial paper in past years consistently provided a yield advantage over other near-cash assets of comparable maturity. The lifting of interest rate ceilings in 1973 by the Federal Reserve Board on certain large CD's, however, has allowed commercial banks to make CD rates fully competitive in the attempt to attract funds. Over any time period, then, CD yields *may* be slightly above the rates available on commercial paper.

REPURCHASE AGREEMENTS

Repurchase agreements (repos) are legal contracts that involve the actual sale of securities by a *borrower* to the *lender,* with a commitment on the part of the borrower to *repurchase* the securities at the contract price plus a stated interest charge. The securities sold to the lender are U. S. government issues or other instruments of the money market such as those described above. The borrower is either a major financial institution—most importantly, a commercial bank—or a dealer in U. S. government securities.

Why might the corporation with excess cash prefer to buy repurchase agreements rather than a given marketable security? There are two major reasons. First, the original maturities of the instruments being sold can, in effect, be adjusted to suit the particular needs of the investing corporation. Funds available for very short time periods, such as one or two days, can be productively employed. The second reason is closely related to the first. The firm could, of course, buy a Treasury bill and then resell it in the market in a few days when cash was required. The drawback here would be the risk involved in liquidating the bill at a price equal to its earlier cost to the firm. The purchase of a repo removes this risk. The contract price of the securities that make up the arrangement is *fixed* for the duration of the transaction. The corporation that buys a repurchase agreement, then, is protected against market price fluctuations throughout the contract period. This makes it a sound alternative investment for funds that are freed up for only very short periods.

These agreements are usually executed in sizes of $500,000 or more. The maturities may be for a specified time period or may have no fixed maturity date. In the latter case either lender or borrower may terminate the contract without advance notice.

The returns that the lender receives on his repurchase agreements are taxed at all governmental levels. Since the interest rates are set by direct negotiation between the lender and borrower, no regular published series of yields is available for direct comparison with other short-term investments. The rates available on repurchase agreements, however, are closely related to, but generally *less* than, Treasury bill rates of comparable maturities.

MONEY MARKET MUTUAL FUNDS

During the summer months of 1974, yields on three-month Treasury bills, three-month CDs, and four-to-six-month commercial paper reached 9.37, 12.48, and 11.85 percent, respectively.[11] Previous to 1974 the opportunity for small firms, and small savers in general, to take advantage of attractive rates of return on short-term securities was extremely limited. Recall that the smallest Treasury bill requires a $10,000 investment. While commercial paper can at times be obtained in $5000 denominations, it lacks the liquidity of Treasuries that is often preferable to financial managers.

The U. S. financial market system is an extraordinarily flexible vehicle of capitalism. This flexibility was again demonstrated in 1974 and 1975. During that time over 25 money market mutual funds, also called liquid-asset funds, began to sell their shares to the public.

Money market funds typically invest in a diversified portfolio of short-term, high-grade debt instruments such as those described above.

---

[11]Federal Reserve Bank of St. Louis, *U. S. Financial Data*, various issues, 1974.

Some such funds, however, will accept more interest rate risk in their portfolios and acquire some corporate bonds and notes.

The money market funds sell their shares to raise cash, and by pooling the funds of large numbers of small savers, they can build their liquid-asset portfolios. Many of these funds allow the investor to start an account with as little as $1000. This small initial investment, coupled with the fact that some liquid-asset funds permit subsequent investments in amounts as small as $100, makes this type of outlet for excess cash suited to the small firm. Furthermore, the management of the small enterprise may not be highly versed in the details of short-term investments. By purchasing shares in a liquid-asset fund, the investor is also buying managerial expertise.

Money market mutual funds offer the investing firm a high degree of liquidity. By redeeming (selling) shares, the investor can quickly obtain cash. Procedures for liquidation vary among the funds, but shares can usually be redeemed by means of (1) special redemption checks supplied by the fund, (2) telephone instructions, (3) wire instructions, or (4) a letter. When liquidation is ordered by telephone or wire, the mutual fund can remit to the investor by the next business day.

The returns earned from owning shares in a money market fund are taxable at all governmental levels. The yields will follow, of course, the returns the investor could receive by purchasing the marketable securities directly.

The Yield Structure of Marketable Securities

What type of returns can the financial manager expect on his marketable securities portfolio? This is a reasonable question. Some insight can be obtained by looking at the past, although we must realize that future returns are not insured by past experience. It is also useful to have some understanding of how the returns on one type of instrument stack up against another. The behavior of yields on short-term debt instruments over the 1965–1976 period is shown by Table 8-4.

An examination of the data in that table permits the following generalizations:

1. The returns from the various instruments are highly correlated in the positive direction over time. That is, the yields tend to rise and fall together.
2. The yields are quite volatile over time. For example, notice the large increases in returns from 1968 to 1969 and from 1972 to 1973. The financial manager, then, cannot plan on any given level of returns prevailing over a long time period. Also, observe the high yields during 1974 that led to the formation of a large number of money market mutual funds.
3. A basic change has occurred in the underlying structure of yields. Between 1966 and 1972, if we ranked the instruments in Table 8-4 from low yield to high yield, we would have

> Treasury bills   (low yield)
> Federal agency securities
> Bankers' acceptances

Table 8-4 ANNUAL YIELDS (PERCENT) ON SELECTED THREE-MONTH
MARKETABLE SECURITIES

YEAR	T-BILLS	AGENCIES	ACCEPTANCES	COMMERCIAL PAPER	CD's
1965	3.93	4.14	4.19	4.25	4.31
1966	4.81	5.22	5.37	5.51	5.43
1967	4.30	4.60	4.81	5.11	4.99
1968	5.27	5.54	5.72	5.92	5.79
1969	6.54	7.12	7.51	7.76	7.66
1970	6.58	6.94	7.50	7.89	7.68
1971	4.39	4.56	4.94	5.12	5.07
1972	4.02	4.22	4.52	4.63	4.61
1973	6.87	7.40	8.03	8.11	8.21
1974	7.78	8.73	9.85	10.06	10.28
1975	5.85	6.03	6.28	6.41	6.61
1976	5.03	5.15	5.18	5.28	5.31

SOURCE: Salomon Brothers, "An Analytical Record of Yields and Yield Spreads," January 1977.

> Certificates of deposit
> Commercial paper   (high yield)

From 1973 to 1976, however, the annual yields available on negotiable certificates of deposit have exceeded those of commercial paper. As mentioned earlier in this chapter, this phenomenon is the direct result of Federal Reserve Board action that removed interest rate limits on large certificates of deposit.

SUMMARY

Modern techniques available to the financial officer for speeding up his firm's cash inflows and for either improving control over, or actually slowing down, the firm's cash outflows were the main subjects of Chapter 7. The important topic of liquid asset management extended into the present chapter. Here we dwelled upon (1) arriving at a prudent split of the company's liquid asset holdings between cash balances and marketable securities and (2) designing the marketable securities portfolio.

Dividing between Cash and Marketable Securities

Three benchmarks were presented that either aid or influence the firm's investment in cash versus its investment in marketable securities. The basic inventory model for cash management suggested by Baumol provides insights into the (1) proper average amount of cash to hold and (2) the proper amount of securities to convert into cash, assuming the need for cash is certain.

The control limit model presented by Miller and Orr is more useful if the firm's cash balances over time follow a random pattern. The control limit model permits the cash balance to wander until it strikes either an upper or a lower limit. When a limit is reached, either a securities purchase or sale is ordered depending on the situation. Both of these models attempt to minimize the total costs of investing in cash, defined as the sum of interest income forgone and the transfer costs of purchasing and selling securities.

A third effect upon the firm's cash investment is the compensating balance requirement at its commercial bank. If the trend toward unit pricing of bank services continues, this influence on company cash balances may decline in the future.

Marketable Securities Portfolio

The factors of (1) financial risk, (2) interest rate risk, (3) liquidity, and (4) taxability affect the yields available on marketable securities. By considering these four factors simultaneously with returns desired from the portfolio, the financial manager can design the mix of near-cash assets most suitable for his firm.

The features of several marketable securities were investigated. Treasury bills and federal agency securities were found to be extremely safe investments. Higher yields are obtainable on bankers' acceptances, CD's, and commercial paper in exchange for greater risk assumption. Unlike the instruments just mentioned, commercial paper enjoys no developed secondary market. The firm can hedge against market-price fluctuations through the use of repurchase agreements. Money market mutual funds, a recent phenomenon of our financial market system, were found to be particularly well suited for the short-term investing needs of small firms.

STUDY QUESTIONS

8-1. Consider the basic inventory model for cash management. If cash is ordered in lot sizes known as the *optimal cash conversion size,* what does the firm minimize by this action?

8-2. What is the major difference in underlying assumptions between the inventory model and the control limit model for cash management?

8-3. Your firm invests in only three different classes of marketable securities: commercial paper, Treasury bills, and federal agency securities. Recently, yields on these money market instruments of three months maturity were quoted at 6.10, 6.25, and 5.90 percent. Match the available yields with the types of instruments that your firm purchases.

8-4. What are compensating balances and under what typical conditions are they imposed on commercial bank customers?

8-5. Your company borrowed $5000 from a commercial bank at a contract rate of interest of 8 percent. The loan contract requires that a compensating balance of 15 percent of the amount borrowed be kept in a demand deposit account at the bank. What is the effective rate of interest on the loan?

8-6. Distinguish between financial risk and interest rate risk as these terms are commonly used in discussions of cash management.

8-7. What is meant when we say, "A money market instrument is highly liquid"?

8-8. Which money market instrument(s):
(a) is generally conceded to have no secondary market?

(b) is largely concentrated in the financing of foreign transactions?

(c) provides returns that are *not* taxable at the state and local levels of government?

(d) are issued to effect the various lending programs of the United States government?

(e) have, at times during recent years, offered yields in excess of those obtainable on commercial paper?

8-9. What two major factors led to the inception of a large number of money market mutual funds during 1974 and 1975?

8-10. What two key factors might induce a firm to invest in repurchase agreements rather than a specific security of the money market?

**STUDY
PROBLEMS**

8-1. The Richard Price Metal Working Company will experience $800,000 in cash payments next month. The annual yield available on marketable securities is 6.5 percent. The company has analyzed the cost of obtaining or investing cash and found it to be equal to $85 per transaction. Since cash outlays for Price Metal Working occur at a constant rate over any given month, the company has decided to apply the principles of the inventory model for cash management to provide answers to several questions.

(a) What is the optimal cash conversion size for the Price Metal Working Company?

(b) What is the total cost of having cash on hand during the coming month?

(c) How often (in days) will the firm have to make a cash conversion? Assume a 30-day month.

(d) What will be Price Metal Working's average cash balance?

8-2. The Edinboro Fabric Company manufactures 18 different final products, which are woven, cut, and dyed for use primarily in the clothing industry. Owing to the whimsical nature of the underlying demand for certain clothing styles, Edinboro Fabric has a most difficult time forecasting its cash balance levels. The company maintains $2000 in its demand deposit account at all times. A detailed study of past cash balance levels has revealed that the standard deviation, σ, in daily cash balance changes has been equal to $600. The nature of the firm is not expected to undergo any structural changes in the foreseeable future, and for this reason the past volatility in cash balance levels is expected to continue in the future. Edinboro has determined that the cost of transacting a marketable securities trade is $85. Marketable securities are yielding 6 percent per annum. The firm always uses a 360-day year in its analysis procedures. Robert Cambridge, Edinboro's treasurer, has just returned from a three-day cash management seminar in New York City. He has decided to apply the control limit model for cash management to his firm's situtation.

(a) What is the optimal cash return point for Edinboro?

(b) What is the upper control limit?

(c) In what lot sizes will marketable securities be purchased? Sold?

(d) Graph your results as obtained above.

8-3. Two years ago your corporate treasurer purchased for the firm a 20-year

bond at its par value of $1000. The coupon rate on this security is 8 percent. Interest payments are made to bondholders once a year. Currently, bonds of this particular risk class are yielding investors 9 percent. A cash shortage has forced you to instruct your treasurer to liquidate this bond.

(a) At what price will your bond be sold?

(b) What will be the amount of your gain or loss over the original purchase price?

(c) What would be the amount of your gain or loss had the treasurer originally purchased a bond with a four-year rather than a 20-year maturity? (Assume all characteristics of the bonds are identical except their maturity periods.)

(d) What do we call this type of risk assumed by your corporate treasurer?

8-4. Red Raider Feedlots has $4 million in excess cash to invest in a marketable securities portfolio. Their broker will charge $10,000 to invest the entire $4 million. The president of Red Raider wants at least half of the $4 million invested at a maturity period of three months or less; the remainder can be invested in securities with maturities not to exceed six months. The relevant term structure of short-term yields follows:

MATURITY PERIOD	AVAILABLE YIELD (ANNUAL)
One month	6.2%
Two months	6.4%
Three months	6.5%
Four months	6.7%
Five months	6.9%
Six months	7.0%

(a) What should be the maturity periods of the securities purchased with the excess $4 million in order to maximize the before-tax income from the added investment? What will be the amount of the income from such an investment?

(b) Suppose that the president of Red Raider relaxes his constraint on the maturity structure of the added investment. What would be your profit-maximizing investment recommendation?

(c) If one-sixth of the excess cash is invested in each of the maturity categories shown above, what would be the before-tax income generated from such an action?

8-5. The corporate treasurer of Aggieland Fireworks is considering the purchase of a BBB-rated bond that carries a 9 percent coupon. The BBB-rated security is taxable, and the firm is in the 48 percent marginal tax bracket. The face value of this bond is $1000. A financial analyst who reports to the corporate treasurer has alerted him to the fact that a municipal obligation is coming to the market with a 5½ percent coupon. The par value of this security is also $1000.

(a) Which one of the two securities do you recommend that the firm purchase? Why?

(b) What must the fully taxed bond yield to make it comparable to the municipal offering?

8-6. A large proportion of the marketable securities portfolio of Edwards Manufacturing is invested in Treasury bills yielding 6.52 percent before consideration of income taxes. Hoosierville Utilities is bringing a new issue of preferred stock to the marketplace. The new preferred issue will yield 9.30 percent before taxes. The corporate treasurer for Edwards wants to evaluate the possibility of shifting a portion of the funds tied up in Treasury bills to the preferred stock issue.

(a) Calculate the ultimate yields available to Edwards from investing in each type of security. Edwards is in the 48 percent tax bracket.

(b) What factors apart from the available yields should be analyzed in this situation?

8-7. The C. K. S. Stove Company manufactures wood-burning stoves in the Pacific Northwest. Despite the recent popularity of this product, the firm has experienced a very erratic sales pattern. Owing to volatile weather conditions and abrupt changes in new housing starts, it has been extremely difficult for the firm to forecast its cash balances. Still, the company president is disturbed by the fact that the firm has never invested in any marketable securities. Instead, the liquid asset portfolio has consisted entirely of cash. As a start toward reducing the firm's investment in cash and releasing some of it to near-cash assets, a historical record and projection of corporate cash holdings is needed. Over the past five years sales have been $10 million, $12 million, $11 million, $14 million, and $19 million, respectively. Sales forecasts for the next two years are $23 and $21 million. Total assets for the firm are 60 percent of sales. Fixed assets are the higher of 50 percent of total assets or $4 million. Inventory and receivables amount to 70 percent of current assets and are held in equal proportions.

(a) Prepare a worksheet that details the firm's balance sheets for each of the past five years and for the forecast periods.

(b) What amount of cash will the firm have on hand during each year for short-term investment purposes?

An Analytical Record of Yields and Yield Spreads. New York: Salomon Brothers, 1977.

ANDERSON, PAUL F., and R. D. BOYD HARMAN, "The Management of Excess Corporate Cash," *Financial Executive*, 32 (October 1964), 26–30, 51.

ARCHER, STEPHEN H., "A Model for the Determination of Firm Cash Balances," *Journal of Financial and Quantitative Analysis*, 1 (March 1966), 1–11.

BACON, PETER W., and RICHARD E. WILLIAMS, "Interest Rate Futures: New Tool for the Financial Manager," *Financial Management*, 5 (Spring 1976), 32–38.

BAUMOL, WILLIAM J., "The Transactions Demand for Cash: An Inventory Theoretic Approach," *Quarterly Journal of Economics*, 65 (November 1952), 545–56.

BUDIN, MORRIS, and ROBERT J. VAN HANDEL, "A Rule-of-Thumb Theory of Cash Holdings by Firms," *Journal of Financial and Quantitative Analysis*, 10 (March 1975), 85–108.

CAMPBELL, TIM, and LELAND BRENDSEL, "The Impact of Compensating Balance Requirements on the Cash Balances of Manufacturing Corporations: An Empirical Study," *Journal of Finance*, 32 (March 1977), 31–40.

COOK, TIMOTHY Q., ed., *Instruments of the Money Market*, 4th ed. Richmond, Va.: Federal Reserve Bank of Richmond, 1977.

DAELLENBACH, HANS G., "Are Cash Management Optimization Models Worthwhile?", *Journal of Financial and Quantitative Analysis*, 9 (September 1974), 607–26.

DESALVO, ALFRED, "Cash Management Converts Dollars into Working Assets," *Harvard Business Review*, 50 (May–June 1972), 92–100.

GITMAN, LAWRENCE J., D. KEITH FORRESTER, and JOHN R. FORRESTER, JR., "Maximizing Cash Disbursement Float," *Financial Management*, 5 (Summer 1976), 15–24.

JONES, REGINALD H., "Face to Face with Cash Management: How One Company Does It," *Financial Executive*, 37 (September 1969), 37–39.

"Lock Box Banking—Key to Faster Collections," *Credit and Financial Management*, 69 (June 1967), 16–21.

LORDAN, JAMES F., "A Profile of Corporate Cash Management," *The Magazine of Bank Administration*, 48 (April 1972), 15–19.

MELTZER, YALE L., *Putting Money to Work: An Investment Primer*. Englewood Cliffs, N.J.: Prentice-Hall, Inc., 1976.

MILLER, MERTON H., and DANIEL ORR, "A Model of the Demand for Money by Firms," *Quarterly Journal of Economics*, 80 (August 1966), 413–35.

————, and DANIEL ORR, "The Demand for Money by Firms: Extension of Analytic Results," *Journal of Finance*, 23 (December 1968), 735–59.

MYERS, STEWART C., *Modern Developments in Financial Management*, Part 4. Praeger Publishers, Inc., 1976.

ORGLER, YAIR E., *Cash Management*, Belmont, Calif.: Wadsworth Publishing Company, Inc., 1970.

SCOTT, DAVID F., JR., LAURENCE J. MOORE, ANDRE SAINT-DENIS, and EDOUARD ARCHER, "Implementation of a Cash Budget Simulator at Air Canada," paper presented to the Annual Meeting of the Financial Management Association, Montreal, Canada (October 14–16, 1976).

SEARBY, FREDERICK W., "Use Your Hidden Cash Resources," *Harvard Business Review*, 46 (March–April 1968), 71–80.

SENCHACK, ANDREW J., and DON M. HEEP, "Auction Profits in the Treasury Bill Market," *Financial Management*, 4 (Summer 1975), 45–52.

SMITH, KEITH V., *Management of Working Capital: A Reader*, Section 2. St. Paul, Minn.: West Publishing Co., 1974.

STONE, BERNELL K., "Cash Planning and Credit-Line Determination with a Financial Statement Simulator: A Case Report on Short-Term Financial Planning," *Journal of Financial and Quantitative Analysis*, 8 (November 1973), 711–30.

————, and ROBERT A WOOD, "Daily Cash Forecasting: A Simple Method for Implementing the Distribution Approach," *Financial Management*, 6 (Fall 1977), 40–50.

The discussion in this chapter on designing the firm's marketable securities portfolio touched upon the essential elements of several near-cash assets. At times it is difficult to sort out the distinguishing features among these short-term investments. To alleviate that problem, Table 8A-1 draws together their principal characteristics.

Table 8A-1 FEATURES OF SELECTED MONEY MARKET INSTRUMENTS

INSTRUMENT	DENOMINATIONS	MATURITIES	BASIS	FORM	LIQUIDITY	TAXABILITY
U. S. Treasury bills—direct obligations of the U. S. government	$ 10,000 15,000 50,000 100,000 500,000 1,000,000	91 days 182 days 365 days 9-month not presently issued	Discount	Bearer	Excellent secondary market	Exempt from state and local income; do not qualify for favorable capital gains rate
Federal agency securities—obligations of corporations and agencies created to effect the federal government's lending programs	Wide variation; from $1000 to $1 million	5 days (Farm Credit consolidated systemwide discount notes) to more than 10 years	Discount or coupon; usually on coupon	Bearer or registered	Good for issues of "big five" agencies	Generally exempt at local level; FNMA issues are not
Bankers' acceptances—drafts accepted for future payment by commercial banks	No set size; typically range from $25,000 to $1 million	Predominantly from 30 to 180 days	Discount	Bearer	Good for acceptances of large, "money market" banks	Taxed at all levels of government
Negotiable certificates of deposit—marketable receipts for funds deposited in a bank for a fixed time period	$25,000 to $10 million	1 to 18 months	Accrued interest	Bearer or registered; bearer is preferable from liquidity standpoint	Fair to good	Taxed at all levels of government
Commercial paper—short-term, unsecured promissory notes	$5000 to $5 million; $1000 and $5000 multiples above the initial offering size are sometimes available	3 to 270 days	Discount	Bearer	Poor; no active secondary market in usual sense	Taxed at all levels of government
Repurchase agreements—legal contracts between a borrower (security seller) and lender (security buyer). The borrower will repurchase at the contract price plus an interest charge.	Typical sizes are $500,000 or more	According to terms of contract	Not applicable	Not applicable	Fixed by the agreement; that is, borrower will repurchase	Taxed at all levels of government

Table 8A-1   FEATURES OF SELECTED MONEY MARKET INSTRUMENTS *(cont.)*

INSTRUMENT	DENOMINATIONS	MATURITIES	BASIS	FORM	LIQUIDITY	TAXABILITY
Money market mutual funds —holders of diversified portfolios of short-term, high-grade debt instruments	Some require an initial investment as small as $1000	Your shares can be sold at any time	Net asset value	Registered	Good; provided by the fund itself	Taxed at all levels of government

Accounts Receivable and Inventory Management

*I*n the three previous chapters we developed a general overview of working-capital management and took an in-depth look at the management of cash and marketable securities. In this chapter we will focus on the management of two more working-capital items, accounts receivable and inventory. Here we will find that determining the desired investment in these assets will center around an analysis of marginal benefits and costs. An increase in accounts receivable—that is, additional extension of trade credit—results not only in higher sales but also requires additional financing to support the increased investment in accounts receivable. The costs of credit investigation and collection efforts and the chance of bad debts also are increased. With respect to inventory management, a larger investment in inventory leads to more efficient production and speedier delivery, hence increased sales. However, additional financing is required to support the increase in inventory and in handling and carrying costs.

In studying the management of these current assets, we will first examine accounts receivable management, focusing on its importance, what determines the investment in it, and what the decision variables are and how we determine them. After examining accounts receivable management, we will turn to inventory management, examining its importance and the order quantity and order point problems, which in combination determine the level of investment in inventory.

All firms by their very nature are involved in selling either goods or services. While some of these sales will be for cash, a large portion will involve the use of credit. Whenever a sale is made on credit, it increases the firm's accounts receivable. Thus, the importance of accounts receivable management depends upon the degree to which the firm sells on credit. Table 9-1 lists, for selected industries, the percentage of total assets made up by accounts receivable.

From Table 9-1 we can see that accounts receivable typically comprise about 24 percent of a firm's assets. In effect, when we discuss management of accounts receivable, we are discussing the management of almost one-quarter of the firm's assets. Moreover, since cash flows from a sale cannot be invested until the account is collected, control of receivables takes on added importance; efficient collection determines both profitability and liquidity of the firm.

The size of the investment in accounts receivable is determined by a number of factors. First, the percentage of credit sales to total sales affects the level of accounts receivable held. Although this factor certainly plays a major role in determining the investment in accounts receivable, it generally is not within the control of the financial manager. In essence, the nature of the business tends to determine the blend between credit sales and cash sales. For a large grocery store, sales tend to be made exclusively on a cash basis, while for most construction-lumber supply firms sales are primarily credit. Thus, the nature of the business, and not the decision of the financial manager, tends to determine what proportion of sales are made on credit.

Table 9-1 ACCOUNTS RECEIVABLE AS A PERCENTAGE OF TOTAL ASSETS FOR MAJOR INDUSTRIES

INDUSTRY	ACCOUNTS RECEIVABLE RELATIVE TO TOTAL ASSETS
All industries	24.11%
Motor vehicles and equipment—manufacturing	41.75
General merchandising stores—retail	32.26
Contract construction	31.60
Building materials, hardware, and farm equipment—retail	26.35
Apparel and accessory stores—retail	19.26
Automotive dealers and service stations—retail	17.90
Agricultural, forestry, and fishery	11.35
Transportation services	9.51
Food stores	7.66
Hotels and other lodging places	6.66

SOURCE: Internal Revenue Service, U. S. Treasury Department, *Statistics of Income, 1972, Corporate Income Tax Returns* (Washington, D. C.: Government Printing Office), 1977, pp. 16–20.

ACCOUNTS
RECEIVABLE
MANAGEMENT

Size
of Investment
in Accounts
Receivable

The level of sales is also a factor in determining the size of the investment in accounts receivable. Very simply, the more sales, the greater will be accounts receivable. As the firm experiences seasonal and permanent growth in sales, the level of investment in accounts receivable will naturally increase. Thus, while the level of sales affects the size of the investment in accounts receivable, it is not a decision variable for the financial manager.

The final determinants of the level of investment in accounts receivable are the credit and collection policies—more specifically, the terms of sale, the quality of customer, and collection efforts. The terms of sale specify both the time period during which the customer must pay and the terms; that is, is there a discount for paying early, and if so, how much? The type of customer or credit policy also affects the level of investment in accounts receivable. For example, the acceptance of poorer risks and their subsequent delinquent payments may lead to an increase in accounts receivable. The strength and timing of the collection efforts can affect the period for which past-due accounts remain delinquent, which in turn affects the level of accounts receivable. Collection and credit policy decisions may further affect the level of investment in accounts receivable by causing changes in the sales level and the ratio of credit sales to total sales. However, the three credit and collection policy variables are the only decision variables under the control of the financial manager. Graphically, this situation is shown in Figure 9-1.

TERMS OF SALE—DECISION VARIABLE

The **terms of sale** identify the possible discount for early payment, the discount period, and the total credit period. They are generally stated in the form *a/b* net *c,* indicating that the customer can deduct *a* percent if the account is paid within *b* days; otherwise, the account must be paid within *c* days. Thus, for example, trade credit terms of 2/10 net 30 indicate

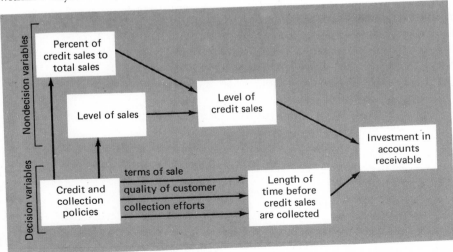

FIGURE 9-1 *Determinants of Investment in Accounts Receivable*

that a 2 percent discount can be taken if the account is paid within 10 days; otherwise, it must be paid within 30 days. What if the customer decides to forgo the discount and not pay until the final payment date? If such a decision is made, the customer has the use of the money for the time period between the discount date and the final payment date. However, failure to take the discount represents a cost to the customer. For instance, if the terms are 2/10 net 30, the annualized opportunity cost of passing up this 2 percent discount in order to withhold payment for an additional 20 days is 36.73 percent. This is determined as follows:

$$\left(\begin{array}{l}\text{annualized opportunity cost} \\ \text{of forgoing the discount}\end{array}\right) = \frac{a}{1-a} \times \frac{360}{c-b} \qquad (9\text{-}1)$$

Substituting the values from the example, we get

$$36.73\% = \frac{.02}{1-.02} \times \frac{360}{30-10} \qquad (9\text{-}2)$$

In industry the typical discount ranges anywhere from one-half percent to 10 percent, while the discount period is generally 10 days and the total credit period varies from 30 to 90 days. Although the terms of credit vary radically from industry to industry, they tend to remain relatively uniform within any particular industry.[1] Moreover, the terms tend to remain relatively constant over time, and they do not appear to be a frequently used decision variable.

TYPE OF CUSTOMER— DECISION VARIABLE

A second decision variable is the firm's **credit policy,** which involves determining the type of customer who is to qualify for trade credit. Quite obviously, several costs are associated with extending credit to lower-quality customers. First, as the probability of customer default increases with the extension of credit to lower-quality customers, it becomes more important to identify which of the possible new customers would be a poor risk. Thus, more time is spent investigating the lower-quality customer, and the costs of credit investigation increase.

Default costs also vary directly with the quality of the customer. As the customer's credit rating declines, the chance that the account will not be paid on time increases. In the extreme case, payment does not occur at all and the account must be written off. Thus, taking on lower-quality customers results in increases in default costs.

Collection costs also increase as the quality of the customer declines. The increase in deliquent accounts will force the firm to spend more time

[1]Theodore N. Beckman and Ronald S. Foster, *Credits and Collections* (New York: McGraw-Hill Book Co., 1969), pp. 697–704.

and money in collecting them. In summary, the decline in customer quality results in increased costs of credit investigation, collection, and default.

In determining whether or not credit should be granted to an individual customer, we are primarily interested in the customer's short-run welfâre. Thus, liquidity ratios, other obligations, and the overall profitability of the firm become the focal point in this analysis. Credit rating services, in particular, Dunn and Bradstreet, provide information on the financial status, operations, and payment history for most firms. Other possible sources of information would include credit bureaus, trade associations, chambers of commerce, competitors, bank references, public financial statements, and, of course, the firm's past relationships with the customer.

COLLECTION EFFORTS— DECISION VARIABLE

The key to maintaining control over the collection of accounts receivable is that the probability of default increases with the age of the account. Thus, control of accounts receivable focuses on the control and elimination of past-due receivables. One common way of evaluating the current situation is **ratio analysis.** By examining the ratio of receivables to sales, receivables to assets, and the amount of bad debts relative to sales over time, the financial manager can determine whether or not receivables are drifting out of control. In addition, an aging of accounts receivable provides a breakdown in both dollars and in percentage terms of the proportion of receivables that are past due. Comparing the current aging of receivables with past data offers further insight into the degree of control that is being maintained over receivables. An example of an **aging account** appears in Table 9-2.

If changes are found in either the ratios or the aging of accounts, the manager should then look for any possible changes in the overall credit policy or laxness in the collection procedures that might have brought on this situation. If changes are found, they should then be reevaluated.

Once the delinquent accounts have been identified, an effort should

Table 9-2 AGING ACCOUNT

AGE OF ACCOUNTS RECEIVABLE (DAYS)	DOLLAR VALUE (IN THOUSANDS)	PERCENT OF TOTAL
0–30	$2340	39%
31–60	1500	25
61–90	1020	17
91–120	720	12
Over 120	420	7
Total	$6000	100%

be made to collect them. For example, past-due letters, called **dunning letters,** should be sent if payment is not received on time, followed by an additional dunning letter in a more serious tone if the account becomes three weeks past due, followed after six weeks by a telephone call. Finally, if the account becomes 12 weeks past due, it might be turned over to a collection agency. Again, a direct tradeoff exists between collection expenses and lost goodwill on one hand and noncollection of accounts on the other. As before, this tradeoff should be seriously evaluated in making the decision.

Thus far, we have discussed the importance and role of accounts receivable in the firm and then examined the determinants of the size of the investment in accounts receivable. Since the credit and collection policies are the only discretionary variables for management, the primary focus has been placed on these determinants. In examining these decision variables, we have merely described their traits. These variables will now be analyzed in a decision-making context, which is termed marginal analysis.

Marginal analysis involves a systematic comparison between the marginal returns and the marginal costs from a change in the discount period, the risk class of customer, or the collection process. Whenever the marginal return from a proposed change in the management of accounts receivable is greater than the marginal costs on the additional investment, the change should be implemented. To illustrate the use of marginal analysis, let us follow through an example of a firm considering extending credit to more risky customers.

Marginal Analysis

Example. Assume that a firm currently has annual sales, all credit, of $8 million and a receivables turnover ratio of six times per year. The current level of bad debt losses is $250,000, and the firm's required rate of return on any new investment in receivables is 20 percent. Further assume that this firm produces only one product, with variable costs equaling 75 percent of the selling price. The company is contemplating a relaxation of its credit policy. The current policy and the expected effects of two proposed policies, X and Y, are compared in Table 9-3.

Determining the marginal profitability from relaxing the credit policy first from the present policy to policy X and then from policy X to policy Y

Table 9-3 EXPECTED EFFECTS OF CREDIT POLICY CHANGES X AND Y

	PRESENT POLICY	POLICY X	POLICY Y
Annual sales (all credit)	$8,000,000	$8,750,000	$9,250,000
Average collection period	2 months	3 months	4 months
Bad debt losses	$250,000	$300,000	$375,000

and comparing this marginal profitability to the required return on the

additional investment in receivables yields the results in Table 9-4.

Examining Table 9-4, we find that the marginal benefit from changing from the present policy to policy X is $137,750. In addition, the required return on the increased investment in accounts receivable, which can be thought of as the marginal cost associated with this change, is $128,125. Thus, since the marginal benefit is $9625 greater than the re-

Table 9-4 MARGINAL ANALYSIS OF RELAXING CREDIT STANDARDS

	PRESENT POLICY	POLICY X	POLICY Y
Annual sales (all credit)	$8,000,000	$8,750,000	$9,250,000
Average collection period	2 months	3 months	4 months
Accounts receivable turnover ratio	6 times	4 times	3 times
Average level of receivables	$1,333,333	$2,187,500	$3,083,333
STEP 1: DETERMINE THE MARGINAL BENEFITS			
Marginal increase in sales (above previous policy)		$750,000	$500,000
Profit on marginal increase in sales (25%)		$187,500	$125,000
Marginal increase in bad debt losses		$50,000	$75,000
Profit on marginal increase in sales (less marginal increase in bad debt loss)		$137,500	$50,000
STEP 2: DETERMINE THE REQUIRED RETURN ON THE MARGINAL INVESTMENT			
Marginal increase in receivables (above previous policy)		$854,167	$895,833
Marginal increase in investment in receivables (above previous policy)[a]		$640,625	$671,875
Required return (20%) on marginal increase in investment in receivables		$128,125	$134,375
STEP 3: COMPARE THE MARGINAL BENEFITS WITH THE REQUIRED RETURN			
Profit on marginal increase in sales (less marginal increase in bad debt loss) less required return (20%) on marginal investment in receivables		$9,375	$-$84,375

[a](Marginal increase in receivables) $\left(\dfrac{\text{variable costs per unit}}{\text{selling price per unit}} \right)$.

quired return (or marginal cost), a change in the credit policy should be made from the current policy to policy X.

With respect to the change from policy X to policy Y, the associated marginal benefit is $50,000. The required rate of return on the increase in accounts receivable or marginal cost associated with this change is $134,375. Thus, since the marginal benefit is $84,375 less than the required return or marginal cost, the credit policy should not be changed from policy X to policy Y.

The logic behind this approach to credit policy is to examine the incremental or marginal benefits, and costs or required returns associated with any change in the credit policy. If the change promises more benefits than costs, the change should be made. If, however, the incremental costs are greater than the benefits, the proposed change should be dropped. Graphically, this logic is shown in Figure 9-2. Under this philosophy investment should continue until marginal costs are equal to marginal revenues, which occurs at credit policy A. This strategy should be used in determining the best values for the accounts receivable decision variables.

INVENTORY MANAGEMENT

Inventory management involves the control of assets being produced to be sold in the normal course of the firm's operations. The general categories of inventory include raw materials inventory, work in process inventory, and finished goods inventory. The importance of inventory management to the firm depends upon the extent of the inventory investment. For

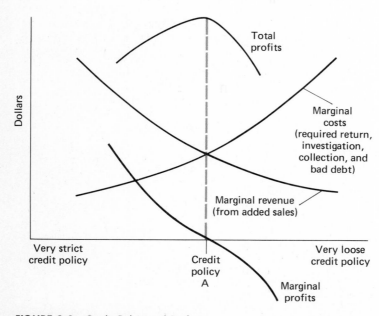

FIGURE 9-2 *Credit Policy and Profits*

an average firm approximately 6.87 percent of all assets are in the form of inventory. However, the percentage varies widely from industry to industry, as can be seen in Table 9-5, and thus the importance of inventory management and control varies from industry to industry also. For example, it is much more important in the automotive dealer and service station trade, where inventories make up 46.50 percent of total assets, than in the hotel business, where the average investment in inventory is only 1.56 percent of total assets.

The purpose of carrying inventories is to uncouple the operations of the firm—that is, to make each function of the business independent of each other function—so that delays or shutdowns in one area no longer affect the production and sale of the final product. Since production shutdowns result in increased costs, and since delays in delivery can lose customers, the management and control of inventory is an important duty of the financial manager.

Actually, the decision-making process with respect to investment in inventory involves a basic tradeoff between risk and return. The risk is that if the level of inventory is too low, the various functions of business are not effectively uncoupled and delays in production and customer delivery can result. The return results because reduced inventory investment saves money. As the size of the inventory increases, the storage and handling costs in addition to the required return on capital invested in inventory will rise. Therefore, as the inventory a firm holds is increased, the risk of running out of inventory is lessened, but the inventory expenses are in-

Table 9-5 INVENTORY AS A PERCENTAGE OF TOTAL ASSETS FOR MAJOR INDUSTRIES

INDUSTRY	INVENTORY RELATIVE TO TOTAL ASSETS
All industries	6.87%
Automotive dealers and service stations—retail	46.50
Building materials, hardware, and farm equipment—retail	40.01
Apparel and accessory stores	39.13
Food stores	31.48
Electrical equipment and supplies	22.92
Contract construction	14.39
Agriculture, forestry, and fishery	14.12
Petroleum refining and related industries	5.79
Eating and drinking places	5.60
Coal mining	3.28
Hotels and other lodging places	1.56

SOURCE: Internal Revenue Service, U. S. Treasury Department, *Statistics of Income, 1972, Corporate Income Tax Returns* (Washington, D.C.: Government Printing Office), 1977, pp. 16–20.

creased. To better illustrate the uncoupling function that inventories perform, we will look at several general types of inventories.

RAW MATERIALS INVENTORY

Raw materials inventory consists of basic materials purchased from other firms to be used in the firm's production operations. These goods may include steel, lumber, petroleum, or manufactured items such as wire, ball bearings, or tires that the firm does not produce itself. Regardless of the specific form the raw materials inventory takes on, all manufacturing firms by definition maintain a raw materials inventory. Its purpose is to uncouple the production function from the purchasing function—that is, to make these two functions independent of each other, so that delays in shipment of raw materials no longer cause production delays. In the event of a delay in shipment, the firm can satisfy its need for raw materials by liquidating its inventory. During the oil embargo of 1973 and the subsequent delays in oil shipments, for example, firms that used petroleum as an input in production and had an adequate supply in their raw materials inventory did not experience the production shutdowns that plagued similar firms with inadequate petroleum inventories.

WORK IN PROCESS INVENTORY

Work in process inventory consists of partially finished goods requiring additional work before they become finished goods. The more complex and longer the production process, the larger will be the investment in work in process inventory. The purpose of work in process inventory is to uncouple the various operations in the production process, so that machine failures and work stoppages in one operation will not affect the other operations. Assume, for example, there are ten different production operations, each one involving the piece of work produced in the previous operation. If the machine performing the first production operation breaks down, a firm with no work in process inventory will have to shut down all ten production operations. Yet, if a firm has such inventory, the remaining nine operations can continue to operate by drawing the input for the second operation from inventory rather than directly from the output of the first operation.

FINISHED GOODS INVENTORY

The **finished goods inventory** consists of goods on which the production has been completed but that are not yet sold. The purpose of a finished goods inventory is to uncouple the production and sales functions, so that it no longer is necessary to produce the good before a sale can occur—sales can be made directly out of inventory. In the auto industry, for example, where periodic strikes are common, if auto dealers did not carry an inventory of cars, sales would virtually cease during a strike period.

STOCK OF CASH

Although we have already discussed cash management at some length in Chapters 7 and 8, it is worthwhile to mention cash again in the light of inventory management. This is because the **stock of cash** carried by a firm is simply a special type of inventory. In terms of uncoupling the various operations of the firm, the purpose of holding a stock of cash is to make the payment of bills independent of the collection of accounts due. When cash is kept on hand, bills can be paid without prior collection of accounts.

The reason we have included cash as a type of inventory is that as we examine and develop inventory economic ordering quantity (EOQ) models, we will see a striking resemblance between the EOQ inventory and EOQ cash model; in fact, except for a minor redefinition of terms, they will be exactly the same.

Inventory Management Techniques

The importance of effective inventory management is directly related to the size of the investment in inventory. Since, on average, approximately 6.87 percent of a firm's assets are tied up in inventory, effective management of these assets is essential to the goal of shareholder wealth maximization. In order to effectively control the investment in inventory, management must solve two problems: the order quantity problem and the order point problem.

THE ORDER QUANTITY PROBLEM

The **order quantity problem** involves determining the optimal order size for an inventory item given its expected usage, carrying costs, and ordering costs. Aside from a change in some of the variable names, it is exactly the same as the inventory model for cash management (EOQ model) presented in Chapter 7.

The EOQ model attempts to determine the order size that will minimize total inventory costs. It assumes that

$$\text{total inventory costs} = \text{total carrying costs} + \text{total ordering costs} \tag{9-3}$$

Assuming that inventory is allowed to fall to zero and then is immediately replenished (this assumption will be lifted when we discuss the order point problem), the average inventory becomes $Q/2$, where Q is inventory order size in units. This can be seen graphically in Figure 9-3.

If the average inventory is $Q/2$ and the carrying cost per unit is C, then carrying costs become:

$$\text{total carrying costs} = (\text{average inventory})(\text{carrying cost per unit}) \tag{9-4}$$

$$= \left(\frac{Q}{2}\right) C \tag{9-5}$$

where Q = the inventory order size in units,

C = carrying costs per unit.

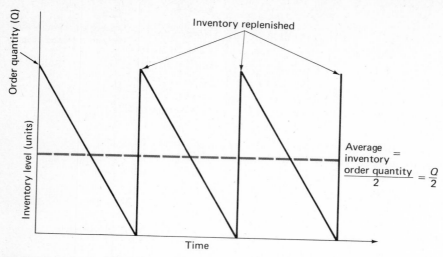

FIGURE 9-3 *Inventory Level and the Replenishment Cycle*

The ordering costs incurred are equal to the ordering costs per order times the number of orders. If we assume total demand over the planning period is S and we order in lot sizes of Q, then S/Q represents the number of orders over the planning period. If the ordering cost per order is O, then

$$\text{total ordering costs} = (\text{number of orders})(\text{ordering cost per order}) \qquad (9\text{-}6)$$

$$= \left(\frac{S}{Q}\right) O \qquad (9\text{-}7)$$

where S = total demand in units over the planning period,

O = ordering cost per order.

Thus, total costs in equation (9-3) become

$$\text{total costs} = \left(\frac{Q}{2}\right) C + \left(\frac{S}{Q}\right) O \qquad (9\text{-}8)$$

Graphically, this equation is illustrated in Figure 9-4.

What we are looking for is the ordering size, Q^*, that provides the minimum total costs. By manipulating equation (9-8), we find that the optimal value of Q—that is, the economic ordering quantity (EOQ)—is[2]

$$Q^* = \sqrt{\frac{2SO}{C}} \qquad (9\text{-}9)$$

The use of the EOQ model can be best illustrated through the use of an example.

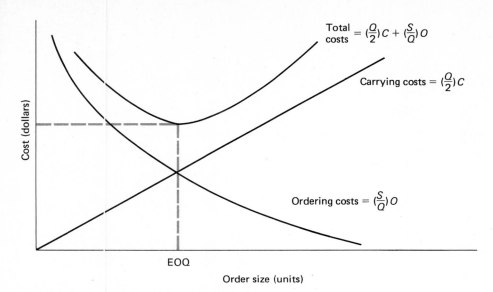

$$\text{Total costs} = \left(\tfrac{Q}{2}\right)C + \left(\tfrac{S}{Q}\right)O$$

$$\text{Carrying costs} = \left(\tfrac{Q}{2}\right)C$$

$$\text{Ordering costs} = \left(\tfrac{S}{Q}\right)O$$

Cost (dollars)

EOQ

Order size (units)

FIGURE 9-4 *Total Cost and EOQ Determination*

Example. Suppose a firm expects total demand (S) for its product over the planning period to be 5000 units, while the ordering cost per order (O) is \$200, and the carrying cost per unit (C) is \$2. Substituting these values into equation (9-9) yields

$$Q^* = \sqrt{\frac{2 \cdot 5000 \cdot 200}{2}} = \sqrt{1,000,000} = 1000 \text{ units}$$

[2]This result can be obtained through calculus.

$$\text{Total cost } (TC) = \left(\frac{Q}{2}\right)C + \left(\frac{S}{Q}\right)O$$

The first derivative with respect to Q defines the slope of the total cost curve. Setting this derivative equal to zero specifies the minimum point (zero slope) on the curve. Thus,

$$\frac{dTC}{dQ} = \frac{C}{2} - \frac{SO}{Q^2} = 0$$

$$Q^2 = \frac{2SO}{C}$$

$$Q^* = \sqrt{\frac{2SO}{C}}$$

To verify that a minimum point is being found, rather than a maximum point where the slope would also equal zero, we check for a positive second derivative:

$$\frac{d^2TC}{dQ^2} = \frac{2SO}{Q^3} \geq 0$$

The second derivative must be positive, since SO and Q can only take on positive values; hence, this is a minimum point.

235

Thus, if this firm orders in 1000-unit lot sizes, it will minimize its total inventory costs.

EXAMINATION OF EOQ ASSUMPTIONS

The major weaknesses of the EOQ model are associated with several of its assumptions, in spite of which, the model tends to yield quite good results. Where its assumptions have been dramatically violated, the EOQ model can generally be easily modified to accommodate the situation. The model's assumptions are as follows:

1. Constant or uniform demand. Although the EOQ model assumes constant demand, demand may vary from day to day. If demand is stochastic—that is, not known in advance—the model must be modified through the inclusion of a safety stock.

2. Constant unit price. The inclusion of variable prices resulting from quantity discounts can be handled quite easily through a modification of the original EOQ model, redefining total costs and solving for the optimum order quantity.

3. Constant carrying costs. Unit carrying costs may vary substantially as the size of the inventory rises, perhaps decreasing because of economies of scale or storage efficiency or increasing as storage space runs out and new warehouses have to be rented. This situation can be handled through a modification in the original model similar to the one used for variable unit price.

4. Constant ordering costs. While this assumption is generally valid, its violation can be accommodated by modifying the original EOQ model in a manner similar to the one used for variable unit price.

5. Instantaneous delivery. If delivery is not instantaneous, which is generally the case, the original EOQ model must be modified through the inclusion of a safety stock.

6. Independent orders. If multiple orders result in cost savings by reducing paperwork and transportation cost, the original EOQ model must be further modified. While this modification is somewhat complicated, special EOQ models have been developed to deal with it.[3]

These assumptions have been pointed out to illustrate the limitations of the basic EOQ model and the ways in which it can easily be modified to compensate for them. Moreover, an understanding of the limitations and assumptions of the EOQ model will provide the financial manager with a strong base for making inventory decisions.

The Order Point Problem

The two most limiting assumptions—those of constant or uniform demand and instantaneous delivery—are dealt with through the inclusion of safety stock. The decision on how much safety stock to hold is generally referred to as the **order point problem;** that is, how low should inventory be depleted before it is reordered?

Two factors go into the determination of the appropriate order point: (1) the procurement or delivery time stock and (2) the safety stock desired.

[3]For example, R. J. Tersire, *Material Management and Inventory Control* (New York: Elsevier-North Holland, 1976).

The inclusion of these stocks is illustrated graphically in Figure 9-5. We observe that the order point problem can be decomposed into its two components, the **delivery time stock,** that is, the inventory needed between the order date and the receipt of the inventory ordered, and the **safety stock,** that is, the inventory held to accommodate any unusually large and unexpected usage during the delivery time. Thus, the order point is reached when inventory falls to a level equal to the delivery time stock plus the safety stock.

In general, several factors simultaneously determine how much delivery time stock and safety stock should be held. First, the efficiency of the replenishment system affects how much delivery time stock is needed. Since the delivery time stock is the expected inventory usage between ordering and receiving inventory, efficient replenishment of inventory would reduce the need for delivery time stock.

The uncertainty surrounding both the delivery time and the demand for the product affects the level of safety stock needed. The more certain the patterns of these inflows and outflows from the inventory, the less safety stock required. In effect, if these inflows and outflows are highly predictable, then there is little chance of any stockout occurring. However, if they are unpredictable, it becomes necessary to carry additional safety stock to prevent unexpected stockouts.

The safety margin desired also affects the level of safety stock held. If it is a costly experience to run out of inventory, then the safety stock held will be larger than it would be otherwise. If running out of inventory and the subsequent delay in supplying customers results in strong customer dissatisfaction and the possibility of lost future sales from that customer, then additional safety stock will be carried. A third determinant is the cost of carrying additional inventory, in terms of both the handling and storage costs and the opportunity cost associated with the investment in additional inventory. Very simply, the greater the costs, the smaller the safety stock.

In summary, the determination of the level of safety stock involves a

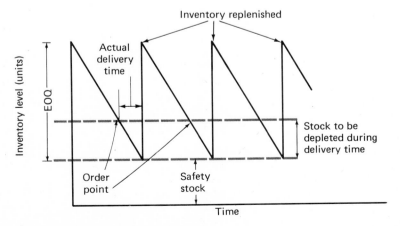

FIGURE 9-5 *Order Point Determination*

basic tradeoff between the risk of stockout, resulting in possible customer dissatisfaction and lost sales, and the increased costs associated with carrying additional inventory.

SUMMARY

The size of the investment in accounts receivable depends upon three factors: the percentage of credit sales to total sales, the level of sales and the credit and collection policies. However, only the credit and collection policies are decision variables open to the financial manager. The policies that the financial manager has control over include the terms of sale, the quality of customer, and the collection efforts. The proper approach in making these policy decisions is through the use of marginal analysis, where the marginal returns from changes in the discount period, the risk class of customer, or the collection process are compared to the marginal costs incurred, including the required return on additional investment.

While the typical firm has less assets tied up in inventory (6.87%) than it does in accounts receivable (24.11%), inventory management and control is still an important function of the financial manager. The purpose of holding inventory is to make each function of the business independent of the other functions—that is, to uncouple the firm's operations. The primary inventory management techniques involve questions of how much inventory should be ordered and when the order should be placed. The answers directly determine the average level of investment in inventory. The EOQ model was employed in answering the first of these questions. This model attempts to calculate the order size that minimizes the sum of the inventory carrying and ordering costs. Then we examined the order point problem, attempting to determine how low inventory should be allowed to drop before it is reordered. The order point was concluded to be reached when the inventory had fallen to a level equal to the delivery time stock plus the safety stock. The determinants of the level of safety stock involve a direct tradeoff between the risk of running out of inventory, thereby engendering customer dissatisfaction, and the increased costs associated with carrying additional inventory.

STUDY QUESTIONS

9-1. What factors determine the size of the investment a firm makes in accounts receivable? Which of these factors are under the control of the financial manager?

9-2. What do the following trade credit terms mean?
(a) 1/20 net 50.   (b) 2/30 net 60.
(c) net 30.   (d) 2/10, 1/30 net 60.

9-3. What is the purpose of the use of an aging account in the control of accounts receivable? Can this same function be performed through ratio analysis? Why or why not?

9-4. If a credit manager experienced no bad debt losses over the past year, would this be an indication of proper credit management? Why or why not?

9-5. What are the risk-return tradeoffs associated with adopting a more liberal trade credit policy?

9-6. Explain the purpose of marginal analysis.

9-7. What is the purpose of holding inventory? Name several types of inventory and describe their purpose.

9-8. Can cash be considered a special type of inventory? If so, what functions does it attempt to uncouple?

9-9. In order to effectively control investment in inventory, what two questions must be answered?

9-10. What are the major assumptions made by the EOQ model?

9-11. What are the risk-return tradeoffs associated with inventory management?

STUDY
PROBLEMS

9-1. Determine the effective annualized cost of forgoing the trade credit discount on the following terms:
(a) 1/10 net 20.   (b) 2/10 net 30.
(c) 3/10 net 30.   (d) 3/10 net 60.
(e) 3/10 net 90.   (f) 5/10 net 60.

9-2. The M. Woodson Corporation is considering relaxing its current credit policy and is in the process of evaluating two proposed policies. Currently the firm has annual sales (all credit) of $5 million and a receivable turnover ratio of 4 times per year. The current level of bad debt losses is $450,000, and the firm's required rate of return on investmznt in new receivables is 25 percent. Woodson produces sports equipment on which the variable costs are 70 percent of the selling price. Given the following information, should they adopt either of the two proposed policies?

	PRESENT POLICY	POLICY 1	POLICY 2
Annual sales (all credit)	$5,000,000	$6,000,000	$6,750,000
Receivables turnover ratio	4 times	3 times	2.4 times
Bad debt losses	$450,000	$600,000	$750,000

9-3. The B. Carter Corporation is considering several major changes in its credit policy. Carter is a major manufacturer of sportswear on which 80 percent of the selling price is variable costs. For any new investments in receivables, the firm would require a return of 30 percent. Given the following information, which policy or policies should Carter adopt?

	PRESENT POLICY	POLICY 1	POLICY 2	POLICY 3
Annual sales (all credit)	$11,000,000	$12,500,000	$13,500,000	$14,250,000
Average collection period	1.5 months	1.7143 months	2.0 months	2.4 months
Bad debt losses	$300,000	$350,000	$450,000	$575,000

9-4. The W. Radford Company currently has annual sales of $2.0 million. All annual sales are on credit, and the credit terms are 30 days. Average collection period has been running 30 days. The company is studying the possibility of relaxing credit terms, which would result in the following estimates: (assume a 360-day year):

CREDIT POLICY	BAD DEBT LOSSES	AVERAGE COLLECTION PERIOD (IN DAYS)	ANNUAL (CREDIT) SALES
1	$ 75,000	40	$2,500,000
2	$100,000	60	$2,700,000
3	$125,000	90	$3,000,000
4	$140,000	120	$3,200,000

Costs are as follows: fixed costs, $250,000; variable costs per unit are 80 percent. Required rate of return on new investment in receivables is 20 percent. Bad debt losses are presently $50,000. Determine which policy Radford should adopt, if any.

9-5. Assuming a 360-day year, calculate what the average investment in inventory would be for a firm, given the following information in each case.
   (a) The firm has sales of $600,000, a gross profit margin of 10 percent, and an inventory turnover rate of 6.
   (b) The firm has a cost of goods sold figure of $480,000 and an average age of inventory of 40 days.
   (c) The firm has a cost of goods sold figure of $1,150,000 and an inventory turnover rate of 5.
   (d) The firm has a sales figure of $25,000,000, a gross profit margin of 14 percent, and an average age of inventory of 45 days.

9-6. A downtown bookstore is trying to determine the optimal order quantity for a popular novel just printed in paperback. The store feels that the book will sell at four times its hardback figures. It would therefore sell approximately 3000 copies in the next year at a price of $1.50. The store buys the book at a wholesale figure of $1. Costs for carrying the book are estimated at $.10 a copy per year, and it costs $10 to order more books.
   (a) Determine what the economic order quantity would be.
   (b) What would the total costs be for ordering the books one, four, five, 10, and 15 times a year?
   (c) What questionable assumptions are being made by the EOQ model?

9-7. The local hamburger fast-food restaurant purchases 20,000 boxes of hamburger rolls every month. Order costs are $50 an order, and it costs $.25 a box for storage.
   (a) What is the optimal order quantity of hamburger rolls for this restaurant?
   (b) What questionable assumptions are being made by the EOQ model?

9-8. A local car manufacturing plant has a $75 per-unit per-year carrying cost

on a certain item in inventory. This item is used at a rate of 50,000 per year. Ordering costs are $500 per order.
(a) What is the economic order quantity for this item?
(b) What are the annual inventory costs for this firm if it orders in this quantity?

AMMER, DEAN S., "Materials Management as a Profit Center," *Harvard Business Review*, 47 (January–February 1969), 72–89.

BERANEK, WILLIAM, "Financial Implications of Lot-Size Inventory Models," *Harvard Business Review*, 47 (January–February 1969), 72–90.

——— , *Working Capital Management*. Belmont, Calif.: Wadsworth, 1966.

BROSKY, JOHN J., *The Implicit Cost of Trade Credit and Theory of Optimal Terms of Sale*. New York: Credit Research Foundation, 1969.

BUFFA, ELWOOD S., *Modern Production Management*, 5th ed., chap. 11. Santa Barbara: John Wiley & Sons, 1977.

GREER, CARL C., "The Optimal Credit Acceptance Policy," *Journal of Financial and Quantitative Analysis*, 2 (December 1967), 399–415.

HERBST, ANTHONY F., "Some Empirical Evidence on the Determinants of Trade Credit at the Industry Level of Aggregation," *Journal of Financial and Quantitative Analysis*, 9 (June 1974), 377–94.

HILLIER, FREDERICK S., and GERALD J. LIEBERMAN, *Introduction to Operations Research*, chap. 11. San Francisco: Holden-Day, Inc., 1974.

LANE, SYLVIA, "Submarginal Credit Risk Classification," *Journal of Financial and Quantitative Analysis*, 7 (January 1972), 1379–85.

MAO, JAMES C. T., "Controlling Risk in Accounts Receivable Management," *Journal of Business Finance & Accounting*, 1 (Autumn 1974), 395–403.

MARRAH, GEORGE G., "Managing Receivables," *Financial Executive*, 38 (July 1970), 40–44.

MEHTA, DILEEP, "The Formulation of Credit Policy Models," *Management Science*, 15 (October 1968), 30–50.

——— , *Working Capital Management*. Englewood Cliffs, N.J.: Prentice-Hall, Inc., 1974.

SCHIFF, MICHAEL, "Credit and Inventory Management," *Financial Executive*, 40 (November 1972), 28–33.

SMITH, DAVID E., *Quantitative Business Analysis*, chap. 14 and 15. Santa Barbara: John Wiley & Sons, 1977.

SMITH, KEITH V., *Management of Working Capital*. New York: West Publishing, 1974.

SNYDER, ARTHUR, "Principles of Inventory Management," *Financial Executive*, 32 (April 1964), 16–19.

SOLDOFSKY, ROBERT M., "A Model for Accounts Receivable Management," *N.A.A. Bulletin*, January 1966, 55–58.

WELSHANS, MERLE T., "Using Credit for Profit Making," *Harvard Business Review*, 45 (January–February 1967), 141–56.

WRIGHTSMAN, DWAYNE, "Optimal Credit Terms for Accounts Receivable," *Quarterly Review of Economics and Business*, 9 (Summer 1969), 59–66.

Short-Term Financing

*T*his chapter is the first of four which discusses sources of financing. For convenience of exposition we will categorize all those sources of financing which must be repaid within one year as short-term, those which must be repaid in one to five years are intermediate term and all those sources with maturities longer than five years are classified long-term. Intermediate term sources are discussed in Chapter 19 in conjunction with financial leases while long term sources are presented in Chapters 20 and 21.

There are two major issues involved in managing the firm's use of short-term financing: (1) How much short-term financing should the firm use? and (2) What specific sources of short-term financing should be selected? Chapter 6 used the *hedging principle* of working capital management to answer the first of these questions. Basically, that involved an attempt to match temporary needs for funds with short-term sources of financing and permanent needs with long-term sources.[1] The objective of this chapter will be to answer the second of the above questions. That is, "How should the financial manager select a source of short-term credit?"

[1]Temporary needs for funds arise in response to the need for temporary assets. These include current assets that the firm does not plan to hold throughout the indefinite future. Permanent needs for funds arise in conjunction with the need for permanent assets. These assets consist of fixed assets plus the firm's minimum level of investment in current assets. Thus, when discussing working-capital management we abandon the current-fixed asset classification in favor of the more useful concept of temporary and permanent assets.

In general there are three basic factors that should be considered in selecting a source of short-term credit: (1) the effective cost of credit, (2) the availability of credit in the amount needed and for the period of time when financing is required, and (3) the influence of the use of a particular credit source on the cost and availability of other sources. We discuss the problem of estimating the cost of short-term credit before introducing the various sources of credit as the procedure used is the same for all. The second and third factors listed above are each discussed as they pertain to the individual sources of short-term credit.

The procedure used in estimating the cost of short-term credit is a very simple one and relies on the basic interest equation:

$$\text{interest} = \text{principal} \times \text{rate} \times \text{time} \qquad (10\text{-}1)$$

ESTIMATING SHORT-TERM CREDIT COST

where *interest* is the dollar amount of interest on a *principal* that is borrowed at some annual *rate* for a fraction of a year (represented by *time*). For example, a six-month loan for $1000 at 8 percent interest would require interest payments of $40:

$$\text{interest} = \$100 \times .08 \times \tfrac{1}{2} = \$40.$$

The problem faced in assessing the cost of a source of short-term financing, however, generally involves estimating the annual effective rate (RATE) where the interest amount, the principal sum, and the time for which financing will be needed are known. Thus, solving the basic interest equation for RATE produces[2]

$$\text{RATE} = \frac{\text{interest}}{\text{principal} \times \text{time}}$$

or $\qquad\qquad\qquad\qquad\qquad\qquad\qquad\qquad\qquad$ (10-2)

$$\text{RATE} = \frac{\text{interest}}{\text{principal}} \times \frac{1}{\text{time}}$$

Example. The SKC Corporation plans to borrow $1000 for a 90-day period. At maturity the firm will repay the $1000 principal amount plus $30 in interest. The effective annual rate of interest for the loan can be estimated using the RATE equation as follows:

$$\text{RATE} = \frac{\$30}{\$1000} \times \frac{1}{90/360}$$

$$= .03 \times \frac{360}{90} = .12 \text{ or } 12 \text{ percent}$$

[2]It will be recalled that a similar expression was used in Chapter 9 to estimate the effective cost of passing up discounts on trade credit.

The effective annual cost of funds provided by the loan is therefore 12 percent.[3]

This simple equation for RATE forms the basis for estimating the effective cost of any source of short-term financing. The remainder of the chapter discusses briefly each of the sources of short-term financing.

Short-term credit sources can be classified into two basic groups: unsecured and secured. **Unsecured** funds include all those sources that have as their security only the lender's faith in the ability of the borrower to repay the funds when due. There are three major sources of unsecured short-term credit: trade credit, unsecured bank loans, and commercial paper. **Secured** funds involve the pledge of specific assets as collateral in the event the borrower defaults in payment of principal or interest. The principal suppliers of secured credit include commercial banks, finance companies, and factors and the primary sources of collateral include accounts receivable and inventories.

Trade credit provides one of the most flexible sources of financing available to the firm. To arrange for credit the firm need only place an order with one of its suppliers. The supplier checks the firm's credit and, if it is good, sends the merchandise. The purchasing firm then pays for the goods in accordance with supplier's credit terms.

CREDIT TERMS AND CASH DISCOUNTS

Very often the credit terms offered with trade credit involve a cash discount for early payment. For example, a supplier might offer terms of 2/10, net 30, which means that a 2 percent discount is offered for payment within 10 days or the full amount is due in 30 days. Thus, a 2 percent penalty is involved for not paying within 10 days. The effective annual cost of not taking the cash discount can be quite severe. Using a $1 invoice amount, the effective cost of passing up the discount period using the above credit terms and our RATE equation can be estimated:

$$\text{RATE} = \frac{\$.02}{\$.98} \times \frac{1}{20/360} = .3673 \text{ or } 36.73\%$$

[3]Compound interest was not considered in the simple RATE calculation. To consider the influence of compounding we can use the following equation:

$$\text{RATE} = (1 + \frac{r}{m})^m - 1 \qquad (10\text{-}3)$$

where r is the nominal rate of interest per year (12 percent in the above example) and m is the number of compounding periods within a year [1/TIME = 1/(90/360) = 4 in the example above.] Thus, the effective rate of interest on the example problem, considering compounding, is

$$\text{RATE} = (1 + \frac{12}{4})^4 - 1 = .126$$

The effect of compounding is to raise the effective cost of short-term credit. Since the differences between the two methods for periods less than one year are usually small, the simple interest version of RATE discussed above will be used.

Note that the 2 percent cash discount is the *interest* cost of extending the payment period an *additional* 20 days. Note also that the principal amount of the credit is $.98. This amount constitutes the full principal amount as of the tenth day of the credit period, after which time the cash discount is lost. The effective cost of passing up the 2 percent discount for 20 days is quite expensive, 36.73%. Furthermore, once the discount period has passed there is no reason to pay before the final due date (the thirtieth day). Table 10-1 lists the effective annual cost of a number of alternative credit terms. Note that the cost of trade credit varies directly with the size of the cash discount and inversely with the length of time between the end of the discount period and the final due date.

STRETCHING ON TRADE CREDIT

Firms utilizing trade credit sometimes engage in *stretching* of their trade accounts. This practice involves not paying within the prescribed credit period. For example, a firm might purchase materials under credit terms of 3/10, net 60; however, when faced with a shortage of cash the firm might extend payment to the eightieth day. Continued violation of trade terms could eventually lead to a loss of credit. However, for short periods, and at infrequent intervals, stretching offers the firm a potentially useful source of short-term credit.

ADVANTAGES OF TRADE CREDIT

As a source of short-term financing, trade credit has a number of advantages. First, trade credit is easily and conveniently obtained as a normal part of the firm's operations. Second, no formal agreements are generally involved in extending credit. Furthermore, the amount of credit extended expands and contracts with the needs of the firm; this is the reason for its earlier classification as a spontaneous source of financing (Chapter 6).

Unsecured Sources: Bank Credit

Commercial banks provide unsecured short-term credit in two basic forms: lines of credit and transaction loans (notes payable). Maturities of both types of loans are usually one year or less, with rates of interest depending on the creditworthiness of the borrower and the level of interest rates in the economy as a whole.

Table 10-1 EFFECTIVE RATES OF INTEREST ON SELECTED TRADE CREDIT TERMS

CREDIT TERMS	EFFECTIVE RATE
2/10, net 60	14.69%
2/10, net 90	9.18%
3/20, net 60	27.84%
6/10, net 90	28.72%

A **line of credit** is generally an informal agreement or understanding between the borrower and the bank as to the maximum amount of credit which the bank will provide the borrower at any one time. Under this type of agreement there is no *legal* commitment on the part of the bank to provide the stated credit. In a **revolving credit agreement,** which is a variant of this form of financing, such a legal obligation is involved. The line of credit agreement generally covers a period of one year corresponding to the borrower's *fiscal* year. Thus, if the borrower is on a July 31 fiscal year, its lines of credit will be based on the same annual period.

Credit Terms. Lines of credit generally do not involve fixed rates of interest but state that credit will be extended *at $\frac{1}{2}$ percent over prime* or some other spread over the bank's prime rate.[4] Furthermore, the agreement usually does not *spell out* the specific use that will be made of the funds

---

[4]The "prime rate of interest" represents the rate that a bank charges its most creditworthy borrowers.

```
                        City National Bank
                          Snook, Texas


                               July 14, 19XX



        Ms. Rebecca Swank
        Vice President and Treasurer
        Nuland Manufacturing Company
        Bryan, Texas

        Dear Ms. Swank:

        Following an analysis of your request, we have decided to extend
        to you a line of credit for working capital purposes in the amount
        of $300,000.  The credit is extended for your current fiscal year
        ending July 31, 19XX.  Borrowings under this line will be at our
        prime rate prevailing at the time.

        This credit is subject only to maintaining the firm's financial
        position.

                               Sincerely,



                               Francis L. Prince
                               Executive Vice President
```

FIGURE 10-1   *Letter of Agreement to Extend a Line of Credit*

beyond some general statement, such as *for working-capital purposes.* Figure 10-1 shows an example letter of agreement to extend a line of credit.

Lines of credit usually require that the borrower maintain a minimum balance in the bank throughout the loan period. This **compensating balance** increases the effective cost of the loan to the borrower (unless such a deposit is ordinarily maintained in the bank).

The effective cost of short-term bank credit can be estimated using the RATE equation. Consider the following example:

Example. M&M Beverage Company has a $300,000 line of credit which requires a 10 percent compensating balance. The rate paid on the loan is 6 percent per annum, $200,000 is borrowed for a six-month period, and the firm does not, at present, have a deposit with the lending bank. The dollar cost of the loan includes the interest expense and, in addition, the cost of maintaining the 10 percent compensating balance. To accommodate the cost of the compensating balance requirement assume that the added funds will have to be borrowed and simply left idle in the firm's checking account. Thus, the amount actually borrowed (B) will be larger than the needed $200,000. In fact, the needed $200,000 will comprise 90 percent of the total borrowed funds, hence $.90B = \$200,000$ such that $B = \$222,222$. The effective annual cost of credit therefore is

$$\text{RATE} = \frac{\$6666.67}{\$200,000} \times \frac{1}{180/360} = 6.67 \text{ percent}$$

Note that interest is paid on a $222,222 loan ($222,222 \times .06 \times 1/2$) of which only $200,000 is available for use by the firm.[5] If the firm normally maintains at least $20,000 (or 10 percent of the borrowed funds) in a demand deposit with the lending bank, then the cost of the credit is

$$\text{RATE} = \frac{\$6000}{\$200,000} \times \frac{1}{180/360} = 6 \text{ percent}$$

TRANSACTION LOANS

Still another form of unsecured short-term bank credit can be obtained in the form of **transaction loans.** Here the loan is made for a specific purpose. This is the type of loan that most individuals associate with bank credit. The loan is obtained by signing a promissory note similar to the one shown in Figure 10-2.

Unsecured transaction loans are very similar to a line of credit with

[5]Although technically incorrect, the same answer could have been obtained by assuming a total loan of $200,000, of which only 90 percent or $180,000 was available for use by the firm; that is,

$$\text{RATE} = \frac{\$6000}{\$180,000} \times \frac{1}{180/360} = 6.67 \text{ percent}$$

January 30 , 19 78

ON DEMAND, or if no demand is made, then ----180 days---- after date, without grace, for value received, I, we, and each of us, as principals, promise to pay to the order of THIRD NATIONAL BANK at Bryan, Texas the sum of --------------FIVE THOUSAND AND NO/100 -------------- DOLLARS, including a/with a **FINANCE CHARGE** of 221.92 which is an **ANNUAL PERCENTAGE RATE** of -9- % from 1/30/78 until maturity, and if not then paid, at the rate of 10% per annum until paid.

In the event of default in the payment of this note, when due, or in the performance of any agreement contained in the security agreement if any is taken to secure payment hereof, or in the event the holder deems itself insecure, then the holder of this note shall have the option, without demand or notice, to declare the principal and interest at once due and payable and to exercise any and all other rights or remedies provided in this note and in the security agreement, if any, including the right to set off against this note and all other liabilities of the undersigned to the holder, all money or other property in its possession held for or owel to the undersigned.

Each maker, surety, endorser, and guarantor of this note hereby waives presentment for payment or acceptance, notice of non-payment or dishonor, protest, notice of protest, and diligence in the collection hereof or in filing suit hereon and agrees that liability for the payment hereof shall not be affected or impaired by any release of or change in the security, if any, or by any extension in the time for payment; and further agrees to pay all costs and expenses of collection incurred by the holder, and if this note is placed in the hands of an attorney for collection after maturity, or is collected by legal proceedings of any kind, to pay a reasonable attorney's fee, which shall not in any event be less than the sum of $50.00 and shall bear interest at the rate of 10% per annum from the date of its accrual.

Payment of this note is secured by all money or other property of the undersigned now or at any time hereafter in the possession of the holder in any capacity and also by_____

INSURANCE AGREEMENT

CREDIT LIFE INSURANCE is not required to obtain this loan. No charge is made for credit insurance and no credit insurance is provided unless the borrower checks the appropriate statement below:

(a) The cost for Credit Life Insurance alone will be $_____ for the term of credit.

☐ I desire Credit Life Insurance.
☐ I do not desire Credit Life Insurance.

1-30-78 _David Marcus_
Date — Signature for Insurance Acknowledgment
Address 36 Nine Street, Bryan, Texas 77800
Phone: Bus. 713-895-2519 Res. 713-693-1707
Age_____ Filing Fee_____

XYZ CORPORATION
By: _David Marcus_

FIGURE 10-2 *Example Short-Term Bank Note*

regard to their cost, term to maturity, and compensating balance requirements. In both instances commercial banks often require that the borrower *clean up* its short-term loans for a 30- to 45-day period during the year. This means, very simply, that the borrower must be free of any bank debt for the stated period. The purpose of such a requirement is to insure that the borrower is not using short-term bank credit to finance a part of its permanent needs for funds.

Only the largest and most creditworthy companies are able to use **commercial paper,** which is simply a short-term *promise to pay* that is sold in the market for short-term debt securities.[6]

Unsecured Sources: Commercial Paper

CREDIT TERMS

The maturity of this credit source is generally six months or less, although some issues carry 270-day maturities. The interest rate on commercial paper is generally slightly lower (one-half to one percent) than the prime rate on commercial bank loans.

New issues of commercial paper are either directly placed (sold by the issuing firm directly to the investing public) or dealer placed. Dealer placement involves the use of a commercial paper dealer, who sells the issue for the issuing firm. Many of the major finance companies, such as General Motors Acceptance Corporation, place their commercial paper directly. The volume of direct versus dealer placements is roughly four to one in favor of direct placements. Dealers are used primarily by industrial firms that make only infrequent use of the commercial paper market or

[6]A limited discussion of commercial paper is presented here as the topic was discussed in detail in Chapter 8.

that, owing to their small size, would have difficulty placing the issue without the help of a dealer.

COMMERCIAL PAPER AS A SOURCE OF SHORT-TERM CREDIT

A number of advantages accrue to the user of commercial paper:

1. *Interest rate.* Commercial paper rates are generally lower than rates on bank loans and comparable sources of short-term financing. Figure 10-3 contains historical rates of interest on short-term bank credit and commercial paper spanning the fifteen month period ended with April 1978.
2. *Compensating balance requirement.* No minimum balance requirements are associated with commercial paper. However, issuing firms usually find it desirable to maintain lines of credit agreements sufficient to *back up* their short-term financing needs in the event that a new issue of commercial paper cannot be sold or an outstanding issue cannot be repaid when due.
3. *Amount of credit.* Commercial paper offers the firm with very large credit needs a single source for all its short-term financing. To obtain the necessary funds from a commercial bank might require dealing with a number of banks, owing to the loan restrictions placed on the banks by the regulatory authorities.[7]
4. *Prestige.* Since it is widely recognized that only the most creditworthy borrowers have access to the commercial paper market, its use signifies a firm's credit status.

Using commercial paper for short-term financing, however, involves a very important *risk.* That is, the commercial paper market is highly impersonal and denies even the most creditworthy borrower any flexibility in terms of repayment. When bank credit is used, the borrower has someone with whom he can work out any temporary difficulties he might encounter in meeting a loan deadline. This flexibility simply does not exist for the user of commercial paper.

Secured sources of short-term credit have certain assets of the firm pledged as collateral to secure the loan. Thus, upon default of the loan agreement the lender has first claim to the pledged assets in addition to his claim as a general creditor of the firm. Hence the secured credit agreement offers an added margin of safety to the lender.

Generally a firm's receivables are among its most liquid assets. For this reason they are considered by many lenders to be prime collateral for a secured loan. Two basic procedures can be used in arranging for financing based on receivables: pledging and factoring.

Secured Sources: Accounts Receivable Loans

PLEDGING ACCOUNTS RECEIVABLE

Under the **pledging** arrangement the borrower simply pledges accounts receivable as collateral for a loan obtained from either a commercial bank or a finance company. The amount of the loan is stated as a percent of

[7]Member banks of the Federal Reserve System are limited to 10 percent of their total capital, surplus, and undivided profits when making loans to a single borrower.

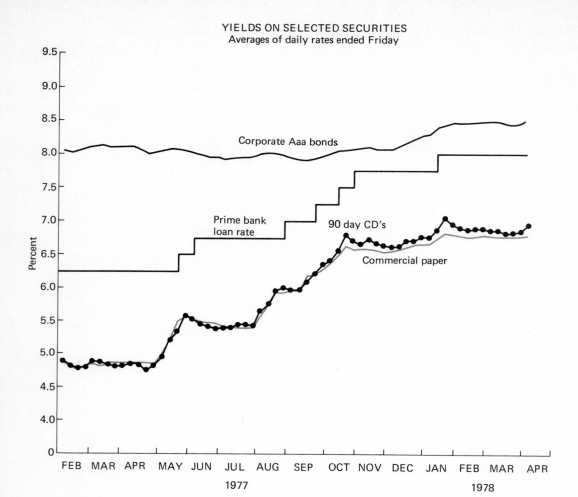

YIELDS ON SELECTED SECURITIES
Averages of daily rates ended Friday

Latest data plotted are averages of rates available for the week ending: April 7, 1978

Data provided by the St. Louis Federal Reserve Bank.

Legend:

Corporate Aaa Bonds: Long-term debt of the most credit worthy firms. (Discussed in Chapter 20.)

Prime Bank Loan Rate: Rate of interest charged to the most creditworthy borrowers on short-term loans.

90-Day CD's: Certificates of deposit carrying a 90-day maturity. (Discussed in Chapter 8.)

FIGURE 10-3 *Historical Rates of Interest on Short-Term Bank Credit and Commercial Paper*

the face value of the receivables pledged. If the firm provides the lender
with a **general line** on its receivables, then all of the borrower's accounts are pledged as security for the loan. This method of pledging is simple and inexpensive. However, since the lender has no control over the quality of the receivables being pledged, he will set the maximum loan at a relatively low percent of the total face value of the accounts, generally ranging downward from a maximum of around 75 percent.

Still another approach to pledging involves the borrower's presenting specific invoices to the lender as collateral for a loan. This method is somewhat more expensive in that the lender must assess the creditworthiness of each individual account pledged; however, given this added knowledge he will be willing to increase the loan as a percent of the face value of the invoices. In this case the loan might reach as high as 85 or 90 percent of the face value of the pledged receivables.

Credit Terms.   Accounts receivable loans generally carry an interest rate 2 to 5 percent higher than the bank's prime lending rate. Finance companies charge an even higher rate. In addition, the lender will usually charge a handling fee stated as a percent of the face value of the receivables processed. This fee may be as much as 1 to 2 percent of the face value.

Example.   The A. B. Good Company sells electrical supplies to building contractors on terms of net 60. The firm's average monthly sales are $100,000; thus, given the firm's two month credit terms, its average receivables balance is $200,000. The firm pledges all of its receivables to a local bank, which in turn advances up to 70 percent of the face value of the receivables at 3 percent over prime and with a 1 percent processing charge on all receivables pledged. A. B. Good follows a practice of borrowing the maximum amount possible, and the current prime rate is 5 percent.

The effective cost of using this source of financing for a full year is computed as follows:

$$\text{RATE} = \frac{\$11,200 + \$12,000}{\$140,000} \times \frac{1}{360/360} = 16.57 \text{ percent}$$

where the total dollar cost of the loan consists of both the annual interest expense ($.08 \times .70 \times \$200,000 = \$11,200$) and the annual processing fee ($.01 \times \$100,000 \times 12$ months $= \$12,000$.) The amount of credit extended is $.70 \times \$200,000 = \$140,000$.

One added point should be made about the cost of loans secured by the pledge of accounts receivable. The lender, in addition to making advances or loans, may be providing certain credit services for the borrower. For example, the lender may provide billing and collection services. The value of these services should *not* be considered a part of the cost of credit. In the preceding example A. B. Good Company may save credit department expenses of $10,000 per year by pledging all its accounts and letting the lender provide those services. In this case the cost of short-term credit is only

$$\text{RATE} = \frac{\$11{,}200 + \$12{,}000 - \$10{,}000}{\$140{,}000} \times \frac{1}{360/360} = 9.43 \text{ percent}$$

Advantages and Disadvantages of Pledging. The primary advantage of pledging as a source of short-term credit relates to the flexibility it provides the borrower. Financing is available on a continuous basis. As new accounts are created through credit sales, they provide the collateral for the financing of new production. Furthermore, the lender may provide credit services that eliminate or at least reduce the need for similar services within the firm. The primary disadvantage associated with this method of financing is its cost, which can be relatively high compared to other sources of short-term credit owing to the level of the interest rate charged on loans and the processing fee on pledged accounts.

FACTORING ACCOUNTS RECEIVABLE

Factoring receivables involves the outright sale of a firm's accounts to a factor.[8] The factor, in turn, bears the risk of collection and, for a fee, services the accounts. The fee is stated as a percent of the face value of all receivables factored (usually from 1 to 3 percent). In addition, the factor provides advances or loans to the borrower (based on the accounts receivable) on which interest is charged for the term of the advance. The effective cost of factoring is estimated the same way that the cost of pledging was estimated earlier.

Inventory loans provide a second source of security for short-term secured credit. The amount of the loan that can be obtained depends on both the marketability and perishability of the inventory. Some items, such as raw materials (grains, oil, lumber, and chemicals), serve as excellent sources of collateral, since they can be easily liquidated. Other items, such as work in process inventories, provide very poor collateral, owing to their lack of marketability.

*Secured Sources:
Inventory Loans*

There are several methods by which inventory can be used to secure short-term financing. These include a *floating* or *blanket lien*, *chattel mortgage*, *field warehouse receipt*, and *terminal warehouse receipt*.

FLOATING LIEN AGREEMENT

Under a **floating lien** agreement the borrower gives the lender a lien against all his inventories. This provides the simplest but least secure form of inventory collateral. The borrowing firm maintains full control of

[8]A **factor** is a financial institution that acquires the receivables of other firms. The factor may be a commercial finance company that engages solely in the factoring of receivables (known as an **old line factor**) or it may be a commercial bank.

the inventories and continues to sell and replace them as it sees fit. Obviously, this total lack of control over the collateral greatly dilutes the value of this type of security to the lender. Correspondingly, loans made with floating liens on inventory as collateral are generally limited to a relatively modest fraction of the value of the inventories covered by the lien. In addition, floating liens usually include future as well as existing inventories.

CHATTEL MORTGAGE AGREEMENTS

The lender can increase his security interest by having specific items of inventory identified (by serial number or otherwise) in the security agreement. Such an arrangement is provided by a **chattel mortgage.** The borrower retains title to the inventory but cannot sell the items without the lender's consent. This type of agreement is very costly to implement, as specific items of inventory must be identified; thus, it is used only for major items of inventory such as machine tools or other capital assets.

FIELD WAREHOUSE FINANCING AGREEMENTS

Increased lender control over inventories used as loan collateral can be obtained through the use of a **field warehouse agreement**. Here the inventories used as collateral are physically separated from the firm's other inventories and placed under the control of a third-party field warehousing firm. Note that the inventories are not removed from the borrower's premises, but they are placed under the control of a third party who is responsible for protecting the security interests of the lender. This arrangement is particularly useful where large bulky items are used as collateral. For example, a refinery might use a part of its inventory of fuel oil to secure a short-term bank loan. Under a field warehousing agreement the oil reserves would be set aside in specific tanks or storage vessels, which would be controlled (monitored) by a field warehousing concern.

The warehousing concern, upon receipt of the inventory, takes full control of the collateral. This means that the borrower is no longer allowed to use or sell the inventory items without the consent of the lender. The warehousing firm issues a **warehouse receipt** for the merchandise, which carries title to the goods represented therein. The receipt may be negotiable, in which case title can be transferred through sale of the receipt, or nonnegotiable, whereby title remains with the lender. With a negotiable receipt arrangement the warehouse concern will release the goods to whomever holds the receipt, whereas with a nonnegotiable receipt the goods may be released only on the written consent of the lender.

The cost of such a loan can be quite high, since the services of the field warehouse company must be paid for by the borrower.

Example. The M. M. Richards Company follows a practice of obtaining short-term credit based on its seasonal finished goods inventory. The firm builds up its inventories of outdoor furniture throughout the winter months for sale in spring and summer. Thus, for the two-month period ended March 31, they use their fall and winter production of furniture as collateral for a short-term bank loan. The bank lends the company up to 70 percent of the value of the inventory at 9 percent interest plus a fixed fee of $2000 to cover the costs of a field warehousing arrangement. During this period the firm usually has about $200,000 in inventories, against which it borrows. The annual effective cost of the short-term credit is therefore

$$\text{RATE} = \frac{\$2100 + \$2000}{\$140,000} \times \frac{1}{60/360} = 17.57 \text{ percent}$$

where the financing cost consists of two months' interest ($140,000 × .09 × $\frac{60}{360}$ = $2100) plus the field warehousing fee of $2000.

TERMINAL WAREHOUSE AGREEMENTS

The **terminal warehouse agreement** differs from the field warehouse agreement just discussed in only one respect. Here the inventories pledged as collateral are transported to a public warehouse that is physically removed from the borrower's premises. An added degree of safety or security is provided to the lender, as the inventory is totally removed from the borrower's control. Once again the cost of this type of arrangement is increased by the necessity for paying the warehouse concern; in addition, the inventory must be transported to and eventually from the public warehouse.

The same warehouse receipt procedure described earlier for field warehouse loans is used. Again, the cost of this type of financing can be quite high.

SUMMARY

There are two basic problems encountered in managing the firm's use of short-term financing. The first of these involves determining the level of short-term financing that the firm should use. This question was addressed in Chapter 6 through the use of the *hedging principle* of working capital management. Basically, this principle suggests the use of short-term financing to finance temporary or short-term investments in assets. In this chapter we have sought to answer the second of the above questions. That is, "How should the financial manager select a source of short-term financing?"

Three basic factors were discussed as providing the key considerations in selecting a source of short-term financing: (1) the effective cost of credit, (2) the availability of financing in the amount and for the time needed and (3) the effect of the use of credit from a particular source on the cost and availability of other sources of credit.

For discussion purposes the various sources of short-term credit were categorized into two groups: unsecured and secured. Unsecured credit, as opposed to secured credit, offers no specific assets as security for the loan agreement. The sources of unsecured short-term credit are many, however. The primary sources include trade credit, lines of credit and unsecured transaction loans from commercial banks, and commercial paper. Secured credit is generally provided to business firms by commercial banks, finance companies, and factors. The most popular sources of security involve the use of accounts receivable and inventories. Loans secured by accounts receivable include pledging agreements wherein a firm merely pledges its receivables as security for a loan, and factoring whereby the firm sells the receivables to a factor. A primary difference in these two arrangements relates to the ability of the lender to seek payment from the borrower in the event that the accounts used as collateral become uncollectible. In a pledging arrangement the lender retains the right of recourse in the event of default whereas factoring generally is without recourse.

Loans secured by inventories can be made using one of several types of security arrangements. Among the most widely used are the floating lien, chattel mortgage, field warehouse agreement, and terminal warehouse agreement. The form of security agreement used will depend largely upon the nature of the inventories being pledged as collateral and the degree of control the lender wishes to exercise over the loan collateral.

STUDY QUESTIONS

10-1. What distinguishes short-term, intermediate-term, and long-term debt?

10-2. What factors should be considered in selecting a source of short-term credit? Discuss each.

10-3. How can the formula "interest = principle × rate × time" be used to estimate the effective cost of short-term credit?

10-4. How can we accommodate the effects of compounding in our calculation of the effective cost of short-term credit?

10-5. There are three major sources of unsecured short-term credit. List and discuss the distinguishing characteristics of each.

10-6. What is meant by the following trade credit terms: 2/10, net 30? 4/20, net 60? 3/15, net 45?

10-7. Define the following:
  (a) Line of credit.
  (b) Commercial paper.
  (c) Compensating balance.
  (d) Prime rate.

10-8. List and discuss four advantages to the use of commercial paper.

10-9. What "risk" is involved in the firm's use of commercial paper as a source short-term credit? Discuss.

10-10. List and discuss the distinguishing features of the principal sources of secured credit based upon accounts receivable.

10-11. List and discuss the distinguishing features of the primary sources of secured credit based upon inventories.

STUDY PROBLEMS

10-1. Calculate the effective cost of the following trade credit terms where payment is made on the net due date.
  (a) 2/10, net 30.
  (b) 3/15, net 30.

(c) 3/15, net 45.

(d) 2/15, net 60.

10-2. Compute the cost of the trade credit terms in problem 1 using the compounding formula discussed in footnote 3, p. 244.

10-3. On July 1, 1978, the Southwest Forging Corporation arranged for a line of credit with the First national Bank of Dallas. The terms of the agreement called for a $100,000 maximum loan with interest set at 1 percent over prime. In addition, the firm has to maintain a 20 percent compensating balance in its demand deposit throughout the year. The prime rate is currently 8 percent.

(a) If Southwest normally maintains a $20,000 to $30,000 balance in its checking account with FNB of Dallas, what is the effective cost of credit through the line of credit agreement where the maximum loan amount is used?

(b) Recompute the effective cost of credit to Southwest if Southwest will have to borrow the compensating balance and they borrow the maximum possible under the loan agreement.

10-4. Tri-state Enterprises plans to issue commercial paper for the first time in the firm's 35-year history. The firm plans to issue $500,000 in 180-day maturity notes. The paper will carry a $7\frac{1}{2}$ percent rate and will cost Tri-State $12,000 to issue.

(a) What is the effective cost of credit to Tri-State?

(b) What other factors should the company consider in analyzing whether to issue the commercial paper?

10-5. Johnson Enterprises, Inc., is involved in the manufacture and sale of electronic components used in small AM-FM radios. The firm needs $300,000 to finance an anticipated expansion in receivables due to increased sales. Johnson's credit terms are 3/20, net 90, and its average monthly credit sales are $250,000. Some of the firm's customers pay within the discount period; others wait until the net period. On the average the firm's accounts receivables are $400,000.

Chuck Idol, Johnson's comptroller, approached the firm's bank with a request for a loan for the $300,000 using the firm's accounts receivable as collateral. The bank offered to make the loan at a rate of 2 percent over prime plus a 1 percent processing charge on the average amount of receivables pledged ($400,000). Furthermore, the bank agreed to loan up to 75 percent of the face value of the receivables pledged.

(a) Estimate the cost of the receivables loan to Johnson where the firm borrows the $300,000. The prime rate is currently 8 percent.

(b) Idol also requested a line of credit for $300,000 from the bank. The bank agreed to grant the necessary line of credit at a rate of 3 percent over prime and required a 15 percent compensating balance. Johnson currently maintains an average demand deposit of $80,000. Estimate the cost of the line of credit to Johnson.

(c) Which source of credit should Johnson select? Why?

10-6. C. H. Linke, Inc., is considering the factoring of its receivables. The firm has an average receivables balance of $500,000. The factor has offered to extend credit equal to 60 percent of the receivables factored at a rate of 1 percent per month. In addition, the factor will charge a fee of $2000 per month plus one-half of 1 percent on each dollar of receivables factored.

If Linke decides to factor its receivables, it will sell them all, so that it can reduce its credit department costs by $1500 a month.

(a) Compute the cost to Linke of borrowing $100,000.

(b) Compute the cost to Linke of borrowing $200,000.

(c) What is the cost of borrowing the maximum amount of credit available to Linke through the factoring agreement?

(d) What factors other than cost should be considered by Linke in determining whether or not to enter the factoring agreement?

10-7. In June of each year the Arlyle Publishing Company builds up its inventories for fall sales. The company has explored the possibility of a field warehouse security agreement as collateral for an inventory loan from its bank during the three summer months. The field warehouse arrangement will cost Arlyle $1500 a month on $400,000 worth of inventory. The bank has agreed to loan up to 60 percent of the value of the inventory at a rate of 9 percent.

(a) If Arlyle borrows $200,000 using the inventory loan for June through August, what is the effective cost of credit?

(b) What is the effective cost of borrowing $280,000 for the June through August period?

10-8. The Sean-Janeow Import Co. needs $500,000 for the three month period ending September 30, 1979. The firm has explored two possible sources of credit.

(1) S-J has arranged with its bank for a $500,000 loan secured by accounts receivable. The bank has agreed to advance S-J 70 percent of the value of its pledged receivables at a rate of 9 percent plus a 1 percent fee based on all receivables pledged.

(2) An insurance company has agreed to loan the $500,000 at a rate of 8 percent a month, using a loan secured by S-J's inventory of salad oil. A field warehouse agreement would be used, which would cost S-J $2000 a month.

Which source of credit should S-J select? Explain.

ABRAHAM, A. B., "Factoring—The New Frontier for Commercial Banks," *Journal of Commercial Bank Lending,* 53 (April 1971), 32–43.

ADDISON, E., "Factoring: A Case History," *Financial Executive,* (November 1963), 32–33.

D'AGOSTINO, R. S., "Accounts Receivable Loans—Worthless Collateral?," *The Journal of Commercial Bank Lending* 52 (July 1970), 34–42.

DANIELS, F., S. LEGG, and E. C. YUEILLE, "Accounts Receivable and Related Inventory Financing," *The Journal of Commercial Bank Lending,* 52 (July 1970), 38–53.

HAYES, D. A., *Bank Lending Policies: Domestic and International.* Ann Arbor, Mich.: University of Michigan, 1971.

QUARLES, J. C., "The Floating Lien," *The Journal of Commercial Bank Lending,* 52 (November 1970), 51–58.

ROGERS, R. W., "Warehouse Receipts and Their Use in Financing," *Bulletin of the Robert Morris Associates,* 46 (April 1964), 317–27.

SELECTED REFERENCES

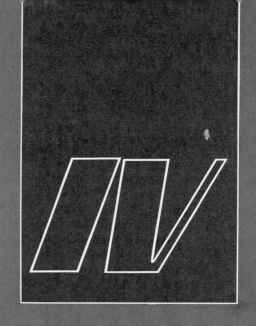

MANAGEMENT OF LONG-TERM ASSETS

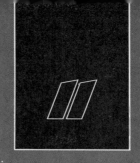

Capital Budgeting

In Chapter 5 we developed tools for making cash flows that occur in different time periods comparable. In the present chapter these techniques are used in conjunction with additional decision rules to determine when to invest money in long-term assets, which has come to be called **capital budgeting.** In evaluating capital investment proposals we will compare the costs and benefits of each in a number of ways. Some of these methods take account of the time value of money, others do not; but each of these methods is used frequently in the real world.

We will look first at the purpose and importance of capital budgeting. Next, since capital budgeting techniques rely on cash flows as inputs, we will study the determination of these cash flows. Five capital budgeting criteria will then be provided for evaluating capital investments. Several advanced topics in capital budgeting will also be examined.

INTRODUCTION TO CAPITAL BUDGETING

Capital budgeting involves the decision-making process with respect to investment in fixed assets; specifically, it involves measuring the incremental cash flows associated with investment proposals and evaluating the attractiveness of these cash flows relative to the project's cost. Typically these investments involve rather large cash outlays at the outset and commit the firm to a particular course of action over a relatively long time horizon. Thus, if a capital budgeting decision is incorrect, reversing it tends to be costly.

For example, the Ford Motor Company's capital budgeting decision to produce the Edsel entailed an outlay of $250 million to bring the car to market and losses of approximately $200 million during the $2\frac{1}{2}$ years it was produced—in all, a $450 million mistake.[1] It is this type of decision that is costly to reverse. Fortunately for Ford, they were able to convert their Edsel production facilities over to produce the Mustang, thereby avoiding an even larger loss.

In order to evaluate investment proposals, we must first set up guidelines by which to measure the value of each proposal. In so doing we will focus our attention on cash flows rather than accounting profits. This choice rests on the fact that cash flows, and not accounting profits, are actually received and reinvested by the firm. Thus, by examining cash flows we are able to correctly analyze the timing of the benefits. In addition, we will examine cash flows on an after-tax basis, as only those flows are available for reinvesting in the firm or for paying shareholders. Moreover, we may find that not all the flows resulting from an investment proposal are incremental in nature. In other words, the total cash flows that result from a project may not be relevant in the analysis. It is only the incremental cash flows that interest us. For example, assume that we are considering a new product line that will compete with one of our current products and reduce its sales. If so, in determining the cash flows associated with the proposed project we would consider only the incremental sales brought to the company as a whole. New product sales achieved at the cost of losing sales of other products in our line would not be considered a benefit of adopting the new product.

In evaluating projects and determining cash flows, we will separate the investment decision from the financing decision. Thus, if accepting this project means we will have to raise new funds by issuing bonds, we will not consider the interest charges associated with raising funds as a relevant cash outflow. When we discount the incremental cash flows back to the present at the required rate of return, we are implicitly accounting for the cost of raising funds to finance the new project. In essence, the required rate of return reflects the cost of funds needed to support the project. In effect, we will first determine the desirability of the project and then determine how best to finance it.

MEASURING CASH FLOWS

In measuring cash flows, we will be interested only in the **incremental,** or differential, **after-tax cash flows** that can be attributed to the investment proposal being evaluated. Obviously, the worth of our capital budgeting decision depends upon the accuracy of our cash flow estimates. In general, a project's cash flows will fall into one of three categories: (1) the initial outlay, (2) the differential flows over the project's life, (3) the termi-

[1] "The Edsel Dies, and Ford Regroups Survivors," *Business Week,* November 28, 1959, p. 27.

nal cash flow. In introducing these cash flow categories, we look first at the actual calculation, which is followed by an illustrative example. This section will then be followed by the development of several capital budgeting criteria that will use these cash flows as inputs.

The **initial outlay** involves the immediate cash outflow necessary to purchase the asset and put it in operating order. This amount includes the cost of installing the asset (the asset's purchase price plus any expenses associated with shipping or installation), and any nonexpense cash outlays, such as increased working-capital requirements. If we are considering a new sales outlet, there might be additional cash flows associated with investment in working capital in the form of increased inventory and cash necessary to operate the sales outlet. While these cash flows are not included in the cost of the asset or even expensed on the books, they must be included in our analysis. The after-tax cost of expense items incurred as a result of new investment must also be included as cash outflows—for example, any training expenses or special engineering expenses that would not have been incurred otherwise. In addition, any cash flow resulting from the investment tax credit should be included. Finally, if the investment decision at hand is a replacement decision, the cash inflow associated with the selling price of the old asset, in addition to any tax effects resulting from its sale, must be accounted for.

Initial Outlay

Obviously, determining the initial outlay is a complex calculation. Table 11-1 summarizes some of the more common calculations involved in determining a project's initial outlay. This list is by no means exhaustive, but it should help simplify the calculations involved in the example that follows.

TAX EFFECTS

Perhaps the most confusing calculation involved occurs when determining the initial outlay of a replacement project and involves the incremental tax payment associated with the sale of the old machine. Although these calculations were examined in Chapter 2, a review is appropriate at this time. There are four possible tax situations dealing with the sale of an old asset.

Table 11-1 SUMMARY OF CALCULATION OF INITIAL OUTLAY INCREMENTAL AFTER-TAX CASH FLOW

1. Installed cost of asset
2. Additional nonexpense outlays incurred (for example, working-capital investments)
3. Additional expenses on an after-tax basis (for example, training expenses)
4. Any cash flow resulting from the investment tax credit
5. In a replacement decision, the *after-tax* cash flow associated with the sale of the old machine

1. The old asset is sold for a price above the depreciated value and also above the original purchase price. In this case, the amount by which the selling price exceeds the original purchase price is considered a capital gain and taxed at the appropriate rate, which for corporations is 30 percent. The amount by which the original purchase price exceeds the depreciated book value is considered recapture of depreciation and taxed at the marginal corporate tax rate, in general, 48 percent. For example, if the old machine had a depreciated book value of $10,000, an original cost of $15,000, and was sold for $17,000, the tax calculation on its sale would be:

Capital gains tax	($17,000 − 15,000) (.30) =	$ 600
Recapture of depreciation	($15,000 − 10,000) (.48) =	2400
Total tax payments		$3000

2. The old asset is sold for a price above the depreciated value, but below or equal to the original cost. Here the difference between the old machine's selling price and its depreciated value is considered recapture of depreciation and taxed at the marginal corporate tax rate. If, for example, the old machine was originally purchased for $15,000, had a book value of $10,000, and was sold for $15,000, the taxes due from recapture of depreciation would be ($15,000 − 10,000) (.48), or $2400.

3. The old asset is sold for its depreciated value. In this case no taxes result, as there is neither a gain nor a loss in the asset's sale.

4. The old asset is sold for less than its depreciated value. In this case the difference between the depreciated book value and the salvage value of the asset is used to offset ordinary income and thus results in tax savings. For example, if the depreciated book value of the asset is $10,000 and it is sold for $7000, assuming the firm's marginal corporate tax rate is 48 percent, the cash inflow from tax savings is ($10,000 − 7,000) (.48), or $1440.[2]

Example. In order to clarify the calculation of the initial outlay, consider an example of a company in the 48 percent marginal tax bracket. This company is considering the purchase of a new machine for $30,000, which will be depreciated using the straight-line method down to a salvage value of zero in 10 years. The new machine will replace an existing machine originally purchased for $15,000 five years ago. The existing machine is being depreciated by the straight-line method down to zero over its expected life of 15 years. In order to put this machine in running order, it is necessary to pay shipping charges of $2000 and installation charges of $3000. Because the new machine will work faster than the old one, it will require an increase in goods in process inventory of $5000. Finally, the old machine can be sold for $15,000 to a scrap dealer.

The installed cost of the new machine would be the $30,000 cost plus

---

[2]The tax treatment on gains or losses has been simplified somewhat for pedagogical purposes. For example, if the asset was not used in business or trade and sold for less than its depreciable value, the loss could be used only to offset capital gains (see Sections 1201, 1211, 1212 of IRS Code). Moreover, in the exchange of *like* assets, the remaining book value is added to the purchase price of the new asset and subsequently depreciated (Section 1031 of IRS Code).

$2000 shipping and $3000 installation fees, for a total of $35,000. Additional outflows are associated with taxes incurred on the sale of the old machine and with increased investment in inventory. Although the old machine had a book value of $10,000, it was sold for $15,000. The increased taxes from recapture of depreciation will be equal to the selling price of the old machine less its depreciated book value times the firm's marginal tax rate, or ($15,000 − 10,000)(.48), or $2400. The increase in goods in process inventory of $5000 must also be considered part of the initial outlay, with an offsetting inflow of $5000 corresponding to the recapture of this inventory occurring at the termination of the project. In effect, the firm invests $5000 in inventory now, resulting in an initial cash outlay, and liquidates this inventory in 10 years, resulting in a cash inflow at the end of the project. The total outlays associated with the new machine are $35,000 for its installed cost, $2400 in increased taxes, and $5000 in investment in inventory, for a total of $42,400. This is somewhat offset by the sale of the old machine for $15,000. Thus, the net initial outlay associated with this project is $27,400. These calculations are summarized in Table 11-2.

The differential cash flows over the project's life involve the incremental after-tax cash flows resulting from increased revenues, plus labor or material savings, and less increased selling expenses. Overhead items, such as utilities, heat, light, and executive salaries, are generally not affected. However, any resultant change in any of these categories must be included. Any increase in interest payments incurred as a result of issuing bonds to finance the project should *not* be included, as the costs of funds needed to support the project are implicitly accounted for by discounting the project back to the present using the **required rate of return**—the rate of return a project must earn to justify raising funds to finance it. Finally, an adjustment for the incremental change in taxes should be made, including any increase in taxes that might result from increased profits or any tax savings from an increase in depreciation expenses. Increased depreciation

Differential Flows over the Project's Life

Table 11-2 CALCULATION OF INITIAL OUTLAY FOR EXAMPLE PROBLEM

Outflows:		
Purchase price	$30,000	
Shipping fee	2,000	
Installation fee	3,000	
Installed cost of machine		$35,000
Increased taxes ($15,000-10,000)(.48)		2,400
Increased investment in inventory		5,000
Total outflows		$42,400
Inflows:		
Salvage value of old machine		15,000
Net initial outlay		$27,400

Table 11-3 SUMMARY OF CALCULATION OF DIFFERENTIAL CASH FLOWS ON AN
AFTER-TAX BASIS

1. Added revenue offset by increased expenses
2. Labor and material savings
3. Increases in overhead incurred
4. Depreciation tax shield on an incremental basis in a replacement decision
5. Do *not* include interest expenses if the project is financed by issuing debt, as this is accounted for in the required rate of return

expenses affect tax-related cash flows by reducing taxable income and thus lowering taxes. Table 11-3 lists some of the factors that might be involved in determining a project's differential cash flows.

Example. Extending the earlier example, which illustrated the calculations of the initial outlay, suppose that purchasing the machine is expected to reduce salaries by $10,000 per year and fringe benefits by $1000 annually, because it will take only one man to operate, whereas the old machine requires two operators. In addition, the cost of defects will fall from $8000 per year to $3000. However, maintenance expenses will increase by $4000 annually. The annual depreciation on this new machine is $3500 per year, while the depreciation expense lost with the sale of the old machine is $1000 for each of the next 10 years. Annual depreciation on the new machine is determined by taking its depreciable value—that is, the cost of the new machine plus any expenses necessary to put it in operating order—subtracting out the salvage value, and dividing by the machine's expected life. For the new machine these calculations are reflected in Table 11-4.

Since the depreciation on the old machine is $1000 per year, the increased depreciation will be from $1000 per year to $3500 per year, or an increase of $2500 per year. Although this increase in depreciation expenses is not a cash flow item, it does affect cash flows by reducing book profits, which in turn reduces taxes.

In order to determine the annual net cash flows resulting from the acceptance of this project, the net savings *before* taxes using both book profit

Table 11-4 CALCULATION OF DEPRECIATION
FOR THE NEW MACHINE

New machine purchase price	$30,000
Shipping fee	2,000
Installation fee	3,000
Total depreciable value	$35,000
Less: Salvage value	0
Divide by expected life	$35,000/10
Equals: Annual depreciation	$3,500/year

Table 11-5 CALCULATION OF THE DIFFERENTIAL CASH FLOWS FOR THE EXAMPLE PROBLEM

		BOOK PROFIT	CASH FLOW
Savings:	Reduced salary	$10,000	$10,000
	Reduced fringe benefits	1,000	1,000
	Reduced defects ($8000 − 3000)	5,000	5,000
Costs:	Increased maintenance expense	−4,000	−4,000
	Increased depreciation expense ($3500 − 1000)	−2,500	
Net savings before taxes		$ 9,500	$12,000
Taxes (48%)		−4,560 ⟶	−4,560
Net cash flow after taxes			$ 7,440

and cash flows must be found. The additional taxes are then calculated based upon the before-tax book profit. For this example, Table 11-5 shows the determination of the differential cash flows on an after-tax basis. Thus, the differential cash flows over the project's life are $7440.

The calculation of the terminal cash flow is in general quite a bit simpler than the previous two calculations. Flows associated with the project's termination generally include the salvage value of the project plus or minus any taxable gains or losses associated with its sale. Here the tax gains or losses would be determined in a manner similar to the tax gains or losses incurred on the sale of the old machine described in the initial outlay. In most cases there will be no forecasted tax gain or loss associated with the termination of the project, because of the common assumption that the salvage value at termination will be equal to the depreciated value at that point in time. In addition to the salvage value, there may be a cash outlay associated with the project termination. For example, at the close of a strip-mining operation, the mine must be refilled in an ecologically acceptable manner. Finally, any working-capital outlay required at the initiation of the project—for example, increased inventory needed for the operation of a new plant—will be recaptured at the termination of the project. In effect the increased inventory required by the project can be liquidated when the project expires. Table 11-6 provides a sample list of some of the factors that might affect a project's terminal cash flow.

Terminal Cash Flow

Table 11-6 SUMMARY OF CALCULATION OF TERMINAL CASH FLOW ON AN AFTER-TAX BASIS

1. The after-tax salvage value of the project
2. Cash outlays associated with the project's termination
3. Recapture of nonexpense outlays that occurred at the project's initiation (for example, working-capital investments)

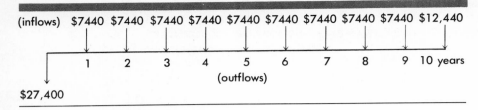

FIGURE 11-1 *Example Cash Flow Diagram*

Example. Extending the example to termination, the depreciated book value of the machine at the termination date will be equal to zero. However, there will be a cash flow associated with the recapture of the initial outlay of work in process inventory of $5000. This flow is generated from the liquidation of the $5000 investment in work in process inventory. Therefore, the expected total terminal cash flow equals $5000.

If we were to construct a cash flow diagram from this example (Figure 11-1), it would have an initial outlay of $27,400, differential cash flows during years 1 through 10 of $7440, and an additional terminal cash flow at the end of year 10 of $5000. The cash flow occurring in year 10 is $12,440, the sum of the differential cash flow in year 10 of $7440 and the terminal cash flow of $5000.

Cash flow diagrams similar to Figure 11-1 will be used through one remainder of this chapter with arrows above the time line indicating cash inflows and arrows below the time line denoting cash outflows.

While the above calculations for determining the incremental after-tax, net cash flows do not cover all possible cash flows, they do set up a framework under which almost any situation can be handled. In order to simplify this framework, and provide an overview of these calculations, Table 11-7 summarizes the rules in Tables 11-1, 11-3, and 11-6.

Table 11-7 SUMMARY OF CALCULATION OF INCREMENTAL AFTER-TAX CASH FLOWS

A. Initial Outlay
   1. Installed cost of asset
   2. Additional nonexpense outlays incurred (for example, working-capital investments)
   3. Additional expenses, on an after-tax basis (for example, training expenses)
   4. Any cash flow resulting from the investment tax credit
   5. In a replacement decision, the *after-tax* flow associated with the sale of the old machine
B. Differential Cash Flows over the Project's Life
   1. Added revenue offset by increased expenses
   2. Labor and material savings
   3. Increases in overhead incurred

4. Depreciation tax shield on an incremental basis in a replacement decision
5. Do *not* include interest expenses if the project is financed by issuing debt, as this is accounted for in the required rate of return

C. Terminal Cash Flow
1. The after-tax salvage value of the project
2. Cash outlays associated with the project's termination.
3. Recapture of nonexpense outlays that occurred at the project's initiation (for example, working-capital investments)

We are now ready to consider the interpretation of cash flows. Cash flows represent the benefits generated from accepting a capital budgeting proposal. In the remainder of this chapter this cash flow information is assumed to be given, and we will examine whether or not the project should be accepted.

We shall consider five commonly used criteria for determining acceptability of investment proposals. The first two are the least sophisticated, in that they do not incorporate the time value of money into their calculations; the final three do take account of it.

The **payback period** is the number of years needed to recover the initial cash outlay. As this criterion measures how quickly the project will return its original investment, it deals with cash flows rather than accounting profits. The accept-reject criterion involves whether or not the project's payback period is less than or equal to the firm's maximum desired payback period. For example, if a firm's maximum desired payback period is three years and an investment proposal requires an initial cash outlay of $10,000 and yields the following set of annual cash flows, what is its payback period? Should the project be accepted?

Nondiscounted Cash Flow Criterion 1: Payback Period

YEAR	AFTER-TAX CASH FLOW
1	$2000
2	4000
3	3000
4	3000
5	1000

In this case, after three years the firm will have recaptured $9000 on an initial investment of $10,000, leaving $1000 of the initial investment to be recouped. During the fourth year a total of $3000 will be returned from this investment, and, assuming it will flow into the firm at a constant rate over the year, it will take one-third of the year ($1000/$3000) to recapture the remaining $1000. Thus, the payback period on this project is $3\frac{1}{3}$ years, which is more than the desired payback period. Hence, using the payback period criterion, the firm would reject this project.

Although the payback period is used frequently, it does have some rather obvious drawbacks, which can be best demonstrated through the use of an example. Consider two investment projects, A and B, which involve an initial cash outlay of $10,000 each and produce the annual cash flows shown in Table 11-8. Both projects have a payback period of two years; therefore, in terms of the payback period criterion both are equally acceptable. However, if we had our choice, it is clear we would select A over B—for at least two reasons. First, regardless of what happens after the payback period, project A returns our initial investment to us earlier within the payback period. Thus, if there is a time value of money, the cash flows occurring within the payback period should not be weighted equally, as they are. In addition, all cash flows that occur after the payback period are ignored. This violates the principle that investors desire more in the way of benefits rather than less—a principle that is hard to deny, especially when we are talking about money.

Although these deficiencies seriously limit the value of the payback period as a tool for investment evaluation, it does have several positive features. First, it deals with cash flows and therefore focuses on the true timing of the project's benefits and costs, although these cash flows are not adjusted for the time value of money. Second, owing to its simplicity, it is easy to visualize, quickly understood, and easy to calculate. Finally, while the payback period method does have serious deficiencies, it is often used as a rough screening device, eliminating projects whose returns do not materialize until later years. This approach emphasizes the earliest returns which in all likelihood are less uncertain and provides for the liquidity needs of the firm. Although these advantages of the payback period are certainly significant, its disadvantages severely limit its value as a discriminating capital budgeting criterion.

The **accounting rate of return (AROR)** compares the average after-tax profits to the average dollar size of the investment. The average profit figure is determined by adding up the after-tax profits generated by the investment over its life and dividing by the number of years. The average investment is determined by adding the initial outlay and the salvage value and dividing by two. This computation assumes that the project is being depreciated by the straight-line method and that the book value is a meaningful investment figure. Thus, the accounting rate of return for an investment with an expected life of n years can be computed as follows:

$$AROR = \frac{\sum_{t=1}^{n} (\text{accounting profit after tax}_t)/n}{(\text{initial investment} + \text{salvage value})/2} \qquad (11\text{-}1)$$

Nondiscounted Cash Flow Criterion 2: Accounting Rate of Return

Table 11-8 PAYBACK PERIOD EXAMPLE PROJECTS

	A	B
Initial cash outlay	−$10,000	−$10,000
Annual net cash inflows:		
Year 1	6,000	5,000
2	4,000	5,000
3	3,000	0
4	2,000	0
5	1,000	0

The accept-reject criterion associated with the accounting rate of return compares the calculated return with a minimum acceptable AROR level. If the AROR is greater than this minimum acceptable level, the project is accepted; otherwise, it is rejected.

Consider an investment in new machinery that requires an initial outlay of $14,000 and has a salvage value of $6000 after five years. Assume that this machine, if acquired, will result in an increase in after-tax profits of $800 each year for five years. In this case the average accounting profit is $800, while the average investment is ($14,000 + 6000)/2 or $10,000. For this example, the AROR would be $800/$10,000 or 8 percent.

While this technique seems straightforward enough, its limitations detract significantly from its value as a discriminating capital budgeting criterion. To examine these limitations, let us first determine the AROR of three mutually exclusive capital budgeting proposals, each with an expected life of five years. Assume that the initial outlay associated with each project is $8000 and it will be depreciated using the straight-line method down to a salvage value of $2000 over the next five years. The minimum acceptable AROR for this firm is 8 percent, and the annual accounting profits from the three proposals are given in Table 11-9. In each case, the average annual accounting profit is $500 and the average investment is $5000—that is, ($8000 + 2000)/2. Therefore, the AROR is 10 percent for each project, which indicates that the AROR method does not do an adequate job of discriminating between these projects. A casual examination leads us to the conclusion that project B is the best, as it yields its

Table 11-9 ANNUAL ACCOUNTING PROFITS AFTER TAX

YEAR	A	B	C
1	$ 0	$500	$ 0
2	1000	500	0
3	500	500	0
4	500	500	0
5	500	500	2500

returns earlier than either project A or C. However, the AROR technique gives equal weight to all returns within the project's life without any regard for the time value of money. The second major disadvantage associated with the AROR method is that it deals with accounting profit figures rather than cash flows. For this reason it does not truly reflect the proper timing of the benefits.

In spite of the forgoing criticisms, the accounting rate of return has been a relatively popular tool for capital budgeting analysis, primarily because it involves familiar terms that are easily accessible. Also it is easily understood.

In summary, the AROR provides a measure of accounting profits per average dollar invested, and the intuitive appeal of this measurement has kept the method alive over the years. For our purposes, the AROR is inadequate, as it does not treat cash flows and does not take account of the time value of money.

The final three capital budgeting criteria to be examined base their decisions on the investment's cash flows after adjusting for the time value of money. For the time being, the problem of incorporating risk into the capital budgeting decision is ignored. This issue will be examined in Chapter 12. In addition, we will assume that the appropriate discount rate, required rate of return, or cost of capital is given. The determination of this rate is studied in Chapters 13 and 14.

We will examine three discounted cash flow capital budgeting techniques—the net present value, the profitability index, and the internal rate of return.

The **net present value (NPV)** of an investment proposal is equal to the present value of its annual net cash flows after tax less the investment's initial outlay. The net present value can be expressed as follows:

$$NPV = \sum_{t=1}^{n} \frac{ACF_t}{(1 + k)^t} - IO \qquad (11\text{-}2)$$

where ACF_t = the annual after-tax cash flow in time period t (this can take on either positive or negative values),

k = the appropriate discount rate, that is the required rate of return or the cost of capital,[3]

IO = the initial cash outlay,

n = the project's expected life.

The project's net present value gives a measurement of the *absolute* value of an investment proposal in terms of today's dollars. Since all cash flows are

DISCOUNTED
CASH FLOW
CRITERIA FOR
CAPITAL
BUDGETING
DECISIONS

Discounted
Cash Flow
Criterion 1: Net
Present Value

[3]The required rate of return or cost of capital is the rate of return necessary to justify raising funds to finance the project or, alternatively, the rate of return necessary to maintain the firm's current market price per share. These terms will be defined in greater detail in Chapter 14.

discounted back to the present, comparing the difference between the present value of the annual cash flows and the investment outlay does not violate the time value of money assumption. The difference between the present value of the annual cash flows and the initial outlay determines the net value of accepting the investment proposal in terms of today's dollars. Whenever there is a positive value associated with the acceptance of a project, we will accept the project; and whenever there is a negative value associated with the acceptance of a project, we will reject the project. If the project's net present value is zero, then we are indifferent as to its acceptance or rejection. This accept-reject criterion is illustrated below:

$$NPV > 0.0 \quad \text{Accept}$$
$$NPV < 0.0 \quad \text{Reject}$$

The following example illustrates the use of the net present value capital budgeting criterion.

Example. A firm is considering new machinery, for which the after-tax cash flows are shown in Table 11-10. If the firm has a 12 percent required rate of return, the present value of the after-tax cash flows is $47,678, as calculated in Table 11-11. Further, the net present value of the new machinery is $7678. Since this value is greater than zero, the net present value criterion indicates that the project should be accepted.

Use Appendix B

Note that the worth of the net present value calculation is a function of the accuracy of cash flow predictions. Before the NPV criterion can be reasonably applied, incremental costs and benefits must first be estimated, including the initial outlay, the differential flows over the project's life, and the terminal cash flow.

In comparing the NPV criterion with those that we have already examined, we find it far superior. First of all, it deals with cash flows rather than accounting profits. In this regard it is sensitive to the true timing of the benefits resulting from the project. Moreover, recognizing the time value of money allows comparison of the benefits and costs in a logical manner. Finally, since projects are accepted only if a positive net present

Table 11-10 NPV ILLUSTRATION OF INVESTMENT IN NEW MACHINERY

	AFTER-TAX CASH FLOW
Initial outlay	−$40,000
Inflow year 1	15,000
Inflow year 2	14,000
Inflow year 3	13,000
Inflow year 4	12,000
Inflow year 5	11,000

Table 11-11 CALCULATION FOR NPV ILLUSTRATION OF INVESTMENT IN NEW MACHINERY

	After-Tax Cash Flow	Present Value Factor at 12 Percent	Present Value
Inflow year 1	$15,000	.893	$13,395
Inflow year 2	14,000	.797	11,158
Inflow year 3	13,000	.712	9,256
Inflow year 4	12,000	.636	7,632
Inflow year 5	11,000	.567	6,237
Present value of cash flows			$47,678
Investment initial outlay			40,000
Net present value			$ 7,678

value is associated with them, the acceptance of a project using this criterion will increase the value of the firm, which is consistent with the goal of maximizing the shareholders' wealth.

The disadvantage of the NPV method stems from the need for detailed, long-term forecasts of the incremental cash flows accruing from the project's acceptance. In spite of this drawback, the net present value is the most theoretically correct criterion that we will examine. The following example provides an additional illustration of its application.

Example. A firm is considering the purchase of a new computer system which will cost $30,000 initially and is to aid in credit billing and inventory management. The incremental after-tax cash flows resulting from this project are provided in Table 11-12. The required rate of return demanded by the firm is 10 percent. In order to determine the system's net present value, the three-year, $15,000 cash flow annuity is first discounted back to present at 10 percent. From the present-value-of-an-annuity table in Appendix D in the back of this book, we find that the appropriate present-value factor is 2.487. Thus, the present value of this $15,000 annuity is $37,305.

Since the cash inflows have been discounted back to the present, they can now be compared with the initial outlay, since both of the flows are now stated in terms of today's dollars. Subtracting the initial outlay ($30,000) from the present value of the cash inflows ($37,305), we find that the system's net present value is $7305. Since the NPV on this project is positive, the project should be accepted.

The **profitability index,** or **benefit/cost ratio,** is the ratio of the present value of the future net cash flows to the initial outlay. While the net present value investment criterion gives a measure of the absolute dollar desirability of a project, the profitability index provides a relative measure of an investment proposal's desirability—that is, the ratio of the

Discounted Cash Flow Criterion 2: Profitability Index (Benefit/Cost) Ratio)

Table 11-12 NPV EXAMPLE PROBLEM
OF A COMPUTER SYSTEM

	AFTER-TAX CASH FLOW
Initial outlay	−$30,000
Year 1	15,000
Year 2	15,000
Year 3	15,000

present value of its future net benefits to its initial cost. The profitability index can be expressed as follows:

$$PI = \frac{\sum\limits_{t=1}^{n} \dfrac{ACF_t}{(1 + k)^t}}{IO} \tag{11-3}$$

where ACF_t = the annual after-tax cash flow in time period t (this can take on either positive or negative values),

k = the appropriate discount rate, that is, the required rate of return or the cost of capital,

IO = the initial cash outlay,

n = the project's expected life.

The decision criterion with respect to the profitability index is to accept the project if the PI is greater than 1.00, and to reject the project if the PI is less than 1.00. However, if the profitability index exactly equals 1.00, we are indifferent between acceptance and rejection of the project. This accept-reject criterion is illustrated below:

$PI > 1.0$ Accept
$PI < 1.0$ Reject

Looking closely at this criterion, we see that it will always yield the same accept-reject decision as does the net present value criterion. Whenever the present value of the project's net cash flow is greater than its initial cash outlay, the project's net present value will be positive, signaling an accept decision. When this is true, then the project's profitability index will also be greater than one, as the present value of the net cash flows (the PI's numerator) is greater than its initial outlay (the PI's denominator). While these two decision criteria will always yield the same accept-reject decision, they will not necessarily rank acceptable projects in the same order. This problem of conflicting ranking will be dealt with at a later point.

Since the net present value and profitability index criteria are essen-

Table 11-13 PROFITABILITY INDEX (PI) ILLUSTRATION OF INVESTMENT IN NEW MACHINERY

	AFTER-TAX CASH FLOW
Initial outlay	−$50,000
Inflow year 1	15,000
Inflow year 2	8,000
Inflow year 3	10,000
Inflow year 4	12,000
Inflow year 5	14,000
Inflow year 6	16,000

tially the same, they have the same advantages over the other criteria examined. They both employ cash flows, recognize the timing of the cash flows, and are consistent with the goal of maximization of shareholders' wealth. The major disadvantage of this criterion, as of the net present value criterion, is that it requires long, detailed cash flow forecasts.

Example.　A firm with a 10 percent required rate of return is considering investing in a new machine with an expected life of six years. The after-tax cash flows resulting from this investment are given in Table 11-13. Discounting the project's future net cash flows back to the present yields a present value of $53,667; dividing this value by the initial outlay of $50,000 gives a profitability index of 1.0733, as shown in Table 11-14. This tells us that the present value of the future benefits accruing from this project is 1.0733 times the level of the initial outlay. Since the profitability index is greater than 1.0, the project should be accepted.

Discounted Cash Flow Criterion 3: Internal Rate of Return

The **internal rate of return (IRR)** attempts to answer the question: What rate of return does this project earn? For computational purposes, the internal rate of return is defined as the discount rate that equates the present value of the project's future net cash flows with the project's initial cash outlay. Mathematically, the internal rate of return is defined as the value *IRR* in the following equation:

$$IO = \sum_{t=1}^{n} \frac{ACF_t}{(1 + IRR)^t} \tag{11-4}$$

where ACF_t = the annual after-tax cash flow in time period t (this can take on either a positive or negative value),

　　IO = the initial cash outlay,

　　n = the project's expected life,

　　IRR = the project's internal rate of return.

Table 11-14 CALCULATION FOR PI ILLUSTRATION OF INVESTMENT IN NEW
MACHINERY

	AFTER-TAX CASH FLOW	PRESENT VALUE FACTOR AT 10 PERCENT	PRESENT VALUE
Initial outlay	−$50,000	1.0	−$50,000
Inflow year 1	15,000	.909	13,635
Inflow year 2	8,000	.826	6,608
Inflow year 3	10,000	.751	7,510
Inflow year 4	12,000	.683	8,196
Inflow year 5	14,000	.621	8,694
Inflow year 6	16,000	.564	9,024

$$PI = \frac{\sum_{t=1}^{n} \frac{ACF_t}{(1+k)^t}}{IO}$$

$$= \frac{\$13,635 + \$6,608 + \$7,510 + \$8,196 + \$8,694 + \$9,024}{\$50,000}$$

$$= \frac{\$53,667}{50,000}$$

$$= 1.0733$$

Intuitively, the internal rate of return is a hard concept to grasp. As another way of viewing it, assume that a project requires an initial outlay of IO and results in annual net cash flows after tax of $ACF_1, ACF_2, \ldots, ACF_n$. If we alternatively took our initial outlay of IO and placed it in a bank where it earned a rate of return equal to the internal rate of return, we could withdraw an amount equal to ACF_1 at the end of the first year, ACF_2 the second year, and so forth; finally, when ACF_n was withdrawn at the end of the nth year, we would have completely exhausted our funds. In other words, a project's internal rate of return is simply the rate of return that the project earns.

The decision criterion associated with the internal rate of return is to accept the project if the internal rate of return is greater than the required rate of return, sometimes called the hurdle rate by investors. Alternatively, we reject the project if its internal rate of return is less than this required rate of return. This accept-reject criterion is illustrated below:

IRR > required rate of return   Accept
IRR < required rate of return   Reject

If the internal rate of return on a project is equal to the shareholders' required rate of return, accepting the project should not result in any change in the firm's stock price. This is because the firm is earning exactly the rate that its shareholders are requiring. On the other hand, if the project yields an internal rate of return greater than the investors' required rate of return, its acceptance should increase the firm's stock price. Similarly, the acceptance of a project with an internal rate of return below the investors' required rate of return will decrease the firm's stock price.

In general, the internal rate of return criterion provides the same accept-reject decision for an investment proposal as the net present value and profitability index criteria. If discounting the future cash flows back to the present at the required rate of return, k, yields a zero net present value, then the profitability index must equal 1.0. In this instance, the internal rate of return will be equal to k, the required rate of return. This happens because the future cash inflows discounted back to present at k must be equal to the initial outlay for the net present value to be zero. Thus k is the internal rate of return because it is the discount rate that equates the initial outlay with the present value of the future cash inflows. Consequently, when one of the discounted cash flow criteria is at its indifference point, they all are. Furthermore, if the net present value is positive, the profitability index must exceed 1.0, and the internal rate of return will be greater than the cost of capital or required rate of return. For this reason, when one of these criteria indicates the project is acceptable, they all suggest that the investment should be made. Finally, if one criterion indicates that a project should be rejected, all three standards will signal a rejection. In essence, if the net present value is negative, the profitability index must be less than 1.0. Also, in this situation, a discount rate less than the required rate of return is required to make the present value of the future flows equal to the initial outlay, which indicates that the internal rate of return is less than the required rate of return.

Thus, in general, all the discounted cash flow criteria are consistent and will give similar accept-reject decisions. In addition, since the internal rate of return is another discounted cash flow criterion, it exhibits the same general advantages and disadvantages as both the net present value and profitability index, and occasionally has an additional disadvantage of being tedious to calculate.

COMPUTING THE IRR
FOR EVEN CASH FLOWS

The calculation of a project's internal rate of return can be either very simple or relatively complicated. As an example of straightforward solution, assume that a firm with a required rate of return of 10 percent is considering a project that involves an initial outlay of $45,555. If the investment is taken, the after-tax cash flows are expected to be $15,000 per annum over the project's four-year life. In this case, the internal rate of return is equal to IRR in the following equation:

$$\$45,555 = \frac{\$15,000}{(1 + IRR)^1} + \frac{\$15,000}{(1 + IRR)^2} + \frac{\$15,000}{(1 + IRR)^3} + \frac{\$15,000}{(1 + IRR)^4}$$

From our discussion of the present value of an annuity in Chapter 5, we know that this equation can be reduced to

$$\$45,555 = \$15,000 \left[\sum_{t=1}^{4} \frac{1}{(1 + IRR)^t} \right]$$

Appendix D gives table values for $\left[\sum_{t=1}^{4} 1/(1 + i)^t \right]$ for various combinations of i and t, which further reduces this equation to

$$\$45,555 = \$15,000 \begin{bmatrix} \text{Table Value} \\ \text{Appendix D} \\ \text{4 years} \\ \text{IRR percent} \end{bmatrix}$$

Dividing both sides by $15,000, this becomes:

$$3.037 = \begin{bmatrix} \text{Table Value} \\ \text{Appendix D} \\ \text{4 years} \\ \text{IRR percent} \end{bmatrix}$$

Hence, we are looking for a table value of 3.037 in the four-year row of Appendix D. This value occurs when i equals 12 percent, which means that 12 percent is the internal rate of return for the investment.

COMPUTING THE IRR
FOR UNEVEN CASH FLOWS

Unfortunately, the internal rate of return can be solved directly in the tables only when the future after-tax net cash flows are in the form of an annuity or a single payment. When these flows are in the form of an uneven series of flows, a trial-and-error approach is necessary. To do this, we first determine the present value of the future after-tax net cash flows using an arbitrary discount rate. If the present value of the future cash flows at this discount rate is larger than the initial outlay, the rate is increased; if it is smaller than the initial outlay, the discount rate is lowered; and the process begins again. This search routine is continued until the present value of the future after-tax cash flows is equal to the initial outlay. The interest rate that creates this situation is the internal rate of return.

To illustrate the procedure, consider an investment proposal that requires an initial outlay of $3817 and returns $1000 at the end of year 1, $2000 at the end of year 2, and $3000 at the end of year 3. In this case, the internal rate of return must be determined using a trial-and-error procedure. This process is shown in Table 11-15, in which an arbitrarily selected discount rate of 15 percent was chosen to begin the process. The trial-and-error search technique slowly centers in on the project's internal rate of return of 22 percent. The project's internal rate of return is then compared

Table 11-15 COMPUTING THE IRR FOR
UNEVEN CASH FLOWS

Initial outlay	−$3817
Flow year 1	1000
Flow year 2	2000
Flow year 3	3000

Solution: Pick an arbitrary discount rate and use it to determine the present value of the inflows. Compare the present value of the inflows with the initial outlay; if they are equal, you have determined the IRR. Otherwise, raise the discount rate if the present value of the inflows is larger than the initial outlay or lower the discount rate if the present value of the inflows is less than the initial outlay. Repeat this process until the IRR is found.

1. Try $i = 15$ percent:

	NET CASH FLOWS	PRESENT VALUE FACTOR AT 15 PERCENT	PRESENT VALUE
Inflow year 1	$1000	.870	$ 870
Inflow year 2	2000	.756	1512
Inflow year 3	3000	.658	1974
Present value of inflows			$4356
Initial outlay			−$3817

2. Try $i = 20$ percent:

	NET CASH FLOWS	PRESENT VALUE FACTOR AT 20 PERCENT	PRESENT VALUE
Inflow year 1	$1000	.833	$ 833
Inflow year 2	2000	.694	1388
Inflow year 3	3000	.579	1737
Present value of inflows			$3958
Initial outlay			−$3817

3. Try $i = 22$ percent:

	NET CASH FLOWS	PRESENT VALUE FACTOR AT 22 PERCENT	PRESENT VALUE
Inflow year 1	$1000	.820	$ 820
Inflow year 2	2000	.672	1344
Inflow year 3	3000	.551	1653
Present value of inflows			$3817
Initial outlay			−$3817

Table 11-16 THREE IRR INVESTMENT PROPOSAL EXAMPLES

	A	B	C
Initial outlay	$10,000	$10,000	$10,000
Inflow year 1	3,362	0	1,000
Inflow year 2	3,362	0	3,000
Inflow year 3	3,362	0	6,000
Inflow year 4	3,362	13,605	7,000

to the firm's required rate of return, and if the IRR is the larger, the project is accepted.

Example. A firm with a required rate of return of 10 percent is considering three investment proposals. Given the information in Table 11-16, management plans to calculate the internal rate of return for each project and determine which projects should be accepted.

Because project A is an annuity, we can easily calculate its internal rate of return by determining the table value necessary to equate the present value of the future cash flows with the initial outlay. This computation is done as follows:

$$IO = ACF_t \left[\sum_{t=1}^{n} \frac{1}{(1 + IRR)^t} \right]$$

$$\$10,000 = \$3362 \left[\sum_{t=1}^{4} \frac{1}{(1 + IRR)^t} \right]$$

$$\$10,000 = \$3362 \begin{bmatrix} \text{Table Value} \\ \text{Appendix D} \\ \text{4 years} \\ \text{IRR percent} \end{bmatrix}$$

$$2.974 = \begin{bmatrix} \text{Table Value} \\ \text{Appendix D} \\ \text{4 years} \\ \text{IRR percent} \end{bmatrix}$$

We are looking for a table value of 2.974, in the four-year row of Appendix D, which occurs in the $i = 13$ percent column. Thus, 13 percent is the internal rate of return. Since this rate is greater than the firm's required rate of return of 10 percent, the project should be accepted.

Project B involves a single future cash flow of $13,605, resulting from an initial outlay of $10,000; thus, its internal rate of return can be determined directly from the present-value table in Appendix B as follows:

$$IO = ACF_t \left[\frac{1}{(1 + IRR)^t} \right]$$

$$\$10,000 = \$13,605 \left[\frac{1}{(1 + IRR)^4} \right]$$

$$\$10,000 = \$13,605 \begin{bmatrix} \text{Table Value} \\ \text{Appendix B} \\ \text{4 years} \\ \text{IRR percent} \end{bmatrix}$$

$$.735 = \begin{bmatrix} \text{Table Value} \\ \text{Appendix B} \\ \text{4 years} \\ \text{IRR percent} \end{bmatrix}$$

This tells us that we should look for a table value of .735 in the four-year row of Appendix B, which occurs in the $i = 8$ percent column. We may therefore conclude that 8 percent is the internal rate of return. Since this rate is less than the firm's required rate of return of 10 percent, project B should be rejected.

The uneven nature of the future cash flows associated with project C necessitates the use of the trial-and-error search method. The internal rate of return for project C is equal to the value of *IRR* in the following equation:

$$\$10,000 = \frac{\$1000}{(1 + IRR)^1} + \frac{\$3000}{(1 + IRR)^2} + \frac{\$6000}{(1 + IRR)^3} + \frac{\$7000}{(1 + IRR)^4} \quad (11\text{-}5)$$

Arbitrarily selecting a discount rate of 15 percent and substituting it into equation (11-5) for IRR reduces the right-hand side of the equation to $11,090, as shown in Table 11-17. Therefore, since the present value of the future cash flows is larger than the initial outlay, we must raise the discount rate in order to find the project's internal rate of return. Substituting 20 percent for the discount rate, the right-hand side of equation (11-5) now becomes $9763. As this is less than the initial outlay of $10,000, we must now decrease the discount rate. In other words, we know that the internal rate of return for this project is between 15 and 20 percent. Since the present value of the future flows discounted back to present at 20 percent was only $237 too low, a discount rate of 19 percent is selected. As shown in Table 11-17, a discount rate of 19 percent reduces the present value of the future inflows down to $10,009, which is approximately the same as the initial outlay. Consequently, project C's internal rate of return is approximately 19 percent.[4] Since the internal rate of return is greater than the

[4]If desired, the actual rate can be more precisely approximated through interpolation as follows:

	DISCOUNT RATE	PRESENT VALUE
	19%	$10,009
	20	9,763
Difference	1%	$ 246

Proportion $9 is of $246 $= \dfrac{\$9}{\$246} = 0.0366\%$ $19\% + .0366\% = 19.0366\%$

Table 11-17 COMPUTING THE IRR FOR PROJECT C

1. Try i = 15 percent:

	NET CASH FLOWS	PRESENT VALUE FACTOR AT 15 PERCENT	PRESENT VALUE
Inflow year 1	$1,000	.870	$ 870
Inflow year 2	3,000	.756	2,268
Inflow year 3	6,000	.658	3,948
Inflow year 4	7,000	.572	4,004
Present value of inflows			$11,090
Initial outlay			$10,000

2. Try i = 20 percent:

	NET CASH FLOWS	PRESENT VALUE FACTOR AT 20 PERCENT	PRESENT VALUE
Inflow year 1	$1,000	.833	$ 833
Inflow year 2	3,000	.694	2,082
Inflow year 3	6,000	.579	3,474
Inflow year 4	7,000	.482	3,374
Present value of inflows			$ 9,763
Initial outlay			$10,000

3. Try i = 19 percent:

	NET CASH FLOWS	PRESENT VALUE FACTOR AT 19 PERCENT	PRESENT VALUE
Inflow year 1	$1,000	.840	$ 840
Inflow year 2	3,000	.706	2,118
Inflow year 3	6,000	.593	3,558
Inflow year 4	7,000	.499	3,493
Present value of inflows			$10,009
Initial outlay			$10,000

firm's required rate of return of 10 percent, this investment should be accepted.

To demonstrate further the computations for the discounted cash flow techniques, assume that a firm is in the 48 percent marginal tax bracket with a 15 percent required rate of return or cost of capital. Management is considering replacing a hand-operated assembly machine with a fully automated assembly operation. Given the information in Table 11-18, we want to determine the cash flows associated with this proposal, the project's net present value, profitability index, and internal rate of return, and then to apply the appropriate decision criteria.

Discounted Cash Flow Criteria: Comprehensive Example

Table 11-18 COMPREHENSIVE CAPITAL BUDGETING EXAMPLE

Existing Situation:	One full-time operator—salary $12,000
	Variable overtime—$1000 per year
	Fringe benefits—$1000 per year
	Cost of defects—$6000 per year
	Original price of hand-operated machine—$20,000
	Expected life—20 years
	Expected salvage value—$0
	Age—10 years
	Depreciation method—straight line
	Current salvage value of old machine—$12,000
	Annual maintenance—$0
	Marginal tax rate—48 percent
	Required rate of return—15 percent
Proposed Situation:	Fully automated operation—no operator necessary
	Cost of machine—$60,000
	Shipping fee—$1000
	Installation costs—$5000
	Expected economic life—10 years
	Depreciation method—straight line
	Salvage value after 10 years—$0
	Annual maintenance—$1000
	Cost of defects—$1000

First, the initial outlay is determined to be $54,960, as reflected in Table 11-19. Next, the differential cash flows over the project's life are calculated as shown in Table 11-20, yielding an estimated $12,048 cash flow per annum. In making these computations, we determine the incremental change in depreciation expenses by first taking the annual depreciation on the new project [($66,000 − $0)/10 years = $6600 per year for the next ten years] and subtracting out the lost depreciation on the old machine [($20,000 − $0)/20 years = $1000 per year for the old machine's remaining 10 years of life]. The depreciable value of the new machine is $66,000

Table 11-19 CALCULATION OF INITIAL OUTLAY FOR THE COMPREHENSIVE EXAMPLE

Outflows:	
Cost of new machine	$60,000
Shipping fee	1,000
Installation cost	5,000
Increased taxes—recapture of depreciation	
($12,000 − 10,000)(.48)	960
Inflows:	
Salvage value—old machine	−12,000
Net initial outlay	$54,960

Table 11-20 CALCULATION OF DIFFERENTIAL CASH FLOWS FOR THE COMPREHENSIVE EXAMPLE

		BOOK PROFIT	CASH FLOW
Savings:	Reduced salary	$12,000	$12,000
	Reduced variable overtime	1,000	1,000
	Reduced fringe benefits	1,000	1,000
	Reduced defects ($6000 − 1000)	5,000	5,000
Costs:	Increased maintenance expense	−1,000	−1,000
	Increased depreciation expense ($6600 − 1000)	−5,600	
Net savings before taxes		$12,400	$18,000
Taxes (48%)		5,952 ⟶	5,952
Net cash flow after taxes			$12,048

rather than just the $60,000 price of the new machine. The additional $6000 represents the charges necessary to put the machine in operating order. Once the change in taxes is determined from the incremental change in book profit, it is subtracted from the net cash flow savings before taxes, yielding the $12,048 net cash flow after taxes.

Finally, the terminal cash flow associated with the project has to be determined. In this case, since the new machine is expected to have a zero salvage value, there will be no terminal cash flow. The cash flow diagram associated with this project is set forth in Figure 11-2.

The net present value for this project is calculated below:

$$NPV = \sum_{t=1}^{n} \frac{ACF_t}{(1 + k)^t} - IO \qquad (11\text{-}2)$$

$$= \sum_{t=1}^{10} \frac{\$12,048}{(1 + .15)^t} - \$54,960$$

$$= \$12,048 \begin{bmatrix} \text{Table Value} \\ \text{Appendix D} \\ 10 \text{ years} \\ 15 \text{ percent} \end{bmatrix} - \$54,960$$

$$= \$12,048(5.019) - \$54,960$$

$$= \$60,469 - \$54,960$$

$$= \$5509$$

FIGURE 11-2 *Cash Flow Diagram for the Comprehensive Example*

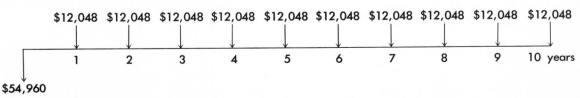

285

Since its net present value is greater than zero, the project should be accepted. The profitability index, which gives a measure of relative desirability of a project, is calculated as follows:

$$PI = \frac{\sum_{t=1}^{n} \frac{ACF_t}{(1 + k)^t}}{IO} \qquad (11\text{-}3)$$

$$= \frac{\$60,469}{\$54,960}$$

$$= 1.100$$

Since the project's PI is greater than one, the project should be accepted.

The internal rate of return can be determined directly from the present-value-of-an-annuity table as follows:

$$IO = \sum_{t=1}^{n} \frac{ACF_t}{(1 + IRR)^t} \qquad (11\text{-}4)$$

$$\$54,960 = \$12,048 \begin{bmatrix} \text{Table Value} \\ \text{Appendix D} \\ \text{10 years} \\ \text{IRR percent} \end{bmatrix}$$

$$4.561 = \begin{bmatrix} \text{Table Value} \\ \text{Appendix D} \\ \text{10 years} \\ \text{IRR percent} \end{bmatrix}$$

Looking in the 10-year row of the present-value-of-an-annuity table in Appendix D, we find that the value of 4.561 occurs between the 17 percent column (4.659) and the 18 percent column (4.494). As a result, the project's internal rate of return is between 17 and 18 percent, and the project should be accepted.

Applying the decision criteria to this example, we find that each of them indicates the project should be accepted, as the net present value is positive, the profitability index is greater than 1.0, and the internal rate of return is greater than the firm's required rate of return of 15 percent.

Up to this point we have focused solely on the accept-reject output of the capital budgeting decision for a single project. Sometimes, however, we must choose among a number of acceptable projects. At other times the number of projects that can be accepted or the total budget is actually limited; that is, capital rationing is imposed. In these cases different rankings may result, depending upon the discounted cash flow criterion being used. Before examining the reasons for these differences, we will explore the

**ADVANCED
TOPICS IN
CAPITAL
BUDGETING**

rationale behind capital rationing and project ranking and the ways in which they affect capital budgeting decisions.

The use of our capital budgeting decision rules implies that the size of the capital budget is determined by the availability of acceptable investment proposals. However, a firm may place a limit on the dollar size of the capital budget. This situation is called **capital rationing.**

Using the internal rate of return as our decision rule, we have accepted all projects with an internal rate of return greater than the firm's required rate of return. This rule is illustrated in Figure 11-3, where projects A through E would be chosen. However, when capital rationing is imposed, the dollar size of the total investment is limited by the budget constraint. In Figure 11-3, the budget constraint of $X precludes the acceptance of an attractive investment, project E. This situation obviously contradicts prior decision rules. Moreover, the solution of choosing the projects with the highest internal rate of return is complicated by the fact that some projects may be indivisible; for example, it is meaningless to recommend that half a computer be acquired.

RATIONALE FOR CAPITAL RATIONING

We will first ask why capital rationing exists and whether or not it is rational. In general, three principal reasons are given for imposing a capital rationing constraint. First, the management may feel that market conditions are temporarily adverse. In the early and mid seventies this reason was frequently given. At that time interest rates were at an all-time high, and stock prices were depressed. Second, there may be a shortage of qualified managers to direct new projects. This circumstance can occur when projects are of such a technical nature that qualified managers are simply not available. Third, there may be intangible considerations. For example,

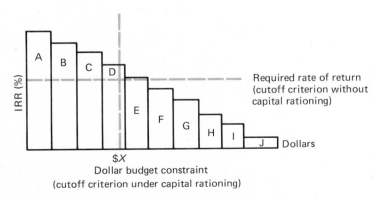

FIGURE 11-3 *Projects Ranked by IRR*

the management may simply fear debt, wishing to avoid interest payments at any cost. Or perhaps the common stock issuance may be limited in order to preserve the current owners' strict voting control over the company or to maintain a stable dividend policy.

Despite strong evidence that capital rationing exists in practice, the question remains as to its effect on the firm. In brief, the effect is negative in direction, and its degree depends upon the severity of the rationing. If the rationing is minor and noncontinuing, then the firm's share price will not suffer to any great extent. In this case capital rationing can probably be excused, although it should be noted that capital rationing entailing rejection of projects with positive net present values is contrary to the firm's goal of maximization of shareholders' wealth. If, on the other hand, the capital rationing is a result of the firm's decision to limit dramatically the number of new projects or to limit total investment to internally generated funds, then this policy will eventually have a significantly negative effect on the firm's share price. For example, a lower share price eventually will result from lost competitive advantage if, owing to a decision to limit arbitrarily its capital budget, a firm fails to upgrade its products and manufacturing process.

CAPITAL RATIONING
AND PROJECT SELECTION

If the firm decides to impose a capital constraint on investment projects, the appropriate decision criterion is to select the set of projects that has the highest net present value subject to the capital constraint. This guideline may preclude merely taking the highest-ranked projects in terms of the profitability index or the internal rate of return. If some or all the projects are indivisible, as shown in Figure 11-3, the last project accepted may be only partially accepted. Although partial acceptances may be possible in some cases, the indivisibility of most capital investments prevents it. If a project is a sales outlet or a truck, it may be meaningless to purchase half a sales outlet or half a truck.

To illustrate this procedure, consider a firm with a budget constraint of $1 million and five indivisible projects available to it, as given in Table 11-21. If the highest-ranked projects were taken, projects A and B would

Table 11-21 CAPITAL RATIONING EXAMPLE OF FIVE INDIVISIBLE PROJECTS

PROJECT	INITIAL OUTLAY	PROFITABILITY INDEX	NET PRESENT VALUE
A	$200,000	2.4	$280,000
B	200,000	2.3	260,000
C	800,000	1.7	560,000
D	300,000	1.3	90,000
E	300,000	1.2	60,000

be taken first. At that point there would not be enough funds available to take project C; hence, projects D and E would be taken. However, a higher total net present value is provided by the combination of projects A and C. Thus projects A and C should be selected from the set of projects available. This illustrates our guideline: to select the set of projects that maximizes the firm's net present value.

In the past, we have proposed that all projects with a positive net present value, a profitability index greater than 1.0, or an internal rate of return greater than the required rate of return be accepted, assuming there is no capital rationing. However, this acceptance is not always possible. In some cases, where two projects are judged acceptable by the discounted cash flow criteria, it may be necessary to select only one of them, as they are mutually exclusive. **Mutually exclusive** projects occur when a set of investment proposals perform essentially the same task; thus, acceptance of one will necessarily mean rejection of the others. For example, a company considering the installation of a computer system may evaluate three or four systems, all of which may have positive net present values; but the acceptance of one system will automatically mean rejection of the others. In general, to deal with mutually exclusive projects, we will merely rank them by means of the discounted cash flow criteria and select the project with the highest ranking. On occasion, unfortunately, problems of conflicting ranking may arise.

PROBLEMS IN PROJECT RANKING

There are three general types of ranking problems—the size disparity problem, the time disparity problem, and the unequal lives problem. Each involves the possibility of conflict in the ranks yielded by the various discounted cash flow capital budgeting criteria. As noted earlier, when one discounted cash flow criterion gives an accept signal, they will all give an accept signal, but they will not necessarily rank all projects in the same order. In most cases this disparity is not critical; however, for mutually exclusive projects the ranking order is important.

SIZE DISPARITY PROBLEM

The **size disparity problem** occurs when mutually exclusive projects of unequal size are examined. This problem is most easily illustrated with the use of an example.

Example.   Suppose that a firm with a cost of capital of 10 percent is considering two mutually exclusive projects, A and B. Project A involves a $200 initial outlay and cash inflow of $300 at the end of one year, while project B involves an initial outlay of $1500 and a cash inflow of $1900 at the end of one year. The net present value, profitability index, and internal rate of return for these projects are given in Figure 11-4.

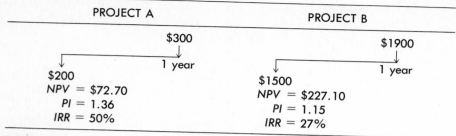

FIGURE 11-4 *Size Disparity Ranking Problem*

In this case, if the net present value criterion is used, project B should be accepted, while if the profitability index or the internal rate of return criterion is used, project A should be chosen. The question now becomes: Which project is better? The answer depends on whether or not capital rationing exists. Without capital rationing, project B is better because it provides the largest increase in shareholders' wealth; that is, it has a larger net present value. If there is a capital constraint, the problem then focuses on what can be done with the additional $1300 that is freed up if project A is chosen (costing $200, as opposed to $1500). If the firm can earn more on project A plus the project financed with the additional $1300 than it can on project B, then project A and the marginal project should be accepted. In effect, we are attempting to select the set of projects that maximize the firm's NPV. Thus, if the marginal project has a net present value greater than $154.40, selecting it plus project A with a net present value of $72.70 will provide a net present value greater than $227.10, the net present value for project B.

In summary, whenever the size disparity problem results in conflicting rankings between mutually exclusive projects, the project with the largest net present value will be selected, provided there is not capital rationing. When capital rationing exists, the firm should select the set of projects with the largest net present value.

TIME DISPARITY PROBLEM

The time disparity problem and the conflicting rankings that accompany it result from the differing reinvestment assumptions made by the net present value and internal rate of return decision criteria. The NPV criterion assumes that cash flows over the life of the project can be reinvested at the required rate of return or cost of capital while the IRR criterion implicitly assumes that the cash flows over the life of the project can be reinvested at the internal rate of return. Again, this problem may be illustrated through the use of an example.

Example.   Suppose a firm with a required rate of return or cost of capital of 10 percent and with no capital constraints is considering the two mutually exclusive projects illustrated in Figure 11-5. The net present

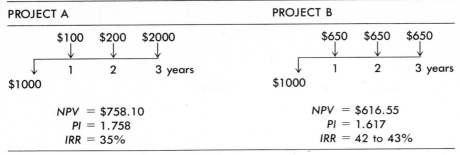

FIGURE 11-5 *Time Disparity Ranking Problem*

value and profitability index indicate that project A is the better of the two, while the internal rate of return indicates that project B is the better. Project B receives its cash flows earlier than project A, and the different assumptions made as to how these flows can be reinvested results in the difference in rankings. Which criterion should be followed depends upon which reinvestment assumption is used. The net present value criterion is preferred in this case because it makes the most acceptable assumption for the wealth-maximizing firm. It is certainly the most conservative assumption that can be made, since the required rate of return can be looked on as the lowest possible reinvestment rate. Moreover, as we have already noted, the net present value method maximizes the value of the firm and the shareholders' wealth.

Like the size disparity problem, the time disparity problem becomes more complicated under capital rationing. As already stated, when a capital constraint is not imposed, net present value is the appropriate decision-making criterion. But when there is a capital constraint, the cutoff rate or actual required rate of return is no longer equal to the firm's normal required rate of return or cost of capital. That is, the firm no longer invests in all projects with returns greater than its required rate of return. Instead, the lowest return on a project accepted is above the normal required rate of return or cost of capital. Hence, owing to the capital rationing constraint, the lowest rate of return accepted is actually the firm's true required rate of return. In other words, under capital rationing the normal required rate of return or cost of capital loses its meaning, and the true required rate of return becomes the lowest rate of return on any project selected. Of course, if a capital constraint is not imposed, these two values will be identical. However, under capital rationing, the reinvestment rate assumptions produce conflicting rankings that can be resolved only through a redetermination of each project's net present value using the actual required rate of return. If capital rationing makes the lowest rate of return earned on any project 20 percent rather than the 10 percent cost of capital, then 20 percent is the firm's true required rate of return under capital rationing. Redetermining the net present value for projects A and B in the example above, using a 20 percent required rate of return, produces a net present value of $380.10 for project A and of $368.90 for project B. Thus, project A should be taken.

UNEQUAL LIVES PROBLEM

The final ranking problem to be examined centers around the question of whether or not it is appropriate to compare mutually exclusive projects with different life spans.

Example. Suppose a firm with a 10 percent required rate of return is faced with the problem of replacing an aging machine and is considering two replacement machines, one with a three-year life and one with a six-year life. The relevant cash flow information for these projects is given in Figure 11-6.

Examining the discounted cash flow criteria, we find the net present value and profitability index criteria indicating that project B is the better project, while the internal rate of return favors project A. This ranking inconsistency is caused by the different life spans of the projects being compared. In this case the decision is a difficult one because the projects are not comparable.

The problem of incomparability of projects with different lives is not merely a result of the different lives; rather, it arises because future profitable investment proposals are affected by the decision currently being made. This can easily be seen in a replacement problem such as the present example, where two mutually exclusive machines with different lives are being considered. In this case, a comparison of the net present values alone on each of these projects would be misleading. If the project with the shorter life were taken, at its termination the firm could replace the machine and receive additional benefits, while acceptance of the project with the longer life would exclude this possibility. The key question thus becomes: Does the investment decision being made today affect future profitable investment proposals? If so, the projects are not comparable. In this case, if project B is taken, then the project that could have been considered after three years when project A terminates can no longer be considered. Thus, acceptance of project B not only forces rejection of project A but also

FIGURE 11-6 *Unequal Lives Ranking Problem*

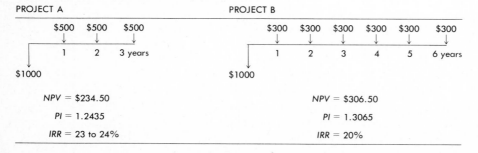

forces rejection of any replacement machine that might have been considered for years 4 through 6.

There are several methods to deal with this situation. The first option is merely to assume that the cash inflows from the shorter-lived investment will be reinvested at the cost of capital until the termination of the longer-lived asset. While this approach is the simplest, merely calculating the net present value, it actually ignores the problem at hand—that of allowing for participation in another replacement opportunity with a positive net present value. The proper solution thus becomes the projection of reinvestment opportunities into the future—that is, making assumptions as to possible future investment opportunities. Unfortunately, while the first method is too simplistic to be of any value, the second is extremely difficult, requiring extensive cash flow forecasts. The final technique for confronting the problem is to assume that reinvestment opportunities in the future will be similar to the current ones. The most common way of doing this is by creating a replacement chain to equalize life spans. The present example would call for the creation of a two-chain cycle for project A—that is, we assume that project A can be replaced with a similar investment at the end of three years. Thus, project A would be viewed as two project A's occurring back to back, as illustrated in Figure 11-7. The net present value on this replacement chain is $426.50, which is comparable with project B's net present value. Thus, project A should be accepted, because the net present value of its replacement chain is greater than the net present value of project B.

In this chapter we examined the process of capital budgeting, which involves decision making with respect to investment in fixed assets. Specifically, we examined the measurement of incremental cash flows associated with such investment proposals and the evaluation of those proposals. In measuring cash flows we focused on the *incremental* or differential *after-tax cash flows* attributed to the investment proposal. In general, a project's cash flows will fall into one of three categories: (1) the initial outlay, (2) the differential flows over the project's life, (3) the terminal cash flow. A summary of the typical entries in each of these categories appeared in Table 11-7.

We examined five commonly used criteria for determining the acceptance or rejection of capital budgeting proposals. The first two methods, the payback period and accounting rate of return, do not incorporate the time value of money into their calculations, while the net present

FIGURE 11-7 *Replacement Chain Illustration: Two Project A's*

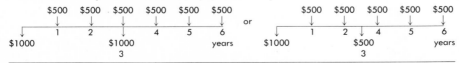

Table 11-22 CAPITAL BUDGETING CRITERIA

Nondiscounted Cash Flow Methods

1. Payback period = number of years required to recapture the initital investment.

   Accept if payback < maximum acceptable payback period
   Reject if payback > maximum acceptable payback period

   Advantages:
   (1) Uses cash flows.
   (2) Is easy to calculate and understand.
   (3) May be used as a rough screening device.

   Disadvantages:
   (1) Ignores the time value of money.
   (2) Ignores cash flows occurring after the payback period.

2. Accounting rate of return =

$$\frac{\sum_{t=1}^{n} (\text{accounting profit after tax}_t)/n}{(\text{initial investment} + \text{salvage value})/2}$$

   where n = project's expected life.

   Accept if $AROR$ > minimum acceptable rate of return
   Reject if $AROR$ < minimum acceptable rate of return

   Advantages:
   (1) Involves familiar, easily accessible terms.
   (2) Is easy to calculate and understand.

   Disadvantages:
   (1) Ignores the time value of money.
   (2) Uses accounting profits rather than cash flows.

Discounted Cash Flow Methods

3. Net present value = present value of the annual cash flows after tax less the investment's initial outlay.

$$NPV = \sum_{t=1}^{n} \frac{ACF_t}{(1 + k)^t} - IO$$

   where ACF_t = the annual after-tax cash flow in time period t (this can take on either positive or negative values),
   k = the appropriate discount rate, that is, the required rate of return or the cost of capital,[a]
   IO = the initial cash outlay,
   n = the project's expected life.

   Accept if NPV > 0.0
   Reject if NPV < 0.0

   Advantages:
   (1) Uses cash flows.
   (2) Recognizes the time value of money.
   (3) Is consistent with the firm goal of shareholder wealth maximization.

   Disadvantages:
   (1) Requires detailed long-term forecasts of the incremental benefits and costs.

Table 11-22 CAPITAL BUDGETING CRITERIA *(cont.)*

4. Profitability index = the ratio of the present value of the future net cash flows to the initial outlay.

$$PI = \frac{\sum_{t=1}^{n} \frac{ACF_t}{(1 + k)^t}}{IO}$$

Accept if $PI > 1.0$
Reject if $PI < 1.0$

Advantages:
(1) Uses cash flows.
(2) Recognizes the time value of money.
(3) Is consistent with the firm firm goal of shareholder wealth maximization.

Disadvantages:
(1) Requires detailed long-term forecasts of the incremental benefits and costs.

5. Internal rate of return = the discount rate that equates the present value of the project's future net cash flows with the project's initial outlay.

$$IO = \sum_{t=1}^{n} \frac{ACF_t}{(1 + IRR)^t}$$

where IRR = the project's internal rate of return.

Accept if $IRR >$ required rate of return
Reject if $IRR <$ required rate of return

Advantages:
(1) Uses cash flows.
(2) Recognizes the time value of money.
(3) Is consistent with the firm goal firm goal of shareholder wealth maximization.

Disadvantages:
(1) Requires detailed long-term forecasts of the incremental benefits and costs.
(2) Can involve tedious calculations.

[a]The cost of capital is discussed in Chapter 14.

value, profitability index, and internal rate of return do. These methods are summarized in Table 11-22. Finally, the problems of capital rationing were introduced, and in particular we examined conflicting rankings caused by the size disparity, the time disparity, and unequal lives problems.

STUDY QUESTIONS

11-1. Why is the capital budgeting decision such an important process? Why are capital budgeting errors so costly?
11-2. Why do we focus on cash flows rather than actual profits in making our capital budgeting decisions? Why are we interested only in incremental cash flows rather than total cash flows?

11-3. If depreciation is not a cash flow expense, does it affect the level of cash flows from a project in any way?

11-4. If a project requires additional investment in working capital, how should this be treated in calculating cash flows?

11-5. How do sunk costs affect the determination of cash flows associated with an investment proposal?

11-6. What are the criticisms of the use of the payback period as a capital budgeting technique? What are its advantages? Why is it so frequently used?

11-7. In some foreign countries, expropriation of foreign investments is a common practice. If you were considering an investment in one of those countries, would the use of the payback period criterion seem more reasonable than it otherwise might? Why?

11-8. What are the criticisms of the use of the accounting rate of return as a capital budgeting technique? What are its advantages?

11-9. Briefly compare and contrast the three discounted cash flow criteria. What are the advantages and disadvantages to the use of each of these methods?

11-10. What are mutually exclusive projects? Why might the existence of mutually exclusive projects cause problems in the implementation of the discounted cash flow capital budgeting criteria?

11-11. What reasons are commonly given for capital rationing? Is capital rationing rational?

11-12. How should the comparison of two mutually exclusive projects of unequal size be dealt with? Would your approach change if capital rationing existed?

11-13. What causes the time disparity ranking problem? What reinvestment rate assumptions are associated with the net present value and internal rate of return capital budgeting criteria?

11-14. When might two mutually exclusive projects having unequal lives be incomparable? How should this problem be dealt with ?

11-15. Often government action to push or slow down the economy is implemented by altering the capital budgeting decision-making process of the firm. How might the following changes affect capital budgeting decisions?

(a) A movement by the Federal Reserve to reduce interest rates.

(b) An increase in the investment tax credit.

(c) A change in the tax laws allowing an increase in the rate of accelerated depreciation.

STUDY PROBLEMS

11-1. The L. Turner Corporation is considering selling one of its old assembly machines. The machine, purchased for $30,000 five years ago, had an expected life of 10 years and an expected salvage value of $10,000. Assume the L. Turner Corporation uses straight-line depreciation and could sell this old machine for $35,000. Also assume a 48 percent marginal tax rate.

(a) What would be the taxes associated with this sale?

(b) If the old machine were sold for $25,000, what would be the taxes associated with this sale?

(c) If the old machine were sold for $20,000, what would be the taxes associated with this sale?

(d) If the old machine were sold for $12,000, what would be the taxes associated with this sale?

11-2. The T. Baker Corporation is considering replacing a hand-operated weaving machine with a new fully automated machine. Given the following information, determine the cash flows associated with this replacement.

Existing Situation:	Two full-time machine operators—salaries $10,000 each per year
	Cost of maintenance—$5000 per year
	Cost of defects—$5000 per year
	Original cost of old machine—$30,000
	Expected life—10 years
	Age—five years old
	Expected salvage value—$0
	Depreciation method—straight line
	Current salvage value—$10,000
	Marginal tax rate—48 percent
Proposed Situation:	Fully automated machine
	Cost of machine—$55,000
	Installation fee—$5000
	Cost of maintenance—$6000 per year
	Cost of defects—$2000 per year
	Expected life—five years
	Salvage value—$15,000
	Depreciation method—straight line

11-3. Given the cash flow information in problem 2, and a required rate of return of 15 percent, compute the following for the automated weaving machine.
(a) Payback period.
(b) Net present value.
(c) Profitability index.
(d) Internal rate of return.
Should this project be accepted?

11-4. Two mutually exclusive projects are being evaluated using the accounting rate of return. Each project has an initial cost of $20,000 and a salvage value of $4000 after six years. Given the following information:

	ANNUAL ACCOUNTING PROFITS AFTER TAX	
Year	Project A	Project B
1	$ 2,000	$10,000
2	2,000	10,000
3	2,000	10,000

Year	Project A	Project B
4	13,000	5,000
5	13,000	5,000
6	14,000	5,000

(a) Determine each project's AROR.

(b) Which project should be selected, using this criterion? Would you support that recommendation? Why or why not?

11-5. Determine the internal rate of return on the following projects:

(a) An initial outlay of $10,000 resulting in a single cash flow of $17,182 after eight years.

(b) An initial outlay of $10,000 resulting in a single cash flow of $48,077 after 10 years.

(c) An initial outlay of $10,000 resulting in a single cash flow of $114,943 after 20 years.

(d) An initial outlay of $10,000 resulting in a single cash flow of $13,680 after three years.

11-6. Determine the internal rate of return on the following projects:

(a) An initial outlay of $10,000 resulting in a cash flow of $1993 at the end of each year for the next 10 years.

(b) An initial outlay of $10,000 resulting in a cash flow of $2054 at the end of each year for the next 20 years.

(c) An initial outlay of $10,000 resulting in a cash flow of $1193 at the end of each year for the next 12 years.

(d) An initial outlay of $10,000 resulting in a cash flow of $2843 at the end of each year for the next five years.

11-7. Determine the internal rate of return to the nearest percent on the following projects:

(a) An initial outlay of $10,000 resulting in a cash flow of $2000 at the end of year 1, $5000 at the end of year 2, and $8000 at the end of year 3.

(b) An initial outlay of $10,000 resulting in a cash flow of $8000 at the end of year 1, $5000 at the end of year 2, and $2000 at the end of year 3.

(c) An initial outlay of $10,000 resulting in a cash flow of $2000 at the end of years 1 through 5 and $5000 at the end of year 6.

11-8. The S. Risley Corporation is considering replacing one of its plastic molding machines with a new more efficient machine. The old machine presently has a book value of $100,000 and could be sold for $60,000. The old machine is being depreciated on a straight-line basis down to a salvage value of zero over the next five years. The replacement machine would cost $300,000 and have an expected life of five years, after which it could be sold for $50,000. Because of reductions in defects and material savings, the new machine would produce cash benefits of

$90,000 per year before depreciation and taxes. Assuming straight-line depreciation, a 48 percent marginal tax rate, and a required rate of return of 15 percent, find:

(a) The payback period.
(b) The net present value.
(c) The profitability index.
(d) The internal rate of return.

11-9. The Robo Corporation is considering replacing a five-year-old machine that originally cost $50,000, presently has a book value of $25,000, and could be sold for $60,000. This machine is currently being depreciated using the straight-line method down to a terminal value of zero over the next five years. The replacement machine would cost $125,000 and have a five-year expected life over which it would be depreciated down to a salvage value of zero using the straight-line method. The new machine would produce savings before depreciation and taxes of $45,000 per year. Assuming a 48 percent marginal tax rate and a required rate of return of 10 percent, calculate:

(a) The payback period.
(b) The net present value.
(c) The profitability index.
(d) The internal rate of return.

11-10. The S. Eells Corporation is considering replacing a 10-year-old machine that originally cost $30,000 and is being depreciated using the straight-line method over its 15-year expected life down to a terminal value of zero in five years. The replacement machine being considered would cost $80,000 and have a five-year expected life and a salvage value of $40,000. Material efficiencies resulting from the replacement would result in savings of $30,000 per year before depreciation and taxes. Currently, the old machine could be sold for $15,000. Assuming straight-line depreciation, a 48 percent marginal tax rate, and a required rate of return of 20 percent, calculate:

(a) The payback period.
(b) The net present value.
(c) The profitability index.
(d) The internal rate of return.

11-11. The L. Bellich Company, a firm in the 48 percent marginal tax bracket, is considering the purchase of a new fully automated machine to replace an older, manually operated one. The machine being replaced, now five years old, originally had an expected life of 10 years, was being depreciated using the straight-line method from $20,000 down to zero, and could be sold for $25,000. It took one man to operate the old machine, and he earned $15,000 per year in salaries and $2000 per year in fringe benefits. The annual costs of maintenance and defects associated with the old machine were $7000 and $3000, respectively. The replacement machine being considered had a purchase price of $50,000 and a salvage value after five years of $10,000 and would be depreciated over this period using the straight-line depreciation method.

In order to get the automated machine in running order, there would be a $3000 shipping fee and a $2000 installation charge. In addition, because the new machine would work faster than the old one, investment in raw materials and goods in process inventories would need to be increased by a total of $5000. The annual costs of maintenance and defects on the new machine would be $2000 and $4000, respectively. The new machine also requires maintenance workers to be specially trained; fortunately, a similar machine was purchased three months ago, and at that time the maintenance workers went through the $5000 training program needed to familiarize themselves with the new equipment. The firm's management is uncertain whether or not to charge half of this $5000 training fee toward the new project. Finally, in order to purchase the new machine, it appears the firm would have to borrow an additional $20,000 at 10 percent interest from its local bank, resulting in additional interest payments of $2000 per year. The required rate of return on projects of this kind is 20 percent.

(a) What is this project's initial outlay?
(b) What are the differential cash flows over the project's life?
(c) What is the terminal cash flow?
(d) Draw a cash flow diagram for this project.
(e) If the firm requires a minimum payback period on projects of this type of three years, should this project be accepted?
(f) Calculate the projects AROR?
(g) What is its net present value?
(h) What is its profitability index?
(i) What is its internal rate of return?
(j) Should the project be accepted? Why or why not?

11-12. The D. Dorner Farms Corporation is considering purchasing one of two fertilizer-herbicides for the upcoming year. The more expensive of the two is the better and will produce a higher yield. Assume these projects are mutually exclusive and that the required rate of return is 10 percent. Given the following after-tax net cash flows:

YEAR	PROJECT A	PROJECT B
0	−$500	−$5000
1	700	6000

(a) Calculate the net present value.
(b) Calculate the profitability index.
(c) Calculate the internal rate of return.
(d) If there is no capital rationing constraint, which project should be selected? If there is a capital rationing constraint, how should the decision be made?

11-13. The R. Tolbert Corporation is considering two mutually exclusive projects. The cash flows associated with those projects are as follows:

YEAR	PROJECT A	PROJECT B
0	−$50,000	−$ 50,000
1	15,625	0
2	15,625	0
3	15,625	0
4	15,625	0
5	15,625	$100,000

The required rate of return on these projects is 10 percent.
(a) What is each project's payback period?
(b) What is each project's net present value?
(c) What is each project's internal rate of return?
(d) What has caused the ranking conflict?
(e) Which project should be accepted? Why?

11-14. The B. T. Knight Corporation is considering two mutually exclusive pieces of machinery that perform the same task. The two alternatives available provide the following set of after-tax net cash flows:

YEAR	EQUIPMENT A	EQUIPMENT B
0	−$20,000	−$20,000
1	12,590	6,625
2	12,590	6,625
3	12,590	6,625
4		6,625
5		6,625
6		6,625
7		6,625
8		6,625
9		6,625

Equipment A has an expected life of three years, while equipment B has an expected life of nine years. Assume a required rate of return of 15 percent.
(a) Calculate each project's payback period.
(b) Calculate each project's net present value.
(c) Calculate each project's internal rate of return.
(d) Are these projects comparable?
(e) Compare these projects using replacement chains. Which project should be selected? Support your recommendation.

ALPIN, RICHARD D., and GEORGE L. CASLER, *Capital Investment Analysis*. Columbus, Ohio: Grid, 1973.
BACON, PETER W., "The Evaluation of Mutually Exclusive Investments," *Financial Management*, 6 (Summer 1977), 55–64.

BERNHARD, RICHARD H., "Mathematical Programming Models for Capital Budgeting—A Survey, Generalization and Critique," *Journal of Financial and Quantitative Analysis,* 4 (June 1969), 111–58.

BIERMAN, HAROLD, JR., "A Reconciliation of Present Value Capital Budgeting and Accounting," *Financial Management,* 6 (Summer 1977), 52–54.

BIERMAN, HAROLD, JR., and SEYMOUR SMIDT, *The Capital Budgeting Decision.* New York: Macmillan, 1971.

DUDLEY, CARLTON L., JR., "A Note on Reinvestment Assumptions in Choosing between Net Present Value and Internal Rate of Return," *Journal of Finance,* 27 (September 1972), 907–15.

FOGLER, H. RUSSELL, "Ranking Techniques and Capital Rationing," *Accounting Review,* 47 (January 1972), 134–43.

ʹEAN, WILLIAM H., *Capital Budgeting: The Economic Evaluation of Investment Projects.* Scranton, Pa.: International Textbook, 1969.

LORIE, JAMES H., and LEONARD J. SAVAGE, "Three Problems in Rationing Capital," *Journal of Business,* 28 (October 1955), 229–39.

MAO, JAMES C. T., "The Internal Rate of Return as a Ranking Criterion," *Engineering Economist,* 11 (Winter 1966), 1–13.

MERRETT, A. J., and ALLEN SYKES, *Capital Budgeting and Company Finance.* London: Longmans, 1966.

OSTERYOUNG, JEROME, *Capital Budgeting: Long-Term Asset Selection.* Columbus, Ohio: Grid, 1974.

PETTY, J. WILLIAM, DAVID F. SCOTT, JR., and MONROE M. BIRD, "The Capital Expenditure Decision-Making Process of Large Corporations," *Engineering Economist,* 20 (Spring 1975), 159–72.

SARNAT, MARSHALL, and HAIM LEVY, "The Relationship of Rules of Thumb to the Internal Rate of Return: A Restatement and Generalization," *Journal of Finance,* 24 (June 1969), 479–90.

SCHNELL, JAMES S., and ROY S. NICHOLOSI, "Capital Expenditure Feedback: Project Reappraisal," *Engineering Economist* 19 (Summer 1974), 253–61.

SCHWAB, BERNHARD, and PETER LUSZTIG, "A Comparative Analysis of the Net Present Value and the Benefit-Cost Ratios as Measures of the Economic Desirability of Investments," *Journal of Finance,* 24 (June 1969), 507–16.

SOLOMON, EZRA, "The Arithmetic of Capital-Budgeting Decisions," *Journal of Business,* 29 (April 1956), 124–29.

TEICHROEW, DANIEL, ALEXANDER A. ROBICHEK, and MICHAEL MONTALBANO, "An Analysis of Criteria for Investment and Financing Decisions under Certainty," *Management Science,* 12 (November 1965), 151–79.

WEAVER, JAMES B., "Organizing and Maintaining a Capital Expenditure Program," *Engineering Economist,* 20 (Fall 1974), 1–36.

WEINGARTNER, H. MARTIN, *Mathematical Programming and the Analysis of Capital Budgeting Problems.* Copyright H. Martin Weingartner, 1963.

————— , "Capital Rationing: *n* Authors in Search of a Plot," *Journal of Finance,* 32 (December 1977), 1403–31.

Capital Budgeting under Uncertainty

In discussing capital budgeting techniques in the previous chapter, we implicitly assumed the level of risk associated with each investment proposal was the same. In this chapter we will lift that assumption and examine various ways in which risk can be incorporated into the capital budgeting decision. To do this we will first discuss the concept of risk, then move on to its measurement, followed by a discussion of various methods for incorporating it into the decision-making process, and conclude the chapter with a discussion of portfolio risk.

Up to this point we have completely ignored risk; that is, we have treated the expected cash flows resulting from an investment proposal as being known with perfect certainty. In reality the future cash flows associated with the introduction of a new sales outlet or a new product are merely estimates of what is expected to happen in the future, not necessarily what will happen in the future. For example, when the Ford Motor Company made its decision to introduce the Edsel, you can bet that the expected cash flows it based its decision on were nothing like the cash flows it realized. In effect, the cash flows we have assumed known with perfect certainty have in actuality merely been our best estimate of the expected future cash flows. A cash flow diagram based on the possible outcomes of an investment propo-

RISK AND THE INVESTMENT DECISION

303

sal rather than the expected values of these outcomes appears in Figure 12-1.

In this chapter we will assume that under risk we do not know beforehand what cash flows will actually result from a new project. However, we do have expectations concerning the possible outcomes and are able to assign probabilities to these outcomes. Stated another way, although we do not know what the cash flows resulting from the acceptance of a new project will be, we can formulate the probability distributions from which the flows will be drawn.

Thus far, we have talked about risk only in a general manner, indicating that risk occurs when there is some question as to what the future outcome of an event will be. Now we will define risk in such a way that statistical measures of risk become possible. We will then proceed with an examination of the logic behind this definition. **Risk** can be defined as a relative measure of the degree of variability of possible outcomes over time. Thus, when risk is applied to the capital budgeting area, we are concerned with the variability or range of possible outcomes for the project's net present value.

The fact that the degree of variability causes the risk can be easily shown by examining a coin toss game. Consider the possibility of flipping a coin—heads you win, tails you lose—for 25 cents with your finance professor. Most likely you would be willing to take on this game, indicating that the utility gained from winning 25 cents is about equal to the utility lost if you lose 25 cents. On the other hand, if the flip is for $1000 you may be willing to play only if you are offered more than $1000 if you win, say $1500 if it comes out heads. That is to say, you will only accept the game if you win $1500 if it turns out heads and lose $1000 if it turns out tails. In each case the probability of winning and losing is the same; that is, there is an equal chance of the coin's landing heads or tails; but the width of the dispersion changes, and that is why the second coin toss is more risky and why it will not be taken unless the payoffs are altered. The key here is the fact that only the dispersion changes; the probability of winning or losing is the same in each case. Thus, the dispersion causes the risk.

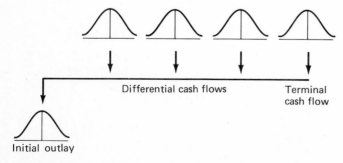

Differential cash flows   Terminal
cash flow

Initial outlay

FIGURE 12-1 *Cash Flow Diagram Based on Possible Outcomes*

The final question to be addressed is whether or not individuals are in fact risk averse given their behavior in state lotteries, at racetracks, and at Las Vegas. While we do see people gambling where the odds of winning are against them, it should be stressed that the monetary return from this action is not the only return they receive. They also receive a nonmonetary, psychic reward when gambling allowing them to fantasize that they will break the bank, never have to work again, and retire to some offshore island. Actually, the heart of the question is how wealth is valued. While these people appear to be acting as risk seekers, they actually attach an additional nonmonetary return to gambling, and if this is considered, their actions seem totally rational. It should also be noted that while these people appear to be pursuing risk on one hand, on the other hand they are also eliminating risk by purchasing insurance and diversifying their investments.

Thus far we have made several points. First, in the previous chapter we made the implicit assumption that the cash flows being evaluated were known with complete certainty, which is not true. In the remainder of this chapter it will be assumed that while future cash flows are not known with certainty, the probability distribution from which they come is known. Second, we have illustrated the fact that it is the dispersion of the probability distribution that causes the risk. Thus, later when we quantify risk, a measure of dispersion will be used. Finally, some behavior, for example, gambling, seems to indicate that not all individuals are risk averse. Yet when the intangible rewards are considered, the behavior of these individuals becomes congruent with that of other, risk-averse individuals.

QUANTITATIVE RISK MEASURES

When risk is considered in the capital budgeting decision, each project must be evaluated with respect to both its return and risk. Before describing two risk measures, we will explore probability distributions and the concept of the expected return, which will serve as our measure of return in this chapter.

Probability Distributions

Probability distributions illustrate the complete set of probabilities over all possible outcomes for that particular event. There are two general types of probability distributions—discrete and continuous. A **discrete probability distribution** is one in which a probability is assigned to each possible outcome in the set of all possible outcomes. For example, if we are considering a coin toss, there would be two possible outcomes, each with a .50 probability of occurring; if we were considering a horse race with ten horses, there would be ten possible outcomes, with the probability of each outcome depending on the speed of each horse. An investment opportunity with five possible outcomes, as shown in Table 12-1, is another example of a discrete distribution.

Table 12-1　A DISCRETE PROBABILITY DISTRIBUTION

POSSIBLE OUTCOME (X_i)	PROBABILITY OF OCCURRENCE $P(X_i)$
$ 5,000	.10
$ 7,000	.25
$ 8,000	.30
$ 9,000	.25
$11,000	.10

This distribution is illustrated graphically in Figure 12-2, giving us a picture of all the possible outcomes and the probabilities associated with them.

Note that the sum of all probabilities attached to all possible outcomes must add up to 1.0. This is because one of these outcomes must occur; otherwise, all possible outcomes have not been identified.

Whereas in a discrete probability distribution probabilities are assigned to specific outcomes, in a **continuous probability distribution** there are an infinite number of possible outcomes, in which the probability of an event is related to a range of possible outcomes. The easiest way to illustrate a continuous distribution is graphically, as in Figure 12-3. Probability in this case is measured by the area under the curve.

Thus, when provided with a continuous distribution, we can answer the question: What is the probability that an outcome will fall within a certain range of values? A discrete distribution, on the other hand, lets us answer the question: What is the probability that a specific outcome will occur? The key to understanding the difference between these questions—and the underlying differences between these classifications of distributions—is that for discrete distributions the number of possible outcomes is finite, while for continuous distributions it is infinite.

While continuous distributions are quite common and valuable, in general they require a degree of calculus that might be confusing. Thus, in

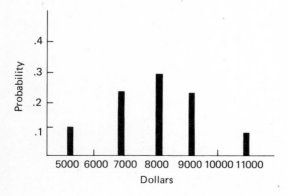

FIGURE 12-2　*A Discrete Probability Distribution*

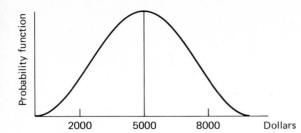

FIGURE 12-3 *A Continuous Probability Distribution*

the remainder of the book we will be concerned primarily with discrete probability distributions.

The expected value of a distribution is the arithmetic mean or average of all possible outcomes, where those outcomes are weighted by the probability that each outcome will occur. Thus, the expected value, $\overline{X}$, can be calculated as follows:

Expected Value

$$\overline{X} = \sum_{i=1}^{N} X_i P(X_i) \qquad (12\text{-}1)$$

where N = the number of possible outcomes,

X_i = the value of the ith possible outcome,

$P(X_i)$ = the probability that the ith outcome will occur.

To illustrate the computation of the expected value, consider the investment opportunity given in Table 12-1. To determine the expected value of this distribution, we need only multiply each possible outcome by its probability of occurrence and sum as follows:

expected value = $5000(.10) + \$7000(.25) + \$8000(.30) + \$9000(.25) +$
            $\$11,000(.10)$
         = $8000

In the previous chapter we ignored risk and took the expected value to be the only possible outcome. Reflecting back on this, it is easy to see that when we are estimating cash flows that are to occur in the future we cannot estimate them with certainty. Therefore, the expected value only provides us with the mean of the probability distribution from which that future cash flow will come. While the expected value provides us with a measure of central tendency, it tells us nothing about the amount of dispersion contained in the probability distribution. To measure dispersion, we will examine the standard deviation and coefficient of variation.

The **standard deviation** provides a measure of the spread of the probability distribution. The larger the standard deviation, the greater the dispersion of the distribution. It is calculated by squaring the difference

***Standard
Deviation***

between each outcome and its expected value, weighing each value by its probability, summing over all possible outcomes, and taking the square root of this sum. Thus, the standard deviation becomes

$$\sigma = \sqrt{\sum_{i=1}^{N} (X_i - \overline{X})^2 P(X_i)} \qquad (12\text{-}2)$$

where N = the number of possible outcomes,

X_i = the value of the ith possible outcome,

$\overline{X}$ = the expected value,

$P(X_i)$ = the probability that the ith outcome will occur.

The calculations for the standard deviation for the distribution given in Table 12-1 are provided in Table 12-2.

In the case of a normal distribution,[1] the standard deviation gives us even more than a measure of the absolute dispersion of that distribution. In this case we can, by consulting a table of areas under the normal curve, determine the probability that the outcome will be above or below a specific value. For example, in a normal distribution there is a 68.3 percent probability that the outcome will be within one standard deviation plus or minus of the expected value and a 95.0 percent probability that it will be within

[1]A **normal distribution** is a special class of bell-shaped distributions with symmetrically decreasing density where the curve approaches but never reaches the X axis.

Table 12-2   CALCULATION OF THE STANDARD DEVIATION
FOR THE DISTRIBUTION IN TABLE 12-1

STEP 1: CALCULATE DIFFERENCES $(X_i - \overline{X})$	STEP 2: SQUARE DIFFERENCES $(X_i - \overline{X})^2$	STEP 3: SQUARED DIFFERENCES TIMES PROBABILITES $(X_i - \overline{X})^2 P(X_i)$
\$ 5,000 − \$8,000 = −3,000	\$9,000,000	\$9,000,000(.10) = \$ 900,000
7,000 − 8,000 = −1,000	1,000,000	1,000,000(.25) = 250,000
8,000 − 8,000 = 0	0	0(.30) = 0
9,000 − 8,000 = 1,000	1,000,000	1,000,000(.25) = 250,000
11,000 − 8,000 = 3,000	9,000,000	9,000,000(.10) = 900,000

STEP 4: $\sum_{i=1}^{N} (X_i - \overline{X})^2 P(X_i)$ = \$2,300,000
SUM

STEP 5: $\sigma = \sqrt{\sum_{i=1}^{N} (X_i - \overline{X})^2 P(X_i)}$ = $\underline{\$1,517}$
TAKE THE
SQUARE ROOT

two standard deviations. Thus, if we are looking at two normal distributions, one with an expected value of $1000 and a standard deviation of $200, the other with an expected value of $2000 and a standard deviation of $300, we can conclude that the second distribution has more dispersion, hence, more absolute risk associated with it. This does not mean that the second distribution is less desirable, just that it has more absolute risk. While the standard deviation gives us a good measure of a distribution's absolute dispersion, it is also desirable to measure dispersion or risk relative to return to provide the manager with a relative measure of risk. This is the purpose of the coefficient of variation.

The **coefficient of variation** provides us with a measure of the relative dispersion of a probability distribution—that is, the risk per unit of return. Mathematically, it is defined as the standard deviation divided by the expected value, or

Coefficient of Variation

$$\gamma = \frac{\sigma}{\overline{X}} \tag{12-3}$$

This measure derives its value from the fact that using the standard deviation to compare the riskiness of two projects can be misleading when the projects are of unequal size.

For example, let us look at two normal distributions given in Table 12-3. In this case distribution B has more absolute risk, as indicated by its standard deviation; however, distribution A has more risk associated with it relative to its expected value. The value of examining the relative risk can easily be seen when examining distributions containing the same level of absolute risk or standard deviation but dramatically different levels of expected value. For example, consider two projects, both with standard deviations of $1000, one having an expected value of $1000 while the other has an expected value of $1,000,000. In each case the absolute risk is the same, as measured by the standard deviation, but the relative risk is not. Thus, the use of the coefficient of variation along with the standard deviation is especially important when two projects of unequal size are being compared. To ignore the coefficient of variation in this case could lead to misconceptions as to the relative level of uncertainty contained in each project.

Table 12-3 COEFFICIENT OF VARIATION

		PROJECT A	PROJECT B
Expected value	$\overline{X}$	$1000	$2000
Standard deviation	σ	200	300
Coefficient of variation	$\sigma/\overline{X}$	0.20	0.15

In the previous chapter we ignored any risk differences between projects. Unfortunately, this assumption was not valid; different investment projects do in fact contain different levels of risk. We will now look at several methods for incorporating risk into the analysis. The first technique, the certainty equivalent approach, attempts to incorporate the manager's utility function into the analysis. The second technique, the risk-adjusted discount rate, is based on the notion that investors require higher rates of return on more risky projects.

The **certainty equivalent approach** involves a direct attempt to allow the decision maker to incorporate his utility function into the analysis. Specifically, the financial manager is allowed to substitute the certain dollar amount that he feels is equivalent to the expected but risky cash flow offered by the investment for that risky cash flow in the capital budgeting analysis. In effect, a set of riskless cash flows is substituted for the original risky cash flows, between both of which the financial manager is indifferent. To a certain extent this process is like the old television program "Let's Make a Deal." On that show Monty Hall asked contestants to trade certain outcomes for uncertain outcomes. In some cases contestants were willing to make a trade, and in some cases they were not; it all depended upon how risk averse they were. The main difference between what we are doing and what was done on "Let's Make a Deal" is that on the TV show contestants were in general not indifferent between the certain outcome and the risky outcome, while in the certainty equivalent approach they are indifferent between the two outcomes.

To illustrate the concept of a certainty equivalent, let us look at a simple coin toss. Assume you can only play the game once and if it comes out heads, you win $10,000, and if it comes out tails you win nothing. Obviously, you have a 50 percent chance of winning $10,000 and a 50 percent chance of winning nothing, with an expected value of $5000. Thus, $5000 is your uncertain expected value outcome. The certainty equivalent then becomes the amount you would demand to make you indifferent between playing and not playing the game. If you are indifferent between receiving $3000 for certain and not playing the game, then $3000 is the certainty equivalent. Relating this back to the "Let's Make a Deal" example, often Monty Hall would offer contestants their choice of money and what was behind door number 2. In doing this he would offer the contestant more and more money until the contestant did not know what to do. At that point, when the contestant was jumping up and down, indifferent between his two choices, Monty had found the "door" or uncertain outcome's certainty equivalent. The dollar value that made the contestant indifferent between the money and what was behind the "door" is the certainty equivalent of the "door."

In order to simplify future calculations and problems, let us define certainty equivalent coefficients (α_t's) that represent the ratio of the certain outcome to the risky outcome, between which the financial manager is indifferent. In equation form, α_t can be represented as follows:

$$\alpha_t = \frac{\text{certain cash flow}_t}{\text{risky cash flow}_t} \tag{12-4}$$

Thus, the α's can vary between 0, in the case of extreme risk, and 1, in the case of certainty. To obtain the value of the equivalent certain cash flow, we need only multiply the risky cash flow and the α_t. When this is done, we are indifferent between this certain cash flow and the risky cash flow. In the previous example of the simple coin toss, the certain cash flow was $3000, while the risky cash flow was $5000, the expected value of the coin toss; thus, the certainty equivalent coefficient is 3000/5000 = .6. Thus, in summary, by multiplying the certainty equivalent coefficient (α_t) times the expected but risky cash flow, we can determine an equivalent certain cash flow.

Once this risk is taken out of the project's cash flows, those cash flows are discounted back to present at the risk-free rate of interest, and the project's net present value or profitability index is determined. If the internal rate of return is calculated, it is then compared to the risk-free rate of interest rather than the firm's required rate of return in determining whether or not it should be accepted or rejected. The certainty equivalent method can be summarized as follows:

$$NPV = \sum_{t=1}^{n} \frac{\alpha_t ACF_t}{(1 + i_F)^t} - IO \tag{12-5}$$

where α_t = the certainty equivalent coefficient,

ACF_t = the annual after-tax expected cash flow in time period t,

IO = the initial cash outlay,

n = the project's expected life,

i_F = the risk-free interest rate.

Let us examine a graphical presentation of the concept of certainty equivalents to illustrate its meaning. Assume that we can plot annual cash flows in risk-return space and that ACF_1 and ACF_2 in Figure 12-4 represent the location of the annual after-tax net cash flows during years 1 and 2. If I_1 and I_2 represent indifference curves of the decision maker, then $\alpha_1 ACF_1$ and $\alpha_2 ACF_2$ represent riskless equivalents of ACF_1 and ACF_2. As is evident from Figure 12-4, ACF_2 is riskier than ACF_1, thus is scaled down more. The degree to which the risky cash flows are scaled down, that is, how small the α_t is, will depend upon (a) the amount of risk or dispersion associated with

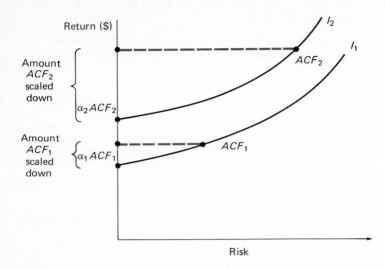

Return ($)

Amount ACF_2 scaled down

$\alpha_2 ACF_2$

Amount ACF_1 scaled down

$\alpha_1 ACF_1$

ACF_2

ACF_1

I_2

I_1

Risk

FIGURE 12-4 *Certainty Equivalents*

the subjective probability distribution assigned to the expected annual cash flow: the more risk, the lower the α_t value; (b) the decision maker's feelings about the attractiveness of the distribution's form: the more attractive the distribution, the higher the α_t values; and (c) to what extent the random variations in the annual cash flows from this project are expected to cancel out with variations in flows from other projects: the more variations that are canceled out, the higher the α_t values.[2]

The certainty equivalent approach can be summarized as follows:

1. Risk is removed from the cash flows through substituting equivalent certain cash flows for the risky cash flows. If the certainty equivalent coefficient (α_t) is given, this is done by multiplying each risky cash flow by the appropriate α_t value.
2. These riskless cash flows are then discounted back to the present at the riskless rate of interest.
3. The normal capital budgeting criteria are then applied, except in the case of the internal rate of return criterion, where the project's internal rate of return is compared to the risk-free rate of interest rather than the firm's required rate of return.

Example. A firm with a 10 percent required rate of return is considering building new research facilities with an expected life of five years. The initial outlay associated with this project involves a certain cash outflow of $120,000. The expected cash inflows and certainty equivalent coefficients, α_t, are as follows:

[2]These last two types of risk—risk associated with nonnormal distributions and risk in a portfolio concept—will be dealt with more fully later in the chapter.

YEAR	EXPECTED CASH FLOW	CERTAINTY EQUIVALENT COEFFICIENT, α_t
1	$10,000	.95
2	20,000	.90
3	40,000	.85
4	80,000	.75
5	80,000	.65

The risk-free rate of interest is 6 percent. What is the project's net present value?

To determine the net present value of this project using the certainty equivalent approach, we must first remove the risk from the future cash flows. We do so by multiplying each expected cash flow by the corresponding certainty equivalent coefficient, α_t.

EXPECTED CASH FLOW	CERTAINTY EQUIVALENT COEFFICIENT, α_t	$\alpha_t \times$ (EXPECTED CASH FLOW) = EQUIVALENT RISKLESS CASH FLOW
$10,000	.95	$ 9,500
20,000	.90	18,000
40,000	.85	34,000
80,000	.75	60,000
80,000	.65	52,000

The equivalent riskless cash flows are then discounted back to the present at the riskless interest rate, not the firm's required rate of return. The required rate of return would be used if this project had the same level of risk as a typical project for this firm. However, these equivalent cash flows have no risk at all; hence, the appropriate discount rate is the riskless rate of interest. The equivalent riskless cash flows can be discounted back to present at the riskless rate of interest, 6 percent, as follows:

YEAR	EQUIVALENT RISKLESS CASH FLOW	PRESENT VALUE FACTOR AT 6 PERCENT	PRESENT VALUE
1	$ 9,500	.943	$ 8,958.50
2	18,000	.890	16,020.00
3	34,000	.840	28,560.00
4	60,000	.792	47,520.00
5	52,000	.747	38,844.00

$$NPV = -\$120,000 + \$8958.50 + \$16,020 + \$28,560 + \$47,520 + \$38,844$$
$$= \$19,902.50$$

Applying the normal capital budgeting decision criteria, we find that the project should be accepted, as its net present value is greater than zero.

The use of risk-adjusted discount rates is based on the concept that investors demand higher returns for more risky projects. This relationship between risk and return is illustrated graphically in Figure 12-5.

The required rate of return on any investment should include compensation for delaying consumption equal to the risk-free rate of return, plus compensation for any risk taken on. If the risk associated with the investment is greater than the risk involved in a typical endeavor, then the discount rate is adjusted upward to compensate for this added risk. Once the firm determines the appropriate required rate of return for a project with a given level of risk, the cash flows are discounted back to present at the risk-adjusted discount rate. Then the normal capital budgeting criteria are applied, except in the case of the internal rate of return, in which case the hurdle rate to which the project's internal rate of return is compared now becomes the risk-adjusted discount rate. Expressed mathematically, the net present value using the risk-adjusted discount rate becomes

$$NPV = \sum_{t=1}^{n} \frac{ACF_t}{(1 + i^*)^t} - IO \qquad (12\text{-}6)$$

where ACF_t = the annual after-tax expected cash flow in time period t,

IO = the initial cash outlay,

i^* = the risk-adjusted discount rate,

n = the project's expected life.

The logic behind the risk-adjusted discount rate stems from the idea that if the level of risk in a project is different from that in the typical firm

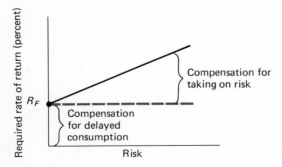

FIGURE 12-5 *Risk-Return Relationship*

project, then the management must incorporate the shareholders' probable reaction to this new endeavor into the decision-making process. If the project has more risk than a typical project, then a higher required rate of return should apply. Otherwise, marginal projects will lower the firm's share price—that is, reduce shareholders' wealth. This will occur as the market raises its required rate of return on the firm to reflect the addition of a more risky project, while the incremental cash flows resulting from the acceptance of the new project are not large enough to fully offset this change. By the same logic, if the project has less than normal risk, a reduction in the required rate of return is appropriate. Thus, the risk-adjusted discount method attempts to apply more stringent standards—that is, require a higher rate of return—to projects that will increase the firm's risk level. This is because these projects will lead shareholders to demand a higher required rate of return to compensate them for the higher risk level of the firm. If this adjustment is not made, the marginal projects containing above-average risk could actually lower the firm's share price.

Example.   A toy manufacturer is considering the introduction of a line of fishing equipment with an expected life of 5 years. In the past, this firm has been quite conservative in its investment in new products, sticking primarily to standard toys. In this context the introduction of a line of fishing equipment is considered an abnormally risky project for the firm. Therefore the management feels that the normal required rate of return for the firm of 10 percent is not sufficient. Instead, the minimally acceptable rate of return on this project should be 15 percent. The initial outlay would be $110,000 and the expected cash flows from this project are as given below:

YEAR	EXPECTED CASH FLOW
1	$30,000
2	30,000
3	30,000
4	30,000
5	30,000

Discounting this annuity back to the present at 15 percent yields a present value of the future cash flows of $100,560. Since the initial outlay on this project is $110,000, the net present value becomes −$9440, and the project should be rejected. Interestingly, if the normal required rate of return of 10 percent had been used as the discount rate, the project would have been accepted with a net present value of $3730.

In practice, when the risk-adjusted discount rate is used, projects are generally grouped according to purpose, or risk class; then the discount rate preassigned to that purpose or risk class is used. For example, a firm with a required rate of return of 12 percent might use the following rate-of-return categorization:

PROJECT	REQUIRED RATE OF RETURN
Replacement decision	12%
Modification or expansion of existing product line	15%
Project unrelated to current operations	18%
Research and development operations	25%

The purpose of this categorization of projects is to make their evaluation easier, but it also introduces an arbitrariness into the calculations that makes the evaluation less meaningful. The tradeoffs involved in the classification above are obvious; time and effort are minimized, but only at the cost of precision.

The primary difference between the certainty equivalent approach and the risk-adjusted discount rate approach involves the point at which the adjustment for risk is incorporated into the calculations. The certainty equivalent penalizes or adjusts downward the value of the expected annual after-tax cash flows, ACF_t, which results in a lower net present value for a risky project. The risk-adjusted discount rate, on the other hand, leaves the cash flows at their expected value and adjusts the required rate of return, i, upward to compensate for added risk. In either case the project's net present value is being adjusted downward to compensate for additional risk. The computational differences are illustrated in Table 12-4.

Certainty Equivalent vs. Risk-adjusted Discount Rate Methods

In addition to the difference in point of adjustment for risk, the risk-adjusted discount rate also makes the implicit assumption that risk becomes greater as we move further out in time. While this is not necessarily a good or bad assumption, we should be aware of it and understand it. In this regard, it should be helpful to look at an example in which the risk-adjusted discount rate is used and then determine what certainty equivalent coefficient, α_t, would be necessary to arrive at the same solution.

Example. Assume that a firm with a required rate of return of 10 percent is considering introducing a new product. This product has an initial outlay of $800,000, an expected life of 15 years, and after-tax cash

Table 12-4 COMPUTATIONAL STEPS IN THE CERTAINTY EQUIVALENT AND RISK-ADJUSTED DISCOUNT RATE METHODS

CERTAINTY EQUIVALENT	RISK-ADJUSTED DISCOUNT RATE
1. Adjust the expected cash flows, ACF_t, downward for risk by multiplying them by the corresponding certainty equivalent coefficient, α_t.	1. Adjust the discount rate upward for risk.
2. Discount the certainty equivalent, riskless, cash flows back to the present using the *risk-free rate of interest*.	2. Discount the expected cash flows back to present using the risk-adjusted discount rate.
3. Apply the normal decision criteria, except in the case of the internal rate of return, where the risk-free rate of interest replaces the required rate of return as the hurdle rate.	3. Apply the normal decision criteria, except in the case of the internal rate of return, where the risk-adjusted discount rate replaces the required rate of return as the hurdle rate.

flows of $100,000 each year during its life. Because of the increased risk associated with this project, the management is requiring a 15 percent rate of return. Also, let us assume that the risk free rate of return is 6 percent.

If the firm chose to use the certainty equivalent method, the certainty equivalent cash flows would be discounted back to the present at 6 percent, the risk-free rate of interest. The present value of the $100,000 cash flow occurring at the end of the first year discounted back to present at 15 percent is $87,000. The present value of this $100,000 flow discounted back to present at the risk-free rate of 6 percent is $94,300. Thus, if the certainty equivalent approach were used, a certainty equivalent coefficient, α_1, of .9226 would be necessary to produce a present value of $87,000. In other words, the same results can be obtained in the first year by using the risk-adjusted discount rate and adjusting the discount rate up to 15 percent or by using the certainty equivalent approach and adjusting the expected cash flows by a certainty equivalent coefficient of .9226. Under the risk-adjusted discount rate, the present value of the $100,000 cash flow occurring at the end of the second year becomes $75,600, and to produce an identical present value under the certainty equivalent approach, a certainty equivalent coefficient of .8494 would be needed. Following this through for the life of the project yields the certainty equivalent coefficients given in Table 12-5.

What does this analysis suggest? It indicates that if the risk-adjusted discount rate method is used, we are adjusting downward the value of future cash flows that occur further out in the future more severely than earlier cash flows. We can easily see this by comparing equations (12-5) and

Table 12-5 CERTAINTY EQUIVALENT COEFFICIENTS YIELDING THE SAME RESULTS AS THE RISK-ADJUSTED DISCOUNT RATE OF 15 PERCENT IN THE ILLUSTRATIVE EXAMPLE

Year:	1	2	3	4	5	6	7	8	9	10
α_t:	.9226	.8494	.7833	.7222	.6653	.6128	.5654	.5215	.4797	.4427

(12-6). The net present value using the risk-adjusted discount rate is expressed as

$$NPV = \sum_{t=1}^{n} \frac{ACF_t}{(1 + i^*)^t} - IO \qquad (12\text{-}6)$$

and the certainty equivalent net present value is measured by

$$NPV = \sum_{t=1}^{n} \frac{\alpha_t ACF_t}{(1 + i_F)^t} - IO \qquad (12\text{-}5)$$

Thus, for the net present values under each approach to be equivalent, the following must be true:

$$\frac{ACF_t}{(1 + i^*)^t} = \frac{\alpha_t ACF_t}{(1 + i_F)^t} \qquad (12\text{-}7)$$

Solving for α_t yields

$$\alpha_t = \frac{(1 + i_F)^t}{(1 + i^*)^t} = \left(\frac{1 + i_F}{1 + i^*} \right)^t \qquad (12\text{-}8)$$

Thus, since i_F and i^* are constants and i^* is greater than i_F, the value of α_t or $[(1 + i_F)/(1 + i^*)]^t$ must decrease as t increases for the present values under each approach to be equivalent. This is exactly what we concluded from Table 12-5.

In summary, the use of the risk-adjusted discount rate assumes that risk increases over time and that cash flows occurring further out in the future should be more severely penalized.

OTHER APPROACHES TO RISK IN CAPITAL BUDGETING

Simulation

Another method for incorporating risk into the investment decision is through the use of **simulation.** Whereas the certainty equivalent and risk-adjusted discount rate approaches provided us with a single value for the risk-adjusted net present value, a simulation approach gives us a probability distribution for the investment's net present value or internal rate of return. The idea behind simulation is to imitate the performance of the project being evaluated. This is done by randomly selecting observations from each of the distributions that affect the outcome of the project, combining those observations to determine the final output of the project, and continuing with this process until a representative record of the project's probable outcome is assembled.

The easiest way to develop an understanding of the computer simulation process is to follow through an example simulation for an investment project evaluation. Suppose a chemical producer is considering an extension to its processing plant. The simulation process is portrayed in Figure 12-6. First the probability distributions are determined for all the factors that affect the project's returns; in this case, let us assume there are nine such variables:

1. Market size.
2. Selling price.
3. Market growth rate.
4. Share of market (which results in physical sales volume).
5. Investment required.
6. Residual value of investment.
7. Operating costs.
8. Fixed costs.
9. Useful life of facilities.

Then the computer randomly selects one observation from each of the probability distributions, according to its chance of actually occurring in the future. These nine observations are combined and a net present value or internal rate of return figure is calculated. This process is repeated as many times as desired, until a representative distribution of possible future outcomes is assembled. Thus, the inputs to a simulation include all the principal factors affecting the project's profitability, and the simulation output is a probability distribution of net present values or internal rates of return for the project. The decision maker bases his decision on the full range of possible outcomes. The project is accepted if the decision maker feels enough of the distribution lies above the normal cutoff criteria ($NPV > 0$, IRR > required rate of return).

Suppose that the output from the simulation of the chemical producer's project is as given in Figure 12-7. The firm's management will examine the probability distribution, and if they consider enough of the distribution of possible net present values to be greater than zero, they will accept the project.

Use of a simulation approach to analyze investment proposals offers two major advantages. First, the financial managers are able to examine and base their decisions on the whole range of possible outcomes rather than just point estimates. Second, they can undertake subsequent sensitivity analysis of the project. That is, by modifying assumptions made about the values and ranges of the input factors and rerunning the simulation, the management can determine how sensitive the outcome of the project is to these changes. If the output appears to be highly sensitive to one or two of the input factors, the management may then wish to spend additional time refining those input estimates.

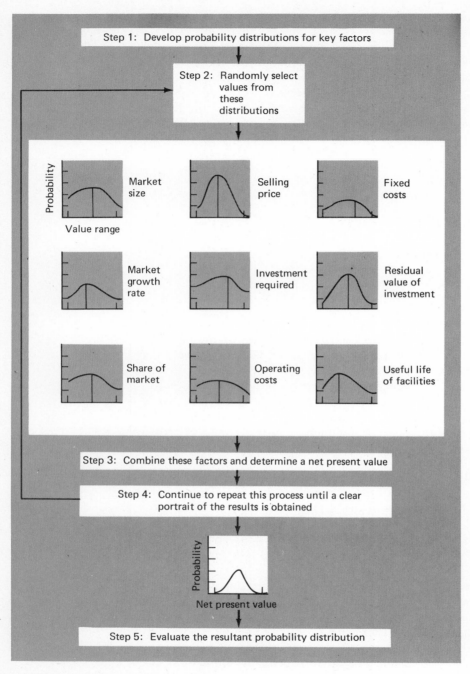

FIGURE 12-6   Capital Budgeting Simulation

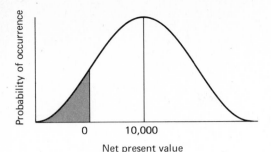

FIGURE 12-7 *Output from Simulation*

A **decision tree** is a graphical exposition of the sequence of possible outcomes, presenting the decision maker with a schematic representation of the problem in which all possible outcomes are graphically displayed. Moreover, the computations and results of the computations are shown directly on the tree, so that the information can easily be understood.

Decision Trees

To illustrate the use of a decision tree, suppose a firm with a required rate of return of 10 percent is considering an investment proposal that requires an initial outlay of $1 million and will yield resultant cash flows for the next two years. During the first year let us assume there are three possible outcomes, as shown in Table 12-6. Graphically, each of these three possible alternatives is represented on the decision tree in Figure 12-8 as one of the three possible branches.

The second step in the decision tree is to continue drawing branches in a similar manner so that each of the possible outcomes during the second year is represented by a new branch. For example, if outcome 1 occurs in year 1, a 20 percent chance of a $300,000 cash flow and an 80 percent chance of a $600,000 cash flow in year 2 have been projected. Two branches would be sent out from the outcome 1 node, reflecting these two possible outcomes. The cash flows that occur if outcome 1 takes place and the probabilities associated with them are called **conditional outcomes** and **conditional probabilities** because they can only occur if outcome 1 occurs during the first year. Finally, to determine the probability of the sequence of a $600,000 flow in year 1 and a $300,000 outcome in year 2, the probability of the $600,000 flow (.5) is multiplied by the conditional probability of the second flow (.2), telling us that this sequence has a 10 percent chance of occurring, which is called its **joint probability.** Letting the values in Table 12-7 represent the conditional outcomes and their respective conditional probabilities, we can complete the decision tree as shown in Figure 12-9.

Table 12-6 POSSIBLE OUTCOMES IN YEAR 1

	PROBABILITY		
	.5 Outcome 1	.3 Outcome 2	.2 Outcome 3
Cash flow	$600,000	$700,000	$800,000

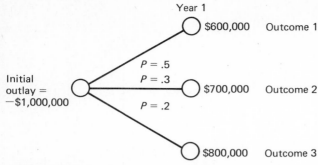

FIGURE 12-8 *First Stage of a Decision Tree Diagram*

The financial manager, by examining the decision tree, is provided with the expected value for the investment, the range of possible outcomes, and a listing of each possible outcome with the probability associated with it. In this case the expected value is $66,634, and there is a 10 percent chance of incurring the worst possible outcome with a net present value of −$206,800. There is also a 2 percent probability of achieving the most favorable outcome, a net present value of $388,000.

Thus, the decision tree allows the manager to quickly visualize the possible future events, their probabilities, and their outcomes. In addition, the calculation of the expected net present value and enumeration of the distribution should aid the financial manager in his decision-making process.

Up to this point, in all approaches other than the decision tree, we have assumed the cash flow in one period is independent of the cash flow in the previous period. While this assumption is appealing because of its simplifying nature, in many cases it is invalid. For example, if a new product is introduced and the initial public reaction is poor, resulting in low initial cash flows, then cash flows in future periods are likely to be low also. An extreme example of this is Ford's experience with the Edsel. Poor consumer acceptance and sales in the first year were followed by even poorer results in the second year. If the Edsel had been received favorably during its first year, it quite likely would have done well in the second year.

OTHER SOURCES AND MEASURES OF RISK

Time Dependence of Cash Flows

Table 12-7 CONDITIONAL OUTCOMES AND PROBABILITIES

YEAR 1	IF OUTCOME 1 $ACF_1 = \$600,000$		IF OUTCOME 2 $ACF_1 = \$700,000$		IF OUTCOME 3 $ACF_1 = \$800,000$	
	ACF_2	Probability	ACF_2	Probability	ACF_2	Probability
Year 2	$300,000	.2	$300,000	.2	$400,000	.2
	600,000	.8	500,000	.3	600,000	.7
			700,000	.5	800,000	.1

322

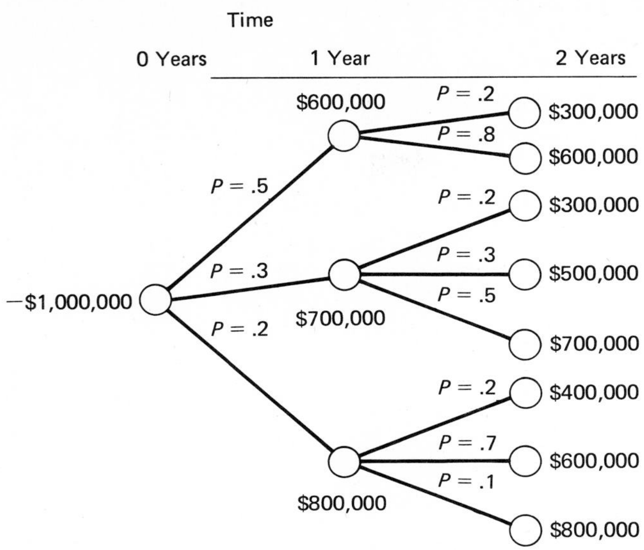

Time			(A) Net present value at 10 percent	(B) Joint probability	(A) × (B)
0 Years	1 Year	2 Years			

Decision tree values:

	(A) Net present value at 10 percent	(B) Joint probability	(A) × (B)
$300,000	−$206,800	.10	−$20,680
$600,000	$ 41,000	.40	$16,400
$300,000	−115,900	.06	−$6,954
$500,000	$49,300	.09	$4,437
$700,000	$214,500	.15	$32,175
$400,000	$57,600	.04	$2,304
$600,000	$222,800	.14	$31,192
$800,000	$388,000	.02	$7,760
		1.00	

Expected net present value = $66,634

FIGURE 12-9 *Decision Tree*

The end effect of time dependence of cash flows is to increase the risk of the project over time. That is, since large cash flows in the first period lead to large cash flows in the second period, and low cash flows in the first period lead to low cash flows in the second period, the probability distribution of possible net present values tends to be wider than if the cash flows were not dependent over time. The greater the degree of correlation between flows over time, the greater will be the dispersion of the probability distribution.

Skewness

In all previous approaches other than simulation and decision trees, we have assumed that the distributions of net present values for projects being evaluated are normally distributed. Unfortunately, this assumption is not always valid. When it is true, the standard deviation provides an adequate measure of the distribution's dispersion; however, when the distribution is not normally distributed, reliance on the standard deviation can be misleading.

A distribution that is not symmetric is said to be **skewed.** In this case the distribution has either a longer "tail" to the right or to the left. For example, if a distribution is skewed to the right, most values will be clustered around the left end, and the distribution will appear to have a long tail on the right end of the range of values. Graphical illustrations of skewed distributions are presented in Figure 12-10.

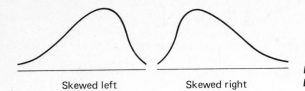

Skewed left   Skewed right

FIGURE 12-10 *Examples of Skewed Distributions*

The difficulty associated with skewed distributions arises from the fact that the use of the expected value and standard deviation alone may not be enough to differentiate properly between two distributions. For example, the two distributions shown in Figure 12-11 have the same expected value and the same standard deviation; however, distribution A is skewed to the left while B is skewed to the right. If a financial manager were given his choice between these two distributions, assuming they are mutually exclusive, he would most likely choose distribution B, because it involves less chance of a negative net present value. Thus, skewness can affect the level of risk and the desirability of a distribution.

Portfolio Risk

Thus far in our analysis we have focused on the risk associated with each individual project under consideration. However, firms do not just invest in a single project but are generally involved in a number of projects at any one time. Therefore, we will now introduce the topic of the risk of projects in a portfolio context; that is, we will examine how the addition of a particular project will affect the overall riskiness of the firm. We will find that the addition of some projects, because of their particular cyclical patterns, is able to lower the overall riskiness of the firm better than the addition of other projects.

In the previous sections we have assumed that the mean and standard deviation were adequate measures of return and risk by which to judge a project. Now we are saying they may not be, provided the firm is involved in other projects. Why? First, some projects are complementary or involve economies of scale with other projects held by the firm. This condition might result when two projects share the same production facilities or the same marketing channels, or when the introduction of the new product may aid sales of a current product. As mentioned in Chapter 11, this

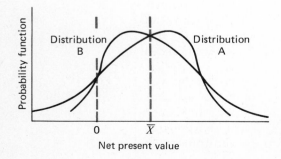

FIGURE 12-11 *Two Distributions with Identical Expected Values and Standard Deviation but Different Skewness*

complementary or economies-of-scale effect should be included in the relevant cash flows as incremental after-tax cash flows to the company as a whole. In other words, if there are any incremental cash flows to the company as a whole from the addition of the new project, even if they show up flowing into a previously existing project, they should be included in the capital budgeting analysis. Thus, although the existence of complementary and economies-of-scale effects may be somewhat difficult to determine, they have already been allowed for in our capital budgeting framework.

A second consideration is the potential diversification effect. If a project's cash flow patterns are cyclically divergent from those of the company, the overall risk of the company may be significantly reduced. In other words, when this project is added to the firm, the resultant risk level of the combination, as measured by the firm's standard deviation, may be less than the sum of the risk levels of the project and the firm held individually.

Before developing the implications of portfolio risk for capital budgeting, we will examine exactly how and why this diversification effect takes place.

PORTFOLIO RISK: A GRAPHICAL ILLUSTRATION

The degree to which the diversification type portfolio effect takes place is a function of the relationship between the pattern of cash flows from the new project and the existing company. For example, let's look at a company that doubles its size by adding a new division. First, assume that the cash flows from both the original company and the new division move directly with the business cycle. If we attach the dollar values given in Table 12-8 to this movement, the situation graphically depicted in Chart A of Figure 12-12 is created. Examining the resultant variability of the combined cash flows, we see that when the cash flows move together, as in this case, their percentage variability remains the same. In this case there is no diversification portfolio effect. If, on the other hand, the new division produced cash flows that were countercyclical, the two series of cash flows would move in opposite directions, and a diversification portfolio effect would take place. If we attach the dollar values in Table 12-9 to this cash flow movement, the situation is as represented in Chart B of Figure 12-12. In this case, because the variabilities of the cash flows of the original firm and the new division move in opposite directions, the variability of their combination is totally eliminated.

Table 12-8   CASH FLOWS

	NORMAL	RECESSION	EXPANSION
Original firm	$1,000,000	$ 500,000	$1,500,000
New division	1,000,000	500,000	1,500,000
Combination	$2,000,000	$1,000,000	$3,000,000

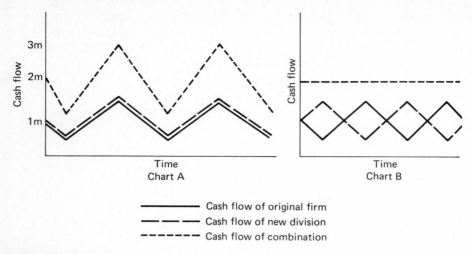

FIGURE 12-12 *Diversification Effects on Cash Flow*

Obviously, the degree to which total risk is reduced becomes a function of how the two sets of cash flows or returns move together. In order to measure this relationship, we use the concept of correlation. **Correlation** measures the linear relationship between any two sets of values. The **correlation coefficient,** a statistical measure, tells us two things about this relationship. First, it can take on either a positive or negative sign. A positive sign indicates that the variables tend to move in the same direction, a negative sign, that they move in opposite directions. Also, the value that the correlation coefficient takes on, ranging from $+1.0$ down to -1.0, provides us with information about the degree or strength of this relationship. If its value is near zero, the linear relationship is weak; however, if the relationship is close to either $+1.0$ or -1.0, there is a strong linear relationship between the two variables. Letting ρ denote the correlation coefficient, R_P the return on the new project, and R_{Firm} the return on the firm, Figure 12-13 graphically illustrates several possible situations.

The degree of correlation between projects takes on importance because it determines the extent to which the diversification portfolio effect will reduce the risk level of the combination. Negatively correlated combinations will provide the greatest level of risk reduction, while perfectly positively correlated projects, those with correlation coefficients of $+1.0$,

Table 12-9 CASH FLOWS

	NORMAL	RECESSION	EXPANSION
Original firm	$1,000,000	$ 500,000	$1,500,000
New division	1,000,000	1,500,000	500,000
Combination	$2,000,000	$2,000,000	$2,000,000

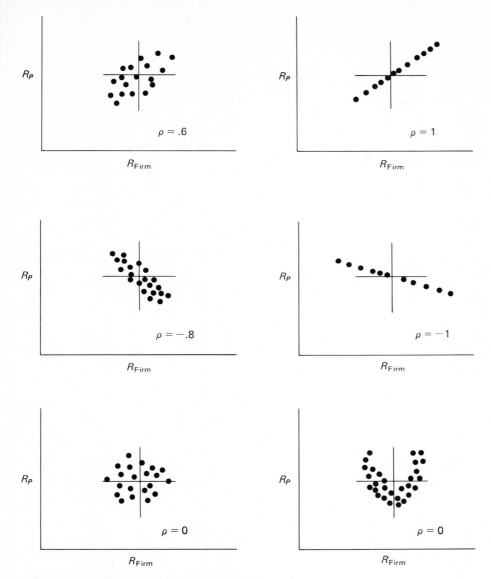

FIGURE 12-13 *Illustrations of Various Degrees of Correlation*

will not provide any diversification effect. If one thinks about it, it makes sense. Any impact from diversification results from combining projects with divergent return or cash flow patterns. If the correlation coefficient is 1.0, these patterns are identical; hence, there is no diversification value present. If, on the other hand, the correlation coefficient is −1.0, then the patterns move in opposite directions; hence, the diversification value is maximum.

PORTFOLIO RISK:
A MATHEMATICAL ILLUSTRATION

To illustrate mathematically, suppose we are considering combining two assets, putting two-thirds of our money in investment A and the remaining third in investment B, and we want to determine the risk or standard deviation of this combination. The mathematical formula for the standard deviation of this two-asset combination is given in equations (12-9) and (12-10).

$$\sigma_{A+B} = \sqrt{\text{Var } (A + B)} \qquad (12\text{-}9)$$

$$\sigma_{A+B} = \sqrt{W_A^2 \sigma_A^2 + W_B^2 \sigma_B^2 + 2W_A W_B \rho_{AB} \sigma_A \sigma_B} \qquad (12\text{-}10)$$

where σ_{A+B} = the standard deviation of the combination of asset A and asset B,

W_A = the weight or fraction of total funds invested in asset A,

W_B = the weight or fraction of total funds invested in asset B,

σ_A = the standard deviation of asset A,

σ_B = the standard deviation of asset B,

ρ_{AB} = the correlation coefficient between asset A and asset B.

Now let us assume that Table 12-10 provides the relevant information about each of these projects. If there is no diversification effect at all—that is, ρ_{AB} = 1.0—the standard deviation of this combination should be equal to its weighted average, 26.66 percent. That is to say that 26.66 percent is the weighted average standard deviation of this portfolio. If we had not discussed portfolio risk, we would expect the risk or standard deviation of this combination to be equal to its weighted average. However, there is a diversification portfolio effect, and its degree depends upon the correlation between the assets being combined. This can be shown mathematically by substituting the values provided in Table 12-10 into equation (12-10). This results in the following reduction in equation (12-10):

$$\sigma_{A+B} = \sqrt{(\tfrac{2}{3})^2(.2)^2 + (\tfrac{1}{3})^2(.4)^2 + 2\rho_{AB}(\tfrac{2}{3})(\tfrac{1}{3})(.2)(.4)}$$

$$\sigma_{A+B} = \sqrt{.0356 + .0356\rho_{AB}}$$

Table 12-10 TWO-ASSET EXAMPLE OF DIVERSIFICATION

ASSET	σ	WEIGHTS (W)	$\sigma \times$ WEIGHTS
A	20%	$\tfrac{2}{3}$	13.33%
B	40%	$\tfrac{1}{3}$	13.33%
		Weighted average σ_{A+B} =	26.66%

The only variable we now need in order to determine the standard deviation for the combination of assets is their correlation coefficient. Letting the correlation coefficient between assets A and B (ρ_{AB}) vary between $+1.0$ and -1.0 results in the following standard deviation for the combination:

	if $\rho_{AB} = 1.0$	if $\rho_{AB} = 0.0$	if $\rho_{AB} = -1.0$
σ_{A+B}	$\sqrt{.0712} = 26.68\%$	$\sqrt{.0356} = 18.9\%$	$\sqrt{0} = 0\%$

Thus, the degree of correlation between projects determines to what extent risk can be eliminated when they are combined. It should be noted that the difference between the weighted average deviation (26.66%) and the one calculated using equation (12-10) and assuming ρ_{AB} equals 1.0 (26.68%) is a result of rounding error.

Unfortunately, in the real world perfectly negatively correlated projects are almost never found. In fact, most projects tend to be positively correlated with each other. Still, as long as positive correlations are not perfect, there will be a reduction in overall risk from these combinations. Historically, this desire to reduce the overall risk of the firm through diversification has led to much of the merger activity of the past.

THE VALUE OF DIVERSIFICATION

How exactly to view the value of a project's risk-reducing ability through diversification with the firm has been a subject of considerable controversy. The central question boils down to, "Is there any value in diversifying among projects for the firm's shareholders when the shareholder may be able to accomplish the same risk reduction by diversifying his personal stockholdings?" Stated another way, "Will the shareholder pay for something (diversification) that he may be able to accomplish at no cost?" This brings us to the question of whether firm diversification achieves some value that stockholder diversification does not.

Firm diversification can reduce the chance of bankruptcy. If there is value in reducing this probability, then there is value to firm diversification. Quite obviously, in the real world there is a cost associated with bankruptcy. First, if a firm fails, its assets in general cannot be sold for their true economic value. Moreover, the amount of money actually available for distribution to stockholders is further reduced by selling costs and legal fees that must be paid. Finally, the opportunity cost associated with the delays related to the legal process further reduces the funds available to the shareholder. Therefore, since costs are associated with bankruptcy, reduction of the chance of bankruptcy has a very real value associated with it.

The risk of bankruptcy also entails indirect costs associated with changes in the firm's debt capacity and the cost of debt. As the firm's cash flow patterns stabilize, the risk of default will decline, giving the firm an increased debt capacity and possibly reducing the cost of this debt. Because interest payments are tax deductible, while dividends are not, debt financing is less expensive than equity financing. Thus, monetary benefits are associated with an increased debt capacity.[3] Since this reduction in default risk cannot be duplicated by stockholder diversification of personal investments, there is a real value associated with it. The question now becomes how to include the benefits from the reduction of bankruptcy risk in our capital budgeting decision.

The most logical way of incorporating these benefits into our capital budgeting framework is to estimate a dollar value associated with them and treat this value as a cash inflow. The guiding logic behind our capital budgeting criteria was to consider the incremental after-tax cash flows to the company as a whole resulting from the acceptance of a project. This being the case, we must estimate the expected value of the reduction in bankruptcy costs, most likely a very small figure, and the expected value associated with expanded debt capacity and debt cost reductions. Quite frankly, there are problems associated with estimating these benefits; however, the benefits should be recognized and incorporated into the capital budgeting process. While their estimation will be deferred to more advanced finance courses, the process of diversification and its value are important concepts and must be understood.

While the subject of risk and capital budgeting is quite complicated and controversial, we should be familiar with the common measures of risk and means of treating it. In addition, we should recognize the limitations of these measures and techniques if we are to use them. In this section we have introduced these limitations and complications in such a manner as to lay a foundation for reexamining them in much greater detail in subsequent finance courses.

In this chapter we removed our assumption of certainty and dealt with the situation in which the firm is not sure exactly what the outcome of any investment will be. We first examined some terminology used to describe probability distributions, their central tendencies, and their level of dispersion. These statistical terms included discrete distribution, continuous distribution, expected value, standard deviation, and coefficient of variation. A discrete distribution is one in which a probability is assigned to each possible outcome in the set of all possible outcomes. A continuous distribution involves the case in which the number of possible outcomes is infinite and the probability of an event is related to a range of possible outcomes. Figure 12-14 depicts examples of each of these distributions. Both of these distributions are valuable; however, because of potential mathematical complications, continuous distributions were dropped and discrete distributions were assumed in the remainder of the chapter. The

---

[3]The benefits associated with debt financing and the relative costs of the various financing alternatives will be dealt with in more detail in Chapter 14.

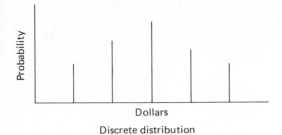

Discrete distribution

Continuous distribution

FIGURE 12-14 *Distributions*

expected value of a distribution is the arithmetic mean or weighted average of all possible outcomes. Mathematically, it is defined as

$$\overline{X} = \sum_{i=1}^{N} X_i P(X_i)$$

The standard deviation provides a measure of absolute risk or dispersion of the distribution. It can be defined as

$$\sigma = \sqrt{\sum_{i=1}^{N} (X_i - \overline{X})^2 P(X_i)}$$

The coefficient of variation provides a relative measure of risk or dispersion. It can be defined as

$$\gamma = \frac{\sigma}{\overline{X}}$$

Four methods were discussed for incorporating risk into the capital budgeting decision: (1) the certainty equivalent method, (2) risk-adjusted discount rates, (3) simulation, and (4) decision trees. The certainty equivalent approach involves a direct attempt to incorporate the decision maker's utility function into the analysis. Under this method, cash flows are adjusted downward by multiplying them by certainty equivalent coefficients,

α_t, which transform the risky cash flows into equivalent certain cash flows in terms of desirability. A project's net present value using the certainty equivalent method for adjusting for risk becomes

$$NPV = \sum_{t=1}^{n} \frac{\alpha_t ACF_t}{(1 + i_F)^t} - IO$$

The risk-adjusted discount rate involves an upward adjustment of the discount rate to compensate for risk. This method is based on the concept that investors demand higher returns for more risky projects.

The simulation and decision-tree methods are used to provide information as to the location and shape of the distribution of possible outcomes. Decisions could be based directly upon these methods, or they could be used to determine input into either the certainty equivalent or risk-adjusted discount method approaches.

The chapter closed with a discussion of diversification and its value to the shareholder. We concluded that if there are bankruptcy costs and if reduction of the possibility of bankruptcy can increase debt capacity, then there is value in firm diversification. In the capital budgeting framework, the value from reduced bankruptcy costs and expanded debt capacity associated with a project's acceptance must be recognized and should be included as cash inflows associated with the acceptance of the project.

12-1. Differentiate between discrete and continuous probability distributions. What information can be gained from each type of distribution?

12-2. Is it possible for the expected value of a probability distribution to differ from the most likely outcome? Why or why not?

12-3. What is the relationship between the standard deviation and the coefficient of variation? Why do we need two measures of risk?

12-4. In the previous chapter we examined the payback period capital budgeting criterion. Often this capital budgeting criterion is used as a risk screening device. Explain the rationale behind its use.

12-5. The use of the risk-adjusted discount rate assumes that risk increases over time. Justify this assumption.

12-6. What are the similarities and differences between the risk-adjusted discount rate and certainty equivalent methods for incorporating risk into the capital budgeting decision?

12-7. What is the value of using the decision-tree technique for evaluating capital budgeting projects?

12-8. Explain how simulation works. What is the value in using a simulation approach?

12-9. What does time dependence of cash flows mean? Why might cash flows be time dependent? Give some examples.

STUDY QUESTIONS

12-10. What does skewness mean? If a distribution is skewed, how does this affect the significance of its standard deviation and mean?

12-11. Through the diversification effect, the total risk of a portfolio can be reduced. How does this happen? How does the correlation between returns on the various projects affect this process?

12-1. Given the information below on projects A and B, calculate:
(a) Their expected values.
(b) Their standard deviations.
(c) Their coefficients of variation.
(d) What do these statistics tell us?

PROJECT A		PROJECT B	
Probability	Outcome	Probability	Outcome
.10	$ 15,000	.15	$ 30,000
.20	25,000	.35	60,000
.40	30,000	.35	80,000
.20	35,000	.15	110,000
.10	45,000		

12-2. The G. Bryan Corporation is considering three projects with their expected outcomes and distributions shown below:

PROJECT A		PROJECT B	
Probability	Outcome	Probability	Outcome
.05	$ 1,000	.10	$ 1,000
.20	6,000	.40	7,000
.50	8,000	.40	9,000
.20	10,000	.10	15,000
.05	15,000		

PROJECT C	
Probability	Outcome
.10	$ 4,000
.40	5,000
.30	10,000
.15	15,000
.05	22,000

Given this information:

(a) Calculate their expected values.

(b) Calculate their standard deviations.

(c) Is the standard deviation a meaningful statistic for the distribution associated with project C? Why or why not?

12-3. The Beatosu Corporation is considering two mutually exclusive projects. Both require an initial outlay of $10,000 and will operate for five years. The probability distributions associated with each project for years 1 through 5 are given below:

CASH FLOWS YEARS 1–5

PROJECT A		PROJECT B	
Probability	Cash Flow	Probability	Cash Flow
.15	$4000	.15	$2000
.70	5000	.70	6000
.15	6000	.15	10,000

Since project B is the riskier of the two projects, the management of Beatosu Corporation has decided to apply a required rate of return of 15 percent to its evaluation but only a 12 percent required rate of return to project A.

(a) Determine the expected value of each project's cash flows.

(b) Determine each project's risk-adjusted net present value.

(c) What other factors might be considered in deciding between these two projects?

12-4. The Goblu Corporation is evaluating two mutually exclusive projects, both of which require an initial outlay of $100,000. Each project has an expected life of five years. The probability distributions associated with the annual cash flows from each project are given below:

CASH FLOWS YEARS 1–5

PROJECT A		PROJECT B	
Probability	Cash Flow	Probability	Cash Flow
.10	$35,000	.10	$10,000
.40	40,000	.20	30,000
.40	45,000	.40	45,000
.10	50,000	.20	60,000
		.10	80,000

The normal required rate of return for Goblu is 10 percent but, since these projects are riskier than most, they are requiring a higher-than-normal rate of return on them. On project A they are requiring a 12 percent and on project B a 13 percent rate of return.

(a) Determine the expected value for each project's cash flows.

(b) Determine each project's risk-adjusted net present value.

(c) What other factors might be considered in deciding between these projects?

12-5. The P. Isenbarger Corp. is considering two mutually exclusive projects. The expected values for each project's cash flows are given below.

YEAR	PROJECT A	PROJECT B
0	−$1,000,000	−$1,000,000
1	500,000	500,000
2	700,000	600,000
3	600,000	700,000
4	500,000	800,000

They have decided to evaluate these projects using the certainty equivalent method. The certainty coefficients for each project's cash flows are given below.

CERTAINTY EQUIVALENT COEFFICIENTS		
Year	Project A	Project B
0	1.00	1.00
1	.95	.90
2	.90	.70
3	.80	.60
4	.70	.50

Given that this company's normal required rate of return is 15 percent and the after-tax risk-free rate is 5 percent, which project should be selected?

12-6. Taylor Toy Company uses the certainty equivalent approach when it evaluates risky investments. The company presently has two mutually exclusive investment proposals, with an expected life of four years each, to choose from with money it received from the sale of part of its toy division to another company. The expected net cash flows are given below:

YEAR	PROJECT A	PROJECT B
0	−$50,000	−$50,000
1	15,000	20,000

YEAR	PROJECT A	PROJECT B
2	15,000	25,000
3	15,000	25,000
4	45,000	30,000

The certainty equivalent coefficients for the net cash flows are as follows:

YEAR	PROJECT A	PROJECT B
0	1.00	1.00
1	.95	.90
2	.85	.85
3	.80	.80
4	.70	.75

Which of the two investment proposals should be chosen, given that the after-tax risk-free rate of return is 6 percent?

12-7. The G. Grunwald Corporation is evaluating an investment proposal with an expected life of two years. This project will require an initial outlay of $1,200,000. The required rate of return on this project is 15 percent. The resultant possible cash flows are given below:

POSSIBLE OUTCOMES IN YEAR 1

	PROBABILITY		
	.6	.3	.1
	Outcome 1	Outcome 2	Outcome 3
Cash flow	$700,000	$850,000	$1,000,000

Conditional Outcomes and Probabilities

IF $ACF_1 = \$700,000$		IF $ACF_1 = \$850,000$		IF $ACF_1 = \$1,000,000$	
ACF_2	Probability	ACF_2	Probability	ACF_2	Probability
$ 300,000	.3	$ 400,000	.2	$ 600,000	.1
700,000	.6	700,000	.5	900,000	.5
1,100,000	.1	1,000,000	.2	1,100,000	.4
		1,300,000	.1		

(a) Construct a decision tree representing the possible outcomes.
(b) Determine the joint probability of each possible sequence of events taking place.

(c) What is the expected NPV of this project?

(d) What is the range of possible NPV's for this project?

12-8. The E. Swank Corporation is considering an investment project with an expected life of two years. Swank Corporation demands a rate of return of 12 percent on projects of this type. The initial outlay on this project would be $600,000, and the resultant possible cash flows are as given below:

POSSIBLE OUTCOMES IN YEAR 1

	PROBABILITY		
	.4 Outcome 1	.4 Outcome 2	.2 Outcome 3
Cash flow	$300,000	$350,000	$450,000

Conditional Outcomes and Probabilities

IF $ACF_1 = \$300,000$		IF $ACF_1 = \$350,000$		IF $ACF_1 = \$450,000$	
ACF_2	Probability	ACF_2	Probability	ACF_2	Probability
$200,000	.3	$250,000	.2	$ 300,000	.2
300,000	.7	450,000	.5	500,000	.5
		650,000	.3	700,000	.2
				1,000,000	.1

(a) Construct a decision tree representing the possible outcomes.

(b) Determine the joint probability of each possible sequence of events taking place.

(c) What is the expected NPV of this project?

(d) What is the range of possible NPV's for this project?

SELECTED REFERENCES

BONINI, CHARLES P., "Capital Investment Under Uncertainty with Abandonment Options," *Journal of Financial and Quantitative Analysis,* 12 (March 1977), 39–54.

BREEN, WILLIAM J., and EUGENE M. LERNER, "Corporate Financial Strategies and Market Measures of Risk and Return," *Journal of Finance,* 28 (May 1973), 339–51.

CARTER, E. EUGENE, *Portfolio Aspects of Corporate Capital Budgeting.* Lexington, Mass.: D. C. Heath, 1974.

GRAYSON, C. JACKSON, JR., *Decisions under Uncertainty: Drilling Decisions by Oil and Gas Operators.* Boston: Division of Research, Harvard Business School, 1960.

GREER, WILLIS R., JR., "Capital Budgeting Analysis with the Timing of Events Uncertain," *Accounting Review,* 45 (January 1970), 103–14.

————— , "Theory versus Practice in Risk Analysis: An Empirical Study," *Accounting Review,* 49 (July 1974), 496–505.

HAYES, ROBERT H., "Incorporating Risk Aversion into Risk Analysis," *Engineering Economist,* 20 (Winter 1975), 99–121.

HERTZ, DAVID B., "Investment Policies That Pay Off," *Harvard Business Review*, 46 (January–February 1968), 96–108.

———— , "Risk Analysis in Capital Investment," *Harvard Business Review*, 42 (January–February 1964), 95–106.

HILLIER, FREDERICK S., "A Basic Model for Capital Budgeting of Risky Interrelated Projects," *Engineering Economist*, 17 (Fall 1971), 1–30.

———— , "The Derivation of Probabilistic Information for the Evaluation of Risky Investments," *Management Science*, 9 (April 1963), 443–57.

JARRETT, JEFFREY E., "An Abandonment Decision Model," *Engineering Economist*, 19 (Fall 1973), 35–46.

KEELEY, ROBERT, and RANDOLPH WESTERFIELD, "A Problem in Probability Distribution Techniques for Capital Budgeting," *Journal of Finance*, 27 (June 1972), 703–709.

LESSARD, DONALD R., and RICHARD S. BOWER, "Risk-Screening in Capital Budgeting," *Journal of Finance*, 28 (May 1973).

LEVY, HAIM, and MARSHALL SARNAT, "The Portfolio Analysis of Multiperiod Capital Investment under Conditions of Risk," *Engineering Economist*, 16 (Fall 1970), 1–19.

LEWELLEN, WILBER G., and MICHAEL S. LONG, "Simulation versus Single-Value Estimates in Capital Expenditure Analysis," *Decision Sciences*, 3 (1972), 19–33.

MAGEE, J. F., "How to Use Decision Trees in Capital Investment," *Harvard Business Review*, 42 (September–October 1964), 79–96.

OSTERYOUNG, JEROME S., ELTON SCOTT, and GORDON S. ROBERTS, "Selecting Projects with the Coefficient of Variation," *Financial Management*, 6 (Summer 1977), 65–70.

PETTY, J. WILLIAM, DAVID F. SCOTT, JR., and MONROE M. BIRD, "The Capital Expenditure Decision-Making Process of Large Corporations," *Engineering Economist*, 20 (Spring 1975), 159–72.

ROBICHEK, ALEXANDER A., "Interpreting the Results of Risk Analysis," *Journal of Finance*, 30 (December 1975), 1384–86.

SALAZAR, RUDOLFO C., and SUBRATA K. SEN, "A Simulation Model of Capital Budgeting under Uncertainty," *Management Science*, 15 (December 1968), 161–79.

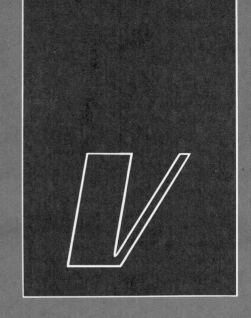

THE COST OF CAPITAL AND FINANCIAL STRUCTURE

Valuation and Rates of Return

In this chapter we examine the **valuation of financial assets,** which includes bonds, preferred stock, and common stock.[1] At first glance, we might wonder why a company's financial management would even be interested in the valuation of financial assets, also known as **security valuation.** However, with further observation, we recognize valuation as a matter of significant importance for a firm's management.

First, in Chapter 1, we indicated that the firm's financial objective should be to maximize the value of the firm's common stock. To implement this objective requires that we understand the factors that underlie valuation. These factors, in a market economy, are the same ones that determine the value of the common stock to its owner. Second, the valuation of a corporation's securities is interrelated with the value of its real assets, such as plant and equipment. That is, the cost of capital used in capital budgeting in Chapters 11 and 12 comes from the rates of return used to value the firm's financial securities.

Thus, we may specify two objectives for studying the valuation of financial assets.

1. The maximization of the firm's common stock value is the objective we follow

[1]Bonds, preferred stock, and common stock are explained in Chapter 20.

in financial decision making. Understanding the valuation of financial securities contributes to our ability to implement this objective.

2. The cost of capital used in making capital budgeting decisions is computed from the required rates of return used by investors in valuing the firm's securities. Hence our discussion of security valuation leads us directly into the estimation of the cost of capital in Chapter 14.

This chapter presents the basic concepts of valuation. It begins by explaining the key determinants of the value of any asset. Next, specific attention is given to the valuation of bonds, preferred stock, and common stock. We then develop the concepts of the investor's *required rate of return* and the *expected rate of return* for a security.

BASIC DETERMINANTS OF VALUE

The value of an asset is based upon its capability to generate future cash flows. However, if "risk" is incurred by accepting the investment, the investor will make the investment only if the possibility of returns overshadows the risk. In this context, value may be expressed as a function of three essential elements: the *asset's expected cash flow,* the *riskiness of these cash flows,* and the *investor's required rate of return* for undertaking the investment. The first two factors are characteristics of the asset, while the investors' required rate of return is the minimum rate necessary to attract an investor to purchase or hold a security. Graphically these three components are depicted in Figure 13-1. Regarding the asset characteristics, the investment is viewed in terms of (1) the timing and amount of potential cash inflows from making the investment, and (2) the level of risk associated with the asset's return. The investor then evaluates the asset in light of his attitude toward the risk-return tradeoff. This attitude is an important element in determining the required rate of return of an investor. Therefore, the

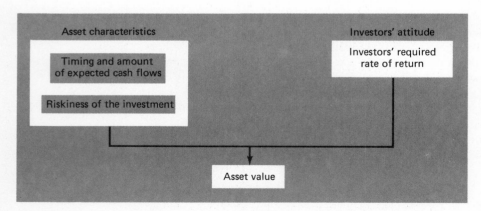

FIGURE 13-1 *Basic Factors Determining an Asset's Value*

value of an asset is determined by the investor's risk-return preferences, which are then reflected in the investor's required rate of return.

The **expected returns** from an investment should be expressed in terms of anticipated cash flows. Certainly, for an investor who is economically motivated, the primary reason, if not the sole reason, for investing is to generate future cash flows. Therefore, throughout this chapter, *cash flows are considered to be the relevant variable to be analyzed in measuring returns.* This viewpoint is applicable regardless of the type of security being analyzed. Whether we are analyzing a debt instrument, preferred stock, common stock, or any special mixture of these categories, the *amount of future cash flows* should be examined in order to estimate the benefits resulting from the investment.

In view of the importance of cash flows in the valuation process, determining their *amount* is a fundamental issue. In a world of uncertainty, the cash flows to be produced from an investment are never precisely known. To illustrate, consider the following possible returns from an investment, where the future cash flows depend upon the state of the economy:

EVENT	PROBABILITY OF THE EVENT	CASH FLOWS FROM THE INVESTMENT
Strong economic growth	50%	$600
Moderate economic growth	30%	400
Economic recession	20%	200

With this information, how should we select the most meaningful cash flow estimate for computing the security's value? One approach would be to compute a weighted expected value, with the weights being the probability of occurrence. (The same approach was used in Chapter 12 to measure expected cash flows for analyzing capital investments under uncertainty.) Let X_i designate the ith possible event (cash flow); N reflect the number of possible events; and $P(X_i)$ indicate the probability that the ith cash flow will occur. The *expected* cash flow, $\overline{X}$, may then be calculated as follows:

$$\overline{X} = \sum_{i=1}^{N} X_i P(X_i) \tag{13-1}$$

For the present illustration,

$$\overline{X} = (.5)(\$600) + (.3)(\$400) + (.2)(\$200) = \$460$$

In addition to computing an expected *dollar* return from an investment, we may also calculate an expected *percentage* return. If in the preceding example the investment cost were $10,000, the $600 cash inflow would represent a 6 percent return ($600 ÷ $10,000). Similarly, the $400 and $200 cash flows could be 4 percent and 2 percent returns, respectively. When we use these percentage returns in place of the dollar amounts, the expected rate of return, $\overline{X}$, is

$$\overline{X} = (.5)(6\%) + (.3)(4\%) + (.2)(2\%) = 4.6 \text{ percent}$$

Having developed a basic measurement for expected returns, let us now consider how we can identify the "riskiness" of an investment.

At this juncture, two questions are important. First, what is meant by the phrase "riskiness of an investment"? Second, given our definition of risk, how should it be measured?

As a tool for understanding the fundamental meaning of risk, consider two prospective investments, A and B. Investment A could conceivably provide a 40 percent return on investment (not bad!). However, a loss as large as 20 percent could result if the project did not develop as planned. In evaluating the respective events that could occur, we estimate the probabilities of the various *percentage* returns on investment A as follows:

*Riskiness
of an Investment*[2]

PROBABILITY	RETURN
5%	−20%
10%	−10%
20%	0%
30%	10%
20%	20%
10%	30%
5%	40%

With this information and from equation (13-1) the **expected rate of return,** $\overline{X}$, is calculated to be 10 percent:

$$\overline{X} = (.05)(-20\%) + (.10)(-10\%) + (.20)(0\%) + (.30)(10\%) + (.20)(20\%) + (.10)(30\%) + (.05)(40\%)$$

$$= 10 \text{ percent}$$

In contrast to this security, investment B is a Treasury bill, offering a "certain" rate of return of 6 percent. Investment A has a higher expected rate of return than investment B, 10 percent versus 6 percent, but which asset is more "risky"—that is, which one results in greater uncertainty as to the final outcome? Defining "risk" or "uncertainty" to be the *possible variation in the return on an investment,* we would have to respond that investment

---

[2]The logic in this section is the same as we used in Chapter 12 when studying capital budgeting under uncertainty.

A is more risky. Therefore, the greater the potential variability in returns, the greater is the risk.[3]

Although the eventual return for investment A is clearly less certain than for investment B, a measurement of risk is useful when the difference between two investments is not so evident. The statistical measure of variability, as suggested in Chapter 12, is the standard deviation (σ), which is computed as follows:

$$\sigma = \sqrt{\sum_{i=1}^{N} (X_i - \overline{X})^2 P(X_i)} \qquad (13\text{-}2)$$

where
N = the number of possible outcomes,

X_i = the value of the ith possible outcome,

$\overline{X}$ = the expected value,

$P(X_i)$ = the probability that the ith outcome will occur.

For investment A, the standard deviation would be 14.49 percent, determined as follows:

$$\sigma = \left[\begin{array}{l} (-20\% - 10\%)^2(.05) + (-10\% - 10\%)^2(.10) + (0\% - 10\%)^2(.20) \\ + (10\% - 10\%)^2(.30) + (20\% - 10\%)^2(.20) + (30\% - 10\%)^2(.10) \\ + (40\% - 10\%)^2(.05) \end{array} \right]^{1/2}$$

$$= \sqrt{210\%} = 14.49 \text{ percent}$$

Although the standard deviation of returns provides a measure of an asset's riskiness, what interpretation should be assigned to the results? Is the 14.49 percentage standard deviation for investment A good or bad? We simply cannot answer this question without comparing another opportunity against investment A. In other words, the attractiveness of a security with respect to its return and risk cannot be determined in isolation. Only by examining other available alternatives can we possibly reach a decision as to the reasonableness of investment A's risk. For example, if another security had an expected return equivalent to that of investment A, but a standard deviation less than 14.49 percent, thereby being *less* risky, we would consider the risk associated with investment A to be excessive.

In addition to the two primary asset characteristics that affect value, those of expected return and risk, we also need to understand the effect of the investor's required rate of return.

We will first examine the concept of the required rate of return for a single investor, then explain how an investor's required rate of return relates to the rates prevailing in the market.

The Required-Rate-of-Return Concept

[3]Alternative definitions of risk have been given in the finance literature. One suggestion, for instance, has been to view as risk only the negative variability in returns from a predetermined minimum acceptable rate of return.

INDIVIDUAL INVESTOR'S
REQUIRED RATE OF RETURN

The investor's **required rate of return** is an important element in valuing an asset. In general, this rate is *the minimum rate of return necessary to attract an investor to purchase or hold a security.* In other words, a prospective investor examines an investment opportunity with the intention of achieving a required rate of return. Only if this rate may be reasonably expected will the investment be made.

In addition to the foregoing definition of the investor's required rate of return, we should understand the underlying factors that determine the *appropriate rate.* In general, this rate is a function of (1) *the time value of money,* (2) *the riskiness (variability in returns) of the asset,* and (3) *the investor's attitude toward risk.* The first element, the time value of money, is represented by a riskless or risk-free rate of return, such as U. S. Treasury securities. Hence, this rate should be used as the required rate of return (discount rate) only for riskless investments. However, as the level of risk increases, investors in the marketplace begin to require additional expected returns to induce them to acquire a security. Thus, the required rate of return, R, is equal to the risk-free rate, R_f, plus a risk premium P.

$$R = R_f + P \qquad (13\text{-}3)$$

REQUIRED RATES OF RETURN
IN THE MARKET

The foregoing perspective is from an *individual* investor's viewpoint; however, the same general principles apply for the market as a whole. The relevant perspective now becomes that of *all investors who are actively involved in buying and selling securities.* A risk-return line may be identified that reflects their attitudes regarding the minimum acceptable rate of return for a given level of risk. One possible description of this relationship, the **security market line (SML),** is represented graphically in Figure 13-2.[4] Although the risk-return relationship in the market (SML) is similar in meaning to the individual's return-risk preferences, the SML provides an extra dimension. Since the SML results from actual market transactions (buying and selling), the relationship represents not only the risk-return demands

[4]Two key assumptions are made in using the *security market line.* First, we assume that the marketplace where securities are bought and sold is highly efficient. Market efficiency indicates that the price of an asset responds quickly to new information, thereby suggesting that the price of a security reflects all available information. As a result, the current price of a security is considered to represent the best estimate of its future price. Second, the model assumes that a perfect market exists. Market perfection is defined as existing when information is readily available to all investors at a nominal cost. Also, securities are assumed to be infinitely divisible, with any transaction costs incurred in purchasing or selling a security being negligible. Furthermore, investors are assumed to be single-period wealth maximizers who agree as to the meaning and the significance of the available information. Finally, within the perfect market, all investors are "price takers," which simply means that no one investor can affect the price of a security.

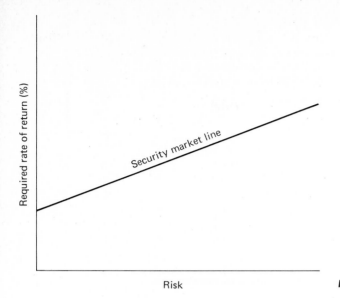

FIGURE 13-2   Security Market Line (SML)

of investors in the market, but also the investor's **opportunity set.** The term *opportunity set* is used to indicate that this risk-return relationship is actually available for an investor interested in purchasing or selling securities.

Before measuring the market risk-return relationship, we need to identify the type of risk that should concern an investor.

IDENTIFYING THE RELEVANT RISK

We have defined the risk of a capital investment in terms of the variability of its anticipated returns, as measured by the standard deviation. However, total variability of returns is not the relevant risk measure for a security in the context of the SML. Total variability can be divided into two components: (1) the risk, or the variability of returns, *unique to the security,* and (2) the comovement or covariation of the security's returns with the *general market.* Thus, the total risk, or the total variability of returns, for a given security can be represented as follows:

$$\boxed{\begin{array}{c}\text{Total}\\\text{risk}\end{array}} = \boxed{\begin{array}{c}\text{Unique security risk}\\\hline\text{Systematic risk}\end{array}} \qquad (13\text{-}4)$$

By investing in different securities, an investor can minimize the impact of the dispersion in returns resulting from events within a single company. Thus, with diversification, the *unique risk* is eliminated from the investor's portfolio. Therefore, the relevant risk for an investor is not total variability of security returns, but rather it is the risk or variability of returns that the security adds to a portfolio. This type of risk is called **nondiversifiable risk** or **systematic risk.** These terms are used to designate the variability in returns that cannot be eliminated by diversification because it results from factors that affect all stocks, such as a change in the general economy.

In measuring a security's systematic risk, we need an indication of the relationship between the security returns and the general market returns. We may calculate this relationship statistically by determining the regression coefficient between security and market returns. This coefficient, frequently called **beta,** β_j, is measured as follows:

$$\beta_j = \frac{\text{Cov}(R_j, R_m)}{\text{Var}(R_m)} \qquad (13\text{-}5)$$

where $\quad \beta_j =$ the systematic risk of security j,

$\text{Cov}(R_j, R_m) =$ the covariance of the returns of the security with the market,

$\text{Var}(R_m) =$ the variance (standard deviation squared) of the market returns.

If beta equals one, then a security's returns will vary in direct proportion with market returns. That is, a 10 percent increase in market returns will produce a 10 percent increase in the security's returns. Correspondingly, a beta of two implies that a 10 percent change in the market return will produce a 20 percent change in the security's returns. Thus, when beta is larger than one, individual security returns are more than proportionately responsive to changes in the market, when returns are both increasing and decreasing. As a consequence, a security with a beta of two is considered to have greater risk than a security having a beta of one.

MEASURING THE MARKET
REQUIRED RATE OF RETURN

Having recognized *nondiversifiable risk* as the relevant risk, we now return to the original equation stating that the required rate of return for a security equals the risk-free rate of return plus a return premium for assuming a given level of risk. In its abbreviated form,

$$R = R_f + P \qquad (13\text{-}3)$$

with P, the risk premium, being a function of the riskiness of the investment. Remember that the risk premium for a security equals the expected return less the riskless rate of return. For example, if the expected return for a security is 14 percent and the risk-free rate is 8 percent, the risk premium is 6 percent. Therefore, if the expected return for the market, R_m, is 12 percent, and the risk-free rate, R_f, is 8 percent, the risk premium for the market portfolio would be 4 percent, or

$$\begin{bmatrix} \text{risk premium in} \\ \text{the market} \end{bmatrix} = \begin{bmatrix} \text{expected market} \\ \text{return} \end{bmatrix} - \begin{bmatrix} \text{risk-free} \\ \text{rate} \end{bmatrix} \qquad (13\text{-}6)$$

This same risk premium would apply to any security having systematic or
nondiversifiable risk equivalent to the general market, or a beta of one. As a
consequence, we would *not* expect an individual to invest in a security
providing a 12 percent return, but having a beta of two. In fact, an investor
would accept an investment with twice the level of risk prevailing in the
market ($\beta = 2$ as opposed to $\beta = 1$) only if the expected risk premium were
also twice as large. Hence, in terms of the security market line, a security
with a beta of two should provide a risk premium of 8 percent, or twice the
4 percent risk premium existing for the market as a whole. At the other
extreme, where a security has a zero beta, the investor should expect no
risk premium, or an expected return equal to the 8 percent risk-free rate.
Thus, adding a security with a zero beta to a portfolio results in no additional risk. Hence, in general, the appropriate required rate of return for
the jth security, R_j, should be determined by

$$R_j = R_f + \beta_j(\overline{R}_m - R_f) \tag{13-7}$$

Equation (13-7) is conventionally defined as the **capital asset pricing
model (CAPM).** This equation designates the risk-return tradeoff existing
in the market, where risk is defined in terms of beta. Figure 13-3 illustrates
graphically the CAPM as the **security market line relationship.** As presented in this figure, securities with betas equal to 0, 1, and 2 should have
required rates of return as follows:

If $\beta_j = 0.0$: $R_j = 8\% + 0.0(12\% - 8\%) = 8$ percent

If $\beta_j = 1.0$: $R_j = 8\% + 1.0(12\% - 8\%) = 12$ percent

If $\beta_j = 2.0$: $R_j = 8\% + 2.0(12\% - 8\%) = 16$ percent

In summary, we cannot formulate a complete concept of valuation
without understanding the nature of the investor's required rate of return. This rate, which serves as the discount rate in the valuation process, represents the investor's minimal acceptable return. In essence, the
required rate of return comprises the return necessary to induce an investor to purchase or hold a security. Finally, a distinct relationship
exists between value and the investor's required rate of return. In the
discussions that follow, this link will be demonstrated clearly as we
examine the valuation of different types of securities. In general, however, we should remember that: *assuming all else to be constant, as the investor's required rate of return decreases, the value of a security increases, or as the
required rate increases, the value decreases.* Simply stated, if we increase our
required rate of return, we are not willing to pay as much for an investment. Reciprocally, as the required rate of return is decreased, value
must increase.

With the foregoing general principles of valuation as a foundation,
we may investigate the procedures for valuing particular types of securi-

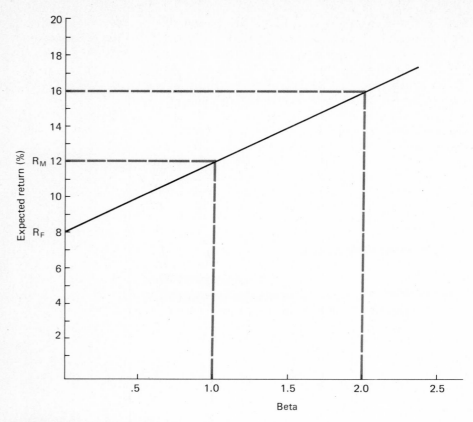

FIGURE 13-3 *Security Market Line*

ties. Specifically, we will examine how to value a bond, preferred stock, and common stock.

The process for valuing a bond is relatively straightforward, provided we understand the terminology and the nature of the security. A more extensive coverage of the contractual provisions of a bond is provided in Chapter 20. We shall consider now several basic terms and provisions that we need in order to understand bond valuation.

Nature of Bonds

When a company, or even a nonprofit institution, has a need for money, one alternative source of financing is **bonds.** This type of financing instrument is simply a long-term promissory note issued by the borrower, promising to pay its holder a predetermined and fixed amount of interest each year. As a form of debt, a contract between the borrower and lender is executed, frequently called an **indenture.** Although the terms of the contract generally are extensive, incorporating detailed protective provisions for the creditor, only three items *directly* affect the value of the security.

1. *Par value.* On the face of a bond is stated the amount the firm is to repay upon the maturity date. This amount, defined as the **par value** or **face value,** is not altered after the bond has been issued. Typically, the par value is set at $1000. Hence, the issuing company contractually agrees to pay the investor this amount when the debt matures. The *par value* is essentially independent of the *market value* of the bond. Thus, while the market value fluctuates in response to changing economic and market conditions, the par value remains constant.

2. *Maturity date.* As already suggested, a bond normally has a maturity date, at which time the borrowing organization is committed to repay the loan. At this time the holder of the security, assuming the company does not default on the obligation, is to receive cash in the amount of the par value.

3. *Coupon interest rate.* Besides paying the owner of the bond a specified amount of money (par value) at the maturity date, the borrower promises to pay a specified amount of interest each year. This annual amount is stated either in terms of dollars, such as $90, or as a percent of the par value. In either instance *the interest to be paid is inflexible.* When the contractual agreement specifies the interest as a percent of par value, this percentage is known as the **coupon interest rate** or the **contractual interest rate.** For instance, if the terms of a $1000 par value bond set the annual interest at $90, the coupon rate is 9 percent, that being $90 divided by $1000. Furthermore, this rate should not be confused with the **current yield** or **yield to maturity,** which represent the expected rate of return to be earned if the bond is purchased at the current market price.

In valuing a bond, we should realize that the preceding provisions (par value, maturity date, and coupon rate) are not subject to change, except possibly when a firm is being reorganized due to financial difficulties. Hence, *the only variable that can cause the value of the bond to increase or decrease is a change in the bondholder's required rate of return.*

Valuation Procedure

The value of a security, including a bond, is equal to the present value of cash flows to be received by the investor. Thus, the terms *value* and *present value* are synonymous. The actual valuation process for a bond, as depicted in Figure 13-4, requires that we know three essential elements: (1) the amount of the cash flows to be received by the investor, (2) the maturity date of the loan, and (3) the investor's required rate of return. The amount of cash flows is dictated by both the periodic interest to be received and the par value to be paid at maturity. Given these cash flows to the bondholder and the maturity date, and using the investor's required rate of return as the discount rate, we may compute the value of the bond, or the **present value.** Thus, the value of a bond, P_0, having a finite maturity date in N years has been defined as the *present value* of the interest payments, I_t, in period t, plus the *present value* of the redemption or par value of the indebt-

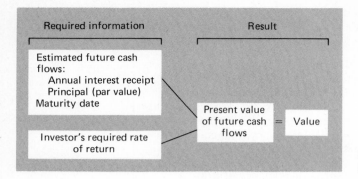

FIGURE 13-4 *Bond Valuation Data Requirements*

edness, M, at the maturity date. If the debtholders' required rate of return is R_d, the value (price) may be calculated as

$$\text{price} = \frac{\$ \text{ interest in year } 1}{(1 + \text{required rate of return})^1} + \frac{\$ \text{ interest in year } 2}{(1 + \text{required rate of return})^2} + \cdots$$

$$+ \frac{\$ \text{ interest in year } N}{(1 + \text{required rate of return})^N} + \frac{\$ \text{ par value}}{(1 + \text{required rate of return})^N}$$

or

$$P_0 = \sum_{t=1}^{N} \frac{\$ \text{ interest in year } t}{(1 + \text{required rate of return})^t} + \frac{\$ \text{ par value}}{(1 + \text{required rate of return})^N}$$

$$P_0 = \underbrace{\phantom{\sum_{t=1}^{N}}\text{present value of interest}} + \underbrace{\text{present value of par value}}$$

$$P_0 = \sum_{t=1}^{N} \frac{\$I_t}{(1 + R_d)^t} + \frac{\$M}{(1 + R_d)^N} \tag{13-8a}$$

If the present value factors in Appendices B and D are used,

$$P_0 = \$I_t \begin{bmatrix} \text{Table Value} \\ \text{Appendix D} \\ N \text{ years} \\ R_d \text{ percent} \end{bmatrix} + \$M \begin{bmatrix} \text{Table Value} \\ \text{Appendix B} \\ N \text{ years} \\ R_d \text{ percent} \end{bmatrix} \tag{13-8b}$$

Example. Consider a bond issued by the Exxon Corporation, having a maturity date of 1998 and a stated coupon rate of $6\frac{1}{2}$ percent.[5] The bonds were originally issued at a price of \$1000. By 1977, however, since the investors' required rate of return had changed, the bond value was less than \$1000. For instance, at one time during 1977 investors were requiring a return of approximately 8 percent for this type of security. At this time the value of the security was approximately \$850.11, which may be calculated in the following steps:

---

[5]In actuality, the company remits the interest to its bondholders on a semi-annual basis on January 15 and July 15. However, for the moment assume the interest is to be received annually. The effect of semiannual payments is to be examined later.

Step 1: Determine the cash flow stream from the investment:

      (a) Annual interest for the 21 years remaining to maturity (1977–1998): $65 per year (6.5 percent × $1000).

      (b) Repayment of the loan at par value in 1998: $1000.

Step 2: Calculate the value (present value) of the cash flows at the prevailing required rate of return. Assume this rate is 8 percent. This computation may be performed from either equation (13-8a) or (13-8b). Using equation (13-8a), we determine the value as follows:[6]

$$P_0 = \sum_{t=1}^{21} \frac{\$65}{(1 + .08)^t} + \frac{\$1000}{(1 + .08)^{21}} = \$850.11$$

Alternatively, by utilizing the present-value tables in Appendices B and D, we may compute the $850.11 value.

YEARS	AMOUNT	PRESENT-VALUE FACTOR AT 8 PERCENT		PRESENT VALUE
1–21 (1977–1998)	$65	10.017	=	$651.11
21 (1998)	$1000	.199	=	199.00
		Value of the security (present value)	=	$850.11

Thus, if investors consider 8 percent to be an appropriate required rate of return in view of the risk level associated with these Exxon bonds, paying a price of $850.11 would satisfy this return requirement.

    In the previous illustration, the interest payments were assumed to be paid annually. However, companies typically forward an interest check to bondholders semiannually. For example, rather than disbursing $65 in interest at the conclusion of each year, Exxon Corporation pays $32.50 (half of $65) on January 15 and July 15.

    In adapting equation (13-8a) to recognize semiannual interest payments, several steps are involved. First, thinking in terms of "periods" instead of years, a bond with a life of N years paying interest semiannually should be thought to have a life of $2N$ periods. In other words, a five-year bond ($N = 5$) that remits its interest on a semiannual basis actually involves 10 payment periods. Yet, while the number of periods has doubled, the *dollar* amount of interest being sent to the investors for each period and the bondholders' required rate of return are half of the equivalent annual

Semiannual Interest Payments[7]

---

[6]A slightly different answer may result from differences in rounding.

[7]The logic for calculating the value of a bond that pays interest semiannually is similar to the material presented in Chapter 5, pp. 125–27, where compound interest with nonannual periods was discussed.

figures. Thus, I_t becomes $I_t/2$ and R_d is changed to $R_d/2$; thus, equation (13-8a) becomes

$$P_0 = \sum_{t=1}^{2N} \frac{\$1_t/2}{\left(1 + \dfrac{R_d}{2}\right)^t} + \frac{\$M}{\left(1 + \dfrac{R_d}{2}\right)^{2N}} \qquad (13\text{-}9a)$$

However, if the present-value tables are used, P_0 is calculated as

$$P_0 = \frac{\$I}{2} \begin{bmatrix} \text{Table Value} \\ \text{Appendix D} \\ 2N \text{ periods} \\ R_d/2 \text{ percent} \end{bmatrix} + \$M \begin{bmatrix} \text{Table Value} \\ \text{Appendix B} \\ 2N \text{ periods} \\ R_d/2 \text{ percent} \end{bmatrix} \qquad (13\text{-}9b)$$

Example. The effect of semiannual interest payments upon the value of a bond, assume the Garrett Corporation has issued a 9 percent, $1000 bond. The debt is to mature in six years, and the **going interest rate** (required rate of return) is currently 8 percent. If interest is paid semiannually, the number of periods is 12 (six years × 2); the dollar interest to be received by the investors at the end of each six-month period is $45 ($90 ÷ 2); and the required rate of return for six months is 4 percent (8 percent ÷ 2). Therefore, the equation is

$$P_0 = \sum_{t=1}^{12} \frac{\$45}{(1 + .04)^t} + \frac{\$1000}{(1 + .04)^{12}} = \$1047.33$$

Equivalently,

$$P_0 = \$45 \begin{bmatrix} \text{Table Value} \\ \text{Appendix D} \\ 12 \text{ periods} \\ 4 \text{ percent} \end{bmatrix} + \$1000 \begin{bmatrix} \text{Table Value} \\ \text{Appendix B} \\ 12 \text{ periods} \\ 4 \text{ percent} \end{bmatrix}$$

$$= \$45(9.385) + \$1000(.625)$$

$$= \$422.33 + \$625.00$$

$$= \$1047.33$$

Thus, the value (present value) of a bond paying $45 semiannually, and $1000 at maturity (6 years), is $1047.33, provided the investor's required rate of return is 8 percent compounded semiannually.

The second basic security type is **preferred stock.** Like a bondholder, the owner of preferred stock should receive a *constant income* from the investment in each period. However, the return from preferred stock comes in the form of *dividends* rather than *interest*. In addition, while bonds generally have a specific maturity date, most preferred stocks are perpetuities (nonmaturing). In this instance, the value (present value) of an equal cash flow stream, P_0, *continuing indefinitely* may be stated as follows:

*PREFERRED
STOCK
VALUATION*

$$P_0 = \frac{\text{dividend in year 1}}{(1 + \text{required rate of return})^1} + \frac{\text{dividend in year 2}}{(1 + \text{required rate of return})^2} + \cdots$$

$$+ \frac{\text{dividend in infinity}}{(1 + \text{required rate of return})^{infinity}}$$

$$= \frac{D_1}{(1 + R_p)^1} + \frac{D_2}{(1 + R_p)^2} + \cdots + \frac{D_\infty}{(1 + R_p)^\infty} \qquad (13\text{-}10)$$

$$= \sum_{t=1}^{\infty} \frac{D_t}{(1 + R_p)^t}$$

If, however, the dividends in each period are equal, as they are with preferred stock, equation (13-10) may be reduced to a relatively simple equation, that being[8]

$$P_0 = \frac{\text{annual dividend}}{\text{required rate of return}} = \frac{D}{R_p} \qquad (13\text{-}11)$$

This equation simply represents a necessary shortcut for computing the present value of an infinite cash flow that does not vary from year to year. Hence, if the value (present value) of an infinite income stream is to be determined, equation (13-11) can be used.

Example. To illustrate the valuation of a preferred stock, American Telephone and Telegraph's outstanding preferred shares provide $3.64 in annual dividends. The *current yield* for the stock, or equivalently, the required rate of return for the stockholders, is 7.28 percent. Thus, given the dividend of $3.64, the value of the stock is $50 per share.

$$P_0 = \frac{\$3.64}{.0728} = \$50$$

[8]To verify this result, consider the following equation

$$P_0 = \frac{D_1}{(1 + R_p)} + \frac{D_2}{(1 + R_p)^2} + \cdots + \frac{D_n}{(1 + R_p)^n}$$

If we multiply both sides of this equation by $(1 + R_p)$, we have

$$P_0(1 + R_p) = D_1 + \frac{D_2}{(1 + R_p)} + \cdots + \frac{D_n}{(1 + R_p)^{n-1}}$$

Subtracting the first equation from the second equation yields

$$P_0(1 + R_p - 1) = D_1 - \frac{D_n}{(1 + R_p)^n}$$

As n approaches infinity, $D_n/(1 + R_p)^n$ approaches zero. Consequently

$$P_0 R_p = D_i \quad \text{and} \quad P_0 = \frac{D_1}{R_p}$$

Since $D_1 = D_2 = \cdots = D_n$, we need not designate the year. Therefore

$$P_0 = \frac{D}{R_p}$$

Common stock is the final type of security to be examined in the present chapter. Like that of both bonds and preferred stock, **common stock** value is equal to the *present value of all future cash inflows expected to be received by the investor owning the stock.* However, in contrast to bonds, the owners of common shares are not promised interest income or a maturity payment at some specified time in the future. Nor does common stock entitle the holder to a predetermined constant dividend, as does preferred stock. For common stock, the dividend is based upon the profitability of the firm and upon management's decision either to pay dividends or to retain the profits for reinvestment purposes. As a consequence, dividend streams tend to increase with the growth in corporate earnings. Thus, estimating the future dividend is extremely difficult.

In addition to dividends, the common stockholder frequently relies upon stock price appreciation as a source of return. If the company is retaining a portion of its earnings to be reinvested, future profits and dividends should grow. This growth should then be reflected in an increased market price of the common stock in future periods. Therefore, in developing a valuation model for common stock, both types of return (dividends and price appreciation) should be recognized.

To explain this process, let us begin by examining how an investor might value a stock that is to be held for only one year.

Single-Period Valuation

For an investor holding a common stock for only a single year, the value of the stock should equal the present value of both the expected dividend to be received in one year, D_1, and the anticipated market price of the share at year end, P_1. If R_c represents an investor's required rate of return, the value of the security would be

$$P_0 = \frac{\text{dividend in one year}}{(1 + \text{required rate of return})} + \frac{\text{market price in one year}}{(1 + \text{required rate of return})}$$

$$= \frac{D_1}{1 + R_c} + \frac{P_1}{1 + R_c} \qquad (13\text{-}12)$$

As an example of single-period valuation, suppose an investor is contemplating the purchase of RCA common stock. The dividend in the forthcoming year is expected to be $1.32 and the market price by year end is projected to be $34. If the individual's required rate of return (sometimes referred to as its capitalization rate) is 12 percent, the value of the security would be

$$P_0 = \frac{\$1.32}{1 + .12} + \frac{\$34}{1 + .12}$$

$$= \$1.18 + \$30.36$$

$$= \$31.54$$

Although single-period valuation is an informative starting point, its departure from reality should be obvious. For this reason a generalized model, not limited to a single year, is definitely preferred. Since common stock has no maturity date, the problem is similar to the valuation of preferred stock where the cash flows extend to infinity, with the *value of the security being the present value of all future dividends.* The general *valuation* model would be

$$P_0 = \frac{D_1}{(1 + R_c)^1} + \frac{D_2}{(1 + R_c)^2} + \cdots + \frac{D_N}{(1 + R_c)^N} + \cdots + \frac{D_\infty}{(1 + R_c)^\infty} \quad (13\text{-}13)$$

This equation simply indicates that we are discounting the dividend in the first year, D_1, back one year, the dividend in the second year, D_2, back two years, . . . , the dividend in the Nth year back N years, . . . , and the dividend in infinity back an infinite number of years. However, a key assumption must be imposed in order to solve the problem: *assume the amount of the dividend is increasing by a constant percent each year.* If this assumption is satisfied, the amount of the dividend in any year is equal to the last dividend plus the amount of the increase in the present year, or

$$\text{dividend in year } t \ (D_t) = \text{dividend received last year } (D_{t-1}) \quad (13\text{-}14)$$
$$+ \text{ growth from last year } (t - 1) \text{ to year } t$$

If the amount of the growth is a constant percent each year, dividends in the future may be expressed quantitatively as a function of last year's dividend. For example, if last year's dividend, D_0, was \$1 and the future dividends are expected to increase by 10 percent each year,

$$\text{dividend in year one } (D_1) = \text{dividend last year } (1 + \text{growth rate})$$
$$= \$1(1 + .10) = \$1.10 \quad (13\text{-}15a)$$

and

$$\text{dividend in year two } (D_2) = \$1(1 + .10)^2 = \$1.21 \quad (13\text{-}15b)$$

In general, the dividend in year t may be represented as

$$D_t = D_0(1 + \text{growth rate})^t \quad (13\text{-}15c)$$
$$= D_0(1 + g)^t$$

By substitution, the valuation model in equation (13-13) may now be revised to be

$$P_0 = \frac{D_0(1 + g)^1}{(1 + R_c)^1} + \frac{D_0(1 + g)^2}{(1 + R_c)^2} + \cdots + \frac{D_0(1 + g)^N}{(1 + R_c)^N} + \cdots + \frac{D_0(1 + g)^\infty}{(1 + R_c)^\infty} \quad (13\text{-}16)$$

However, if g is the same each year, and R_c is greater than g, equation (13-16) may be modified to a much simpler format:[9]

$$\text{value} = \frac{\text{dividend in year 1}}{(\text{required rate of return}) - (\text{growth rate})} \qquad (13\text{-}17)$$

$$P_0 = \frac{D_1}{R_c - g}$$

Consequently, the value (present value) of a security where the receipts continue to infinity and increase at a constant annual compound growth rate may be easily calculated by equation (13-17). Although this equation may not be intuitively appealing, we should remember that its end result equals the present value of the future dividend stream growing at a rate, g, to infinity.

To illustrate, compute the value (present value) of a common stock that paid $2 in dividends last year. The stockholders' required rate of return is 15 percent, and a 10 percent growth rate in earnings and dividends is anticipated into the indefinite future. In this case, the value of the security is

$$P_0 = \frac{D_1}{R_c - g} \qquad (13\text{-}17)$$

$$= \frac{D_0(1 + g)}{R_c - g}$$

$$= \frac{\$2(1 + 10\%)}{15\% - 10\%}$$

$$= \$44$$

Having analyzed the valuation process on the assumption that the investor's required rate of return is known, let us consider next how to measure this rate of return.

[9] If both sides of equation (13-16) are multiplied by $(1 + R_c)/(1 + g)$ and then equation (13-16) is subtracted from the product, the result is

$$\frac{P_0(1 + R_c)}{1 + g} - P_0 = D_0 - \frac{D_0(1 + g)^\infty}{(1 + R_c)^\infty}$$

If $R_c > g$, which normally should hold, $[D_0(1 + g)^\infty/(1 + R_c)^\infty]$ approaches zero. As a result,

$$\frac{P_0(1 + R_c)}{1 + g} - P_0 = D_0$$

$$P_0\left(\frac{1 + R_c}{1 + g}\right) - P_0\left(\frac{1 + g}{1 + g}\right) = D_0$$

$$P_0\left(\frac{(1 + R_c) - (1 + g)}{1 + g}\right) = D_0$$

$$P_0(R_c - g) = D_0(1 + g)$$

$$P_0 = \frac{D_1}{R_c - g}$$

Earlier in this chapter we examined the general concept of an investor's required rate of return, emphasizing the primary factors determining this required rate without serious concern for actually *measuring* it. Until the valuation procedures for bonds, preferred stock, and common stock had been individually presented, we could not gain a clear understanding of the technique for calculating required rates of return. However, with these valuation procedures now in hand, we may investigate the computation of the required rate of return.

MEASURING THE REQUIRED RATE OF RETURN

To begin with, we need to develop a general perspective. As already indicated, the value of a security is determined from (1) the timing and amount of the cash flows to be received from the investment, and (2) the investor's required rate of return. These relationships may be specified as follows:

Valuation from a Different Perspective

KNOWN VARIABLES	UNKNOWN VARIABLE
Cash flows	Value
Required rate of return	
(discount rate)	

Thus, two variables are known, and the unknown variable, value, is computed. For the investment with cash flows (CF) terminating within a finite period, and a required rate of return of R, the general valuation model was

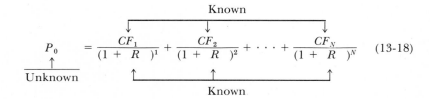

$$P_0 = \frac{CF_1}{(1 + R)^1} + \frac{CF_2}{(1 + R)^2} + \cdots + \frac{CF_N}{(1 + R)^N} \quad (13\text{-}18)$$

This equation has as its sole objective the determination of value. Yet, if the value of the security is already known, but the required rate of return is not known, we may solve for this rate. Thus, only the status of the variables is different, as reflected below:

KNOWN VARIABLES	UNKNOWN VARIABLES
Cash flows	Required rate of return
Value	(discount rate)

Restated within the equation,

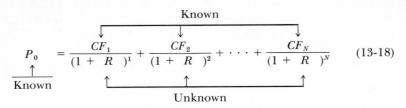

$$P_0 = \frac{CF_1}{(1+R)^1} + \frac{CF_2}{(1+R)^2} + \cdots + \frac{CF_N}{(1+R)^N} \qquad (13\text{-}18)$$

Known

Known

Unknown

Hence, the equation is not changed. Only the perspective is different, in that previously we were given the cash flows and the appropriate discount rate, and asked to ascertain value. Now the cash flows and the value are provided, and the desired result is to compute the required rate of return (discount rate). In brief, *the required rate of return is the discount rate that equates the present value of future cash flows with the current market price of the security.*

Computing the bondholder's required rate of return results in the following framework:

Bondholder's Required Rate of Return

$$\text{value} = \left(\begin{array}{c}\text{present value of}\\ \text{the interest receipts}\end{array}\right) + \left(\begin{array}{c}\text{present value of}\\ \text{maturity value}\end{array}\right) \qquad (13\text{-}19)$$

More specifically, we "find" the required rate of return for bondholders, R_b, that equates the value of the security, P_0, with the present value of both interest receipts, I_t, and the par or maturity value of the security, M. As provided previously in valuing a bond, the appropriate equation is

$$P_0 = \frac{\$I_1}{(1+R_b)^1} + \frac{\$I_2}{(1+R_b)^2} + \cdots + \frac{\$I_N}{(1+R_b)^N} + \frac{\$M}{(1+R_b)^N} \qquad (13\text{-}8a)$$

"Find" R_b

A slight difficulty arises in that R_b cannot be solved directly. Instead, a *trial-and-error* procedure, similar to solving for an *internal rate of return* in capital budgeting, must be used. We simply have to keep trying a rate until the equality is satisfied.

Example.   To demonstrate the computation of a bondholder's required rate of return, assume that a person is willing to pay *no more than* $900 for a bond. (He would always be agreeable to paying less.) The $1000 par value security, which matures in five years, is to pay 8 percent in annual interest. At the $900 value, what rate of return is the investor implicitly requiring? We answer this question by solving the following equation:

$$\$900 = \frac{\$80}{(1+R_b)^1} + \frac{\$80}{(1+R_b)^2} + \frac{\$80}{(1+R_b)^3} + \frac{\$80}{(1+R_b)^4} + \frac{\$80}{(1+R_b)^5} + \frac{\$1000}{(1+R_b)^5}$$

At this point, we select a rate and either (1) insert the rate into the above equation or (2) rely upon the appropriate present-value factors in the tables in Appendices B and D. Selecting the second approach, we now face the question: What discount rate should be used as a starting point? No precise answer may be given; however, the investor is evidently requiring a return in excess of 8 percent, since he is not amenable to paying the full $1000 par value. Hence, we might arbitrarily select 12 percent. Trying this rate, we find that the present value of the bond's annual interest and principal is $855.40, which is determined as follows:

YEARS	CASH RECEIVED	PRESENT-VALUE FACTOR AT 12 PERCENT	PRESENT VALUE
1–5	$ 80	3.605[a]	$288.40
5	$1000	.567[b]	567.00
		Present value at 12 percent:	$855.40

[a]For years 1 through 5 at 12 percent.
[b]For year 5 at 12 percent.

Since an $855.40 present value results from discounting the receipts at a 12 percent rate, we may conclude that purchasing the security at the $900 market value does not provide a 12 percent rate of return on investment. In essence, to achieve at least 12 percent return stipulates that no more than $855.40 be paid for the investment. Since the investor is agreeable to paying $900, the required return must be less than 12 percent. Arbitrarily selecting a lower rate of 10 percent results in a present value of $924.28 [$80(3.791) + $1000(.621)]. A reversed conclusion would now appear justified, in that the $900 investment could be expected to produce a rate in excess of 10 percent. The mere fact that the present value is now larger than the acceptable $900 suggests that an investor who is not willing to pay more than $900 must not be satisfied with a 10 percent rate of return. Consequently, the required rate of return must be between 10 and 12 percent. To be more accurate requires interpolation between these two rates.

Since the difference between 10 percent and 12 percent is 2 percent, we may restate the problem as follows: The required rate of return (R_d) is 10 percent plus some part of the 2 percent difference between 10 percent and 12 percent. In this example, increasing the discount rate from 10 percent to 12 percent resulted in a $68.88 reduction in the present value ($924.28 − $855.40). However, since a present value of $900 (the security's value to the investor) is the desired present value, the discount rate should only be increased enough to reduce the present value by $24.28 ($924.28 − $900). With this rationale, the required rate of return may be estimated by the following equation:[10]

[10]Although interpolation provides increased accuracy in identifying the rate, the final answer is not precise. This slight inaccuracy is due to the nonlinearity of the present-value equation.

$$\begin{bmatrix} \text{required rate} \\ \text{of return} \end{bmatrix} = 10\% + \left(\frac{\begin{array}{c}\text{desired decrease} \\ \text{in the present value}\end{array}}{\begin{array}{c}\text{actual decrease in} \\ \text{the present value}\end{array}} \right) 2\% \qquad (13\text{-}20)$$

or

$$R_d = 10\% + \left(\frac{\$24.28}{\$68.88} \right) 2\% = 10\% + (.352)2\%$$

$$= 10.70 \text{ percent}$$

Thus, an investor who purchases the bond for $900 is requiring a yield to maturity of 10.70 percent.

Preferred Stockholder's Required Rate of Return

Determining the required rate of return for a preferred stockholder is equivalent in principle to measuring the bondholder's minimum acceptable rate of return. As before, the required rate of return is the discount rate that equates the present value of the future cash flows (dividends) and the value the investor is willing to pay for the security. Hence, if we know what an investor would pay for a stock and the amount of the expected dividends, we can determine his required rate of return.

In computing the preferred stockholder's required rate we should return to the valuation equation for preferred stock. Earlier, equation (13-11) specified the value of a preferred stock, or P_o, as

$$P_0 = \frac{\text{annual dividend}}{\text{required rate of return}} = \frac{D}{R_p} \qquad (13\text{-}11)$$

Clearly, this equation may be restructured to be

$$R_p = \frac{\text{annual dividend}}{\text{value}} = \frac{D}{P_0} \qquad (13\text{-}21)$$

which simply indicates that the required rate of return of a preferred security equals the **dividend yield** (dividend/price). For example, if an investor would be willing to pay at least, but no more than, $50 for AT&T's preferred stock ($3.64 dividend), the required rate of return would be

$$R_p = \frac{D}{P_0} = \frac{\$3.64}{\$50} = 7.28 \text{ percent}$$

Therefore, investors who pay $50 per share for a preferred security paying $3.64 in annual dividends are requiring a 7.28 percent rate of return.

Common Stockholder's Required Rate of Return

As already explained for bonds and preferred stock, the present-value equation may be used in solving for value if the investor's required rate of return is known. Alternatively, if the value is already provided, but the required rate of return is unknown, the valuation equation is useful in solving for the required rate of return. Continuing with this same logic, the common stockholder's required rate of return may likewise be calculated.

The valuation equation for common stock was given earlier as

$$\text{value} = \frac{\text{dividend in year 1}}{(1 + \text{required rate of return})^1} + \frac{\text{dividend in year 2}}{(1 + \text{required rate of return})^2}$$

$$+ \cdots + \frac{\text{dividend in year } \infty}{(1 + \text{required rate of return})^\infty}$$

$$P_0 = \frac{D_1}{(1 + R_c)^1} + \frac{D_2}{(1 + R_c)^2} + \cdots + \frac{D_\infty}{(1 + R_c)^\infty}$$

$$= \sum_{t=1}^{\infty} \frac{D_t}{(1 + K_c)^t} \tag{13-13}$$

Owing to the difficulty in discounting to infinity, a key assumption was made that the dividends, D_t, increase at a constant annual compound growth rate of g. If this assumption is valid, equation (13-13) was shown to be equivalent to

$$\text{value} = \frac{\text{dividend in year 1}}{\text{required rate of return} - \text{the growth rate}} \tag{13-17}$$

$$P_0 = \frac{D_1}{R_c - g}$$

Thus, P_0 represents the maximum value that an investor having a required rate of return of R_c would pay for a security having an anticipated dividend in year one of D_1 that is expected to grow in future years at rate g. By restructuring equation (13-17), we may compute the required rate of return for a common investor directly as

$$R_c = \left(\frac{D_1}{P_0}\right) + g \tag{13-22}$$

$\uparrow$ $\uparrow$

| Dividend yield | Annual growth rate |

From this equation, the common stockholders' required rate of return is equal to the *dividend yield* plus a *growth* factor. *Although the growth rate, g, applies to the growth in the company's dividends, the firm's earnings and the stock price may also be expected to increase at the same rate.* For this reason, g represents the annual percentage growth in the stock price. In other words, the investor's required rate of return is satisfied by receiving *dividends,* expressed as a percentage of the price of the stock (dividend yield), and *capital gains,* as reflected by the percentage growth rate.

Example. As an example of computing the required rate of return for a common stock, where dividends are anticipated to grow at a constant rate to infinity, assume that the common stock of RCA has been valued by an investor to be worth $33. If the expected dividend at the conclusion of this year is $1.32 and dividends and earnings are growing at an 8 percent annual rate, the investor's required rate of return, R_c, would be computed as

$$R_c = \frac{\$1.32}{\$33} + 8\% = 12 \text{ percent}$$

The preceding section sought to measure the individual investor's *required* rate of return. However, as explained earlier by the *security market line,* a single investor's required rate of return may not be in agreement with the returns available in the market. For instance, at a given risk level, a particular investor may require a 12 percent return while the *going rate of return,* or the *expected return,* for the same risk may only be 10 percent.

In actual calculation of the expected rate of return, the logic is quite similar to that used in the measurement of the required rate of return. However, instead of the price at which a particular investor would *prefer* to purchase the security, the relevant figure is the price at which the security is actually selling in the market. Thus, the distinction between the required and the expected rate is based entirely upon whether the "value" is determined by a sole investor or by the interaction of many investors in the market.[11] The *expected rate of return is found by determining the discount rate that sets the present value of the future cash flows equal to the current market price of the security.*

Example. To illustrate, consider the bonds of the McIlroy Corporation, which are selling for $1140. The bonds carry a coupon interest rate of 9 percent and mature in 10 years. Although they are selling for $1140, Talley, a potential investor, considers them to be worth only $1067. What are the *expected rate of return* for the bonds and Talley's *required rate of return?*

In determining the *expected rate,* we need to find the rate that discounts the anticipated cash flows back to a present value of $1140, the existing market price for the bond. Trying 7 percent, we find the present value of future cash flows to be $1140.16, computed as follows:

YEARS	CASH FLOW	PRESENT-VALUE FACTORS AT 7 PERCENT	PRESENT VALUE
1–10	$90 per year	7.024	$632.16
10	$1000 in year 10	.508	508.00
		Present value at 7 percent:	$1,140.16

[11]In other words, the expected rate of return in the market is the required rate of return for all investors actively buying and selling the security.

$$\text{value} = \frac{\text{dividend in year one}}{(\text{required rate of return} - \text{growth rate})} \qquad (13\text{-}17)$$

The investor's **required rate of return** is a cornerstone in valuation. Computing this minimum acceptable return requires knowing the value of the security to the investor and the cash flows expected from the investment. Hence, the only change in the problem is one of perspective. Either (1) we know the cash flows expected from the investment and the required rate of return, and are asked to compute value, or (2) we are given the cash flows and the value, and are asked to ascertain the required rate of return. If the rate of return is the unknown variable, we find this rate by determining the discount rate that equates the present value of future cash flows with the price acceptable to the investor. Moreover, a distinction between the *required rate of return* and the *expected rate of return* should be maintained, with the *required rate* being a function of the price that the individual investor deems reasonable. In contrast, the *expected rate of return* is what may be expected given that the investor pays the current market price of the security. The market is in equilibrium when the expected rate of return and the required rate of return are equal.

13-1. Explain the three factors that determine the value of an asset.

13-2. (a) Define risk.

   (b) How have we measured the riskiness of an asset?

   (c) How should the proposed measurement of risk be interpreted?

13-3. (a) What is meant by the phrase "the investor's required rate of return"?

   (b) What key factors determine the appropriate required rate of return?

13-4. Define the security market line. What does it represent?

13-5. Explain the relationship between an investor's required rate of return and the value of a security.

13-6. (a) How does a bond's par value differ from its market value?

   (b) Explain the difference between the coupon interest rate and a bond-holder's required interest rate.

13-7. What is a general definition for the value of a security regardless of its type?

13-8. The common stockholders receive two types of return from their investment. What are they?

13-9. State how the investor's required rate of return is computed.

13-10. Distinguish between the *required* and the *expected* rate of return.

STUDY QUESTIONS

13-1. Universal Corporation is planning to invest in a security that has several possible rates of return. Given the following probability distribution of returns, what is the expected rate of return on the investment? Also compute the standard deviation of the returns. What do the resulting numbers represent?

STUDY PROBLEMS

PROBABILITY	RETURN
.10	−10%
.20	5%
.30	10%
.40	25%

13-2. Syntex, Inc., is considering an investment in one of two common stocks. Given the information below, which investment is better, based upon risk and return?

COMMON STOCK A		COMMON STOCK B	
Probability	Return	Probability	Return
		.20	−5%
.30	11%	.30	6%
.40	15%	.30	14%
.30	19%	.20	22%

13-3. Trico bonds have a coupon rate of 8 percent, a par value of $1000, and will mature in 20 years. If you require a return of 7 percent, what price would you be willing to pay for the bond? What happens if you pay *more* for the bond? What happens if you pay *less* for the bond?

13-4. Friedman Manufacturing, Inc., has prepared the following information regarding two investments under consideration. Which investment should be accepted?

SECURITY A		SECURITY B	
Probabilities	Returns	Probabilities	Returns
.2	−2%	.1	4%
.5	18%	.3	6%
.3	27%	.4	10%
		.2	15%

13-5. Sunn Co.'s bonds, maturing in seven years, pay 8 percent interest semiannually on a $1000 face value. If your required rate of return is 10

percent, what is the value of the bond? How would your answer change
if the interest were paid annually?

13-6. Sharp Co. bonds are selling in the market for $1045. These 15-year
bonds pay 7 percent interest on a $1000 par value. If they are pur-
chased at the market price, what is the expected rate of return? What is
your required rate of return? Compare and interpret the two returns.

13-7. Enterprise, Inc., bonds pay 9 percent interest semiannually until they
mature in eight years. Their par value is $1000. If your required rate of
return is 8 percent, what is the value of the bond? What is its value if the
interest is paid annually?

13-8. You are willing to pay $900 for a 10-year bond ($1000 par value) that
pays 8 percent interest semiannually. What is your required rate of
return?

13-9. The preferred stock of Armlo pays a $2.75 dividend. What is the value
of the stock if your required return is 9 percent?

13-10. Solitron's preferred stock is selling for $42.16 and pays $1.95 in dividends. What is your required rate of return if you purchase the security
at the market price?

13-11. Crosby Corporation's common stock paid $1.32 in dividends last year
and is expected to grow indefinitely at an annual 7 percent rate. What is
the value of the stock if you require an 11 percent return?

13-12. The common stock of Zaldi Co. is selling for $32.84. The stock paid
dividends of $2.94 per share last year and has a projected growth rate
of 9.5 percent. If you purchase the stock at the market price, what is
your required rate of return?

13-13. Honeywag common stock is expected to pay $1.85 in dividends next
year, and the market price is projected to be $42.50 by year end. If the
investor's required rate of return is 11 percent, what is the current value
of the stock?

13-14. The market price for Hobart common stock is $43. The price at the end
of one year is expected to be $48, and dividends for next year should be
$2.84. What is the capitalization rate?

13-15. Esson 20-year bonds pay 9 percent interest annually on a $1000 par
value. If you buy the bonds at $945, what is your required rate of
return?

13-16. Zerith Co.'s bonds mature in 12 years and pay 7 percent interest annually. If you purchase the bonds for $1150, what is your required rate of
return?

13-17. National Steel 15-year $1000 par value bonds pay 8 percent interest
annually. The market price of the bonds is $1085, and your required
rate of return is 10 percent.
(a) Compute the bond's expected rate of return.
(b) Determine the value of the bond to you, given your required rate of
return.
(c) Should you purchase the bond?

13-18. Pioneer's preferred stock is selling for $33 in the market and pays $3.60
annual dividend.

(a) What is the expected rate of return on the stock?

(b) If an investor's required rate of return is 10 percent, what is the value of the stock for that investor?

(c) Should the investor acquire the stock?

13-19. The common stock of NCP paid $1.32 in dividends last year. Dividends are expected to grow at an 8 percent annual rate for an indefinite number of years.

(a) If NCP's current market price is $23.50, what is the stock's expected rate of return?

(b) If your required rate of return is 10.5 percent, what is the value of the stock for you?

(c) Should you make the investment?

13-20. Johnson Manufacturing, Inc., is considering several investments. The rate on Treasury bills is currently 6.75 percent, and the expected return for the market is 12 percent. What should be the required rates of return for each investment?

SECURITY	BETA
A	1.50
B	.82
C	.60
D	1.15

13-21. CSB, Inc., has a beta of .765. If the expected market return is 11.5 percent and the risk-free rate is 7.5 percent, what is the appropriate required return of CSB (using the CAPM)?

13-22. The expected return for the general market is 12.8 percent, and the risk premium in the market is 4.3 percent. Tasaco, LBM, and Exxos have betas of .864, .693, and .575, respectively. What are the appropriate required rates of return of the three securities?

SELECTED REFERENCES

APPLEYARD, A. R., and G. K. YARROW, "The Relationship Between Take-Over Activity and Share Valuation," *Journal of Finance,* 30 (December 1975), 1239–49.

ARDITTI, FRED D., "Risk and the Required Return of Equity," *Journal of Finance,* 22 (March 1967), 19–36.

BAKER, H. KENT, and JOHN A. HASLEM, "Toward the Development of Client-Specified Valuation Models," *Journal of Finance,* 29 (September 1974), 1255–63.

BARNEA, AMIR, and DENNIS E. LOGUE, "The Evaluation Forecasts of a Security Analyst," *Financial Management,* 2 (Summer 1973), 38–45.

BAUMAN, W. SCOTT, "Investment Returns and Present Values," *Financial Analysts Journal,* 25 (November–December 1969), 107–18.

BEIDLEMAN, CARL R., "Limitation of Price-Earnings Ratios," *Financial Analysts Journal,* 27 (September–October 1971), 86–91.

BOUDREAUX, KENNETH J., "Divestiture of Share Price," *Journal of Financial and Quantitative Analysis,* 10 (November 1975), 619–26.

BOWER, RICHARD S., and DOROTHY H. BOWER, "Risk and Valuation of Common Stock," *Journal of Political Economy,* 77 (May–June 1969), 349–62.

BRIGHAM, EUGENE F., and JAMES L. PAPPAS, "Duration of Growth, Changes in Growth Rates, and Corporate Share Prices," *Financial Analysts Journal,* 24 (May–June 1966), 157–62.

CARLETON, WILLARD T., and IRWIN H. SILBERMAN, "Joint Determination of Rate of Return and Capital Structure: An Econometric Analysis," *Journal of Finance,* 32 (June 1977), 811–21.

ELTON, EDWIN J., and MARTIN J. GRUBER, "Earnings Estimates and the Accuracy of Expectional Data," *Management Science,* 18 (April 1972), 409–24.

————, and MARTIN J. GRUBER, "Valuation and Asset Selection Under Alternative Investment Opportunities," *Journal of Finance,* 31 (May 1976), 525–39.

FOSTER, EARL M., "Price-Earnings Ratio and Corporate Growth," *Financial Analysts Journal* (January–February 1970), 96–99.

FRIEND, IRWIN, and MARSHALL BLUME, "The Demand for Risky Assets," *American Economic Review,* 75 (December 1975), pp. 900–22.

GOODING, ARTHUR E., "Quantification of Investors' Perceptions of Common Stocks: Risk and Return Dimensions," *Journal of Finance* 30 (December 1975), 1301–16.

GORDON, MYRON, *The Investment, Financing and Valuation of the Corporation* (Homewood, Ill.: Richard D. Irwin, Inc., 1963).

GRANGER, CLIVE W. J., "Some Consequences of the Valuation Model When Expectations Are Taken to be Optimum Forecasts," *Journal of Finance,* 30 (March 1975), 135–45.

HAGERMAN, ROBERT L., and E. HAN KIM, "Capital Asset Pricing with Price Level Changes," *Journal of Financial and Quantitative Analysis,* 11 (September 1976), 381–93.

HAUGEN ROBERT A., "Expected Growth, Required Return, and the Variability of Stock Prices," *Journal of Financial and Quantitative Analysis,* 5 (September 1970), 297–308.

HAUGEN, ROBERT A., and DEAN W. WICHERN, "The Elasticity of Financial Assets," *Journal of Finance,* 29 (September 1974), 1229–40.

HENDERSON, GLENN V., JR., "Shareholder Taxation and the Required Rate of Return of Internally Generated Funds," *Financial Management,* 5 (Summer 1976), 25–31.

LAUGHHUN, DAN J., and C. RONALD SPRECHER, "Probability of Loss and the Capital Asset Pricing Model," *Financial Management,* 6 (Spring 1977), 18–25.

LEE, CHENG F., and WILLIAM P. LLOYD, "The Capital Asset Pricing Model Expressed as a Recursive System: An Empirical Investigation," *Journal of Financial and Quantitative Analysis,* 11 (June 1976), 237–49.

LOGUE, DENNIS E., and LARRY J. MERIVILLE, "Financial Policy and Market Expectations," *Financial Management,* 1 (Summer 1972), 37–44.

McENALLY, RICHARD W., "A Note on the Return of High Risk Common Stocks," *Journal of Finance,* 29 (March 1974), 199–202.

MYERS, STEWART C., and STUART M. TURNBULL, "Capital Budgeting and the Capital Asset Pricing Model: Good News and Bad News," *Journal of Finance,* 32 (May 1977), 321–33.

NELSON, CHARLES R., "Inflation and Rates of Return on Common Stocks," *Journal of Finance,* 31 (May 1976), 471–83.

NORGAARD, RICHARD L., "An Examination of the Yields of Corporate Bonds and Stocks," *Journal of Finance,* 29 (September 1974), 1275–86.

OFER, AHARON R., "Investors' Expectations of Earnings Growth, Their Accuracy and Effects on the Structure of Realized Rate of Return," *Journal of Finance,* 30 (May 1975), 509–23.

PRINGLE, JOHN J., "Price-Earnings Ratios, Earnings Per Share, and Financial Management," *Financial Management,* 2 (Spring 1973), 34–40.

REILLY, FRANK K., and THOMAS J. ZELLER, "An Analysis of Relative Industry Price-Earnings Ratios," *Financial Review,* 1974.

RICKETTS, DONALD E., and MICHAEL J. BARRET, "Corporate Operating Income Forecasting Ability," *Financial Managment,* 2 (Summer 1973), 53–62.

Cost of Capital

*T*he "cost of capital" represents a critical link between management's financial decisions and the value of the firm. In Chapter 11, the cost of capital was seen to be an important element in *capital budgeting* analysis. In this context, the **cost of capital** represents the rate of return that the company must earn on its investments in order to meet the required rates of return of the firm's investors. Furthermore, the firm's optimal *financial structure* is determined by finding the capital structure that minimizes the firm's cost of capital. In this chapter we present the concept of the cost of capital and the procedures involved in its calculation. Specifically, the chapter objectives include the following:

1. Develop an understanding of the principles underlying the firm's cost of capital.
2. Determine the key factors influencing a corporation's cost of capital.
3. Specify the assumptions generally required in measuring the firm's cost of capital.
4. Provide a procedure for calculating a corporation's weighted cost of capital.
5. Investigate (in the appendix) a required rate of return for an individual project as an alternative to the firm's weighted cost of capital.

There are two reasons for computing a firm's cost of capital. First, the financial manager might wish to examine the cost of capital for different capital structures. In this context, the objective would be to determine the financial mix that has the lowest cost of capital. By financing at the lowest cost of capital, the value of the firm would be maximized.[1] However, measuring the cost of capital for various financial structures is not simple in practice. Therefore, this objective has little practical significance for the financial manager.

The second reason for estimating a company's cost of capital relates to its use in making investment decisions. In Chapters 11 and 12 we looked closely at the evaluation of capital investments. The criterion for accepting or rejecting a capital expenditure was presented in two contexts: accept the investment (1) if the present value of future cash inflows discounted at the firm's *cost of capital* exceeds the cost of the project, or (2) if the internal rate of return is greater than the firm's *cost of capital*. (Both approaches result in the same accept-reject decision for any given analysis.) The cost of capital is the standard against which prospective investments are compared.

If a firm's cost of capital is 12 percent, what interpretation should be given to this rate? How was the cost determined? To answer these questions, we must first define the term **cost of capital.** *A company's cost of capital is the rate that must be earned in order to satisfy the required rate of return of the firm's investors.* Stated somewhat differently, the cost of capital is the minimum acceptable rate of return for capital investments. At first glance it may seem that if the company exactly earns the investors' required rate of return, management may in turn use this return for completely satisfying the investors' required rate of return. However, such is not the case. When new securities are issued by a corporation, the total amount paid by the investors is seldom received by the firm. Instead, the investment bankers selling the issue generally receive their compensation by retaining a portion of the receipts from the investors.[2] For example, a company might contract with an investment banker to underwrite a stock issue for the firm, with the banker keeping 15 percent of the sales.[3] If the stock sells for $100, the issuing corporation would net only $85 per share. Yet, if an investor purchases the stock, and expects to receive a 10 percent return, or $10, on the $100 investment, the company has to earn 11.76 percent ($10 ÷ $85) on its investment. *Thus, the objective of the cost of capital calculation is to determine the rate of return that must be achieved on the company's investments so as to earn the required rate of return of the firm's investors.*

THE CONCEPT OF THE COST OF CAPITAL

Defining the Cost of Capital

---

[1]The relationship between the firm's capital structure and its cost of capital is provided in Chapter 16.

[2]An investment banker is an individual who assists companies in selling new securities. The functions of an investment banker are provided in Chapter 18.

[3]This process is explained more thoroughly in Chapter 18.

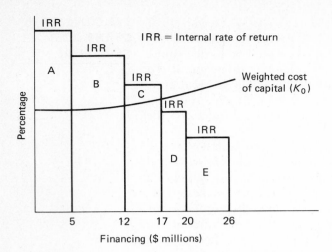

IRR = Internal rate of return

Weighted cost of capital (K_0)

Percentage

Financing ($ millions)

5   12   17 20   26

FIGURE 14-1 *Investment and Financing Schedules*

If the firm exactly earned its cost of capital, we would expect the price of its common stock to remain unchanged. However, if a rate different from the cost of capital were attained, we could anticipate the price of the stock to change. For example, in Figure 14-1, the internal rates of return for projects A, B, and C exceed the firm's cost of capital, and accepting these projects would increase the value of the firm's common stock. In contrast, investing in projects D and E would lower the stock value. For this reason, the best level of capital expenditures equals $17 million. *Therefore, the cost of capital may also be defined as the rate of return on investments at which the price of the firm's common stock will remain unchanged.*

In determining the cost of capital for a firm, which investors should be considered? A company generally has different types of investors, such as creditors, preferred stockholders, and common stockholders. When a variety of sources of financing exist, should only one type of investor be considered? To illustrate, the Alfred Corporation's capital structure is presented in Table 14-1. The company is using three primary sources of capital: debt, preferred stock, and common stock. The company's management is considering a $200,000 investment opportunity with an expected internal rate of return of 14 percent. The *current* cost of the firm's

Types of Investors and the Cost of Capital

Table 14-1   ALFRED CORPORATION: CAPITAL STRUCTURE

Bonds (8%)		$ 600,000
Preferred stock (10%)		200,000
Common stock:		
Par ($1 per share)	$100,000	
Paid-in capital	600,000	
Retained earnings	500,000	1,200,000
Total liabilities and equity		$2,000,000

Cost of debt capital	10%
Cost of preferred stock	12%
Cost of common stock	16%

Given this information, should the investment be made? The creditors and preferred stockholders would probably encourage management to undertake the project. Yet, since the 14 percent internal rate of return is less than the cost of common stock, the common stockholders might argue that the investment should be foregone. Who is right?

This question cannot be answered without additional information. Specifically, what percentage of the $200,000 is to be provided by each type of investor? If the corporation's financial manager intends to finance 30 percent by debt, 10 percent by preferred stock, and 60 percent by common stock, we could *compute a weighted cost of capital,* where the weights equal the percentage of capital to be financed by each source. For our example, this computation is made in Table 14-2, with the weighted cost of the individual sources of capital being 13.8 percent. From this calculation we would conclude that an investment offering a 13.8 percent return would be acceptable to the company's investors. In this illustration, the investment should be undertaken, since the 14 percent rate of return more than satisfies all investors. *In summary, each type of capital (debt, preferred stock, and common stock) should be incorporated into the cost of capital, with the relative importance of a particular source being based upon the percentage of the financing provided by each source of capital.*

To gain further insight into the meaning of the firm's cost of capital, we should consider the elements in the business environment that cause a company's cost of capital to be high or low. Looking at Figure 14-2, we see four primary factors. The first is general economic conditions. This factor determines the demand for and supply of capital within

FACTORS DETERMINING THE COST OF CAPITAL

Table 14-2 ALFRED CORPORATION: WEIGHTED COST OF CAPITAL

	WEIGHTS (PERCENTAGE OF FINANCING)	COST OF INDIVIDUAL SOURCES	WEIGHTED COST
Debt	30%	10%	3.0%
Preferred stock	10%	12%	1.2%
Common stock	60%	16%	9.6%
	100%	Weighted cost of capital:	13.8%

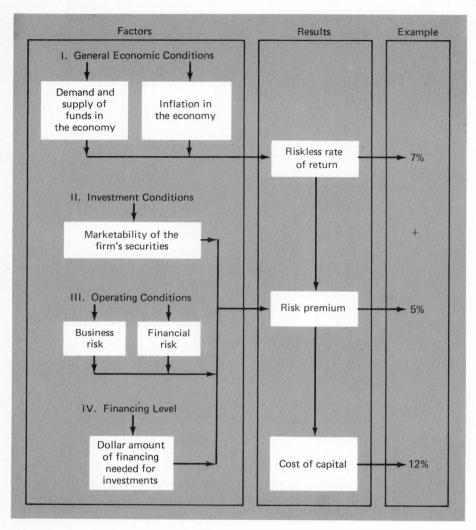

Factors	Results	Example

I. General Economic Conditions

Demand and supply of funds in the economy   Inflation in the economy

Riskless rate of return → 7%

II. Investment Conditions

Marketability of the firm's securities

+

III. Operating Conditions

Business risk   Financial risk

Risk premium → 5%

IV. Financing Level

Dollar amount of financing needed for investments

Cost of capital → 12%

FIGURE 14-2 *Primary Factors Influencing the Cost of a Particular Source of Capital*

the economy, as well as the level of expected inflation. This economic variable is reflected in the riskless rate of return. This rate represents the rate of return on risk-free investments, such as the interest rate on short-term U. S. government securities. In principle, as the demand for money in the economy changes relative to the supply, investors alter their required rate of return. For example, if the demand for money increases without an equivalent increase in the supply, lenders will raise their required interest rate. At the same time, if inflation is expected to deteriorate the purchasing power of the dollar, investors require a higher rate of return to compensate for this anticipated loss.

To this point, risk has had no impact upon the cost of capital. However, if an investor is purchasing a security where the *risk* of the investment is significant, the opportunity for additional returns is necessary to make the investment attractive. Essentially, as risk increases, the investor requires a higher rate of return.

Risk being defined as the potential variability of returns, the investor may encounter risk from two sources. First, the security may not be readily marketable when the investor wants to sell; or, even if a continuous demand for the security exists, the price may vary significantly.[4] Second, risk results from the decisions made within the company. This risk is generally divided into two classes, **business risk** and **financial risk.** Business risk is the variability in returns on assets and is affected by the company's investment decisions. Financial risk is the increased variability in returns to the common stockholders as a result of using debt and preferred stock.

The last factor determining the corporation's cost of funds is the amount of financing required. This relationship is demonstrated graphically in Figure 14-1, where the weighted cost of capital increases as the financing requirements of the firm for a given period become larger. This increase may be attributable to one of several factors. For instance, as increasingly larger security issues are floated in the market, additional flotation costs (costs of issuing the security) and underpricing will affect the percentage cost of the funds to the firm. Also, as management approaches the market for large amounts of capital relative to the firm's size, the investors' required rate of return may rise. Suppliers of capital become hesitant to grant relatively large amounts of funds without evidence of management's capability to absorb this capital into the business. This concern is reflected in the proverbial "too much too soon." Also, as the size of the issue increases, the investment advisor has greater difficulty in placing the issue without reducing the price of the security, which also increases the firm's cost of capital.

As an example of the cost of a particular source of capital, Figure 14-2 gives an illustration in the right-hand margin. The risk-free rate, determined by the general economic conditions, is 7 percent. However, owing to the additional risks associated with the security, the firm has to earn an additional 5 percent to satisfy the investors' required rate of return of 12 percent.

In summary, the important variables influencing a corporation's cost of capital, K, are represented in Figure 14-3. However, while these factors are useful for conceptual purposes, they offer us little assistance in actually estimating the cost of capital.

[4]For additional explanation of this issue see Chapter 18.

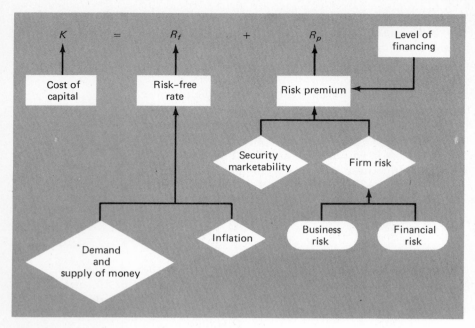

FIGURE 14-3 *An Overview of the Cost of Capital*

In a complex business world difficulties quickly arise in computing a corporation's cost of capital. For this reason, several simplifying assumptions are made.

Since business risk is defined as the potential variability of returns on an investment, the level of business risk within a firm is determined by management's investment policies. An investor's required rate of return for a company's securities and therefore *the firm's cost of capital is a function of the firm's current business risk*. If this risk level is altered, the corporation's investors will naturally change their required rates of return, which in turn modifies the cost of capital. However, the amount of change in the cost of capital resulting from a given increase or decrease in business risk is difficult to assess. For this reason, the cost of capital calculation assumes that any investment being considered will not significantly change the firm's business risk. In other words, *the cost of capital is an appropriate investment criterion only for an investment having a risk level similar to existing assets*.

Financial risk has been defined as the increased variability in returns on common stock resulting from the increased use of debt and preferred stock financing.[5] Also, financial risk relates to the threat of bank-

[5]This concept is explained in Chapter 15.

ASSUMPTIONS OF THE COST OF CAPITAL MODEL

Constant Business Risk

Constant Financial Risk

ruptcy. As the percentage of debt in the capital structure increases, the possibility that the firm will be unable to meet contractual interest and principal payments is also increased. As a result, the level of financial risk in a company has an impact upon the investors' required rate of return. For instance, as debt comprises a larger portion of the capital structure, the common stockholders will increase their required rate of return. In essence, the costs of individual sources of capital are a function of the current financial structure. For this reason, the data used in computing the cost of capital are appropriate only if management continues to use the same financial mix. If the present capital structure consists of 40 percent debt, 10 percent preferred stock, and 50 percent common stock, this capital structure is assumed to be maintained in the financing of future investments.

A third assumption required in estimating the cost of capital relates to the corporation's dividend policy. For ease of computation it is generally assumed that the firm's dividends are increasing at a constant annual growth rate. Also, this growth is assumed to be a function of the firm's earning capabilities and not merely the result of paying out a larger percentage of the company's earnings. Thus, it is implicitly assumed that the dividend payout ratio (dividends/net income) is constant. The rationale for this simplifying assumption is explained later.

Constant Dividend Policy

The preceding assumptions are quite restrictive. Thus, management should be aware of the underlying assumptions of the cost of capital computation before using it in investment analyses. In a practical setting the financial executive may need an estimate of a range of possible cost of capital values rather than a single-point estimate. For example, it may be more appropriate to take a 10 to 12 percent range as an *estimate* of the firm's cost of capital, rather than to presume that a precise number can be determined. However, in this chapter the principal concern will be with calculating a single cost of capital figure.

A firm's weighted cost of capital is a composite of the individual costs of financing, weighted by the percentage of financing provided by each source. Therefore, a firm's weighted cost of capital is a function of (1) the individual costs of capital, (2) the makeup of the capital structure mix, and (3) the level of financing necessary to make the investment.

COMPUTING THE WEIGHTED COST OF CAPITAL

A large variety of financing instruments have been created by companies attempting to attract new investors. However, our interest will be restricted to three types of securities: debt, preferred stock, and common stock. In calculating these costs, remember that the end objective is to determine *the rate of return that the company must earn on its investmens so as*

Determining Individual Costs of Capital

to satisfy the investors' required rate of return. Also, since the cash flows used in capital budgeting analysis (net present value, profitability index, and internal rate of return) are on an after-tax basis, the required rates of return should also be expressed on an after-tax basis for comparability.

THE COST OF CAPITAL
AND FINANCIAL
STRUCTURE

COST OF DEBT

The **cost of debt** *may be defined as the rate that has to be received from an investment in order to achieve the required rate of return for the creditors.* In Chapter 13, the required rate of return for debt capital was found by solving for R_d in

$$P_0 = \sum_{t=1}^{N} \frac{\$I_t}{(1 + R_d)^t} + \frac{\$M}{(1 + R_d)^N} \qquad (14\text{-}2)$$

$$P_0 = \$I_t \begin{bmatrix} \text{Table Value} \\ \text{Appendix D} \\ N \text{ years} \\ R_d \text{ percent} \end{bmatrix} + \$M \begin{bmatrix} \text{Table Value} \\ \text{Appendix B} \\ N \text{ years} \\ R_d \text{ percent} \end{bmatrix}$$

where P_0 = the market price of the debt,

$\$I_t$ = the annual dollar interest paid to the investor each year,

$\$M$ = the maturity value of the debt,

R_d = the required rate of return of the debtholder, and

N = the number of years to maturity.

Example.   Assume that an investor is willing to pay $908.24 for a bond. The security has a $1000 par value, pays 8 percent in annual interest, and matures in 20 years. The investor's required rate of return is 9 percent, which is the rate that sets the present value of the future interest payments and the maturity value equal to the value of the bond, or

$$\$908.24 = \sum_{t=1}^{20} \frac{\$80}{(1 + .09)^t} + \frac{\$1000}{(1 + .09)^{20}}$$

However, if brokerage commissions and legal and accounting fees are incurred in issuing the security, the company will not receive the full $908.24 market price. As a result, the effective cost of these funds is larger than the investor's 9 percent required rate of return. To adjust for this difference, we would simply use the *net price* after flotation costs in place of the market price in equation (14-2). Thus, the equation becomes

$$NP_0 = \sum_{t=1}^{N} \frac{\$I_t}{(1 + k_d)^t} + \frac{\$M}{(1 + k_d)^N} \qquad (14\text{-}3)$$

where NP_0 represents the net amount received by the company from issuing the debt, k_d equals the *before-tax* cost of debt, and the remaining vari-

ables retain their meaning from equation (14-2). If in the present example
the company nets $850 after issuance costs, the equation should read

$$\$850 = \sum_{t=1}^{20} \frac{\$80}{(1 + k_d)^t} + \frac{\$1000}{(1 + k_d)^{20}}$$

$$= \$80 \begin{bmatrix} \text{Table Value} \\ \text{Appendix D} \\ 20 \text{ years} \\ k_d \text{ percent} \end{bmatrix} + \$1000 \begin{bmatrix} \text{Table Value} \\ \text{Appendix B} \\ 20 \text{ years} \\ k_d \text{ percent} \end{bmatrix}$$

Solving for k_d in equation (14-3) can be achieved only by trial and error. If *10 percent* is selected as a trial discount rate, a present value of $829.73 results. This approach suggests that the before-tax cost of the debt capital is between 9 and 10 percent. Since the rate falls between 9 and 10 percent, we may approximate it by interpolating. The logic of interpolation was explained in Chapter 13 (page 361). Following that rationale, we may find the before-tax cost of debt as follows:

RATE	VALUE	DIFFERENCES IN VALUES
9%	$908.24	$58.24
k_d	850.00 Net proceed	$78.12
10%	830.12	

Based upon the foregoing information,

$$k_d = .09 + \left(\frac{\$58.24}{\$78.12}\right)(.10 - .09) = .0975 = 9.75 \text{ percent}$$

Thus, the company's cost of debt, before recognizing the tax deductibility of interest, is 9.75 percent. However, the *after-tax* interest cost is found by multiplying the before-tax interest rate by a factor equal to $[1 - (\text{tax rate})]$. Thus, defining t as the company's marginal tax rate and letting k_d equal the before-tax cost of debt, the after-tax cost of new debt financing K_d is found as follows:

$$K_d = k_d(1 - t) \tag{14-4}$$

If in the present example the corporation's tax rate is 40 percent, the after-tax cost of debt is 5.85 percent:

$$K_d = 9.75\%(1 - .40) = 5.85 \text{ percent}$$

In summary, the firm must earn 5.85 percent on its borrowed capital *after the payment of taxes*. In doing so, it can achieve the investor's 9 percent required rate of return on his $908.24 investment.

COST OF PREFERRED STOCK

Determining the cost of preferred stock follows the same logic as the cost of debt. *The objective is to find the rate of return that must be earned on the preferred stockholders' investment that will satisfy the required rate of return on their investment.*

In Chapter 13, it was shown that the value of a security, P_0, that is nonmaturing and promising a constant dividend per year can be defined as follows:

$$P_0 = \frac{\text{dividend}}{\text{required rate of return}} = \frac{D}{R_p} \qquad (14\text{-}5)$$

From this equation, the required rate of return, R_p, is defined as

$$R_p = \frac{\text{dividend}}{\text{market price}} = \frac{D}{P_0} \qquad (14\text{-}6)$$

If, for example, a preferred stock pays $1.50 in annual dividends and sells for $15, the investors' required rate of return is 10 percent:

$$R_p = \frac{\$1.50}{\$15} = 10 \text{ percent}$$

Yet, even if these preferred stockholders have a 10 percent required rate of return, the effective cost of this capital will be greater, owing to the flotation costs incurred in issuing the security. If a firm were to net $13.50 per share after issuance costs, rather than the full $15 market price, the cost of preferred stock, K_p, should be calculated using the net price received by the company. Therefore,

$$K_p = \frac{\text{dividend}}{\text{net price}} = \frac{D}{NP_0} \qquad (14\text{-}7)$$

For the previous example, the cost would be

$$K_p = \frac{\$1.50}{\$13.50} = 11.11 \text{ percent}$$

No adjustment for taxes is required, since preferred stock dividends are not tax-deductible. The firm has to earn the cost of preferred capital after taxes have been paid, which in the preceding example was 11.11 percent.

COST OF COMMON STOCK

In measuring the cost of capital for funds provided by common stockholders, the end objective is the same as when the cost of debt and preferred stock are considered. However, a special distinction exists for common stock, since common stockholders can provide additional capital in one of two ways. First, new common stock may be issued. Second, the earnings available to common stockholders can be retained, in whole or in part, within the company and used to finance future investments. This latter source of financing, which does not require a new common issue, represents the largest single source of capital for most U. S. corporations. To distinguish between these two sources of common stock financing, the term **internal common equity** is used to designate the profits retained within the business for investment purposes, and **external common equity** to represent a new issue of common stock.

> *Cost of Internal Common Equity.* When managers are considering the retention of earnings as a means for financing an investment, they are serving in a *fiduciary* capacity. That is, the common stockholders have entrusted the company assets to management. If the company's objective is wealth maximization for its common stockholders, management should retain the profits *only if* the company's investments within the firm are at least as attractive as the stockholders' next best investment opportunity.[6] Otherwise, the profits should be paid out in dividends, thereby permitting the investor to invest more profitably elsewhere.

Yet, how can management know the stockholders' alternative investment opportunities? Certainly the specific identification of these investments is not feasible. However, the investors' required rate of return should be a function of competing investment opportunities. If the only other investment alternative of similar risk has a 12 percent return, one would expect a rational investor to set a minimum acceptable return on his investment (his required rate of return) at 12 percent. In other words, *the investors' required rate of return should equal the rate of the best competing investment available.* Thus, if the common stockholder's required rate of return is used as a threshold return for investments financed by common stock investors, management may be assured that their investment policies are acceptable to the common stockholder.

In actually measuring the common investors' required rate of return, we shall use the presentation from Chapter 13. There, the value of a common stock was defined as being equal to the present value of the expected future dividends, discounted at the common stockholders' *required rate of return*. Since the stock has no maturity date, these dividends extend to infinity. Thus, for an investor with a required rate of return of R_c, the value of a common stock, P_0, promising dividends of D_t in year t would be

$$P_0 = \frac{D_1}{(1 + R_c)^1} + \frac{D_2}{(1 + R_c)^2} + \cdots + \frac{D_n}{(1 + R_c)^n} + \cdots + \frac{D_\infty}{(1 + R_c)^\infty} \quad (14\text{-}8)$$

If, however, the market for the security, P_0, is known, then the required rate of return of an investor purchasing the security at this price can be

[6]Other factors may justify management's not adhering completely to this principle. These issues are examined when we discuss dividend policy in Chapter 17.

determined by estimating future dividends, D_t, and solving for R_c. Further, if it may be assumed that the dividends are increasing at a constant annual growth, g, that is less than R_c, the required rate, R_c, may be measured as follows:[7]

$$R_c = \left(\frac{\text{dividend in year 1}}{\text{market price}}\right) + \left(\begin{array}{c}\text{annual growth rate} \\ \text{in dividends}\end{array}\right) = \frac{D_1}{P_0} + g \qquad (14\text{-}9)$$

Furthermore, no adjustment is required for taxes. Dividends paid to the firm's common stockholders are *not* tax deductible; therefore, the cost is already on an after-tax basis. Finally, flotation costs are not involved in computing the cost of internal common, since the funds are already within the business and no issuance of securities is necessary. Thus, the investor's required rate of return, R_c, is the same as the cost of internal common equity, K_c.

Example. To demonstrate the foregoing computation, the Talbot Corporation's common stockholders recently received a $2 dividend per share, and they expect dividends to grow at an annual rate of 10 percent into the indefinite future. If the market price of the security is $50, the investors' required rate of return is

$$R_c = K_c = \frac{D_1}{P_0} + g \qquad (14\text{-}9)$$

$$= \frac{\$2\,(1 + .10)}{\$50} + .10$$

$$= \frac{\$2.20}{\$50} + .10 = .144$$

$$= 14.4 \text{ percent}$$

Note that the forthcoming dividend, D_1, is estimated by taking the past dividend, $2, and increasing it by 10 percent, the expected growth rate. For example $D_1 = D_0\,(1.10)$ or $D_1 = \$2\,(1.10) = \$2.20$.

Cost of New Common Stock. If **internal common equity** does not provide sufficient equity capital for the amount of investments under consideration, the firm may need to issue new common stock. Again, this capital should not be acquired from investors unless the expected returns on the prospective investments exceed a rate sufficient to satisfy the stockholders' required rate of return. Since the required rate of return of common stockholders has already been measured in equation (14-9), the only adjustment to this equation is to recognize the potential flotation costs incurred from issuing the stock. These market flotation costs may be appropriately considered by reducing the market price of the stock by the amount of these costs. Thus, the cost of new common stock, K_{nc}, is

[7]For additional explanation, see Chapter 13.

where NP_0 equals the net proceeds per share received by the company. If, in the previous example, flotation costs are 15 percent of the market price, the cost of capital for the new common stock, or **external common,** would be 15.18 percent, calculated as follows:

$$K_{nc} = \frac{\$2.20}{\$50 - .15\,(\$50)} + .10$$

$$= \frac{\$2.20}{\$42.50} + .10 = .1518$$

$$= 15.18 \text{ percent}$$

In this example, if management achieves a 15.18 percent return on the net capital received from common stockholders, the 14.4 percent required rate of return of these investors, as determined in equation (14-9), will be satisfied.

The individual costs of capital will be different for each source of capital in the firm's capital structure. Thus, to use the cost of capital in investment analyses, we must compute a composite or overall cost of capital. *The weights for computing this overall cost should reflect the corporation's financing mix.* For instance, if the creditors are expected to finance 30 percent of the forthcoming investments, and the common stockholders are to provide the remaining 70 percent, the weighted cost should recognize this financing mix.

In selecting the financing weights for a composite cost of capital, several choices are available. Theoretically, it is recommended that the actual financial mix used in financing the proposed investments be used as the weights. This approach, while quite attractive, presents two problems. First, the interdependency between investment policies and financing decisions creates difficulties in anticipating the future financial mix. Second, the costs of capital for the individual sources depend upon the firm's financial risk, which is dictated by the current capital structure. If management significantly alters the present financial structure, the individual costs are no longer appropriate. Thus, it will be assumed that the company's financial mix is relatively stable and that these weights will closely approximate future financing patterns. Although this assumption will not be strictly met in any particular year, firms frequently have a **target capital structure** (desired debt-equity mix), which is maintained over the long term.

Assuming the present capital structure is a reasonable weighting scheme still does not resolve the entire issue. It is also necessary to choose between **book value** and **market value** weights as the basis for describing the firm's present capital structure. For instance, the capital structure for Menielle, Inc., in terms of both the book values and the market values, is

Selection of Weights

depicted in Table 14-3. The book value weights come from the company's balance sheet, while the market value weights are determined from the current market price of the firm's bonds and preferred and common stock. Although book values are easy to calculate, market value weights are to be used in measuring the firm's composite cost of capital, since they are consistent with the theoretical definition of cost of capital.

In summary, calculating a firm's weighted cost of capital entails the use of market required rates of returns, adjusted for taxes and flotation costs, and the market value weights of each source of financing.

Example: The Weighted Cost of Capital. The computation of a company's weighted cost of capital is demonstrated using the example of Menielle, Inc., from Table 14-3. Assume that the individual costs of each source of capital have been determined as shown in Table 14-4. For the moment, equity financing is restricted to the retained earnings available for reinvestment, or **internally generated common equity.** If only internal common is used, the weighted cost of capital equals 10.04 percent. This calculation is set forth in Table 14-5, where the market weights and the individual cost for each of the Menielle, Inc., securities are combined into a single weighted cost of capital. Given that the assumptions of the weighted cost of capital concept are met and that common equity requirements can be satisfied internally, the 10.08 percent is a reasonable estimate of the firm's minimum acceptable rate of return for new investments.

Table 14-3   MENIELLE, INC., CAPITAL STRUCTURE

| | BALANCE SHEET DATA | | MARKET VALUE DATA[a] | |
	$ Amount	Percentage	$ Amount	Percentage
Bonds:[a]				
(8%, $1000 par value maturing in 1981)	$1,000,000	20%	$980,000	14%
(10%, $1000 par value maturing in 1997)	750,000	15%	840,000	12%
Preferred stock (3000 shares outstanding, 12%, $100 par value)	300,000	6%	350,000	5%
Common stock:				
Par value (100,000 shares outstanding, $1 per share)	$ 100,000			
Paid-in capital	1,000,000			
Retained earnings	1,850,000			
Total common value				
	2,950,000	59%	4,830,000	69%
Total	$5,000,000	100%	$7,000,000	100%

[a]Market prices: $980 for bonds maturing in 1981, $1120 for bonds maturing in 1997, $116.67 per share for preferred stock, and $48.30 per share for common stock.

Table 14-4 COMPONENT COSTS OF CAPITAL FOR MENIELLE, INC.

INVESTOR GROUP	COMPONENT COSTS
Bonds (8%, 1981)	4.5%
Bonds (10%, 1997)	4.8%
Preferred stock	11.0%
Common stock	
Internally generated common	12.0%
New common	14.0%

LEVEL OF
FINANCING AND
THE WEIGHTED
COST OF CAPITAL

Impact of a New
Common Stock
Issue

In the previous illustration, the weighted cost of capital was determined under the assumption that the size of the firm's investment budget did not require any new common stock. If the new investments necessitate an increase in common stock, the firm's weighted cost of capital will increase. This change results from using *external* equity capital, which has a higher cost. Thus, a company's weighted cost of capital may be a function of the size of its total investment outlay.

Example. To illustrate this relationship, the Crisp Corporation, an independent oil company, is contemplating three major capital investments in 1979. The first proposal is the acquisition of equipment used in examining geological formations. This new equipment should improve the success ratio in discovering productive oil and gas reserves. The second investment under consideration is water flooding equipment, which involves injecting large amounts of water into underground oil reserves. This process permits more efficient recapture of the minerals. Third, new and advanced drilling equipment appears to offer significant cost savings in drilling for oil and gas. The costs and expected returns for these three investments are shown in Table 14-6. If these projects are accepted, the financing will consist of 50 percent debt and 50 percent common. Based upon the antici-

Table 14-5 WEIGHTED COST OF CAPITAL FOR MENIELLE, INC,
IF ONLY INTERNAL COMMON IS USED

(1) SECURITY TYPE	(2) MARKET WEIGHT[a]	(3) INDIVIDUAL COSTS[b]	(4) WEIGHTED COSTS [COLS. (2) × (3)]
Bonds (8%, 1981)	14%	4.5%	0.63%
Bonds (10%, 1997)	12%	4.8%	0.58%
Preferred stock	5%	11.0%	0.55%
Common stock (internal only)	69%	12.0%	8.28%
	Weighted cost of capital (K_0):		10.04%

[a]Taken from the market weights computed in Table 14-3.
[b]Taken from Table 14-4.

Table 14-6 CRISP CORPORATION'S INVESTMENT OPPORTUNITIES

	COST	EXPECTED INTERNAL RATE OF RETURN
Geological equipment	$1,500,000	14%
Water flooding equipment	2,000,000	18%
Drilling equipment	2,500,000	11%

pated profits during 1979, the company should have $1,500,000 available for reinvestment (internal common). The costs of capital for each source of financing have been computed and are presented in Table 14-7.

In this simplified illustration, the weighted cost of capital, K_0, is calculated as

$$K_0 = \left[\left(\begin{array}{c} \text{percentage of} \\ \text{debt financing} \end{array} \right) \times \left(\begin{array}{c} \text{cost of} \\ \text{debt} \end{array} \right) \right] + \left[\left(\begin{array}{c} \text{percentage of} \\ \text{common financing} \end{array} \right) \times \left(\begin{array}{c} \text{cost of} \\ \text{common} \end{array} \right) \right]$$
(14-11)

If only internally generated common is utilized, the weighted cost of capital is 10 percent:

$$K_0 = [50\% \times 6\%] + [50\% \times 14\%] = 10 \text{ percent}$$

However, when only new common stock is used, the weighted cost of capital is 12 percent:

$$K_0 = [50\% \times 6\%] + [50\% \times 18\%] = 12 \text{ percent}$$

Which weighted cost of capital should be used in evaluating the three investments?

To answer this question, two procedures should be used. First, rank the projects in descending order by their internal rate of return. Second, the firm should use its cheapest funds prior to acquiring more expensive capital, while maintaining the target debt ratio. In other words, internally generated common should be blended with debt until fully exhausted.

Table 14-7 CRISP CORPORATION'S INDIVIDUAL COSTS OF CAPITAL

SOURCE	COST
Debt (after-tax cost)	6%
Internally generated common	14%
Cost of new common stock	18%

Only then should new common stock be issued. In the Crisp Corporation illustration, $3 million in new investments may be financed with the combined debt and *internal* common. This investment level is computed as

$$\text{total financing from all sources} = \frac{\text{internally generated common}}{\text{percentage of common financing}} \qquad (14\text{-}12)$$

$$= \frac{\$1,500,000}{.50}$$

$$= \$3,000,000$$

Therefore, for a total investment level of $3 million or less, the firm's weighted cost of capital is expected to be 10 percent. Beyond this point, the weighted cost of capital increases, since the firm has to rely on new common stock for its equity financing. The weighted cost of capital for any funds exceeding the $3 million in total financing is 12 percent. This relationship between the weighted cost of capital and the amount of financing being sought is portrayed graphically in Figure 14-4. The graph depicts the firm's **weighted marginal cost of capital.** The term *marginal* is used because the computed cost of capital specifies the composite cost for each *additional* dollar of financing. This marginal cost of capital represents the appropriate criterion for making investment decisions. Thus, the firm should continue to invest up to the point where the marginal rate of return earned on new investment (IRR) equals the marginal cost of new capital. This comparison is reflected in Figure 14-5, where the firm's optimal capital budget is found to be $3,500,000. The company should invest in water flooding machinery and the geological equipment. However, since the weighted marginal cost of capital is greater than the expected internal rate of return of the drilling equipment, this investment should be rejected.

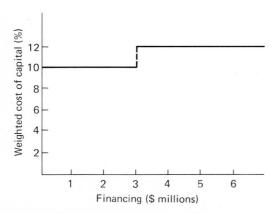

FIGURE 14-4 *Crisp Corporation's Weighted Marginal Cost of Capital*

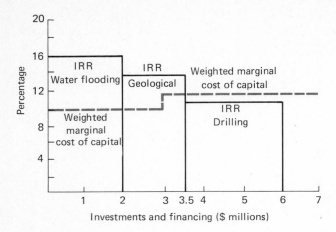

FIGURE 14-5 *Crisp Corporation: Comparison of Investment Returns and the Weighted Marginal Cost of Capital*

Thus far, only the effect of increases in the cost of common stock on the firm's weighted marginal cost of capital has been noted. Similar effects may occur as the cost of any source of financing increases with the level of funds raised. If the 6 percent cost of debt capital for Crisp Corporation increased to 8 percent after the firm issued $2 million in bonds, an increase in the weighted marginal cost of capital would have occurred at the $4 million financing level from all sources. This **break** in the marginal cost of capital curve is determined as

$$\frac{\text{total financing}}{\text{from all sources}} = \frac{\text{maximum amount of lower-cost debt}}{\text{percentage of debt financing}} \qquad (14\text{-}13)$$

$$= \frac{\$2,000,000}{.50}$$

$$= \$4,000,000$$

Therefore, as a general rule, *changes in the weighted marginal cost of capital will take place when the cost of an individual source increases.* The break in the marginal cost of capital curve will occur at the dollar financing level where

$$\frac{\text{total financing}}{\text{from all sources}} = \frac{\substack{\text{maximum amount of a} \\ \text{cheaper source of capital}}}{\substack{\text{percentage financing} \\ \text{provided by the source}}} \qquad (14\text{-}14)$$

An example will help us bring together the principles for computing a firm's weighted cost of capital. Phifer Instruments is a manufacturer of medical and surgical instruments. The right-hand portion of the firm's most recent balance sheet along with the market values of each source of

General Effect of New Financing on Marginal Cost of Capital

MARGINAL COST OF CAPITAL: A Case Study

Table 14-8 PHIFER MEDICAL INSTRUMENTS, DECEMBER 31, 1978

TOTAL LIABILITIES AND EQUITY	BALANCE SHEET DATA		MARKET VALUE DATA[a]	MARKET VALUE PERCENTAGES
Bonds (4000 bonds, 7%, $1000 par, maturing in 1998)		$4,000,000	$3,600,000	30.0%
Preferred stock (9%, 20,000 shares outstanding, $50 par)		1,000,000	900,000	7.5
Common stock:				
Par value ($2 par, 100,000 shares outstanding)	$ 200,000			
Paid-in capital	1,800,000			
Retained earnings	3,000,000	5,000,000	7,500,000	62.5
Total liabilities and equity		$10,000,000	$12,000,000	100.0%

[a]Market price: $900 for bonds; $45 per share for preferred stock; and $75 per share for common stock.

financing are presented in Table 14-8. The management attempts to maintain a relatively constant capital structure mix in terms of the market value of the securities. The most recent earnings per share (1978) was $5, which was twice the earnings per share in 1972, and this represents a growth rate of 12 percent.[8] Dividends and the market price of the firm's common stock have grown at the same rate. The dividend payout ratio, which equals the ratio of common dividends to earnings available to common, has been 50 percent, and management intends to hold to this dividend policy in the future.[9] Five potential investments are being examined by the company for 1979. The costs and the expected internal rates of return for these projects are provided in Table 14-9. To finance these investments, Phifer expects to have $500,000 from 1979 retained earnings available for reinvestment. Also, management has conferred with representatives from investment companies, and it is believed that the following issues can be sold:

1. *Bonds.* An amount not exceeding $240,000 could be issued in new bonds. The issue, after considering the effect of flotation costs, would have an effective before-tax cost of 7 percent. If additional debt is required, the effective yield would have to be increased to 9 percent.

2. *Preferred stock.* New preferred stock could be issued by Phifer with a par value of $50, paying $4.50 in annual dividends. The market price of the security is $45, but $1.80 per share in flotation costs would be incurred for an issue size

[8]This growth rate is computed by dividing the 1972 earnings per share by the 1978 earnings per share, $2.50/$5, or .50, which is the present value interest factor for six years at 12 percent.

[9]Dividend policy is discussed in Chapter 17.

Table 14-9   PHIFER INSTRUMENTS: 1979 INVESTMENT OPPORTUNITIES

INVESTMENT	ESTIMATED COST	PROJECTED INTERNAL RATES OF RETURN
A	$ 450,000	15.0%
B	500,000	12.0%
C	300,000	13.0%
D	250,000	11.5%
E	500,000	14.5%
Total proposed budget	$2,000,000	

of $105,000 or less. Additional preferred stock could be sold at $45; however, the flotation costs would be $3.33 per share.

3. *Common stock.* Common stock can be sold at the existing $75 market price. If the issue size is not greater than $375,000, a 10 percent flotation cost would result. For any additional common stock, the flotation costs would increase to 15 percent of the market price.

With the foregoing information, a weighted marginal cost of capital curve can be constructed. Relying upon the market weights in Table 14-8 and the amount of capital available at each cost, we can compute the points at which breaks in the marginal cost curve will occur. These calculations are shown in Table 14-10, with the results indicating two breaks in the curve. The increases in the marginal cost of capital arise as the amount of total financing raised reaches (1) $800,000 (cost of debt and common equity simultaneously increase), and (2) $1,400,000 (cost of preferred stock increases and cost of common equity increases again).

The next step in determining the weighted cost of capital requires computing the individual costs of capital from the various sources of financing. This procedure is presented in Table 14-11, with the amount of capital and the costs for these funds being provided. For debt, the costs need only to be adjusted by Phifer's marginal income tax rate. For a 40 percent income tax rate the 8 percent and 9 percent costs of debt have an effective after-tax cost of 4.2 percent [(1 − .4) 8%] and 5.4 percent [(1 − .4) 9%], respectively. The cost of preferred stock, which equals the dollar dividend relative to the *net price* per share received by the company, equals 10.4 percent for the first $105,000 and 10.8 percent for any greater amounts. The cost of internally generated common equals the dividend yield (the forthcoming dividend per share/price) plus the expected growth in dividends. An annual compound growth rate of 12 percent is estimated from the past growth in earnings per share. The dividend yield plus the 12 percent growth rate produces a 15.73 percent cost of internally generated common. The costs of new common stock are easily determined by adjusting the required rate of return of the common stockholders by the flotation costs in issuing the stock.

Table 14-10 PHIFER INSTRUMENTS: DOLLAR BREAKS IN MARGINAL COST OF CAPITAL CURVE

I. *Debt*

$$\frac{\text{total financing available with}}{\text{the cheaper debt}} = \frac{\text{total debt available at lower cost}}{\text{percentage of debt financing}}$$

$$= \frac{\$240,000}{.30}$$

$$= \$800,000$$

II. *Preferred stock*

$$\frac{\text{total financing available with}}{\text{cheaper preferred stock}} = \frac{\text{total preferred stock available at lower cost}}{\text{percentage of preferred stock financing}}$$

$$= \frac{\$105,000}{.075}$$

$$= \$1,400,000$$

III. *Common stock*

$$\frac{\text{total financing available with}}{\text{internal common}} = \frac{\text{total internal common available}}{\text{percentage of common financing}}$$

$$= \frac{\$500,000}{.625}$$

$$= \$800,000$$

$$\frac{\text{total financing available with}}{\text{both internal common and}}_{\text{with cheaper new common}} = \frac{\text{total internal common plus new}}{\text{common stock at cheaper cost}}_{\text{percentage of common financing}}$$

$$= \frac{\$500,000 + \$375,000}{.625}$$

$$= \$1,400,000$$

With the preceding information the weighted marginal costs of capital relative to the funds raised may be determined. The necessary calculations are provided in Table 14-12. The first portion of the table identifies the weighted marginal cost of capital, provided that the total amount of capital does not exceed $800,000. The remaining parts of the table reflect the incremental weighted costs as the individual costs increase. For example, the difference between the 11.87 and the 12.49 percent weighted costs of capital results from the simultaneous increases in the cost of debt and the

Table 14-11 PHIFER INSTRUMENTS: AMOUNT AND COSTS OF INDIVIDUAL SOURCES, DECEMBER 1978

SOURCE	AMOUNT AVAILABLE	COST CALCULATIONS
I. Debt	(a) $240,000 (b) Over $240,000	$\left[\begin{array}{c}\text{after-tax} \\ \text{cost of bonds}\end{array}\right] = \left(\begin{array}{c}\text{before-tax} \\ \text{cost}\end{array}\right)(1 - \text{tax rate})$ $K_d = 7\% (1 - .40) = 4.2\%$ $K_d = 9\% (1 - .40) = 5.4\%$
II. Preferred stock	(a) $105,000 (b) Over $105,000	$\left[\begin{array}{c}\text{cost of} \\ \text{preferred}\end{array}\right] = \left[\dfrac{\text{dividend per share}}{\begin{array}{c}\text{market price less} \\ \text{flotation costs}\end{array}}\right]$ $K_p = \dfrac{\$4.50}{\$45 - \$1.80} = 10.4\%$ $K_p = \dfrac{\$4.50}{\$45 - \$3.33} = 10.8\%$
III. Common financing A. Internal common	$500,000	$\left[\begin{array}{c}\text{cost of} \\ \text{internal common}\end{array}\right] = \left[\dfrac{\text{dividend in one year}}{\text{market price}}\right] + \text{growth}$ $K_c = \dfrac{\$2.50 (1 + .12)}{\$75} + .12 = 15.73\%$
B. New common stock	(a) $375,000 (b) Over $375,000	$\left[\begin{array}{c}\text{cost of} \\ \text{common} \\ \text{stock}\end{array}\right] = \left[\dfrac{\text{dividend in one year}}{\begin{array}{c}\text{market price less} \\ \text{flotation costs}\end{array}}\right] + \text{growth}$ $K_{nc} = \dfrac{\$2.50 (1 + .12)}{\$75 - \$7.50} + .12 = 16.15\%$ $K_{nc} = \dfrac{\$2.50 (1 + .12)}{\$75 - \$11.25} + .12 = 16.39\%$

Table 14-12 PHIFER INSTRUMENTS: WEIGHTED MARGINAL COST OF CAPITAL

Weighted Marginal Cost of Capital for $0–$800,000 Funds Raised

(1) SOURCE	(2) MAXIMUM AMOUNT OF CAPITAL	(3) PROPORTIONS	(4) COST OF CAPITAL	(5) WEIGHTED COST OF CAPITAL
Bonds	$240,000[a]	30.0%	4.20%	1.26%
Preferred stock	60,000	7.5%	10.40%	.78%
Common equity	500,000[a]	62.5%	15.73%	9.83%
	$800,000	100.0%		11.87%

Weighted Marginal Cost of Capital for $800,000–$1,400,000 Funds Raised

(1) SOURCE	(2) MAXIMUM AMOUNT OF CAPITAL	(3) PROPORTIONS	(4) COST OF CAPITAL	(5) WEIGHTED COST OF CAPITAL
Bonds	$420,000	30.0%	5.40%[b]	1.62%
Preferred stock	105,000[a]	7.5%	10.40%	.78%
Common equity	875,000[a]	62.5%	16.15%[b]	10.09%
	$1,400,000	100.0%		12.49%

Weighted Marginal Cost of Capital for More Than $1,400,000 Funds Raised

(1) SOURCE	(2) MAXIMUM AMOUNT OF CAPITAL	(3) PROPORTIONS	(4) COST OF CAPITAL	(5) WEIGHTED COST OF CAPITAL
Bonds	$420,000	30.0%	5.40%	1.62%
Preferred stock	105,000	7.5%	10.80%[b]	.81%
Common equity	875,000	62.5%	16.39%[b]	10.24%
	$1,400,000	100.0%		12.67%

[a]Maximum amount without an increase in the cost.

[b]Cost increased from the previous weighted cost of capital computation.

cost of common equity. The third weighted cost of capital in Table 14-12, 12.67 percent, corresponds to new financing in excess of $1,400,000.

The weighted marginal costs of capital in Table 14-12 are to be used in determining whether to accept any or all of the investment prospects being reviewed by Phifer Instruments. A ranking of the projects, taken from Table 14-9, and a comparison of the returns against the weighted costs of capital are given in Figure 14-6. As evident from the figure, Phifer Instrument's *optimal* capital budget for 1979 is $1,250,000. The particular investments that should be included in the budget are projects A, E, and C, with the returns for projects B and D falling short of the weighted cost of capital hurdle rate.

Cost of capital is an important concept within financial management. For investment purposes, the cost of capital is the rate of return that must

SUMMARY

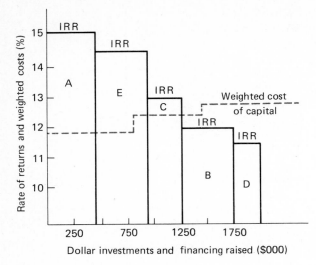

FIGURE 14-6 *Phifer Instruments: Comparison of Returns on Investment and Weighted Marginal Cost of Capital*

be achieved on the company's investments in order to satisfy the investor's required rate of return. If the rate of return from the corporation's investments equals the cost of capital, the price of the stock should remain unchanged. In other words, the firm's cost of capital may be defined as the rate of return from an investment that will leave the company's stock price unchanged. Therefore, the cost of capital, if certain assumptions are met, represents the minimum acceptable rate of return for new corporate investments.

The factors that affect a firm's cost of capital were shown to consist of four components. First, the general economic conditions (as reflected in the demand and supply of funds in the economy), as well as inflationary pressures, affect the general level of interest rates. Second, the marketability of the firm's securities have an impact on the cost of capital. Any change in the marketability of a firm's stock will affect investors' required rate of return. These changes then directly influence the firm's cost of capital. Third, the firm's operating and financial risks are reflected in its cost of capital. Finally, a relationship exists between a firm's cost of capital and the dollar amount of financing needed for future investments.

The cost of debt is equal to the effective interest rate on new debt adjusted for the tax deductibility of the interest expense. The cost of preferred stock is equal to the effective dividend yield on new preferred stock. In making this computation, we should use the net price received by the company from the new issue. Thus, **Cost of Individual Sources of Financing**

$$\text{cost of preferred stock} = \frac{\text{annual dividend}}{\text{net price of preferred stock}} \qquad (14\text{-}7)$$

In calculating the cost of common equity, we distinguished between the costs of internally generated funds and of new common stock. If historical data reasonably reflect the expectations of the investors, the cost of internally generated capital is equal to the dividend yield on the common stock plus the anticipated percentage increase in dividends (and in the price of the stock) during the forthcoming year. If, however, the common equity is to be acquired by issuing new common stock, the cost of common should recognize the effect of flotation costs. This alteration results in the following equation for the cost of new common stock:

$$\left(\begin{matrix}\text{cost of new} \\ \text{common}\end{matrix}\right) = \left(\frac{\text{dividend in year one}}{\text{market price} - \text{flotation cost}}\right) + \left(\begin{matrix}\text{annual growth rate} \\ \text{in dividends}\end{matrix}\right) \quad (14\text{-}10)$$

A firm's *weighted* cost of capital is a composite of the individual costs of financing weighted by the percentage of financing provided by each source. In this chapter we have assumed that the firm is to finance future investments in the same manner as past investments. The problem of defining the best set of weights is addressed in Chapter 16. Hence, the existing capital structure has been used for developing the weighting scheme.

Weighted Cost of Capital

Since the *amount of financing* has an impact upon the firm's weighted cost of capital, the expected return from an investment has to be compared with the cost of financing the project. If the cost of capital does rise as the level of financing increases, we should be interested in the marginal cost of capital, and not the average cost of all funds raised. Following the basic economic principle of marginal analysis, investments should be made to the point where marginal revenue (internal rate of return) equals marginal cost (marginal cost of capital). The internal rate of return is simply the marginal revenue on the last dollar invested in a project, and the marginal cost of that dollar is the weighted cost of capital.

Marginal Cost of Capital

14-1. Why do we calculate a firm's cost of capital?

14-2. Define the term *cost of capital*.

14-3. In computing the cost of capital, which sources of capital should be recognized?

14-4. In general, what factors determine a firm's cost of capital? In answering this question, identify the factors that are and those that are not within management's control.

14-5. What limitations exist in using the firm's cost of capital as an investment hurdle rate?

14-6. How do the corporation's tax rate and the flotation costs associated with a new security issue affect a firm's cost of capital?

14-7. (a) Distinguish between *internal common equity* and *new common stock*.
(b) Why is a cost associated with internal common equity?

STUDY QUESTIONS

14-8. Define the expression *marginal cost of capital*. Why is the marginal cost of capital the appropriate investment criterion?

14-9. (a) How might we adjust the required rate of return for an individual project where the risk level of the project is significantly different from the risk associated with the existing assets? (See Appendix 14A.)

   (b) What limitations result from this method? (See Appendix 14A.)

14-1. Compute the cost for the following sources of financing:

   (a) A bond selling to yield 9 percent after flotation cost, but prior to adjusting for the marginal corporate tax rate of 48 percent. In other words, 9 percent is the rate that equates the net proceeds from the bond with the present value of the future cash flows (principal and interest).

   (b) A preferred stock selling for $105 with an annual dividend payment of $9. If the company sells a new issue, the flotation cost will be $10 per share. The company's marginal tax rate is 22 percent.

   (c) A $1000 par value bond with a market price of $960 and a coupon interest rate of 10 percent. Flotation costs for a new issue would be approximately 5 percent. The bonds mature in 10 years and the corporate tax rate is 48 percent.

   (d) New common stock where the most recent dividend was $3. The company's dividends per share should continue to increase at an 8 percent growth rate into the indefinite future. The market price of the stock is currently $55; however, flotation costs of $6 per share are expected if the new stock is issued.

   (e) A preferred stock paying an 8 percent dividend on a $100 par value. If a new issue is offered, the company can expect to net $90 per share.

   (f) Internal common equity where the current market price of the common stock is $40. The expected dividend this forthcoming year should be $2.50, increasing thereafter at a 6 percent annual growth rate. The corporation's tax rate is 48 percent.

   (g) A new common stock issue that paid a $1 dividend last year. The par value of the stock is $2, and the earnings per share have grown at a rate of 5 percent per year. This growth rate is expected to continue into the forseeable future. The company maintains a constant dividend/earnings ratio of 50 percent. The price of this stock is presently $25, but 10 percent flotation costs are anticipated.

   (h) A bond that has a $1000 par value and a contract interest rate of 12 percent. A new issue would net the company 92 percent of the present $1100 market value. The bonds mature in 20 years, and the firm's tax rate is 48 percent.

   (i) Internally generated common totaling $5 million. The price of the common stock is $80 per share, and the dividends per share were $4 last year. These dividends are not expected to increase.

14-2. Xeros is issuing a $1000 par value bond that pays 7 percent annual interest and matures in 15 years. Investors are willing to pay $968.50 for the bond. Flotation costs will be 12 percent of market value. The company is in a 48 percent tax bracket. What will be the firm's after-tax cost of debt on the bond?

14-3. The preferred stock of Jensen Industries sells for $34 and pays $2.10 in dividends. The net price of the security after issuance costs is $31.75. What is the cost of capital for the preferred stock?

14-4. Sharpe Corporation is issuing new common stock at a market price of $24. Dividends last year were $1.53 and are expected to grow at an annual rate of 9 percent forever. Flotation costs will be 7½ percent of market price. What is Sharpe's cost of the equity?

14-5. Bendir Co.'s common stock is currently selling for $18.75. Dividends paid last year were $1.23. The dividends and earnings per share are projected to have an annual growth rate of 11 percent. What is the cost of internal common equity for Bendir?

14-6. Brenco, Inc.'s, capital structure is provided below. Flotation costs would be (1) 11½ percent of market value for a new bond issue; (2) $1.15 per share for common stock, and (3) $1.85 per share for preferred stock. The dividends for common stock were $2.75 last year and are projected to have an annual growth rate of 7 percent. The firm is in a 53 percent tax bracket. What is the weighted cost of capital if Brenco uses only internal common equity? Use market weights.

BALANCE SHEET

Bonds (8%, $1000 par, 16-year maturity)		$1,500,000
Preferred stock (5000 shares outstanding, $75 par, $2 dividend)		375,000
Common stock:		
Par value (150,000 shares, $2 par value)	$300,000	
Paid-in capital	200,000	
Retained earnings	500,000	
Total common value		1,000,000
Total		$2,875,000

Market prices: $1015 for bonds; $86 for preferred stock, and $38 for common stock.

14-7. The Argus Company has the following capital structure mix (based upon market values):

Debt	30%
Preferred stock	15%
Common	55%
	100%

Assuming that management intends to maintain the above financial structure, what amount of *total* investments may be financed by (a) $100,000 of debt, (b) $150,000 of debt, (c) $40,000 of preferred stock, (d) $90,000 of preferred stock, (e) $200,000 of internally generated common equity, (f) $200,000 of internally generated common equity plus $300,000 in new common stock?

14-8. The Holt Manufacturing Corporation has determined the company's marginal costs of capital for debt, preferred stock, and common equity as follows:

SOURCE	AMOUNT OF CAPITAL	COST
Debt	$0–$200,000	5.0%
	$200,001–$300,000	5.5%
	over $300,000	7.0%
Preferred stock	$0–$50,000	9.0%
	$50,001–$75,000	12.0%
	over $75,000	14.0%
Common stock	$0–$400,000[a]	14.0%
	$400,001–$1,000,000	16.0%
	over $1,000,000	20.0%

[a]$400,000 is available from internally generated common equity.

The firm maintains a capital mix consisting of 40 percent debt, 10 percent preferred stock, and 50 percent common. Construct Holt's weighted marginal cost of capital curve.

14-9. Rickard Ski, Inc., is a regional manufacturer of ski equipment. The firm's capital structure appears as follows:

		BOOK VALUE	MARKET VALUE
Debt		$ 750,000	$ 900,000
Preferred stock		300,000	300,000
Common stock:			
Par $4	$100,000		
Paid-in capital	400,000		
Retained earnings	500,000	1,000,000	1,800,000
		$2,050,000	$3,000,000

The corporation's management is currently involved in evaluating the capital budget. Six investments are under consideration. The costs and the expected internal rates of return for these projects are given below:

INVESTMENT	COST	INTERNAL RATE OF RETURN
A	$175,000	16%
B	100,000	14%
C	125,000	12%
D	200,000	10%
E	250,000	9%
F	150,000	8%

As the accept-reject criterion, Darrell Rickard, president of the firm, has compiled the necessary data for computing the firm's weighted marginal cost of capital. The cost information indicates the following:

(1) Debt can be raised at the following before-tax costs:

AMOUNT	COST
$0–$150,000	8.0%
$150,001–$225,000	9.0%
over $225,000	10.5%

(2) Preferred stock can be issued paying an annual dividend of $8.50. The par value of the stock is $100. Also, the market price of the stock is $100. If new stock were issued, the company would receive a net price of $80 on the first $75,000. Thereafter, the net amount received would be reduced to $75.

(3) Common equity is provided first by internally generated funds. Profits for the year that should be available for reinvestment purposes are projected at $150,000. Additional common stock can be issued at the current $72 market price less 15 percent in flotation costs. However, if more than $225,000 in new common stock is required, a 20 percent flotation cost is expected. The dividend per share was $2.75 last year, and the long-term growth rate for dividends is 9 percent.

(a) Given that the firm's marginal tax rate is 50 percent, compute the company's weighted marginal cost of capital at a financing level up to $1 million.

(b) Construct a graph that presents the firm's weighted marginal cost of capital relative to the amount of financing.

(c) What is the appropriate size of the capital budget, and which projects should be accepted?

14-10. Stauffer Chemical Co. is considering five investments. The cost of each is shown below. $650,000 in retained earnings will be available for investment purposes, and management can issue the following securities:

(1) *Bonds*. $270,000 can be issued at an after-flotation, before-tax cost of 8.5 percent. Above $270,000 the cost will be 9.75 percent.

(2.) *Preferred stock*. The stock can be issued at the prevailing market price. Issuance will cost $1.55 per share up to an issue size of $90,000; thereafter costs will be $2.80 per share.

(3) *Common stock*. The stock will be issued at the market price. For an issue of $250,000, flotation costs will be $1 per share. The flotation costs should then be $1.75 per share.

The tax rate for the firm is 40 percent. Common dividends last year were $1.80 and are expected to grow at an annual rate of 9 percent. Market prices are $975 for bonds, $39 for preferred stock, and $23 for common stock. Determine which projects should be accepted, based upon a comparison of the internal rates of return (IRR) of the investments and the weighted marginal cost of capital.

INVESTMENT	COST	IRR
A	$ 200,000	16%
B	650,000	12%
C	115,000	9%
D	875,000	10%
E	180,000	15%
Total	$2,020,000	

CAPITAL STRUCTURE		
Bonds (9%, $1000 par, 18-year maturity)		$3,000,000
Preferred stock (10%, $45 par, 30,000 shares outstanding)		1,350,000
Common stock:		
Par value ($3 par, 100,000 shares)	$ 300,000	
Paid-in capital	950,000	
Retained earnings	1,350,000	2,600,000
Total		$6,950,000

ANG, JAMES S., "Weighted Average Versus True Cost of Capital," *Financial Management*, 2 (Autumn 1973), 56–60.

ARDITTI, FRED D., "The Weighted Average Cost of Capital: Some Questions on Its Definition, Interpretation and Use," *Journal of Finance*, 28 (September 1973), 1001–08.

———— and HAIM LEVY, "The Weighted Average Cost of Capital as a Cutoff Rate: A Critical Analysis of the Classical Textbook Weighted Average," *Financial Management*, 6 (Fall 1977), 24–34.

———— and MILFORD S. TYSSELAND, "Three Ways to Present the Marginal Cost of Capital," *Financial Management*, 2 (Summer 1973), 63–67.

BARGES, A., *The Effect of Capital Structure on the Cost Capital* (Englewood Cliffs, N. J.: Prentice-Hall, Inc., 1963).

BERANEK, WILLIAM, "The Cost of Capital, Capital Budgeting, and the Maximization of Shareholder Wealth," *Journal of Financial and Quantitative Analysis*, 5 (March 1975), 1–20.

———— "A Little More on the Weighted Average Cost of Capital," *Journal of Financial and Quantitative Analysis*, 5 (December 1975), 892–96.

———— "The Weighted Average Cost of Capital and Shareholder Wealth Maximization," *Journal of Financial and Quantitative Analysis*, 12 (March 1977), 17–31.

BONESS, JAMES A., and GEORGE M. FRANKFURTER, "Evidence of Non-Homogeneity of Capital Costs Within 'Risk Classes'," *Journal of Finance* 32 (June 1977), 775–87.

BOWER, RICHARD S., and J. M. JENKS, "Divisional Screening Rates," *Financial Management*, 4 (Autumn 1975), 42–49.

———— and D. R. LESSARD, "An Operational Approach to Risk Screening," *Journal of Finance*, 28 (May 1973), 321–28.

BRENNAN, J. B., "A New Look at the Weighted Average Cost of Capital," *Journal of Business Finance*, 5 (1973), 24–30.

BRIGHAM, EUGENE F., and MYRON J. GORDON, "Leverage, Dividend Policy and the Cost of Capital," *Journal of Finance*, 23 (March 1968), 85–103.

DONALDSON, GORDAN, "Strategic Hurdle Rates for Capital Investment," *Harvard Business Review*, 50 (March–April 1972), 50–55.

EZZELL, JOHN R., and R. BURR PORTER, "Flotation Costs and the Weighted Average Cost of Capital," *Journal of Financial and Quantitative Analysis*, 11 (September 1976), 403–13.

GORDON, MYRON J., and PAUL J. HALPERN, "Cost of Capital for a Division of a Firm," *Journal of Finance*, 29 (September 1974), 1153–63.

HALEY, CHARLES, "Taxes, the Cost of Capital, and The Firm's Investment Decisions," *Journal of Finance*, 20 (September 1971), 901–17.

HIGGINS, ROBERT C., "Growth, Dividend Policy and Capital Costs in the Electric Utility Industry," *Journal of Finance*, 29 (September 1974), 1189–1201.

JOHNSON, KEITH B., T. GREGORY MORTON, and M. CHAPMAN FINDLAY, III, "An Analysis of the Flotation Cost of Corporate Quasi-Equity Securities, 1971–72," *Financial Management*, 4 (Winter 1975), 12–17.

LAWRENZ, DAVID W., "The Effects of Corporate Taxation on the Cost of Equity Capital," *Financial Management*, 5 (Spring 1976), 53–57.

LEWELLEN, WILBUR G., "A Conceptual Reappraisal of Cost of Capital," *Financial Management*, 3 (Winter 1974), 63–70.

————, "A Conceptual Reappraisal of Cost of Capital," *Financial Management*, 3 (Winter 1974), 63–70.

————, *The Cost of Capital* (Belmont, Calif.: Wadworth Publishing Company, Inc., 1969).

LINTNER, J., "The Cost of Capital and Optimal Financing of Corporate Growth," *Journal of Finance*, 18 (May 1963), 292–310.

MODIGLIANI, F., and M. MILLER, "The Cost of Capital, Corporation Finance, and the Theory of Investment," *American Economic Review*, 48 (June 1958), 261–96.

————, "Dividend Policy, Growth and the Valuation of Shares," *Journal of Business*, 34 (October 1961), 411–32.

————, "Taxes and the Cost of Capital: A Correction," *American Economic Review*, 53 (June 1963), 433–44.

MOSSIN, J., "Equilibrium in a Capital Asset Market," *Econometrica* 34 (4), (October 1966), 768–75.

MYERS, STEWART C., "Interactions of Corporate Financing and Investment Decisions— Implications for Capital Budgeting," *Journal of Finance*, 29 (March 1974), 1–25.

NANTELL, TIMOTHY J., and C. ROBERT CARLSON, "The Cost of Capital as a Weighted Average," *Journal of Finance*, 30 (December 1975), 1343–55.

PETRY, GLENN H., "Empircal Evidence on Cost of Capital Weights," *Financial Management*, 4 (Winter 1975), 58–70.

QUIRIN, G. DAVID, and WILLIAM R. WATERS, "Market Efficiency and the Cost of Capital: The Strange Case of Fire and Casualty Insurance Companies," *Journal of Finance*, 30 (May 1975), 427–50.

REILLY, RAYMOND R., and WILLIAM E. WECKER, "On the Weighted Average Cost of Capital," *Journal of Financial and Quantitative Analysis*, 8 (January 1973), 123–26.

WEST, DAVID A., and ARTHUR A. EUBANK, "An Automatic Cost of Capital Adjustment Model for Regulating Public Utilities," *Financial Management*, 5 (Spring 1976), 23–31.

WESTON, J. FRED, "Investment Decisions Using the Capital Asset Pricing Model," *Financial Management*, 2 (Spring 1973), 25–33.

APPENDIX 14A

REQUIRED RATE OF RETURN FOR INDIVIDUAL PROJECTS

Two basic assumptions are required in computing and using the firm's *weighted cost of capital*. First, the riskiness of the project being evaluated was presumed to be similar to the riskiness of the company's existing assets. In other words, acceptance of the investment would not alter the firm's overall business risk. In practice, however, most investment opportunities have different levels of risk. Since an investor's required rate of return is equal to the risk-free rate plus a risk premium which reflects the project riskiness, a single required rate of return (such as the weighted cost of capital) is not always applicable. Second, we assumed that future investments would be financed in the same proportions of debt, preferred stock, and common stock as past investments. However, in practice, different financing arrangements are made for different projects, with the nature and the size of the investment frequently dictating the financing strategy. Although the financial mix may influence the accept-reject decision for an individual project, this issue is beyond the scope of this book. Consequently, we will examine only the first issue, that of differing levels of project riskiness.[1]

---

[1]For further explanation, see Ezra Solomon, "Measuring a Company's Cost of Capital," *Journal of Business* (October 1955), pp. 95–117; Stewart C. Myers, "Interactions of Corporate Financing and Investment Decision—Implications for Capital Budgeting," *Journal of Finance* (March 1974), pp. 1–25; Richard S. Bower and Jeffery M. Jenks, "Divisional Screening Rates," *Financial Management* (Autumn 1975), pp. 42–49; Donald L. Tuttle and Robert H. Litzenberger, "Leverage Diversification and Capital Market Effects on a Risk-Adjusted Capital Budgeting Framework," *Journal of Finance* (June 1968), pp. 427–43; and John D. Martin and David F. Scott, Jr., "Debt Capacity and the Capital Budgeting Decision," *Financial Management* (Summer 1976), pp. 7–14.

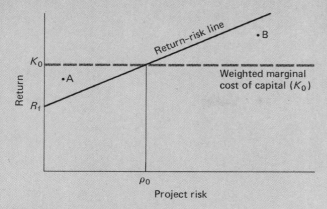

FIGURE 14A-1   *Return-Risk Relationship*

The general limitation of the weighted cost of capital is illustrated in Figure 14 A-1, where the dashed line represents the firm's weighted marginal cost of capital, K_0. This cost of capital, as computed earlier in the chapter, does not allow for varying levels of project risk. In Figure 14 A-1, this investment hurdle rate is appropriate only for a project with ρ_0 amount of risk. However, the *return-risk line* in the figure specifies the appropriate required rates of return for investments having different amounts of risk. In addition, investments A and B in the figure may be used to illustrate incorrect decisions that would result from the use of the firm's cost of capital as the sole acceptance criterion. In this example, investment A would be rejected and investment B accepted if the required rate being used were the weighted marginal cost of capital. However, if the return-risk line accurately measures the market return-risk relationship, investment A should be accepted and investment B rejected. Although the expected return for investment A is below the firm's weighted marginal cost of capital, the reduction in company risk sufficiently justifies acceptance of the investment's lower expected return.

In identifying the relationship between the required rate of return and project risk, the *price* of risk in the market, or the risk premium, may be measured as

$$
\begin{pmatrix} \text{risk} \\ \text{premium} \end{pmatrix} = \begin{pmatrix} \text{companywide marginal} \\ \text{cost of capital} \end{pmatrix} - \begin{pmatrix} \text{risk-free} \\ \text{rate} \end{pmatrix} \qquad (14A\text{-}1)
$$
$$
P = K_0 - R_f
$$

Yet, this risk premium applies only to the firm's investments with an average level of risk. Only if this risk premium is standardized relative to the riskiness of the firm's average project is it relevant for other investments of different risk levels. The firm's excess return relative to the risk for a typical project would be

$$\left(\begin{array}{c}\text{excess return per}\\ \text{unit of risk}\end{array}\right) = \frac{\left(\begin{array}{c}\text{companywide marginal}\\ \text{cost of capital}\end{array}\right) - \left(\begin{array}{c}\text{risk-free}\\ \text{rate}\end{array}\right)}{\text{risk for average project}} \quad (14\text{A-2})$$

$$EP = \frac{K_0 - R_f}{\rho_0}$$

This excess return-risk relationship holds not only for the firm but for individual investments. Therefore, if K_j is the required rate of return for investment j, and ρ_j is the risk for project j,

$$\frac{K_j - R_f}{\rho_j} = \frac{K_0 - R_f}{\rho_0} \quad (14\text{A-3})$$

Restructuring equation (14A-3), we have

$$K_j - R_f = [K_0 - R_f]\frac{\rho_j}{\rho_0} \quad (14\text{A-4})$$

Therefore,

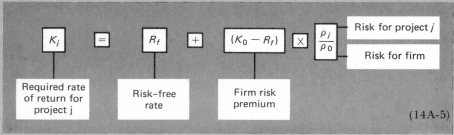

$$(14\text{A-5})$$

Thus, equation (14A-5) defines the return-risk line in Figure 14A-1.

Even though equation (14A-5) has been developed in such a way that it conceptually represents the return-risk relationship for the corporation's investments, several implementation problems arise. As may be recalled from prior sections, computing the weighted cost of capital, K_0, is at best an approximation. Also, since use of the weighted cost of capital necessitates the assumption that the firm's capital structure will not change as a result of financing new investments, equation (14A-5) also requires that the financing of the jth asset not result in a change in the company's existing financial mix.[2]

To this point, no suggestion has been offered as to how project risk is to be measured. Although we would generally concur that the appropriate concept of risk comes in terms of variability of returns, how this dispersion should be measured is still open to some question. Earlier the standard deviation statistic was used to represent risk.[3]

[2]As previously mentioned, this limitation in theory may be avoided; however, in reality, the necessary adjustments are difficult and beyond the scope of the text. See references in footnote 1.

[3]The basis for this risk measurement is explained with respect to capital budgeting under uncertainty (Chapter 12) and valuation (Chapter 13).

Example. To demonstrate the necessary calculations, assume that

the cost of capital for Petroleum Exploration, Inc., is 14 percent, and the standard deviation of the returns for an average project is 6 percent.

The riskless interest rate on long-term U. S. government bonds, R_f, is 8 percent. In developing a return-risk relationship for investments, management has used the foregoing information for determining the minimum acceptable return for a project. Specifically, for project j the required rate of return is determined as follows:

$$K_j = R_f + (K_0 - R_f) \frac{\rho_j}{\rho_0} \qquad (14A\text{-}5)$$

$$= .08 + (.14 - .08) \frac{\rho_j}{.06}$$

Several investments, which are set forth in Table 14A-1, are currently being considered by the firm. Using equation (14A-5), we may determine the acceptability of the proposed investments. These computations, shown in Table 14A-2, indicate that investments B, D, and E should be accepted and investments A and C should be rejected. This analysis of whether to accept or reject these projects is also presented in Figure 14A-2. The decision rule should be to accept all projects that are on or above the return-risk line.

Table 14A-1 PETROLEUM EXPLORATION, INC., INVESTMENT OPPORTUNITIES

PROJECT	EXPECTED RETURNS	STANDARD DEVIATION OF RETURNS
A	10.0%	5.0%
B	12.0%	2.0%
C	14.0%	7.5%
D	16.0%	8.0%
E	17.0%	7.0%

Table 14A-2 COMPUTATION OF REQUIRED RATES OF RETURN

PROJECT	STANDARD DEVIATION OF RETURNS (COL. 3, TABLE 14A-1)	COMPUTATION OF THE REQUIRED RATE OF RETURN [EQUATION (14A-5)]	REQUIRED RATE OF RETURN	EXPECTED RETURN (COL. 2, TABLE 14A-1)	DECISION
A	.050	$.08 + (.14 - .08)(.05/.06) =$	.130	.10	Reject
B	.020	$.08 + (.14 - .08)(.02/.06) =$	.100	.12	Accept
C	.075	$.08 + (.14 - .08)(.075/.06) =$	.155	.14	Reject
D	.080	$.08 + (.14 - .08)(.08/.06) =$	.160	.16	Accept
E	.070	$.08 + (.14 - .08)(.07/.06) =$	.150	.17	Accept

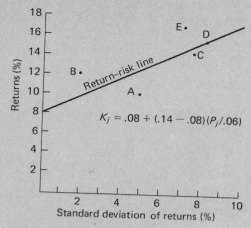

$$K_j = .08 + (.14 - .08)(P_j/.06)$$

FIGURE 14A-2 *Petroleum Exploration, Inc., Investment Opportunities*

The previous explanation of the market return-cisk relationship considered only one investment in isolation. However, if investors find risk distasteful—that is, if they are risk averse—diversification can be used to reduce risk relative to the expected return of a portfolio of assets or to increase the expected return relative to the riskiness of the portfolio of investments. When a firm and/or investors make a variety of investments, we are concerned about the effect of a new project on the riskiness of the total portfolio of assets.

In examining the effect of diversification upon the market risk-return relationship, we note that the ability to diversify occurs at two levels. First, the firm can diversify its holdings in capital investments, thereby reducing the variability of the cash flows within the company. Alternatively, the firm's investors can diversify their own investments. Considerable controversy has developed regarding the advantage of the firm's diversifying its investments. In essence, since investors can diversify, is there any benefit to be gained by the firm's also diversifying? This issue is quite complex and extends beyond the purpose and scope of this text.[4] However, for simplicity, investors are assumed to hold diversified portfolios. Also, perfect markets are assumed to exist, where (1) information is readily available to all investors at no cost, (2) there are no transaction costs, (3) investment opportunities are readily accessible to all prospective investors, and (4) financial distress and bankruptcy costs are nonexistent. In this situation, the **capital-asset pricing model** provides the appropriate criterion for accepting or rejecting the jth project. In other words, the required rate of return for the jth project, K_j, should be[5]

Effect of Diversification

[4]See Chapter 12 for a brief explanation of this issue.
[5]For an explanation of the *correlation* between the returns of two investments, r_{jm}, see Chapter 12.

$$\begin{pmatrix} \text{required rate} \\ \text{for project } j \end{pmatrix} = \begin{pmatrix} \text{risk-free} \\ \text{rate} \end{pmatrix} + \begin{pmatrix} \text{risk premium for a} \\ \text{widely diversified} \\ \text{portfolio} \\ \hline \text{standard deviation} \\ \text{of the returns for a} \\ \text{widely diversified} \\ \text{portfolio} \end{pmatrix} \begin{pmatrix} \text{correlation} \\ \text{of project } j \\ \text{returns with} \\ \text{portfolio} \\ \text{returns} \end{pmatrix} \begin{pmatrix} \text{standard} \\ \text{deviation} \\ \text{of the } j\text{th} \\ \text{project} \end{pmatrix}$$

$$K_j = R_f + \left(\frac{R_m - R_f}{\rho_m} \right) r_{jm}\, \rho_j \qquad (14\text{A-}6)$$

The capital-asset pricing model [equation (14A-6)] is similar to equation (14A-5). However, the excess return-risk relationship, $(R_m - R_f)/\rho_m$, is for the *market portfolio* and not simply that of the firm. The expression $r_{jm}\,\rho_j$ measures the portion of the standard deviation for project j that cannot be eliminated through investor diversification, or the *undiversifiable risk* for project j. Equation (14A-6), may be restated as

$$K_j = R_f + (R_m - R_f) \left(\frac{r_{jm}\, \rho_j}{\rho_m} \right) \qquad (14\text{A-}7)$$

Letting

$$\beta_j = \frac{r_{jm}\, \rho_j}{\rho_m}, \qquad (14\text{A-}8)$$

we have

$$K_j = R_f + (R_m - R_f)\, \beta_j \qquad (14\text{A-}9)$$

where β_j (beta) identifies the volatility of the jth project returns relative to the investor's widely diversified portfolio. Thus, β_j represents the effect of the jth project upon the riskiness of the investor's portfolio, which should identify the relevant *risk* in the market.

Example. To illustrate the use of the capital-asset pricing model for determining the required rate of return for a project, suppose that a capital investment is being considered with an expected return of 16 percent. Management believes that the riskiness of the project should be analyzed in terms of its contribution to the risk of a diversified investor's portfolio. The expected return for a diversified portfolio of assets, R_m, is 14 percent, and the risk-free rate, R_f, is 6 percent. The standard deviation of returns for the portfolio, ρ_m, is 5 percent, while the standard deviation of the project returns, ρ_j, is estimated to be 7 percent. The correlation coefficient between the two returns, r_{jm}, is anticipated to be .8. With this information, the beta for the investment is

$$\beta_j = \frac{r_{jm}\, \rho_j}{\rho_m}$$

$$= \frac{(.8)\,(.07)}{.05}$$

$$= 1.12$$

which indicates that a 1 percent change in the market portfolio's rate of return will produce an expected 1.12 precent change in the investment's rate of return. Thus, the project returns and the market portfolio returns encounter approximately the same amount of variability. As a result, we would expect the required rate of return for the project to be roughly equal to the expectedreturn for the market portfolio. To verify, equation (14A-9) may be used to compute the appropriate required rate of return for the project.

$$K_j = R_f + (R_m - R_f)\, \beta_j \qquad\qquad (14A\text{-}9)$$

$$= .06 + (.14 - .06)\, 1.12 = .1496$$

$$= 14.96 \text{ percent}$$

Since the 16 percent expected return for the investment exceeds the required rate of return, the investment should be made.

While conceptually sound, the use of the capital-asset pricing model in calculating a project required rate of return is difficult, owing to measurement problems. The primary difficulty lies in the determination of r_{jm}, the relationship between the market returns and the project returns. Also, the model maintains that the relevant risk is limited to the portion of the risk that the *investor* cannot eliminate through diversification. For this premise to hold, bankruptcy costs are assumed to equal zero if the firm fails. In reality, bankruptcy costs are generally significant. Therefore, if a project increases significantly the probability of firm bankruptcy, total variability of project returns is the appropriate risk measure.

Evaluation of CAPM

In summary, owing to the limiting assumptions associated with an overall cost of capital for the firm, this single hurdle rate is not generally appropriate for all the investments a firm will analyze. In particular if the risk associated with a particular investment is significantly different from the firm's existing assets, the weighted cost of capital should not be employed. In this context, a minimum acceptable rate of return that recognizes the different risk levels has to be used. To implement such an approach, financial management has to identify the relevant measure for risk. Several alternatives are available. First, the variability in returns for a single project, without any regard for the effect of diversification, could be used. Second, if management considers diversification to be a worthwhile activity, the riskiness of an individual project must be viewed in terms of its contribution to the risk of the firm's existing assets. Third, if the capital-asset pricing model is used, the appropriate risk measurement should recognize the portion of the risk that the investor cannot eliminate by diversifying among different securities.

14A-1. Hastings, Inc., is analyzing several investments. The expected returns and standard deviations of each project are tabulated below. The firm's cost of capital is 16.5 percent, and the standard deviation of the average project is 7 percent. The current rate on long-term U. S. government securities is 8.5 percent. Which investments should the firm accept?

PROJECT	INVESTMENT'S EXPECTED RETURN	STANDARD DEVIATIONS OF RETURNS
A	18.0%	7.0%
B	13.8%	6.0%
C	15.3%	7.8%
D	11.4%	5.0%

14A-2. Scudder Corporation is evaluating three investments, which have the expected returns and standard deviations listed below. The management of the firm wants to determine the required rates of return of the projects using the capital-asset pricing model. The expected return of a diversified portfolio with a standard deviation of 6 percent is 15 percent. The rate on U. S. government securities is 8 percent. Which investments should be made?

INVESTMENT	EXPECTED RETURNS	STANDARD DEVIATION	CORRELATION WITH THE MARKET
A	18.8%	8.9%	.65
B	13.5%	7.0%	.80
C	15.0%	6.5%	.75

14A-3. Two capital investments are being examined by Wellton Corporation. Management wants to analyze the riskiness of the projects in terms of their effect on the riskiness of a diversified portfolio. The standard deviation of returns of project A is 9.82 percent and of B, 6.79 percent. The expected return for a diversified portfolio is 16 percent, and its standard deviation is 5 percent. The correlation coefficient between project A and the portfolio is estimated to be .536, and between project B and the portfolio, .742. The risk-free rate is 7 percent. Project A is expected to return 15.7 percent; project B, 17.5 percent. Which investments should the company accept?

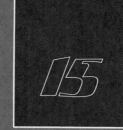

Analysis
and Impact of Leverage

*O*ur work in the previous two chapters allowed us to develop an understanding of how financial assets are valued in the marketplace. Drawing on the tenets of valuation theory, we then presented various approaches to measuring the cost of funds to the business organization. The concepts to be covered in this chapter relate closely to those discussions of the valuation process and the cost of capital, and also extend to the crucial problem of planning the firm's financing mix.

The cost of capital provides a direct link between the formulation of the firm's asset structure and its financial structure. This is illustrated in Figure 15-1. Recall that the cost of capital is a basic input to the time-adjusted capital budgeting models. It affects, therefore, the asset selection process that we have called "capital budgeting." The cost of capital is affected, in turn, by the composition of the right-hand side of the firm's balance sheet—that is, its financial structure.

The tools to be examined in this chapter can be useful aids to the financial manager in determining his firm's proper financial structure. Although these tools can certainly be applied in other settings, such as the product-pricing process, it is their application in designing a prudent financing mix that is stressed. First, the technique of breakeven analysis will be reviewed. This provides the foundation for the relationships to be high-

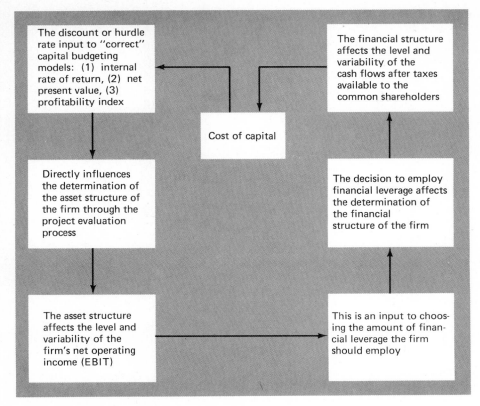

The discount or hurdle rate input to "correct" capital budgeting models: (1) internal rate of return, (2) net present value, (3) profitability index

Cost of capital

The financial structure affects the level and variability of the cash flows after taxes available to the common shareholders

Directly influences the determination of the asset structure of the firm through the project evaluation process

The decision to employ financial leverage affects the determination of the financial structure of the firm

The asset structure affects the level and variability of the firm's net operating income (EBIT)

This is an input to choosing the amount of financial leverage the firm should employ

FIGURE 15-1 *Cost of Capital as a Link between the Firm's Asset Structure and Financial Structure*

lighted in the remainder of the chapter. We will then examine, second, the concept of operating leverage, third, some consequences of the firm's use of financial leverage, and fourth, the impact on the firm's earnings stream from combining operating and financial leverage in various degrees. Our immediate tasks are to distinguish two types of risk that confront the firm and to clarify some other terminology that will be used throughout this and the subsequent chapter.

In studying capital budgeting techniques we referred to **risk** as the likely variability associated with expected revenue streams. As our attention is now focused on the firm's financing decision rather than its investment decision, it is useful to separate the income-stream variations attributable to (1) the company's exposure to business risk and (2) its decision to incur financial risk.

Business risk refers to the relative dispersion (variability) in the firm's expected earnings before interest and taxes (EBIT).[1] Figure 15-2(a) shows a subjectively estimated probability distribution of next year's EBIT for the Pierce Grain Company. Figure 15-2(b) shows the same type of projection for Pierce's larger competitor, The Blackburn Seed Company. The expected value of EBIT for Pierce is $100,000, with an associated standard deviation of $20,000. If next year's EBIT for Pierce fell one standard deviation short of the expected $100,000, then the actual EBIT would equal $80,000. Blackburn's expected EBIT is $200,000, and the size of the associated standard deviation is $20,000. The standard deviation about the expected level of EBIT is the same for both firms. We would say that Pierce's degree of business risk exceeds Blackburn's owing to its larger coefficient of variation of expected EBIT, as follows:

$$\text{Pierce's coefficient of variation of expected EBIT} = \frac{\$20,000}{\$100,000} = 0.20$$

$$\text{Blackburn's coefficient of variation of expected EBIT} = \frac{\$20,000}{\$200,000} = 0.10$$

It is to be emphasized that the relative dispersion in the firm's EBIT stream, measured here by its expected coefficient of variation, is the *residual*

[1]If what the accountants call "other income" and "other expenses" are equal to zero, then EBIT is equal to net operating income. These terms will be used interchangeably.

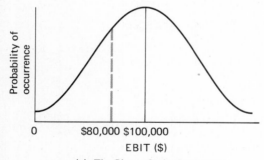

(a) The Pierce Grain Company

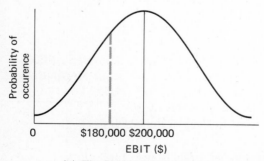

(b) The Blackburn Seed Company

FIGURE 15-2 *Subjective Probability Distribution of Next Year's EBIT*

effect of several causal influences. Dispersion in operating income does not cause business risk; such dispersion, which we call business risk, is the result of several influences. Some of these are listed in Table 15-1, along with an example of each particular attribute. Notice that the company's cost structure, product demand characteristics, and intraindustry competitive position all affect its business risk posture. Such business risk is a direct result of the firm's investment decision. It is the firm's asset structure, after all, that gives rise to both the level and variability of its operating profits.

Financial risk, on the other hand, is a direct result of the firm's financing decision. In the context of selecting a proper financing mix it refers to (1) the additional variability in earnings available to the firm's common shareholders, and (2) the additional chance of insolvency borne by the common shareholder caused by the use of financial leverage.[2] **Financial leverage** means financing a portion of the firm's assets with securities bearing a fixed (limited) rate of return in hopes of increasing the ultimate return to the common stockholders. The decision to use debt or preferred stock in the financial structure of the corporation means that

[2]Note that the concept of financial risk used here differs from that used in our examination of cash and marketable securities management in Chapters 7 and 8.

Table 15-1 THE CONCEPT OF BUSINESS RISK

BUSINESS RISK ATTRIBUTE	EXAMPLE[a]
1. Sensitivity of the firm's product demand to general economic conditions	If GNP declines, does the firm's sales level decline by a greater percent?
2. Degree of competition	Is the firm's market share small in comparison to other firms that produce and distribute the same product(s)?
3. Product diversification	Is a large proportion of the firm's sales revenue derived from a single major product or product line?
4. Operating leverage	Does the firm utilize a high level of operating leverage resulting in a high level of fixed costs?
5. Growth prospects	Are the firm's product markets expanding and (or) changing, making income estimates and prospects highly volatile?
6. Size	Does the firm suffer a competitive disadvantage due to lack of size in assets, sales, or profits that translates into (among other things) difficulty in tapping the capital market for funds?

[a]Affirmative responses indicate greater business risk exposure.

those who own the common shares of the firm are exposed to financial risk. Any given level of variability in EBIT will be magnified by the firm's use of financial leverage, and such additional variability will be embodied in the variability of earnings available to the residual owner and earnings per share. If these magnifications are negative, the common stockholder endures a higher change of insolvency than would have existed had the use of fixed-charge securities (debt and preferred stock) been avoided.

The closely related concepts of business and financial risk are crucial to the problem of financial structure design. This follows from the impact of these types of risk on the variability of the earnings stream flowing to the company's residual owners. In the rest of this chapter we will study techniques that permit a precise assessment of the earnings-stream variability caused by (1) operating leverage and (2) financial leverage. We have already defined financial leverage. In Table 15-1 it was observed that the business risk of the enterprise is influenced by the use of what is called operating leverage. **Operating leverage** refers to the incurrence of fixed operating costs in the firm's income stream. To fully understand the nature and importance of operating leverage, we need to draw upon the basics of cost-volume-profit analysis (breakeven analysis).

BREAKEVEN ANALYSIS

The technique of breakeven analysis is familiar to legions of businessmen. It is usefully applied in a wide array of business settings, including both small and large organizations. The fact that this tool is based on straightforward assumptions explains a portion of its acceptance by the business community. It should not be overlooked, however, that companies have found the information gained from application of the breakeven model to be of positive benefit in decision-making situations.

Objective and Uses

The objective of breakeven analysis is to determine the breakeven quantity of output by studying the relationships among the firm's cost structure, volume of output, and profit. Alternatively, the breakeven level of sales dollars that corresponds to the breakeven quantity of output can be ascertained. We will develop the fundamental relationships by concentrating on units of output and then extend the procedure to permit direct calculation of the breakeven sales level.

What is meant by the breakeven quantity of output? It is that quantity of output, denominated in units, that results in an EBIT level equal to zero. Use of the breakeven model, therefore, enables the financial officer (1) to determine the quantity of output that must be sold to cover all operating costs, as distinct from financial costs, and (2) to calculate the EBIT that will be achieved at various output levels.

Actual and potential applications of the breakeven approach are wide in scope. Some of these include:

1. Capital expenditure analysis. As a *complementary* technique to discounted cash

flow evaluation models, the breakeven model locates in a rough way the sales volume needed to make a project economically beneficial to the firm. It should *not* be used to replace the time-adjusted evaluation techniques.

2. Pricing policy. The sales price of a new product can be set to achieve a target EBIT level. Further, should market penetration be a prime objective, the price could be set that would cover slightly more than the variable costs of production and provide only a partial contribution to the recovery of fixed costs. The negative EBIT at several possible sales prices can then be studied.

3. Labor contract negotiations. The effect of increased variable costs resulting from higher wages on the breakeven quantity of output can be analyzed.

4. Cost structure. The choice of reducing variable costs at the expense of incurring higher fixed costs can be evaluated. Management might decide to become more capital intensive by performing tasks in the production process through use of equipment rather than laborers. Application of the breakeven model can indicate what the effects of this tradeoff will be on the breakeven point for the given product.

5. Financing decisions. Analysis of the firm's cost structure will reveal the proportion that fixed operating costs bear to sales. If this proportion is high, the firm might reasonably decide not to add any fixed financing costs on top of the high fixed operating costs.

ASSUMED BEHAVIOR OF COSTS

To implement the breakeven model we must separate the production costs of the company into two mutually exclusive categories: (1) fixed costs and (2) variable costs. You will recall from your study of basic economics that in the *long run* all costs are variable. Breakeven analysis, therefore, is a short-run concept.

Essential Elements of the Breakeven Model

Fixed Costs. **Fixed costs,** also referred to as **indirect costs,** do not vary in total amount as sales volume or the quantity of output changes over some *relevant* range of output. Total fixed costs are independent of the quantity of product produced and equal some constant dollar amount. Obviously, as production volume increases, fixed cost per unit of product falls. The reason is that total fixed costs are being spread over larger and larger quantities of output. The behavior of total fixed costs with respect to the company's relevant range of output is depicted in Figure 15-3. This total is shown to be unaffected by the quantity of product that is manufactured and sold. Over some other relevant output range the amount of total fixed costs might be higher or lower for the same company.

In a manufacturing setting some specific examples of fixed costs are:

1. Administrative salaries.
2. Depreciation.
3. Insurance.
4. Lump sums spent on intermittent advertising programs.
5. Property taxes.
6. Rent.

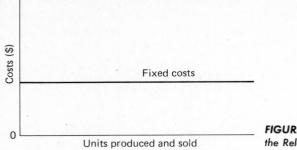

FIGURE 15-3 *Fixed Cost Behavior over the Relevant Range of Output*

Variable Costs.   **Variable costs** are sometimes referred to as **direct costs.** Variable costs are fixed per unit of output, but vary in total as output changes. Total variable costs are computed by taking the variable cost per unit and multiplying it by the quantity produced and sold. The breakeven model assumes proportionality between total variable costs and sales. Thus, if sales rise by 10 percent, it is assumed that variable costs will rise by 10 percent. The behavior of total variable costs with respect to the company's relevant range of output is depicted in Figure 15-4. Total variable costs are seen to depend on the quantity of product that is manufactured and sold. Notice that if zero units of the product are manufactured, then variable costs are zero, but fixed costs are greater than zero. This implies that some contribution to the coverage of fixed costs occurs as long as the selling price per unit exceeds the variable cost per unit. This helps explain why some firms will operate a plant even when sales are *temporarily* depressed—that is, to provide some increment of revenue toward the coverage of fixed costs.

For a manufacturing operation some examples of variable costs include:

1. Direct labor.
2. Direct materials.
3. Energy costs (fuel, electricity, natural gas) associated with the production area.
4. Freight costs on products leaving the plant.

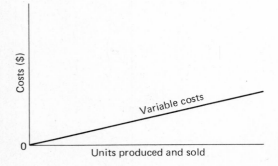

FIGURE 15-4 *Variable Cost Behavior over the Relevant Range of Output*

418

5. Packaging.

6. Sales commissions.

More on Behavior of Costs. No one really believes that *all* costs behave as neatly as we have illustrated the fixed and variable costs in Figures 15-3 and 15-4. Neither does any law or accounting principle dictate that a certain element of the firm's total costs always be classified as fixed or variable. This will depend on the set of circumstances associated with the specific firm. In one firm utility costs may be predominantly fixed, whereas in another they may vary with output.[3]

Furthermore, some costs may be fixed for a while, then rise sharply to a higher level as a higher output is reached, remain fixed, and then rise again with further increases in production. Such costs may be termed either (1) **semivariable** or (2) **semifixed.** The nomer is your choice, since both are used in industrial practice. An example might be the salaries paid production foremen. Should output be cut back by 15 percent for a short period, the management of the organization are not likely to lay off 15 percent of their foremen. Similarly, commissions paid to salesmen often follow a stepwise pattern over wide ranges of success. This sort of cost behavior is shown in Figure 15-5.

To implement the breakeven model and deal with such "difficult" costs, it is necessary that the financial manager (1) identify the most relevant output range for his planning purposes and then (2) approximate the cost effect of semivariable items over this range by segregating a portion of them to fixed costs and a portion to variable costs. In the actual business setting this procedure is not fun, but it must be faced. It would not be unusual for the analyst who deals with the figures to spend considerably more time on allocating costs to fixed and variable categories than to carrying out the breakeven calculations shortly to be described.

[3]In a greenhouse operation, where plants are grown (manufactured) under very strictly controlled temperatures, heat costs will tend to be fixed whether the building is full or only half full of seedlings. In a metal stamping operation, where levers are being produced, there is no need to heat the plant to as high a temperature when the machines are stopped and the workers are sent home. In this latter case the heat costs will tend to be variable.

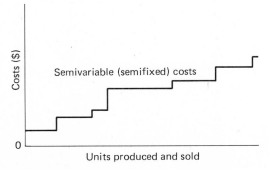

FIGURE 15-5 *Semivariable Cost Behavior over the Relevant Range of Output*

Besides fixed and variable costs the essential elements of the break-even model include (1) total revenue from sales and (2) volume of output. **Total revenue** means sales dollars and is equal to the selling price per unit multiplied by the quantity sold. The **volume of output** refers to the firm's level of operations and may be indicated as (1) a unit quantity, or (2) as sales dollars.

FINDING THE BREAKEVEN POINT

Finding the breakeven point in terms of units of production can be accomplished in several ways. All approaches require use of the essential elements of the breakeven model just described. The breakeven model is just a simple adaption of the firm's income statement expressed in the following analytical format:

$$\text{sales} - (\text{total variable cost} + \text{total fixed cost}) = \text{profit} \qquad (15\text{-}1)$$

On a units of production basis, it is necessary to introduce (1) the price at which each unit is sold and (2) the variable cost per unit of output. Because the profit item studied in breakeven analysis is EBIT, we will use that acronym instead of the word "profit." In terms of units the income statement shown in equation (15-1) becomes the breakeven model by setting EBIT equal to zero:

$$\left(\begin{array}{c}\text{sales price}\\ \text{per unit}\end{array}\right)\left(\begin{array}{c}\text{units}\\ \text{sold}\end{array}\right) - \left[\left(\begin{array}{c}\text{variable cost}\\ \text{per unit}\end{array}\right)\left(\begin{array}{c}\text{units}\\ \text{sold}\end{array}\right) + \left(\begin{array}{c}\text{total fixed}\\ \text{cost}\end{array}\right)\right] = \text{EBIT} = \$0$$
$$(15\text{-}2)$$

Our task now becomes that of finding the number of units that must be produced and sold in order to satisfy equation (15-2)—that is, to arrive at an EBIT = $0. This can be done by use of (1) trial-and-error analysis, (2) contribution margin analysis, or (3) algebraic analysis. Each approach will be illustrated using the same set of circumstances.

Even though The Pierce Grain Company manufactures several different products, it has observed over a lengthy period that the product mix is rather constant. This allows the firm's management to conduct its financial planning by use of a "normal" sales price per unit and "normal" variable cost per unit. The selling price is $10 and the variable cost is $6. Total fixed costs for the firm are $100,000 per year. What is the breakeven point in units produced and sold for the company during the coming year?

The most cumbersome approach to determining the firm's breakeven point is to employ the trial-and-error technique illustrated in Table 15-2. The process simply involves (1) the arbitrary selection of an output level, and (2) the calculation of a corresponding EBIT amount. When the level of output is found that results in an EBIT = $0, the breakeven point has been

Table 15-2 THE PIERCE GRAIN COMPANY: SALES, COST, AND PROFIT SCHEDULE

(1) UNITS SOLD	(2) UNIT SALES PRICE	(3) = (1) × (2) SALES	(4) UNIT VARIABLE COST	(5) = (1) × (4) TOTAL VARIABLE COST	(6) TOTAL FIXED COST	(7) = (5) + (6) TOTAL COST	(8) = (3) − (7) EBIT	
1. 10,000	$10	$100,000	$6	$ 60,000	$100,000	$160,000	$−60,000	1.
2. 15,000	10	150,000	6	90,000	100,000	190,000	−40,000	2.
3. 20,000	10	200,000	6	120,000	100,000	220,000	−20,000	3.
4. 25,000	10	250,000	6	150,000	100,000	250,000	0	4.
5. 30,000	10	300,000	6	180,000	100,000	280,000	20,000	5.
6. 35,000	10	350,000	6	210,000	100,000	310,000	40,000	6.

Input Data

Unit sales price = $10
Unit variable cost = $6
Total fixed cost   = $100,000

Output Data

Breakeven point in units = 25,000 units produced and sold
Breakeven point in sales = $250,000

---

located. Notice that Table 15-2 is just equation (15-2) in worksheet form. For The Pierce Grain Company total operating costs will be covered when 25,000 units are manufactured and sold. This tells us that if sales equal $250,000, the firm's EBIT will equal $0.

Unlike trial-and-error analysis, use of the contribution margin technique permits direct computation of the breakeven quantity of output. The **contribution margin** is the difference between the unit selling price and unit variable costs as follows:

Contribution Margin Analysis

Unit sales price
− Unit variable cost
= Unit contribution margin

The use of the word "contribution" in the present context means contribution to the coverage of fixed operating costs. For The Pierce Grain Company the unit contribution margin is:

Unit sales price	$10
Unit variable cost	6
Unit contribution margin	$ 4

If the annual fixed costs of $100,000 are divided by the unit contribution margin of $4, we find the breakeven quantity of output for Pierce Grain is 25,000 units. With much less effort we have arrived at the identical result found by application of the trial-and-error approach. Figure 15-6 portrays the contribution margin technique for finding the breakeven point.

Explanation of the algebraic method for finding the breakeven output level can be facilitated by adoption of some notation. Let

Q = the number of units sold,

Q_B = the breakeven level of Q,

P = the unit sales price,

F = total fixed costs anticipated over the planning period,

V = the unit variable cost.

Equation (15-2), the breakeven model, is repeated below as equation (15-2a) with the model symbols used in place of words. The breakeven model is then solved for Q, the number of units that have to be sold in order that EBIT will equal $0. We label this breakeven point quantity as Q_B.

$$(P \cdot Q) - [(V \cdot Q) + (F)] = \text{EBIT} = \$0 \qquad (15\text{-}2a)$$
$$(P \cdot Q) - (V \cdot Q) - F = \$0$$
$$Q(P - V) = F$$
$$Q_B = \frac{F}{P - V} \qquad (15\text{-}3)$$

Observe that equation (15-3) says: divide total fixed operating costs, F, by the unit contribution margin, $P - V$, and the breakeven level of output, Q_B, will be obtained. The contribution margin analysis is nothing more than equation (15-3) in different garb.

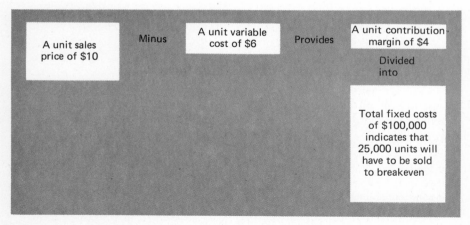

FIGURE 15-6 *Contribution Margin Approach to Breakeven Analysis*

Application of equation (15-3) permits direct calculation of Pierce Grain's breakeven point as follows:

$$Q_B = \frac{F}{P - V} = \frac{\$100{,}000}{\$10 - \$6} = 25{,}000 \text{ units}$$

In dealing with the firm that produces several products, it is convenient to compute the breakeven point in terms of sales dollars rather than units of output. Sales, in effect, become a common denominator associated with a particular product mix. Furthermore, the outside analyst may not have access to internal unit cost data. He may, however, be able to obtain annual reports for the firm. If the analyst can separate the firm's total costs as identified from its annual reports into their fixed and variable components, he can calculate a general breakeven point in sales dollars.

We will illustrate the procedure using The Pierce Grain Company's cost structure, contained in Table 15-2. Suppose that the information on line 5 of Table 15-2 is arranged in the format shown in Table 15-3. We will refer to this type of financial statement as an **analytical income statement.** This distinguishes it from audited income statements published, for example, in the annual reports of public corporations. If we are aware of the simple mathematical relationships upon which cost-volume-profit analysis is based, Table 15-3 can be employed to find the breakeven point in sales dollars for The Pierce Grain Company.

First, let us explore the logic of the process. Recall from equation (15-1) that

$$\text{sales} - (\text{total variable cost} + \text{total fixed cost}) = \text{EBIT}$$

If we let total sales $= S$, total variable cost $= VC$, and total fixed cost $= F$, the above relationship becomes

$$S - (VC + F) = \text{EBIT}$$

Since variable cost per unit of output and selling price per unit are *assumed* constant over the relevant output range in breakeven analysis, the ratio of total sales to total variable cost, VC/S, is a constant for any level of sales. This permits us to rewrite the previous expression as

Table 15-3 THE PIERCE GRAIN COMPANY:
ANALYTICAL INCOME STATEMENT

Sales	$300,000
Less: Total variable costs	180,000
Revenue before fixed costs	$120,000
Less: Total fixed costs	100,000
EBIT	$ 20,000

$$S - \left[\left(\frac{VC}{S}\right) S\right] - F = \text{EBIT}$$

and

$$S\left(1 - \frac{VC}{S}\right) - F = \text{EBIT}$$

At the breakeven point, however, EBIT = 0, and the corresponding breakeven level of sales can be represented as S*. At the breakeven level of sales we have

$$S^*\left(1 - \frac{VC}{S}\right) - F = 0$$

or

$$S^*\left(1 - \frac{VC}{S}\right) = F$$

Therefore,

$$S^* = \frac{F}{1 - \frac{VC}{S}} \tag{15-4}$$

The application of equation (15-4) to Pierce Grain's analytical income statement in Table 15-3 permits the breakeven sales level for the firm to be directly computed as follows:

$$S^* = \frac{\$100,000}{1 - \frac{\$180,000}{\$300,000}}$$

$$= \frac{\$100,000}{1 - 0.60} = \$250,000$$

Notice that this is indeed the same breakeven sales level for Pierce Grain that is indicated on line 4 of Table 15-2.

GRAPHIC REPRESENTATION, ANALYSIS OF INPUT CHANGES, AND CASH BREAKEVEN POINT

In making a presentation to management it is often more effective to display the firm's cost-volume-profit relationships in the form of a chart, rather than merely in figures and equations. Even those individuals who truly enjoy analyzing financial problems find figures and equations dry material at times. Furthermore, by quickly scanning the basic breakeven chart, the manager can approximate the EBIT amount that will prevail at different sales levels.

Such a chart has been prepared for The Pierce Grain Company. Figure 15-7 has been constructed for this firm using the input data contained in Table 15-2. Total fixed costs of $100,000 are added to the total variable costs that are associated with each production level to form the total costs line. When 25,000 units of product are manufactured and sold, the sales line and total costs line intersect. This means, of course, that the EBIT that would exist at that volume of output is zero. Beyond 25,000 units of output, notice that sales revenues exceed the total costs line. This causes a positive EBIT. This positive EBIT or profit is labeled "original EBIT" in Figure 15-7.

The unencumbered nature of the breakeven model makes it possible to quickly incorporate changes in the requisite input data and generate the revised output. Suppose that a favorable combination of events might cause Pierce Grain's fixed costs to decrease by $25,000. This would put their total fixed costs for the planning period at a level of $75,000 rather than the $100,000 originally being forecast. Total costs, being the sum of fixed and variable costs, would be lower by $25,000 at all output levels. The revised total costs line in Figure 15-7 reflects Pierce Grain's reduction in fixed costs. Under these revised conditions the new breakeven point in units would be

$$Q_B = \frac{\$75,000}{\$10 - \$6} = 18,750 \text{ units}$$

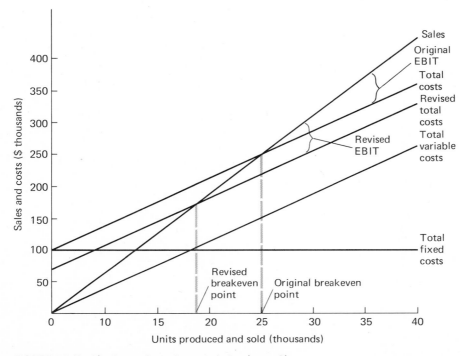

FIGURE 15-7 *The Pierce Grain Company's Breakeven Chart*

The revised breakeven point of 18,750 units is identified in Figure 15-7 along with the revised EBIT amounts that would prevail at differing output and sales amounts. Note that the chart clearly indicates that at any specific production and sales level, the revised EBIT would exceed the original EBIT. This must be the case, as the revised total costs line lies below the original total costs line over the entire relevant output range. The effect upon the breakeven point caused by other changes in (1) the cost structure or (2) the pricing policy can be analyzed in a similar fashion.

The data in Figure 15-7 can be used to demonstrate another version of basic cost-volume-profit analysis. This can be called **cash breakeven analysis.** If the company's fixed or variable cost estimates contain allowance for any noncash expenses, then the resultant breakeven point is higher on an accounting profit basis than on a cash basis. This means the firm's production and sales levels do not have to be as great to cover the cash costs of manufacturing the product.

What are these noncash expenses? The largest and most significant is depreciation expense. Another category is prepaid expenses. Insurance policies are at times paid to cover a three-year cycle. Thus, the time period for which the breakeven analysis is being performed might *not* involve an actual cash outlay for insurance coverage.

For purposes of illustration assume that noncash expenses for Pierce Grain amount to $25,000 over the planning period, and that all of these costs are of a fixed nature. We can compare the revised total costs line in Figure 15-7, which implicitly assumes a lower fixed *cash* cost line, with the sales revenue line to find the cash breakeven point. Provided that Pierce Grain can produce and sell 18,750 units over the planning horizon, revenues from sales will be equal to cash operating costs.

LIMITATIONS OF BREAKEVEN ANALYSIS

Earlier we identified some of the several applications of breakeven analysis. This technique is a useful tool in many settings. It must be emphasized, however, that breakeven analysis provides a *beneficial guide* to managerial action, not the final answer. The use of cost-volume-profit analysis has drawbacks, which should be kept in mind. These include the following:

1. The cost-volume-profit relationship is assumed to be linear. This is realistic only over narrow ranges of output.
2. The total revenue curve (sales curve) is presumed to increase linearly with the volume of output. This implies *any* quantity can be sold over the relevant output range at that *single* price. To be more realistic it is necessary in many situations to compute *several* sales curves and corresponding breakeven points at differing prices.
3. A constant production and sales mix is assumed. Should the company decide to produce more of one product and less of another, a new breakeven point would have to be found. Only if the variable cost to sales ratios were identical for products involved, would the new calculation be unnecessary.
4. The breakeven chart and the breakeven computation are static forms of

analysis. Any alteration in the firm's cost structure or price structure dictates that a new breakeven point be calculated. Breakeven analysis is more helpful, therefore, in stable industries than in dynamic ones.

OPERATING LEVERAGE

If fixed operating costs are present in the firm's cost structure, *operating leverage* results. Fixed operating costs do *not* include interest charges incurred from the firm's use of debt financing. Those costs will be incorporated into the analysis when financial leverage is discussed.

So operating leverage *arises* from the firm's use of fixed operating costs. But what is operating leverage? **Operating leverage** is the responsiveness of the firm's EBIT to fluctuations in sales. By continuing to draw upon our data for The Pierce Grain Company, we can illustrate the concept of operating leverage. Consider Table 15-4, where a possible fluctuation in the firm's sales level is being studied. It is assumed here that Pierce Grain is currently operating at an annual sales level of $300,000. This is referred to in the tabulation as the base sales level at t_0 (time period zero). The question being asked is: how will Pierce Grain's EBIT level respond to a positive 20 percent change in sales? A sales volume of $360,000, referred to as the forecast sales level at $t + 1$, reflects the 20 percent sales rise anticipated over the planning period. Assume that the planning period is one year.

Operating leverage relationships are derived within the mathematical assumptions of cost-volume-profit analysis. In the present example, this means that Pierce Grain's variable cost to sales ratio of .6 will continue to hold during time period $t + 1$, and the fixed costs will hold steady at $100,000.

Given the forecasted sales level for Pierce Grain and its cost structure, we can measure the responsiveness of EBIT to the upswing in volume. Notice in Table 15-4 that EBIT is expected to be $44,000 at the end of the planning period. The percentage change in EBIT from t_0 to $t + 1$ can be measured as follows:

$$\text{percentage change in EBIT} = \frac{\$44,000_{t+1} - \$20,000_{t_0}}{\$20,000_{t_0}}$$

$$= \frac{\$24,000}{\$20,000}$$

$$= 120 \text{ percent}$$

Table 15-4 THE CONCEPT OF OPERATING LEVERAGE: AN INCREASE IN PIERCE GRAIN COMPANY SALES

ITEM	BASE SALES LEVEL, t_0	FORECAST SALES LEVEL, $t + 1$
Sales	$300,000	$360,000
Less: Total variable costs	180,000	216,000
Revenue before fixed costs	$120,000	$144,000
Less: Total fixed costs	100,000	100,000
EBIT	$ 20,000	$ 44,000

We know that the projected fluctuation in sales amounts to 20 percent of the base period, t_0, sales level. This is verified below:

$$\text{percentage change in sales} = \frac{\$360,000_{t+1} - \$300,000_{t_0}}{\$300,000_{t_0}}$$

$$= \frac{\$60,000}{\$300,000}$$

$$= 20 \text{ percent}$$

By relating the percentage fluctuation in EBIT to the percentage fluctuation in sales, we can calculate a specific measure of operating leverage. Thus, we have

$$\begin{array}{l}\text{degree of operating}\\ \text{leverage from the} \\ \text{base sales level}\end{array} = \text{DOL}_s = \frac{\text{percentage change in EBIT}}{\text{percentage change in sales}} \qquad (15\text{-}5)$$

Applying equation (15-5) to our Pierce Grain data gives

$$\text{DOL}_{\$300,000} = \frac{120\%}{20\%} = 6 \text{ times}$$

Unless we understand what the specific measure of operating leverage tells us, the fact that we may know it is equal to six times is nothing more than sterile information. For Pierce Grain the inference is that for *any* percentage fluctuation in sales from the base level, the percentage fluctuation in EBIT will be six times as great.

If Pierce Grain, therefore, expected only a 5 percent rise in sales over the coming period, a 30 percent rise in EBIT would be anticipated as follows:

$$(\text{percentage change in sales}) \times (\text{DOL}_s) = \text{percentage change in EBIT}$$

$$(5\%) \times (6) = 30 \text{ percent}$$

We will return, now, to the postulated 20 percent change in sales. What if the direction of the fluctuation is expected to be negative rather than positive? What is in store for Pierce Grain? Unfortunately for Pierce Grain, but fortunately for the analytical process, we will see that the operating leverage measure holds in the negative direction as well as the positive. This situation is displayed in Table 15-5.

At the $240,000 sales level, which represents the 20 percent decrease from the base period, Pierce Grain's EBIT is expected to be $-4000. How sensitive is EBIT to this sales change? The magnitude of the EBIT fluctuation is calculated as

$$\text{percentage change in EBIT} = \frac{\$-4000_{t+1} - \$20,000_{t_0}}{\$20,000_{t_0}}$$

Table 15-5 THE CONCEPT OF OPERATING LEVERAGE:
A DECREASE IN PIERCE GRAIN COMPANY SALES

ITEM	BASE SALES LEVEL, t_0	FORECAST SALES LEVEL, $t + 1$
Sales	$300,000	$240,000
Less: Total variable costs	180,000	144,000
Revenue before fixed costs	$120,000	$ 96,000
Less: Total fixed costs	100,000	100,000
EBIT	$ 20,000	$ −4,000

$$= \frac{\$-24,000}{\$20,000}$$

$$= -120 \text{ percent}$$

Making use of our knowledge that the sales change was equal to -20 percent permits us to compute the specific measure of operating leverage as

$$DOL_{\$300,000} = \frac{-120\%}{-20\%} = 6 \text{ times}$$

What we have seen, then, is that the degree of operating leverage measure works in either the positive or negative direction. A negative change in production volume and sales can be magnified severalfold when the effect on EBIT is calculated.

To this point our calculations of the degree of operating leverage have required two analytical income statements: one for the base period and a second for the subsequent period that incorporates the possible sales alteration. This cumbersome process can be simplified. If unit cost data are available to the financial manager, the relationship can be expressed directly in the following manner:

$$DOL_s = \frac{Q(P - V)}{Q(P - V) - F} \tag{15-6}$$

Observe in equation (15-6) that the variables were all previously defined in our algebraic analysis of the breakeven model. Recall that Pierce sells its product at $10 per unit, the unit variable cost is $6, and total fixed costs over the planning horizon are $100,000. Still assuming that Pierce is operating at a $300,000 sales volume, which means output (Q) is 30,000 units, we can find the degree of operating leverage by application of equation (15-6):

$$DOL_{\$300,000} = \frac{30,000(\$10 - \$6)}{30,000(\$10 - \$6) - \$100,000} = \frac{\$120,000}{\$20,000} = 6 \text{ times}$$

Whereas equation (15-6) requires us to know unit cost data to carry out the computations, the next formulation we examine does not. If we have an analytical income statement for the base period, then equation (15-7) can be employed to find the firm's degree of operating leverage:

$$DOL_s = \frac{\text{revenue before fixed costs}}{\text{EBIT}} = \frac{S - VC}{S - VC - F} \qquad (15\text{-}7)$$

Use of equation (15-7) in conjunction with the base period data for Pierce Grain shown in either Table 15-4 or 15-5 gives

$$DOL_{s300,000} = \frac{\$120,000}{\$20,000} = 6 \text{ times}$$

The three versions of the operating leverage measure all produce the same result. Data availability will sometimes dictate which formulation can be applied. The crucial consideration, though, is that you grasp what the metric tells you. For Pierce Grain a 1 percent change in sales will produce a 6 percent change in EBIT.

Implications

As the firm's scale of operations moves in a favorable manner above the breakeven point, the degree of operating leverage at each subsequent (higher) sales base will decline. In short, the greater the sales level, the lower will be the degree of operating leverage. This is demonstrated in Table 15-6 for The Pierce Grain Company. At the breakeven sales level for Pierce Grain the degree of operating leverage is *undefined,* since the denominator in any of the computational formulas is zero. Notice that beyond the breakeven point of 25,000 units, the degree of operating leverage declines. It will decline at a decreasing rate and asymptotically approach a value of 1.00. As long as some fixed operating costs are present in the firm's cost structure, however, operating leverage exists, and the degree of operating leverage (DOL_s) will exceed 1.00. Operating leverage is present, then, whenever the firm faces the following situation:

$$\frac{\text{percentage change in EBIT}}{\text{percentage change in sales}} > 1.00$$

The data in Table 15-6 are presented in graphic form in Figure 15-8.

The greater the firm's degree of operating leverage, the more its profits will vary with a given percentage change in sales. Thus, operating leverage is definitely an attribute of the business risk that confronts the company. From Table 15-6 and Figure 15-8 we have seen that the degree of operating leverage falls as sales increase past the firm's breakeven point. The sheer size of the firm, therefore, affects and can lessen its business risk exposure.

An understanding of the operating leverage concept can assist the manager who is contemplating an alteration in the firm's cost structure. It

Table 15-6 THE PIERCE GRAIN COMPANY: DEGREE OF OPERATING LEVERAGE
RELATIVE TO DIFFERENT SALES BASES

UNITS PRODUCED AND SOLD	SALES DOLLARS	DOL$_s$
25,000	$ 250,000	Undefined
30,000	300,000	6.00
35,000	350,000	3.50
40,000	400,000	2.67
45,000	450,000	2.25
50,000	500,000	2.00
75,000	750,000	1.50
100,000	1,000,000	1.33

might be possible to replace part of the labor force with capital equipment (machinery). A possible result is an increase in fixed costs associated with the new machinery and a reduction in variable costs attributable to a lower

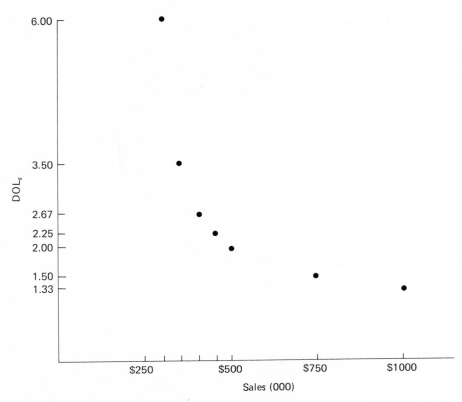

FIGURE 15-8 *The Pierce Grain Company:*
Degree of Operating Leverage Relative to Different Sales Bases

labor bill. This conceivably could raise the firm's degree of operating leverage at a specific sales base. If the prospects for future sales increases are high, then increasing the degree of operating leverage might be a prudent decision. The opposite conclusion will be reached if the firm's sales prospects are unattractive.

FINANCIAL LEVERAGE

We have defined **financial leverage** as the practice of financing a portion of the firm's assets with securities bearing a fixed rate of return in hopes of increasing the ultimate return to the common stockholders. In the present discussion we focus upon the responsiveness of the company's earnings per share to changes in its EBIT. For the time being, then, the sort of return to the common stockholder being concentrated upon is earnings per share. We are *not* saying that earnings per share is the appropriate criterion for all financing decisions. In fact, the weakness of such a contention will be examined in the next chapter. Rather, a certain type of *effect* is caused by the use of financial leverage. This effect can be clearly illustrated by concentrating upon an earnings per share criterion.

Let us assume that The Pierce Grain Company is in the process of getting started as a going concern. The firm's potential owners have calculated that $200,000 is needed to purchase the necessary assets to conduct the business. Three possible financing plans have been identified for raising the $200,000; they are presented in Table 15-7. In plan A no financial risk is assumed: the entire $200,000 is raised by selling 2000 common shares, each with a $100 par value. In plan B a moderate amount of financial risk is assumed: 25 percent of the assets are financed with a debt issue that carries an 8 percent annual interest rate. Plan C would use the most financial leverage: 40 percent of the assets would be financed with a debt issue costing 8 percent.[4]

Table 15-8 presents the impact of financial leverage on earnings per share associated with each fund-raising alternative. If EBIT should increase from $20,000 to $40,000, then earnings per share would rise by 100 percent under plan A. The same positive fluctuation in EBIT would occasion an earnings per share rise of 125 percent under plan B, and 147 percent under plan C. In plans B and C the 100 percent increase in EBIT (from $20,000 to $40,000) is magnified to a greater than 100 percent increase in earnings per share. The firm is employing financial leverage, and exposing its owners to financial risk, when the following situation exists:

$$\frac{\text{percentage change in earnings per share}}{\text{percentage change in EBIT}} > 1.00$$

By following the same general procedures that allowed us to analyze the firm's use of operating leverage, we can lay out a precise measure of finan-

[4]In actual practice moving from a 25 to a 40 percent debt ratio would probably result in a higher interest rate on the additional bonds. That effect is ignored, here, to let us concentrate on the ramifications of using different proportions of debt in the financial structure.

Table 15-7 THE PIERCE GRAIN COMPANY: POSSIBLE FINANCIAL STRUCTURES

Plan A: 0% debt

		Total debt	$ 0
		Common equity	200,000[a]
Total assets	$200,000	Total liabilities and equity	$200,000

Plan B: 25% debt at 8% interest rate

		Total debt	$ 50,000
		Common equity	150,000[b]
Total assets	$200,000	Total liabilities and equity	$200,000

Plan C: 40% debt at 8% interest rate

		Total debt	$ 80,000
		Common equity	120,000[c]
Total assets	$200,000	Total liabilities and equity	$200,000

[a]2000 common shares outstanding.
[b]1500 common shares outstanding.
[c]1200 common shares outstanding.

Table 15-8 THE PIERCE GRAIN COMPANY: ANALYSIS OF FINANCIAL LEVERAGE AT DIFFERENT EBIT LEVELS

(1)	(2)	(3) = (1) − (2)	(4) = (3) × .5	(5) = (3) − (4) NET INCOME	(6)
EBIT	INTEREST	EBT	TAXES	TO COMMON	EARNINGS PER SHARE

Plan A: 0% debt; $200,000 common equity; 2000 shares

(1)	(2)	(3)	(4)	(5)	(6)	
$ 0	$ 0	$ 0	$ 0	$ 0	$ 0	
20,000	0	20,000	10,000	10,000	5.00	} 100%
40,000	0	40,000	20,000	20,000	10.00	
60,000	0	60,000	30,000	30,000	15.00	
80,000	0	80,000	40,000	40,000	20.00	

Plan B: 25% debt; 8% interest rate; $150,000 common equity; 1500 shares

(1)	(2)	(3)	(4)	(5)	(6)	
$ 0	$4,000	$ (4,000)	$ (2,000)[a]	$ (2,000)	$ (1.33)	
20,000	4,000	16,000	8,000	8,000	5.33	} 125%
40,000	4,000	36,000	18,000	18,000	12.00	
60,000	4,000	56,000	28,000	28,000	18.67	
80,000	4,000	76,000	38,000	38,000	25.33	

Plan C: 40% debt; 8% interest rate; $120,000 common equity; 1200 shares

(1)	(2)	(3)	(4)	(5)	(6)	
$ 0	$6,400	$ (6,400)	$ (3,200)[a]	$ (3,200)	$ (2.67)	
20,000	6,400	13,600	6,800	6,800	5.67	} 147%
40,000	6,400	33,600	16,800	16,800	14.00	
60,000	6,400	53,600	26,800	26,800	22.33	
80,000	6,400	73,600	36,800	36,800	30.67	

[a]The negative tax bill recognizes the credit arising from the carryback and carryforward provision of the tax code. See Chapter 2.

cial leverage. Such a measure deals with the sensitivity of earnings per share to EBIT fluctuations. The relationship can be expressed as

$$\begin{array}{l}\text{degree of financial}\\ \text{leverage from the}\\ \text{base EBIT level}\end{array} = \text{DFL}_{EBIT} = \frac{\text{percentage change in}}{\text{percentage change in EBIT}} \quad (15\text{-}8)$$

Use of equation (15-8) with each of the financing choices outlined for Pierce Grain is shown below. The base EBIT level is $20,000 in each case.

$$\text{Plan A:} \quad \text{DFL}_{\$20,000} = \frac{100\%}{100\%} = 1.00 \text{ time}$$

$$\text{Plan B:} \quad \text{DFL}_{\$20,000} = \frac{125\%}{100\%} = 1.25 \text{ times}$$

$$\text{Plan C:} \quad \text{DFL}_{\$20,000} = \frac{147\%}{100\%} = 1.47 \text{ times}$$

Like operating leverage, the degree of financial leverage concept performs in the negative direction as well as the positive. Should EBIT fall by 10 percent, The Pierce Grain Company would suffer a 12.5 percent decline in earnings per share under plan B. If plan C were chosen to raise the necessary financial capital, the decline in earnings would be 14.7 percent. Observe that the greater the degree of financial leverage, the greater the fluctuations (positive or negative) in earnings per share. The common stockholder is required to endure greater variations in returns when the firm's management chooses to use more financial leverage rather than less. The degree of financial leverage measure allows the variation to be quantified.

Rather than taking the time to compute percentage changes in EBIT and earnings per share, the degree of financial leverage can be found directly as follows:

$$\text{DFL}_{EBIT} = \frac{\text{EBIT}}{\text{EBIT} - I} \quad (15\text{-}9)$$

In equation (15-9) the variable, I, represents the total interest expense incurred on *all* of the firm's contractual debt obligations. If six bonds are outstanding, I is the sum of the interest expense on all six bonds. If the firm has preferred stock in its financial structure, the dividend on such issues must be inflated to a before-tax basis and included in the computation of I.[5] In this latter instance, I is in reality the sum of all fixed financing costs.

---

[5]Suppose (1) preferred dividends of $4000 are paid annually by the firm, and (2) it faces a 40 percent marginal tax rate. How much must the firm earn *before taxes* to make the $4000 payment out of after-tax earnings? Since preferred dividends are not tax-deductible to the paying company, we have $4000/(1 − 0.40) = $6666.67.

Equation (15-9) has been applied to each of Pierce Grain's financing plans (Table 15-8) at a base EBIT level of $20,000. The results are as follows:

$$\text{Plan A:} \quad \text{DFL}_{\$20,000} = \frac{\$20,000}{\$20,000 - 0} = 1.00 \text{ time}$$

$$\text{Plan B:} \quad \text{DFL}_{\$20,000} = \frac{\$20,000}{\$20,000 - \$4000} = 1.25 \text{ times}$$

$$\text{Plan C:} \quad \text{DFL}_{\$20,000} = \frac{\$20,000}{\$20,000 - \$6400} = 1.47 \text{ times}$$

As you probably suspected, the measures of financial leverage shown above are identical to those obtained by use of equation (15-8). This will always be the case.

COMBINING OPERATING AND FINANCIAL LEVERAGE

Changes in sales revenues cause greater changes in EBIT. Additionally, changes in EBIT translate into larger variations in both earnings per share (EPS) and total earnings available to the common shareholders (EAC), if the firm chooses to use financial leverage. It should be no surprise, then, to find out that combining operating and financial leverage causes rather large variations in earnings per share. This entire process is visually displayed in Figure 15-9.

Since the risk associated with possible earnings per share is affected by the use of combined or total leverage, it is useful to quantify the effect. For an illustration, we refer once more to The Pierce Grain Company. The cost structure identified for Pierce Grain in our discussion of breakeven analysis still holds. Furthermore, assume that plan B, which carried a 25 percent debt ratio, was chosen to finance the company's assets. Turn your attention to Table 15-9.

In Table 15-9 an increase in output for Pierce Grain from 30,000 to 36,000 units is analyzed. This represents a 20 percent rise in sales revenues. From both our earlier discussion of operating leverage and the data in Table 15-9 we can see that this 20 percent increase in sales is magnified into a 120 percent rise in EBIT. From this base sales level of $300,000 the degree of operating leverage is six times.

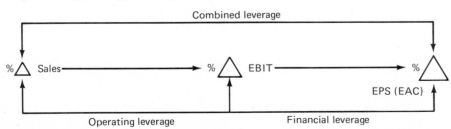

FIGURE 15-9 *Leverage and Earnings Fluctuations*

Table 15-9 THE PIERCE GRAIN COMPANY: COMBINED LEVERAGE ANALYSIS

ITEM	BASE SALES LEVEL, t_0	FORECAST SALES LEVEL, $t + 1$	SELECTED PERCENTAGE CHANGES
Sales	$300,000	$360,000	+20
Less: Total variable costs	180,000	216,000	
Revenue before fixed costs	$120,000	$144,000	
Less: Total fixed costs	100,000	100,000	
EBIT	$ 20,000	$ 44,000	+120
Less: Interest expense	4,000	4,000	
Earnings before taxes (EBT)	$ 16,000	$ 40,000	
Less: Taxes at 50%	8,000	20,000	
Net income	$ 8,000	$ 20,000	+150
Less: Preferred dividends	0	0	
Earnings available to common	$ 8,000	$ 20,000	+150
Number of common shares	1,500	1,500	
Earnings per share (EPS)	$ 5.33	$ 13.33	+150

$$\text{Degree of operating leverage} = \text{DOL}_{\$300,000} = \frac{120\%}{20\%} = 6 \text{ times}$$

$$\text{Degree of financial leverage} = \text{DFL}_{\$20,000} = \frac{150\%}{120\%} = 1.25 \text{ times}$$

$$\text{Degree of combined leverage} = \text{DCL}_{\$300,000} = \frac{150\%}{20\%} = 7.50 \text{ times}$$

The 120 percent rise in EBIT induces a change in earnings per share and earnings available to the common shareholders of 150 percent. The degree of financial leverage is, therefore, 1.25 times.

The upshot of the analysis is that the 20 percent rise in sales has been magnified to 150 percent, as reflected by the percentage change in earnings per share. The formal measure of combined leverage can be expressed as

$$\begin{pmatrix} \text{degree of combined} \\ \text{leverage from the} \\ \text{base sales level} \end{pmatrix} = \text{DCL}_s = \left(\frac{\text{percentage change in}}{\text{percentage change in sales}} \right) \quad (15\text{-}10)$$

This equation was used in the bottom portion of Table 15-9 to determine that the degree of combined leverage from the base sales level of $300,000 is 7.50 times. Pierce Grain's use of both operating and financial leverage will cause any percentage change in sales (from the specific base level) to be magnified by a factor of 7.50 when the effect on earnings per share is computed. A 1 percent change in sales, for example, will result in a 7.50 percent change in earnings per share.

Notice that the degree of combined leverage is actually the *product* (not the simple sum) of the two independent leverage measures. Thus, we have

or

$$(DOL_s) \times (DFL_{EBIT}) = DCL_s \qquad (15\text{-}11)$$

$$(6) \times (1.25) = 7.50 \text{ times}$$

It is possible to ascertain the degree of combined leverage in a direct fashion, without determining any percentage fluctuations or the separate leverage values. We need only substitute the appropriate values into equation (15-12):[6]

$$DCL_s = \frac{Q(P - V)}{Q(P - V) - F - I} \qquad (15\text{-}12)$$

The variable definitions in equation (15-12) are the same ones that have been employed throughout this chapter. Use of equation (15-12) with the information in Table 15-9 gives

$$DCL_{\$300,000} = \frac{30,000(\$10 - \$6)}{30,000(\$10 - \$6) - \$100,000 - \$4000}$$

$$= \frac{\$120,000}{\$16,000}$$

$$= 7.5 \text{ times}$$

Implications

The total risk exposure that the firm assumes can be managed by combining operating and financial leverage in different degrees. Knowledge of the various leverage measures we have examined aids the financial officer in his determination of the proper level of overall risk that should be accepted. If a high degree of business risk is inherent to the specific line of commercial activity, then a low posture with regard to financial risk would minimize *additional* earnings fluctuations stemming from sales changes. On the other hand, the firm that by its very nature incurs a low level of fixed operating costs might choose to use a high degree of financial leverage in hopes of increasing earnings per share and the rate of return on the common equity investment.

SUMMARY

In this chapter we began to study the process of arriving at an appropriate financial structure for the firm. Tools that can assist the financial manager in this task were examined. We were mainly concerned with as-

---

[6]As was the case with the degree of financial leverage metric, the variable, I, in the combined leverage measure must include the before-tax equivalent of any preferred dividend payments when preferred stock is in the financial structure.

sessing the variability in the firm's residual earnings stream (either earnings per share or earnings available to the common shareholders) induced by the use of operating and financial leverage. This assessment built upon the tenets of breakeven analysis.

Breakeven analysis permits the financial manager to determine the quantity of output or the level of sales that will result in an EBIT level of zero. The effect of price changes, cost structure changes or volume changes upon profits (EBIT) can be studied. To make the technique operational it is necessary that the firm's costs be classified as fixed or variable. We recognized that not all costs fit neatly into one of these two categories. Over short planning horizons, though, the preponderance of costs can be assigned to either the fixed or variable classification. Once the cost structure has been identified, the breakeven point can be found by use of (1) trial-and-error analysis, (2) contribution margin analysis, or (3) algebraic analysis. If the major limitations of this breakeven analysis are recognized, it can be a useful financial planning tool.

Breakeven Analysis

Operating leverage is the responsiveness of the firm's EBIT to changes in sales revenues. It arises from the firm's use of fixed operating costs. When fixed operating costs are present in the company's cost structure, changes in sales are magnified into even greater changes in EBIT. The firm's degree of operating leverage from a base sales level is the percentage change in EBIT divided by the percentage change in sales. All types of leverage are two-edged swords. When sales decrease by some percentage, the negative impact upon EBIT will be even larger.

Operating Leverage

A firm employs financial leverage when it finances a portion of its assets with securities bearing a fixed rate of return. The presence of debt and/or preferred stock in the company's financial structure means that it is using financial leverage. When financial leverage is used, changes in EBIT translate into larger changes in earnings per share. The concept of the degree of financial leverage dwells on the sensitivity of earnings per share to changes in EBIT. The degree of financial leverage from a base EBIT level is defined as the percentage change in earnings per share divided by the percentage change in EBIT. All other things equal, the more fixed-charge securities the firm employs in its financial structure, the greater its degree of financial leverage. Clearly, EBIT can rise or fall. If it falls, and financial leverage is used, the firm's shareholders endure negative changes in earnings per share that are larger than the relative decline in EBIT. Again, leverage is a two-edged sword.

Financial Leverage

Firms use operating and financial leverage in various degrees. The joint use of operating and financial leverage can be measured by computing the degree of combined leverage, defined as the percentage change in earnings per share divided by the percentage change in sales. This

Combining Operating and Financial Leverage

metric allows the financial manager to ascertain the effect on total leverage caused by adding financial leverage on top of operating leverage. Effects can be dramatic, because the degree of combined leverage is the product of the degrees of operating and financial leverage.

15-1. Distinguish between business risk and financial risk. What gives rise to, or causes, each type of risk?

15-2. Define the term *financial leverage*. Does the firm use financial leverage if preferred stock is present in the capital structure?

15-3. Define the term *operating leverage*. What type of effect occurs when the firm uses operating leverage?

15-4. What is the difference between the (ordinary) breakeven point and the cash breakeven point? Which will be the greater?

15-5. A manager in your firm decides to employ breakeven analysis. Of what shortcomings should he be aware?

15-6. What is meant by total risk exposure? How may a firm move to reduce its total risk exposure?

15-7. If a firm has a degree of combined leverage of 3.0 times, what does a negative sales fluctuation of 15 percent portend for the earnings available to the firm's common-stock investors?

15-8. Breakeven analysis assumes linear revenue and cost functions. In reality these linear functions over large output and sales levels are highly improbable. Why?

15-1. Wilbur's Quik-Stop Party Store expects to earn $3600 next year after taxes. Sales will be $100,000. The store is located near the fraternity-row district of Cambridge Springs State University and sells only kegs of beer for $20 a keg. The variable cost per keg is $15. The store experiences a 40 percent tax rate.

   (a) What are the Party Store's fixed costs expected to be next year?

   (b) Calculate the firm's breakeven point both in units and dollars.

15-2. Rodney's Tool and Die Company will produce 100,000 units next year. All of this production will be sold as finished goods. Fixed costs will total $275,000. Variable costs for this firm are relatively predictable at 70 percent of sales.

   (a) If Rodney's Tool and Die wants to achieve an earnings before interest and taxes level of $160,000 next year, at what price per unit must it sell its product?

   (b) Based upon your answer to part (a), set up an analytical income statement that will verify your solution.

15-3. A recent business graduate of Midwestern State University is planning to open a new wholesaling operation. His target operating profit margin is 28 percent. His unit contribution margin will be 50 percent of sales. Average annual sales are forecast to be $3,750,000.

(a) How large can fixed costs be for the wholesaling operation and still allow the 28 percent operating profit margin to be achieved?

(b) What is the breakeven point in dollars for the firm?

15-4. The Portland Recreation Company manufactures a full line of lawn furniture. The average selling price of a finished unit is $25. The associated variable cost is $15 per unit. Fixed costs for Portland average $50,000 per year.

(a) What is the breakeven point in units for the company?

(b) What is the dollar sales volume the firm must achieve in order to reach the breakeven point?

(c) What would be the company's profit or loss at the following units of production sold: 4000 units; 6000 units; 8000 units?

(d) Find the degree of operating leverage for the production and sales levels given in part (c) above.

(e) What is the effect on the degree of operating leverage as sales rise above the breakeven point?

15-5. Detroit Heat Treating projects that next year its fixed costs will total $120,000. Its only product sells for $12 per unit, of which $7 is a variable cost. The management of Detroit is considering the purchase of a new machine that will lower the variable cost per unit to $5. The new machine, however, will add to fixed costs through an increase in depreciation expense. How large can the *addition* to fixed costs be in order to keep the firm's breakeven point in units produced and sold unchanged?

15-6. The management of Detroit Heat Treating did not purchase the new piece of equipment (see problem 15-5 above). Using the existing cost structure, calculate the degree of operating leverage at 30,000 units of output. Comment upon the meaning of your answer.

15-7. An analytical income statement for Detroit Heat Treating is shown below. It is based upon an output (sales) level of 40,000 units. You may refer to the original cost structure data in problem 15-5.

Sales	$480,000
Variable costs	280,000
Revenue before fixed costs	$200,000
Fixed costs	120,000
EBIT	$ 80,000
Interest expense	30,000
Earnings before taxes	$ 50,000
Taxes	25,000
Net income	$ 25,000

(a) Calculate the degree of operating leverage at this output level.

(b) Calculate the degree of financial leverage at this level of EBIT.

(c) Determine the combined leverage effect at this output level.

15-8. You are employed as a financial analyst for a single-product manufacturing firm. Your supervisor has made the following cost structure information available to you, all of which pertains to an output level of 1,600,000 units.

Return on operating assets = 15 percent
Operating asset turnover = 5 times
Operating assets = $3 million
Degree of operating leverage = 8 times

Your task is to find the breakeven point in units of output for the firm.

15-9. You are supplied with the following analytical income statement for your firm. It reflects last year's operations.

Sales	$16,000,000
Variable costs	8,000,000
Revenue before fixed costs	$ 8,000,000
Fixed costs	4,000,000
EBIT	$ 4,000,000
Interest expense	1,500,000
Earnings before taxes	$ 2,500,000
Taxes	1,250,000
Net income	$ 1,250,000

(a) At this level of output, what is the degree of operating leverage?
(b) What is the degree of financial leverage?
(c) What is the degree of combined leverage?
(d) If sales should increase by 20 percent, by what percent would earnings before taxes (and net income) increase?
(e) What is your firm's breakeven point in sales dollars?

15-10. Toledo Components produces four lines of auto accessories for the major Detroit automobile manufacturers. The lines are known by the code letters A, B, C, and D. The current sales mix for Toledo and the contribution margin ratio (unit contribution margin divided by unit sales price) for these product lines are given below:

PRODUCT LINE	PERCENT OF TOTAL SALES	CONTRIBUTION MARGIN RATIO
A	$33\frac{1}{3}$	40%
B	$41\frac{2}{3}$	32%
C	$16\frac{2}{3}$	20%
D	$8\frac{1}{3}$	60%

Total sales for next year are forecast to be $120,000. Total fixed costs will be $29,400.

(a) Prepare a table showing (1) sales, (2) total variable costs, and (3) the total contribution margin associated with each product line.
(b) What is the aggregate contribution margin ratio indicative of this sales mix?
(c) At this sales mix, what is the breakeven point in dollars?

15-11. Because of production constraints Toledo Components (see problem 15-10, above) may have to adhere to a different sales mix for next year. The alternative plan is outlined below.

PRODUCT LINE	PERCENT OF TOTAL SALES
A	25
B	$36\frac{2}{3}$
C	$33\frac{1}{3}$
D	5

(a) Assuming all other facts in problem 15-10 remain the same, what effect will this different sales mix have on Toledo's breakeven point in dollars?

(b) Which sales mix will Toledo's management prefer?

SELECTED REFERENCES

GHANDI, J. K. S., "On the Measurement of Leverage," *Journal of Finance*, 21 (December 1966), 715–26.

HASLEM, JOHN A., "Leverage Effects on Corporate Earnings," *Arizona Business Review*, 19 (March 1970), 7–11.

HELFERT, ERICH A., *Techniques of Financial Analysis*, 4th ed., chap. 6. Homewood, Ill: Richard D. Irwin, Inc., 1977.

HUNT, PEARSON, "A Proposal for Precise Definitions of Trading on the Equity and Leverage," *Journal of Finance*, 16 (September 1961), 377–86.

JAEDICKE, ROBERT K., and ALEXANDER A. ROBICHEK, "Cost-Volume-Profit Analysis Under Conditions of Uncertainty," *Accounting Review*, 39 (October 1964), 917–26.

LEV, BARUCH, "On the Association Between Operating Leverage and Risk," *Journal of Financial and Quantitative Analysis*, 9 (September 1974), 627–42.

PERCIVAL, JOHN R., "Operating Leverage and Risk," *Journal of Business Research*, 2 (April 1974), 223–27.

REINHARDT, U. E., "Break Even Analysis for Lockheed's Tri Star: An Application of Financial Theory," *Journal of Finance*, 28 (September 1973), 821–38.

SHALIT, SOL S., "On the Mathematics of Financial Leverage," *Financial Management*, 4 (Spring 1975), 57–66.

SULLIVAN, TIMOTHY G., "Market Power, Profitability and Financial Leverage," 29 (December 1974), 1407–14.

VISCIONE, JERRY A., *Financial Analysis: Principles and Procedures*, chap. 4. Boston: Houghton Mifflin Company, 1977.

Planning the Firm's Financing Mix

In this chapter we direct our attention to the determination of an appropriate financing mix for the firm. It will facilitate the discussion to distinguish between financial structure and capital structure. **Financial structure** is the mix of all items that appear on the right-hand side of the company's balance sheet. **Capital structure** is the mix of the *long-term* sources of funds used by the firm. In equation form, the relationship between financial and capital structure can be expressed as

$$\text{(financial structure)} - \text{(current liabilities)} = \text{capital structure} \qquad (16\text{-}1)$$

Prudent **financial-structure design** requires answers to the following two questions:

1. What should be the maturity composition of the firm's sources of funds?
2. In what proportions relative to the total should the various forms of *permanent* financing be utilized?

The first of these questions concerns the division of total funds sources into short-term and long-term components. The major influence on the maturity structure of the financing plan is the nature of the assets owned by the

firm. A company heavily committed to real capital investment, represented
primarily by fixed assets on its balance sheet, *should* finance those assets with
permanent (long-term) types of financial capital. Furthermore, the permanent portion of the firm's investment in current assets should likewise be
financed with permanent capital. Alternatively, assets held on a temporary
basis are to be financed with temporary funds sources. The present discussion assumes that the bulk of the company's current liabilities are financed
with temporary capital.

 If this elaboration seems familiar to you—it should. It is a review of
what was called the *hedging concept* in both Chapters 6 and 10. Accordingly,
our central focus in this chapter is upon the second of the two questions
noted above—what is usually called capital-structure management.

The *objective* of capital-structure management is to mix the permanent
sources of funds used by the firm in a manner that will maximize the
company's common stock price. Alternatively, this objective may be viewed
as a search for the funds mix that will minimize the firm's composite cost of
capital. We can call this proper mix of funds sources the **optimal capital
structure.**

Table 16-1 looks at Equation (16-1) in terms of a simplified balance
sheet format. It helps us visualize the overriding problem of capital-
structure management. The sources of funds that give rise to financing
fixed costs (long-term debt and preferred equity) must be combined with
common equity in the proportions most suitable to the investing marketplace. If that proper mix can be found, then holding all other factors
constant, the firm's common stock price will be maximized.

While Equation (16-1) quite accurately indicates that the corporate
capital structure may be viewed as an absolute dollar *amount*, the *real*
capital-structure problem is one of balancing the array of funds sources in a
proper manner. Thus, our use of the term capital structure emphasizes this
latter problem of relative magnitude, or proportions.

The rest of this chapter will cover three main areas. First, we discuss
the theory of capital structure in order to provide a perspective for the
subsequent material. Second, we examine the basic tools of capital-

Table 16-1 BALANCE SHEET

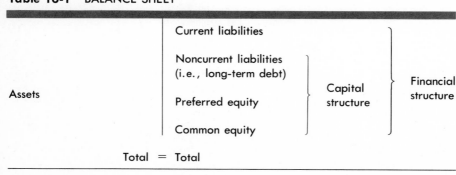

structure management. Third, we conclude with a few comments on actual capital-structure management and a summary.

An enduring controversy within the arena of financial theory concerns the effect of financial leverage on the overall cost of capital to the enterprise. The heart of the argument may be stated in the form of a question:

> Can the firm affect its overall cost of funds, either favorably or unfavorably, by varying the mixture of financing sources used?

This controversy has taken many elegant forms in the finance literature. Most of these presentations appeal to academics as opposed to practitioners of the financial management art. In the present discussion we will purposely pursue a nonmathematical approach to obtain a basic understanding of the underpinnings of this **cost of capital–capital structure argument.** By so doing, we can emphasize the ingredients of capital-structure theory that have practical implications for business financial management.

The Importance of Capital Structure

It makes economic sense for the firm to strive to minimize the cost of using financial capital just as it strives to minimize any cost of doing business, such as labor or material expenses. Both capital costs and other costs, such as manufacturing costs, share a common characteristic in that they potentially reduce the size of the cash dividend that could be paid to the firm's common stockholders.

We saw in Chapters 13 and 14 that the ultimate value of a share of common stock depends in part on the amount of the returns that investors expect to receive from holding the stock. Cash dividends comprise all (in the case of an infinite holding period) or part (in the case of a holding period less than infinity) of these expected returns. Now, hold constant all factors that could affect share price except capital costs. If these capital costs could be kept at a minimum, the dividend stream flowing to the common stockholders would be maximized. This, in turn, would maximize the firm's common stock price.

If the firm's cost of capital can be affected by its capital structure, then capital-structure management is clearly an important subset of business financial management. The extent of this importance comprises the capital-structure controversy.

The Analytical Setting

The essentials of the capital-structure controversy are best highlighted within a framework that economists would call a "partial equilibrium analysis." In a partial equilibrium analysis changes that *do* occur in a number of factors and have an impact upon a certain key item are *ignored* in order to study the effect of changes in a main factor upon that same item of interest. Here, two items are simultaneously of interest: (1) K_0, the firm's composite cost of capital and (2) P_0, the market price of the firm's common stock. The firm's use of financial leverage is the main factor that is allowed to vary in the analysis. This means that obviously important financial decisions, such as investing policy and dividend policy, are held constant throughout this discussion. So, we are concerned with the effect of changes in the financing mix on share price and capital costs.

Our analysis will be facilitated if we adopt a *simplified* version of the basic dividend valuation model presented as Equation (13-12) in our earlier study of valuation principles and as Equation (14-8) in our assessment of the cost of capital. That model is shown below as Equation (16-2).

$$P_0 = \sum_{t=1}^{\infty} \frac{D_t}{(1 + K_c)^t} \tag{16-2}$$

where P_0 = the current price of the firm's common stock,

$\quad D_t$ = the cash dividend per share expected by investors during period t,

$\quad K_c$ = the cost of common equity capital.

We can strip away some needless complications by making the following assumptions concerning the valuation process implicit in Equation (16-2).

1. Cash dividends paid will not change over the infinite holding period. Thus, $D_1 = D_2 = D_3 = \cdots = D_\infty$. There is no expected growth by investors in the dividend stream.

2. The firm retains none of its current earnings. This means that *all* of each period's per-share earnings are paid to the stockholders in the form of cash dividends. The firm's dividend payout ratio is 100 percent. Cash dividends per share in Equation (16-2), then, also equal earnings per share for the same time period.

Under these assumptions the cash dividend flowing to investors can be viewed as a level payment over an infinite holding period. The payment stream is perpetual, and according to the mathematics of perpetuities, Equation (16-2) reduces to Equation (16-3) below, where E_t represents earnings per share during time period t:

$$P_0 = \frac{D_t}{K_c} = \frac{E_t}{K_c} \tag{16-3}$$

In addition to the suppositions noted above, the analytical setting for the discussion of capital-structure theory includes the following assumptions:

1. Initially, assume that corporate income is not subject to any taxation. The major implication of removing this assumption is discussed later.

2. Capital structures consist of only stocks and bonds. Furthermore, the degree of financial leverage used by the firm is altered by the issuance of common stock with the proceeds used to retire existing debt, or the issuance of debt with the proceeds used to repurchase stock. This permits leverage use to vary but maintains constancy of the total book value of the firm's capital structure.

3. The expected values of all investors' forecasts of the future levels of net operating income (EBIT) for each firm are identical. Say that you forecast the average level of EBIT to be achieved by General Motors over a very long period of time ($n \to \infty$). Your forecast will be the same as our forecast, and they both will be equal to the forecasts of all other investors interested in General Motors common stock. Additionally, we do not expect General Motors' EBIT to grow over time. Each year's forecast is the same as any other year's. This is consistent with our assumption underlying Equation (16-3), where the firm's dividend stream is not expected to grow.

4. Securities are traded in perfect or efficient financial markets. This means that transaction costs and legal restrictions do not impede any investor's incentive to execute portfolio changes that he expects will increase his wealth. Information is freely available. Moreover, corporations and individuals that are equal credit risks can borrow funds at the same rates of interest.

This completes our construction of the analytical setting. We can now discuss three differing views on the relationship between financial leverage use and common stock value.

Extreme Position 1: The Independence Hypothesis (NOI Theory)[1]

The crux of this position is that the firm's composite cost of capital, K_0, and common stock price, P_0, are both *independent* of the degree to which the company chooses to use financial leverage. In other words, no matter how *modest* or *excessive* the firm's use of debt financing, its common stock price will not be affected by such capital-structure management. Let's illustrate the mechanics of this point of view.

Suppose that Rix Camper Manufacturing Company has the following financial characteristics:

Shares of common stock outstanding = 2,000,000 shares

Common stock price, P_0 = \$10 per share

Expected level of net operating income (EBIT) = \$2,000,000

Dividend payout ratio = 100 percent

Currently the firm uses no financial leverage; the capital structure, then, consists entirely of common equity. Earnings per share and dividends per share equal \$1 each. When the capital structure is all common equity, the cost of common equity, K_c, and the weighted cost of capital, K_0, are

---

[1]The net-operating-income and net-income-capitalization methods, which are referred to here as "extreme positions 1 and 2," were first presented in comprehensible form by Durand. See David Durand, "Costs of Debt and Equity Funds for Business: Trends and Problems of Measurement," *Conference on Research in Business Finance* (New York: National Bureau of Economic Research, 1952), reprinted in *The Management of Corporate Capital*, Ezra Solomon, ed. (New York: Free Press, 1959), pp. 91–116. The leading proponents of the independence hypothesis in its various forms are Professors Modigliani and Miller. See Franco Modigliani and Merton H. Miller, "The Cost of Capital, Corporation Finance and the Theory of Investment," *American Economic Review*, 48 (June 1958), 261–97; Franco Modigliani and Merton H. Miller, "Corporate Income Taxes and the Cost of Capital: A Correction," *American Economic Review*, 53 (June 1963), 433–43; and Merton H. Miller, "Debt and Taxes," *The Journal of Finance*, 32 (May 1977), 261–75.

equal. If equation (16-3) is restated in terms of the cost of common equity, we have for Rix Camper

$$K_c = \frac{D_t}{P_0} = \frac{\$1}{\$10} = 10 \text{ percent}$$

Now, the management of Rix Camper decides to use some debt capital in its financing mix. The firm sells $8 million worth of long-term debt at an interest rate of 6 percent. With no taxation of corporate income this 6 percent interest rate is the cost of debt capital, K_d. The firm uses the proceeds from the sale of the bonds to repurchase 40 percent of its outstanding common shares. After the capital-structure change has been accomplished, Rix Camper Manufacturing Company has the financial characteristics displayed in Table 16-2.

Based on the data above we notice that the recapitalization (capital-structure change) of Rix Camper will result in a dividend paid to owners that is 26.7 percent higher than it was when the firm used no debt in its capital structure. Will this higher dividend result in a lower composite cost of capital to Rix and a higher common stock price? According to the principles of the independence hypothesis, the answer is "No."

The independence hypothesis suggests that the total market value of the firm's outstanding securities is *unaffected* by the manner in which the right-hand side of the balance sheet is arranged. That is, the sum of the market value of outstanding debt plus the sum of the market value of outstanding common equity will always be the *same* regardless of how much or little debt is actually used by the company. If capital structure has no impact on the total market value of the company, then that value is arrived at by the marketplace's capitalizing (discounting) the firm's expected net operating income stream. Therefore, the independence hypothesis rests

Table 16-2 RIX CAMPER COMPANY: FINANCIAL DATA REFLECTING THE CAPITAL-STRUCTURE ADJUSTMENT

Capital-Structure Information
Shares of common stock outstanding = 1,200,000
Bonds at 6 percent = $8,000,000

Earnings Information

Expected level of net operating income (EBIT) =	$2,000,000
Less: Interest expense	480,000
Earnings available to common stockholders	$1,520,000
Earnings per share (E_t)	$1.267
Dividends per share (D_t)	$1.267
Percentage change in both earnings per share and dividends per share relative to the unlevered capital structure	26.7 percent

upon what is called the **net-operating-income (NOI) approach to valuation.**

The format is a very simple one, and the market value of the firm's common stock turns out to be a residual of the valuation process. Recall that before Rix Camper's recapitalization, the total market value of the firm was $20 million (2,000,000 common shares times $10 per share). The firm's cost of common equity, K_c, and its weighted cost of capital, K_0, were each equal to 10 percent. The composite discount rate, K_0, is used to arrive at the market value of the firm's securities. After the recapitalization, we have for Rix Camper

Expected level of net operating income	$2,000,000
Capitalized at K_0 = 10 percent	
= Market value of debt and equity	$20,000,000
− Market value of the new debt	8,000,000
= Market value of the common stock	$12,000,000

Under this valuation format, what is the market price of each share of common stock? Since we know that 1,200,000 shares of stock are outstanding after the capital-structure change, the market price per share is $10 ($12,000,000/1,200,000). This is exactly the market value per share, P_0, that existed *before* the capital-structure change was effected.

Now, if the firm is using some debt that has an *explicit cost* of 6 percent, K_d, and the weighted (composite) cost of capital, K_0, is still 10 percent, then it stands to reason that the cost of common equity, K_c, has risen above its previous level of 10 percent. What will the cost of common equity be in this situation? As we did previously, we can take Equation (16-3) and restate it in terms of K_c, the cost of common equity. After the recapitalization, the cost of common equity for Rix Camper is shown to *rise* to 12.67 percent:

$$K_c = \frac{D_t}{P_0} = \frac{\$1.267}{\$10} = 12.67 \text{ percent}$$

The cost of common equity for Rix Camper is 26.7 percent higher than it was before the capital-structure shift. Notice in Table 16-2 that this is *exactly* equal to the percentage increase in earnings and dividends per share that accompanies the same capital-structure adjustment. This highlights a fundamental relationship that is an integral part of the independence hypothesis. It concerns the perceived behavior in the firm's cost of common equity as expected dividends (earnings) increase relative to a financing mix change:

$$\text{percentage change in } K_c = \text{percentage change in } D_t$$

In this framework the use of a greater degree of financial leverage may result in greater earnings and dividends, but the firm's cost of common equity will rise at precisely the same rate as the earnings and dividends do.

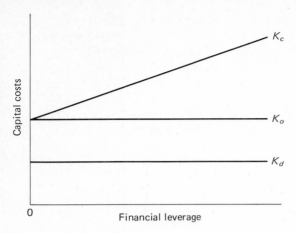

FIGURE 16-1 *Capital Costs and Financial Leverage: No Taxes—The Independence Hypothesis (NOI Theory)*

Thus, the inevitable tradeoff between the higher expected return in dividends and earnings (D_t and E_t) and increased risk that accompanies the use of debt financing manifests itself in a linear relationship between the cost of common equity (K_c) and financial leverage use. This view of the relationship between the firm's cost of funds and its financing mix is shown graphically in Figure 16-1. Figure 16-2 relates the firm's stock price to its financing mix under the same set of assumptions.

In Figure 16-1 the firm's overall cost of capital, K_0, is shown to be unaffected by an increased use of financial leverage. If more debt is used in the capital structure, the cost of common equity will rise at the same rate additional earnings are generated. This will keep the composite cost of capital to the corporation unchanged. Figure 16-2 shows that since the cost of capital will not change with leverage use, neither will the firm's stock price.

Debt financing, then, has two costs—its **explicit cost of capital, K_d,** calculated according to the formats outlined in Chapter 14, and an implicit cost. The **implicit cost of debt** is the change in the cost of common equity brought on by using financial leverage (additional debt). The real cost of debt is the sum of these explicit and implicit costs. In general, the real cost

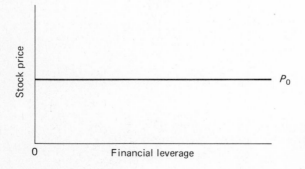

FIGURE 16-2 *Stock Price and Financial Leverage: No Taxes—The Independence Hypothesis (NOI Theory)*

450

of *any* source of capital is its explicit cost plus the change that it induces in the cost of any other source of funds.

Followers of the independence hypothesis argue that the use of financial leverage brings about a change in the cost of common equity large enough to offset the benefits of higher dividends to investors. Debt financing is not as cheap as it first appears to be. This will keep the composite cost of funds constant. The implication for management is that one capital structure is as good as any other. Financial officers should not waste much time in searching for an optimal capital structure. One capital structure, after all, is as beneficial as any other, because they all result in the same weighted cost of capital.

This position is at the opposite pole from the independence hypothesis. The dependence hypothesis suggests that both the weighted cost of capital, K_0, and common stock price, P_0, are *affected* by the firm's use of financial leverage. No matter how modest or excessive the firm's use of debt financing, both its cost of debt capital, K_d, and cost of equity capital, K_c, will not be affected by capital-structure management. Since the cost of debt is less than the cost of equity, greater financial leverage use will lower the firm's composite cost of capital indefinitely. Greater use of debt financing will, thereby, have a favorable effect on the company's common stock price. By returning to the Rix Camper situation, we can illustrate this point of view.

Extreme Position 2: The Dependence Hypothesis (NI Theory)

The same capital-structure shift is being evaluated. That is, management will market $8 million of new debt at a 6 percent interest rate and use the proceeds to purchase its own common shares. Under this approach the market is assumed to capitalize (discount) the expected earnings available to the common stockholders in order to arrive at the aggregate market value of the common stock. The market value of the firm's common equity is *not* a residual of the valuation process. After the recapitalization, the firm's cost of common equity, K_c, will still be equal to 10 percent. Thus, a 10 percent cost of common equity is applied in the following format:

Expected level of net operating income	$2,000,000
− Interest expense	480,000
= Earnings available to common stockholders	$1,520,000
capitalized at K_c = 10 percent	
= Market value of the common stock	$15,200,000
+ Market value of the new debt	8,000,000
= Market value of debt and equity	$23,200,000

When we assume that the firm's capital structure consists only of debt and common equity, earnings available to the common stockholders is synonymous with net income. In the valuation process outlined above, it is net income that is actually capitalized to arrive at the market value of the common equity. Because of this, the dependence hypothesis is also called the **net-income approach to valuation.**

Notice that the total market value of the firm's securities has risen to $23,200,000 from the $20 million level that existed before the firm moved from the unlevered to the levered capital structure. The per-share value of the common stock is also shown to rise under this valuation format. With 1,200,000 shares of stock outstanding, the market price per share is $12.67 ($15,200,000/1,200,000).

This increase in the stock price to $12.67 represents a 26.7 percent rise over the previous level of $10 per share. This is exactly equal to the percentage change in earnings per share and dividends per share calculated in Table 16-1. This permits us to characterize the dependence hypothesis in a very succinct fashion:

Percentage change in K_c (overall degrees of leverage) = 0 percent < percentage change in D_t

percentage change in P_0 = percentage change in D_t

The dependence hypothesis suggests that the *explicit* and *implicit* costs of debt are one and the same. The use of more debt does *not* change the firm's cost of common equity. Using more debt, which is explicitly cheaper than common equity, will lower the firm's composite cost of capital, K_0. If you take the market value of Rix Camper's common stock according to the net-income theory of $15,200,000 and express it as a percent of the total market value of the firm's securities, you get a market-value weight of .655 ($15,200,000/$23,200,000). In a similar fashion the market-value weight of Rix Camper's debt is found to be .345 ($8,000,000/$23,200,000). After the capital-structure adjustment the firm's weighted cost of capital becomes:

$$K_0 = (.345)(6.00\%) + (.655)(10.00\%) = 8.62 \text{ percent}$$

So, changing the financing mix from all equity to a structure including both debt and equity lowered the composite cost of capital from 10 percent to 8.62 percent. The ingredients of the dependence hypothesis are illustrated in Figures 16-3 and 16-4.

The implication for management from Figures 16-3 and 16-4 is that the firm's cost of capital, K_0, will decline as the debt-to-equity ratio increases. This also implies that the company's common stock price will rise with increased leverage use. Since the cost of capital decreases continuously with leverage, the firm should use as much financial leverage as is possible. Next, we will move toward reality in the analytical setting of our capital-structure discussion. This is accomplished by relaxing some of the major assumptions that surrounded the independence and dependence hypotheses.

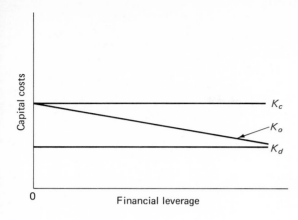

FIGURE 16-3 *Capital Costs and Financial Leverage: No Taxes—The Dependence Hypothesis (NI Theory)*

In general, an analysis of extreme positions may be useful in that you are forced to sharpen up your thinking about not only the poles, but also the situations that span the poles. In microeconomics the study of pure competition and monopoly provides a better understanding of the business activity that takes place in the wide area between these two model markets. In a similar fashion the study of the independence and dependence hypotheses of the importance of capital structure helps us formulate a more informed view of the possible situations between those polar positions.

We turn now to a description of the cost of capital–capital structure relationship that has rather wide appeal to both business practitioners and academics. This moderate view (1) admits to the fact that interest expense is tax deductible and (2) acknowledges that the probability of the firm's suffering bankruptcy costs is directly related to the company's use of financial leverage.

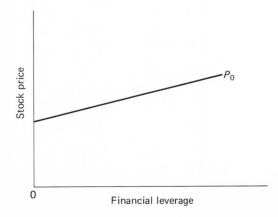

FIGURE 16-4 *Stock Price and Financial Leverage: No Taxes—The Dependence Hypothesis (NI Theory)*

TAX DEDUCTIBILITY
OF INTEREST EXPENSE

This portion of the analysis recognizes that corporate income is subject to taxation by governmental authorities. Furthermore, we assume that interest expense is tax deductible for purposes of computing the firm's tax bill. In this environment the use of debt financing should result in a higher total market value for the firm's outstanding securities. We will see why, below.

We continue with our example data concerning the Rix Camper Manufacturing Company. First, consider the total cash payments made to all security holders (holders of common stock plus holders of bonds). In the no-tax case the sum of cash dividends paid to common shareholders plus interest expense amounted to $2 million both (1) when financing was all by common equity and (2) after the proposed capital-structure adjustment to a levered situation was accomplished. The *sum* of the cash flows that Rix Camper could pay to its contributors of debt and equity capital was not affected by its financing mix.

When corporate income is taxed by the government, however, the sum of the cash flows made to all contributors of financial capital *is affected* by the firm's financing mix. Table 16-3 illustrates this point.

If Rix Camper makes the capital-structure adjustment identified in the previous sections of this chapter, the total payments to equity and debt holders will be $240,000 *greater* than under the all-common-equity capitalization. Where does this $240,000 come from? The government's take, through taxes collected, is lower by that amount. This difference, which flows to the Rix Camper security holders, is called the **tax shield** on interest. In general, it may be calculated by Equation (16-4), where r_d is the interest rate paid on the debt, M is the principal amount of the debt, and t is the firm's marginal tax rate:

$$\text{tax shield} = r_d(M)(t) \qquad (16\text{-}4)$$

Table 16-3 RIX CAMPER COMPANY: CASH FLOWS TO ALL INVESTORS—THE CASE OF TAXES

	UNLEVERED CAPITAL STRUCTURE	LEVERED CAPITAL STRUCTURE
Expected level of net operating income	$2,000,000	$2,000,000
Less: Interest expense	0	480,000
Earnings before taxes	$2,000,000	$1,520,000
Less: Taxes at 50%	1,000,000	760,000
Earnings available to common stockholders	$1,000,000	$ 760,000
Expected payments to *all* security holders	$1,000,000	$1,240,000

The moderate position on the importance of capital structure presumes that the tax shield must have value in the marketplace. Accordingly, this tax benefit will increase the total market value of the firm's outstanding securities relative to the all-equity capitalization. Financial leverage does affect firm value. Because the cost of capital is just the other side of the valuation coin, financial leverage also affects the firm's composite cost of capital. Can the firm increase firm value indefinitely and lower its cost of capital continuously by using more and more financial leverage? Common sense would tell us, "No!" So would most financial managers and academicians. The acknowledgment of bankruptcy costs provides the rationale.

THE LIKELIHOOD OF FIRM FAILURE

The probability that the firm will be unable to meet the financial obligations identified in its debt contracts increases as more debt is employed. The highest costs would be incurred if the firm actually went into bankruptcy proceedings. Here, assets would be liquidated. If we admit that these assets might sell for something less than their perceived market values, equity investors and debt holders could both suffer monetary losses. Other problems accompany bankruptcy proceedings. Lawyers and accountants have to be hired and paid. Managers must spend time in preparing lengthy reports for those involved in the legal action.

Milder forms of financial distress also have their costs. As the firm's financial condition weakens, creditors may take action to restrict normal business activity. Suppliers may not deliver materials on credit. Profitable capital investments may have to be forgone, and dividend payments may even be interrupted. At some point the expected cost of default will be large enough to outweigh the tax-shield advantage of debt financing. The firm will turn to other sources of financing, mainly common equity. At this point the real cost of debt is thought to be higher than the real cost of common equity.

This moderate view of the relationship between financing mix and the firm's cost of capital is depicted in Figure 16-5. The result is a saucer-shaped (or U-shaped) average cost of capital curve, K_0. The firm's average cost of equity, K_c, is seen to rise over all positive degrees of financial-leverage use. For a while the firm can borrow funds at a relatively low cost of debt, K_d. Even though the cost of equity is rising, it does not rise at a fast enough rate to offset the use of the less expensive debt financing. Thus, between points 0 and A on the financial-leverage axis, the average cost of capital declines and stock price rises.

Eventually, the threat of financial distress causes the cost of debt to rise. In Figure 16-5 this increase in the cost of debt shows up in the average cost of debt curve, K_d, at point A. Between points A and B, mixing debt and equity funds produces an average cost of capital that is (relatively) flat. The firm's **optimal range of financial-leverage use** lies between points A and B.

The Moderate View: The Saucer-Shaped Cost of Capital Curve

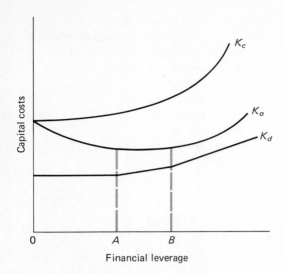

FIGURE 16-5 *Capital Costs and Financial Leverage: The Moderate View, Considering Taxes and Financial Distress*

All capital structures between these two points are *optimal* because they produce the firm's lowest composite cost of capital. As we said in the introduction to this chapter, finding this optimal range of financing mixes is the *objective of capital-structure management*.

Point *B* signifies the firm's debt capacity. **Debt capacity** is the maximum proportion of debt that the firm can include in its capital structure and still maintain its lowest composite cost of capital. Beyond point *B*, additional fixed-charge capital can be attracted only at very costly interest rates. At the same time this excessive use of financial leverage would cause the firm's cost of equity to rise at a faster rate than previously. The composite cost of capital would then rise quite rapidly, and the firm's stock price would decline.

This version of the moderate view as it relates to the firm's stock price is characterized below. The notation is the same as that found in our discussion of the independence and dependence hypotheses.

1. Between points 0 and *A*:
   $0 <$ percentage change in $P_0 <$ percentage change in D_t
2. Between points *A* and *B*:
   percentage change in $P_0 = 0$
3. Beyond point *B*:
   percentage change in $P_0 < 0$

Where does this examination of capital-structure theory leave us? The upshot is that the determination of the firm's financing mix is centrally important to the financial manager. The firm's stockholders *are* affected by capital-structure decisions.

At the very least, and before bankruptcy costs become detrimental,

Managerial Implications

456

the tax-shield effect will cause the shares of a levered firm to sell at a higher price than they would if the company had avoided debt financing. Owing to the risk of failure, however, that accompanies the excessive use of leverage, the financial manager must exercise caution in the use of fixed-charge capital. This problem of searching for the optimal range of use of financial leverage comprises the rest of the chapter.

Recall from Chapter 15 that the use of financial leverage has two effects upon the earnings stream flowing to the firm's common stockholders. For clarity of exposition Tables 15-7 and 15-8 are repeated here as Tables 16-4 and 16-5. Three possible financing mixes for the Pierce Grain Company are contained in Table 16-4, and an analysis of the corresponding financial leverage effects is displayed in Table 16-5.

The **first financial-leverage effect** is the added variability in the earnings-per-share stream that accompanies the use of fixed-charge securities in the company's capital structure. By means of the degree-of-financial-leverage measure (DFL_{EBIT}) we explained how this variability can be quantified. The firm that uses more financial leverage (rather than less) will experience larger relative changes in its earnings per share (rather than smaller) following EBIT fluctuations. Assume that Pierce Grain elected financing plan C rather than plan A. Plan C is highly levered and plan A is unlevered. A 100 percent increase in EBIT from $20,000 to $40,000 would cause earnings per share to rise by 147 percent under plan C, but only 100

BASIC TOOLS OF CAPITAL-STRUCTURE MANAGEMENT

Table 16-4   THE PIERCE GRAIN COMPANY: POSSIBLE CAPITAL STRUCTURES

Plan A: 0% debt

		Total debt	$ 0
		Common equity	200,000[a]
Total assets	$200,000	Total liabilities and equity	$200,000

Plan B: 25% debt at 8% interest rate

		Total debt	$ 50,000
		Common equity	150,000[b]
Total assets	$200,000	Total liabilities and equity	$200,000

Plan C: 40% debt at 8% interest rate

		Total debt	$ 80,000
		Common equity	120,000[c]
Total assets	$200,000	Total liabilities and equity	$200,000

[a] 2000 common shares outstanding.
[b] 1500 common shares outstanding.
[c] 1200 common shares outstanding.

Table 16-5 THE PIERCE GRAIN COMPANY: ANALYSIS OF FINANCIAL LEVERAGE AT DIFFERENT EBIT LEVELS

(1) EBIT	(2) INTEREST	(3) = (1) − (2) EBT	(4) = (3) × .5 TAXES	(5) = (3) − (4) NET INCOME TO COMMON	(6) EARNINGS PER SHARE
Plan A: 0% debt; $200,000 common equity; 2000 shares					
$ 0	$ 0	$ 0	$ 0	$ 0	$ 0
20,000	0	20,000	10,000	10,000	5.00 ⎫
40,000	0	40,000	20,000	20,000	10.00 ⎬ 100%
60,000	0	60,000	30,000	30,000	15.00 ⎭
80,000	0	80,000	40,000	40,000	20.00
Plan B: 25% debt; 8% interest rate; $150,000 common equity; 1500 shares					
$ 0	$4,000	$ (4,000)	$ (2,000)[a]	$ (2,000)	$ (1.33)
20,000	4,000	16,000	8,000	8,000	5.33 ⎫
40,000	4,000	36,000	18,000	18,000	12.00 ⎬ 125%
60,000	4,000	56,000	28,000	28,000	18.67 ⎭
80,000	4,000	76,000	38,000	38,000	25.33
Plan C: 40% debt; 8% interest rate; $120,000 common equity; 1200 shares					
$ 0	$6,400	$ (6,400)	$ (3,200)[a]	$ (3,200)	$ (2.67)
20,000	6,400	13,600	6,800	6,800	5.67 ⎫
40,000	6,400	33,600	16,800	16,800	14.00 ⎬ 147%
60,000	6,400	53,600	26,800	26,800	22.33 ⎭
80,000	6,400	73,600	36,800	36,800	30.67

[a]The negative tax bill recognizes the credit arising from the carryback and carryforward provision of the tax code. See Chapter 2.

percent under plan A. Unfortunately, the effect would operate in the negative direction as well. A given change in EBIT is *magnified* by the use of financial leverage. This magnification is reflected in the variability of the firm's earnings per share. Figure 16-6 illustrates for some firm a possible probability distribution for EBIT and earnings per share. It shows that a given change in EBIT will be magnified by the use of financial leverage. A greater-than-proportionate change in earnings per share will result.

The **second financial leverage effect** concerns the level of earnings per share at a given EBIT under a given capital structure. Refer to Table 16-5. At the EBIT level of $20,000, earnings per share would be $5, $5.33, and $5.67 under financing arrangements A, B, and C, respectively. Above a critical level of EBIT the firm's earnings per share will be higher if greater degrees of financial leverage are employed. Conversely, below some critical level of EBIT earnings per share will suffer at greater degrees of financial leverage. Whereas the first financial-leverage effect is quantified by the degree-of-financial-leverage measure (DFL_{EBIT}), the second is quantified by what is generally referred to as "EBIT-EPS" analysis. EPS refers, of course, to earnings per share. The rationale underlying this sort

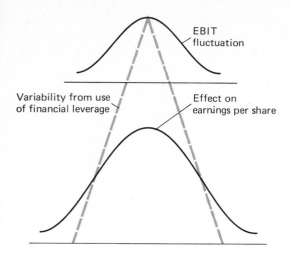

EBIT
fluctuation

Variability from use
of financial leverage

Effect on
earnings per share

FIGURE 16-6 *Variability in Residual Earnings Due to Use of Financial Leverage*

of analysis is simple. Earnings is one of the key variables that influences the market value of the firm's common stock. The effect of a financing decision on EPS, then, should be understood because the decision will probably affect the value of the stockholders' investment.

Example. Assume that plan B in Table 16-5 is the existing capital structure for the Pierce Grain Company. Furthermore, the asset structure of the firm is such that EBIT is expected to be $20,000 per year for a very long time. A capital investment is available to Pierce Grain that will cost $50,000. Acquisition of this asset is expected to raise the projected EBIT level to $30,000, permanently. The firm can raise the needed cash by (1) selling 500 shares of common stock at $50 each or (2) selling new bonds that will net the firm $50,000 and carry an interest rate of 8.5 percent. These capital structures and corresponding EPS amounts are summarized in Table 16-6.

At the projected EBIT level of $30,000, the EPS for the common stock and debt alternatives are $6.50 and $7.25, respectively. Both are considerably above the $5.33 that would occur if the new project were rejected and the additional financial capital were not raised. Based on a criterion of selecting the financing plan that will provide the highest EPS, the bond alternative is favored. But what if the basic business risk to which the firm is exposed causes the EBIT level to vary over a considerable range? Can we be sure that the bond alternative will *always* have the higher EPS associated with it? The answer, of course, is "No." When the EBIT level is subject to uncertainty, a graphic analysis of the proposed financing plans can provide useful information to the financial manager.

GRAPHIC ANALYSIS

The EBIT-EPS analysis chart allows the decision maker to visualize the impact of different financing plans on EPS over a range of EBIT levels.

Table 16-6 THE PIERCE GRAIN COMPANY: ANALYSIS OF FINANCING CHOICES

Part A: Capital Structures

EXISTING CAPITAL STRUCTURE		WITH NEW COMMON STOCK FINANCING		WITH NEW DEBT FINANCING	
Long-term debt at 8%	$ 50,000	Long-term debt at 8%	$ 50,000	Long-term debt at 8%	$ 50,000
Common stock	150,000	Common stock	200,000	Long-term debt at 8.5%	50,000
				Common stock	150,000
Total liabilities and equity	$200,000	Total liabilities and equity	$250,000	Total liabilities and equity	$250,000
Common shares outstanding	1,500	Common shares outstanding	2,000	Common shares outstanding	1,500

Part B: Projected EPS Levels

	EXISTING CAPITAL STRUCTURE	WITH NEW COMMON STOCK FINANCING	WITH NEW DEBT FINANCING
EBIT	$20,000	$30,000	$30,000
Less: Interest expense	4,000	4,000	8,250
Earnings before taxes (EBT)	$16,000	$26,000	$21,750
Less: Taxes at 50%	8,000	13,000	10,875
Net income	$ 8,000	$13,000	$10,875
Less: Preferred dividends	0	0	0
Earnings available to common	$ 8,000	$13,000	$10,875
EPS	$5.33	$6.50	$7.25

The relationship between EPS and EBIT is linear. All we need, therefore, to construct the chart is two points for each alternative. Part B of Table 16-6 already provides us with one of these points. The answer to the following question for each choice gives us the second point: At what EBIT level will the EPS for the plan be exactly zero? If the EBIT level *just covers* the plan's financing costs (on a before-tax basis), then EPS will be zero. For the stock plan, an EPS of zero is associated with an EBIT of $4000. The $4000 is the interest expense incurred under the existing capital structure. If the bond plan is elected, the interest costs will be the present $4000 plus $4250 per year arising from the new debt issue. An EBIT level of $8250, then, is necessary to provide a zero EPS with the bond plan.

The EBIT-EPS analysis chart representing the financing choices available to the Pierce Grain Company is shown as Figure 16-7. EBIT is charted on the horizontal axis and EPS on the vertical axis. The intercepts on the horizontal axis represent the before-tax equivalent financing

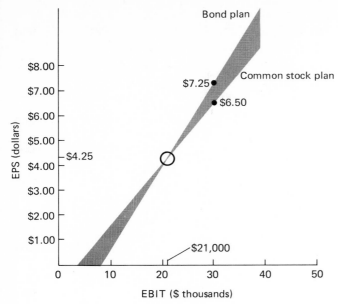

FIGURE 16-7 *EBIT-EPS Analysis Chart*

charges related to each plan. The straight lines for each plan tell us the EPS amounts that will occur at different EBIT amounts.

Notice that the bond-plan line has a *steeper slope* than the stock-plan line. This ensures that the lines for each financing choice will *intersect*. Above the intersection point, EPS for the plan with greater leverage will exceed that for the plan with lesser leverage. The intersection point, encircled in Figure 16-7, occurs at an EBIT level of $21,000 and produces EPS of $4.25 for each plan. When EBIT is $30,000, notice that the bond plan produces EPS of $7.25 and the stock plan, $6.50. Below the intersection point, EPS with the stock plan will *exceed* that with the more highly levered bond plan. The steeper slope of the bond-plan line indicates that with greater leverage, EPS is more sensitive to EBIT changes. This same concept was discussed in Chapter 15, when we derived the degree-of-financial-leverage measure.

COMPUTING INDIFFERENCE POINTS

The point of intersection in Figure 16-7 is called the **EBIT-EPS indifference point.** It identifies the EBIT level at which the EPS will be the same regardless of the financing plan chosen by the financial manager. This indifference point, sometimes called the breakeven point, has major implications for financial planning. At EBIT amounts in excess of the EBIT indifference level, the more heavily levered financing plan will generate a higher EPS. At EBIT amounts below the EBIT indifference level, the financing plan involving less leverage will generate a higher EPS. It is important, then, to know the EBIT indifference level.

We can find it graphically, as in Figure 16-7. At times it may be more efficient, though, to calculate the EBIT-EPS indifference point directly. This can be done by using the following equation:

$$\underset{S_s}{\underbrace{\frac{(\text{EBIT} - I)(1 - t) - P}{S_s}}_{\textit{EPS: Stock Plan}}} = \underset{S_b}{\underbrace{\frac{(\text{EBIT} - I)(1 - t) - P}{S_b}}_{\textit{EPS: Bond Plan}}} \tag{16-5}$$

where S_s and S_b are the number of common shares outstanding under the stock and bond plans, respectively, I is interest expense, t is the firm's income tax rate, and P is preferred dividends paid. In the present case P is zero, because there is no preferred stock outstanding. If preferred stock is associated with one of the financing alternatives, keep in mind that the preferred dividends, P, are not tax deductible. Equation 16-5 *does* take this fact into consideration.

For the present example, we calculate the indifference level of EBIT as

$$\frac{(\text{EBIT} - \$4000)(1 - 0.5) - 0}{2000} = \frac{(\text{EBIT} - \$8250)(1 - 0.5) - 0}{1500}$$

When the expression above is solved for EBIT, we obtain \$21,000. If EBIT turns out to be \$21,000, then EPS will be \$4.25 under both plans.

UNCOMMITTED EARNINGS PER SHARE AND INDIFFERENCE POINTS

The calculations that permitted us to solve for Pierce Grain's EBIT-EPS indifference point made no explicit allowance for the repayment of the bond principal. This procedure is not that unrealistic. It only presumes the debt will be perpetually outstanding. This means that when the current bond issue matures, a new bond issue will be floated. The proceeds from the newer issue would be used to pay off the maturity value of the older issue.

Many bond contracts, however, require that **sinking-fund payments** be made to a bond trustee. A **sinking fund** is a real cash reserve that is used to provide for the orderly and early retirement of the principal amount of the bond issue. Most often the sinking-fund payment is a mandatory fixed amount and is required by a clause in the bond indenture. Sinking-fund payments can represent a sizable cash drain on the firm's liquid resources. Moreover, sinking-fund payments are a return of borrowed principal, so they are *not* tax deductible to the firm.

Because of the potentially serious nature of the cash drain caused by sinking-fund requirements, the financial manager might be concerned with the uncommitted earnings per share (UEPS) related to each financing plan. The calculation of UEPS recognizes that sinking-fund commitments have been honored. UEPS can be used, then, for discretionary spending—such as the payment of cash dividends to common stockholders or investment in capital facilities.

If we let *SF* be the sinking fund payment required in a given year, the EBIT-UEPS indifference point can be calculated as

$$\underset{UEPS:\ Stock\ Plan}{\frac{(\text{EBIT} - I)(1 - t) - P - SF}{S_s}} = \underset{UEPS:\ Bond\ Plan}{\frac{(\text{EBIT} - I)(1 - t) - P - SF}{S_b}} \qquad (16\text{-}6)$$

If several bond issues are already outstanding, then *I* in Equations (16-5) and (16-6) for the stock plan consists of the sum of their related interest payments. For the bond plan, *I* would be the sum of existing plus new interest charges. In Equation (16-6) the same logic applies to the sinking-fund variable, *SF*. The indifference level of EBIT based on UEPS will always exceed that based on EPS.

A WORD OF CAUTION

Above the EBIT-EPS indifference point, a more heavily levered financial plan promises to deliver a larger EPS. Strict application of the criterion of selecting the financing plan that produces the highest EPS might have the firm issuing debt most of the time it raised external capital. Our discussion of capital-structure theory taught us the dangers of that sort of action.

The primary weakness of EBIT-EPS analysis is that it disregards the implicit costs of debt financing. The effect of the specific financing decision on the firm's cost of common equity capital is totally ignored. Investors should be concerned with both the *level* and *variability* of the firm's expected earnings stream. EBIT-EPS analysis considers only the level of the earnings stream and ignores the variability (riskiness) inherent in it. Thus, this type of analysis must be used in conjunction with other basic tools in reaching the objective of capital-structure management.

Comparative Leverage Ratios

In Chapter 3 we explored the overall usefulness of financial ratio analysis. Leverage ratios were one of the categories of financial ratios identified in that chapter. We emphasize here that the computation of leverage ratios comprises one of the basic tools of capital-structure management.

Two types of leverage ratios must be computed when a financing decision faces the firm. We have called these *balance sheet leverage ratios* and *coverage ratios*. The inputs to the balance sheet leverage ratios come from the firm's balance sheet. In various forms these balance sheet metrics compare the firm's use of funds supplied by creditors to those supplied by owners.

Inputs to the coverage ratios *generally* come from the firm's income statement. At times the external analyst may have to consult balance sheet information to construct some of these needed estimates. On a privately placed debt issue, for example, some fraction of the current portion of the firm's long-term debt might have to be used as an estimate of that issue's sinking fund. Coverage ratios provide estimates of the firm's ability to service its financing contracts. High coverage ratios, compared to a standard, imply unused debt capacity.

A WORKSHEET

Table 16-7 is a sample worksheet used to analyze financing choices. The objective of the analysis is to determine the effect each financing plan will have on key financial ratios. The financial officer can compare the existing level of each ratio with its projected level, taking into consideration the contractual commitments of each alternative.

In reality we know that EBIT might be expected to vary over a considerable range of outcomes. For this reason the coverage ratios should be calculated several times, each at a different level of EBIT. If this is accomplished over all possible values of EBIT, a probability distribution for each coverage ratio can be constructed. This provides the financial manager with much more information than simply calculating the coverage ratios based on the expected value of EBIT.

INDUSTRY NORMS

The comparative leverage ratios calculated according to the format laid out in Table 16-7, or in a similar format, have additional utility to the decision maker if they can be compared to some standard. Generally, corporate financial analysts, investment bankers, commercial bank loan officers, and bond rating agencies rely upon industry classes from which to compute "normal" ratios. Although industry groupings may actually contain firms whose basic business risk exposure differs widely, the aforementioned practice is entrenched in American business behavior.[2] At the very least, then, the financial officer must be interested in *industry standards* because almost everybody else is.

Several published studies indicate that capital-structure ratios vary in a significant manner among industry classes.[3] For example, random samplings of the common equity ratios of large retail firms seem to differ statistically from those of major steel producers. The major steel producers use financial leverage to a lesser degree than do the large retail organizations. On the whole, firms operating in the *same* industry tend to exhibit capital structure ratios that cluster around a central value, which we call a

---

[2]An approach to grouping firms based on several component measures of business risk, as opposed to ordinary industry classes, is reported in John D. Martin, David F. Scott, Jr., and Robert F. Vandell, "Equivalent Risk Classes: A Multidimensional Examination," *Journal of Financial and Quantitative Analysis*, 13 (December 1978), forthcoming.

[3]See, for example, Eli Schwartz and J. Richard Aronson, "Some Surrogate Evidence in Support of the Concept of Optimal Financial Structure," *Journal of Finance*, 22 (March 1967), 10–18; David F. Scott, Jr., "Evidence on the Importance of Financial Structure," *Financial Management*, 1 (Summer 1972), 45–50; and David F. Scott, Jr., and John D. Martin, "Industry Influence on Financial Structure," *Financial Management*, 4 (Spring 1975), 67–73.

Table 16-7 COMPARATIVE LEVERAGE RATIOS: WORKSHEET FOR ANALYZING FINANCING PLANS

RATIOS	COMPUTATION METHOD	EXISTING RATIO	RATIO WITH NEW COMMON STOCK FINANCING	RATIO WITH NEW DEBT FINANCING
Balance sheet leverage ratios				
1. Debt ratio	$\dfrac{\text{Total liabilities}}{\text{Total assets}}$	_____ %	_____ %	_____ %
2. Long-term debt to total capitalization	$\dfrac{\text{Long-term debt}}{\text{Long-term debt} + \text{net worth}}$	_____ %	_____ %	_____ %
3. Total liabilities to net worth	$\dfrac{\text{Total liabilities}}{\text{Net worth}}$	_____ %	_____ %	_____ %
4. Common equity ratio	$\dfrac{\text{Common equity}}{\text{Total assets}}$	_____ %	_____ %	_____ %
Coverage ratios				
1. Times interest earned	$\dfrac{\text{EBIT}}{\text{Annual interest expense}}$	_____ times	_____ times	_____ times
2. Times burden covered	$\dfrac{\text{EBIT}}{\text{Interest} + \dfrac{\text{sinking fund}}{1-t}}$	_____ times	_____ times	_____ times
3. Cash flow overall coverage ratio	$\dfrac{\text{EBIT} + \text{lease expense} + \text{depreciation}}{\text{Interest} + \text{lease expense} + \dfrac{\text{preferred dividends}}{1-t} + \dfrac{\text{principal payments}}{1-t}}$	_____ times	_____ times	_____ times

norm. Business risk will vary from industry to industry. As a consequence, the capital-structure norms will vary from industry to industry.

This is not to say that all companies in the industry will maintain leverage ratios "close" to the norm. There will always be outliers. For instance, firms that are very profitable may display *high* coverage ratios and *high* balance sheet leverage ratios. The moderately profitable firm, though, might find such a posture unduly risky. Here the usefulness of industry normal leverage ratios is clear. If the firm chooses to deviate in a material manner from the accepted values for the key ratios, it must have a sound reason for so doing.

In Chapter 3 we stated that liquidity ratios are designed to measure the ability of the firm to pay its bills on time. Financing charges are just another type of bill that eventually comes due for payment. Interest charges, preferred dividends, lease charges, and principal payments all must be paid on time, or the company risks being caught in bankruptcy proceedings. To a lesser extent, dispensing with financing charges on an other-than-timely basis can result in severely restricted business operations. We have just seen that coverage ratios provide a measure of the safety of one general class of payment—financing charges. Coverage ratios, then, and liquidity ratios are very close in concept.

A more comprehensive method is available for studying the impact of capital-structure decisions on corporate cash flows. The method is simple but nonetheless very valuable. It involves the preparation of a series of cash budgets under (1) different economic conditions and (2) different capital structures.[4] The net cash flows under these different situations can be examined to determine if the financing requirements expose the firm to a degree of default risk too high to bear.

In work that has been highly acclaimed, Donaldson has suggested that the firm's debt-carrying capacity (defined in the broad sense here to include preferred dividend payments and lease payments) ought to depend upon the net cash flows that the firm could expect to receive during a recessionary period.[5] In other words, *target capital-structure proportions* could be set by planning for the "worst that could happen." An example will be of help.

Suppose that a recession is expected to last for one year.[6] Moreover, the end of the year represents the bottoming-out, or worst portion of the recession. Equation (16-7) defines the cash balance, CB_r, that the firm could expect to have at the end of the recession period:[7]

Companywide Cash Flows: What Is the Worst that Could Happen?

---

[4]Cash budget preparation is discussed in Chapter 4.

[5]Refer to Gordon Donaldson, "New Framework for Corporate Debt Policy," *Harvard Business Review*, 40 (March-April 1962), 117–31; Gordon Donaldson, *Corporate Debt Capacity* (Boston: Division of Research, Graduate School of Business Administration, Harvard University, 1961), Chap. 7; and Gordon Donaldson, "Strategy for Financial Emergencies," *Harvard Business Review*, 47 (November-December 1969), 67–79.

[6]The analysis can readily be extended to cover a recessionary period of several years. All that is necessary is to calculate the cash budgets over a similar period.

[7]For the most part, the present notation follows that of Donaldson.

$$CB_r = C_0 + (C_s + OR) - (P_a + RM + \cdots + E_n) - FC \qquad (16\text{-}7)$$

where C_0 = the cash balance at the beginning of the recession,

$\quad C_s$ = collection from sales,

$\quad OR$ = other cash receipts,

$\quad P_a$ = payroll expenditures,

$\quad RM$ = raw material payments,

$\quad E_n$ = the last of a long series of expenditures over which management
has little control (nondiscretionary expenditures),

$\quad FC$ = fixed financial charges associated with a specific capital structure.

If we let the net of total cash receipts and nondiscretionary expenditures be represented by NCF_r, then Equation (16-7) can be simplified to

$$CB_r = CB_0 + NCF_r - FC \qquad (16\text{-}8)$$

The inputs to Equation (16-8) come from a detailed cash budget. The variable representing financing costs, FC, can be changed in accordance with several alternative financing plans to ascertain if the net cash balance during the recession, CB_r, might fall below zero.

Suppose that some firm typically maintains \$500,000 in cash and marketable securities. This amount would be on hand at the start of the recession period. During the economic decline, the firm projects that its net cash flows from operations, NCF_r, will be \$2 million. If the firm currently finances its assets with an unlevered capital structure, its cash balance at the worst point of the recession would be

$$CB_r = \$500,000 + \$2,000,000 - \$0 = \$2,500,000$$

This procedure allows us to study many different situations.[8] Assume that the same firm is considering a shift in its capitalization such that annual interest and sinking-fund payments will be \$2,300,000. If a recession occurred, the firm's cash balance at the end of the adverse economic period would be

$$CB_r = \$500,000 + \$2,000,000 - \$2,300,000 = \$200,000$$

The firm ordinarily maintains a liquid asset balance of \$500,000. Thus, the effect of the proposed capital structure on the firm's cash balance during adverse circumstances might seem too risky for management to accept. When the chance of being out of cash is too high for management to bear,

[8] It is not difficult to improve the usefulness of this sort of analysis by applying the technique of simulation to the generation of the various cash budgets. This facilitates the construction of probability distributions of net cash flows under differing circumstances. Simulation was discussed in Chapter 12.

then the use of financial-leverage has been pushed beyond a reasonable level. According to this tool, the appropriate level of financial-leverage use is reached when the chance of being out of cash is exactly equal to that which management will assume.

In this chapter we have spent much time discussing (1) the concept of an optimal capital structure, (2) the search for an appropriate range of financial-leverage use, and (3) the fundamental tools of capital-structure management. The opinions and practices of financial executives lead us to believe that the present emphasis is a reasonable one.

A GLANCE AT ACTUAL CAPITAL-STRUCTURE MANAGEMENT

The Conference Board has surveyed 170 senior financial officers with respect to their capital-structure practices.[9] Of these 170 executives, 102 or 60 percent stated that they *do* believe there is an optimum capital structure for the corporation. Sixty-five percent of the responding practitioners worked for firms with annual sales in excess of $200 million. One executive who subscribed to the optimal-capital-structure concept stated:

> In my opinion, there is an optimum capital structure for companies. However, this optimum capital structure will vary by individual companies, industries, and then is subject to changing economies, by money markets, earnings trends, and prospects . . . the circumstances and the lenders will determine an optimum at different points in time.[10]

This survey and others consistently point out that (1) financial officers set target debt ratios for their companies, and (2) the values for those ratios are influenced by a conscious evaluation of the basic business risk to which the firm is exposed.

Target Debt Ratios

Selected comments from financial executives point to the widespread use of target debt ratios. A vice-president and treasurer of the American Telephone and Telegraph Company (AT&T) described his firm's debt ratio policy in terms of a range:

> All of the foregoing considerations led us to conclude, and reaffirm for a period of many years, that the proper range of our debt was 30% to 40% of total capital. Reasonable success in meeting financial needs under the diverse market and economic conditions that we have faced attests to the appropriateness of this conclusion.[11]

In a similar fashion the president of Fibreboard Corporation identified his

[9]Francis J. Walsh, Jr., *Planning Corporate Capital Structures* (New York: The Conference Board, Inc., 1972).

[10]Walsh, *Planning Corporate Capital Structures*, p. 14.

[11]John J. Scanlon, "Bell System Financial Policies," *Financial Management*, 1 (Summer 1972), 16–26.

468

firm's target debt ratio and noted how it is related to the uncertain nature of the company's business:

> Our objective is a 30% ratio of debt to capitalization. We need that kind of flexibility to operate in the cyclical business we are in.[12]

In the Conference Board survey mentioned earlier, 84 of the 102 financial officers who subscribed to the optimal-capital-structure concept stated that their firm *has* a target debt ratio.[13] The most frequently mentioned influence on the level of the target debt ratio was the firm's ability to adequately meet its financing charges. Other factors identified as affecting the target were (1) maintaining a desired bond rating, (2) providing an adequate borrowing reserve, and (3) exploiting the advantages of financial leverage.

In our opinion the single most important factor that should affect the firm's financing mix is the underlying nature of the business in which it operates. In Chapter 15 we defined business risk as the relative dispersion in the firm's expected stream of EBIT. If the nature of the firm's business is such that the variability inherent in its EBIT stream is high, then it would be unwise to impose a high degree of financial risk on top of this already uncertain earnings stream.

Business Risk

Corporate executives are likely to point this out in discussions of capital-structure management. A financial officer in a large steel firm related:

> The nature of the industry, the marketplace, and the firm tend to establish debt limits that any prudent management would prefer not to exceed. Our industry is capital intensive and our markets tend to be cyclical. . . . The capability to service debt while operating in the environment described dictates a conservative financial structure.[14]

Notice how that executive was concerned with both his firm's business risk exposure and its cash flow capability for meeting any financing costs. The AT&T financial officer referred to earlier also has commented on the relationship between business and financial risk:

> In determining how much debt a firm can safely carry, it is necessary to consider the basic risks inherent in that business. This varies considerably among industries and is related essentially to the nature and demand for an industry's product, the operating characteristics of the industry, and its ability to earn an adequate return in an unknown future.[15]

[12]*Business Week*, December 6, 1976, p. 30.
[13]Walsh, *Planning Corporate Capital Structures*, p. 17.
[14]*Ibid*., p. 18.
[15]Scanlon, "Bell System Financial Policies," p. 19.

It appears clear that the firm's capital structure cannot be properly designed without a thorough understanding of its commercial strategy.

This chapter dealt with the design of the firm's financing mix. The particular focus was upon the management of the firm's permanent sources of funds—that is, its capital structure. The objective of capital-structure management is to arrange the company's sources of funds in such a manner that its common stock price will be maximized, all other factors held constant.

SUMMARY

Capital-Structure Theory

Can the firm affect its composite cost of capital by altering its financing mix? Attempts to answer that question have comprised a significant portion of capital-structure theory for over two decades. Extreme positions show that the firm's stock price is either (1) unaffected or (2) continually affected as the firm increases its reliance upon leverage-inducing funds. In an operating environment where interest expense is tax deductible and market imperfections operate to restrict the amount of fixed-income obligations a firm can issue, most financial officers and financial academics subscribe to the concept of an optimal capital structure. The optimal capital structure minimizes the firm's composite cost of capital. Searching for a proper range of financial-leverage use, then, is an important financial management activity.

The Tools of Capital-Structure Management

The decision to use senior securities in the firm's capitalization causes two types of financial-leverage effects. The first is the added variability in the earnings-per-share stream that accompanies the use of fixed-charge securities. We explained in Chapter 15 how this could be quantified by use of the degree-of-financial-leverage metric. The second financial-leverage effect relates to the level of earnings per share (EPS) at a given EBIT under a specific capital structure. We rely upon *EBIT-EPS analysis* to measure this second effect. Through EBIT-EPS analysis the decision maker can inspect the impact of alternative financing plans on EPS over a full range of EBIT levels.

A second tool of capital-structure management is the calculation of *comparative leverage ratios.* Balance sheet leverage ratios and coverage ratios can be computed according to the contractual stipulations of the proposed financing plans. Comparison of these ratios with industry standards enables the financial officer to determine if his firm's key ratios are materially out of line with accepted practice.

A third tool involves the *analysis of corporate cash flows.* This process involves the preparation of a series of cash budgets that consider different economic conditions and different capital structures. Useful insight into the identification of proper *target capital structure ratios* can be obtained by analyzing projected cash flow statements that assume adverse operating circumstances.

Surveys indicate that the majority of financial officers in large firms believe in the concept of an optimal capital structure. The optimal capital structure is approximated by the identification of *target debt ratios*. The targets reflect the firm's ability to service fixed financing costs and also consider the *business risk* to which the firm is exposed.

16-1. Define the following terms:
    (a) Financial structure.
    (b) Capital structure.
    (c) Optimal capital structure.
    (d) Debt capacity.
16-2. What is the primary weakness of EBIT-EPS analysis as a financing-decision tool?
16-3. What is the objective of capital-structure management?
16-4. Distinguish between (a) balance sheet leverage ratios and (b) coverage ratios. Give two examples of each and indicate how they would be computed.
16-5. Why might firms whose sales levels change drastically over time choose to use debt only sparingly in their capital structures?
16-6. What condition would cause capital-structure management to be a meaningless financial management activity?
16-7. What does the term "independence hypothesis" mean as it applies to capital-structure theory?
16-8. Who have been the foremost advocates of the independence hypothesis?
16-9. A financial manager might say that the firm's composite cost of capital is saucer-shaped or U-shaped. What does this mean?
16-10. Define what is called the "EBIT-EPS indifference point."
16-11. What is uncommitted earnings per share (UEPS)?
16-12. Explain how industry norms might be used by the financial manager in the design of his company's financing mix.

16-1. A group of college professors have decided to form a small manufacturing corporation. The company will produce a full line of contemporary furniture. Two financing plans have been proposed by the investors. Plan A is an all-common-equity alternative. Under this arrangement 1,400,000 common shares will be sold to net the firm $10 per share. Plan B involves the use of financial leverage. A debt issue with a 20-year maturity period will be privately placed. The debt issue will carry an interest rate of 8 percent and the principal borrowed will amount to $4 million. The corporate tax rate is 50 percent.

(a) Find the EBIT indifference level associated with the two financing proposals.

(b) Prepare an analytical income statement that *proves* EPS will be the same regardless of the plan chosen at the EBIT level found in part (a).

(c) Prepare an EBIT-EPS analysis chart for this situation.

(d) If a detailed financial analysis projects that long-term EBIT will always be close to $1,800,000 annually, which plan will provide for the higher EPS?

16-2. The professors in problem 16-1 contracted a financial consultant to provide them with some additional information. They felt that in a few years the stock of the firm would be publicly traded over-the-counter, so they were interested in the consultant's opinion as to what the stock price would be under the financing plan outlined in problem 16-1. The consultant agreed that the projected long-term EBIT level of $1,800,000 was reasonable. He also felt that if plan A were selected, the marketplace would apply a price/earnings ratio of 12 times to the company's stock; for plan B he estimated a price/earnings ratio of ten times.

(a) According to this information, which financing alternative would offer a higher stock price?

(b) What price/earnings ratio applied to the EPS related to plan B would provide the same stock price as that projected for plan A?

(c) Comment upon the results of your analysis of problems 16-1 and 16-2.

16-3. Cavalier Agriculture Supplies is undertaking a thorough cash flow analysis. It has been proposed by management that the firm expand by raising $5 million in the long-term debt markets. All of this would be immediately invested in new fixed assets. The proposed bond issue would carry an 8 percent interest rate and have a maturity period of 20 years. The bond issue would have a sinking-fund provision that one-twentieth of the principal would be retired annually. Next year is expected to be a poor one for Cavalier. The firm's management feels, therefore, that the upcoming year would serve well as a model for the worst possible operating conditions that the firm can be expected to encounter. Cavalier ordinarily carries a $500,000 cash balance. Next year sales collections are forecast to be $3 million. Miscellaneous cash receipts will total $200,000. Wages and salaries will amount to $1 million. Payments for raw materials used in the production process will be $1,400,000. Additionally, the firm will pay $500,000 in nondiscretionary expenditures including taxes. The firm faces a 50 percent tax rate.

(a) Cavalier currently has no debt or preferred stock outstanding. What will be the total fixed financial charges that the firm must meet next year?

(b) What is the expected cash balance at the end of the recessionary period (next year), assuming the debt is issued?

(c) Based on this information, should Cavalier issue the proposed bonds?

16-4. Some financial data for three corporations are displayed below:

	FIRM A	FIRM B	FIRM C	INDUSTRY NORM
Debt ratio	20%	25%	40%	20%
Times burden covered	8 times	10 times	7 times	9 times
Price/earnings ratio	9 times	11 times	6 times	10 times

(a) Which firm appears to be excessively levered?

(b) Which firm appears to be employing financial leverage to the most appropriate degree?

(c) What explanation can you provide for the higher price/earnings ratio enjoyed by firm B as compared to firm A?

16-5. Boston Textiles has an all-common-equity capital structure. Pertinent financial characteristics for the company are shown below:

$$\text{Shares of common stock outstanding} = 1,000,000$$
$$\text{Common stock price, } P_0 = \$20 \text{ per share}$$
$$\text{Expected level of EBIT} = \$5,000,000$$
$$\text{Dividend payout ratio} = 100 \text{ percent}$$

In answering the following questions, assume that corporate income is not taxed.

(a) Under the present capital structure, what is the total value of the firm?

(b) What is the cost of common equity capital, K_c? What is the composite cost of capital, K_0?

(c) Now, suppose that Boston Textiles sells $1 million of long-term debt with an interest rate of 8 percent. The proceeds are used to retire outstanding common stock. According to *net-operating-income theory* (the independence hypothesis), what will be the firm's cost of common equity *after* the capital structure change?

   (1) What will be the dividend per share flowing to the firm's common shareholders?

   (2) By what percent has the dividend per share changed owing to the capital-structure change?

   (3) By what percent has the cost of common equity changed owing to the capital-structure change?

   (4) What will be the composite cost of capital after the capital-structure change?

16-6. Albany Golf Equipment is analyzing three different financing plans for a newly formed subsidiary. The plans are described below:

PLAN A	PLAN B	PLAN C
Common stock: $100,000	Bonds at 9%: $20,000 Common stock: 80,000	Preferred stock at 9%: $20,000 Common stock: 80,000

In all cases the common stock will be sold to net Albany $10 per share.
The subsidiary is expected to generate an average EBIT per year of
$22,000. The management of Albany places great emphasis on EPS
performance. Income is taxed at a 50 percent rate.
  (a) Where feasible, find the EBIT indifference levels between the alterna-
      tives.
  (b) Which financing plan do you recommend that Albany pursue?

**SELECTED
REFERENCES**

ALTMAN, EDWARD I., "Corporate Bankruptcy Potential, Stockholder Returns, and Share
  Valuation," *Journal of Finance*, 24 (December 1969), 887–900.
BARGES, ALEXANDER, *The Effect of Capital Structure on the Cost of Capital*. Englewood Cliffs,
  N.J.: Prentice-Hall, Inc., 1963.
BAUMOL, WILLIAM, and BURTON G. MALKIEL, "The Firm's Optimal Debt-Equity Combination
  and the Cost of Capital," *Quarterly Journal of Economics*, 81 (November 1967), 547–78.
BAXTER, NEVINS D., "Leverage, Risk of Ruin, and the Cost of Capital," *Journal of Finance*, 22
  (September 1967), 395–404.
BELKAOUI, AHMED, "A Canadian Survey of Financial Structure," *Financial Management*, 4
  (Spring 1975), 74–79.
BRIGHAM, EUGENE F., and MYRON J. GORDON, "Leverage, Dividend Policy, and the Cost of
  Capital," *Journal of Finance*, 23 (March 1968), 85–104.
DONALDSON, GORDON, *Corporate Debt Capacity*. Boston: Division of Research, Graduate
  School of Business Administration, Harvard University, 1961.
————, "New Framework for Corporate Debt Policy," *Harvard Business Review*, 40 (March-
  April 1962), 117–31.
————, "Strategy for Financial Emergencies," *Harvard Business Review*, 47 (November-
  December 1969), 67–79.
————, *Strategy for Financial Mobility*. Boston: Division of Research, Graduate School of
  Business Administration, Harvard University, 1969.
DURAND, DAVID, "Costs of Debt and Equity Funds for Business: Trends and Problems of Mea-
  surement," *Conference on Research in Business Finance*. New York: National Bureau of
  Economic Research, 1952, 215–47.
ELLIS, CHARLES D., "New Framework for Analyzing Capital Structure," *Financial Executive*, 37
  (April 1969), 75–86.
HAMADA, ROBERT S., "The Effect of the Firm's Capital Structure on the Systematic Risk of
  Common Stocks," *Journal of Finance*, 27 (May 1972), 435–52.
LEWELLEN, WILBUR G., *The Cost of Capital*. Dubuque, Iowa: Kendall/Hunt Publishing Company,
  1976.
MARTIN, JOHN D., and DAVID F. SCOTT, JR., "A Discriminant Analysis of the Corporate
  Debt-Equity Decision," *Financial Management*, 3 (Winter 1974), 71–79.
————, "Debt Capacity and the Capital Budgeting Decision," *Financial Management*, 5
  (Summer 1976), 7–14.
MELNYK, Z. LEW, "Cost of Capital as a Function of Financial Leverage," *Decision Sciences*, 1
  (July-October 1970), 327–56.
MILLER, MERTON H., "Debt and Taxes," *The Journal of Finance*, 32 (May 1977), 261–75.
MODIGLIANI, FRANCO, and MERTON H. MILLER, "The Cost of Capital, Corporation Finance
  and the Theory of Investment," *American Economic Review*, 48 (June 1958), 261–97.
————, "Corporate Income Taxes and the Cost of Capital: A Correction," *American Economic
  Review*, 53 (June 1963), 433–43.

PRINGLE, JOHN J., "Price/Earnings Ratios, Earnings per Share, and Financial Management," *Financial Management*, 2 (Spring 1973), 34–40.

SCHALL, LAWRENCE D., "Firm Financial Structure and Investment," *Journal of Financial and Quantitative Analysis*, 6 (June 1971), 925–42.

SCHWARTZ, ELI, and J. RICHARD ARONSON, "Some Surrogate Evidence in Support of the Concept of Optimal Capital Structure," *Journal of Finance*, 22 (March 1967), 10–18.

SCOTT, DAVID F., JR., "Evidence on the Importance of Financial Structure," *Financial Management*, 1 (Summer 1972), 45–50.

——————, and JOHN D. MARTIN, "Industry Influence on Financial Structure," *Financial Management*, 4 (Spring 1975), 67–73.

SOLOMON, EZRA, "Leverage and the Cost of Capital," *Journal of Finance*, 18 (May 1963), 273–79.

——————, *The Theory of Financial Management*. New York: Columbia University Press, 1963.

TAGGART, ROBERT A., "Capital Budgeting and the Financing Decision: An Exposition," *Financial Management*, 6 (Summer 1977), 59–64.

WALSH, FRANCIS J., JR., *Planning Corporate Capital Structures*. New York: The Conference Board, Inc., 1972.

Dividend Policy and Internal Financing

*M*aximization of the value (price) of the firm's common stock was established in Chapter 1 as the appropriate goal in financial decision making. In other words, the "success" or "failure" of a decision by management should be judged by its impact upon the common stock price. We observed that the company's investment (Chapters 7, 8, 9, 11, and 12) and financing (Chapters 10, 14, 15, and 16) can increase the value of the firm. As we approach the firm's *dividend* and *internal financing* policies, the same framework is adopted. Toward that end, five objectives are established for this chapter:

1. *Examine the relationship between a corporation's dividend policy and the market price of its common stock.* Extensive controversy has developed on this issue, with the key question being, "Can dividend policy affect the value that investors place upon a company's stock?" Consequently, we look at the theoretical basis for the relationship between dividend policy and the market price of the stock.

2. *Present practical considerations that must be resolved in establishing the firm's dividend policy.*

3. *Review the types of dividend policy frequently used by corporations.* Here we examine the rationale underlying a stable dollar dividend policy.

4. *Study the procedures followed by a company in administering the dividend payment.*

5. *Examine the use of noncash dividends (stock dividends and stock splits).*

Before studying the particular issues relating to a firm's dividend policy, **INTRODUCTION**
we must understand several key terms and interrelationships.

A firm's dividend policy has two basic characteristics. First, the **dividend payout ratio** indicates the amount of dividends relative to the company's earnings per share. For instance, if the dividends per share is $2 and the earnings per share is $4, the payout ratio is 50 percent ($2 ÷ $4). A second feature of a firm's dividend policy relates to the *stability* of the dividends over time. As will be observed later in the chapter, dividend stability may be as important to the investors as the amount of dividends received.

The decision to pay a cash dividend involves a simultaneous decision *not* to reinvest the requisite cash in the firm. As a firm pays greater amounts in *dividends* to its common stockholders, less *internally generated capital* is available for reinvestment purposes. Alternatively, if management increases the amount of profits to be retained and reinvested within the business, the common stockholders' dividends must be reduced. Thus, a tradeoff exists between retaining internally generated funds and paying cash dividends.

This portion of the chapter examines the balance between paying **DIVIDEND POLICY**
dividends and retaining funds for future investments. At present, we will **AND COMMON**
be interested only in understanding the *theoretical issues*. Although this **STOCK PRICES**
approach may appear to be abstract and removed from the real world, the
basic theory is a prerequisite to understanding the practical issues involved
in establishing the firm's dividend policy.

To investigate the importance of dividend policy, we begin our study
in the *Land of Ez* (pronounced "Ease"), where the environment is quite
simple. First, the king has imposed *no income taxes*. Second, in the Land of
Ez investors can buy and sell securities without paying any sales *commissions*.
In addition, when a company issues new securities (stock or bonds), there
are no *flotation costs*. Furthermore, the Land of Ez is completely computerized, so that all information about firms is *instantaneously available* to the
public at *no cost*. Finally, all investors realize that the value of a company is a
function of its investment opportunities and its financing decisions. Therefore, the dividend policy offers *no new information* about either the firm's
ability to generate earnings or the riskiness of its earnings. To summarize,
in the beautiful Land of Ez:

1. There is no income tax on the investor's income nor is there a tax on gains
   realized from holding shares of common stock.
2. Security markets are considered to be perfect, where:
   (a) The investors incur no brokerage commissions.
   (b) Firms can issue securities at no cost.
   (c) Information is free and equally available to all investors.

(d) No informational content is assigned to a particular policy in determining the firm's capability to generate profits.

(e) Security prices reflect the present value of the expected future cash flows accruing to their owners.

Within this financial utopia, would a change in a corporation's dividend stream have any effect upon the price of the firm's stock? The answer is, "No." An example should help demonstrate why the investors in Ez would be indifferent as to which dividend payment policy the firm adopts.

Example: Dividend Policy in Perfect Markets. To illustrate the principles being set forth, consider King Venture, Inc., a corporation that received a charter at the end of 1978 to conduct business in the Land of Ez. The firm is to be financed by common stock only. Its life is to extend for only two years (1979 and 1980), at which time it will be liquidated.

The balance sheet at the time of King Venture's formation, as well as the projected cash flows from the short-term venture, are presented in Table 17-1. The anticipated cash flows are based upon an expected return on investment of 20 percent, which corresponds exactly with the common shareholders' required rate of return.

At the end of 1979 an additional investment of $300,000 will be required, which may be financed by retaining $300,000 of the 1979 profits or issuing new common stock or some combination of both. In fact, two dividend plans for 1979 are under consideration. The investors would receive either $100,000 or $250,000 in dividends. If $250,000 were paid, the company would be required to issue $150,000 in new stock. These two dividend plans and the corresponding new stock issue are depicted in Table 17-2. Our objective in analyzing the data is to answer the question, "Is either dividend plan preferable to the investors?" In answering this question, we must take three steps: (1) Calculate the amount and timing of the dividend stream for the *original* investors. (2) Determine the present

Table 17-1 KING VENTURE, INC., FINANCIAL DATA

	DECEMBER 31, 1978
Total assets	$2,000,000
Common stock (100,000 shares)	$2,000,000

	1979	1980
Projected cash available from operations for paying DIVIDENDS or for REINVESTING	$400,000	$460,000

Table 17-2 KING VENTURE, INC., 1979 PROPOSED DIVIDEND PLANS

	PLAN 1	PLAN 2
Internally generated cash flow	$400,000	$400,000
Dividend for 1979	100,000	250,000
Cash available for reinvestment	$300,000	$150,000
Amount of investment in 1979	300,000	300,000
Additional external financing required	$ 0	$150,000

Table 17-3 KING VENTURE, INC.: STEP 1—MEASUREMENT OF THE PROPOSED DIVIDEND STREAMS

	PLAN 1		PLAN 2	
	Total Amount	Amount Per Share[a]	Total Amount	Amount Per Share[a]
Year 1 (1979)				
(1) Dividend	$100,000	$1.00	$250,000	$2.50
Year 2 (1980)				
Total dividend consisting of:				
(2) *Original investment:*				
(a) Old investors	$2,000,000		$2,000,000	
(b) New investors	0		150,000	
(3) Retained earnings	300,000		150,000	
(4) Profits for 1980	460,000		460,000	
(5) Total dividend to all investors in 1980	$2,760,000		$2,760,000	
(6)				
Less dividends to new investors:				
(a) Original investment	0		(150,000)	
(b) Profits for new investors (20% of $150,000 investment)	0		(30,000)	
(7) Dividends available to original investors in 1980	$2,760,000	$27.60	$2,580,000	$25.80

[a]Number of original shares outstanding equals 100,000.

value of the dividend stream for each dividend plan. (3) Select the dividend alternative providing the higher value to the investors.

Step 1: Computing the dividend streams. The first step in this process is presented in Table 17-3. The dividends in 1979 (line 1, Table 17-3) are readily apparent from the data in Table 17-2. The amount of the dividend to be paid to the present shareholders in 1980 has to be calculated. In doing so, we assume that investors receive (1) their original investments (line 2, Table 17-3), (2) any funds retained within the business in 1979 (line 3, Table 17-3), and (3) the profits for 1980 (line 4, Table 17-3). However, if additional stockholders invest in the company, as with plan 2, the dividends to be paid to these investors must be subtracted from the total available dividends (line 6, Table 17-3). The remaining dividends (line 7, Table 17-3) represent the amount to be received in 1980 by the current stockholders. Therefore, the amounts of the dividend may be summarized as follows:

DIVIDEND PLAN	YEAR 1	YEAR 2
1	$1.00	$27.60
2	2.50	25.80

Step 2: Determining the present value of the cash flow streams. For each of the dividend payment streams the resulting common stock value is:[1]

$$\text{stock price (plan 1)} = \frac{\$1.00}{(1 + .20)} + \frac{\$27.60}{(1 + .20)^2} = \$20$$

$$\text{stock price (plan 2)} = \frac{\$2.50}{(1 + .20)} + \frac{\$25.80}{(1 + .20)^2} = \$20$$

Therefore, the two approaches provide the same end product; that is, the market price of King Venture's common stock is $20 regardless of the dividend policy chosen.

Step 3: Select the best dividend plan. If the objective is to maximize the shareholders' wealth, either plan is equally acceptable. Alternatively, shifting the dividend stream by a different dividend policy does not affect the value of the security. Thus, only if investments are made with expected returns exceeding 20 percent will the value of the stock increase. In other words, the only *wealth-creating activity* in the Land of Ez, where companies are financed entirely by equity, is the management's investment decisions.

The foregoing presentation of the firm's dividend decision is unquestionably deficient as a description of reality. However, from this meager beginning, a better understanding can be developed of the factors that affect dividend payment decisions. While the theory may not provide an accurate description of reality, we have learned that dividend policy is not

TRANSITION FROM THEORY TO PRACTICE

[1]Remember that in our perfect capital market security prices equal the present value of expected future cash flows.

inherently a wealth-creating activity for the firm's owners. In this setting, dividend policy is a passive factor, which has no impact upon the value of the firm. Only as the assumptions are relaxed to allow for *imperfections* in the market does dividend policy become a relevant policy variable for the firm. Specifically, recognition should be given to the following:

1. Flotation costs.
2. Income taxes.
3. Transaction costs in buying and selling securities and in acquiring information regarding the securities.
4. The potential informational content of a particular dividend policy.

Flotation Costs

Flotation costs represent the fees paid to investment bankers, lawyers, and accountants involved in selling a security issue to investors. If a company incurs flotation costs, they have a direct bearing upon the dividend decision. Owing to these costs, a firm must issue a larger amount of securities in order to receive the amount required for investments. For example, if $300,000 is needed to finance proposed investments, an amount exceeding the $300,000 will have to be issued to offset the flotation costs. This means, very simply, that new equity capital raised through the sale of common stock will be more expensive than capital raised through the retention of earnings.

The effect of flotation costs upon our simplified world has been to eliminate our indifference between financing by internal capital and by new common stock. Earlier, the company could either pay dividends and issue common stock or retain profits. However, where flotation costs exist, internal financing is preferred. Flotation costs add an extra dimension to the theory. Dividend policy, however, is still not a wealth-creating activity.

With the flotation cost assumption now removed, the firm's dividend policy would be as follows:

1. Maintain the optimum debt ratio in financing future investments.
2. Accept an investment if the net present value is positive. That is, the expected rate of return exceeds the cost of capital.
3. Finance the equity portion of new investments *first* by internally generated funds. Only after this capital is fully utilized should the firm issue new common shares.
4. If any internally generated funds still remain after making all investments, pay dividends to the investors. However, if all internal capital is needed for financing the equity portion of proposed investments, pay no dividend.

Example.   Assume that the KLP Corporation finances 40 percent of its investments by debt and the remaining 60 percent by common equity. Two million dollars have been generated from operations and may be used to finance the common equity portion of new investments or to pay common dividends. The firm's management is considering five investment opportunities. The expected rate of return for these investments, along with the firm's weighted marginal cost of capital curve, are presented graphically in Figure 17-1. From the information contained in the figure, we would accept projects A, B, and C, requiring $2.5 million in total financing. Therefore, $1 million in new debt (40% of $2.5 million) would be needed, with common equity having to provide $1.5 million (60% of $2.5 million). In this instance, the dividend payment decision would be to pay $500,000 in dividends, which is the **residual** or remainder of the $2 million internally generated capital after $1.5 million has been used for investment purposes.

To demonstrate further, what would have been the dividend decision if project D had been acceptable? If this investment is added to the firm's portfolio of proposed capital expenditures, $4 million in financing is needed. The debt financing would be $1.6 million (40% × $4 million) and common equity would provide $2.4 million (60% × $4 million). Since only $2 million is available internally, $400,000 in new common stock would be issued. Thus, the residual available for dividends would be zero, and no dividend would be paid.

In summary, dividend policy is influenced by: (1) the company's investment opportunities, (2) the capital-structure mix, and (3) the availability of the capital generated internally. In the KLP Corporation example, dividends were paid *only* after all acceptable investments had been financed. This logic, termed the **residual dividend theory,** implies that the dividends to be paid should equal the equity capital *left over* after financing investments. By this theory, dividend policy is a passive influence, having by itself no direct influence on the market price of the common stock. In this context, dividend policy is still insignificant when decisions are being

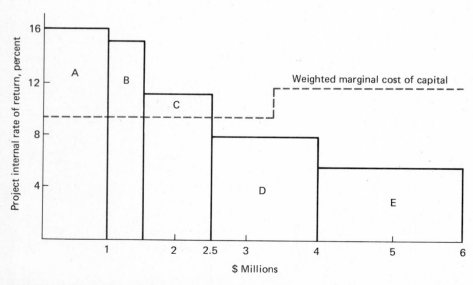

FIGURE 17-1 *KLP Corporation Investment Schedule*

made to maximize the shareholders' wealth. However, the amount of dividends may be less under the residual theory, where flotation costs are recognized, than in the Land of Ez, where flotation costs are nonexistent.

Personal Income
Taxes

Unlike the investors in the great Land of Ez, most investors do pay income taxes. For these taxpayers, the objective is to maximize the after-tax return on investment relative to the risk being assumed. This objective is realized by *minimizing* the effective tax rate on the income and whenever possible by *deferring* the payment of taxes. For investors who are subject to tax, the tax on the gain from the sale of stock is usually only 50 percent of the tax for dividend income.[2] For example, if an individual is in a 40 percent tax bracket, the tax rate on a gain from a stock price increase (capital gains) is 20 percent (half of 40%.) Also, taxes on dividend income are paid when the dividend is received, while taxes on price appreciation (capital gains) are deferred until the stock is actually sold. For these reasons, a preference may be created for the retention of a firm's earnings as opposed to the payment of cash dividends. If earnings retention is selected, there will be an increase in stock price, which in turn is taxed at the lower capital gains tax rate, and not until the stock is sold.

Although the majority of investors are subject to taxes, certain investment companies, trusts, and pension plans are exempt from taxes on their dividend income. Also, for tax purposes, a corporation may exclude 85 percent of the dividend income received from another corporation. For these investors, a bias exists for dividend income as opposed to capital gains.

In summary, the existence of taxes can directly affect a common shareholder's preference for capital gains or dividend income. This preference could in turn have a direct bearing upon a company's dividend policy.

Investor
Transaction Costs

The investors in the Land of Ez could exactly satisfy their personal income preferences by purchasing or selling securities when the dividends received did not comply with their current needs for income. If the investor did not view the dividends to be sufficient, he could simply sell a portion of stock, thereby creating a "dividend." However, if the dividend exceeded the desired amount, the investor would purchase stock with any "excess dividend."

As real-world considerations are inserted into our theory, we quickly realize that altering a firm's dividend policy by buying and selling the stock can be accomplished only at a cost. When an investor makes a stock transaction, brokerage fees are incurred. These commissions range from approximately 1 to 10 percent, depending upon the dollar size of the transaction. Additionally, when a stock is bought or sold, it must be reevaluated. Acquisition of the information needed to make the decision to buy or sell the stock may be time consuming and entail investigation costs. Therefore,

[2]See Chapter 2.

transaction costs discourage investors from adjusting common stockholdings to achieve a desired dividend. However, the net effect of transaction costs is not clear. Whether a low dividend–high retention or a high dividend–low retention is a better choice is a function of the investors' circumstances.

Informational Content

The financial theorist in the Land of Ez would adamantly maintain that a firm's value is strictly a function of its investment and financing decisions. A change in dividend policy has no impact upon the value of the stock. However, without any great effort, we may identify instances where companies have altered their dividend policy, and the market price of the stock reacted immediately. A prime example is Consolidated Edison. Investors were aware of the problems within the firm. Yet, when Con Ed eliminated its dividend in the second quarter of 1974, the stock price fell from $18 to $8 in a two-week period.

Why did the Con Ed investors react negatively to the modification in dividend policy? Does a decrease in dividends always produce a stock price reduction? In answering this question, we need to understand two basic principles. First, when investors are caught by *surprise* by the altered dividend policy, a change in the common stock market price will probably ensue. If the change had been expected, the price of the stock would have already adjusted before the formal announcement. Second, a constant relationship between the direction of the change in the level of a firm's dividends and its stock price movement does not exist. A decrease in the dividends can produce price increases or price decreases. The key determinant is not the direction of change in the dividend policy, but rather the perceived rationale or basis for the change. The Con Ed dividend reduction produced a sharp decrease in the stock price. Investors evidently perceived the dividend reduction to imply lower expectations for future earnings on the part of management. However, different conditions accompanying a dividend reduction could generate a higher price. For example, when a company is expanding into new investments, a short-term shortage in cash flows may develop. This problem may require a temporary reduction in dividends in order to provide adequate financing of the investments. If the stockholders consider the investment opportunities attractive, the price of the shares could very well rise, even though dividends have been cut.

To summarize, when an unexpected change in dividend policy develops, investors may attach *informational content* to the event. They simply perceive the managerial decision as a reflection of management's belief regarding the firm's earnings capacity.

SUMMARY OF DIVIDEND THEORY

Beginning from an idealistic world, we have seen that if income taxes and frictions within the marketplace are nonexistent, dividend policy is of no consequence to the financial manager. In this hypothetical world, dividend policy is a *passive* variable, and has no effect on the value of the firm's common stock. However, real-world considerations were shown to provide the stockholder with a distinct preference for either capital gains or dividend income. Therefore, as reflected in Figure 17-2, the amount of a firm's dividend payment depends upon two factors.

1. *The profitability of investment opportunities.* As a firm's investment opportunities increase, the dividend payout ratio should decrease. In other words, an inverse relationship should exist between the amount of investments having an expected rate of return that exceeds the cost of capital and the dividends remitted to investors. Owing to the flotation costs associated with raising external capital, the retention of internally generated equity financing is preferable to selling stock in terms of the wealth of the current common shareholders.

2. *The investor's preference and perceptions.* In the perfect market of the Land of Ez, stockholders were found to be indifferent between dividends and capital gains. However, a firm's dividend policy decisions may have an impact upon the value of the stock where (1) flotation costs are encountered in issuing new securities; (2) a tax advantage exists for capital gains over dividend income; (3) positive transaction costs are encountered when purchasing or selling securities; and (4) a dividend policy provides informational content.

DIVIDEND POLICY DECISION

In selecting a dividend policy for a firm, management should certainly be aware of the basic principles set forth by the residual dividend theory and the impact of potential market imperfections. In addition, *other practical considerations* that are generally unique to the firm should be included in the decision. After specifying these factors, we may then examine alternate dividend policies available to a company. Finally, we present an overview of the dividend policy decision.

Other Practical Considerations

To this point, we have indicated that the profitability of a corporation's investment opportunities and the "frictions" within the marketplace

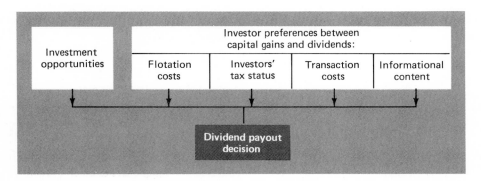

FIGURE 17-2 *Primary Factors Influencing the Firm's Dividend Payment*

(which affect investor preferences for dividend versus capital gains) are the key determinants of dividend policy. However, a number of secondary considerations should also be incorporated into the decision.

LEGAL RESTRICTIONS

Certain legal restrictions may limit the amount of the dividends that a firm may pay. These legal constraints fall into two categories. First, **statutory restrictions** prevent a company from paying dividends under certain conditions. While these specific limitations vary by state, generally a corporation may not pay a dividend (1) if the firm's liabilities exceed its assets; (2) if the amount of the dividend exceeds the accumulated profits (retained earnings); and (3) if the dividend is being paid from capital invested in the firm.

The second type of legal restrictions is unique to each firm and results from restrictions in debt and preferred stock contracts. To minimize their risk, debtholders and preferred stockholders frequently impose restrictive provisions upon management as a condition to their investment in the company. These constraints placed upon management may include the provision that dividends may not be paid from earnings prior to the debt contract. The corporation may also be required to maintain a given amount of working capital. Preferred stockholders may stipulate that dividends may not be paid if any past or present preferred dividends have gone unpaid.

LIQUIDITY POSITION

Contrary to common opinion, the mere fact that a company has a large amount of retained earnings shown in the balance sheet does not indicate that any cash is available. The firm's current position in liquid assets, including cash, is basically independent of the retained earnings account. Certainly, a company with sizable retained earnings has historically been successful in generating cash from operations. Yet, these funds are typically either reinvested in the company within a short time period or used to pay maturing indebtedness. Thus, a firm may be extremely profitable and still be *cash poor*. Since dividends are paid with cash, *and not with retained earnings*, the firm must have cash available if dividends are to be paid. Hence, the firm's liquidity position has a direct bearing upon its ability to pay dividends.

AVAILABILITY OF OTHER SOURCES OF FINANCING

As already noted, a firm may (1) retain profits for investment purposes, and/or (2) pay dividends and issue new debt or equity securities to finance investments. However, for numerous small or new companies this second option is not realistic. These firms just do not have access to the capital markets, so they must rely more heavily upon internally generated funds. As a consequence, the dividend payout ratio is generally much less for a small or newly established firm than for a large, publicly-owned corporation.

EARNINGS PREDICTABILITY

A company's dividend payout ratio depends to some extent upon the predictability of the firm's profits over time. If earnings fluctuate significantly, management has greater difficulty in consistently relying upon internally generated funds to meet future needs. In this situation, when profits are realized, larger amounts may be retained to ensure that money is available when needed. Conversely, a firm that experiences a stable trend in earnings typically will pay a larger portion of its earnings out in dividends. For this company, less concern has to be given to the availability of profits to meet future capital requirements.

OWNERSHIP CONTROL

For many large corporations, control through the ownership of common stock is not an issue. However, for many small and medium-sized companies, maintaining voting control takes a high priority. If the present common shareholders are unable to participate in a new offering, issuing new stock is unattractive, in that the control of the current stockholders is diluted. The owners would prefer that management finance new investments by debt and through profits rather than by issuing new common stock. Thus, the firm's growth is constrained by the amount of debt capital available and by the company's capability to generate profits.

INFLATION

In recent years, inflationary pressures have become a problem for both consumers and businesses. The deterioration of the dollar's purchasing power has had a direct impact upon the replacement of fixed assets. Ideally, as these assets become worn and obsolete, the funds generated from depreciation are used to finance the replacements. However, as the cost of equivalent equipment continues to increase, the depreciation funds are insufficient. As a consequence, greater retention of profits may be required, which in turn implies that dividends may be inversely affected.

Regardless of a firm's long-term dividend policy, one of several year-to-year dividend payment patterns is generally followed:

Alternate Dividend Policies

1. *Constant dividend payout ratio.* If this policy is chosen, the percentage of earnings paid out in dividends is held constant. Although the dividend-to-earnings ratio is stable with this policy, the dollar amount of the dividend naturally fluctuates from year to year as profits vary.
2. *Stable dollar dividend per share.* This policy maintains a relatively stable dollar dividend over time. An increase in the dollar dividend usually does not occur until management is convinced that the higher dividend level can be maintained in the future. Management also will not reduce the dollar dividend

until the evidence clearly indicates that a continuation of the present dividend cannot be supported.

3. *Small, low, regular dividend plus a year-end extra.* A corporation following this policy pays a small regular dollar dividend plus a year-end *extra dividend* in prosperous years. The extra dividend is declared toward the end of the fiscal year, when the company's profits for the period can at least be estimated. Management's objective is to avoid the connotation of a permanent dividend. However, this purpose may be defeated if *recurring* "extra" dividends come to be expected by the investors. General Motors is an example of a firm that employs the low stable dividend plus an extra dividend at the end of the year.

Of the three dividend policies, the stable dollar dividend is by far the most popular. Figure 17-3 depicts the general tendency of companies to pay stable, but increasing, dividends. This practice is maintained even though the profits fluctuate significantly. In a study by Lintner, corporate managers were found to be reluctant to change the dollar amount of the dividend in response to "temporary" fluctuations in earnings from year to year. This aversion was particularly evident when it came to decreasing the amount of the dividend from the previous level.[3] More recently, Smith explained this process in terms of his "increasing-stream hypothesis of

---

[3]John Lintner, "Distribution of Income of Corporations among Dividends, Retained Earnings, and Taxes," *American Economic Review*, 46 (May 1956), 97–113.

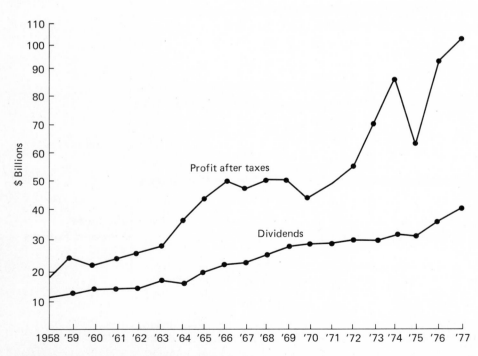

FIGURE 17-3 *Corporate Earnings and Dividends*

dividend policy."[4] He proposed that dividend stability is essentially a smoothing of the dividend stream in order to minimize the effect of other types of company reversals. Thus, corporate managers make every effort to avoid a dividend cut, attempting instead to develop a gradually increasing dividend series over the long-term future. However, if a dividend reduction is absolutely necessary, the cut will be sufficiently large to reduce the probability of future decreases.

As an example of a stable dividend policy, Figure 17-4 compares W. R. Grace & Co.'s earnings per share and dividends per share for 1967 through 1977. On average, the firm has paid approximately 56 percent of its earnings out in dividends. This percentage, however, has varied from 31.6 percent in 1975 to 107.1 percent in 1971. The contrasts clearly demonstrate management's hesitancy to change dividends in response to short-term fluctuations in earnings. When profits were decreasing between 1968 and 1971, the dollar dividends were essentially held constant. On the other hand, when profits rose sharply in 1975, dividends were increased only slightly.

Basis for Stable Dividends

While a stable dividend policy is certainly prevalent among many corporations, does an economic basis exist for this policy? In essence, is a stable dividend policy of value to investors? At present, no empirical evidence provides conclusive results. However, on an intuitive basis, several reasons have been offered to explain why an investor might prefer a stable dividend.

[4]Keith V. Smith, "Increasing Stream Hypothesis of Corporate Dividend Policy," *California Management Review*, 15 (Fall 1971), 56–64.

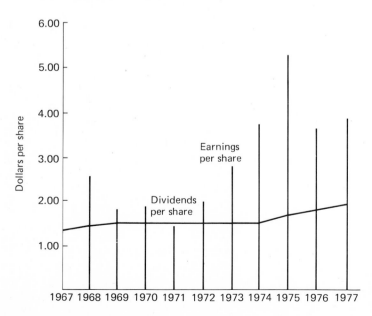

FIGURE 17-4 *Dividends Per Share and Earnings Per Share, W. R. Grace & Co.*

First, investors are thought to assign informational content to a firm's dividend policy. Since we have returned from the Land of Ez, the acquisition of information regarding a company's future prospects is no longer free of cost. To minimize these costs, investors may use the dividend policy as a surrogate for information that is not as easily accessible. If the investors of a particular company know that the board of directors will not change the dividend payment without being confident that the change reflects the company's *long-term* earnings prospects, this piece of information is useful in assessing the value of the corporate earnings. However, if dividends fluctuate randomly from year to year, investors are unable to glean any information from this policy in terms of the firm's long-term prospects. With this increased uncertainty, the dividends may be valued at a lower price; that is, the stock price may be less.

The second reason for an investor's preferring a stable dividend is related to the potential need for *current income*. Many investors rely upon dividends to satisfy personal needs. These needs are relatively constant over time and are best satisfied by a stable dividend. If the dividend payments fluctuate substantially, the investor who depends on them for personal living expenses may have to sell or purchase the stock for the purpose of synchronizing cash flows. For instance, if the dividend payment is decreased, many personal investors may have to sell a portion of their stock to make up the difference. On the other hand, if dividends were increased sizably, the investor would have to reinvest the excess funds. Either action, that of buying or selling the security, involves both investor time and brokerage commissions. For these investors, a stable dividend would no doubt be a better policy.

A third basis for a stable dividend policy is the existence of **legal listing.** Many states stipulate that financial institutions, such as insurance companies, mutual funds, and pension funds, may invest only in companies with a regular dividend payment. Also, the recent federal legislation controlling qualified pension plans *encourages* the investment managers of these plans to invest in stock with stable dividends.

In summary, we can expect, at least intuitively, that investors prefer stable dividends. An investor preferring dividend stability will have a lower required rate of return for a firm's stock that maintains a stable dividend policy than for a similar stock where the dividend is subject to erratic fluctuations. Hence, a stable dividend means a *lower required rate of return*, which in turn results in a *higher market price of the stock*.

After studying the relevance of a firm's dividend policy, what conclusions may we reach? Is the determination of a dividend policy a wealth-creating activity? In other words, does the dividend-policy decision have any bearing upon the common stock market price? Definitive answers to these questions are lacking. Market imperfections definitely suggest that the theoretician does not provide a complete picture. Even so, we may not unequivocally state that dividend policy is relevant in maximizing share price. The omissions and oversimplifications may be counterproductive.

Dividend Policy: A Scenario

That is, as we relax one assumption, the implications may favor a larger dividend payment. Yet, the simultaneous relaxation of a second assumption could suggest a lower dividend. Consequently, the net result on the stock price may be insignificant. Even so, several intuitive conclusions appear appropriate.

The residual dividend theory is definitely infeasible in the short term. The year-to-year variability in dividend payments resulting from a strict compliance to the residual theory would place undue hardship on investors who depend on dividend income. The increased personal transactions costs and the loss of potential informational content would probably be detrimental to the stockholders' welfare. However, the firm's dividend policy could effectively be treated as a *long-term residual.* Rather than projecting investment requirements for a single year, management should anticipate financing needs for several years. Based upon the expected investment opportunities during the planning horizon, the firm's debt-equity mix, and the funds generated from operations, the target dividend payout ratio could be established. If internal funds remained after projection of the necessary equity financing, dividends would be paid. However, a dividend stream should be planned by which the residual capital would be distributed evenly to the investors over the planning period. Conversely, if over the long term the entire amount of internally generated capital is needed for reinvestment in the company, then no dividend should be paid. The only reason for a small dividend in this circumstance is the possible interest by management in institutional investors who require a stable dividend as a criterion for investment.

In summary, the residual dividend theory is operational, but only in the long term. An effort has to be made to avoid short-term fluctuations in the dividend per share.

DIVIDEND-PAYMENT PROCEDURES

After the firm's dividend policy has been structured, several procedural details must be arranged. For instance, how frequently are dividend payments to be made? If a stockholder sells the shares during the year, who is entitled to the dividend? To answer these questions, we need to understand the dividend-payment procedures.

Generally, companies pay dividends on a quarterly basis. To illustrate, Sherwin Williams, Inc., has for several years paid $2.20 per share in annual dividends. However, the firm actually issues a $.55 quarterly dividend for a total yearly dividend of $2.20 ($.55 × 4).

The final approval of a dividend payment comes from the board of directors. As an example, Phillips Petroleum on January 9, 1978, announced that holders of record on February 3 would receive a $.30 dividend. The dividend payment was to be made on March 1. January 9 is the **declaration date**—the date when the dividend is formally declared by the board of directors. The **date of record,** February 3, designates when the stock transfer books are to be closed. Investors shown to own the stock on this date receive the dividend. If a notification of a transfer is recorded subsequent to February 3, the new owner is not entitled to the dividend. However, a problem could develop if the stock were sold on February 2, one day prior to the record date. Time would not permit the sale to be reflected on the stockholder list by the February 3 date of record. To avoid this problem, stock brokerage companies have uniformly decided to terminate the right of ownership to the dividend four working days prior to the record date. This prior date is the **ex-dividend date.** Therefore, any acquirer of the Phillips stock on January 30 or thereafter does not receive the dividend. Finally, the company mails the dividend check to each investor on March 1, the **payment date.**

An integral part of dividend policy is the use of **stock dividends** and **stock splits.** Both involve issuing new shares of stock on a pro rata basis to the current shareholders, while the firm's assets, its earnings, and the risk being assumed and the investor's percentage ownership in the company remain unchanged. The only *definite* result from either a stock dividend or stock split is the increase in the number of shares of stock outstanding.

STOCK DIVIDENDS AND STOCK SPLITS

To illustrate the effect of a stock dividend, assume that the KMP Corporation has 100,000 shares outstanding.[5] The firm's after-tax profits are $500,000, or $5 in earnings per share. At present, the company's stock is selling at a price/earnings multiple of ten, or $50 per share. Management is planning to issue a 20 percent stock dividend, so that a stockholder owning ten shares would receive two additional shares. We might immediately conclude that this investor is being given an asset (two shares of stock) worth $100; consequently, his personal worth should increase by $100. This conclusion is erroneous. The firm will be issuing 20,000 new shares (100,000 shares × 20 percent). Since the $500,000 in after-tax profits do not change, the new earnings per share will be $4.167 ($500,000 ÷ 120,000 shares). If the price/earnings multiple remains at ten, the market price of the stock after the dividend should fall to $41.67 ($4.167 earnings per share × 10). The investor now owns 12 shares worth $41.67, which provides a $500 total value; thus he is neither better nor worse off than before the stock dividend.

This example may make us wonder why a corporation would even bother with a stock dividend or stock split, if no one is benefited. However, before we study the rationale for such distributions, we should first understand the differences between a stock split and a stock dividend.

The only difference between a stock dividend and a stock split relates to their respective accounting treatment. Stated differently, *there is absolutely no difference on an economic basis between a stock dividend and a stock split.* Both represent a proportionate distribution of additional shares to the

Stock Dividend vs. Split

[5]The logic of this illustration is equally applicable for a *stock split.*

present stockholders. However, the stock split *for accounting purposes* has been defined as a stock dividend exceeding 25 percent.[6] Thus, a stock dividend is arbitrarily defined as a distribution of shares up to 25 percent of the number of shares currently outstanding.

The accounting treatment for a stock dividend requires the issuing firm to capitalize the "market value" of the dividend. In other words, the dollar amount of the dividend is transferred from retained earnings to the capital accounts. This procedure may best be explained by an example. Assume that the L. Bernard Corporation is preparing to issue a 15 percent stock dividend. The equity portion of the firm's balance sheet prior to the distribution is presented in Table 17-4. The market price for the stock has been $14. Thus, the 15 percent stock dividend increases the number of shares by 150,000 (1,000,000 shares × 15 percent). The "market value" of this increase is $2,100,000 (150,000 shares × $14 market price). To record this transaction, $2,100,000 would be transferred from retained earnings, resulting in a $300,000 increase in total par value (150,000 shares × $2 par value) and a $1,800,000 increment to paid-in capital. The $1,800,000 is the residual difference between $2,100,000 and $300,000. The revised balance sheet is reflected in Table 17-5.

What if the management of L. Bernard Corporation changed their plans, deciding rather to split the stock two-for-1? In other words, a *100*

---

[6]The 25 percent standard applies only to corporations listed on the New York Stock Exchange. The American Institute of Certified Public Accountants states that a stock dividend greater than 20 or 25 percent is for all practical purposes a stock split.

Table 17-4 L. BERNARD CORPORATION: BALANCE SHEET BEFORE STOCK DIVIDEND

Common stock:	
Par value (1,000,000 shares outstanding; $2 par value)	$2,000,000
Paid-in capital	8,000,000
Retained earnings	15,000,000
Total equity	$25,000,000

Table 17-5 L. BERNARD CORPORATION: BALANCE SHEET AFTER STOCK DIVIDEND

Common stock:	
Par value (1,150,000 shares outstanding; $2 par value)	$2,300,000
Paid-in capital	9,800,000
Retained earnings	12,900,000
Total equity	$25,000,000

percent increase in the number of shares would result. In accounting for the split, the changes to be recorded are (1) the increase in the number of shares, and (2) the decrease in the per-share par value from $2 to $1. The dollar amounts of each account do not change. The new balance sheet is shown in Table 17-6.

Thus, for a stock dividend, an amount equal to the market value of the stock dividend is transferred from retained earnings to the capital stock accounts. When stock is split, only the number of shares changes, and the par value of each share is decreased proportionately. Yet, despite this dissimilarity in accounting treatment, we should remember that no intrinsic difference exists between a split and a dividend.

Although *stock* dividends and splits occur far less frequently than *cash* dividends, a significant number of companies choose to use these share distributions either with or in lieu of cash dividends. In view of our earlier conclusion that no economic benefit results, how do corporations justify these distributions?

Proponents of stock dividends and splits frequently maintain that a key benefit is received by the stockholder because the price of the stock will not fall precisely in proportion to the share increase. For a two-for-one split, the price of the stock would not decrease by a full 50 percent, thereby leaving the stockholder with a higher total value. Two reasons are given for this disequilibrium condition. First, many financial executives believe that an optimal price range exists. Within this range the total market value of the common stockholders is thought to be maximized. As the price exceeds this range, fewer investors can purchase the stock, thereby constraining the demand for the stock. Consequently, a downward pressure is placed upon its price.[7] The second explanation relates to the *informational content* of the dividend/split announcement. Stock dividends and splits have generally been associated with growth companies. The connotation of a stock dividend or split has therefore been perceived as favorable, which suggests that this information will be received favorably in the market. However, the empirical evidence fails to verify these conclusions. Most studies indicate

[7]The "optimal price range" concept is a stronger incentive for stock splits than for stock dividends. As an example of a firm using a stock split to reduce the stock price, IBM in 1973 declared a three-for-two stock split.

Table 17-6 L. BERNARD CORPORATION: BALANCE SHEET AFTER STOCK SPLIT

Common stock:	
Par value (2,000,000 shares outstanding; $1 par value)	$2,000,000
Paid-in capital	8,000,000
Retained earnings	15,000,000
Total equity	$25,000,000

Rationale for a Stock Dividend or Split

that investors are perceptive in identifying the true meaning of a share distribution. If the stock dividend or split is not accompanied by a positive trend in earnings and increases in cash dividends, price increases surrounding the stock dividend or split are insignificant.[8] Therefore, we should be suspicious of the assertion that a stock dividend or split is beneficial in terms of increasing the investors worth.

A second reason cited for stock dividends or splits is the conservation of corporate cash. If a company is encountering cash problems, it can substitute a stock dividend for a cash dividend. However, as before, investors will probably look beyond the dividend to ascertain the underlying reason for the attempt to conserve cash. If the stock dividend results from an effort to conserve cash for attractive investment opportunities, the shareholder may bid up the stock price. However, if the move to conserve cash relates to financial difficulties within the firm, the market price will most likely react adversely.

SUMMARY

In determining the firm's dividend policy, two issues are important. First, the dividend payout ratio (the percentage of the earnings paid out in dividends) must be decided. This decision has an immediate impact upon the firm's financial mix. As the dividend payment is increased, less funds are available internally for financing investments. Consequently, if additional equity capital is needed, the company has to issue new common stock. Keeping in mind this interaction between the level of dividends and financing, management has to determine the *best* dividend policy for the company's investors. As with investment and capital-structure decisions, the *best* policy is defined as the one that maximizes the price of the common stock. The decision requires close scrutiny of the firm's financing needs and the investors' preference for dividend income or capital gains. However, selection of the most beneficial dividend payment is not easily accomplished. Management cannot apply an equation to resolve the question; rather, considerable judgment is required.

In its simplest form, the dividend payment is a *residual* factor. In this context, the dividend equals the remaining internal capital after financing of the equity portion of investments. However, this single criterion fails to recognize (1) the tax benefit of capital gains, (2) the investor's transaction costs associated with buying and selling stock, (3) the company's cost of issuing new stock, and (4) the informational content of a given policy. Furthermore, other factors to be considered include the firm's liquidity position, the accessibility to capital markets, inflation, legal restrictions, the stability of earnings, and the desire of investors to maintain control of the company.

[8]See James A. Millar and Bruce D. Fielitz, "Stock Split and Stock-Dividend Decisions," *Financial Management* (Winter 1973), pp. 35–45; and Eugene Fama, Lawrence Fisher, Michael Jensen, and Richard Roll, "The Adjustment of Stock Prices to New Information," *International Economic Review* (February 1969), pp. 1–21.

The second issue relating to dividend policy is the stability of dividends over time. All else remaining constant, most investors are thought to prefer a stable dollar dividend. This desire for stability relates to the need for current income, the informational content provided by a stable policy, and the requirement of many institutional investors that a regular dividend be paid.

Given the firm's investment opportunities, the imperfections in the market, and the perceived preference for stable dividends, the financial manager should apply the residual dividend theory over the long term. In essence, the firm's investment opportunities are to be projected throughout a multiple-year planning horizon. Given these investment needs, the target debt mix, and the anticipated internally generated funds, the amount of money available to pay dividends for the planning period may be determined. The dividend payments should then be made so that large and unexpected changes in the dividend per share are avoided.

Stock dividends and stock splits have been used by numerous corporations either in lieu of or to supplement cash dividends. At the present, no empirical evidence conclusively identifies a relationship between stock dividends and splits and the market price of the stock. Yet, conceivably a stock dividend or split could be used to keep the stock price within an optimal trading range. Also, if the investors perceived that the stock dividend contained favorable information about the firm's operations, the price of the stock could increase.

17-1. What is meant by the term *dividend payout ratio*?

17-2. Explain the tradeoff between retaining internally generated funds and paying cash dividends.

17-3. (a) What are the assumptions of a perfect market?
   (b) What effect does dividend policy have on the share price in a perfect market?

17-4. What is the impact of flotation costs on the financing decision?

17-5. (a) What is the *residual dividend theory*?
   (b) Why is this theory operational only in the long term?

17-6. Why might investors prefer capital gains over the same amount of dividend income?

17-7. What legal restrictions may limit the amount of dividends to be paid?

17-8. How does a firm's liquidity position affect the payment of dividends?

17-9. How can *ownership control* constrain the growth of a firm?

17-10. (a) Why is a stable dollar dividend policy popular from the viewpoint of the corporation?
   (b) Is it also popular with investors? Why?

17-11. Explain declaration date, date of record, and ex-dividend date.

17-12. What are the advantages of a stock split or dividend over a cash dividend?

17-1. United, Inc., maintains a constant dividend payout ratio of 40 percent. Earnings per share this year are $5.80 and are expected to grow indefinitely at a rate of 12 percent. What will be the dividend per share in one year? In five years?

17-2. If flotation costs for a common stock issue are 15 percent, how large must the issue be so that the firm will net $450,000?

17-3. Irwin Co. finances new investments by 35 percent debt and 65 percent equity. The firm needs $4,200,000 for financing new investments. If retained earnings equal $3,000,000, how much money will be available for dividends in accordance with the residual dividend theory?

17-4. RCB has 175,000 shares of common stock outstanding. Net income is $485,000, and the P/E ratio for the stock is eight. Management is planning a 15 percent stock dividend. What will be the price of the stock after the stock dividend? If an investor owns 100 shares prior to the stock dividend, does the total value of his shares change?

17-5. The management of Harris, Inc., is considering two dividend policies for the years 1979 and 1980. In 1980, the management is planning to liquidate the firm. One plan would pay a dividend of $1.75 in 1979 and a liquidating dividend of $25.40 in 1980. The alternative would be to pay out $4.25 in dividends in 1979 and a final dividend of $22.45 in 1980. The required rate of return for the common stockholders is 18 percent. Management is concerned about the effect of the two dividend streams on the value of the common stock.
(a) Assuming perfect markets, what would be the effect?
(b) What factors in the real world might change your conclusion reached in part (a)?

17-6. Britton Corporation is considering four investment opportunities. The required investment outlays and expected rates of return for these investments are shown below. The firm's cost of capital is 12 percent. The investments are to be financed 35 percent debt and 65 percent common equity. Internally generated funds totaling $850,000 are available for reinvestment.
(a) Which investments should be accepted? According to the residual dividend theory, what amount should be paid out in dividends?
(b) How would your answer change if the cost of capital were 9 percent?

STUDY PROBLEMS

INVESTMENT	INVESTMENT COST	INTERNAL RATE OF RETURN
A	$150,000	16.73%
B	600,000	14.25
C	300,000	12.50
D	250,000	9.65

17-7. Smead's, Inc., has projected its investment opportunities over a five-year planning horizon. The cost of each year's investment and the amount of internal funds available for reinvestment for that year are given below. The firm's debt-equity mix is 40 percent debt and 60 percent equity. There are currently 100,000 shares of common stock outstanding.

(a) What would be the dividend each year if the residual dividend theory were used on a year-to-year basis?

(b) What target stable dividend can Smead's establish by using the long-term residual dividend theory over the future planning horizon?

(c) Why might a residual dividend policy applied to the five years as opposed to individual years be preferable?

YEAR	COST OF INVESTMENTS	INTERNAL FUNDS AVAILABLE FOR REINVESTMENT OR FOR DIVIDENDS
1	$ 150,000	$300,000
2	650,000	450,000
3	200,000	400,000
4	1,000,000	600,000
5	300,000	650,000

17-8. The debt and equity section of the Randolph Corporation balance sheet is shown below. The current market price of the common shares is $25. Reconstruct the financial statement assuming that (a) a 10 percent stock dividend is issued, and (b) a 3 for 2 stock split is declared.

RANDOLPH CORPORATION

Debt	$1,000,000
Common	
Par ($2)	200,000
Paid in capital	400,000
Retained earnings	900,000
	$2,500,000

ARDITTI, FRED D., HAIM LEVY and MARSHALL SARNAT, "Taxes, Uncertainty and Optimal Dividend Policy," *Financial Management*, 1 (Spring 1976), 46–52.

BAKER, H. KENT and JOHN A. HASLEM, "Toward the Development of Client-Specified Valuation Models," *Journal of Finance*, 29 (September 1974), 1255–63.

BLACK, FISHER, and MYRON SCHOLES, "The Effects of Dividend Yield and Dividend Policy on Common Stock Prices and Returns," *Journal of Financial Economics*, 1 (May 1974), 1–22.

BRENNAN, MICHAEL, "A Note on Dividend Irrelevance and the Gordon Valuation Model," *Journal of Finance*, 26 (December 1971), 85–103.

SELECTED REFERENCES

BRIGHAM, EUGENE F., and MYRON J. GORDON, "Leverage, Dividend Policy, and the Cost of Capital," *Journal of Finance*, 23 (March 1968), 85–104.

FAMA, EUGENE F., "The Empirical Relationships between the Dividend and Investment Decisions of Firms," *American Economic Review*, 64 (June 1974), 304–18.

FAMA, EUGENE, LAWRENCE FISHER, MICHAEL JENSEN, and RICHARD ROLL, "The Adjustment of Stock Prices to New Information," *International Economic Review*, February 1969, pp. 1–21.

FRIEND, IRWIN, and MARSHALL PUCKETT, "Dividends and Stock Prices," *American Economic Review*, 54 (September 1964), 656–82.

GORDON, MYRON J., "Dividends, Earnings, and Stock Prices," *Review of Economic Statistics*, 41 (May 1959), 99–105.

HIGGINS, ROBERT C., "The Corporate Dividend-Saving Decision," *Journal of Financial and Quantitative Analysis*, 7 (March 1972), 1527–41.

————, "Dividend Policy and Increasing Discount Rate: A Clarification," *Journal of Financial and Quantitative Analysis*, 7 (June 1972), 1757–62.

KEANE, SIMON M., "Dividends and the Resolution of Uncertainty," *Journal of Finance and Accounting*, 1 (Autumn 1974), 389–93.

LAUB, P. MICHAEL, and ROSS WATTS, "On the Information Content of Dividends," *Journal of Business*, 49 (January 1976), 73–80.

LEASE, RONALD C., WILBUR C. LEWELLEN, and GARY G. SCHLARBAUM, "The Individual Investor: Attributes and Attitudes," *Journal of Finance*, May 1974, pp. 413–33.

LINTER, JOHN, "Distribution of Income of Corporations among Dividends, Retained Earnings, and Taxes," *American Economic Review*, 46 (May 1956), 97–113.

————, "Dividends, Earnings, Leverage, Stock Prices and the Supply of Capital to Corporations," *Review of Economics and Statistics*, 44 (August 1962), 243–69.

MEHTA, DILEEP R., "The Impact of Outstanding Convertible Bonds on Corporate Dividend Policy," *Journal of Finance*, 2 (May 1976), 489–506.

MILLAR, JAMES A., and BRUCE D. FIELITZ, "Stock Split and Stock Dividend Decisions," *Financial Management*, 2 (Winter 1973), 35–45.

MILLER, MERTON H., and FRANCO MODIGLIANI, "Dividend Policy, Growth, and the Valuation of Shares," *Journal of Business*, 34 (October 1961), 411–33.

PETTIT, R. RICHARDSON, "Dividend Announcements, Security Performance, and Capital Market Efficiency," *Journal of Finance*, 27 (December 1972), 993–1007.

PETTWAY, RICHARD H., and R. PHIL MALONE, "Automatic Dividend Reinvestment Plans of Nonfinancial Corporations," *Financial Management*, 2 (Winter 1973), 11–18.

POTTER, ROGER E., "An Empirical Study of Motivations of Common Stock Investors," *The Southern Journal of Business*, 6:3 (July 1971), 41–48.

SMITH, KEITH V., "Increasing Stream Hypothesis of Corporate Dividend Policy," *California Management Review*, 14 (Fall 1971), 56–64.

WALTER, JAMES E., "Dividend Policies and Common Stock Prices," *Journal of Finance*, 11 (March 1956), 29–41.

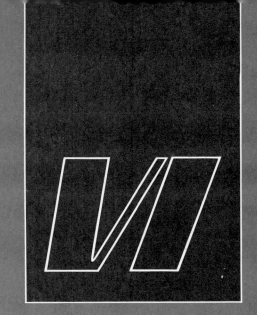

VI

LONG-TERM FINANCING

Raising Funds in the Capital Market

*A*t times internally generated funds will not be sufficient to finance all of the firm's proposed expenditures. In these situations the corporation may find it necessary to attract large amounts of financial capital externally.[1] The focus of this chapter is on the market environment in which long-term capital is raised. Ensuing chapters discuss the distinguishing features of the instruments by which long-term funds are raised.

The sums involved in tapping the capital markets can be vast. In November of 1975 Diamond Shamrock Corporation sold $100 million of 25-year sinking-fund debentures.[2] At the same time Phillips Petroleum Company marketed $250 million of 25-year debentures. In March of 1978 Texas Utilities Company offered $100 million of new common stock to the public. In two separate issues sold in October 1975 and June 1976, American Telephone and Telegraph Company (AT&T) sold a combined total of $1.2 billion of common stock.

To be able to distribute and absorb security offerings of this size, an economy must have a well-developed financial market system. To effec-

---

[1]By externally, we mean that the funds are "obtained" *other* than through retentions or depreciation. These latter two "sources" are commonly called internally generated funds.

[2]Debentures are long-term, unsecured promissory notes. The detailed features of corporate debt instruments are discussed in Chapter 20.

tively use that system, the financial officer must have a basic understanding of its structure. Accordingly, this chapter explores the rudiments of raising funds in the capital market.

Financial markets are institutions and procedures that facilitate transactions in all types of financial claims. The purchase of your home, the common stock that you may own, and your life insurance policy all took place in some type of financial market. Why do financial markets exist? What would the economy lose if our complex system of financial markets were not developed? We will address these questions here.

Some economic units spend *more* during a given period of time than they earn. Other economic units spend *less* on current consumption than they earn. For example, business firms in the aggregate usually spend more during a specific time period than they earn. Households in the aggregate usually spend less on current consumption than they earn. As a result, some mechanism is needed to facilitate the transfer of savings from those economic units with a savings surplus to those with a savings deficit. That is precisely the function of financial markets. Financial markets exist in order to *allocate* savings in the economy to the demanders of those savings. The central characteristic of a financial market is that it acts as the vehicle through which the forces of demand and supply for a specific type of financial claim (such as a corporate bond) are brought together.

Now, why would the economy suffer without a developed financial market system? The answer is simple. The wealth of the economy would be lessened without the financial markets. The rate of capital formation would not be as high if financial markets did not exist. This means that the net additions during a specific period to the stocks of (1) dwellings, (2) productive plant and equipment, (3) inventory, and (4) consumer durables would occur at lower rates. The rationale behind this assertion can be clarified through the use of Figure 18-1. The abbreviated balance sheets in the figure refer to firms or any other type of economic units that operate in the private as opposed to governmental sectors of the economy. This means that such units cannot issue money to finance their activities.

At stage 1 in Figure 18-1 only real assets exist in the hypothetical economy. **Real assets** are tangible assets like houses, equipment, and inventories. They are distinguished from **financial assets,** which represent claims for future payment on other economic units. Common and preferred stocks, bonds, bills, and notes all are types of financial assets. If only real assets exist, then savings for a given economic unit, such as a firm, must be accumulated in the form of real assets. If the firm has a great idea for a new product, that new product can be developed, produced, and distributed only out of company savings (retained earnings). Furthermore, all investment in the new product must occur simultaneously as the savings are generated. If you have the idea, and we have the savings, there is no mechanism to transfer our savings to you. This is not a good situation.

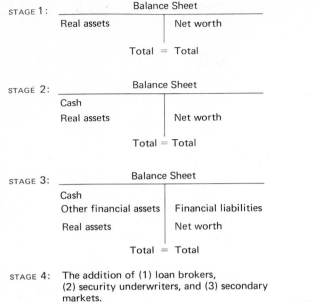

STAGE 1:

Balance Sheet	
Real assets	Net worth

Total = Total

STAGE 2:

Balance Sheet	
Cash	
Real assets	Net worth

Total = Total

STAGE 3:

Balance Sheet	
Cash	
Other financial assets	Financial liabilities
Real assets	Net worth

Total = Total

STAGE 4: The addition of (1) loan brokers, (2) security underwriters, and (3) secondary markets.

STAGE 5: The addition of financial intermediaries.

FIGURE 18-1 *The Development of a Financial Market System*

At stage 2 paper money comes into existence in the economy. Here, at least, you can *store* your own savings in the form of money. Thus, you can finance your great idea by drawing down your cash balances. This is an improvement over stage 1, but there is still no effective mechanism to transfer our savings to you. You see, we will not just hand you our dollar bills. We will want a receipt.

The concept of a receipt that represents the transfer of savings from one economic unit to another is a monumental advancement. The economic unit with excess savings can lend the savings to an economic unit that needs them. To the lending unit these receipts are identified as "other financial assets" in stage 3 of Figure 18-1. To the borrowing unit, the issuance of financial claims (receipts) shows up as "financial liabilities" on the stage 3 balance sheet. The economic unit with surplus savings will earn a rate of return on those funds. The borrowing unit will pay that rate of return, but it has been able to finance its great idea.

In stage 4 the financial market system moves further toward full development. Loan brokers will come into existence. These brokers help locate pockets of excess savings and channel such savings to economic units needing the funds. Some economic units will actually purchase the financial claims of borrowing units and sell them at a higher price to other investors; this process is called **underwriting.** Underwriting will be discussed in more detail later in this chapter. Additionally, **secondary markets** will develop. Secondary markets just represent trading in already-existing financial claims. If you buy your brother's General Motors common stock, that is a secondary market transaction. Secondary markets reduce the risk of investing in financial claims. Should you need cash, you can liquidate your claims in the secondary market. This induces savers to invest in securities.

The progression toward a developed and complex system of financial markets ends with stage 5. Here, financial intermediaries come into existence. You can think of financial intermediaries as the major financial institutions with which you are used to dealing. These include commercial banks, savings and loan associations, credit unions, life insurance companies, and mutual funds. Financial intermediaries all share a common characteristic: they offer their own financial claims, called **indirect securities,** to economic units with excess savings. The proceeds from selling their indirect securities are then used to purchase the financial claims of other economic units. These latter claims can be called **direct securities.** Thus, a mutual fund might sell mutual fund shares (their indirect security) and purchase the common stocks (direct securities) of some major corporations. A life insurance company sells life insurance policies and purchases huge quantities of corporate bonds. Financial intermediaries thereby involve many small savers in the process of capital formation. This means there are more "good things" for everybody to buy.

A developed financial market system provides for a greater level of wealth in the economy. In the absence of financial markets, savings are not transferred to the economic units most in need of those funds. It is difficult, after all, for a household to build its own automobile. The financial market system makes it easier for the economy to build automobiles and all of the other goods that economic units like to accumulate.

Numerous approaches exist for classifying the securities markets. At times, the array can be confusing. An examination, however, of four sets of dichotomous terms can help provide a basic understanding of the structure of the U. S. financial markets.

When a corporation decides to raise external capital, those funds can be obtained by making a public offering or a private placement. In a **public offering** both individual and institutional investors have the opportunity to purchase the securities. The securities are usually made available to the public at large by a managing investment banking firm and its underwriting syndicate. In the public offering the firm does not meet the ultimate purchasers of the securities. The public market is an impersonal market.

In a **private placement,** also called a **direct placement,** the securities are offered and sold to a limited number of investors. The firm will usually hammer out, on a face-to-face basis with the prospective buyers, the details of the offering. In this setting the investment banking firm may act as a finder by bringing together the potential lenders and borrower. The private placement market is a more personal market than its public counterpart. Both investment banking and private placements are explored in more detail later in this chapter.

Primary markets are those where securities are offered for the *first* time to potential investors. A new issue of common stock by AT&T is a primary market transaction. This type of transaction *increases* the total stock of financial assets outstanding in the economy.

As mentioned in our discussion of the development of the financial market system, **secondary markets** represent transactions in currently outstanding securities. If the first buyer of the AT&T stock subsequently sells it, he does so in the secondary market. All transactions after the initial purchase take place in the secondary market. These sales do *not* affect the total stock of financial assets that exist in the economy. Both the money market and the capital market, described next, have primary and secondary sides.

MONEY MARKET

The key distinguishing feature between the money and capital markets is the maturity period of the securities traded in them. The **money market** refers to all institutions and procedures that provide for transactions in short-term debt instruments generally issued by borrowers with very high credit ratings. By financial convention, "short-term" means maturity periods of one year or less. Notice that equity instruments, either common or preferred, are not traded in the money market. The major instruments issued and traded are U. S. Treasury bills, various federal agency securities, bankers' acceptances, negotiable certificates of deposit, and commercial paper. Detailed descriptions of these instruments as elements of the firm's marketable securities portfolio are given in Chapter 8. Commercial paper as a short-term financing vehicle is discussed in Chapter 10. Keep in mind that the money market is an intangible market. You do not walk into a building on Wall Street that has the words "Money Market" etched in stone over its arches. Rather, the money market is primarily a telephone market where trading does not occur at any specific location. Most agree, however, that New York City is the center of this market.

CAPITAL MARKET

The **capital market** refers to all institutions and procedures that provide for transactions in long-term financial instruments. Long-term, here, means having maturity periods that extend beyond one year. In the broad sense this encompasses term loans and financial leases, corporate equities, and bonds. All of these financing modes are discussed in Chapters 19, 20, and 21. The funds that comprise the firm's capital structure are raised in the capital market. Important elements of the capital market are the organized security exchanges and the over-the-counter markets.

Organized security exchanges are tangible entities; they physically occupy space (such as a building or part of a building), and financial instruments are traded on their premises. The **over-the-counter markets** include all security markets *except* the organized exchanges. The money market, then, is an over-the-counter market. Because both of these markets are important to financial officers concerned with raising long-term capital, some additional discussion is warranted.

Organized Security Exchanges and Over-the-Counter Markets

ORGANIZED SECURITY EXCHANGES

For practical purposes there are seven major security exchanges in the United States.[3] These are the (1) New York Stock Exchange, (2) American Stock Exchange, (3) Midwest Stock Exchange, (4) Pacific Coast Stock Exchange, (5) Philadelphia Stock Exchange, (6) Boston Stock Exchange, and the (7) Cincinnati Stock Exchange. The New York Stock Exchange (NYSE) and the American Stock Exchange (AMEX) are called *national* exchanges, while the others are loosely described as *regionals.*

All of these seven active exchanges are registered with the Securities and Exchange Commission (SEC). Firms whose securities are traded on the registered exchanges must comply with reporting requirements of both the specific exchange and the SEC. In excess of 80 percent of the annual dollar volume of transactions on the registered exchanges takes place on the NYSE. In 1977 the dollar trading volume on the Midwest exchange actually exceeded that of the AMEX, which usually runs second to the NYSE.[4] Together, the NYSE, the AMEX, and the Midwest account for over 90 percent of the annual dollar volume transacted on the registered exchanges.

The business of an exchange, including securities transactions, is conducted by its **members.** Members are said to occupy "seats." There are 1366 seats on the NYSE, a number that has remained constant since 1953. Major stock brokerage firms own seats on the exchanges. An officer of the firm is designated to be the member of the exchange, and this membership permits the brokerage house to use the facilities of the exchange to effect securities trades. During 1976 the prices of seats that were exchanged for cash ranged from a low of $40,000 to a high of $104,000. The highest price paid in recent times was $515,000 in 1969.[5]

Stock-Exchange Benefits. Both corporations and investors enjoy

[3]Others include (1) the Honolulu Stock Exchange, which is unregistered; (2) the Board of Trade of the City of Chicago, which does not now trade stocks; and (3) the Chicago Board Options Exchange, Inc., which deals in options rather than stocks.
[4]Jonathan R. Laing, "Shaky Floor: Problems Multiply at Midwest Exchange, but Chief is Optimistic," *The Wall Street Journal*, April 4, 1978, pp. 1, 20.
[5]New York Stock Exchange, *Fact Book* (New York, 1977), p. 58.

several benefits provided by the existence of organized security exchanges.[6]

These include:

1. *Providing a continuous market.* This may be the most important function of an organized security exchange. A continuous market provides a series of continuous security prices. Price changes from trade to trade, then, tend to be smaller than they would be in the absence of organized markets. The reasons are that there is a relatively large sales volume in each security, trading orders are quickly executed, and the range between the price asked for a security and the offered price tends to be narrow. The result is that price volatility is reduced. This enhances the liquidity of security investments and thereby makes them more attractive to potential investors. While it is difficult to prove, it seems logical to offer that this market feature probably reduces the cost of capital to corporations.

2. *Establishing and publicizing fair security prices.* An organized exchange permits security prices to be freely set by competitive forces. They are not set by negotiations off the floor of the exchange, where one party might have a bargaining advantage over the other. A bidding process is followed that flows from the supply and demand underlying each security. This means the specific price of a security is determined in the manner of an auction. Additionally, the security prices determined at each exchange are widely publicized. Just read the pages of most newspapers and the information is available to you. By contrast, the prices and resulting yields on the private placements of securities are more difficult to obtain.

3. *Helping business raise new capital.* Because a continuous secondary market exists where prices are competitively determined, it is easier for firms to successfully float new security offerings. This continuous pricing mechanism also facilitates the determination of the offering price of a new issue. This means that comparative values are easily observed.

Listing Requirements. To directly receive the benefits provided by an organized exchange, the firm must seek to have its securities listed on the exchange. An application for listing must be filed and a fee paid. The requirements for listing vary from exchange to exchange; those of the NYSE are the most stringent. The general criteria for listing fall into these categories: (1) profitability, (2) size, (3) market value, and (4) public ownership. To give you the flavor of an actual set of listing requirements, those set forth by the NYSE are displayed in Table 18-1.[7]

OVER-THE-COUNTER MARKETS

Many publicly held firms do not meet the listing requirements of major stock exchanges. Others may want to avoid the (1) reporting re-

---

[6]A more detailed discussion on stock-exchange functions can be found in Frederick Amling, *Investments: An Introduction to Analysis and Management*, 4th ed. (Englewood Cliffs, N.J.: Prentice-Hall, Inc., 1978), Chap. 8.

[7]New York Stock Exchange, *Fact Book*, 1977, p. 31.

Table 18-1 NYSE LISTING REQUIREMENTS

Profitability

Earnings before taxes (EBT) for the most recent year must be at least $2.5 million. For the two years preceding that, EBT must be at least $2.0 million.

Size

Net tangible assets must be at least $16.0 million.

Market Value[a]

The market value of publicly held stock must be at least $16.0 million.

Public Ownership

There must be at least 1.0 million publicly held common shares. There must be at least 2000 holders of 100 shares or more.

[a]The market value test is tied to the level of common stock prices prevailing in the marketplace at the time of the listing application. From time to time the $16.0 requirement noted above may be lessened. Under current regulations of the NYSE, the requirement can never be less than $8.0 million.

quirements and (2) fees required to maintain listing. As an alternative their securities may trade in the over-the-counter markets. On the basis of sheer numbers (not dollar volume), more stocks are traded over-the-counter than on organized exchanges. As far as secondary trading in corporate bonds is concerned, the over-the-counter markets are "where the action is." In a typical year, upwards of 90 percent of corporate bond business takes place over-the-counter.

Most over-the-counter transactions take place through a loose network of security traders who are known as broker-dealers and brokers. Brokers do not purchase securities for their own account, whereas dealers do. Broker-dealers stand ready to buy and sell specific securities at selected prices. They are said to "make a market" in those securities. Their profit is the spread or difference between the price they will pay for a security (bid price) and the price at which they will sell the security (asked price).

Price Quotes. The availability of prices is not as continuous in the over-the-counter market as it is on an organized exchange. Since February 8, 1971, however, when a computerized network called NASDAQ came into existence, the availability of prices in this market has improved substantially. NASDAQ stands for National Association of Security Dealers Automated Quotation System. It is a telecommunications system that serves to provide a national information linkup among the brokers and dealers operating in the over-the-counter markets. Subscribing traders have in their offices a cathode-ray terminal that allows them to obtain representative bid and ask prices for thousands of securities traded over-the-counter. NASDAQ is a quotation system, not a transactions system. The final trade is still consummated by direct negotiation between traders.

NASDAQ price quotes for many stocks are published daily in *The Wall Street Journal.* This same financial newspaper also publishes prices on hundreds of other stocks traded over-the-counter. Local papers supply prices on such stocks of regional interest. Finally, the National Quotation Bureau publishes daily "pink sheets," which contain prices on about 8000 securities; these sheets are available in the offices of most security dealers.

Most corporations raise long-term capital on an infrequent basis. Whereas the activities of working-capital management go on daily, the attracting of long-term capital is, by comparison, episodic. The monetary sums involved can be huge, so these situations are considered of great importance to financial managers. Since most financial managers are unfamiliar with the subtleties of raising long-term funds, they will enlist the help of an expert. That expert is an investment banker.

The **investment banker** is a financial specialist involved as an intermediary in the merchandising of securities. He acts as a middleman by facilitating the flow of savings from those economic units that want to invest to those units that want to raise funds. We use the term "investment banker" to refer both to a given individual and to the organization for which he works, variously known as an **investment banking firm** or an **investment banking house.** Although these firms are called "investment bankers," they are bankers in name only. They perform no depository or lending functions. The activities of commercial banking and investment banking as we know them today were separated by the Banking Act of 1933 (also known as the Glass-Steagall Act of 1933). Just what does this middleman role consist of? That is most easily understood in terms of the basic functions of investment banking.

The investment banker performs three basic functions: (1) underwriting, (2) distributing, and (3) advising. Each of these activities will be discussed briefly.

UNDERWRITING

The term **underwriting** is borrowed from the field of insurance. It means "assuming a risk." The investment banker assumes the risk of selling a security issue at a satisfactory price. A satisfactory price is one that will generate a profit for the investment banking house.

The procedure goes like this. The managing investment banker and his syndicate will buy the security issue from the corporation that is in need of funds. The **syndicate** is just a group of other investment bankers who are invited to help buy and resell the issue. The managing house is the investment banking firm that originated the business because its corporate client decided to raise external funds. So, on a specific day, the firm that is raising capital is presented with a check in exchange for the securities being issued. At this point the investment banking syndicate owns the securities. The fund-raising corporation has its cash and can proceed to use it in the predetermined manner. The firm is now immune from the possibility that the state of the security markets might turn sour. If the price of the newly issued security falls below that paid to the firm by the syndicate, then the syndicate will suffer a loss on this underwriting effort. The syndicate, of course, hopes that the opposite situation will result. Its objective is to sell the new issue to the investing public at a price per security greater than its cost.

DISTRIBUTING

Once the syndicate owns the new securities, it must get them into the hands of the ultimate investors. This is the distribution or selling function of investment banking. The investment banker may have branch offices across the United States or it may have an informal arrangement with several security dealers who regularly buy a portion of each new offering for final sale. It is not unusual to have 300 to 400 dealers involved in the selling effort. The syndicate can properly be viewed as the security wholesaler, while the dealer organization can be viewed as the security retailer.

ADVISING

The investment banker is an expert in the issuance and marketing of securities. A sound investment banking house will be aware of prevailing market conditions and can relate those conditions to the particular type of security that should be sold at a given time. Business conditions may be pointing to a future increase in interest rates. The investment banker might advise the firm to issue its bonds in a timely fashion to avoid the higher yields that are forthcoming. He can analyze the firm's capital structure and make recommendations as to what general source of capital should be issued. In many instances the firm will invite its investment banker to sit on the board of directors. This permits him to observe corporate activity and make recommendations on a regular basis.

Several methods are available to the corporation for placing new security offerings into the hands of final investors. The investment banker's role is different in each of these. Sometimes, in fact, it is possible to bypass completely the use of an investment banker. These methods are described in this section. Private placements, because of their importance, are treated separately later in the chapter.

Distribution Methods

NEGOTIATED PURCHASE

In a negotiated underwriting the firm that needs funds makes contact with an investment banker, and deliberations concerning the new issue begin. If all goes well, a *method* is negotiated for determining the price the investment banker and his syndicate will pay for the securities. For example, the agreement might state that the syndicate will pay $2 less than the closing price of the firm's common stock on the day before the offering date of a new stock issue. The negotiated purchase is the most prevalent method of securities distribution in the private sector. It is generally thought to be the most profitable technique as far as investment bankers are concerned.[8]

COMPETITIVE-BID PURCHASE

The method by which the underwriting group is determined distinguishes the competitive-bid purchase from the negotiated purchase. In a competitive underwriting several underwriting groups bid for the right to purchase the new issue from the corporation that is raising funds. The firm does not directly select the investment banker. The investment banker that underwrites and distributes the issue is in effect chosen by an auction process. The syndicate willing to pay the greatest dollar amount per new security will win the competitive bid.[9]

Most competitive-bid purchases are confined to three situations, compelled by legal regulations. These are (1) railroad issues, (2) public utility issues, and (3) state and municipal bond issues. The argument in favor of competitive bids is that any undue influence of the investment banker over the firm is mitigated and the price received by the firm for each security should be higher. Thus, we would intuitively suspect that the cost of capital in a competitive-bid situation would be less than in a negotiated-purchase situation. Evidence on this question, however, is mixed.[10] One problem with the competitive-bid purchase as far as the fund-raising firm is concerned is that the benefits gained from the advisory function of the investment banker are lost. It may be necessary to use an investment banker for advisory purposes and then exclude him from the competitive-bid process. In this regard many utilities have in the 1960s and 1970s obtained exemptions from the Federal Power Commission that permit them to raise capital by negotiated underwriting.

COMMISSION OR BEST-EFFORTS BASIS

Here, the investment banker acts as an agent rather than as a principal in the distribution process. The securities are *not* underwritten. The investment banker attempts to sell the issue in return for a fixed commission on each security that is actually sold. Unsold securities are returned to the corporation. This arrangement is typically used for more speculative issues. The issuing firm may be smaller or less established than the investment banker would like in order to assume the underwriting risk. Because

[8]Samuel L. Hayes, III, "Investment Banking: Power Structure in Flux," *Harvard Business Review*, 49 (March-April 1971), 138.

[9]An excellent description of this process is found in Ernest Bloch, "Pricing a Corporate Bond Issue: A Look Behind the Scenes," *Essays in Money and Credit*, Federal Reserve Bank of New York (December 1964), pp. 72–76.

[10]Gary D. Tallman, David F. Rush, and Ronald W. Melicher, "Competitive Versus Negotiated Underwriting Cost of Regulated Industries," *Financial Management*, 3 (Summer 1974), 49–55.

the underwriting risk is not passed on to the investment banker, this distribution method is less costly to the issuer than either a negotiated or competitive-bid purchase. On the other hand, the investment banker only has to give it his "best effort." A successful sale is not guaranteed.

PRIVILEGED SUBSCRIPTION

Occasionally, the firm may feel that a distinct market already exists for its new securities. When a new issue is marketed to a definite and select group of investors, it is called a **privileged subscription.** Three target markets are typically involved: (1) current stockholders, (2) employees, or (3) customers. Of these, distributions directed at current stockholders are the most prevalent. Such offerings, called "rights" offerings, are discussed in detail in Chapter 20. In a privileged subscription the investment banker may act only as a selling agent. It is also possible that the issuing firm and the investment banker might sign a **standby agreement,** which would obligate the investment banker to underwrite the securities that are *not* accepted by the privileged investors.

DIRECT SALE

In a **direct sale** the issuing firm sells the securities directly to the investing public without involving an investment banker in the process. Even among established corporate giants this procedure is relatively rare. A variation of the direct sale, though, has been used more frequently in the 1970s than in previous decades. This involves the private placement of a new issue by the fund-raising corporation *without* the use of an investment banker as an intermediary. Texaco, Mobil Oil, and International Harvester are examples of large firms that have followed this procedure.[11]

The negotiated purchase is the distribution method most likely to be used by the private corporation. It makes sense, then, to cover in some detail the *sequence of events* that comprise the negotiated underwriting.

The Negotiated-Purchase Sequence

1. *Selection of an investment banker.* The firm will initiate the fund-raising process by choosing an investment banker. On some occasions a third party, called a **finder,** may direct the firm to a specific investment banker. Typically the finder will receive a fee from the fund-raising firm if an underwriting agreement is eventually signed. Use of a finder is one way of gaining access to a quality investment banker.
2. *Preunderwriting conferences.* A series of preunderwriting conferences will be held between the firm and the investment banker. Key items discussed are (1) the amount of capital to be raised, (2) whether the capital markets seem to be especially receptive at this time to one type of financing instrument over another, and (3) whether the proposed use of the new funds appears reasonable. At these conferences it will be confirmed that a flotation will, in fact, take

[11] See Wyndham Robertson, "Future Shock at Morgan Stanley," *Fortune*, 97 (February 27, 1978), 88, 90.

place, and that this particular investment banker will manage the underwriting. The investment banker will then undertake a complete financial analysis of the corporation and assess its future prospects. The final outcome of the preunderwriting conferences is the **tentative underwriting agreement.** This will detail (1) the approximate price the investment banker will pay for the securities and (2) the **upset price.** The upset price is a form of escape mechanism for the benefit of the issuing firm. If the market price of the firm's securities should drop in a significant fashion just before the new securities are to be sold, the price that the investment banker is to pay the firm might drop below the upset price. In this situation the new offering would be aborted.

3. *Formation of the underwriting syndicate.* An underwriting syndicate is a temporary association of investment bankers formed to purchase a security issue from a corporation for subsequent resale, hopefully at a profit to the underwriters. The syndicate is formed for very sound reasons. First, the originating investment banker probably could not finance the entire underwriting himself. Second, the use of a syndicate reduces the risk of loss to any single underwriter. Third, the use of a syndicate widens the eventual distribution effort. Each underwriter has his own network of security dealers who will purchase a portion of his participation in the offering. Most syndicates will contain ten to sixty investment banking houses. Since each house will have its own distribution network, the selling group can often consist of 100 to 600 dealers. An agreement signed by all members of the syndicate will bind them to certain performance standards. This will detail their participation (amount they can purchase) in the offering and their liability for any portion of the issue unsold by their fellow underwriters.

4. *Registering the securities.* Before a new public issue can be offered to prospective investors, it must be registered with the Securities and Exchange Commission (SEC). Securities that are exempt from registration will be discussed later in this chapter when we examine the regulation of the securities markets. Most new issues must comply with the requirements of the **Securities Act of 1933.** This dictates that a **registration statement** must be submitted to the SEC aimed at disclosing all facts relevant to the new issue that will permit an investor to make an informed decision. The SEC itself does *not* judge the investment quality of securities. The registration statement is a lengthy document containing (1) historical, (2) financial, and (3) administrative facts about the firm. The details of the new offering are presented, as well as the proposed use of the funds that are being raised. During a 20-day waiting period the SEC examines the registration statement for any errors or omissions. While this examination process is being carried out, the investment banking syndicate *cannot* offer the security for sale. Part of the package presented to the SEC for scrutiny is a document called a **prospectus.** Once approved, it is the official advertising vehicle for the security offering. During the waiting period a **preliminary prospectus,** outlining the important features of the new issue, may be distributed to potential investors. The preliminary prospectus contains no selling-price information or offering date. In addition, a stamped red-ink statement on the first page tells the reader that the document is *not* an official offer to sell the securities. In the jargon of finance, this preliminary prospectus is called a **red herring.** Once the registration statement is approved by the SEC, the security can be offered for sale provided the prospectus is made available to all concerned parties.

5. *Formation of the selling group.* In order to distribute the securities to final investors, a selling group is formed. The dealers comprising the selling group will purchase portions of the new issue from the syndicate members with whom they regularly do business. They will pay for each security a price higher than that paid by the syndicate member, but less than the offering price to the investing public. The responsibilities and rewards of the selling group are contained in the **selling group agreement.** Formation of the selling group completes the distribution network for the new offering. The structure of such a network is diagrammed in Figure 18-2.

6. *The due diligence meeting.* This is a "last-chance" gathering to get everything in order before taking the offering to the public. Usually, all members of the syndicate are present along with key officers of the issuing firm. Any omissions from the prospectus should be caught at this meeting. Most importantly, the final price to be paid by the syndicate to the firm will be settled. As we said earlier in this chapter, if the issue is additional common stock, the underwriting price may be a fixed amount below the closing price of the firm's outstanding stock on the day prior to the new offering. Capital-market conditions will be discussed, and the offering price of the security to the public will be set in light of those conditions. The "go ahead" will be given to print the final prospectus, which now will contain all relevant price information. The offering will usually be made the next day.

7. *Price-pegging.* Once the issue has been offered for sale, the managing underwriter will attempt to mitigate downward price movements in the secondary market for the security. He will do this by placing orders to buy at the agreed-upon public offering price. The objective of this activity is to stabilize the market price of the issue so that it can be sold at the initial offering price.

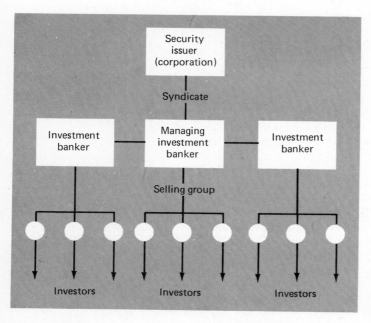

FIGURE 18-2 *Distributing New Securities*

The syndicate manager's intent to perform this price-maintenance operation must be disclosed in the registration statement.

8. *Syndicate termination.* A contractual agreement among the underwriters identifies the duration of the syndicate. Pragmatically, the syndicate is dissolved when the issue has been fully subscribed. If the demand for the issue is great, it may be sold out in a few days. If the issue lingers on the market, without much buyer interest, the remaining inventory may be sold at the existing secondary market price. The name of the game in investment banking is not margin, but turnover. Should the issue go sour, the underwriters will quickly absorb their loss and get on to the next underwriting.

All industries have their leaders. Investment banking is no exception. We have talked at some length in this chapter about investment bankers in general, without identifying any specific firms; Table 18-2 fills this gap. It shows the top ten houses in 1977 based upon the dollar volume of new security issues that were either managed or comanaged.

Industry Leaders

Private placements are an alternative to the sale of securities to the public or to a restricted group of investors through a privileged subscription. Any type of security can be privately placed (directly placed). This market, however, is clearly dominated by debt issues. Thus, we restrict this discussion to debt securities. From year to year the volume of private placements will vary. Table 18-3 shows, though, that the private placement market is always a significant portion of the U. S. capital market.

PRIVATE PLACEMENTS

The major investors in private placements are large financial institutions. Based on the volume of securities purchased, the three most important investor groups are (1) life insurance companies, (2) state and local retirement funds, and (3) private pension funds.

In arranging a private placement the firm may (1) avoid the use of an investment banker and work directly with the investing institutions or (2)

Table 18-2 LEADING U. S. INVESTMENT BANKERS, 1977

FIRM	UNDERWRITING VOLUME ($ BILLIONS)
1. Morgan Stanley	5.24
2. Merrill Lynch	3.73
3. Salomon Brothers	3.54
4. Goldman Sachs	2.76
5. First Boston	2.70
6. Blyth Eastman Dillon	2.33
7. Lehman Brothers	1.60
8. Dean Witter	1.27
9. Kidder, Peabody	1.19
10. Bache Halsey Stuart Shields	1.16

SOURCE: *Fortune*, 97 (February 27, 1978), 90.

Table 18-3 PUBLIC AND PRIVATELY PLACED CORPORATE DEBT
(GROSS PROCEEDS OF ALL NEW U. S. CORPORATE DEBT ISSUES)

YEAR	TOTAL VOLUME $ MILLIONS	PERCENT PUBLICLY PLACED	PERCENT PRIVATELY PLACED
1976	42,262	62.6	37.4
1975	42,756	76.2	23.8
1974	32,066	80.8	19.2
1973	21,049	62.9	37.1
1972	26,132	66.7	33.3

SOURCE: *Federal Reserve Bulletin*, various issues.

engage the services of an investment banker. If the investment banker is not used, of course, the firm does not have to pay him a fee. On the other hand, the investment banker can provide valuable advice in the private placement process. He will usually be in contact with several major institutional investors, he will know if they are in a position to invest in the firm's proposed offering, and he can help the firm evaluate the terms of the new issue.

Private placements have both advantages and disadvantages compared to public offerings. The financial manager must carefully evaluate both sides of the question. The advantages associated with private placements are:

1. *Speed.* The firm usually obtains funds more quickly through a private placement than a public offering. The major reason is that registration of the issue with the SEC is *not* required.

2. *Reduced flotation costs.* These savings result because the lengthy registration statement for the SEC does not have to be prepared, and the investment banking underwriting and distribution costs do not have to be absorbed.

3. *Financing flexibility.* In a private placement the firm deals on a face-to-face basis with a small number of investors. This means that the terms of the issue can be precisely tailored to meet the specific needs of the company. For example, all of the funds need not be taken by the firm at once. In exchange for a commitment fee the firm can "draw down" against the established amount of credit with the investors. This provides some insurance against capital-market uncertainties, and the firm does not have to borrow the funds if the need does not arise. There is also the possibility of *renegotiation.* The terms of the debt issue can be altered. The term to maturity, the interest rate, or any restrictive covenants can be discussed among the affected parties.

The disadvantages of private placements that must be evaluated include:

1. *Interest costs.* It is generally conceded that interest costs on private placements exceed those of public issues. Whether this disadvantage is enough to offset the reduced flotation costs associated with a private placement is a determina-

tion that the financial manager must make. There is some evidence that on smaller issues, say $500,000 as opposed to $30 million, the private placement alternative would be preferable.[12]

2. *Restrictive covenants.* Dividend policy, working-capital levels, and the raising of additional debt capital may all be affected by provisions in the private placement debt contract. That is not to say that such restrictions are always absent in public debt contracts. Rather, the financial officer must be alert to the tendency for these covenants to be especially burdensome in private contracts.

3. *The possibility of future SEC registration.* If the lender (investor) should decide to sell the issue to a public buyer before maturity, it must be registered with the SEC. Some lenders, then, require that the issuing firm agree to a future registration at their option.

FLOTATION COSTS

The firm raising long-term capital incurs two types of **flotation costs:** (1) the underwriter's spread and (2) issuing costs. Of these two costs, the underwriter's spread is the larger. The **underwriter's spread** is simply the difference between the gross and net proceeds from a given security issue expressed as a percent of the gross proceeds. The **issue costs** include (1) printing and engraving, (2) legal fees, (3) accounting fees, (4) trustee fees, and (5) several other miscellaneous components. The two most significant issue costs are printing and engraving and legal fees.

Data published by the SEC have consistently revealed two relationships about flotation costs. First, the costs associated with issuing common stock are notably greater than the costs associated with preferred stock offerings. In turn, preferred stock costs exceed those of bonds. Second, flotation costs (expressed as a percent of gross proceeds) decrease as the size of the security issue increases.

In the first instance, the stated relationship reflects the fact that issue costs are sensitive to the risks involved in successfully distributing a security issue. Common stock is riskier to own than corporate bonds. Underwriting risk is, therefore, greater with common stock than with bonds. Thus, flotation costs just mirror these risk relationships. In the second case, a portion of the issue costs are fixed. Legal fees and accounting costs are good examples. So, as the size of the security issue rises, the fixed component is spread over a larger gross proceeds base. As a consequence, total flotation costs vary inversely with the size of the issue.

REGULATION

Following the severe economic downturn of 1929–1932, congressional action was taken to provide for federal regulation of the securities markets. State statutes (blue sky laws) also govern the securities markets where

[12]John D. Rea and Peggy Brockschmidt, "The Relationship Between Publicly Offered and Privately Placed Corporate Bonds," *Monthly Review, Federal Reserve Bank of Kansis City,* (November 1973), p. 15.

applicable, but the federal regulations are clearly the more pressing and important. The major federal regulations are reviewed here.

The new issues market is governed by the **Securities Act of 1933.** The intent of the Act is important. It aims to provide potential investors with accurate, truthful disclosure about the firm and the new securities being offered to the public. This does *not* prevent firms from issuing highly speculative securities. The SEC says nothing whatsoever about the possible investment worth of a given offering. It is up to the investor to separate the junk from the jewels. The SEC does have the legal power and responsibility to enforce the 1933 Act.

Primary Market Regulations

Full public disclosure is achieved by the requirement that the issuing firm file a registration statement with the SEC containing requisite information. The statement details particulars about the firm and the new security being issued. During a minimum 20-day waiting period, the SEC will examine the submitted document. In numerous instances the 20-day wait has been extended by several weeks. The SEC can ask for additional information that was omitted in order to clarify the original document. The SEC can also order that the offering be stopped.

During the registration process a preliminary prospectus (the red herring) may be distributed to potential investors. When the registration is approved, the prospective investors must have available to them the final prospectus. The prospectus is actually a condensed version of the full registration statement. If, at a later date, the information in the registration statement and the prospectus is found to be lacking, purchasers of the new issue who incurred a loss can sue for damages. Officers of the issuing firm and others who took part in the registration and marketing of the issue may suffer both civil and criminal penalties.

Generally the SEC defines public issues as those which are sold to more than 25 investors. Some public issues need not be registered. These include:

1. Relatively small issues of less than $500,000
2. Issues that are sold entirely intrastate.
3. Issues that are basically short-term instruments. This translates into maturity periods of 270 days or less.
4. Issues that are already regulated or controlled by some other federal agency. Examples here are the Federal Power Commission (public utilities) and the Interstate Commerce Commission (railroads).

Secondary market trading is regulated by the **Securities Exchange Act of 1934.** This act created the SEC to enforce federal securities laws. The Federal Trade Commission enforced the 1933 Act for one year. The major aspects of the 1934 Act can be best presented in outline form.

Secondary Market Regulations

1. Major security exchanges must register with the SEC. This regulates the

exchanges and places reporting requirements upon the firms whose securities are listed on them.

2. Insider trading is regulated. Insiders can be officers, directors, employees, relatives, major investors, or anyone having information about the operation of the firm that is not public knowledge. If an investor purchases the security of the firm in which he is an insider, he must hold it for at least six months before disposing of it. Otherwise, profits made from trading the stock within a period of less than six months must be returned to the firm. Furthermore, insiders must file with the SEC a monthly statement of holdings and transactions in the stock of their corporation.

3. Manipulative trading of securities by investors to affect stock prices is prohibited.

4. The SEC is given control over proxy procedures.

5. The Board of Governors of the Federal Reserve System is given responsibility for setting margin requirements. This affects the flow of credit into the security markets. Buying securities on margin simply means using credit to acquire a portion of the subject financial instruments.

SUMMARY

This chapter centered upon the market environment in which corporations raise long-term funds. Topics explored include the structure of the U. S. financial markets, the institution of investment banking, and the various methods for distributing securities.

Why Financial Markets Exist

The function of financial markets is to allocate savings efficiently in the economy to the ultimate demander (user) of the savings. In a financial market the forces of supply and demand for a specific financial instrument are brought together. The wealth of an economy would not be as great as it is without a fully-developed financial market system.

Components of the U. S. Financial Market System

Corporations can raise funds through either public offerings or private placements. The public market is impersonal in that the security issuer does not meet the ultimate investors in the financial instruments. In a private placement, the securities are sold directly to a limited number of institutional investors.

The primary market is the market for new issues. The secondary market represents transactions in currently outstanding securities. Both the money and capital markets have primary and secondary sides. The money market refers to transactions in short-term debt instruments. The capital market, on the other hand, refers to transactions in long-term financial instruments. Trading in the money and capital markets can take place on either the organized security exchanges or the over-the-counter market. The money market is exclusively an over-the-counter market.

Using an Investment Banker

The investment banker is a financial specialist involved as an intermediary in the merchandising of securities. He performs the functions of (1) underwriting, (2) distributing, and (3) advising. Major methods for the public distribution of securities include (1) the negotiated purchase, (2) the competitive-bid purchase, (3) the commission or best-efforts basis, (4) privileged subscriptions, and (5) direct sales. The direct sale bypasses the use of an investment banker. The negotiated purchase is the most profitable distribution method to the investment banker. It also provides for the greatest amount of investment banking services to the corporate client.

Privately placed debt provides an important market outlet for corporate bonds. Major investors in this market are (1) life insurance firms, (2) state and local retirement funds, and (3) private pension funds. Several advantages and disadvantages are associated with private placements. The financial officer must weigh these attributes and decide if a private placement is preferable over a public offering.

Private Placements

Flotation costs consist of the underwriter's spread and issuing costs. The flotation costs of common stock exceed those of preferred stock, which, in turn, exceed those of debt. Moreover, flotation costs as a *percent* of gross proceeds are inversely related to the size of the security issue.

Flotation Costs

The new-issues market is regulated at the federal level by the Securities Act of 1933. It provides for the registration of new issues with the SEC. Secondary market trading is regulated by the Securities Exchange Act of 1934.

Regulation

STUDY QUESTIONS

18-1. What are financial markets? What function do they perform? How would an economy be worse off without them?

18-2. Define in a technical sense what we mean by a "financial intermediary." Give an example of your definition.

18-3. Distinguish between the money and capital markets.

18-4. What major benefits do corporations and investors enjoy because of the existence of organized security exchanges?

18-5. What are the general categories examined by an organized exchange in determining whether an applicant firm's securities can be listed on it? (Specific numbers are not needed here, but rather "areas" of investigation.)

18-6. Why do you think most secondary market trading in bonds takes place over-the-counter?

18-7. What is an investment banker and what major functions does he perform?

18-8. What is the major difference between a negotiated purchase and a competitive-bid purchase?

18-9. Why is an investment banking syndicate formed?

18-10. Why might a large corporation want to raise long-term capital through a private placement rather than a public offering?

18-11. As a recent business school graduate, you work directly for the corporate treasurer. Your corporation is going to issue a new security and is concerned with the probable flotation costs. What tendencies about flotation costs can you relate to the treasurer?

18-12. You own a group of five clothing stores, all located in southern California. You are about to market $200,000 worth of new common stock. Your stock trades over-the-counter. The stock will be sold only to California residents. Your financial adviser informs you that the issue must be registered with the SEC. Is he correct?

SELECTED REFERENCES

AMLING, FREDERICK, *Investments: An Introduction to Analysis and Management*, 4th ed. Englewood Cliffs, N.J.: Prentice-Hall, Inc., 1978.

BLOCH, ERNEST, "Pricing a Corporate Bond Issue: A Look Behind the Scenes," *Essays in Money and Credit*, pp. 72–76. New York: Federal Reserve Bank of New York, 1964.

COHAN, A. B., *Private Placements and Public Offerings: Market Shares Since 1945*. Chapel Hill, N.C.: University of North Carolina Press, 1961.

DOUGALL, HERBERT E., and JACK E. GAUMNITZ, *Capital Markets and Institutions*, 3d ed. Englewood Cliffs, N.J.: Prentice-Hall, Inc., 1975.

EDERINGTON, LOUIS H., "Negotiated Versus Competitive Underwritings of Corporate Bonds," *Journal of Finance*, 31 (March 1976), 17–28.

FURST, RICHARD W., "Does Listing Increase the Market Price of Common Stocks?," *Journal of Business*, 43 (April 1970), 174–80.

GOULET, WALDEMAR M., "Price Changes, Managerial Actions and Insider Trading at-the Time of Listing," *Financial Management*, 3 (Spring 1974), 30–36.

HAYES, SAMUEL L., III, "Investment Banking: Power Structure in Flux," *Harvard Business Review*, 49 (March–April 1971), 136–52.

HENNING, CHARLES N., WILLIAM PIGOTT, and ROBERT H. SCOTT, *Financial Markets and the Economy*, 2d ed. Englewood Cliffs, N.J.: Prentice-Hall, Inc., 1978.

JOHNSON, KEITH B., GREGORY T. MORTON, and M. CHAPMAN FINDLAY, III, "An Empirical Analysis of the Flotation Cost of Corporate Securities, 1971–1972," *Journal of Finance*, 30 (June 1975), 1129–33.

LOGUE, DENNIS E., and JOHN R. LINDVALL, "The Behavior of Investment Bankers: An Econometric Investigation," *Journal of Finance*, 29 (March 1974), 203–15.

RATNER, DAVID L., *Securities Regulation In a Nutshell*. St. Paul, Minn.: West Publishing Co., 1978.

TALLMAN, GARY D., DAVID F. RUSH, and RONALD W. MELICHER, "Competitive Versus Negotiated Underwriting Cost of Regulated Industries," *Financial Management*, 3 (Summer 1974), 49–55.

VAN HORNE, JAMES C., *Financial Market Rates and Flows*. Englewood Cliffs, N.J.: Prentice-Hall, Inc., 1978.

WEST, RICHARD R., and SEHA M. TINIC, "Corporate Finance and the Changing Stock Market," *Financial Management*, 3 (Autumn 1974), 14–23.

WIESEN, JEREMY L., *Regulating Transactions in Securities*. St. Paul, Minn.: West Publishing Co., 1975.

Term Loans and Leases

For discussion purposes we generally categorize the sources of financing available to the business firm into three groups, distinguished on the basis of the maturity of the financing agreement. Short-term sources of financing, which have a maturity of one year or less, were discussed in Chapter 10. Intermediate-term financing, which includes all financing arrangements having final maturities longer than one year but no longer than ten years, is the subject of this chapter. Long-term financing, which includes all forms of financing with final maturities longer than ten years, is discussed in Chapters 20 and 21.

The principal sources of intermediate-term financing include term loans and leases. We shall look first at the primary sources of term loans and their characteristics. Then we shall discuss lease financing, including (1) the types of leasing arrangements, (2) the accounting treatment of financial leases, (3) the lease versus purchase decision, and (4) the potential benefits from leasing.

TERM LOANS

Term loans generally share three common characteristics: they (1) have maturities of one to ten years, (2) are repaid in periodic installments (such as quarterly, semiannual, or annual payments) over the life of the loan, and (3) are usually secured by either a chattel mortgage on equipment or a mortgage on real property. The principal suppliers of term credit include commercial banks, insurance companies, and to a lesser extent pension funds.

We shall consider briefly some of the more common characteristics of term-loan agreements.

Commercial banks generally restrict their term lending to one- to five-year maturities. Insurance companies and pension funds with their longer-term liabilities generally make loans with five- to 15-year maturities. Thus, the term-lending activities of commercial banks actually complement rather than compete with those of insurance companies and pension funds. In fact, commercial banks very often cooperate with both insurance companies and pension funds in providing term financing for very large loans.

Maturities

Term loans are almost always backed by some form of collateral. Shorter-maturity loans are frequently secured with a chattel mortgage on machinery and equipment or with securities such as stocks and bonds. Longer-maturity loans are frequently secured by mortgages on real estate.

Collateral

In addition to collateral the lender in a term-loan agreement will often place restrictions on the borrower that, when violated, make the loan immediately payable and due. These restrictive covenants are designed to maintain the borrower's financial condition on a par with that which existed at the time the loan was made. Thus, the lender seeks to prohibit the borrower from engaging in any activities that would increase the likelihood of loss on the loan. Some commonly used restrictions are discussed below.

Restrictive Covenants

WORKING-CAPITAL REQUIREMENT

One such restriction involves maintaining a minimum amount of working capital. Very often this restriction takes the form of a minimum current ratio, such as 2 to 1 or 3½ to 1, or a minimum dollar amount of net working capital. The actual requirement would reflect the norm for the borrower's industry, as well as the lender's desires.

ADDITIONAL BORROWING

Generally, this type of restriction requires the lender's approval before any additional debt can be issued. Furthermore, the restriction is often extended to long-term lease agreements, which are discussed later in this chapter.

PERIODIC FINANCIAL STATEMENTS

A standard covenant in most term-loan agreements involves supplying the lender with periodic financial statements. These generally include annual or perhaps quarterly income statements and balance sheets.

Term-loan agreements will sometimes include a provision requiring prior approval by the lender of major personnel changes. In addition, the borrower may be required to insure the lives of certain *key* personnel, naming the lender as beneficiary.

We have discussed here only a partial listing of restrictions commonly found in term-loan agreements. The number and form of such provisions is limited only by the imagination of the parties involved. It should be noted, however, that restrictive convenants are subject to negotiation. Thus, the specific agreement that results will reflect the relative bargaining strengths of the borrower and lender. For this reason the marginal borrower is likely to find his loan agreement more burdened with restrictive covenants than a more creditworthy borrower.

Term-loan agreements can be very technical and are generally tailored to the specific situation involved. For this reason it is difficult to generalize too much about their content. However, many banks utilize *work sheets* or *check sheets* to aid in the preparation of the document.

Repayment Schedules

Term loans are generally repaid with periodic installments, which include both an interest and a principal component. Thus, the loan is repaid over its life with equal annual, semiannual, or quarterly payments.

To illustrate how the repayment procedure works, let us assume that a firm borrows $6000, which is to be repaid in five annual installments. The loan will carry an 8 percent rate of interest, and payments will be made at the end of each of the next five years. Visually, the loan will involve the following cash flows to the lender:

0	1	2	3	4	5
$(6000)	A_1	A_2	A_3	A_4	A_5

The $6000 cash flow at time period zero is placed in parenthesis to indicate an outflow of cash by the lender, whereas the annual installments, A_1 through A_5, represent cash inflows (of course the opposite is true for the borrower). The lender then needs to determine the annual installments that will give him his 8 percent return on the outstanding loan balance over the life of the loan. This problem is very similar to the internal-rate-of-return problem encountered in Chapter 11, where we discussed capital-budgeting decisions. There we had to determine the rate of interest that would make the present value of a stream of future cash flows equal to some present sum. Here we want to determine the future cash flows whose present value, when discounted at 8 percent, is equal to the $6000 loan amount. Thus, we must solve for those values of A_1 through A_5 whose present value when discounted at 8 percent is $6000. In equation form,

$$\$6000 = \sum_{t=1}^{5} \frac{A_t}{(1 + .08)^t} \qquad (19\text{-}1)$$

Where we assume equal annual installments, A, for all five years, we can solve for A as follows:

$$A = \frac{\$6000}{\sum\limits_{t=1}^{5} \dfrac{1}{(1 + .08)^t}} \qquad (19\text{-}2)$$

We recognize the term being divided into the $6000 loan as the present-value factor for a five-year annuity carrying an 8 percent rate of interest; thus, using the present-value-of-an-annuity table in Appendix D and solving for A,

$$A = \frac{\$6000}{3.993} = \$1502.63$$

Therefore, if the borrower repays $1502.63 each year, then the lender will receive an 8 percent return on the outstanding loan balance. To verify this assertion Table 19-1 contains the principal and interest components of the

Table 19-1   TERM-LOAN AMORTIZATION SCHEDULE

END OF YEAR, t	INSTALLMENT PAYMENT,[a] A	INTEREST,[b] I_t	PRINCIPAL REPAYMENT,[c] P_t	REMAINING BALANCE,[d] RB_t
0	—	—	—	$6000.00
1	$1502.63	$480.00	$1022.63	4977.37
2	1502.63	399.19	1104.44	3872.93
3	1502.63	309.83	1192.80	2680.13
4	1502.63	214.41	1288.22	1391.91
5	1502.63	111.35	1391.28	.63[e]

[a] The annual installment payment, A, is found as follows:

$$A = \frac{\$6000}{\sum\limits_{t=1}^{5} \dfrac{1}{(1 + .08)^t}} = \$1502.63$$

[b] Annual interest expense is equal to 8 percent of the outstanding loan balance. Thus, for year 1 the interest expense, I_1, is found as follows:

$$I_1 = .08(\$6000) = \$480$$

[c] Principal repayment for year t, P_t, is the difference in the loan payment, A, and interest for the year. Thus, for year 1 we compute:

$$P_1 = A - I_1 = \$1502.63 - \$480 = \$1022.63$$

[d] The remaining balance at the end of year 1, RB_1, is the difference in the remaining balance for the previous year, RB_0, and the principal payment in year 1, P_1. Thus, at the end of year 1,

$$RB_1 = RB_0 - P_1 = \$6000 - \$1022.63 = \$4977.37$$

[e] The $.63 difference in RB_4 and P_5 is due to rounding error.

annual loan payments. Here we see that the $1502.63 installments truly provide the lender with an 8 percent return on the outstanding balance of his $6000 loan.

Leasing provides an alternative to buying an asset in order to acquire its services. Although some leases involve maturities of more than ten years, most do not. Thus, lease financing is classified as a source of intermediate-term credit. Today, virtually any type of asset can be acquired through a lease agreement. The recent growth in lease financing has been phenomenal, with over $60 billion in assets (based on original cost) presently under lease in the United States.[1] Furthermore, the total value of outstanding leases has been growing at a rate of roughly 20 percent per year.[2]

We begin our discussion by defining the major types of lease arrangements. Next we consider the history and present status of the accounting treatment of leases. We examine the lease-versus-purchase decision, and we conclude by investigating the potential benefits of leasing.

There are three major types of lease agreements: direct leasing, sale and leaseback, and leveraged leasing. Most lease agreements fall into one of these categories. However, the particular lease agreement can take one of two forms. (1) The **financial lease** constitutes a noncancelable contractual commitment on the part of the firm leasing the asset (the lessee) to make a series of payments to the firm that actually owns the asset (the lessor) for use of the asset. (2) The **operating lease** differs from the financial lease only with respect to its cancelability. An operating lease can be canceled after proper notice to the lessor any time during its term. The balance of this chapter is concerned with the financial lease, which provides the firm with a form of intermediate-term financing most comparable to debt financing.

DIRECT LEASING

In a **direct lease** the firm acquires the services of an asset it did not previously own. Direct leasing is available through a number of financial institutions, including manufacturers, banks, finance companies, independent leasing companies, and special-purpose leasing companies.[3] Basically, the lease arrangement involves the lessor's purchasing the asset and leasing it to the lessee. In the case of the manufacturer lessor, however, the acquisition step is not necessary.

---

[1] For an excellent discussion of the rationale underlying the growth in lease financing the interested reader is referred to P. Vanderwicken, "The Powerful Logic of the Leasing Boom," *Fortune,* November 1973, pp. 132–36, 190, 194–95.

[2] *Ibid.,* p. 136.

[3] Many leasing companies specialize in the leasing of a single type of asset. For example, a number of firms lease computers exclusively, and others lease only automobiles.

SALE AND LEASEBACK

A **sale and leaseback** arrangement arises when a firm sells land, buildings, or equipment that it already owns to a lessor and simultaneously enters into an agreement to lease the property back for a specified period under specific terms. The lessor involved in the sale and leaseback varies with the nature of the property involved and the lease period. Where land is involved and the corresponding lease is long term, the lessor is generally a life insurance company. If the property consists of machinery and equipment, then the maturity of the lease will probably be intermediate term and the lessor could be an insurance company, commercial bank, or leasing company.

The lessee firm receives cash in the amount of the sales price of the assets sold and the use of the asset over the term of the lease. In return the lessee must make periodic rental payments throughout the term of the lease and give up any salvage or residual value to the lessor.

LEVERAGED LEASING

In the leasing arrangements discussed thus far only two participants have been identified: the lessor and lessee. In a **leveraged lease** a third participant is added. The added party is the lender who helps finance the acquisition of the asset to be leased. From the point of view of the lessee there is no difference in a leveraged lease, direct lease, or sale and lease-back arrangement. However, with a leveraged lease specific consideration is given to the method of financing used by the lessor in acquiring the asset. The lessor will generally supply equity funds of 20 to 30 percent of the purchase price and borrow the remainder from a third-party lender, which may be a commercial bank or insurance company. In some arrangements the lessor firm sells bonds, which are guaranteed by the lessee. This guarantee serves to reduce the risk and thus the cost of the debt.

Before January 1977 most financial leases were not included in the balance sheets of lessee firms. Instead, they were reported in the footnotes to the balance sheet.[4] However, in November 1976 the Financial Accounting Standards Board reversed its long-standing position with *Statement of Financial Accounting Standards No. 13*, "Accounting for Leases."[5] The board adopted the position that the economic effect of the transaction should

Accounting for Leases

[4]Prior to January 1977 the guiding accounting principles regarding the treatment of leases were *Opinion No. 5* and *Opinion No. 31* of the Accounting Principles Board (APB). Opinion No. 5 stated that only in the case in which a lease "is in substance a purchase" should an asset and a liability appear on the lessee's balance sheet. In response to requests from various groups of statement users, the APB expanded its disclosure requirements in Opinion No. 31. See American Institute of Certified Public Accountants, *Accounting Principles Board Opinion No. 5*, "Reporting of Leases in Financial Statements of Lessee" (New York: AICPA, September 1964), and *Accounting Principles Board Opinion No. 31*, "Disclosure of Lease Commitments by Lessees" (New York: AICPA, June 1973).

[5]Financial Accounting Standards Board, *Statement of Accounting Standards No. 13*, "Accounting for Leases" (Stanford, Conn.: FASB, November 1976).

govern its accounting treatment.[6] In this regard, the FASB asserted that "a lease that transfers substantially all the benefits and risks incident to the ownership of property should be accounted for as the acquisition of an asset and the incurrence of an obligation by the lessee."[7] Specifically, Statement No. 13 requires that any lease that meets one or more of the following criteria be included in the body of the balance sheet of the lessee:

1. The lease transfers ownership of the property to the lessee by the end of the lease term.
2. The lease contains a bargain repurchase option.
3. The lease term is equal to 75 percent or more of the estimated economic life of the leased property.
4. The present value of the minimum lease payments equals or exceeds 90 percent of the excess of the fair value of the property over any related investment tax credit retained by the lessor.[8]

The last two requirements are the most stringent elements in the board's statement. The first two have been applicable to most leases for many years because of the Internal Revenue Service's "true" lease requirements.[9] However, the last two apply to the majority of the financial leases written in the United States. As a result, most financial leases entered into after 1976 will appear in the body of the lessee's balance sheet. Moreover, the board encourages immediate retroactive application of the standards, and it requires such application after December 31, 1980.

The Lease-Versus-Purchase Decision

The lease-versus-purchase problem is a hybrid capital-budgeting problem that forces the analyst to consider the consequences of alternative forms of financing on the investment decision. When we discussed capital budgeting in Chapter 11 and the cost of capital in Chapter 14, we assumed that all new financing would be undertaken in accordance with the firm's optimal capital structure. When analyzing an asset that is to be leased, the analysis must be altered to consider financing through leasing as opposed to the use of the more traditional debt and equity sources of funds. Thus, the lease-versus-purchase decision requires a standard capital-budgeting type of analysis, as well as an analysis of two alternative financing *packages*.

Thus, the lease-purchase decision can be viewed as consisting of two separate issues:

[6]*Ibid.,* p. 49.
[7]*Ibid.,* p. 49.
[8]*Ibid.,* pp. 9–10.
[9]The full amount of the annual rentals paid under a lease agreement is tax deductible, provided the Internal Revenue Service agrees that a particular contract is a true lease and not simply an installment loan called a lease. The interested reader is referred to Rev. Rul. 55–540, 1955 C.B. 41.

1. Should the asset be purchased using the firm's optimal financing mix?
2. Should the asset be leased?

The answer to the first question can be obtained through an analysis of the project's net present value (*NPV*) following the methodology laid out in Chapter 11. However, regardless of whether the asset should or should not be purchased, it may be advantageous for the firm to lease it. That is, the cost savings accruing through leasing might be so great as to offset a negative net present value or add to a positive one. For example, the Alpha Mfg. Co. is considering the acquisition of a new computer-based inventory and payroll system. The computed net present value of the new system based upon normal purchase financing is $-40, indicating that acquisition of the system through purchasing or ownership is not warranted. However, an analysis of the cost savings resulting from leasing the system (referred to here as the net advantage of leasing—*NAL*) indicates that the lease alternative will produce a present value cost saving of $60 over normal purchase financing. Therefore, the net present value of the system if leased is $20 ($-40 + $60), which indicates that the system's services should be acquired via the lease agreement.

In the pages that follow we will (1) review briefly the concept of a project's net present value, which we will refer to as the net present value of purchase or *NPV(P)*; (2) introduce a model for estimating the net present value advantage of leasing over normal purchase financing, which we will refer to as the net advantage of lease financing or *NAL*; (3) present a flow chart that can be used in performing lease-purchase analyses based upon *NPV(P)* and *NAL*; and (4) provide a comprehensive example of a lease-purchase analysis.

THE LEASE-PURCHASE ALGORITHM

Answers to each of the questions posed earlier can be obtained using the two equations found in Table 19-2. The first equation is simply the net present value of the proposed project, discussed earlier in Chapter 11. The second equation represents the net present value advantage of leasing (*NAL*). *NAL* represents an accumulation of the cash flows (both inflows and outflows) that are associated with leasing as opposed to purchasing the asset. Specifically, through leasing the firm avoids certain operating expenses, O_t, but incurs the after-tax rental expense, $R_t(1 - T)$. By leasing, furthermore, the firm loses the tax deductible expense associated with interest, $T \cdot I_t$, depreciation, $T \cdot D_t$, and the interest on repaid debt or lost debt capacity, $T \Delta I_t$. Finally, the firm does not receive the salvage value from the asset, V_n, if it is leased, but it does not have to make the initial cash outlay to purchase the asset, *IO*. Thus, *NAL* reflects the cost savings associated with leasing net of the opportunity costs of not purchasing.

Note that the cost of new debt is used to discount the *NAL* cash flows other than the salvage value, V_n. This is justified because the affected cash

Table 19-2 THE LEASE-PURCHASE MODEL

Equation One—Net present value of purchase [NPV(P)]:

$$NPV(P) = \sum_{t=1}^{n} \frac{ACF_t}{(1 + K)^t} - IO \tag{19-3}$$

where ACF_t = the annual after-tax cash flow resulting from the asset's purchase in period t,

K = the firm's cost of capital applicable to the project being analyzed and the particular mix of financing used to acquire the project,

IO = the initial cash outlay required to purchase the asset in period zero (now), and

n = the productive life of the project.

Equation Two—Net Advantage of Leasing (NAL):

$$\tag{19-4}$$

$$NAL = \sum_{t=1}^{n} \frac{O_t(1 - T) - R_t(1 - T) - T \cdot I_t - T \cdot \Delta I_t - T \cdot D_t}{(1 + r)^t} - \frac{V_n}{(1 + K_s)^n} + IO$$

where O_t = any operating cash flows incurred in period t that are incurred only where the asset is purchased. Most often this consists of maintenance expenses and insurance that would be paid by the lessor.

R_t = the annual rental for period t.

T = the marginal tax rate on corporate income.

I_t = the tax-deductible interest expense forfeited in period t if the lease option is adopted.

ΔI_t = the interest on debt that must be repaid in the event the asset is leased so as to maintain the firm's desired capital structure. That is, since leasing involves 100 percent levered financing, the firm uses up more than the leased asset's allotment of levered financing by leasing it. If, for example, the firm's financial policy were to finance 60 percent of its assets with owner funds, then by leasing the asset it would have to repay outstanding debt equal to 60 percent of the cost of the lease asset to maintain its desired leverage ratio.[a] Thus, $T \cdot \Delta I_t$ reflects the lost interest tax shield from the repayment of debt.[b]

D_t = depreciation expense in period t for the asset.

V_n = the after-tax salvage value of the asset expected in year n.

K_s = the discount rate used to find the present value of V_n. This rate should reflect the risk inherent in the estimated V_n. For simplicity the after-tax cost of capital is often used as a proxy for this rate.

IO = the purchase price of the asset, which is not paid by the firm in the event the asset is leased.

r = the rate of interest on borrowed funds. This rate is used to discount the relatively certain, after-tax cash flow savings that accrue through the leasing of the asset.

---

[a] For simplicity of exposition, it is assumed that a dollar of lease is equivalent to a dollar of loan. This form of equivalence is only one of several that might be used. The interested reader is referred to A. H. Ofer, "The Evaluation of the Lease Versus Purchase Alternatives," *Financial Management*, 5 (Summer 1976), 67–74.

[b] Debt may not actually be repaid; however, by leasing the asset the firm uses more levered financing than the asset will support. Thus, to maintain its target debt-equity ratio the firm will have to use less levered financing on future projects. The term ΔI_t represents the lost interest tax shield on the debt "displaced" by the lease.

flows are very nearly riskless and certainly no more risky than the interest and principal accruing to the firm's creditors (which underlie the rate of interest charged to the firm for its debt).[10]

Figure 19-1 contains a flow chart that can be used in performing lease purchase analyses. The analyst first calculates $NPV(P)$. If the resulting project net present value is positive, then the left-hand branch of Figure 19-1 should be followed. Tracing through the left branch we now compute NAL. If NAL is positive, this indicates that the lease alternative offers a positive present value cost advantage over normal purchase financing in which case the asset should be leased. Should NAL be negative, then the purchase alternative should be selected. Return to the top of Figure 19-1 once again. This time we assume that $NPV(P)$ is negative such that the analyst's attention is directed to the right hand side of the flow chart. The only hope for the project's acceptance is a favorable set of lease terms. In this circumstance the project would be acceptable and thus leased only if NAL were large enough to offset the negative $NPV(P)$ [that is, where NAL was greater than the absolute value of $NPV(P)$ or, equivalently, where $NAL + NPV(P) \geq 0$].[11]

CASE PROBLEM
IN LEASE-PURCHASE ANALYSIS

The Waynesboro Plastic Molding Company (WPM) is presently deciding whether to purchase an automatic casting machine. The machine will cost $15,000 and has an expected life of five years, at which time its after-tax salvage value will be $1050.[12] The firm has a marginal tax rate of 50 percent and utilizes the sum-of-the-years' digits depreciation method to depreciate the $15,000 asset toward a zero salvage value. Further, the project is expected to generate annual cash revenues of $5000 per year over the next five years (net of cash operating expenses but before depreciation and taxes). WPM has a target debt ratio of 40 percent for projects of

[10]The argument for using the firm's borrowing rate to discount these tax shelters goes as follows: The tax shields are relatively free of risk in that their source (depreciation, interest rental payments) can be estimated with a high degree of certainty. There are, however, two sources of uncertainty with regard to these tax shelters: (1) the possibility of a change in the firm's tax rate and (2) the possibility that the firm might become bankrupt at some future date. If we attach a very low probability to the likelihood of a reduction in the tax rate then the prime risk associated with these tax shelters is the possibility of bankruptcy wherein they would be lost forever (certainly all tax shelters after the date of bankruptcy would be lost). We now note that the firm's creditors also faced the risk of the firm's bankruptcy when they loaned the firm funds at the rate r. If this rate, r, reflects the market's assessment of the firm's bankruptcy potential as well as the price of time then it offers an appropriate rate for discounting the interest tax shelters generated by the firm. Note also that the O_t cash flows are generally estimated with a high degree of certainty (in the case where they represent insurance premiums they may be contractually set) such that r is appropriate as a discount rate here also.

[11]That is, the sum of $NPV(P)$ and NAL is the net present value of the asset if leased. See Lawrence D. Schall, "The Lease-or-Buy and Asset Acquisition Decisions," *Journal of Finance,* 29 (September 1974), 1203–14, for a development of the net present value of leasing and purchasing equations upon which our discussion is based.

[12]The problem example is a modification of the well-known example from R. W. Johnson and W. G. Lewellen, "Analysis of the Lease or Buy Decision," *Journal of Finance,* 27 (September 1972), 815–23.

Note that we depreciate the asset toward a zero salvage value for tax and analytical purposes although we estimate (for cash flow purposes) an after tax salvage value of $1050 or a before tax salvage value of $2100.

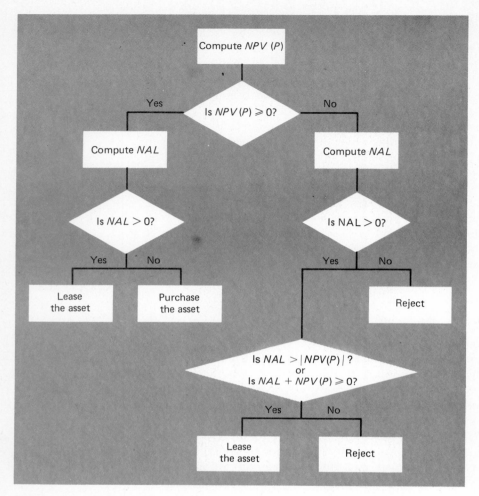

FIGURE 19-1 *Lease-Purchase Analysis*

this type and estimates its after-tax cost of capital at 12 percent. Finally, WPM can borrow funds at a before-tax rate of 8 percent.

Step 1: Computing NPV(P)—Should the asset be purchased? The first step in analyzing the lease-purchase problem involves computing the net present value under the purchase alternative. The relevant cash flow computations are presented in Table 19-3.

The $NPV(P)$ is found by discounting the annual cash flows (ACF_t) in Table 19-3 back to the present at the firm's after-tax cost of capital of 12 percent, adding this sum to the present value of the salvage value, and subtracting the initial cash outlay. These calculations are shown in Table 19-4. The project's $NPV(P)$ is a positive \$421.85, indicating that the asset should be acquired.

Table 19-3 COMPUTING PROJECT ANNUAL AFTER-TAX CASH FLOWS (ACF$_t$)

YEAR

	1 Book Profits	1 Cash Flow	2 Book Profits	2 Cash Flow	3 Book Profits	3 Cash Flow	4 Book Profits	4 Cash Flow	5 Book Profits	5 Cash Flow
Annual cash revenues	$5000	$5000	$5000	$5000	$5000	$5000	$5000	$5000	$5000	$5000
Less: Depreciation	(5000)	—	(4000)	—	(3000)	—	(2000)	—	(1000)	—
Net revenues before taxes	0	$5000	$1000	$5000	$2000	$5000	$3000	$5000	$4000	$5000
Less: Taxes (50%)	0 →	0	(500) →	(500)	(1000) →	(1000)	(1500) →	(1500)	(2000) →	(2000)
Annual after-tax cash flow		$5000		$4500		$4000		$3500		$3000

Table 19-4 CALCULATING NPV(P)

YEAR, t	ANNUAL CASH FLOW, ACF_t	DISCOUNT FACTOR FOR 12 PERCENT	PRESENT VALUE
1	$5000	.893	$4465.00
2	4500	.797	3586.50
3	4000	.712	2848.00
4	3500	.636	2226.00
5	3000	.567	1701.00
5 (Salvage—V_n)	1050	.567	595.35

$$\text{Present value of } ACF\text{'s and } V_n = \$15,421.85$$
$$NPV(P) = \$15,421.85 - \$15,000 = \$421.85$$

The second question concerns whether the asset should be leased. This can be answered by considering the net advantage to leasing (*NAL*).

Step 2: Computing NAL—Should the asset be leased? The computation of *NAL* is shown in Table 19-5. The resulting *NAL* is a positive $139, which indicates that leasing is preferred to the normal debt-equity method of financing. In fact, WPM will be $139 better off in present-value terms if it chooses to lease rather than purchase the asset.

Calculating *NAL* involves solving equation 19-4 presented earlier in Table 19-2. To do this, we first estimate all those cash flows that are to be discounted at the firm's cost of debt, *r*. These include $O_t(1 - T), R_t(1 - T), I_t \cdot T, T \cdot \Delta I_t$ and $T \cdot D_t$.

The operating expenses associated with the asset that will be paid by the lessor if we lease—that is, the O_t, generally consist of certain maintenance expenses and insurance. WPM estimates them to be $1000 per year over the life of the project. The annual rental or lease payments, R_t, are given and equal $4200.

The interest tax shelters lost because the asset is leased and not purchased must now be estimated. These tax shelters are lost because the firm's normal debt financing is not used and also because the firm uses more than its target debt ratio allotment when it finances the asset with a lease equal to 100 percent of the asset's purchase price. Both these sets of lost tax shelters involve determining the principal and interest components on a loan.

Table 19-1, discussed earlier, contains the principal and interest for the $6000 (.40 × $15,000) loan used to finance the project under the purchase alternative. Note that the interest column supplies the needed information for the interest tax shelter that is lost if the asset is leased, I_t. To compute ΔI_t the analyst estimates the interest on that amount of debt which must be repaid so as to maintain the firm's target debt ratio. Since the target debt ratio is 40 percent, WPM must repay a loan equal to 60 percent of the purchase price of the asset, or .60 × $15,000 = $9000. Thus, ΔI_t is found just as we found I_t, except that the calculations are based on a $9000 rather than a $6000 loan. The relevant values for ΔI_t are shown below:

YEAR, t	INTEREST, ΔI_t	YEAR, t	INTEREST, ΔI_t
1	$720.00	4	$321.59
2	596.81	5	168.65
3	464.17		

Note that both I_t and ΔI_t constitute lost tax shelters when the asset is leased. Also, I_t and ΔI_t correspond to loans equal to 40 and 60 percent, respectively, of the purchase price of the asset. Thus, the sum of I_t and ΔI_t is simply the interest expense on a loan equal to 100 percent of the asset's purchase price. A direct and less tedious way to estimate the interest tax shelters lost through leasing would be to compute the annual interest expense on a loan equal to the full purchase price of the asset ($15,000 in the present example).

The next step in calculating NAL involves finding the present value of the after-tax salvage value. Earlier when we computed $NPV(P)$, we

Table 19-5   COMPUTING THE NET ADVANTAGE TO LEASING (NAL)

(1) Solving for $\displaystyle\sum_{t=1}^{n} \frac{O_t(1-T) - R_t(1-T) - I_t \cdot T - \Delta I_t \cdot T - D_t \cdot T}{(1+r)^t}$

YEAR	AFTER-TAX OPERATING EXPENSES PAID BY LESSOR[a]	AFTER-TAX RENTAL EXPENSE[b]	TAX SHELTER ON LOAN INTEREST[c]	TAX SHELTER ON DEPRECIATION[d]	TOTAL	DISCOUNT FACTOR AT 8 PERCENT	PRESENT VALUE
t	$O_t(1-t)$ $-$	$R_t(1-t)$ $-$	$(I_t T + \Delta I_t T)$ $-$	$D_t T$	$=$ SUM	$\times$ DF	$=$ PV
1	$500	$2100	$600	$2500	$-4700	.926	$-4352
2	500	2100	498	2000	-4098	.857	-3512
3	500	2100	387	1500	-3487	.794	-2769
4	500	2100	268	1000	-2868	.735	-2108
5	500	2100	140	500	-2240	.681	-1525
							-14,266

(2) Solving for $-\left[\dfrac{V_n}{(1+K_s)^n}\right]$: $-\dfrac{\$1050}{(1+.12)^5} = \$-1050 \times .567^e =$ -595

(3) Adding the purchase price of the asset (IO) =   15,000

(4) Net advantage of leasing (NAL) = $\underline{\$\ \ \ \ 139}$

[a] After-tax lessor-paid operating expenses are found by $O_t(1-T) = \$1000(1-.5) = \$500$.
[b] After-tax rent expense for year 1 is computed as follows: $R_t(1-T) = \$4200(1-.5) = \$2100$.
[c] This includes interest on the loan that is not used if the lease is undertaken plus interest on the amount of debt that must be repaid to maintain the target debt ratio. Thus for year 1, $(I_t + \Delta I_t)T = (\$480 + 720).5 = \$600$.
[d] For the first year the tax shelter from depreciation is found as follows: $D_1 T = \$5000 \times .5 = \$2500$.
[e] K_s was estimated to be the same as the firm's after-tax cost of capital, 12 percent.

found this to equal $421.85. Now, substituting the results of our calculations into equation 19-4 produces the *NAL* of $139.

To summarize the lease-purchase analysis, first the project's net present-value was computed. This analysis produced a positive *NPV(P)* equal to $421.85, which indicated that the asset should be acquired. Upon computing the net advantage to leasing, we found that the financial lease was the preferred method of financing the acquisition of the asset's services. Thus, the asset should be leased.

A number of purported advantages have been associated with leasing as opposed to debt financing. These benefits include flexibility and convenience, lack of restrictions, avoiding the risk of obsolescence, conservation of working capital, 100 percent financing, tax savings, and availability of credit. Each is discussed below in an effort to assess its merit.

Potential Benefits from Leasing[13]

FLEXIBILITY AND CONVENIENCE

A variety of potential benefits are often included under the rubric of flexibility and convenience. It is argued, for example, that leasing provides the firm with flexibility because it allows for piecemeal financing of relatively small asset acquisitions. It is pointed out that debt financing of such acquisitions can be costly and difficult to arrange. Leases, on the other hand, may be arranged more quickly and with less documentation.

Another flexibility argument notes that leasing may allow a division or subsidiary manager to acquire equipment without the approval of the corporate capital-budgeting committee. Depending upon the firm, the manager may be able to avoid the time-consuming process of preparing and presenting a formal acquisition proposal.

A third purported flexibility advantage relates to the fact that some lease payment schedules may be structured to coincide with the revenues generated by the asset, or they may be timed to match seasonal fluctuations in a given industry. Thus, the firm is able to synchronize its lease payments with its cash cycle—an option that is rarely available with debt financing.

Arguments for the greater convenience of leasing take many forms. It is sometimes stated that leasing simplifies bookkeeping for tax purposes because it eliminates the need to prepare time-consuming depreciation tables and subsidiary fixed asset schedules. It is also pointed out that the fixed-payment nature of lease rentals allows more accurate forecasting of cash needs. Finally, it is frequently noted that leasing allows the firm to avoid the "problems" and "headaches" associated with ownership. For example, executives often note that leasing "keeps the company out of the real estate business." Implicit in this argument is the assumption that the firm's human and material resources may be more profitably allocated to its primary line of business and that it is better to allow the lessor to deal with the nuances associated with ownership.

[13]The contributions of Paul F. Anderson in the preparation of this discussion are gratefully acknowledged.

It is difficult to generalize about the validity of the various arguments
for greater flexibility and convenience in leasing. Some companies, under
specific conditions, may find leasing advantageous for some of the reasons
listed above. In practice, the tradeoffs are likely to be different for every
firm. With regard to a number of the arguments, the relevant issue is that
of shifting functions. By leasing a piece of capital equipment, the firm may
effectively shift bookkeeping, disposal of used equipment, and other functions to the lessor. The lessee will benefit in these situations if the lessor is
able to perform the functions at a lower cost than the lessee and is willing to
pass on the savings in a lower lease rate.

The remaining arguments should be viewed in a similar vein. Any
lessee must attempt to determine the price it is paying for greater flexibility
and convenience. In many cases, the benefits the firm is able to attain are
not worth the cost. Compounding the problem is the fact that it is often
difficult for a lessee firm to quantify such cost-benefit tradeoffs.

LACK OF RESTRICTIONS

Another suggested advantage relates to the lack of restrictions associated with a lease. Unlike term-loan agreements or bond indentures,
lease contracts generally do not contain protective-covenant restrictions.
Furthermore, in calculating financial ratios under existing covenants, it is
sometimes possible to exclude lease payments from the firm's debt commitments. Once again, the extent to which the lack of restrictions benefits a
lessee will depend on the price it must pay. If a lessor views his security
position to be superior to that of a lender, he may not require a higher
return on the lease to compensate for the lack of restrictions on the lessee.
On the other hand, if the prospective lessee is viewed as a marginal credit
risk, a higher rate may be charged.

AVOIDING THE RISK
OF OBSOLESCENCE

Similar reasoning applies to another popular argument for leasing.
This argument states that a lease is advantageous because it allows the firm
to avoid the risk that the equipment will become obsolete. In actuality, the
risk of obsolescence is passed on to the lessee in any financial lease. Since
the original cost of the asset is fully amortized over the basic lease term, all
of the risk is borne by the lessee. Only in a cancelable operating lease is it
sometimes possible to avoid the risk of obsolescence.

A related argument in favor of leasing states that a lessor will generally provide the firm with better and more reliable service in order to
maintain the resale value of the asset. The extent to which this is true will
depend on the lessor's own cost-benefit tradeoff. If the lessor is a manufacturing or a leasing company that specializes in a particular type of equipment, it may be profitable to maintain the equipment's resale value by
insuring that it is properly repaired and maintained. Because of their technical and marketing expertise, these types of lessors may be able to operate
successfully in the secondary market for the equipment. On the other

hand, bank lessors or independent financial leasing companies would probably find it too expensive to follow this approach. Thus, it is difficult to generalize with regard to this potential advantage.

CONSERVATION OF WORKING CAPITAL

One of the oldest and most widely used arguments in favor of leasing is the assertion that a lease conserves the firm's working capital. Indeed, many within the leasing industry still consider this to be the number one advantage of leasing.[14] The conservation argument runs as follows: since a lease does not require an immediate outflow of cash to cover the full purchase price of the asset, funds are retained in the business.

It is clear that a lease does require a lower initial outlay than a cash purchase. However, the cash outlay associated with the purchase option can be reduced or eliminated by borrowing the down payment from another source. This argument leads us directly into the next purported advantage of lease financing.

100 PERCENT FINANCING

Another alleged benefit of leasing is embodied in the argument that a lease provides the firm with 100 percent financing. It is pointed out that the borrow-and-buy alternative generally involves a down payment, whereas leasing does not. Given that investors and creditors are reasonably intelligent, however, it is reasonable to conclude that they consider similar amounts of lease and debt financing to be equivalent from the standpoint of the amount of risk they add to the firm. Thus, a firm uses up less of its capacity to raise nonequity funds with debt than with leasing. In theory, it could issue a second debt instrument to make up the difference—that is, the down payment.

TAX SAVINGS

It is also argued that leasing offers an economic advantage in that the tax shield generated by the lease payments usually exceeds the tax shield from depreciation that would be available if the asset were purchased. The extent to which leasing provides a tax-shield benefit will be a function of many factors. The *NAL* equation (19-4), discussed earlier, provided the basis for weighing these differences in tax shields.

EASE OF OBTAINING CREDIT

Another alleged advantage of leasing is that firms with poor credit ratings are able to obtain assets through leases when they are unable to finance the acquisitions with debt capital. The obvious counterargument is that the firm will most certainly face a high lease rate in order to compensate the lessor for bearing the risk of default.

[14]For example, see L. Rochwarger, "The Flexible World of Leasing," *Fortune*, 39 (November 1974), 56–59.

In this chapter the various sources of intermediate-term credit were discussed. **Intermediate**, or simply **term credit**, was defined as encompassing any source of financing with a final maturity greater than one year but less than ten. The two major sources of term credit discussed were term loans and financial leases.

Term loans are available from commercial banks, life insurance companies, and pension funds. Although the specifics of each term loan agreement vary, they were found to share a common set of general characteristics. These included:

1. A final maturity of one to ten years.
2. A requirement of some form of collateral.
3. A body of "restrictive covenants" designed to protect the security interests of the lender.
4. A loan amortization schedule whereby periodic loan payments, comprised of both principal and interest components, are made over the life of the loan.

There are three basic types of lease arrangements:

1. Direct lease.
2. Sale and leaseback.
3. Leveraged lease.

The lease agreement can further be classified as a financial or operating lease, with the former comprising the basis for our discussion. Recent statements by the Financial Accounting Standards Board virtually assure the inclusion of all financial leases in the body of the lessee firm's balance sheet.

The lease-versus-purchase decision was presented as a hybrid capital-budgeting problem wherein the analyst must consider both the investment and financing aspects of the decision. Finally, we discussed the many and varied factors often claimed as "advantages" of leasing as opposed to the use of the firm's usual debt-equity financing mix. Many of the arguments were found to be either wholly or partially fallacious. However, a complete lease-purchase analysis using a model similar to the one discussed here should provide a rational basis for ferreting out the true advantages of lease financing.

19-1. What characteristics distinguish intermediate-term debt from other forms of debt instruments?

19-2. List and discuss the major types of restrictions generally found in the covenants of term-loan agreements.

19-3. Define each of the following:
   (a) Direct leasing.

(b) Sale and leaseback arrangement.
(c) Leveraged leasing.
(d) Operating lease.

19-4. How are financial leases handled in the financial statements of the lessee firm?

19-5. List and discuss each of the potential benefits from lease financing.

19-1. Compute the annual payments for an installment loan carrying an 8 percent rate of interest, a five-year maturity, and a face amount of $80,000.

19-2. Compute the annual principal and interest components of the loan in problem 19-1.

19-3. The J. B. Marcum Company needs $250,000 to finance a new mini-computer. The computer sales firm has offered to finance the purchase with a $50,000 down payment followed by five annual installments of $55,481.95 each. Alternatively, the firm's bank has offered to lend the firm $200,000 to be repaid in five annual installments based on an annual rate of interest of 10 percent. Finally, the firm has arranged to finance the needed $200,000 through a loan from an insurance company requiring a lump-sum payment of $337,011.63, in five years.

(a) What is the effective annual rate of interest on the loan from the computer sales firm?

(b) What will the annual payments on the bank loan be?

(c) What is the annual rate of interest for the insurance company term loan?

(d) Based upon cost considerations only, which source of financing should Marcum select?

19-4. Early in the spring of 1978 the Jonesboro Steel Corporation (JSC) decided to purchase a small computer. The computer is especially designed to handle the inventory, payroll, shipping, and general clerical functions for small manufacturers like JSC. The firm estimates that the computer will cost $60,000 to purchase and will last four years, at which time it can be salvaged for $10,000. The firm's marginal tax rate is 50 percent, and the firm's cost of capital for projects of this type is estimated to be 12 percent. Over the next four years the management of JSC feel the computer will reduce operating expenses by $20,000 a year before depreciation and taxes. JSC utilizes straight-line depreciation.

JSC is also considering the possibility of leasing the computer. The computer sales firm has offered JSC a four-year lease contract with annual payments of $18,000. In addition, if JSC leases the computer, the lessor will absorb insurance and maintenance expenses valued at $2000 per year.

(a) Evaluate the net present value of the computer purchase. Should the computer be acquired via purchase?

(b) If JSC uses a 40 percent target debt-to-total-assets ratio, evaluate the net present value advantage of leasing. JSC can borrow at a rate of 8 percent with annual installments paid over the next four years.

(c) Should JSC lease the asset?

19-5. S. S. Johnson Enterprises (SSJE) is evaluating the acquisition of a heavy-duty forklift with 20,000 to 24,000 pound lift capacity. SSJE can either purchase the forklift through the use of its normal financing mix (30 percent debt and 70 percent common equity) or lease it. Pertinent details are found below:

Acquisition price of the forklift	$20,000
Useful life	4 years
Salvage value	$4000
Depreciation method	straight life
Annual before-tax and depreciation cash savings from the forklift	$6000
Rate of interest on a four-year installment loan	10 percent
Marginal tax rate	50 percent
Annual rentals (four-year lease)	$6000
Annual operating expenses included in the lease	$1000
Cost of capital	12 percent

(a) Evaluate whether the forklift's acquisition is justified through purchase.

(b) Should SSJE lease the asset?

SELECTED REFERENCES

BOWER, RICHARD S., "Issues in Lease Financing," *Financial Management*, 2 (Winter 1973), 25–34.

COOPER, KERRY, and ROBERT H. STRAWSER, "Evaluation of Capital Investment Projects Involving Asset Leases," *Financial Management*, 4 (Spring 1975), 44–49.

DOENGES, R. CONRAD, "The Cost of Leasing," *Engineering Economist*, 17 (Fall 1971), 31–44.

JOHNSON, ROBERT W., and WILBUR G. LEWELLEN, "Analysis of the Lease-or-Buy Decision," *Journal of Finance*, 27 (September 1972), 815–23.

MIDDLETON, J. WILLIAM, "Term-Lending—Practical and Profitable," *Journal of Commercial Banking Lending*, 50 (August 1968), 31–43.

ROENFELDT, RODNEY L., and JEROME S. OSTERYOUNG, "Analysis of Financial Leases," *Financial Management*, 2 (Spring 1973), 74–87.

ROGERS, DEAN E., "An Approach to Analyzing Cash Flow for Term Loan Purposes," *Bulletin of the Robert Morris Associates*, 48 (October 1965), 79–85.

SCHALL, LAWRENCE D., "The Lease-or-Buy and Asset Acquisition Decisions," *Journal of Finance*, 29 (September 1974), 1203–14.

Long-Term Debt, Preferred Stock, and Common Stock

*I*n this chapter we will concern ourselves with the three major sources of long-term and permanent funds for the firm: long-term debt, preferred stock, and common stock. In Chapters 13 and 16 we discussed the valuation and theory behind their use. In this chapter we will devote our attention to the terminology and basic features common to these securities, focusing on their similarities and differences, as well as their advantages and disadvantages as sources of financing to the firm.

A **bond** is any long-term (ten years or more) promissory note issued by the firm. In examining bonds we will first acquaint ourselves with bond terminology and features, then examine types of bonds (both secured and unsecured), methods of retiring debt, bond refunding, and advantages and disadvantages of financing with long-term debt.

BONDS OR LONG-TERM DEBT

PAR VALUE

The **par value** of a bond is the face value appearing on it that is returned to the bondholder at maturity. In general, most corporate bonds are issued in denominations of $1000, although there are some exceptions to this rule.

Basic Bond Terminology, Features, and Characteristics

COUPON INTEREST RATE

The **coupon interest rate** on a bond indicates what percentage of the par value of the bond will be paid out annually in the form of interest. Thus, regardless of what happens to the price of a bond with an 8 percent coupon interest rate and a $1000 par value, it will pay out $80 annually in interest until maturity.

MATURITY

The **maturity** of a bond indicates the length of time until the bond issuer returns the par value to the bondholder and terminates the bond.

INDENTURE

An **indenture** is the legal agreement between the firm issuing the bonds and the bond trustee who represents the bondholders. The indenture provides the specific terms of the loan agreement, including a description of the bonds, the rights of the bondholders, the rights of the issuing firm, and the responsibilities of the trustees. This legal document may run 100 pages or more in length, with the majority of it devoted to defining protective provisions for the bondholder. The bond trustee, usually a banking institution or trust company, is then assigned the task of overseeing the relationship between the bondholder and the issuing firm, protecting the bondholder, and seeing that the terms of the indenture are carried out.

Typically, the restrictive provisions included in the indenture attempt to protect the bondholder's position relative to that of other outstanding securities. Common provisions involve: (1) prohibitions on the sale of accounts receivable, (2) constraints on the issuance of common stock dividends, (3) restrictions on the purchase or sale of fixed assets, and (4) constraints on additional borrowing. Prohibitions on the sale of accounts receivable result because such sales would benefit the firm's short-run liquidity position at the expense of its future liquidity position. Constraints on the issuance of common stock dividends generally take the form of limiting them when working capital falls below a specified level, or simply limiting the maximum dividend payout to 50 or 60 percent of earnings under any circumstance. Fixed asset restrictions generally require lender permission before the liquidation of any fixed asset or prohibit the use of any existing fixed asset as collateral on new loans. Constraints on additional borrowing are usually in the form of restrictions or limitations on the amount and type of additional long-term debt that can be issued. All these restrictions have one thing in common: they attempt to prohibit action that would improve the status of other securities at the expense of bonds and to protect the status of bonds from being weakened by any managerial action.

CURRENT YIELD

The **current yield** on a bond refers to the ratio of the annual interest payment to the bond's market price. If, for example, we are examining a bond with an 8 percent coupon interest rate, a par value of $1000, and a market price of $700, it would have a current yield of

$$\text{current yield} = \frac{\text{annual interest payments}}{\text{market price of the bond}} \qquad (20\text{-}1)$$

$$= \frac{.08 \times \$1000}{\$700} = \frac{\$80}{\$700} = 11.4 \text{ percent}$$

YIELD TO MATURITY

The **yield to maturity** refers to the bond's internal rate of return. It incorporates into the analysis both the annual interest payments and capital gains or losses. Mathematically, the yield to maturity is the discount rate that equates the present value of the interest and principal payments with the current market price of the bond.[1]

BOND RATINGS

John Moody first began to rate bonds in 1909; since that time three rating agencies, Moody's, Standard and Poor's, and Fitch Investor Services, have provided **ratings** on corporate bonds. These ratings involve a judgment about the future risk potential of the bond. Although they deal with expectations, several historical factors appear to play a significant role in their determination.[2] Bond ratings are favorably affected by: (1) a low utilization of financial leverage, (2) profitable operations, (3) a low variability in past earnings, (4) large firm size, and (5) little use of subordinated debt. In turn, the rating a bond receives affects the rate of return demanded on the bond by the investors. The poorer the bond rating, the higher the rate of return demanded in the capital markets. An example of these ratings and their description is given in Table 20-1.

DETERMINANTS OF THE COST OF LONG-TERM DEBT

In Chapter 13 we computed an investor's required rate of return for debt financing to the firm. We now focus on the factors that determine the required rate of return that investors demand on this debt. The total cost of debt that the firm will pay depends primarily upon five factors: (1) the size of the issue, (2) the issue's maturity, (3) the issue's riskiness or rating, (4) the restrictive requirements of the issue, and (5) the current riskless interest rate. To a large extent the administrative costs of issuing debt are fixed, and they will decrease in percentage terms as the size of the issue increases. In effect, economies of scale are associated with the issuance of debt. The

---

[1] See Chapter 13 for illustrative example.
[2] See Thomas F. Pogue and Robert M. Soldofsky, "What's in a Bond Rating?," *Journal of Financial and Quantitative Analysis*, 4 (June 1969), 201–228, and George E. Pinches and Keut A. Mingo, "A Multivariate Analysis of Industrial Bond Ratings," *Journal of Finance*, 28 (March 1973), 1–18.

Table 20-1 STANDARD AND POOR'S CORPORATE BOND RATINGS

AAA   This is the highest rating assigned by Standard and Poor's debt obligation and indicates an extremely strong capacity to pay principal and interest.

AA   Bonds rated AA also qualify as high-quality debt obligations. Their capacity to pay principal and interest is very strong, and in the majority of instances they differ from AAA issues only in small degree.

A   Bonds rated A have a strong capacity to pay principal and interest, although they are somewhat more susceptible to the adverse effects of changes in circumstances and economic conditions.

BBB   Bonds rated BBB are regarded as having an adequate capacity to pay principal and interest. Whereas they normally exhibit adequate protection parameters, adverse economic conditions or changing circumstances are more likely to lead to a weakened capacity to pay principal and interest for bonds in this category than for bonds in the A category.

BB
B
CCC
CC   Bonds rated BB, B, CCC, and CC are regarded, on balance, as predominantly speculative with respect to the issuer's capacity to pay interest and repay principal in accordance with the terms of the obligation. BB indicates the lowest degree of speculation and CC the highest. While such bonds will likely have some quality and protective characteristics, these are outweighed by large uncertainties or major risk exposures to adverse conditions.

C   The rating C is reserved for income bonds on which no interest is being paid.

D   Bonds rated D are in default, and payment of principal and/or interest is in arrears.

Plus (+) or Minus (−): To provide more detailed indications of credit quality, the ratings from "AA" to "BB" may be modified by the addition of a plus or minus sign to show relative standing within the major rating categories.

Provisional Ratings: A provisional rating assumes the successful completion of the project being financed by the issuance of the bonds being rated and indicates that payment of debt service requirements is largely or entirely dependent upon the successful and timely completion of the project. This rating, however, while addressing credit quality subsequent to completion, makes no comment on the likelihood of, or the risk of default upon failure of, such completion. Accordingly, the investor should exercise his own judgment with respect to such likelihood and risk.

SOURCE: *Standard and Poor's Fixed Income Investor*, Vol. 6 (1978). Reprinted by permission.

issue's maturity also affects the cost of debt. Borrowers prefer to borrow for long periods in order to lock in their interest costs and avoid the problem of frequent refinancing, while lenders would rather not tie up their money for long periods. In order to bring about equilibrium between supply and demand for funds, long-term debt generally carries a higher interest rate than does short-term debt. This tends to encourage some borrowers to borrow for shorter periods and some investors to lend for longer periods, bringing about equilibrium between supply and demand.

Investors also desire additional return for taking on added risk. Thus the less risky the bond or the higher the bond rating, the lower will be the interest rate. We can see this by looking at the movement of bond yields for four different ratings during 1977, as shown in Table 20-2.

The restrictive requirements and rights of both the issuer and holder also affect the interest rate paid on the bond. The more the bondholder requires in the way of protection and rights, the lower will be rate of return earned. On the other hand, the more rights the issuer demands—for example, the right to repurchase the debt at a predetermined price (called a call provision and discussed later in detail)—the higher will be the rate that the issuer will have to offer in order to convince investors to purchase the bond.

Finally, the current riskless interest rate plays a major role in determining the cost of debt. As the riskless rate of interest moves up and down, parallel movements are produced for corporate bond rates. The determination of the riskless interest rate is generally deferred to courses on money and banking and financial institutions. We may note here that one of the major factors affecting it is the anticipated inflation rate.

CLAIMS ON ASSETS AND INCOME

In the case of insolvency the claims of debt are honored prior to those of both common stock and preferred stock. However, different types of debt may also have a hierarchy among themselves as to the order of their claim on assets.

Bonds also have a claim on income prior to that of common and

Table 20-2   COMPARISON OF CORPORATE BOND YIELDS OF VARIOUS RATINGS, MONTHLY AVERAGES, 1977

	RATINGS			
	LEAST RISK AAA	AA	A	MOST RISK BBB
January	8.04%	8.17%	8.34%	8.81%
February	8.14	8.27	8.42	8.88
March	8.17	8.28	8.42	8.91
April	8.12	8.15	8.40	8.92
May	8.16	8.28	8.40	8.85
June	8.03	8.15	8.28	8.73
July	8.06	8.18	8.30	8.74
August	8.04	8.17	8.29	8.82
September	7.97	8.07	8.25	8.93
October	8.11	8.24	8.36	8.93
November	8.14	8.27	8.40	9.05
December	8.24	8.37	8.53	9.00
Monthly averages	8.10%	8.21%	8.36%	8.89%

SOURCE: Standard and Poor's Corporation, *Bond Guide* (January 1978).

preferred stock. If interest on bonds (other than income bonds, to be discussed later) is not paid, the bond trustees can classify the firm insolvent and force it into bankruptcy. Thus, the bondholder's claim on income is more likely to be honored than that of common and preferred stock-holders, whose dividends are paid at the discretion of the firm's management.

DEBENTURES

The term **debentures** applies to any unsecured long-term debt. Because these bonds are unsecured, the earning ability of the issuing corporation is of great concern to the bondholder. Often the issuing firm attempts to provide some protection to the holder through the prohibition of any additional encumbrance of assets. This prohibits the future issuance of secured long-term debt that would further tie up the firm's assets and leave the bondholders less protected. To the issuing firm the major advantage of debentures is that no property is secured by them. This allows the firm to issue debt and still preserve some future borrowing power.

SUBORDINATED DEBENTURES

Many firms have more than one issue of debentures outstanding. In this case a hierarchy may be specified, in which some debentures are given subordinated standing in the case of insolvency. The claims of the **subordinated debentures** are honored only after the claims of secured debt and unsubordinated debentures have been satisfied.[3]

INCOME BONDS

An **income bond** requires interest payments only if earned, and failure to meet these interest payments does not lead to firm bankruptcy. In this sense income bonds are more like preferred stock (which is discussed in a later section) than bonds. They are generally issued during the reorganization of a firm facing financial difficulties. The maturity of income bonds is usually much longer than that of other bonds in order to relieve pressure associated with the repayment of principal. While interest payments may be passed, unpaid interest is generally allowed to accumulate for some period of time and must be paid prior to the payment of any common stock dividends. This cumulative-interest feature provides the bondholder with some security. Several income bonds and their characteristics are shown in Table 20-3.

MORTGAGE BONDS

A **mortgage bond** is a bond secured by a lien on real property. Typically the value of the real property being secured is greater than that of the mortgage bonds issued. This provides the mortgage bondholders

---

[3]See Chapter 23 for an illustrated example.

Table 20-3 EXAMPLES OF INCOME BONDS, THEIR CUMULATIVE FEATURES AND INTEREST STATUS

BOND	STANDARD AND POOR'S RATING	CUMULATIVE FEATURE	INTEREST STATUS
Central of Georgia, $4\frac{1}{2}$ percent interest paid semiannually, due in 2020	BB	Cumulative up to 13.5 percent with interest payable only after first-mortgage interest and sinking-fund payment	Currently paying
Chicago & Eastern Illinois Railroad Co., 5 percent interest paid semiannually, due in 2054	BB	Noncumulative	Currently paying
Chicago, Milwaukee, St. Paul & Pacific, 5 percent interest paid semiannually, due in 2055	D	Noncumulative	No interest paid since Sept. 1969
Chicago, Indianapolis & Louisville, 4 percent interest paid semi-annually, due in 1983	BB	Fully cumulative	Currently paying
Chicago, Rock Island & Pacific, 4 percent interest paid semi-annually, due in 1995	D	Cumulative up to 18 percent	No interest paid since Sept. 1967
Missouri Pacific Railroad Co., $4\frac{3}{4}$ percent interest paid semi-annually, due in 2030	BB	Cumulative up to 13.5 percent	Currently paying
Western Pacific Railroad, 5 percent paid semi-annually, due in 1984	B	Cumulative up to 20 percent	Currently paying

Source: Standard and Poor's Corporation, *Bond Guide* (January 1978).

with a margin of safety in the event the market value of the secured property declines. In the case of foreclosure, the trustees have the power to sell the secured property and use the proceeds to pay the bondholders. In the event that the proceeds from this sale do not fully cover the bonds, the bondholders become general creditors, similar to debenture bondholders, for the unpaid portion of the debt. While a mortgage bond is a general classification for bonds secured by real property, they can be further differentiated among themselves to include subclassifications of mortgage bonds, blanket mortgage bonds, and closed-, open-, and limited open-end mortgage bonds.

First Mortgage Bonds.   The same property may be pledged on more than one mortgage bond. In this case, the first mortgage bond has the senior claim on the secured assets.

Second Mortgage Bonds. The second mortgage bond has the second claim on assets and is serviced only after the claims of the first mortgage bonds have been satisfied. Obviously, second mortgage bonds are much less secure than are first mortgage bonds, and they are not extremely popular. They are seldom issued except by firms experiencing financial difficulties. When they are issued, buyers generally demand a relatively high return because of their risky position.

Blanket or General Mortgage Bonds. Under a blanket or general mortgage bond, all the assets of the firm act as security.

Closed-End Mortgage Bonds. A closed-end mortgage bond forbids the use of the assets being secured by this bond as security in the issuance of any future mortgage bonds of the same priority. This type of mortgage assures bondholders that their claim on assets will not be diluted by the issuance of any future mortgage bonds. Although this type of mortgage bond restricts the financial manager's future financing options, it is extremely well liked by bondholders.

Open-End Mortgage Bonds. An open-end mortgage bond does not preclude the issuance of additional mortgage bonds of the same priority that use the same secured asset as security. Generally a restriction is placed upon the borrower, requiring that additional assets be added to the secured property if new debt is issued.

Limited Open-End Mortgage Bonds. Limited open-end mortgage bonds are a hybrid of the open- and closed-end mortgage bonds. Although they allow the issuance of additional bonds at the same priority level using the already mortgaged assets as security, they also limit the amount of these additional bonds that can be issued.

COLLATERAL TRUST BONDS

Collateral trust bonds are secured by common stock and/or bonds, which are held by a trustee who has the power to liquidate them in the event of default. Generally, to assure that collateral trust bonds are amply covered, the indenture contains a clause that the market value of the collateral must be at least 20 to 50 percent greater than the value of the bonds. An example of a collateral trust bond is the Pennsylvania Co. collateral trust $5\frac{1}{2}$s (paying $5\frac{1}{2}$ percent interest semiannually) due in 1985, which is secured by Norfolk and Western common stock. The bond indenture states that the market value of the Norfolk and Western common stock must equal at least 150 percent of the principal value of the bonds outstanding.

EQUIPMENT TRUST CERTIFICATES

Equipment trust financing, a cross between lease financing and debt financing, is used primarily by railroads and some airlines and oil companies to finance the purchase of rolling stock or planes. Under this financing method the railroad or issuing firm first orders the railroad cars or equipment. When the equipment is received, the title is transferred to a newly formed trust company. The manufacturer is then paid in full by the trust company, which obtains funds primarily through the issuance of **equipment trust certificates.**

The equipment trust certificates have minimal risk because they are secured by the equipment being purchased, and this is generally quite standardized. The railroad company also adds to the safety of these bonds by guaranteeing the payment of principal and interest. The equipment is then leased to the railroad in such a way that the interest payments and amortization of the certificates are completely covered. When these certificates are retired, the ownership of the equipment is passed to the railroad.

Through the use of equipment trust certificates, railroads, which have fallen upon hard times, are able to secure funds to purchase much-needed equipment at a reasonable cost. This cost is generally lower than it would be otherwise, because the quality and standardness of the assets used as collateral make equipment trust certificates less risky than the railroad bonds would be. Table 20-4 compares the ratings of equipment trust certificates and the best rating assigned to any bonds issued by the parent company. This comparison shows that the certificates were consistently rated higher than were the corporation's typical bonds. The minimal risk associated with

Table 20-4 COMPARISON OF RATINGS BETWEEN EQUIPMENT TRUST CERTIFICATES AND THE HIGHEST RATING RECEIVED BY ANY BOND IN THE SAME SYSTEM, JANUARY 1978

	EQUIPMENT TRUST CERTIFICATE	HIGHEST RATED BOND
Atchison, Topeka & Santa Fe	AAA	AA
Atlantic Coast Line	AA	BBB
Baltimore & Ohio	A	BB
Canadian Pacific	AA	A
Chicago & Eastern Illinois	AA	BB
Chicago North Western	A	B
Chicago Rock Island & Pacific	BBB	D
Denver & Rio Grande Western	AAA	A
Louisville & Nashville Railroad	A	BBB
New York, Chicago & St. Louis	AA+	A
Wabash Railroad	AA+	BBB

SOURCE: Standard and Poor's Corporation, *Bond Guide* (January 1978)

equipment trust certificates has been historically illustrated by their record. In June 1970, for example, when Penn Central defaulted on much of its debt, it did not default on its $1.2 billion worth of equipment trust certificates.

Because bonds have a maturity date, their retirement is a crucial matter. Bonds may be retired at maturity, at which time the bondholder receives the par value of the bond, or they can be retired prior to maturity. Early redemption is generally accomplished through the use of a call provision or a sinking fund. *Retiring Debt*

CALL PROVISION

A **call provision** entitles the corporation to repurchase or "call" the bonds from their holders at stated prices over specified periods. This feature provides the firm with the flexibility to recall its debt and replace it with lower-cost debt if interest rates fall. The terms of the call provision are provided in the indenture and generally state the call price above the bond's par value. The difference between the call price and the par value is referred to as the **call premium.** The size of this premium often changes over time, becoming smaller as the date of call approaches the bond's scheduled maturity. It is also common to prohibit calling the bond during its first years. Obviously a call provision works to the disadvantage of the bondholder, who for this reason is generally compensated by a higher rate of return on the bond.

SINKING FUND

A **sinking fund** allows for the periodic repayment of debt, thus reducing the total amount of debt outstanding. When a sinking fund is set up, the firm makes annual payments to the trustee, who can then purchase the bonds in the capital markets or use the call provision. The advantage is that the annual retirement of debt through a sinking fund reduces the amount needed to retire the remaining debt at maturity. Otherwise, the firm would face a major payment at maturity. If the firm were experiencing temporary financial problems when the debt matured, both the repayment of the principal and the firm's future could be jeopardized. The use of a sinking fund and its periodic retirement of debt eliminates this potential danger.

The **bond-refunding** decision—that is, whether or not to call an entire issue of bonds—is similar to the capital-budgeting decision. The present value of the stream of benefits from the refunding decision is compared with the present value of its costs, and if the benefits outweigh the costs, the refunding is done. *Bond Refunding*

The benefits from refunding generally involve interest savings, achieved by replacing older, high-cost debt with less expensive debt as interest rates drop. In addition, tax benefits come about because the unamortized flotation costs and discount on the old bonds, if any, and the call premium are treated as expenses during the year of the refunding. The costs include issuing and recalling expenses and any interest expenses during the bond overlap period. An **overlap period,** when the new bonds have been issued and the old bonds have not yet been called, generally occurs because firms wish to obtain the funds from the new issue before calling the old bonds. This eliminates the risk of a rise in interest rates or a drying up of funds in the capital markets after the old debt has been called but before the new debt has been issued. Thus, the cost associated with the additional interest payment can be viewed as the cost of elimination of this risk.

While the calculations associated with a bond-refunding decision appear to be quite complex, it should be remembered that we are merely determining the net present value of this decision. The major difference between the refunding decision and capital budgeting, as presented in Chapter 11, is that the discount rate used in refunding is the after-tax cost of borrowing on the new bonds rather than the firm's cost of capital. This is because in a refunding decision, as opposed to a normal investment decision, the costs and benefits are known with complete certainty. In effect, a refunding decision is an example of a riskless investment. The only risk involved is the risk of the firm's defaulting on the interest or principal payments. Thus, because the after-tax cost of borrowing on the new bonds takes into account this default risk, it is the appropriate discount rate. The following example will illustrate and explain these calculations.

Example. Suppose that interest rates have just fallen and that a firm in the 50 percent tax bracket has a $50 million, 9 percent debenture issue outstanding with 20 years remaining to maturity. The unamortized flotation costs and discount on the old bonds total $3 million. These bonds contain a call provision and can be called at $104 (that is, $104 for each $100 of par). Let us assume that they could be replaced with a $50 million issue of 8 percent 20-year bonds providing the firm with $48 million after flotation costs. That is to say, the discount on the new bonds is $2 million ($50 million − $48 million). Let us further assume that an additional $400,000 in issuing expenses would be incurred. The overlap period during which both issues will be outstanding is expected to be one month. Finally, since the marginal corporate tax rate is 50 percent, the appropriate discount rate is 8%(1 − .5) = 4 percent.

The procedure for arriving at a decision involves first determining the initial outlay and the differential cash flows. Then all the flows are discounted back to the present, and the net present value of the refunding decision is determined. These calculations are illustrated in Table 20-5. In this example the net present value of the refunding decision is $1,106,150. Since this is positive, the refunding proposal should be accepted.

Table 20-5 CALCULATIONS ILLUSTRATING THE BOND-REFUNDING DECISION

STEP 1: Calculate the *initial outlay*.

    (a) Determine the difference between the inflow from the new issue and the outflow from retiring the old issue:

Cost of calling old bonds ($50,000,000 × 1.04)	$52,000,000
Proceeds, after flotation costs, from new issue	48,000,000
Difference between inflow and outflow	$ 4,000,000

    (b) Determine total issuing and overlap expenses:

Issuing expense on new bonds	$ 400,000	
Interest expense on old bonds during overlap period	375,000	775,000

    (c) Add the items above to determine the gross initial outlay $ 4,775,000

    (d) Determine tax-deductible expenses incurred:

Interest expenses during overlap period	$ 375,000
Unamortized flotation costs and discount on the old bonds	3,000,000
Call premium (call price less par value)	2,000,000
Total tax-deductible expenses	$5,375,000

    (e) Less tax savings:

Marginal tax rate (50%) × total tax-deductible expenses	×.50	2,687,500

    (f) Equals net *initial* cash outflow $ 2,087,500

STEP 2: Calculate the *annual cash benefit* from eliminating the old bonds through refunding.

    (a) Determine annual interest expense:

9% interest on $50,000,000	$4,500,000

    (b) Determine tax deductible expenses incurred:

Annual interest expense	$4,500,000
Annual amortization of flotation costs and discount on old bonds ($3,000,000/20)	150,000
Total annual tax-deductible expenses	$4,650,000

    (c) Less annual tax savings:

Marginal tax rate (50%) × total annual tax-deductible expenses	×.50	2,325,000

    (d) Equals annual cash benefit from elimination of old bonds $2,175,000

STEP 3: Calculate the *annual cash outflow* from issuing the new bonds.

    (a) Determine the annual interest expense:

8% interest on $5,000,000	$4,000,000

    (b) Determine tax deductible expenses incurred:

Annual interest expense	$4,000,000
Annual amortization of bond discount ($2,000,000/20)	100,000

Table 20-5 (*cont.*)

STEP 3: Calculate the annual cash outflow. (cont.)

Annual amortization of issuing expenses ($400,000/20)	20,000	
Total annual tax-deductible expenses	$4,120,000	
(c) Less annual tax savings:		
Marginal tax rate (50%) × total annual tax-deductible expenses	×.50	2,060,000
(d) Equals annual net cash outflow from issuing new bonds		$1,940,000

STEP 4: Calculate the *annual net cash benefits* (that is, difference between the annual benefits and costs) from the refunding decision.

(a) Add benefits:	
Annual cash benefits from eliminating the old bonds	$2,175,000
(b) Less costs:	
Annual cash outflows from issuing the new debt	1,940,000
(c) Equals annual net cash benefits	$ 235,000

STEP 5: Calculate the *present value of the annual net cash benefits*.

(a) Discount the 20-year $235,000 annuity back to the present at the after-tax cost of borrowing on the new bonds of 4 percent ($235,000 × 13.590)	$3,193,650

STEP 6: Calculate the *refunding decision's net present value*.

(a) Present value of the annual net cash benefits	$3,193,650
(b) Less present value of initial outlay	2,087,500
(c) Equals net present value	$1,106,150

The corporate financing decision is complicated by the various tradeoffs between alternative financial instruments. In order to better understand the role of long-term debt in this decision process, we will examine its advantages and disadvantages.

Advantages and Disadvantages of Long-Term Debt

ADVANTAGES

1. Long-term debt is generally less expensive than other forms of financing, because (a) investors view debt as a relatively safe investment alternative and demand a lower rate of return, and (b) interest expenses are tax deductible.
2. Bondholders do not participate in extraordinary profits; thus the payments are limited to interest.
3. Bondholders do not have voting rights.
4. Flotation costs on bonds are generally lower than those on common stock.

DISADVANTAGES

1. Debt (other than income bonds) results in interest payments that, if not met, can force the firm into bankruptcy.
2. Debt (other than income bonds) produces fixed charges, increasing the firm's financial leverage. Although this may not be a disadvantage to all firms, it certainly is for some firms with unstable earnings streams.
3. Debt must be repaid at maturity and thus at some point involves a major cash outflow.
4. The typically restrictive nature of indenture covenants may limit the firm's future financial flexibility.

Preferred stock is often referred to as a hybrid security, because it has many characteristics of both common stock and bonds. Preferred stock is similar to common stock in that it has no fixed maturity date, the nonpayment of dividends does not bring on bankruptcy, and dividends are not deductible for tax purposes. On the other hand, preferred stock is similar to bonds in that dividends are limited in amount.

The size of the preferred stock dividend is generally fixed either as a dollar amount or as a percentage of the par value. For example, Texas Power and Light has issued $4 preferred stock, while Toledo Edison has some 4.25% preferred stock outstanding. The par value on the Toledo Edison preferred stock is $100, hence each share pays 4.25% × $100 or $4.25 in dividends annually. Since these dividends are fixed, preferred stockholders do not share in the residual earnings of the firm but are limited to their stated annual dividend.

In examining preferred stock we will first discuss several features common to almost all preferred stock. Next we will investigate several less frequently included features and take a brief look at methods of retiring preferred stock. We will close by examining its advantages and disadvantages.

*PREFERRED
STOCK*

Although each issue of preferred stock is unique, several characteristics are common to almost all issues. These traits include the ability to issue multiple classes of preferred stock, the claim on assets and income, and the cumulative and protective features.

*Features
Common to
Preferred Stock*

MULTIPLE CLASSES
OF PREFERRED STOCK

If a company desires, it can issue more than one series or class of preferred stock, and each class can have different characteristics. In fact it is quite common for firms that issue preferred stock to issue more than one series. For example, Tenneco Inc. has 19 different issues of preferred stock outstanding with dividend rates ranging from 4.50 to 7.94 percent. These issues are further differentiated by the fact that some are convertible into common stock while others are not, and they have varying priority status with respect to assets in the event of bankruptcy.

CLAIM ON ASSETS AND INCOME

Preferred stock has priority over common stock with respect to claims on assets in the case of bankruptcy. The preferred stock claim is honored after that of bonds and before that of common stock. Multiple issues of preferred stock may be differentiated within themselves with respect to the priority of their claim. Preferred stock also has a claim on income prior to common stock. That is, the firm must pay its preferred stock dividends before it issues common stock dividends. Thus, in terms of risk, preferred stock is safer than common stock because it has a prior claim on assets and income. By the same token it is riskier than long-term debt because its claims on assets and income come after those of bonds.

CUMULATIVE FEATURE

Most preferred stock carries a **cumulative feature,** requiring that all past unpaid preferred stock dividends be paid before any common stock dividends are declared. The purpose is to provide some degree of protection for the preferred stock shareholder. Without a cumulative feature there would be no reason why preferred stock dividends would not be omitted or passed when common stock dividends were passed. Since preferred stock does not have the dividend enforcement power of interest from bonds, the cumulative feature is necessary to protect the rights of preferred stockholders.

Occasionally, if a firm does not pay preferred stock dividends for a number of years, dividends in arrears may become extremely large and virtually unpayable. In this case an arrangement is usually made to clear unpaid preferred stock dividends by exchanging other securities and cash, or securities alone, for the old preferred stock. This rids the firm of its built-up cumulative obligation and allows it to issue common stock dividends. The preferred stockholder is protected because the exchange is, of course, subject to his approval. An example occurred in 1973 with ASG Industries, which was faced with $2.1 million in dividend arrearages on its 5 percent preferred stock. To rid itself of the obligation, ASG exchanged three shares of common stock for each share of preferred. The value of the common stock received in the exchange was substantial, indicating that the cumulative feature had indeed served its purpose and protected the preferred shareholders.

PROTECTIVE FEATURES

Protective provisions in addition to the cumulative feature are common to preferred stock. These protective provisions generally allow for voting rights in the event of nonpayment of dividends, or they restrict the payment of common stock dividends if sinking-fund payments are not met or if the firm is in financial difficulty. In effect the protective features included with preferred stock are similar to the restrictive provisions included with long-term debt.

To examine typical protective provisions, let us look at Tenneco Inc. and Reynolds Metals preferred stock. The Tenneco preferred stock has a protective provision that provides the preferred stockholders with voting rights whenever six quarterly dividends are in arrears. At that point the preferred shareholders are given the power to elect a majority of the board of directors. The Reynolds Metals preferred stock includes a protective provision that precludes the payment of common stock dividends during any period in which the preferred stock sinking fund is in default. Both of these provisions, which yield protection beyond that provided for by the cumulative provision and thereby reduce shareholder risk, are desired by investors. Thus, they reduce the cost of preferred stock to the issuing firm.

Although convertibility and participating features are infrequent to preferred stock, their inclusion can greatly affect its desirability and cost.

**Infrequent
Features to
Preferred Stock**

CONVERTIBILITY FEATURE

Some preferred stock is **convertible** at the discretion of the holder into a predetermined number of shares of common stock. In this case, it takes on value as both preferred stock and common stock. The convertibility feature is, of course, desirable and thus reduces the cost of the preferred stock to the issuer. The characteristics common to convertible preferred stock will be discussed in detail in Chapter 21.

PARTICIPATION FEATURE

The **participation** feature allows the preferred stockholder to participate in earnings beyond the payment of the stated dividend. This is usually done in accordance with some set formula. For example, Borden Series A preferred stock currently provides for a dividend of no less than 60 cents per share, to be determined by the board of directors. Preferred stock of this sort actually resembles common stock as much as it does normal preferred stock. Although a participating feature is certainly desirable from the point of view of the investor, it is infrequently included in preferred stock.

Although preferred stock does not have a set maturity associated with it, issuing firms generally provide for some method of retirement. If preferred stock could not be retired, issuing firms could not take advantage of falling interest rates.

**Retirement of
Preferred Stock**

CALL PROVISIONS

Most preferred stock has some type of call provision associated with it. In fact the Securities Exchange Commission discourages the issuance of preferred stock without some call provision. The SEC has taken this stance on the ground that if a method of retirement is not provided, the issuing firm will not be able to replace its preferred stock if interest rates fall.

The call feature on preferred stock usually involves an initial premium above the par value or issuing price of the preferred of approximately 10 percent. Then, over time, the call premium generally falls. For example, Quaker Oats in 1976 issued $9.56 cumulative preferred stock with no par value for $100 per share. This issue is not callable until 1980 and then is callable at $109.56. After that the call price gradually drops to $100 in the year 2000, as shown in Table 20-6.

By setting the initial call price above the initial issue price and allowing it to decline slowly over time, the firm protects the investor from an early call that carries no premium. A call provision also allows the issuing firm to plan the retirement of its preferred stock at predetermined prices.

SINKING FUNDS

A sinking-fund provision allows the firm to periodically set aside an amount of money for the retirement of its preferred stock. This money is then used to purchase the preferred stock either in the open market or through the use of the call provision, whichever method is cheapest. Although preferred stock does not have a maturity date associated with it, the use of a call provision in addition to a sinking fund can effectively create a maturity date for the preferred stock. For example, the Quaker Oats issue we just examined has associated with it an annual sinking fund, operating between the years 1981 and 2005, which requires the annual elimination of a minimum of 20,000 shares and a maximum of 40,000. The minimum payments are designed so that the entire issue will be retired by the year 2005. If any sinking-fund payments are made above the minimum amount, the issue will be retired prior to 2005. Thus the Quaker Oats issue of preferred stock has a maximum life of 30 years, and the size of the issue outstanding will decrease each year after 1981.

Because preferred stock is a hybrid of bonds and common stock, it offers the firm several advantages and disadvantages by comparison with bonds and common stock.

Advantages and Disadvantages of the Use of Preferred Stock

Table 20-6 CALL PROVISION OF QUAKER OATS
$9.56 CUMULATIVE PREFERRED STOCK

DATE		CALL PRICE
Date of issue	until 7/19/80	not callable
7/20/80	until 7/19/85	$109.56
7/20/85	until 7/19/90	107.17
7/20/90	until 7/19/95	104.78
7/20/95	until 7/19/00	102.39
After 7/19/00		100.00

ADVANTAGES

1. Preferred stock does not have any default risk to the issuer. That is, the nonpayment of dividends does not force the firm into bankruptcy as does the nonpayment of interest on debt.

2. The dividend payments are generally limited to a stated amount. Thus, preferred stock does not participate in excess earnings as does common stock.

3. Preferred stockholders do not have voting rights except in the case of financial distress. Therefore, the issuance of preferred stock does not create a challenge to the owners of the firm.

4. Although preferred stock does not carry a specified maturity, the inclusion of call features and sinking funds provides the firm with the ability to replace the issue if interest rates decline.

DISADVANTAGES

1. Because preferred stock is riskier than bonds and because its dividends are not tax deductible, its cost is higher than that of bonds.

2. Although preferred stock dividends can be omitted, their cumulative nature makes their payment almost mandatory.

COMMON STOCK

Common stock involves the ownership position in the corporation. In effect bondholders and preferred stockholders can be viewed as creditors, with the common stockholders being the true owners of the firm. Common stock does not have a maturity date but exists as long as the firm does. Nor does common stock have an upper limit on its dividend payments. Dividend payments must be declared by the firm's board of directors before they are issued. In the event of bankruptcy the common stockholders, as owners of the corporation, cannot exercise claims on assets until the bondholders and preferred shareholders have been satisfied.

In examining common stock we will first look at several of its features or characteristics. Then we will focus on the process of raising funds through rights offerings. Finally, we will investigate the advantages and disadvantages of the use of common stock.

Features or Characteristics of Common Stock

We will now examine common stock's claim on income and assets, its voting rights, and the meaning and importance of its limited-liability feature.

CLAIM ON INCOME

As the owners of the corporation, the common shareholders have the right to the residual income after bondholders and preferred stockholders have been paid. This income may be paid directly to the shareholders in the form of dividends or retained and reinvested by the firm. While it is obvious the shareholder benefits immediately from the distribution of income in the form of dividends, the reinvestment of earnings also benefits the shareholder. Plowing back earnings into the firm results in an increase in the value of the firm, in its earning power, and in its future dividends. This action then results in an increase in the value of the stock. In effect residual income is directly distributed to shareholders in the form of dividends or indirectly in the form of capital gains on their common stock.

The right to residual income has both advantages and disadvantages for the common stockholder. The advantage is that the potential return is limitless. Once the claims of the most senior securities—that is, bonds and preferred stock—have been satisfied, the remaining income flows to the common stockholders in the form of dividends or capital gains. The disadvantage is that if the bond and preferred stock claims on income totally absorb the firm's earnings, the common shareholders receive nothing. Thus, in years when earnings fall it is the common shareholder who suffers first.

CLAIMS ON ASSETS

Just as common stock has the residual claim on income, it also has a residual claim on assets in the case of liquidation. Only after the claims of debt holders and preferred stockholders have been satisfied do the claims of common shareholders receive attention. Unfortunately, when bankruptcy does occur, the claims of the common shareholders generally go unsatisfied. In effect, this residual claim on assets adds to the risk of common stock. Thus, while common stock has historically provided a large return, averaging 9 percent annually since the late 1920s, it also has large risks associated with it.

VOTING RIGHTS

The common stock shareholders, as owners of the corporation, are entitled to elect the board of directors. Early in this century it was not uncommon for a firm to issue two classes of common stock, which were identical except that only one carried voting rights. For example, both the Parker Pen Co. and the Great Atlantic and Pacific Tea Co. (A&P) had two such classes of common stock. This practice has been virtually eliminated by (1) the Public Utility Holding Company Act of 1935, which gave the Securities and Exchange Commission the power to require that newly issued common stock carry voting rights, (2) the New York Stock Exchange's refusal to list common stock without voting privileges, and (3) investor demand for the inclusion of voting rights.

Although there are exceptions, each share of common stock is entitled to one vote, and common stock is the only security that carries the right to vote. Common shareholders not only have the right to elect the board of directors, they also must approve any change in the corporate charter. A typical charter change might involve the authorization to issue new stock or perhaps a merger proposal.

Voting for directors and charter changes occurs at the corporation's annual meeting, and while shareholders may vote in person, the majority generally vote by proxy. A **proxy** gives a designated party the temporary power of attorney to vote for the signee at the corporation's annual meeting. The firm's management generally solicits proxy votes and, if the shareholders are satisfied with its performance, has little problem securing them. However, in times of financial distress or when management takeovers are threatened, **proxy fights**—battles between rival groups for proxy votes—occur.

While each share of stock carries the same number of votes, the voting procedure is not always the same from company to company. The two procedures commonly used are majority and cumulative voting. Under **majority voting** each share of stock allows the shareholder one vote, and each position on the board of directors is voted on separately. Since each member of the board of directors is elected by a simple majority, a majority of shares has the power to elect the entire board of directors.

With **cumulative voting,** each share of stock allows the shareholder a number of votes equal to the number of directors being elected. The shareholder can then cast all his votes for a single candidate or split them among the various candidates. The advantage of a cumulative voting procedure is that it allows minority shareholders the power to elect a director.

LIMITED LIABILITY

Although the common stock shareholders are the actual owners of the corporation, their liability in the case of bankruptcy is limited to the amount of their investment. The advantage is that investors who might not otherwise invest their funds in the firm become willing to do so. Thus, this limited-liability feature aids the firm in raising funds.

PREEMPTIVE RIGHTS

The **preemptive right** entitles the common shareholder to maintain his proportionate share of ownership in the firm. When new shares are issued, the common shareholders have the first right of refusal. If a shareholder owns 25 percent of the corporation's stock, then he is entitled to purchase 25 percent of the new shares. Certificates issued to the shareholders giving them an option to purchase a stated number of new shares of stock at a specified price during a two- to ten-week period are called **rights.** These rights can be exercised, generally at a price below the common stock's current market price, can be allowed to expire, or can be sold in the open market. We will now explore the terminology and theoretical relationships involved in raising new funds through a rights offering.

Rights Offering

We will first look at the dates surrounding a rights offering and then examine the process of raising funds and the value of a right.

DATES SURROUNDING A RIGHTS OFFERING

Let us examine the announcement of a rights offering by a hypothetical corporation. On March 1 the firm announces that all "holders of record" as of April 6 will be issued rights, which will expire on May 30 and will be mailed to them on April 25. In this example March 1 is the **announcement date,** April 6 the **holder-of-record date,** and May 30 the **expiration date.** While this seems rather straightforward, it is complicated by the fact that if the stock is sold a day or two before the holder-of-record date, the corporation may not have time to record the transaction and replace the old owner's name with that of the new owner; the rights might then be sent to the wrong person. To deal with this problem an additional date has been created, the **ex rights date.** The ex rights date occurs four trading days prior to the holder-of-record date. On or after the ex rights date the stock sells without the rights. Whoever owns the stock on the day prior to the ex rights date receives the rights. Thus, if the holder-of-record date is April 6 and four trading days earlier is April 2, anyone purchasing the stock on or before April 1 will receive the rights, while anyone purchasing the stock on or after April 2 will not. The price of the stock prior to the ex rights date is referred to as the **rights-on price,** while the price on or after the ex rights date is the **ex rights price.** The timing of this process and the terminology are shown in Table 20-7.

RAISING FUNDS THROUGH RIGHTS OFFERINGS

Three questions and theoretical relationships must be dealt with if we are to fully understand rights offerings. First, how many rights are required to purchase a share of new stock? Second, what is the theoretical value of a right? Finally, what effect do rights offerings have on the value of the common stock outstanding?

Let us continue with the example of our hypothetical corporation and assume it has 600,000 shares of stock outstanding, currently selling for $100 per share. In order to finance new projects this firm needs to raise an additional $10,500,000 and wishes to do so with a rights offering.

Table 20-7 ILLUSTRATION OF THE TIMING OF A RIGHTS OFFERING

Stock sells rights on	March 1	– Announcement date
	April 1	– The owner of the stock as of this date receives the rights
Stock sells ex rights	April 2	– Ex rights date
	April 6	– Holder-of-record date } four trading days
	April 25	– Mailing date
	May 30	– Expiration date

Moreover, the subscription price on the new stock is $70 per share. The subscription price is set below the current market price of the stock in order to insure a complete sale of the new stock. To determine how many shares must be sold to raise the desired funds, we merely divide the desired funds by the subscription price:

$$\text{new shares to be sold} = \frac{\text{desired funds to be raised}}{\text{subscription price}} \quad (20\text{-}2)$$

$$= \frac{\$10,500,000}{\$70}$$

$$= 150,000 \text{ shares}$$

We know each share of common stock receives one right, and 150,000 new shares of common stock must be sold. Therefore, to determine the number of rights necessary to purchase one share of stock we merely divide the original number of shares outstanding by the new shares to be sold:

$$\text{number of rights necessary to purchase one share of stock} = \frac{\text{original number of shares outstanding}}{\text{new shares to be sold}} \quad (20\text{-}3)$$

$$= \frac{600,000 \text{ shares}}{150,000 \text{ shares}}$$

$$= 4 \text{ rights}$$

This indicates that if a current shareholder wishes to purchase a share of the new stock, he needs four rights plus $70:

$$\text{price of a share of new stock} = \text{subscription price} + \text{number of rights necessary to purchase one share of stock} \quad (20\text{-}4)$$

$$= \$70 + 4 \text{ rights}$$

Since the subscription price is well below the current market value, there is clearly some value to a right.

The precise value of the right obviously depends upon: (1) the relationship between the market price of the stock and the subscription price and (2) the number of rights necessary to purchase one share of stock. To determine the value of a right in the previous example, first let us determine the market value of the corporation. Originally the firm had 600,000 shares of stock outstanding, selling at $100 each, for a total value of $60,000,000. Let us now assume that the market value of the firm went up by exactly the amount raised by the rights offering, $10,500,000, making the new market value of the firm $70,500,000. In reality the market value of the firm will go up by more than this amount if investors feel the firm will earn more than its required rate of return on these funds.

Taking the new market value for the firm, $70,500,000, and dividing by the total number of shares outstanding, 750,000, we find that the new market value for the stock will be $94 per share. That is to say, after all the new stock has been subscribed to, the market value of the stock will fall to $94 per share. Since it takes four rights and $70 in order to purchase one share of stock that will end up worth $94, the value of a right is equal to the savings made ($24—that is, you can buy a $94 share of stock for $70) divided by the number of rights necessary to purchase one share of stock:

$$\text{value of one right} = \frac{\left(\begin{array}{c}\text{market price of stock}\\ \text{ex rights}\end{array}\right) - \left(\begin{array}{c}\text{subscription}\\ \text{price}\end{array}\right)}{\begin{array}{c}\text{number of rights necessary to}\\ \text{purchase one share of stock}\end{array}} \quad (20\text{-}5)$$

$$R = \frac{P_{ex} - S}{N} \quad (20\text{-}6)$$

$$= \frac{\$94 - \$70}{4}$$

$$= \$6$$

where R = value of one right,
P_{ex} = ex rights price of the stock,
S = subscription price,
N = number of rights necessary to purchase one share of stock.
    If the stock were selling rights-on—that is, prior to the ex rights date—the value of a right could be determined from the following equation:[4]

$$R = \frac{P_{on} - S}{N + 1} \quad (20\text{-}12)$$

where P_{on} is the rights-on price of the stock. Substituting in the values from our example, we find:

[4]This equation is derived from the previous equation as follows. We know that

$$P_{ex} = P_{on} - R \quad (20\text{-}7)$$

Substituting $(P_{on} - R)$ for P_{ex} in equation (20-6) yields

$$R = \frac{P_{on} - R - S}{N} \quad (20\text{-}8)$$

Simplifying,

$$RN = P_{on} - R - S \quad (20\text{-}9)$$
$$RN + R = P_{on} - S \quad (20\text{-}10)$$
$$R(N + 1) = P_{on} - S \quad (20\text{-}11)$$
$$R = \frac{P_{on} - S}{N + 1} \quad (20\text{-}12)$$

$$R = \frac{\$100 - \$70}{4 + 1} = \$6$$

We found the same value for the right from both equations, because the second equation is derived directly from the first.

If we think about the mathematical operations we have just performed, it should be evident that a stockholder does not benefit or lose from a rights offering. He receives something of value, the right, but loses exactly that amount in the form of a stock price decline. Of course, if he does not exercise or sell his rights, he loses, but if the rights are not ignored, then he neither loses nor gains from a rights offering. Examination of the behavior of stockholders shows that only a small percentage of them neglect to exercise or sell their rights.

The primary benefit for the firm is that issuing new stock via a rights offering has a high probability of success. The rights must be exercised or sold to someone who will exercise them or else the shareholder will lose money. Another advantage is that the flotation costs associated with a rights offering are lower than on a public flotation.

Therefore, while rights offerings are not of direct value to the stockholder, they offer advantages to the financial manager.

Advantages and Disadvantages of Common Stock

The raising of new funds with common stock offers the firm several advantages and disadvantages by comparison with bonds and preferred stock.

ADVANTAGES

1. The firm is not legally obligated to pay common stock dividends. Thus in times of financial distress there need not be a cash outflow associated with common stock, while there must be with bonds.

2. Because common stock has no maturity date, the firm does not have a cash outflow associated with its redemption. If the firm desires, it can repurchase its stock in the open market, but it is under no obligation to do so.

3. By issuing common stock the firm increases its financial base and thus its future borrowing capacity. On the other hand, issuing debt increases the financial base of the firm but it also cuts into the firm's borrowing capacity. If the firm's capital structure is already overburdened with debt, a new debt offering may preclude any future debt offering until the existing equity base is enlarged. Thus, financing with common stock increases the firm's financing flexibility.

DISADVANTAGES

1. Because dividends are not tax deductible as are interest payments, and because flotation costs on equity are larger than those on debt, common stock has a higher cost than does debt.

2. The issuance of new common stock may result in a change in the ownership and control of the firm. While the owners have a preemptive right to retain

their proportionate control, they may not have the funds to do so. If this is the case, the original owners may see their control diluted by the issuance of new stock.

SUMMARY

This chapter dealt with the terminology, basic features, advantages, and disadvantages of long-term debt, preferred stock, and common stock.

Bonds are any long-term promissory note issued by the firm. The legal agreement between the issuing firm and the bond trustee who represents the bondholders is called the indenture. The indenture states the specific terms of the issue, the rights of the bondholders and issuing firm, and the responsibilities of the trustee. In the case of insolvency the claims of debt are honored before those of both common and preferred stock. Bonds also have a claim on income before those of common and preferred stock.

The major types of unsecured debt include debentures, subordinated debentures, and income bonds, while the major types of secured debt include mortgage, first mortgage, second mortgage, blanket mortgage, closed-end mortgage, open-end mortgage, and collateral trust bonds, in addition to equipment trust certificates. Because bonds have a maturity date, we examined the problem of their retirement. Bonds may be retired at maturity, or they may be retired prior to maturity through the use of a call provision or a sinking fund. We also examined the bond refunding decision.

Preferred stock is referred to as a hybrid security because it possesses many characteristics of both common stock and bonds. With respect to its claim on assets in the case of bankruptcy and its claim to income for dividends, it takes priority over common stock and yields priority to debt. Most preferred stock also has a cumulative feature, requiring that all past unpaid preferred stock dividends be paid before any common stock dividends be declared. While preferred stock does not have a maturity date, its retirement is usually provided for through the use of call provisions and sinking funds.

While debt holders and preferred stockholders can be viewed as creditors, the common stockholders are the true owners of the company. As such, they cannot exercise a claim on assets in the event of bankruptcy until the bondholders and preferred stockholders have been satisfied. The common stockholders have the right to elect the board of directors. They have the further right to maintain their proportionate share in the firm, called the preemptive right. In order to allow them to maintain this proportionate ownership, new funds often are raised through rights offerings.

STUDY QUESTIONS

20-1. Explain the difference between mortgage bonds and debentures.
20-2. Why are income bonds regarded as more risky than debentures?
20-3. Under what circumstances will a bond's current yield equal its yield to

maturity? How is it possible for a bond's current yield to be greater than its yield to maturity? How is it possible for a bond's current yield to be less than its yield to maturity?

Long-Term Debt, Preferred Stock, and Common Stock

20-4. What factors affect the cost of long-term debt?

20-5. Explain the mechanics of issuing railroad equipment trust certificates. Why do they generally have a higher rating than other bonds issued by the same railroad?

20-6. Bondholders often prefer the inclusion of a sinking fund in their bond issue. Why?

20-7. Although the bond-refunding decision is analyzed in much the same way as the capital-budgeting decision, one major difference is the discount rate used. What discount rate is used in the refunding decision, and what is the rationale behind this?

20-8. Why is preferred stock referred to as a hybrid security? It is often said to combine the worst features of common stock and bonds. What is meant by this statement?

20-9. Since preferred stock dividends in arrears must be paid before common stock dividends, should they be considered a liability and appear on the right-hand side of the balance sheet?

20-10. What are the advantages and disadvantages of the common stockholders' residual claim on income from the point of view of the investor?

20-11. What is a proxy? What is a proxy fight? Why do they occur?

20-12. Explain the difference between majority voting and cumulative voting. If you were a majority shareholder, which would you favor? Why? If you were a minority shareholder, which would you favor? Why?

20-13. Since a rights offering allows the common shareholders to purchase common stock at a price below the current market price, why is it not of value to the common shareholder?

STUDY PROBLEMS

20-1. The Hayes Corporation is facing bankruptcy. The market value of its mortgaged assets is $30 million and of all other assets $50 million. Hayes currently has outstanding $40 million in mortgaged bonds, $20 million in subordinated debentures, and $20 million in preferred stock, and the par value of the common stock outstanding is $40 million. If the corporation goes bankrupt, how will the distribution be made?

20-2. The T. Kitchel Corporation currently has outstanding a 20-year $10 million bond issue with a $9\frac{1}{4}$ percent interest rate callable at $103. The unamortized flotation costs and the discount on these bonds currently total $600,000. Because of a decline in interest rates, Kitchel would be able to refund the issue with a $10 million issue of 8 percent 20-year bonds, providing the firm with $9.3 million after flotation costs. The issuing expenses would claim an additional $200,000. The overlap period during which both issues would be expected to be outstanding is one month. Assuming a 50 percent marginal corporate tax rate, determine whether or not this bond issue should be refunded.

20-3. Three years ago the R. Wittman Corporation issued a 30-year $50 million bond issue with a 7 percent interest rate callable at $108. Because of the discount and flotation costs this issue initially raised only $48 million. The discount and flotation costs are being amortized using the straight-line method. During the past three years interest rates have fallen, allowing the Wittman corporation to replace this bond issue with a 27-year $50 million bond issue with a coupon rate of 6 percent. The new issue will provide the firm with $49 million after flotation costs. Issuing expenses will drain an additional $400,000. The overlap period during which both issues are expected to be outstanding is one month. Assuming a 50 percent marginal corporate tax rate, determine whether or not the refunding decision should be made. (NOTE: The present value of an annuity of $1 for 27 years at 3 percent is 18.327.)

20-4. As a research project obtain several bond indentures. These can be obtained directly from the corporation issuing the bond or perhaps through a local stock broker. Examine the restrictive covenants—in particular, prohibitions on the sale of accounts receivable, constraints on common stock dividends, fixed asset restrictions, and constraints on additional borrowing—and determine the reason for their inclusion.

20-5. The L. Turner Corporation is considering raising $12 million through a rights offering. They have one million shares of stock outstanding, currently selling for $84 per share. The subscription price on the new stock will be $60 per share.

(a) How many shares must be sold to raise the desired funds?
(b) How many rights are necessary to purchase one share of stock?
(c) What is the value of one right?

20-6. The E. Muransky Corporation is considering a rights offering to raise $35 million to finance new projects. They currently have two million shares of stock outstanding, selling for $50 per share. The subscription price on the new shares would be $35 per share.

(a) How many shares must be sold to raise the desired funds?
(b) How many rights are necessary to purchase one share of stock?
(c) What is the value of one right?

SELECTED
REFERENCES

ANG, JAMES S., "The Two Faces of Bond Refunding," Journal of Finance, 30 (June 1975), 869–74.

BACON, PETER W., and EDWARD L. WINN, JR., "The Impact of Forced Conversion on Stock Prices," Journal of Finance, 24 (December 1969), 871–74.

BIERMAN, HAROLD, JR., and AMIR BARNEA, "Expected Short-Term Interest Rates in Bond Refunding," Financial Management, 3 (Spring 1974), 75–79.

BILDERSEE, JOHN S., "Some Aspects of the Performance of Non-Convertible Preferred Stocks," Journal of Finance, 28 (December 1973), 1187–1202.

BOWLIN, OSWALD D., "The Refunding Decision: Another Special Case in Capital Budgeting," Journal of Finance, 21 (March 1966), 55–68.

DUVALL, RICHARD M., and DOUGLAS V. AUSTIN, "Predicting the Results of Proxy Contests," Journal of Finance, 20 (September 1965), 467–71.

EIBOTT, PETER, "Trends in the Value of Individual Stockholdings," *Journal of Business*, 47 (July 1974), 339–48.

ELSAID, HUSSEIN H., "The Function of Preferred Stock in the Corporate Financial Plan," *Financial Analysts Journal* (July–August 1969), 112–17.

FISHER, DONALD E., and GLENN A. WILT, JR., "Nonconvertible Preferred Stock as a Financing Instrument, 1950–1965," *Journal of Finance*, 23 (September 1968), 611–24.

HALFORD, FRANK A., "Income Bonds," *Financial Analysts Journal*, 20 (January–February 1964), 73–79.

JEN, FRANK C., and JAMES E. WERT, "The Deferred Call Provision and Corporate Bond Yields," *Journal of Financial and Quantitative Analysis*, 3 (June 1968), 157–69.

————, "The Effect of Call Risk on Corporate Bond Yields," *Journal of Finance*, 22 (December 1967), 637–51.

JOHNSON, RODNEY, and RICHARD KLEIN, "Corporate Motives in Repurchases of Discounted Bonds," *Financial Management*, 3 (Autumn 1974), 44–49.

KEANE, S. M., "The Significance of Issue Price in Rights Issues," *Journal of Business Finance*, 4 (September 1972), 40–45.

KOLODNY, RICHARD, "The Refunding Decision in Near Perfect Markets," *Journal of Finance*, 29 (December 1974), 1467–78.

MAYOR, THOMAS H., and KENNETH G. McCOIN, "The Rate of Discount in Bond Refunding," *Financial Management*, 3 (Autumn 1974), 54–58.

PINCHES, GEORGE E., and KENT A. MINGO, "The Role of Subordination and Industrial Bond Ratings," *Journal of Finance*, 30 (March 1975), 201–206.

SIBLEY, A. M., "Some Evidence on the Cash Flow Effects of Bond Refunding," *Financial Management*, 3 (Autumn 1974), 50–53.

STEVENSON, RICHARD A., "Retirement of Non-Callable Preferred Stock," *Journal of Finance*, 25 (December 1970), 1143–52.

WINN, WILLIS J., and ARLEIGH HESS, JR., "The Value of the Call Privilege," *Journal of Finance*, 14 (May 1959), 182–95.

Convertibles and Warrants

In earlier chapters we concerned ourselves with methods of raising long-term funds through the use of common stock, preferred stock, and short- and long-term debt. In this chapter we will examine how convertibles and warrants can be used to increase the attractiveness of these securities. We have grouped convertibles and warrants together in our discussion because they both can be exchanged at the owner's discretion for a specified number of shares of common stock. In investigating each financing alternative we will first look at its specific characteristics and purpose; then we will focus on any special considerations that should be examined before it is issued. We will close by discussing valuation of convertibles and warrants.

A **convertible security** is a preferred stock or a debt issue that can be exchanged for a specified number of shares of common stock at the will of the owner. It provides the stable income associated with preferred stock and bonds in addition to the possibility of capital gains associated with common stock. This combining of features has led convertibles to be called hybrid securities.

When the convertible is initially issued, the firm receives the proceeds from the sale less whatever flotation costs occur. This is the only time the

CONVERTIBLE SECURITIES

firm receives any proceeds at all from issuing convertibles. The firm then treats this convertible as if it were normal preferred stock or debentures, paying dividends or interest regularly. If the security owner wishes to exchange the convertible for common stock, he may do so at any time according to the terms specified when the convertible was originally issued. The desire to convert generally follows an increase in the price of the common stock. Once the convertible owner trades his convertibles in for common stock, he can never trade the stock back for convertibles. From then on he is treated as any other common stockholder and receives only common stock dividends.

CONVERSION RATIO

The number of shares of common stock for which the convertible security can be exchanged is set out when the convertible is initially issued. On some convertible issues this **conversion ratio** is stated directly. For example, the convertible may state that it is exchangeable for 15 shares of common stock. Some convertibles give only a **conversion price,** stating, for example, that the security is convertible at $39 per share. This tells us that for every $39 of par value of the convertible security one share of common stock will be received.

$$\text{Conversion ratio} = \frac{\text{par value of convertible security}}{\text{conversion price}} \qquad (21\text{-}1)$$

For example, Burlington Industries has issued $1000 par value, 5 percent semiannual convertible debentures that mature in 1991 and have a conversion price of $39. Thus the conversion ratio—the number of shares to be received upon conversion—is $1000/$39 = 25.641 shares. In effect, the security owner has his choice of holding the 5 percent convertible debenture or trading it in for 25.641 shares of Burlington Industries common stock. In this case, the bond indenture states how the fractional shares are to be dealt with, either by issuing fractional shares, allowing the security holder to purchase the unissued fractional share, or paying the investor for the fractional share.

CONVERSION VALUE

The **conversion value** of a convertible security is the total market value of the common stock for which it can be exchanged. This can be calculated as follows:

$$\text{conversion value} = (\text{conversion ratio}) \times \left(\begin{array}{c}\text{market value per share} \\ \text{of the common stock}\end{array}\right) \qquad (21\text{-}2)$$

If the Burlington Industries common stock were selling, say, for $19.375 per share, as it was on a given date, then the conversion value for the Burlington Industries convertible would be (25.641)($19.375) = $496.79;

that is, the market value of the common stock for which the convertible could be exchanged would be $496.79. Thus, regardless of what this convertible debenture was selling for, it could be converted into $496.79 worth of common stock.

BOND VALUE

The **bond value** of a security is the price that the convertible security would sell for in the absence of its conversion feature. This is calculated by determining the required rate of return on a straight (nonconvertible) issue of the same quality and then determining the present value of the bond payments at this rate of return. For example, the Burlington Industries convertible has a Standard and Poor's BBB rating, and on a given day straight BBB issues were yielding approximately 10 percent. Thus, in determining the bond value of this issue, we are answering the question: What must this Burlington Industries bond, which pays 5 percent semiannually and is rated BBB with (at that time) 13 years to maturity, sell at in order to yield 10 percent? Since this bond pays 5 percent semiannually, it gives the investor $25 every six months for the next 13 years for a total of 26 $25 payments, and at the end of 13 years (after 26 six-month periods) it pays the investor its par value of $1000. As shown in equation (5-7), in determining the present value of this bond we use a discount rate of 10/2 or 5 percent. Thus the value of a bond with semiannual payments is determined as follows:

$$BV = \sum_{t=1}^{2n} \frac{\frac{IP}{2}}{\left(1 + \frac{i}{2}\right)^t} + \frac{P}{\left(1 + \frac{i}{2}\right)^{2n}} \qquad (21\text{-}3)$$

where BV = the bond value
I = the coupon interest rate
P = the par value
n = the number of years to maturity
i = the required rate of return on a straight issue of the same quality

Then the value of the Burlington security as a straight debenture yields the following:

$$BV = \sum_{t=1}^{26} \frac{\$25}{(1 + .05)^t} + \frac{\$1000}{(1 + .05)^{26}}$$

$$= \$359.38 + \$281.25 = \$640.63$$

Thus, regardless of what happens to the value of Burlington's common stock, the lowest value the convertible can drop to, assuming there is no change in interest rates, is its value as a straight bond, which is $640.63.

CONVERSION PERIOD

On some issues the time period during which the convertible can be exchanged for common stock is limited. Many times conversion is not allowed until a specified number of years have passed, or is limited by a terminal conversion date. Still other convertibles may be converted at any time during their life. In either case the **conversion period** will be specified when the convertible is originally issued.

CONVERSION PARITY PRICE

The **conversion parity price** is the price at which the investor in effect buys the company's stock:

$$\text{conversion parity price} = \frac{\text{market price of convertible security}}{\text{conversion ratio}} \quad (21\text{-}4)$$

If the Burlington Industries bond is selling for $757.50 and the investor can exchange this bond for 25.641 shares of Burlington Industries common stock, then the conversion parity price is ($757.50/25.641) = $29.54. Thus, if the investor purchases this convertible and converts it into common stock, he is in effect buying that stock for $29.54 per share.

CONVERSION PREMIUM

The **conversion premium** is the difference between the convertible's market price and the higher of its bond value and its conversion value. It can be expressed as an absolute dollar value, in which case it is defined as

$$\begin{matrix} \text{conversion} \\ \text{premium} \end{matrix} = \begin{pmatrix} \text{market price of} \\ \text{the convertible} \end{pmatrix} - \begin{pmatrix} \text{higher of the bond value} \\ \text{and conversion value} \end{pmatrix} \quad (21\text{-}5)$$

Alternatively, the conversion premium can be expressed as a percentage, in which case it is defined as

$$\begin{matrix} \text{percentage} \\ \text{conversion} \\ \text{premium} \end{matrix} = \frac{\begin{pmatrix} \text{market price of} \\ \text{convertible bond} \end{pmatrix} - \begin{pmatrix} \text{higher of the bond value} \\ \text{and the conversion value} \end{pmatrix}}{(\text{higher of the bond value and the conversion value})} \quad (21\text{-}6)$$

In the case of the Burlington Industries convertible, on a given date its market price was $757.50 while its bond value was $640.63 and its conversion value $496.79. Thus its conversion premium was

$$\frac{\$757.50 - 640.63}{\$640.63} = 18.24 \text{ percent}$$

In effect, an investor was willing to pay an 18.24 percent premium over the higher of its bond and conversion value in order to have the possibility of capital gains from stock price advances coupled with the security of the fixed interest payments associated with a debenture.

Table 21-1 SUMMARY OF CONVERTIBLE TERMINOLOGY

Conversion ratio: the number of shares for which the convertible security can be exchanged.

$$\text{Conversion ratio} = \frac{\text{par value of convertible security}}{\text{conversion price}} \qquad (21\text{-}1)$$

Conversion value: the total market value of the common stock for which the convertible can be exchanged.

$$\text{Conversion value} = (\text{conversion ratio}) \times \left(\begin{array}{c} \text{market value per} \\ \text{share of the common stock} \end{array} \right) \quad (21\text{-}2)$$

Bond value: the price the convertible security would sell for in the absence of its conversion feature.

Conversion period: the time period during which the convertible can be exchanged for common stock.

Conversion parity price: the price the investor is in effect paying for the common stock.

$$\text{Conversion parity price} = \frac{\text{market price of convertible security}}{\text{conversion ratio}} \qquad (21\text{-}4)$$

Conversion premium: the difference between the convertible's market price and the higher of its bond value and its conversion value.

$$\begin{array}{c} \text{Conversion} \\ \text{premium} \end{array} = \left(\begin{array}{c} \text{market price} \\ \text{of the} \\ \text{convertible} \end{array} \right) - \left(\begin{array}{c} \text{higher of the} \\ \text{bond value and} \\ \text{conversion value} \end{array} \right) \quad (21\text{-}5)$$

In describing convertibles, we have introduced a number of terms, and in order to eliminate confusion, Table 21-1 summarizes them.

There are several major reasons why firms choose to issue convertibles rather then straight debt, preferred stock, or common stock. These reasons include "sweetening" the long-term debt issue to make it more attractive, delayed equity financing, raising temporarily inexpensive funds, and financing corporate mergers.

Reasons for Issuing Convertibles

SWEETENING LONG-TERM DEBT

Before World War II the major reason for adding a convertible feature to preferred stock or debt was to make the security attractive enough to insure a market for it. At that time convertibles were primarily limited to firms of lower credit standings who would have had a difficult time issuing straight debt or preferred stock. Consequently, a convertible feature would be added to increase the attractiveness of the issue and thereby guarantee its success. Since World War II firms of higher credit standing have also entered the convertible market, citing other reasons for issuing convertibles, while weaker firms have continued to use convertibles as sweeteners.

DELAYED EQUITY FINANCING

Many times a company would rather issue common stock than either preferred stock or debentures; however, because they feel the current stock price is temporarily depressed or are worried that issuing additional common stock will temporarily drive the stock's earnings per share down and result in a lower stock price, they resort to convertible securities. Management's hope is that, after a short period of time, the common stock price will rise and investors will trade their convertibles in for common stock. Thus, for example, if the price of Burlington's common stock rose and investors subsequently exchanged their convertibles for common stock, they would have in effect purchased the common stock for the conversion parity price, $29.54. That is, for every share of stock Burlington exchanged for convertibles, they originally received $29.54. Since Burlington has set its conversion parity price above the stock's market price, the firm will have to give up fewer shares of common stock when the securities are converted than if it raised funds via a common stock offering originally. In effect, equity financing is provided only if the market value of the common stock rises. If it does not, financing remains in the form of lower-cost debt or preferred stock.

RAISING TEMPORARILY INEXPENSIVE FUNDS

If the firm is raising funds for a large expansion it wishes to finance with common stock, it may instead choose to issue a convertible. By this means funds needed during the building stage can be accumulated at a lower cost (as debt, because of its tax advantage, is cheaper than common stock) without diluting the firm's earnings per share by increasing the number of shares of common stock outstanding.[1] When the expansion is completed, the firm's earnings will rise, increasing the common stock share price and allowing convertible holders to exchange their securities for common stock. In this manner, the firm is given access to relatively inexpensive funds during the expansion period; its common stock earnings per share does not drop, since there is no increase in common shares outstanding unaccompanied by an increase in earnings; and the expansion is financed through a delayed issue of common stock, provided the common price rises enough to support conversion.

FINANCING CORPORATE MERGERS

If the stockholders of an acquired company take cash or debt in exchange for their common stock, they incur an immediate tax liability on

---

[1]Where potential dilution is in excess of 3 percent, the earnings per share are shown on two bases, unadjusted and adjusted for potential conversion.

any capital gains on their investment. If, however, the exchange is made for common, preferred, or convertible preferred stock, the tax liability is postponed, since the transaction is regarded as a tax-free exchange. Thus, many mergers are financed with common or convertible preferred stock.

Convertible preferred stock is frequently used in order to provide the most attractive terms possible for the exchange. Holders of stock in the company being acquired can be offered the stable income and limited risk of preferred stock, plus the chance for capital gains afforded by the convertible feature. The issuing company also benefits from the use of convertible preferred stock rather than common stock in that less dilution of earnings occurs. The reason is that investors would have demanded additional common stock if the exchange had been made for straight common stock.

OVERHANGING ISSUE

An **overhanging issue** is one in which the firm cannot force conversion because the common stock has not risen sufficiently to justify it. The overhanging issue's major disadvantage to the firm is that it limits financing flexibility. Not only does it make additional financing with convertible securities practically impossible, but it may also make long-term debt unacceptable to investors if the firm has been relying on a successful conversion to bring its financial structure back to normal. If this is the case, and the conversion has been thwarted by an insufficient rise in the common stock price, the only available alternative may be a common stock offering. However, this too may be unacceptable or at least undesirable to the firm's management if they feel the common stock price is temporarily depressed.

FORCED CONVERSION

While the investor has full legal control over the exercise of his convertible security, the firm can often force him into conversion by either calling the convertible or establishing step-up conversion prices. If, for example, the conversion value of the security exceeds its call price, the firm need only call the security to force any rational investor to convert. A second way of inducing conversion is to provide for increasingly larger conversion prices and thus lower conversion ratios over the years. A convertible debenture with a $1000 par value could have a conversion price of $50 per share for the first five years and $60 per share after that. In this case if the price of the common stock had risen to $100 per share after five years an investor would have his choice of converting the security into 20 shares of common stock worth $2000 or not converting and watching the conversion value of the security drop to $1666.67 as the conversion price is increased to $60 per share. In most cases a step-up conversion price will provide enough incentive to induce conversion as long as the conversion value is greater than the bond value of the convertible.

VALUATION OF A CONVERTIBLE

The valuation of a convertible depends primarily upon two factors:

the value of the straight debenture or preferred stock and the value of the security if it were converted into common stock. Complicating the valuation is the fact that investors are in general willing to pay a premium for the conversion privilege, which allows them to hedge against the future. If the price of the common stock should rise, the investor would participate in capital gains; if it should decline, the convertible security will fall only to its value as a straight debenture or preferred stock.

In examining the Burlington Industries convertible debenture we found that if it were selling as a straight debenture, its price would be $640.63. Thus, regardless of what happens to its common stock, the lowest the value of the convertible can drop to is $640.63, the value of the security as a straight debenture. The convertible value of the security was only $496.79; however, the convertible was selling for $757.50. Why is such a large conversion premium attached to this security? Quite simply because investors are willing to pay for the chance for large gains without large risk of loss.

If we look at the relationship between the value of the convertible and the price of its common stock, we find it to be as depicted graphically in Figure 21-1. The bond value of the convertible serves as a floor for the value of the investment: when the market price of the common stock approaches the conversion price (point A), the value of the convertible becomes dependent upon its conversion value. In effect the convertible security is valued as a bond when the price of the common stock is low and as common stock when the price of the common stock rises. While the minimum price of the convertible is determined by the higher of either the straight bond or preferred stock price or the conversion value, investors also pay a premium for the conversion option. Again, this premium results because convertible securities offer investors stable income from debentures or preferreds and thus less risk of price decline due to adverse stock conditions, while retaining capital gains prospects from stock price gains. In effect, downside stock price variability is hedged away while upside variability is not.

WARRANTS

A **warrant** provides the investor with an option to purchase a fixed number of shares of common stock at a predetermined price during a specified time period. Warrants have been used in the past primarily by weaker firms as "sweetener" attachments to bonds or preferred stock to improve their marketability. However, in April of 1970 when AT&T included them as a part of a major financing package, warrants achieved a new level of respectability.

While warrants are similar to convertibles in that they both provide investors with a chance to participate in capital gains, the mechanics of the two instruments differ greatly. From the standpoint of the issuing firm there are two major differences. First, when convertibles are exchanged for common stock there is an elimination of debt and a reduction in fixed financing charges, while when warrants are exchanged there is no reduc-

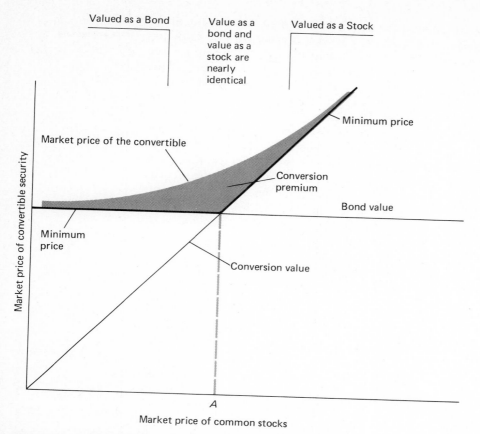

Valued as a Bond

Value as a bond and value as a stock are nearly identical

Valued as a Stock

Minimum price

Market price of the convertible

Conversion premium

Bond value

Market price of convertible security

Minimum price

Conversion value

A

Market price of common stocks

FIGURE 21-1 *Relationship between the market price of the common stock and the market price of the convertible security*

tion in fixed charges. Second, when convertibles are exchanged there is no cash inflow into the firm—the exchange is merely one type of security for another, but with warrants, since they are merely an option to buy the stock at a set price, a cash flow accompanies the exchange.

EXERCISE PRICE

The **exercise price** is that at which the warrant allows its holder to purchase the firm's common stock. The investor trades a warrant plus the exercise price for common stock. Typically, when warrants are issued the exercise price is set above the current market price of the stock. Thus, if the stock price does not rise above the exercise price, the warrant will never be converted.

Characteristics and Features of Warrants

EXPIRATION DATE

While some warrants are issued with no **expiration date**, most warrants are set to expire after a number of years. In issuing warrants as opposed to convertibles, the firm gives up some control over when the warrants will be exercised. With convertibles the issuing company can force conversion by calling the issue or using step-up conversion prices, whereas with warrants only the approach of the expiration date can encourage conversion.

DETACHABILITY

Most warrants are said to be **detachable** in that they can be sold separately from the bond or preferred stock to which they were originally attached. Thus if an investor purchases a primary issuance of a corporate bond with a warrant attached, he has the option of selling the bond alone, selling the warrant alone, or selling the combination intact. **Nondetachable warrants** cannot be sold separately from the bond or preferred stock to which they were originally attached. Such a warrant can be separated from the senior security only by being exercised.

EXERCISE RATIO

The **exercise ratio** states the number of shares that can be obtained at the exercise price with one warrant. If the exercise ratio on a warrant were 1.5, one warrant would entitle its owner to purchase one and one-half shares of common stock at its exercise price.

SWEETENING LONG-TERM DEBT

Warrants attached to debt offerings provide a feature whereby investors can participate in capital gains while holding debt. The firm thereby can increase the demand for the issue, increase the proceeds, and lower the interest costs.

Reasons for Issuing Warrants

ADDITIONAL CASH INFLOW

If warrants are added to sweeten a debt offering, the firm will receive an eventual cash inflow when and if the warrants are exercised; a conversion feature would not provide this additional inflow.

NONEXTINGUISHMENT OF DEBT

When warrants are exercised, the debt to which they were originally attached remains in existence. The warrant exercise process provides an additional cash inflow but does not provide for the elimination of the original security. Thus the decision between convertible and warrant financing becomes one partially of tradeoffs, elimination of debt versus additional cash inflows.

Other Factors to Be Considered with Warrants

DILUTION AND FLEXIBILITY

Since present accounting standards provide that earnings per share be stated as if all the warrants outstanding had been exercised, warrants have the effect of reducing the firm's reported earnings per share. This potential dilution of earnings per share may reduce the firm's financing flexibility. Because of previously issued warrants, the issuance of additional common stock may be hindered or even prohibited. The market's reluctance to accept further equity offerings may be due not only to the potential earnings-per-share dilution effect of the outstanding warrants, but also to a feeling that only weaker firms have to resort to warrant financing to sweeten their senior security offerings.

VALUATION OF A WARRANT

Since the warrant is an option to purchase a specified number of shares of stock at a specified price for a given length of time, the market value of the warrant will be primarily a function of the common stock price. To understand the valuation of warrants we must define two additional terms, the minimum price and the premium. Let us look at a specific example. In March of 1977 American Airlines issued warrants in conjunction with a preferred stock offering with an expiration date of 4/1/82, an exercise ratio of 1.0, and an exercise price of $14. This means that at any time between then and April 1, 1982, an investor could with one warrant and $14 purchase a share of American Airlines stock regardless of what that stock was selling for. On a given date the American Airlines warrants were selling for $3.625, while the American Airlines stock was selling for $10.25 per share.

Minimum Price. The **minimum price** of a warrant is determined as follows:

$$\text{minimum price} = \left(\begin{matrix} \text{market price of} \\ \text{common stock} \end{matrix} - \begin{matrix} \text{exercise} \\ \text{price} \end{matrix} \right) \times \text{exercise ratio} \qquad (21\text{-}7)$$

In the American Airlines example the exercise price is greater than the price of the common stock ($14 as opposed to $10.25). In this case the minimum price of the warrant is considered to be zero, because things simply do not sell for negative prices [($10.25 − $14) × 1 = −$3.75]. If, for example, the price of the American Airlines common stock rose to $16 per share, the minimum price on the warrant would become ($16 − $14) × 1 = $2. This would tell us that this warrant could not fall below a price of $2, because if it did, investors could realize immediate trading profits by purchasing the warrants and converting them along with the $14 exercise price into common stock until the price of the warrant was pushed up to the minimum price. This process of simultaneously buying and selling equivalent assets for different prices is called **arbitrage,** a process we have previously examined.

Premium. The **premium** is the amount above the minimum price for which the warrant sells:

$$\text{premium} = \left(\begin{matrix} \text{market price} \\ \text{of warrant} \end{matrix} \right) - \left(\begin{matrix} \text{minimum price} \\ \text{of warrant} \end{matrix} \right) \qquad (21\text{-}8)$$

In the case of the American Airlines warrant the premium is $3.625 − $0 = $3.625. Investors are paying a premium of $3.625 above the minimum price for the warrant. They are willing to do so because the possible loss is small, in that the warrant price is only about one-third that of the common stock, and the possible return is large, since, if the price of the common stock climbs, the value of the warrant also will climb.

The relationships among the warrant price, the minimum price, and the premium are illustrated graphically in Figure 21-2. Point A represents the exercise price on the warrant. Once the price of the stock is above the exercise price, the warrant's minimum price takes on positive (or nonzero) values.

A hypothetical numerical example based upon Figure 21-2 is provided in Table 21-2. Looking at the graphical representation of the warrant and the example, we find that the warrant premium tends to drop off as the ratio of the stock price to the exercise price climbs. Why? As the stock price climbs, the warrant loses its leverage ability. Looking at the numerical example, assume an investor purchased $1000 worth of warrants and $1000 worth of common stock, when the common stock price was $40 and the warrant price was $10; then the price of the stock went up 50 percent to $60 per share, which caused the price of the warrant to go up 150 percent to $25 per share. This leverage feature—small investment with high possible returns—encourages investors to purchase warrants. However, as the stock price rises, the leverage ability of the warrant declines. This can be shown by assuming an investor purchases $1000 worth of common stock selling at $110 per share and $1000 worth of warrants selling for $71 per share; if the stock price went up to $130, the stock investment would have returned 18 percent while the warrant price would have risen to $90 for a return of 27 percent. In the first example when the stock price rose from $40 to $60 per share, the warrant resulted in profits three times greater than on the common stock. In the second example the warrant provided profits only about one and one-half times larger than the common stock. Thus the warrant premium tends to drop off as the ratio of the stock price

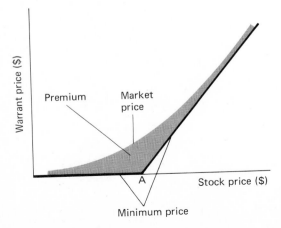

FIGURE 21-2 *Valuation of Warrants*

Table 21-2 HYPOTHETICAL WARRANT EXAMPLE

STOCK PRICE, SP	EXERCISE PRICE, EP	EXERCISE RATIO, ER	MINIMUM PRICE: SP − (EP × ER) = MP	HYPOTHETICAL WARRANT PRICE, WP	PREMIUM, WP − MP	STOCK PRICE/ EXERCISE PRICE RATIO, SP/EP
$ 30	$40	1	$ 0	$ 5	$ 5	75%
40	40	1	0	10	10	100
50	40	1	10	16	6	125
60	40	1	20	25	5	150
70	40	1	30	34	4	175
80	40	1	40	43	3	200
90	40	1	50	52	2	225
100	40	1	60	62	2	250
110	40	1	70	71	1	275
120	40	1	80	81	1	300
130	40	1	90	90	0	325

to the exercise price climbs and the leverage ability of the warrant declines.

While the stock price/exercise price ratio is one of the most important factors in determining the size of the premium, several other factors also affect it. One such factor is the time left to warrant expiration date. As the warrant's expiration date approaches, the size of the premium begins to shrink, approaching zero. A second factor is investors' expectation concerning the capital gains potential of the stock. If they feel favorably about the prospects for price increases in the common stock, a large warrant premium will result, because a stock price increase will result in a warrant price increase. Finally, the degree of price volatility on the underlying common stock affects the size of the warrant premium. The more volatile the common stock price, the higher the warrant premium. As price volatility increases, so does the probability of and potential size of profits.

SUMMARY

Convertible securities are preferred stock or debentures that can be exchanged for a specified number of shares of common stock at the will of the owner. They are issued by corporations in order to sweeten debt and thereby make it more marketable, as a form of delayed equity financing, and as a source of temporarily inexpensive funds during expansions. While these reasons can justify the use of convertibles, the risks involved in the possibility of an overhanging issue should also be weighed. With an overhanging issue conversion does not occur, and the firm cannot force it, because the common stock price has not risen sufficiently; financing flexibility is reduced in that, depending upon the firm's financial structure, investors might react negatively toward an additional offering of either debt or equity. The valuation of convertible securities is a function of both its value as a straight bond and its value if converted into common stock. Since the convertible provides the security of debt with the capital gains potential of common stock, it generally sells for a premium above the higher of its bond or conversion value.

Warrants are an option to purchase a fixed number of shares of common stock at a predetermined price during a specified period. While in general they are issued in association with debt, most warrants are detachable in that they can be bought and sold separate from the debt to which they were originally attached. They are generally issued as a sweetener to debt in order to make it more marketable and lower the interest costs. In addition, unlike convertibles, warrants provide for an additional cash inflow when they are exercised. On the other hand the exercise of convertibles results in the elimination of debt while the exercise of warrants does not. Thus there is a tradeoff—additional cash inflow versus elimination of debt—involved in the warrants-versus-convertibles decision. Since a warrant is an option to purchase a specified number of shares of stock during a given period, its market value is primarily a function of the price of the common stock. Warrants generally sell above their minimum price, the size of the premium being determined by the degree of leverage they provide, the time left to their expiration, investors' expectations as to the future movement of the stock price, and the stock's price volatility.

21-1. Define the following terms:
  (a) Conversion ratio.
  (b) Conversion value.
  (c) Conversion parity price.
  (d) Conversion premium.

21-2. What are some reasons commonly given for issuing convertible securities?

21-3. Why does a convertible bond sell at a premium above its value as a bond or common stock?

21-4. Convertible bonds are said to provide the capital gains potential of common stock and the security of bonds. Explain this statement both verbally and graphically. What happens to the graph when interest rates rise? When they fall?

21-5. Convertible bonds generally carry lower coupon interest rates than do nonconvertible bonds. If this is so, does it mean that the cost of capital on convertible bonds is lower than on nonconvertibles? Why or why not?

21-6. Since convertible securities allow for the conversion price to be set above the current common stock price, is it true that the firm is actually issuing its common stock at a price above the current market price?

21-7. In the light of our discussion of the common stockholders' preemptive right in Chapter 20, explain why convertibles are often sold on a rights basis.

21-8. Although only the holder of a convertible has the right to convert the security, firms often are able to force conversion. Comment on this statement.

21-9. Explain the difference between a convertible security and a warrant.

21-10. How do firms force the exercising of warrants?

21-11. Explain both verbally and graphically the valuation of warrants.

21-12. What factors affect the size of the warrant premium? How?

21-1. In 1978 the G. Bryan Corporation issued some $1000 par value, 6 percent convertible debentures that come due in 1998. The conversion price on these convertibles is $40 per share. The price of the common stock is presently $27.25 per share. These convertibles have a BBB rating, and straight BBB debentures are presently yielding 9.00 percent. The market price of the convertible is presently $840.25. Determine the following (assume bond interest payments are made annually):

(a) Conversion ratio.

(b) Conversion value.

(c) Bond value.

(d) Conversion parity price.

(e) Conversion premium in absolute dollars.

(f) Conversion premium in percentage.

21-2. The L. Padis, Jr., Corporation has an issue of 5 percent convertible preferred stock outstanding. The conversion price on these securities is $27 per share to 9/30/85. The price of the common stock is presently $13.25 per share. The preferred stock is selling for $17.75. The par value of the preferred stock is $25 per share. Similar quality preferred stock without the conversion feature are currently yielding 8 percent. Determine the following:

(a) The conversion ratio.

(b) The conversion value.

(c) The conversion premium (in both absolute dollars and percentages).

21-3. The T. Kitchel Corporation has a warrant that allows the purchase of one share of common stock at $30 per share. The warrant is currently selling at $4 and the common stock is priced at $25 per share. Determine the minimum price and the premium of the warrant.

21-4. Frontier Airlines has some warrants outstanding that allow the purchase of common stock at the rate of one warrant for each share of common stock at $11.71 per share. These warrants expire on March 1, 1987.

(a) On March 17, 1978, the warrants were selling for $3 each, and the common stock was selling for $10 per share. Determine the minimum price and the warrant premium as of that date.

(b) Determine the minimum price and the warrant premium for the Frontier Airlines warrant as of today. To do this you will have to look up the prices of the Frontier Airlines common stock and the Frontier Airlines warrant. They are both listed on the American Stock Exchange (AMEX) under the names Front A and Front A wt.

21-5. Braniff International Corporation has some warrants outstanding that allow the purchase of common stock at the price of $22.94 per share. These warrants are somewhat unusual in that one warrant allows for the purchase of 3.1827 shares of common stock at the exercise price of $22.94 per share. These warrants expire on December 1, 1986.

(a) On March 17, 1978, the warrants were selling for $8.375 each, and the common stock was selling for $11.50 per share. Determine the minimum price and the warrant premium as of that date.

(b) Determine the minimum price and the warrant premium for the Braniff warrant as of today. To do this you will have to look up the prices of the Braniff common stock and the Braniff warrant. The common stock is listed on the New York Stock Exchange (NYSE), while the warrant is listed on the American Stock Exchange (AMEX).

SELECTED REFERENCES

ALEXANDER, GORDON J., and ROGER D. STOWER, "Pricing in the New Issue Convertible Debt Market," *Financial Management*, 6 (Fall 1977), 35–39.

BACON, PETER W., and EDWARD L. WINN, JR., "The Impact of Forced Conversion on Stock Prices," *Journal of Finance*, 24 (December 1969), 871–74.

BAUMOL, WILLIAM J., BURTON G. MALKIEL, and RICHARD E. QUANDT, "The Valuation of Convertible Securities," *Quarterly Journal of Economics*, 80 (February 1966), 48–59.

BRIGHAM, EUGENE F., "An Analysis of Convertible Debentures: Theory and Some Empirical Evidence," *Journal of Finance*, 21 (March 1966), 35–54.

CHEN, A. H. Y., "A Model of Warrant Pricing in a Dynamic Market," *Journal of Finance*, 25 (December 1970), 1041–59.

FRANK, WERNER G., and CHARLES O. KRONCKE, "Classifying Conversions of Convertible Debentures over Four Years," *Financial Management*, 3 (Summer 1974), 33–42.

HAYES, SAMUEL L., III, and HENRY B. REILING, "Sophisticated Financing Tool: The Warrant," *Harvard Business Review*, 47 (January-February 1969), 137–50.

JENNINGS, EDWARDS H., "An Estimate of Convertible Bond Premiums," *Journal of Financial and Quantitative Analysis*, 9 (January 1974), 33–56.

LEWELLEN, WILBUR G., and GEORGE A. RACETTE, "Convertible Debt Financing," *Journal of Financial and Quantitative Analysis*, 7 (December 1973), 777–92.

PINCHES, GEORGE E., "Financing with Convertible Preferred Stocks, 1960–1967," *Journal of Finance*, 25 (March 1970), 53–64.

RUSH, DAVID F., and RONALD W. MELICHER, "An Empirical Examination of Factors Which Influence Warrant Prices," *Journal of Finance*, 29 (December 1974), 1449–66.

SAMUELSON, PAUL A., "Rational Theory of Warrant Pricing," *Industrial Management Review*, 6 (Spring 1965), 13–31.

SHELTON, JOHN P., "The Relation of the Price of a Warrant to the Price of Its Associated Stock," *Financial Analysts Journal*, 23 (May-June and July-August 1967), 88–99 and 143–51.

SOLDOFSKY, ROBERT M., "Yield-Risk Performance of Convertible Securities," *Financial Analysts Journal*, 39 (March-April 1971), 61–65.

VAN HORNE, JAMES C., "Warrant Valuation in Relation to Volatility and Opportunity Costs," *Industrial Management Review*, 10 (Spring 1969), 19–32.

WEIL, ROMAN L., JR., JOEL E. SEGALL, and DAVID GREEN, JR., "Premiums on Convertible Bonds," *Journal of Finance*, 23 (June 1968), 445–63.

EXTERNAL GROWTH AND CONTRACTION

Business Combinations: Mergers and Acquisitions

*T*hroughout this chapter the terms **merger** and **acquisition** are used interchangeably to represent a combination of two or more businesses into a single operational entity. Although these two terms have different legal implications, we are concerned only with the financial consequences of a combination. Our objectives are three:

1. Identify and explain the basic factors that determine the value of a business.
2. Examine the techniques used in financing an acquisition.
3. Explain the use of *tender offers* in acquiring a new business.

Company growth through the merging of two firms has been a part of the United States economic scene for many years. At the beginning of the twentieth century many basic industries came under the control of large, publicly owned corporations. During the 1920s a second surge of business combinations developed; big business expanded into new industries, creating numerous vertically integrated companies. The latter 1960s witnessed more activity in mergers than ever before. This last period, the **conglomerate** age, peaked in 1968 when the nation's largest 200 corporations acquired 94 large firms with aggregate assets in excess of $8 billion.

This latest merger phase, which began in 1964 and ebbed in 1969, saw an emphasis on science-related firms, accounting techniques that produced "instant growth" in earnings, and a market psychology that encouraged a speculative fever. Also, a concept developed that a good corporate executive could effectively manage a firm, regardless of its nature. This philosophy spurred the development of multifaceted corporations involved in various, often unrelated, products and services. This select group of corporations came to be known as conglomerates.

The 1960s merger phenomenon grew almost without restraint until the 1969–1970 recession set in and the business combination process began to be more closely scrutinized. Simultaneously, the accounting profession tightened the guidelines associated with its treatment of mergers, which significantly reduced the attractiveness of many combinations. Finally, the federal government intervened with a relatively strong antimerger position, protesting the potential loss in competition. As these influences came to be felt, along with sharp declines in the market prices of conglomerate stocks, the merger excitement quickly dissipated. Recently, the interest in growth through external acquisitions has again increased. However, cautiousness has permeated the latest interest. The acquiring companies have relied more on basic economic analysis, rather than merely a concern for the accounting effects on the firm's earnings. In essence, while the current merger volume is certainly far short of the 1967–1969 era, business combinations continue to represent a potentially viable avenue for company growth.

One of the first problems in analyzing a potential merger involves placing a value on the acquired firm. This task is not easy. The value of a firm depends not only upon its earnings capabilities but also upon the operating and financial characteristics of the acquiring firm. As a result, no single value may be thought to exist for a company. Instead, a range of values are determined that would be economically feasible to the prospective acquirer, and the final price within this range is established by the negotiating talents of the two firms' managements.

To determine an acceptable price for a corporation, a number of factors are carefully evaluated. In this valuation process, the final objective is to maximize the stockholders' wealth (stock price) of the acquiring firm. However, quantifying the relevant variables for this purpose is difficult at best. For instance, the primary reason for a merger might be to acquire managerial talent, or to complement a strong sales staff with an excellent production department. This potential **synergistic effect** is difficult to measure using the historical data of either company. Even so, several quantitative variables are frequently used in an effort to determine a firm's value. These factors include (1) book value, (2) appraisal value, (3) market price of the firm's common stock, and (4) earnings per share.

The **book value** of a firm's net worth is the depreciated value of its assets (original cost less accumulated depreciation) less its outstanding

DETERMINING A FIRM'S VALUE

Book Value

liabilities. For example, if a firm's historical cost less accumulated depreciation is $10 million, and the firm's debt totals $4 million, the aggregate book value of net worth is $6 million. Further, if 100,000 shares of common stock are outstanding, the book value per share is $60 ($6 million ÷ 100,000 shares).

Book value alone does not measure the market value of a company's net worth because it is based on the historical cost of the firm's assets. Such costs bear little relationship to the value of the organization or to its ability to produce earnings.[1]

Although the book value of an enterprise is clearly not the most important factor, it should not be completely overlooked. It can be used as a starting point to be compared with other analyses. Also, a study of the firm's working capital is particularly appropriate and necessary in acquisitions involving a business consisting primarily of liquid assets. Furthermore, in industries where the ability to generate earnings requires large investments in such items as steel, cement, and petroleum, the book value could be a critical factor, especially where plant and equipment are relatively new.

Appraisal Value

An **appraised value** of a company may be acquired from an independent appraisal firm. The techniques used by appraisers vary widely; however, this value is often tied closely to replacement cost. This method of analysis is not adequate by itself, since the value of individual assets may have little relation to the firm's overall ability to generate earnings, and thus the going concern value of the firm. However, the appraisal value of an enterprise may be considered useful in conjunction with other methods. Also, the appraisal value may be an important factor in special situations, such as in financial companies, natural resource enterprises, and organizations that have been operating at a loss.[2]

The use of appraisal values does yield several additional advantages. The appraisal by independent appraisers may permit the reduction of accounting goodwill by increasing the recognized worth of specific assets. Goodwill results when the purchase price of a firm exceeds the value of the individual assets. For example, assume a company having a book value of $60,000 is purchased for $100,000 (the $40,000 difference is goodwill). The $60,000 book value consists of $20,000 in working capital and $40,000 in fixed assets. However, an appraisal might suggest that the current values of these assets are $25,000 and $55,000 respectively. The $15,000 increase ($55,000−$40,000) in fixed assets permits the acquiring firm to record a larger depreciation expense than would otherwise be possible, thereby reducing taxes. A second reason for an appraisal is to provide a test of the

[1]See Appendix 3A.
[2]The assets of a financial company and a natural resources firm largely consist of securities and natural reserves, respectively. The value of these individual assets have a direct bearing on the firm's earning capacity. Also, a company operating at a loss may only be worth its liquidation value, which would approximate the appraisal value.

reasonableness of results obtained through methods based upon the going-concern concept. Third, the appraiser may uncover strengths and weaknesses that otherwise might not be recognized, as in the valuation of patents, secret processes, and partially completed research and development expenditures.

Thus, the appraisal-value procedure is generally worthwhile, if performed with additional evaluation processes. In specific instances it may be an important instrument for valuing a corporation.

The **stock market value,** as expressed by stockmarket quotations, comprises another approach for estimating the net worth of a business. If the stock is listed on a major securities exchange, such as the New York Stock Exchange, and is widely traded, an approximate value can be established on the basis of the market value. The justification is based upon the fact that the market quotations indicate the different opinions of investors as to a firm's earnings potential and the corresponding risk.

Stock Market Value

The market-value approach is the one most frequently used in valuing large corporations. However, this value can change abruptly. Table 22-1 depicts the various factors influencing the market value. As the table shows, computations by market analysts are not the sole determinant of value. Analytical factors compete with purely speculative influences and are subject to people's sentiments and personal decisions. Thus,

> [T]he market is not a weighing machine, on which the value of each issue is recorded by an exact and impersonal mechanism, in accordance with the specific qualities. Rather should we say that the market is a voting machine, whereon countless individuals register choices which are the product partly of reason and partly of emotion.[3]

In summary, the market-value approach is probably the one most widely used for determining the worth of a firm, with a 10- to 20-percent premium above the market price often being required as an inducement for the current owners to sell their stock. Even so, executives who place their entire reliance upon this method are subject to an inherent danger of market psychology.

In practice, the purchase of another business normally has one primary objective—to increase the acquiring firm's earnings, usually expressed in earnings per share. This increase in earnings per share hopefully will have a favorable impact upon the purchasing company's common stock price. The acquiring firm is, in fact, purchasing future earnings. Therefore, the value of the prospective acquisition is frequently considered to be a function of the merger's impact upon earnings per share.

Earnings Per Share

[3]Benjamin Graham, David L. Dodd, and Sidney Cottle, *Security Analysis,* 4th ed. (New York: McGraw-Hill Book Company, Inc., 1962), p. 42.

Example. As an illustration of the earnings effect of an acquisition, suppose that company A is contemplating the purchase of company B. Company A has 100,000 shares of common stock outstanding with a $100 market value per share, while company B has issued 50,000 shares selling at $75. The earnings per share for the corporations are $6.25 for company A and $5 for company B. The two managements have agreed that the company B shareholders are to receive company A stock in exchange for their shares. The swap is to be based upon the relative earnings per share of the two firms. Therefore, the company B owners should receive .8 shares of company A stock for each share owned of company B ($5 ÷ $6.25), or 40,000 shares of company A. Consequently, company B shareholders are receiving securities with a total market value of $4 million (40,000 shares at a $100 market price), which is greater than their original $3,750,000 value in company B. At the same time, the company A stockholders incur no loss in value.

What causes the increase in value for the company B stockholders without an offsetting reduction in value for the company A owners? In answering this question, we must examine the relative price/earnings ratios of the two firms. For company A the price/earnings multiple is 16 ($100 price ÷ $6.25 earnings per share), while for company B it is only 15 ($75 price ÷ $5 earnings per share). Our computations implicitly assume that company B's earnings will be valued at the higher price/earnings ratio of 16. If the price/earnings relationship were to decrease after the merger, the value of company A shares would fall proportionately.

Table 22-1 RELATIONSHIP OF INTRINSIC-VALUE FACTORS TO MARKET PRICE

I. General market factors

II. Individual factors

A. Speculative
  1. Market factors
    (a) Technical
    (b) Manipulative
    (c) Psychological

B. Investment
  2. Future-value factors
    (a) Management and reputation
    (b) Competitive conditions and prospects
    (c) Possible and probable changes in volume, price, and costs

  3. Intrinsic-value factors
    (a) Earnings
    (b) Dividends
    (c) Assets
    (d) Capital structure
    (e) Terms of the issue
    (f) Others

Attitude of public toward the issue } Bids and offers } Market price

SOURCE: Benjamin Graham, David L. Dodd, and Sidney Cottle, *Security Analysis,* 4th ed. (New York: McGraw-Hill Book Company, Inc., 1962), p. 43.

EFFECT OF EARNINGS DILUTION

In the preceding example, no dilution (or reduction) in earnings per share for either group of shareholders resulted. This fact is verified in Table 22-2, where the total earnings for the new firm (company A+B) is $875,000. Since 140,000 shares will be outstanding after the combination, the earnings per share is $6.25, which equals the premerger company A earnings per share. Although the earnings per share has increased from $5 to $6.25 for company B stockholders, these shareholders only have 80 percent of their original number of shares. Therefore, the $6.25 *postmerger* earnings per share should not be compared with the $5 *premerger* earnings per share for company B stockholders. Instead, the *equivalent* earnings per share on a *premerger* basis is 80 percent of $6.25, or $5. Alternatively, the equivalent earnings per share on a *postmerger* basis is $5 divided by 80 percent, or $6.25. In other words, $5 in earnings per share prior to the merger is the same as $6.25 after the merger for company B stockholders. Therefore, the effective earnings position for company B stockholders is not changed as a result of the merger.

What if the final share exchange ratio were not based upon the relative earnings per share? Instead, assume that company B shareholders would agree to the merger only if they received .9 share of company A for one share of company B. In this circumstance, a dilution in earnings per share would be felt by the company A stockholders, with the company B

Table 22-2   MERGER EFFECT ON EARNINGS (.8:1 EXCHANGE RATIO)

COMPANY	(a) ORIGINAL NUMBER OF SHARES	(b) EARNINGS PER SHARE	(c) NET INCOME (a) × (b)
A	100,000	$6.25	$625,000
B	50,000	5.00	250,000
		Total postmerger earnings	$875,000

Number of shares after the merger:
100,000 + (.8)50,000 — 140,000

Earnings per share for company A stockholders after the merger:
$875,000 ÷ 140,000 shares — $6.25

Equivalent earnings per share for company B stockholders:

1. Before the merger:
   (Earnings per share *after* the merger)
   × (share exchange ratio) = $6.25 × .8 — $5.00

2. After the merger:
   (Earnings per share *before* the merger)
   ÷ (share exchange ratio) = $5 ÷ .8 — $6.25

investors receiving an addition in earnings per share. As shown in Table 22-3, the earnings per share for company A immediately decreases from $6.25 to $6.03, or a $.22 *dilution* in earnings per share. Conversely, the equivalent earnings per share increases by $.47 for the company B stockholders ($5.56 to $6.03).

For many managements, a merger that results in a dilution in earnings per share is to be avoided. However, the fact that a merger immediately dilutes a firm's current earnings per share need not make the transaction undesirable. Such a criterion places undue emphasis upon the immediate effects of a prospective merger upon the earnings per share.

In examining the consequences of a merger upon the surviving concern's earnings per share, we should extend the analysis into future periods. Therefore the investigation should include all of the variables affecting future earnings per share, which include (1) the share exchange ratio, (2) the firms' relative sizes, and (3) their relative expected future growth rates in earnings.

Continuing the previous illustration, assume that the anticipated growth rate in earnings is 8 percent for company A and 14 percent for company B. Under these conditions the $.22 dilution in company A's earnings per share (Table 22-3) is gradually eliminated in future years. In other words, company A earnings per share is reduced in the current year, but company B's growth rate will benefit company A's stockholders in future years. As shown in Table 22-4, the combined earnings per share for company A+B (column d) is lower than company A's earnings per share (col-

Table 22-3 MERGER EFFECT ON EARNINGS (.9:1 EXCHANGE RATIO)

Total postmerger earnings	$875,000
Number of shares after the merger: 100,000 + (.9)50,000	$145,000
Earnings per share: $875,000 ÷ 145,000	$6.03
Company A stockholders: Earnings per share before the merger	$6.25
Earnings per share after the merger: ($875,000 ÷ 145,000 shares)	6.03
Dilution in earnings per share	($0.22)
Company B stockholders: Equivalent earnings per share after the merger: (Earnings per share before the merger) ÷ (share exchange ratio) = $5 ÷ .9	$5.56
Earnings per share after the merger	6.03
Accretion in earnings per share	$0.47

Table 22-4 PROJECTION OF EARNINGS PER SHARE

YEAR	(a) COMPANY A EARNINGS (8% GROWTH)	(b) COMPANY B EARNINGS (14% GROWTH)	(c) COMPANY A+B POSTMERGER COMBINED EARNINGS [(a) + (b)]	(d) COMPANY A+B EARNINGS PER SHARE [(c) ÷ 145,000 SHARES[a]]	(e) COMPANY A PRE-MERGER EARNINGS PER SHARE [(a) ÷ 100,000 SHARES]	(f) COMPANY B EARNINGS PER SHARE WITHOUT THE MERGER [(b) ÷ 45,000 SHARES[b]]	(g) ACCRETION (DILUTION) EARNINGS PER SHARE — A	(g) ACCRETION (DILUTION) EARNINGS PER SHARE — B
1979	$625,000	$250,000	$ 875,000	$6.03	$6.25	$5.56	($.22)	$.47
1980	675,000	285,000	960,000	6.62	6.75	6.33	(.13)	.29
1981	729,000	324,900	1,053,900	7.26	7.29	7.22	(.03)	.04
1982	787,320	370,386	1,157,706	7.98	7.87	8.23	.11	(.25)
1983	850,306	422,240	1,272,546	8.78	8.50	9.38	.28	(.60)
1984	918,330	481,354	1,399,684	9.65	9.18	10.70	.47	(1.05)

[a] 100,000 company A shares + (.9)50,000 company B shares = 145,000 company A+B shares.

[b] (.9)50,000 company B shares = 45,000 equivalent shares in company A+B.

umn e) during the 1979–1981 period, after which the earnings per share is greater for the merged company. On the other hand, the impact on the *equivalent* earnings per share for company B is favorable for 1979 through 1981 (compare columns d and f). For all subsequent years, company B's earnings per share are diluted.

Based upon the data in Table 22-4, should company A's management undertake the merger? No concrete answer can be reached from the limited information available. In general, the terms of the merger must be developed so as to provide a mutually satisfactory earnings pattern for the shareholders of both firms. Also, if any lesson is to be learned from the merger activities of the 1960s, certainly the fallacy of placing a large emphasis upon earnings per share at the expense of other considerations should not go unnoticed. A prime example of potential problems is Litton Industries. During the mid 1960s, Litton's earnings per share grew at an annual compound growth rate of 24 percent. This growth was the result principally of its acquisitions. However, when the 1969–1970 recession materialized, Litton's earnings fell sharply, completely eliminating the growth from the previous years. Eventually, in 1973 Litton disposed of the unprofitable product lines not considered to be in its main area of operations.

FINANCING TECHNIQUES IN MERGERS

After a value has been placed on a firm, the method of payment must be determined. The choice of financial instruments and techniques in acquiring a firm usually has an effect on the purchase agreement. The payment may take the form of either cash or securities. The securities are generally common and preferred stock, with the preferred securities normally being convertible into common stock. Also, recognition of advantages to be gained by using deferred payment plans has resulted in their increased utilization.

Common Stock Financing

When a company is deciding whether to use common stock to finance a merger, the relative price/earnings ratios of the two businesses become an important consideration. Although the price/earnings multiple should not be the only criterion, it is important in determining the method of payment. For a firm having a high stock price relative to its earnings per share, common stock represents a primary tool for negotiating a merger or acquisition. In addition, the common stock route becomes more advantageous for both companies when the firm being acquired has a low price/earnings ratio. This fact may best be explained by an illustration.

Assume that Tajos, Inc.'s, common stock is selling for $36, and the firm is earning $2 per share. Negotiations are underway to acquire the Old Dominion Corporation, with a stock price of $10 and earnings per share of $1. Both firms have 300,000 shares outstanding. The management of Tajos has agreed to exchange one share for every three shares of Old Dominion. The resulting earnings per share for Tajos, Inc., after the merger is $2.25, as shown in Table 22-5. Therefore, the Old Dominion shareholders are receiving one share of stock valued at $36, while relinquishing three shares of stock with a total value of $30 ($10 per share × 3). This exchange represents a 20 percent premium ($36 relative to $30) to the Old Dominion stockholders. Furthermore, provided that the price/earnings multiple of 18 ($36 ÷ $2) is sustained for Tajos, Inc., shares, the value of the Tajos shares will increase to $40.50 ($2.25 earnings per share × 18). This price increase is the result of converting a firm with relatively low growth expectations into one with high growth expectations, thereby increasing the market value of the Old Dominion shares.

In summary, a corporation with a high price/earnings ratio has a distinct advantage in the business of mergers and acquisitions. Use of this ratio may prove beneficial to the acquiring business as well as to the firm being acquired. However, because some companies cannot attain a high price/earnings multiple, and because different types of investors must be recognized, other types of securities may need to be used in conjunction with or in lieu of common stock.

Debt and Preferred Stock Financing

Since some investors prefer growth stocks, while others seek substantial dividend or interest income, an acquiring company must at times offer a combination of securities in settlement with the new stockholders. In an attempt to tailor a security for such investors, convertible debentures and convertible preferred stock have frequently been used.

The phenomenon of convertible securities has had a decided impact upon acquisitions and mergers. Although requirements established by the

Table 22-5 TAJOS, INC., POSTMERGER EARNINGS

COMPANY	NUMBER OF SHARES	EARNINGS PER SHARE	TOTAL EARNINGS
Tajos, Inc.	300,000	$2	$600,000
Old Dominion	300,000	$1	300,000
			$900,000

Total shares after the merger:

Tajos, Inc., shares + (exchange ratio × company B shares)
= 300,000 + $\left(\frac{1}{3}\right)$ 300,000
= 400,000 postmerger shares

Postmerger earnings per share:

$900,000 earnings ÷ 400,000 shares = $2.25

accounting and securities profession have diminished the benefits of convertible securities, the following primary advantages still remain.[3]

1. Potential earnings dilution may be partially minimized by issuing a convertible security. If such a security is designed to sell at a premium over its conversion value, fewer common shares will ultimately be issued. For example, if the acquirer's stock currently has a market price of $50 per share, and the price of the acquisition is $10 million, using common stock would require issuing 200,000 shares. In comparison, a convertible preferred issue could be designed to sell at $100 with a 1.7 conversion ratio, which would mean a conversion value of $85. The $10 million price would be realized by issuing 100,000 preferred shares convertible into 170,000 shares of common stock. The purchaser would have decreased the eventual number of shares to be issued, thereby reducing the dilution in earnings per share that could ultimately result.

2. A convertible issue may allow the acquiring company to comply with the seller's income objectives without changing its own dividend policy. If the two firms have different dividend payout policies and the acquirer does not want to commit his common stock to a dividend rate that suits the seller, convertible preferred stock may be an appropriate solution.

3. Convertible preferred stock also represents a possible way of lowering the voting power of the acquired company. This reduction of voice in management can be important, especially if the seller is a closely held corporation.

4. The convertible preferred debenture or stock may appear more attractive to the firm being acquired because it combines senior security protection with a portion of the growth potential of common stock.

In summary, debt and preferred stock are often compatible with the needs and purposes of a merger. The need for altering financial leverage and for a variety of securities is resolved, at least in part, by the use of senior securities.

Earn-Outs

The **deferred payment plan,** which has come to be called an **earn-out,** represents a relatively recent approach to merger financing. The acquiring firm agrees to make a specified initial payment of cash or stock and, if it can maintain or increase earnings, to pay additional compensation.

An earn-out has several benefits for the acquiring organization. It provides a logical method of adjusting the difference between the amount of stock the purchaser is willing to issue and the amount the seller is agreeing to accept for the business. Second, the merging company will immediately be able to report higher earnings per share because fewer shares of stock will become outstanding at the time of the acquisition. In addition, the acquiring company is provided with downside protection in the event that the merged business does not fulfill its earnings expectations. Finally,

[3]Anthony H. Meyer, "Designing a Convertible Preferred Issue," *Financial Executive* (April 1968), pp. 53–55.

the earn-out diminishes the guesswork in establishing an equitable purchase price, because the price is based upon the actual performance of the
prospective acquisition after the merger.

Even though several advantages exist for earn-outs, potential problems must also be recognized. First, the acquired corporation must be
capable of being operated as an autonomous business entity. Second, the
acquiring firm must be willing to allow freedom of operation to the management of the newly acquired business. Third, the seller must be willing to
contribute toward the future growth of the acquiring company, realizing
that only by working together will the two firms attain success.

Numerous types of earn-outs have been devised; the various arrangements are limited only by the imagination of the management of the
two firms involved. However, the **base-period earn-out** may be used as an
illustration. Under this plan the stockholders of the acquired company are
to receive additional stock in each future year if the firm improves its
earnings above the base-period profits—that is, the earnings in the last year
before the acquisition. The amount of the future payments will be determined by three factors: (1) the amount of earnings in the forthcoming
years in excess of the base-period profits, (2) the capitalization rate (discount rate) agreed upon by the parties, and (3) the market value of the
acquiring organization at the end of each year. For example, the compensation in shares in the future years might be computed by using the following
formula:

$$\frac{\text{excess earnings} \times \text{price/earnings multiple}}{\text{stock market price}}$$

To illustrate, company A acquired company B in 1975, which had base-
period earnings of $400,000. At the time of the merger, company B stock-
holders received 300,000 shares of company A stock. Annual profits subsequent to the merger have been $475,000, $550,000, $650,000, and
$500,000. The market value of company A's stock is $30 per share and the
price/earnings ratio is 8. Based upon the formula above, the additional
shares to be paid to company B stockholders would be:

1976:	$\dfrac{\$ 75,000 \times 8}{\$30}$	=	20,000 shares
1977:	$\dfrac{\$150,000 \times 8}{\$30}$	=	40,000 shares
1978:	$\dfrac{\$250,000 \times 8}{\$30}$	=	66,667 shares
1979:	$\dfrac{\$100,000 \times 8}{\$30}$	=	26,667 shares
Total			153,334 shares

Therefore, in addition to the down payment of 300,000 company A shares, company B stockholders would receive a total of 153,334 shares during the ensuing four years.

The foregoing example is oversimplified, since other variables must also be recognized in the development of an earn-out plan. Such factors include (1) a specified limitation as to the maximum amount of stock that can be transferred in any one year; (2) an established range for the stock price employed in the computations; (3) the recognition of yearly earnings increments over the prior year; (4) the determination of an equitable down payment; and (5) the succinct definition of earnings for the earn-out computations.

In conclusion, the earn-out technique provides a means by which the acquiring business can eliminate part of the guesswork involved in purchasing a firm. In essence, it allows the acquiring management the privilege of hindsight.

TENDER OFFER

As an alternative approach in purchasing another firm, the acquiring corporation may consider using a **tender offer.** This technique has received extensive recognition during recent years. In fact, from 1972 to 1975 the number of major tender offers reported by the Securities and Exchange Commission more than doubled, increasing from 50 in 1972 to 113 in 1975.

A tender offer involves a bid by an interested party, usually a corporation, for controlling interest in another corporation. The prospective purchaser approaches the stockholders of the firm, rather than the management, to encourage them to sell their shares, typically at a premium over the current market price. For instance, Lowe offered to purchase 20 million shares of CNA common stock at $5, which had been selling for $4.25 the week prior to the offer. A larger premium was offered by Tesoro Petroleum for Commonwealth Oil Refining common stock: the tender price was $11.50 compared to $8.75 the day before the offer.

Since the tender offer is a direct appeal to the stockholders, prior approval is not required by the management of the target firm. However, the acquiring firm may choose to approach the management of the target firm. If the two managements are unsuccessful in negotiating the terms, a tender offer may then be attempted. Alternatively, a firm's management interested in acquiring control of a second corporation may try a surprise takeover without contacting the management of the latter company.

In response to a tender offer, the management of the firm under attack will frequently strike back zealously. Owing to tender offer abuses, Congress in 1968 established requirements that must be satisfied by the firm making the offer. For instance, the management of the acquiring firm has to provide notice to the target corporation and to the Securities and Exchange Commission 30 days prior to the takeover bid. More recently, managements under attack have occasionally relied upon state statutes existing in a minority of states to block or at least delay tender offers. In addition to stipulating a waiting period, these state statutes provide the target firm the opportunity to request court hearings. This legal process, while intended for the protection of the stockholders, works to the advantage of the target firm's management. The statutes increase the legal costs of a tender offer and afford the target management additional time for developing a counterattack to the takeover bid.

As an example, in 1977 Societe Imetal, a French holding company, announced its intent to make a tender offer to the shareholders of Copperweld Corporation. Executives within Copperweld initiated a strategy in the federal courts for delaying the offer. At the same time, Ohio state officials issued a *cease and desist* order requesting delay until the tender offer could be evaluated for any violations of state regulations. The court ruled that Imetal could not make the offer until after the hearings were completed. A second example of a tender offer would be United Technologies Corporation's takeover of Otis Elevator Company. The Otis management quickly acted to delay the offering in the courts. During the time thus gained, Otis management mailed letters to the firm's stockholders in an effort to develop sentiment against the tender offer. Among other tactics they suggested a dividend increase, as well as a search for other merger partners. Finally, when United Technologies raised the offering price, Otis management terminated their opposition. When the offer expired, United had acquired 73 percent of the outstanding Otis shares.

The disadvantages of the tender offer are readily apparent from the preceding examples. If the target firm's management attempts to block it, the costs of executing the offer may increase significantly. Also, the purchasing company may fail to acquire a sufficient number of shares to meet the objective of controlling the firm. On the other hand, if the offer is not strongly contested, it may possibly be less expensive than the normal route for acquiring a company, in that it permits control by purchasing a smaller portion of the firm. Also, the tender offer has proven somewhat less susceptible to judicial inquiries regarding the fairness of the purchase price, since each stockholder individually decides the fairness of the price.

SUMMARY

Business combinations historically have represented a major influence in the growth of firms within the United States. This avenue for growth has been particularly important during selected periods, such as the latter part of the 1960s. In recent years the number of mergers and acquisitions has again increased, but with greater caution than in the 1960s, when conglomerates played a big part in the merger activity.

Valuing a Firm

Determining the worth of a firm is a difficult task. In addition to projecting the firm's future profitability, which is a cornerstone in valuation, the acquirer must consider the effects of joining two businesses into a single operation. What may represent a "good investment" may not be a good merger.

In estimating a firm's worth several factors are frequently considered.

1. The **book value** represents the historical investment of the common stock-holders in the firm. By itself, book value is not an effective measure of a company's present value.

2. An **appraisal value** may or may not be a good indicator of the price to be paid for a company. The merits of an appraisal depend upon the approach taken and the nature of the business.

3. The **stock market value** of a firm's common shares is a key element in valuing a firm, particularly if the securities are actively traded in the market. However, care should be taken not to lean too heavily on this single factor.

4. **Earnings per share** is the *bottom line* for a company's operations and financing decisions. Although excessive reliance upon this single figure is often criticized, most business people view it as an important criterion for investment decisions, and they consider seriously how a merger may affect it. However, we should look at a merger's impact not only on present but also on future earnings.

Financing the Merger

The price to be paid for a company is seldom uninfluenced by the method of financing the purchase. Generally, the acquiring firm issues common stock or securities that are eventually convertible into common stock in payment for the acquisition. For this reason, a firm with a high price/earnings multiple is at an advantage in acquiring other businesses. More recently, deferred payment plans have been used.

Tender Offers

Normally, the interested purchaser approaches the management of the firm to be acquired. Alternatively, the purchasing firm can directly approach the stockholders of the firm under consideration. This bid for ownership, called a tender offer, has been used with increasing frequency. This approach may be cheaper, provided that the managers of the target firm do not attempt to block it.

STUDY QUESTIONS

22-1. What factors contributed to the reduction in the number of mergers in 1969 and 1970?

22-2. Why is book value alone not a significant measure of the worth of a company?

22-3. What advantages are provided by the use of an appraisal value in valuing a firm?

22-4. Why is the price/earnings ratio a significant factor in determining the method of financing a merger?

22-5. What are the advantages of using convertible securities as a method of financing mergers?

22-6. What is meant by the term "earn-out"?

22-7. What are the prerequisites for an earn-out plan to be effective?

22-8. Under the base-period earn-out, the amount of future payments depends on what factors?

22-9. What are the disadvantages of the tender offer?

22-1. Company X has negotiated the purchase of company Y. The two firms have agreed that the company Y shareholders are to receive common stock of company X in exchange for their shares. The exchange is to be based on the relative earnings per share of the two firms. Company X currently has 125,000 shares of common stock outstanding with an $84 market value, and earnings per share of $5.25. Company Y has issued 45,000 shares, which are selling for $46.20; earnings per share are $4.20. What will be the share exchange ratio for the merger? Will any dilution in earnings occur for either group of shareholders?

22-2. Company A has agreed to purchase company B. Company A currently has 150,000 shares of common stock outstanding; the market value is $115, and earnings per share is $7.85. Company B's common stock has a market value of $45, and earnings per share of $5.15, with 30,000 shares outstanding. The two firms have agreed that company B stockholders will receive company A common stock in exchange for their shares at a ratio of .75 to 1. What will be the effect on the earnings position of each company's stockholders?

22-3. Norton Industries has negotiated an acquisition at a price of $37.5 million. Norton's common stock is currently selling at $75. A convertible preferred stock could be issued to sell at $120 with a 1.25 conversion ratio. Compare the financing of the acquisition by common stock and by the convertible preferred issue. If Norton's management wants to minimize the impact of dilution, which financing method should be chosen?

22-4. Premier Chemical, Inc., agreed to purchase Mocatta Laboratories under a base-period earn-out plan. Mocatta's base-period profits were $325,000, and its earnings subsequent to the merger are shown below, as are Premier's common stock market value and earnings. What would be the total number of shares received by Mocatta's stockholders at the end of the fourth year if the initial down payment were 250,000 shares?

YEAR	MOCATTA'S EARNINGS	PREMIER'S STOCK PRICE	PREMIER'S EPS
1	$400,000	$48	$3.25
2	475,000	56	5.10
3	535,000	63	7.25
4	495,000	59	6.85

SELECTED REFERENCES

AUSTIN, DOUGLAS V., "The Financial Management of Tender Offer Takeovers," *Financial Management*, 3 (Spring 1974), 37–43.

CHENEY, RICHARD E., "What's New on the Corporate Takeover Scene," *Financial Executive*, 40 (April 1972), 18–21.

COHEN, MANUEL F., "Takeover Bids," *Financial Analysts Journal*, 26 (January–February 1970), 26–31.

CROWTHER, JOHN F., "Peril Point Acquisitions Prices," *Harvard Business Review*, 47 (September–October 1969), 58–62.

CUNTIZ, JONATHAN A., "Valuing Potential Acquisitions," *Financial Executive*, 39 (April 1971), 16–28.

GORT, MICHAEL, and THOMAS E. HOGART, "New Evidence on Mergers," *Journal of Law and Economics*, 13 (April 1970), 167–84.

HAUGEN, ROBERT A., and TERENCE C. LANGETIEG, "An Empirical Test for Synergism in Merger," *Journal of Finance*, 30 (September 1975), 1003–15.

HEATH, ROBERT A., "Valuation Factors and Techniques in Mergers," *Journal of Law and Economics*, 40 (April 1972), 34–44.

HIGGINS, ROBERT C., and LAWRENCE D. SCHALI, "Corporate Bankruptcy and Conglomerate Merger," *Journal of Finance*, 30 (March 1975), 93–115.

HOGARTY, THOMAS F., "The Profitability of Corporate Mergers," *Journal of Business*, 44 (July 1970), 317–27.

JOEHNK, MICHAEL D., and JAMES F. NIELSEN, "The Effects of Conglomerate Merger Activity on Systematic Risk," *Journal of Financial and Quantitative Analysis*, 9 (March 1974), 215–27.

KIM, E. HAN, and JOHN J. McCONNELL, "Corporate Merger and the Co-insurance of Corporate Debt," *Journal of Finance*, 32 (May 1977), 349–66.

LEE, LI WAY, "Co-Insurance and Conglomerate Merger," *Journal of Finance*, 32 (December 1977), 1527–39.

LEV, BARUCH, and GERSHON MADELKER, "The Microeconomic Consequences of Corporate Mergers," *Journal of Business*, 45 (January 1972), 85–104.

LEWELLEN, WILBUR G., "A Pure Financial Rationale for the Conglomerate Merger," *Journal of Finance*, 26 (May 1971), 521–37.

MACDOUGAL, GARY E., and FRED V. MALEK, "Master Plan for Merger Negotiations," *Harvard Business Review*, 7 (December 1969), 295–306.

MEAD, WALTER J., "Instantaneous Merger Profit as a Conglomerate Merger Motive," *Western Economic Review*, 7 (December 1969), 295–306.

MELICHER, RONALD W., and DAVID F. RUSH, "Evidence of the Acquisition-Related Performance of Conglomerate Firms," *Journal of Finance*, 29 (March 1974), 141–49.

————, and THOMAS R. HARTER, "Stock Price Movements of Firms Engaging in Large Acquisitions," *Journal of Financial and Quantitative Analysis*, 7 (March 1972), 1469–75.

————, and D. F. RUSH, "The Performance of Conglomerate Firms: Recent Risk and Return Experience," *Journal of Finance*, 28 (May 1973), 381–88.

MUELLER, DENNIS C., "A Theory of Conglomerate Mergers," *Quarterly Journal of Economics*, 83 (November 1969), 643–59.

SCOTT, JAMES H., JR., "On the Theory of Conglomerate Mergers," *Journal of Finance*, 32 (September 1977), 1235–51.

SHICK, RICHARD A., and F. C. JEN, "Merger Benefits to Shareholders of Acquiring Firms," *Financial Management*, 3 (Winter 1974), 45–53.

————, "The Analysis of Mergers and Acquisitions," *Journal of Finance*, 27 (May 1972), 495–502.

WESTON, J. FRED, KEITH V. SMITH, and RONALD E. SHRIEVES, "Conglomerate Performance Using the Capital Asset Pricing Model," *Review of Economics and Statistics* (November 1972), 357–63.

————, and SURENDRA K. MANSINGHKA, "Tests on the Efficiency of Conglomerate Firms," *Journal of Finance*, 26 (September 1971), 919–36.

WOODS, DONALD H., and THOMAS A. CAVERLY, "Development of a Linear Programming Model for the Analysis of Merger/Acquisition Situations," *Journal of Financial and Quantitative Analysis*, 4 (January 1970), 627–42.

Failure
and Reorganization

The financial manager interacts with risk on a daily basis. At the extreme, risk can result in the entire company's becoming dysfunctional—ineffective in generating profits or unable to pay maturing financial obligations. Even if a firm does not face serious financial embarrassment itself, occasionally the financial manager will be required to work with a customer who is having severe financial problems; consequently he should be aware of the financial and legal implications of business failure.

The present chapter has several objectives:

1. Explain the general terms of business failure.
2. Identify frequent causes of company failures.
3. Specify the financial characteristics that generally develop within a firm facing possible bankruptcy.
4. Explain the procedural aspects for reorganizing or liquidating a business.

The term *failure* is used in a variety of contexts. **Economic failure** suggests that the company's costs exceed its revenues. Stated differently, the internal rates of return on investments are less than the firm's cost of capital. *Insolvency* also is frequently used to specify serious financial prob-

WHAT FAILURE IS

lems. A firm is **technically insolvent** when it can no longer honor its financial obligations. Although the book value of assets may exceed total liabilities, indicating a positive net worth, the company simply does not have sufficient liquidity to pay its debts. This condition may be temporary or irreversible. Another term used is **insolvency in bankruptcy.** Here the company's liabilities are actually greater than the fair valuation of its assets, which means a negative net worth. Regardless of the liquidity of its assets, the company is completely and unquestionably unable to meet maturing obligations. This situation generally indicates that liquidation rather than a reorganization of the firm is necessary.

Although causes of business failure vary from firm to firm, we may identify several common ones. The predominant cause of firm failure is management incompetence. Also, the following key structural problems within management may appear.[1]

FREQUENT CAUSES OF FAILURE

1. An imbalance of skills within the top echelon. A manager tends to attract other managers of similar skills. For example, the corporate management may consist principally of individuals having a background in sales, without anyone having production experience.
2. A chief executive who dominates a firm's operations without regard for the inputs of peers.
3. An inactive board of directors. For instance, the board of directors for Penn Central, even including the members who were bankers, supposedly did not become aware of the firm's impending financial disaster until a few weeks before its declaration of insolvency.
4. A deficient finance function within the firm's management. Not infrequently, the only substantial input provided by the financial officer occurs when the budget is submitted to the board. A company may have an effective financial information system; however, this information is of no avail if it does not flow to the board through a strong financial officer.
5. The absence of responsibility for the chief executive officer. Although all other managers with a company are responsible to a superior, the chief executive seldom must account for his actions. Conceptually, this person is responsible to the stockholders. However, with the increased separation of management and stockholders, this link is tenuous or even missing altogether.

The foregoing deficiencies render the firm vulnerable to several mistakes. First, management may be negligent in developing effective accounting systems. Second, the company may be unresponsive to change—unable to adjust to a general recession and unfavorable industry developments. Third, management may be inclined to undertake an investment project that is disproportionately large relative to firm size. If the project fails, the probability of insolvency is greatly increased. Finally, management may

[1]John Argenti, *Corporate Collapse: The Causes and Symptoms* (New York: John Wiley & Sons, 1976), pp. 123–26.

come to rely so heavily on debt financing that even a minor problem can place the firm in a dangerous position.

Dun & Bradstreet, Inc., each year samples a large number of companies that have experienced failure.[2] The reasons given for these business casualties are shown in Table 23-1. Clearly, the primary causes relate to the weakness of the firm's management.

As a company enters the final stages prior to failure, a pattern may develop in terms of a changing financial profile. Although bankruptcy or insolvency cannot be predicted with certainty, several financial ratios have proven to be useful indicators of impending disaster. A study by Altman[3] developed a statistical model that found the financial ratios best predicting bankruptcy. The study yielded an equation that used five ratios to predict bankruptcy:

SYMPTOMS OF BANKRUPTCY

$$\text{Bankruptcy score} = .012X_1 + .014X_2 + .033X_3 + .006X_4 + .999X_5$$

where $X_1 = $ (net working capital $\div$ total assets) $\times$ 100,

$X_2 = $ (retained earnings $\div$ total assets) $\times$ 100,

$X_3 = $ (earnings before interest and taxes $\div$ total assets) $\times$ 100,

[2]Dun & Bradstreet, Inc., *The Failure Record Through 1976* (New York, 1977), p. 12.
[3]Edward L. Altman, *Corporate Bankruptcy in America* (Lexington, Mass.: Heath Lexington Books, 1971).

Table 23-1 CAUSES OF BUSINESS FAILURE IN 1976

UNDERLYING CAUSES	MANUFACTURERS	WHOLESALERS	RETAILERS	CONSTRUCTION	COMMERCIAL SERVICES	ALL-FIRM TOTAL
Neglect	0.8%	0.9%	0.9%	1.0%	0.5%	0.8%
Fraud	0.9	0.5	0.4	0.3	0.6	0.5
Lack of experience in the Line	10.8	13.3	16.7	10.9	11.9	13.8
Lack of managerial experience	12.5	11.7	13.6	13.4	12.3	13.0
Unbalanced experience[a]	20.5	25.5	23.2	23.4	22.2	23.0
Incompetence	48.9	43.4	39.2	44.4	41.8	42.3
Disaster	1.2	0.6	0.7	0.9	0.6	0.8
Reason unknown	4.4	4.1	5.3	5.7	10.1	5.8

[a]Experience not well rounded in sales, finance, purchasing, and production on the part of the individual in case of a proprietorship, or of two or more partners or officers constituting a management unit.

SOURCE: Dun & Bradstreet, Inc., *The Business Failure Record Through 1976* (New York, 1977), p. 12.

$X_4 =$ (total market value of stock ÷ book value of total debt) ×
100,

$X_5 =$ sales ÷ total assets.

With the above equation, the criterion for separating firms with a strong likelihood of bankruptcy from those that probably will not fail should be as follows. If the score exceeds 2.99, no concern should exist that the company is facing bankruptcy in the foreseeable future. On the other hand, a score less than 1.81 suggests that the firm is a likely candidate for failure. Values between 1.81 and 2.99 are difficult to assign to either a "successful" or "failure" classification. However, although a firm in this "gray area" can be easily misclassified in terms of the final outcome, the best way to set up a dividing line is to predict that a company will fail if its score is less than 2.675. Alternatively, a score exceeding 2.675 may be used as an indicator that success is more likely than failure. These guidelines are shown in Table 23-2. We may conclude that a potentially failing corporation begins to invest less in current assets (X_1). Since X_2 is a cumulative indicator of profitability relative to time, the findings suggest that younger companies have a greater chance of bankruptcy. Variable X_3 reflects the firm's general earnings power. Deterioration in this factor was shown to be the best single indicator that bankruptcy may be forthcoming. Variable X_4 depicts the firm's financial leverage position. Finally, X_5, the asset turnover ratio, measures management's ability to generate sales from the firm's assets.

Although the financial information flowing from a firm helps us identify problems, the predictions we make with it certainly are not perfect. Owing to factors unique to the firm as well as to the tendency for management of problem firms to do some "window dressing" of the financial statements, the ratios will not always effectively identify corporations that face bankruptcy within the near future. Even so, they will help us assess the likelihood of bankruptcy.

When a firm faces severe problems, either the problems must be resolved or the firm must be liquidated. The question has to be answered, "Is the firm worth more dead or alive?" A decision to continue operating has to be based upon the feasibility and fairness of reorganizing the firm as opposed to the benefits of liquidating the business. As shown in Figure

Table 23-2 ALTMAN'S BANKRUPTCY CRITERION

BANKRUPTCY SCORE		
Less than 1.81	Between 1.81 and 2.99	Greater than 2.99
Probability of failure is high	Probability of failure is difficult to determine	Probability of failure is remote
Predict failure	2.615	Predict success

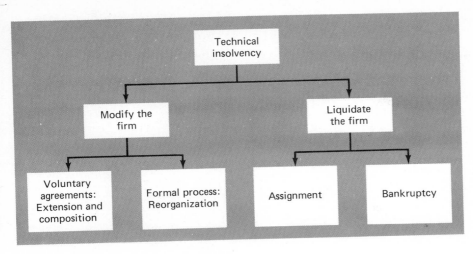

FIGURE 23-1 *Choices Resulting from Technical Insolvency*

23-1, when technical insolvency occurs, management must either modify the operating and financial conditions or terminate the firm's life. If the decision is made to alter the company in the hopes of revitalizing its operations, either voluntary agreements with the investors or a formal court-arranged reorganization must be used. If, on the other hand, the difficulties are believed to be insurmountable, a liquidation will take place, either by assignment of the assets to an independent party for liquidation or by formal bankruptcy proceedings.

If a company finds itself in financial distress, the management may need to seek a remedy that is acceptable to the creditors. If the evidence suggests that the company's going-concern value is larger than its liquidation value, the management may attempt to arrange for a voluntary reorganization. These arrangements may allow the firm an extension of time to pay the debts, or even reduce the amount ultimately to be paid. **VOLUNTARY REMEDIES TO INSOLVENCY**

Voluntary remedies avoid the necessity of a court settlement. However, any creditor who refuses to participate may legally prohibit the arrangement for the remaining creditors. Such action may result in a smaller settlement if the courts become involved; thus, general agreement by the creditors is a key prerequisite to the success of a voluntary remedy. Whether a reasonable chance exists for the creditors to finalize such a plan is based upon (1) the debtor's proven honesty and integrity, (2) the firm's potential for recovery, and (3) the economic prospects for the industry. *Prerequisites*

Most frequently, the debtor confers with the creditors to explain the firm's financial condition and to request that they consider developing a plan that would be most beneficial to all parties involved. This meeting is *Procedure* generally planned under the guidance of an adjustment bureau associated with either a local credit association or a trade association. The creditors appoint a committee to represent both the large and small claimants. If it decides a feasible plan can be developed, the committee, in conjunction with the firm and the adjustment bureau, constructs an agreement. Typically, this voluntary agreement may be classified as an extension, a composition, or some combination thereof.

EXTENSION

An **extension** requires that the debtor pay the amount owed in full. However, an extension in time is provided. For instance, the agreement may stipulate that all new purchases are to be made on a cash basis, with the outstanding balance from prior purchases to be paid over an extended period. Also, the contract may place the existing debt in subordination to new liabilities during the extension period. Clearly, the creditors must have confidence in the company's management and in the economic conditions affecting the firm; otherwise they would not agree to such concessions.

Although the creditors' basis for an extension is largely a function of their trust in the present management, several control mechanisms may be used during this period of uncertainty. For example, the plan may prohibit any dividend payments to the stockholders. In fact, the stockholders may have to place their shares in escrow with the creditors' committee. Also, the agreement may require that the firm's assets be assigned to the creditors' committee for the duration of the extension period. Finally, a requirement may be incorporated into the contract stipulating that a member of the creditors' committee countersign checks.

COMPOSITION

A **composition** permits the debtor to pay less than the full balance owed the creditors. In other words, the creditors receive a pro rata share of their claim. The amount received is to represent final settlement of the indebtedness. The creditors' reason for agreeing to a partial payment is that the only remaining option available is bankruptcy proceedings, the costs of which can quickly deplete the firm's resources. Negotiations between the debtor and creditors hinge on the savings that may be expected by avoiding the legal costs associated with bankruptcy. Also, the debtor is benefited by avoiding the stigma attached to bankruptcy.

Evaluation of Voluntary Remedies

The primary advantages of voluntary remedies relate to the minimization of costs and the informality of the process. A significant amount of legal, investigative, and administrative expenses may be avoided, resulting in a higher return to the creditors. Also, the bargaining process is greatly simplified, and a more congenial atmosphere typically prevails than in the bankruptcy courts.

One of the difficulties in arranging a voluntary remedy is that a creditor may refuse to participate. For this reason, a composition generally allows for the payment in full of small claims. For instance, the terms of the agreement may state that all creditors are to receive $50 plus a pro rata share of the remaining claim. This provision eliminates the small claimants. However, essentially it means that the larger creditors partially underwrite the amounts payable to small creditors.

Another disadvantage, particularly for the extension, is that the debtor maintains control of the business. If the underlying problems confronting the business are not corrected, the company's assets may continue to erode in value, which clearly works to the detriment of the creditors. However, as already explained, controls may be initiated to minimize any potential losses due to continued inefficient management.

REORGANIZATION

If a voluntary remedy, such as an extension or composition, is not workable, a company can declare or be forced by its creditors into bankruptcy. As a part of this process, the firm is either reorganized or dissolved. Reorganization under the Bankruptcy Act is similar to an extension or composition, the objective being to revitalize the firm by changing its operating procedures and the capital structure; however, the procedure is more formal and it is administered by the courts. Two chapters within the Bankruptcy Act are particularly important in providing for an orderly reorganization of a business.

Chapter XI

Under **Chapter XI** of the Bankruptcy Act, the debtor may file a reorganizational plan. The plan, termed an **arrangement,** is a petition to the court requesting that the firm be required to make only partial or a delayed payment to its creditors. Implementation of the arrangement is then subject to court assent and the approval of a majority of the creditors, both in number and in dollar claims. If the arrangement is initiated, all creditors are compelled to accept it. However, the agreement is applicable only to unsecured creditors, with the secured lenders having the right to full payment. In implementing the arrangement, the court may either appoint a receiver to manage the firm or, more typically, permit management to maintain control.

The primary advantage of a Chapter XI reorganization is that legal and administrative costs are lower than in the more involved Chapter X proceedings. Also, usually the court permits the present management to continue providing the corporate leadership.

If the firm's financial position has deteriorated to the point where no mutually beneficial agreement can be reached, the creditors may file for a reorganization under Chapter X of the Bankruptcy Act. As an example, in July 1977, when United Merchants and Manufacturers filed a petition for reorganization, the Securities and Exchange Commission quickly recommended that the proceeding be transferred into Chapter X, so that a trustee could be appointed for the protection of the stockholders and the owners of the firm's debentures.

When the debtor and creditors cannot resolve the terms of an arrangement under the Chapter XI provisions, the creditors can request a reorganization through **Chapter X.** In this instance, three or more creditors having a combined claim totaling at least $5000 may request that the court appoint a trustee for the purposes of managing the company during the proceedings and developing a reorganization plan. If the company's liabilities exceed $3 million, the trustee must also submit the plan to the Securities and Exchange Commission for advisory purposes. After receiving court approval, the plan is presented to the creditors and stockholders. Consent is required from two-thirds of the creditors and a simple majority of the stockholders, provided that the stockholders are to participate in the reorganization. Stockholder involvement occurs only when the firm's value after the reorganization exceeds the outstanding liabilities.

In the reorganization process, the trustee has to establish the going-concern value for the debtor's business after the reorganization. This procedure requires an estimation of the company's future earnings. With this projection in hand, a capitalization rate (or equivalently a price/earnings ratio) for a similar but prosperous firm is determined. When this rate is applied to the earnings, a going-concern value may be approximated. For example, assume that a corporation may reasonably expect to make $1 million in earnings after the reorganization. If the price/earnings multiple for a comparable firm is 8, the going-concern value is $8 million ($1 million earnings × 8 price/earnings).

After a going-concern value has been estimated, the trustee devises a reorganization plan, including a way of reformulating the capital structure to meet the criteria of fairness and feasibility. In developing this recommendation, the trustee carefully evaluates what changes are necessary to place the company in a more profitable posture. Also, in revamping the capital structure, concern is given to the firm's ability to cover the financial fixed charges: interest, principal repayments, and preferred dividends.

If the facts indicate that a reorganization is fair and feasible to the respective creditors and the stockholders, new securities are issued to reflect the revised capital structure. The principal guideline in this procedure is the **rule of absolute priority,** which simply indicates that the company must completely honor senior claims on assets before settling junior claims.

Example. To illustrate the rule of absolute priority, consider the Paine Corporation which is currently undergoing a reorganization. The firm's balance sheet as of June 30, 1979, is presented in Table 23-3. The creditors have filed a petition for reorganization. The court has named a trustee, who is serving to develop a possible plan of reorganization. Based upon the trustee's evaluation, an internal reorganization is considered to be both fair and feasible to the existing investors. The trustee has projected the company's earnings, and by using an appropriate price/earnings multi-

Table 23-3 PAINE CORPORATION: BALANCE SHEET, JUNE 30, 1979

Assets	
Current assets	$ 2,000,000
Net plant and equipment	15,500,000
Other assets	1,000,000
Total assets	$18,500,000
Liabilities and equity	
Current liabilities	
Accounts payable	$ 1,000,000
Notes payable	3,000,000
Total current liabilities	$ 4,000,000
Long-term liabilities	
Mortgage bonds (8% due in 1985)	$ 4,000,000
Subordinated debentures ($9\frac{1}{2}$% due in 1983)[a]	8,000,000
Total long-term liabilities	$12,000,000
Total liabilities	$16,000,000
Equity	
Common stock (par $5)	500,000
Paid-in capital	14,000,000
Retained earnings	(12,000,000)
Total equity	$ 2,500,000
Total liabilities and equity	$18,500,000

[a]Subordinated to the mortgage bonds.

ple has estimated the firm's going-concern value to be $8 million, as compared to a $6 million liquidation value (the approximate amount that would be received if the business were terminated and the assets sold individually).

The proposed plan for reorganizing the company is shown in Table 23-4. The first portion of the table specifies the amounts of the distribution to be made to each group of creditors. Since the going-concern value is $8 million, only 50 percent of the $16 million in debt can be honored. As a result, the common stockholders will not be entitled to any of the distribution. Also, the subordinated debentures are not to participate in the reorganization until the mortgage bondholders have been repaid in full. Consequently, the $4 million in securities that would have been distributed to the owners of the debentures has to be reduced by $2 million. The final distribution, after recognizing the subordination, is shown in the last column of Table 23-4.

The lower section of Table 23-4 reflects the trustee's proposed changes in the firm's capital structure. The objective is to reduce the financial leverage to a point commensurate with the company's ability to cover the fixed financial charges from earnings. For example, the original ac-

617

Table 23-4 PAINE CORPORATION: REORGANIZATION PLAN

CREDITORS	AMOUNT OF CLAIM	50 PERCENT OF CLAIM	NEW CLAIM AFTER SUBORDINATION
Accounts payable	$ 1,000,000	$ 500,000	$ 500,000
Notes payable	3,000,000	1,500,000	1,500,000
Mortgage bonds	4,000,000	2,000,000	4,000,000
Subordinated debentures[a]	8,000,000	4,000,000	2,000,000
	$16,000,000	$8,000,000	$8,000,000

[a]Subordinated to the mortgage bonds.

NEW SECURITIES ISSUED IN THE REORGANIZATION

OLD SECURITY	NEW SECURITIES	
Accounts payable	Accounts payable	$ 250,000
	Common stock	250,000
Notes payable	Preferred stock	750,000
	Common stock	750,000
Mortgage bonds	Mortgage bonds (8%)	2,000,000
	Subordinated debentures ($9\frac{1}{2}$%)	1,000,000
	Preferred stock (10%)	1,000,000
Subordinated debentures	Common stock	2,000,000

counts payable balance is reduced to $500,000, with these creditors having a short-term claim of $250,000 and receiving $250,000 in new common stock. The final capital structure, if the trustee's plan is adopted, is provided in Table 23-5.

THE PENN CENTRAL REORGANIZATION

As an illustration of an actual reorganization, we will briefly look at the failure and the impending reorganization of the Penn Central Transportation Company. For a number of years the company had encountered serious difficulties; however, not until several weeks before the request for bankruptcy did the severity of the problems emerge. The cash drain from

Table 23-5 PAINE CORPORATION: LIABILITIES AND EQUITY AFTER REORGANIZATION

Accounts payable	$ 250,000
Mortgage bonds (8%)	2,000,000
Subordinated debentures ($9\frac{1}{2}$%)	1,000,000
Preferred stock (10%)	1,750,000
Common stock	3,000,000
	$8,000,000

railroad operations resulted in Penn Central's having to borrow heavily on a short-term basis. When it was unable to refinance these short-term liabilities, the firm collapsed and filed a petition of bankruptcy on June 21, 1970. At that time Penn Central had more than $5 billion in liabilities outstanding. By 1978 the reorganization plan for revitalizing the firm had been eight years in the making, with heavy assistance by the federal government through loans and guarantees. The plan in a simplified format is shown in Table 23-6. Liabilities to the federal government are to be partially paid, with the remaining amounts deferred until a later date. State and local governments are given a choice between a reduced payment in cash or a full settlement in the form of notes. Small unsecured creditors are to be paid in full. Large unsecured creditors are to receive a mixture of common stock and certificates of beneficial interest. The **certificate of beneficial interest** entitles the holder to receive cash only if any money remains after other claims have been paid. The secured creditors are to receive a mixture of cash, bonds, preferred stock, and common stock.

To make the company profitable, the trustees see three primary steps

Table 23-6 THE PENN CENTRAL REORGANIZATION

Claims to Be Resolved

Federal government's claims ($500 million) would be paid in cash and secured notes. State and local governments ($385 million) would be offered either 50% of their claims in cash or 100% in secured notes. Small unsecured claimants would be paid in full.

Secured creditors ($1.8 billion) would be paid as follows:
10% of the face amount (principal and interest) of their claims in cash,
30% in general mortgage bonds,
30% in preferred stock, and
30% in common stock.

Unsecured creditors ($521 million) would be paid 30% of their claims in certificates of beneficial interest, the rest in common stock.

Common stockholders: Penn Central Co. would be given 10% of the reorganized company's 25 million shares.

Plan of Action for Correcting Problems

I. *Dispose of property.* Sell over $1 billion worth of property, including real estate, coal properties, the Pittsburgh & Lake Erie Railroad and other remaining rail facilities.
II. *Run ongoing operations.* Pennsylvania Co., a subsidiary, will generate earnings and make acquisitions. The subsidiary currently includes Buckeye Pipe Line, Edgington Oil, Arvida Corp., and Great Southwest Corp.
III. *Prosecute a lawsuit.* Sue the U. S. government for just compensation for the rail properties Conrail acquired. Proceeds could be anywhere from $525 million to several billions of dollars.

SOURCE: *Forbes,* May 1, 1977, p. 53.

as essential. First, the firm's subsidiary, the Pennsylvania Company, is to be charged with the company's operational aspects, including future acquisitions. Second, over $1 billion in assets, particularly in real estate and rail operations, are to be liquidated. Finally, the trustees view a lawsuit as necessary in recovering a fair compensation for the railroad operations that the federal government required the firm to sell to Conrail. The trustees maintain that the government grossly undervalued the property.

LIQUIDATION

If the likelihood is small that reorganization of an insolvent firm would result in a profitable business, the firm should be dissolved. In this situation the liquidation value exceeds the going-concern value, and it is to the investor's advantage to terminate the business. Continuing the operation at this point generally results only in further losses. Complete termination of the company can be accomplished either through assignment or by declaring bankruptcy. The end objective of either procedure is to distribute any proceeds from the liquidation to the creditors.

Liquidation by Assignment

If an **assignment** is used to liquidate the business, the final settlement is done privately with a minimum amount of court involvement. The debtor transfers title of the firm's assets to a third party, who has been appointed either by the creditors or by the court. This individual, known as an **assignee** or **trustee,** administers the liquidation process and sees that an appropriate distribution is made of the proceeds. Under an assignment, the debtor is not automatically discharged of the remaining balance due a creditor. When the liquidation funds are distributed to the creditors, a notation on the checks should be made indicating that endorsement of the check represents the creditor's acceptance of the money as full settlement of the claim. However, even then a creditor can refuse to accept the payment, considering that his interests would be better served by a court-administered liquidation.

Owing to the possible nonacceptance of the assignment by one or more creditors, the debtor may attempt to reach a prior agreement with the creditors that the assignment will represent a complete settlement of claims. If the agreement is made, a creditors' committee will usually recommend that the debtor be released from all claims after the final execution of the assignment.

An assignment has several advantages over a formal bankruptcy procedure. The assignment is usually quicker, less expensive, and requires less legal formality. The assignee is provided greater discretion and flexibility than a court-appointed trustee in bankruptcy in liquidating the assets. He can take quicker action to avoid further depletion in the value of inventories and equipment, and typically he is more familiar with the debtor's business, which should improve the final results. However, the assignment does not legally discharge the debtor from the responsibility of unpaid balances, and the creditor is not protected against fraud; consequently, formal bankruptcy proceedings may be preferred by either the debtor or creditors.

THE LIQUIDATION PROCESS

A petition for a company to be declared bankrupt may be filed in Federal District Court. Subject to the provisions of the Bankruptcy Act, the petition can be initiated either by the debtor (voluntary) or by the creditors (involuntary). A voluntary declaration of bankruptcy by the debtor is usually taken when management considers further delays as being detrimental to the stockholders' position. Involuntary bankruptcy proceedings may be initiated by creditors if three conditions are satisfied:

1. The firm's total debts equal or exceed $1000.
2. If fewer than 12 creditors are involved in the liquidation, only one claimant has to file the petition, provided that the amount owed is at least $500. If the total number of creditors is 12 or more, the petition must be filed by three or more creditors, individually having claims of at least $500.
3. The debtor has committed an act of bankruptcy within the past four months.

The Bankruptcy Act specifically designates actions on the part of a debtor that represent **acts of bankruptcy.** First, an act of bankruptcy occurs if the debtor, through a written document, admits an inability to repay outstanding loans and a willingness to be judged bankrupt. Second, the appointment of a trustee or assignee for the benefit of the creditors is an act of bankruptcy. Finally, the debtor commits an act of bankruptcy by concealing or improperly transferring assets for the purpose of defrauding any or all of the firm's creditors.

After the filing and approval of the bankruptcy petition, the court adjudges the debtor bankrupt and names a **referee in bankruptcy.** In turn, the referee may appoint a **receiver** to serve as the interim caretaker of the company's assets until a trustee can be designated by the creditors. The referee then requests from the debtor a list of assets and liabilities.

A meeting of the creditors is called by the referee. At the meeting, a trustee is elected by the creditors, and a creditors' committee is appointed. Also, the debtor may be questioned for additional information relevant to the proceedings.

The trustee and the creditors' committee initiate plans to liquidate the company's assets. As a part of this conversion process, individuals owing money to the debtor are contacted in an effort to collect these outstanding balances. Appraisers are selected to determine a value for the property, and these values are used as guidelines in liquidating assets. Specifically, the trustee may not sell an asset at less than 75 percent of its appraised value, without the approval of the court. After all assets have been converted into cash through private sales or public auctions, all expenses incurred in the bankruptcy process are paid. The remaining cash is distributed on a pro rata basis to the creditors. The trustee provides a final accounting to the creditors and the referee. The bankruptcy filing is then discharged, and the debtor is relieved of all responsibility for prior debts.

PRIORITY OF CLAIMS

Following the rule of absolute priority, claims are honored in the following order:

1. Expenses incurred in administering the bankrupt estate.
2. Salaries and commissions not exceeding $600 per employee that were earned within the three months preceding the bankruptcy petition.
3. Federal, state, and local taxes.
4. Secured creditors, with the proceeds from the sale of the specific property going first to these creditors. If any portion of the claim remains unpaid, the balance is treated as an unsecured loan.
5. Unsecured creditors.
6. Preferred stocks.
7. Common stock.

An example will illustrate the order of payments from a liquidation. The Poverty Stricken Corporation has been judged bankrupt; its balance sheet is shown in Table 23-7. Although the historical cost of the assets was $100 million, the trustee in bankruptcy was able to realize only $44 million from their sale. In addition, costs of $8 million were incurred in administering the bankruptcy.

Table 23-7 POVERTY STRICKEN CORPORATION: BALANCE SHEET

Current assets		
Net plant and equipment		$20,000,000
Total assets		80,000,000
		$100,000,000
Accounts payable	$22,000,000	
Accrued wages[a]	600,000	
Notes payable	20,000,000	
Federal taxes	2,500,000	
State taxes	500,000	
Current debt		$45,600,000
First mortgage bonds[b]	$12,000,000	
Subordinated debentures[c]	10,000,000	
Long-term debt		22,000,000
Preferred stock	$ 4,000,000	
Common stock	28,400,000	
Equity		32,400,000
Total debt and equity		$100,000,000

[a]No single claim exceeds $600.
[b]These bonds have a first lien on the building.
[c]Subordinated to the notes payable.

The order of settling the claims is presented in Table 23-8. As the table shows, the administrative costs associated with filing and executing the bankruptcy petition, employee salaries, and the tax liabilities receive first priority. Also, the first mortgage bondholders are entitled to receive the net proceeds resulting from the sale of the specific property identified in the lien. We are assuming that the sale price of this property is $10 million, which leaves an unpaid balance of $4 million to be treated as an unsecured claim.

After all payments have been made for prior claims, $22,400,000 is available for general unsecured creditors, whose claims total $56 million; dividing 22.4 by 56, we find that the claimants are entitled to 40 percent of the original loan. This percentage is computed from the amount available for general creditors, $22,400,000, relative to the total claims of $56 million. However, an adjustment must be made to recognize the subordination of the debentures to the notes payable. In essence, the owners of debentures must relinquish their right to any money until the notes payable have been settled in full. In this situation, $12 million of the note balance remains unpaid. As a consequence, the $4 million originally shown to be received by the debentures must be paid to the investors owning the note payable. The actual distributions to the unsecured creditors are shown in the last column at the bottom of Table 23-9.

SUMMARY

Facing financial adversity is never easy. For this reason, management should be aware of the implications and consequences of financial embarrassment. This information may prove useful if reorganization or liquidation is required for the firm or if similar action becomes necessary for one of the firm's customers.

Business failure is principally the result of incompetent management. In a related sense, a deficiency in the management structure, such as an imbalance of skills, may pose serious problems. The symptoms of these

Table 23-8 POVERTY STRICKEN CORPORATION: PRIORITY OF CLAIMS

DISTRIBUTION OF PROCEEDS		
Liquidation value of assets		$44,000,000
Priority of claims:		
1. Administrative expenses	$10,000,000	
2. Salaries due employees	600,000	
3. Taxes	3,000,000	
4. First mortgage receipts from the sale of the building	8,000,000	
Total prior claims		21,600,000
Amount available for settling claims of general creditors		$22,400,000

Table 23-9 POVERTY STRICKEN CORPORATION: CLAIMS OF GENERAL CREDITORS

GENERAL CLAIMS	CLAIM	PERCENTAGE OF CLAIMS AVAILABLE	ADJUSTMENT FOR SUBORDINATION
Accounts payable	$22,000,000	$8,800,000	$8,800,000
Notes payable	20,000,000	8,000,000	12,000,000
Remaining portion of first mortgage bond	4,000,000	1,600,000	1,600,000
Subordinated debenture	10,000,000	4,000,000	-0-
Totals	$56,000,000	$22,400,000	$22,400,000

weaknesses are often readily identifiable in the firm's financial statements. The company will generally decrease its investment in liquid assets, while profitability declines. Also, the use of financial leverage increases significantly. Finally, management's efficient use of assets, as depicted by the asset turnover ratio, may deteriorate.

When a business becomes technically insolvent, one of two choices must be accepted. The firm has to be either reorganized or liquidated. In either case, the process may be relatively informal or closely controlled by the court. In the reorganization of a firm, voluntary agreements may be arranged, taking the form of either an extension or a compostion. If, however, these plans are not acceptable to the creditors, a court-administered reorganization may be necessary. If the company's liquidation value is thought to exceed its going-concern value, the firm should be dissolved.

If liquidation is required, the assets may be assigned to a third party for the purpose of selling them and distributing the funds according to the rule of absolute priority. Such an assignment aims to avoid the more costly court-ordered bankruptcy filing. Yet, if the debtor or creditors consider formal bankruptcy proceedings preferable, voluntary or involuntary bankruptcy may be requested. For this petition to be executed, certain conditions must exist; for instance, an *act of bankruptcy* must have been committed by the debtor. If the debtor is judged to be bankrupt, a referee is selected to liquidate the firm's assets and distribute the proceeds in accordance with the rule of absolute priority.

STUDY QUESTIONS

23-1. Explain the following terms: economic failure, technical insolvency, and insolvency in bankruptcy.

23-2. What are the most frequent causes of business failure?

23-3. To what potential mistakes is a firm vulnerable if it is experiencing any of the deficiencies cited in question 23-2?

23-4. What are the prerequisites to a successful voluntary remedy?

23-5. What procedure is usually followed in arranging a voluntary agreement?

23-6. Compare an extension with a composition.

23-7. What are the advantages and disadvantages of voluntary remedies?

23-8. Why may a Chapter XI reorganization be advantageous to the firm?

23-9. Explain the process of liquidation by assignment.

23-10. What acts of bankruptcy are designated by the Bankruptcy Act?

23-1. You are studying five companies and have decided to use Altman's model to predict the probability of bankruptcy for each. The five ratios needed are given below. What are the bankruptcy scores for these companies and how are they interpreted?

	VARIABLES				
COMPANY	X_1	X_2	X_3	X_4	X_5
A	15%	20%	35%	335%	1.60×
B	25	45	40	175	1.95
C	20	25	15	125	.75
D	15	12	10	110	.55
E	40	35	30	175	1.50

23-2. You are considering investing in the securities of three companies. Using the Altman model and the information given below, compute the bankruptcy score for each company. Which companies would you invest in?

	COMPANY		
	A	B	C
Sales	$1,500,000	$ 800,000	$3,000,000
Total assets	4,000,000	1,000,000	4,500,000
Net working capital	1,100,000	650,000	2,000,000
Earnings before interest and taxes	1,000,000	500,000	1,000,000
Retained earnings	800,000	350,000	1,500,000
Stock market value	1,250,000	500,000	2,200,000
Debt book value	750,000	100,000	1,250,000

23-3. Brogham, Inc., is currently undergoing a reorganization. The trustee has estimated the firm's going-concern value to be $1,260,000. Given the liabilities and equity from the balance sheet, formulate the plan for reorganization under the rule of absolute priority.

BROGHAM, INC. OCTOBER 30, 1978

Liabilities and equity

Current liabilities

Accounts payable	$ 120,000
Notes payable	300,000
Total current liabilities	$ 420,000

Long-term liabilities

Mortgage bonds	$ 420,000
Subordinated debentures	1,260,000
Total long-term liabilities	$1,680,000
Total liabilities	$2,100,000

Equity

Common stock (par $10)	$ 500,000
Paid-in capital	2,000,000
Total equity	$2,500,000
Total liabilities and equity	$4,600,000

23-4. The trustee for the reorganization of Warner Corporation has established the going-concern value at $7.5 million. The creditors and the amounts owed are given below. As part of the reorganization plan, the accounts payable are to be settled by renewal of $500,000 of the accounts, with a due date of six months. Any remaining amount to be received by these claimants is to be realized in the form of long-term notes payable. The current owners of the firm's notes are to be paid in preferred stock. The mortgage bondholders will receive half of their adjusted claim under the reorganization in the form of newly issued bonds, with the remainder being common stock. The investors owning the subordinated debentures are to receive common stock in settlement of their claim. What will Warner's liabilities and equity be after reorganization?

WARNER CORPORATION

CREDITORS	AMOUNT OF CLAIMS
Accounts payable	$ 2,000,000
Notes payable	1,000,000
Mortgage bonds	4,000,000
Subordinated debentures[a]	3,000,000
	$10,000,000

[a] Subordinated to the mortgage bonds.

23-5. Pioneer Enterprises is bankrupt and being liquidated. The liabilities and equity portion of its balance sheet is given below. The book value of the assets was $60 million, but the realized value when liquidated was only

$31.58 million, of which $7.55 million was from the sale of the firm's office building. Administrative expenses associated with the liquidation were $4.8 million. Determine the distribution of the proceeds.

PIONEER ENTERPRISES LIABILITIES AND EQUITIES

Accounts payable	$ 6,500,000	
Accrued wages[a]	400,000	
Notes payable	15,000,000	
Federal taxes	3,000,000	
State taxes	1,250,000	
Current debt		$26,150,000
First mortgage bonds[b]	$14,000,000	
Subordinated debentures[c]	8,500,000	
Long-term debt		$22,500,000
Preferred stock	$ 2,350,000	
Common stock	9,000,000	
Equity		$11,350,000
Total		$60,000,000

[a] No single claim exceeds $600.
[b] Have first lien on office building.
[c] Subordinated to the first mortgage bonds.

23-6. Loggins Industries has filed bankruptcy and is in the process of being liquidated. Its liabilities and equity are shown below. The book value of the assets is $80 million, but the liquidation value is $42 million. Administrative expenses of the liquidation procedures were $2 million. What is the distribution of proceeds?

LOGGINS INDUSTRIES LIABILITIES AND EQUITIES

Accounts payable	$10,000,000	
Accrued wages[a]	1,000,000	
Notes payable	17,000,000	
Federal taxes	3,000,000	
State taxes	1,000,000	
Current debt		$32,000,000
Bonds (10-year 8%)	$25,000,000	
Subordinated debentures[b]	18,000,000	
(7-year 10%)		
Long-term debt		$43,000,000
Preferred stock	$ 1,000,000	
Common stock	4,000,000	
Equity		$ 5,000,000
Total		$80,000,000

[a] No single claim exceeds $600.
[b] Subordinated to notes payable.

ALTMAN, EDWARD I., "Corporate Bankruptcy Potential, Stockholder Returns and Share Valuation," *Journal of Finance*, 24 (December 1969), 887–900.

————, "Equity Securities of Bankrupt Firm," *Financial Analysts Journal*, 25 (July–August 1969), 129–33.

————, and ARNOLD W. SANCHEZ, eds., *Financial Crises: Institutions and Markets in a Fragile Environment*. New York: John Wiley & Sons, Inc., 1977.

————, "Financial Ratios, Discriminant Analysis and the Prediction of Corporate Bankruptcy," *Journal of Finance*, 23 (September 1968), 589–609.

ARGENTI, JOHN, *Corporate Collapse; The Causes and Symptoms*. New York: Halsted Press, 1976.

CHRISTIAN, ROGER W. and ROBERT A. WIENER, *Insolvency Accounting*. New York: McGraw-Hill Book Company, 1977.

EDMISTER, ROBERT O., "An Empirical Test of Financial Ratio Analysis for Small Business Failure Prediction," *Journal of Financial and Quantitative Analysis*, 7 (March 1972), 1477–93.

GORDON, MYRON J., "Towards a Theory of Financial Distress," *Journal of Finance*, 26 (May 1971), 347–56.

HANNA, MARK, "Corporate Bankruptcy Potential, Stockholder Returns and Share Valuation: Comment," *Journal of Finance*, 27 (June 1977), 711–18.

HIGGINS, ROBERT C., and LAWRENCE D. SCHALL, "Corporate Bankruptcy and Share Conglomerate Merger," *Journal of Finance*, 30 (March 1975), 93–115.

JOHNSON, CRAIG G., "Ratio Analysis and the Prediction of Firm Failure," *Journal of Finance*, 25 (December 1970), 1166–68.

MOYER, ROGER F., "Forecasting Financial Failure: A Re-examination," *Financial Management*, 6 (Spring 1977), 11–18.

MURRAY, ROGER F., "The Penn Central Debacle: Lessons for Financial Analysis," *Journal of Finance*, 26 (May 1971), 327–32.

SCOTT, JAMES H., JR., "Bankruptcy, Secured Debt, and Optimal Capital Structure," *Journal of Finance*, 32 (March 1977), 1–21.

WARNER, JEROLD B., "Bankruptcy Costs: Some Evidence," *Journal of Finance*, 32 (May 1977), 339–49.

WESTON, J. FRED, "The Industrial Economics Background of the Penn Central Bankruptcy," *Journal of Finance*, 26 (May 1971), 311–26.

SELECTED REFERENCES

APPENDIXES

Appendix A COMPOUND SUM OF $1

n	1%	2%	3%	4%	5%	6%	7%	8%	9%	10%
1	1.010	1.020	1.030	1.040	1.050	1.060	1.070	1.080	1.090	1.100
2	1.020	1.040	1.061	1.082	1.102	1.124	1.145	1.166	1.188	1.210
3	1.030	1.061	1.093	1.125	1.158	1.191	1.225	1.260	1.295	1.331
4	1.041	1.082	1.126	1.170	1.216	1.262	1.311	1.360	1.412	1.464
5	1.051	1.104	1.159	1.217	1.276	1.338	1.403	1.469	1.539	1.611
6	1.062	1.126	1.194	1.265	1.340	1.419	1.501	1.587	1.677	1.772
7	1.072	1.149	1.230	1.316	1.407	1.504	1.606	1.714	1.828	1.949
8	1.083	1.172	1.267	1.369	1.477	1.594	1.718	1.851	1.993	2.144
9	1.094	1.195	1.305	1.423	1.551	1.689	1.838	1.999	2.172	2.358
10	1.105	1.219	1.344	1.480	1.629	1.791	1.967	2.159	2.367	2.594
11	1.116	1.243	1.384	1.539	1.710	1.898	2.105	2.332	2.580	2.853
12	1.127	1.268	1.426	1.601	1.796	2.012	2.252	2.518	2.813	3.138
13	1.138	1.294	1.469	1.665	1.886	2.133	2.410	2.720	3.066	3.452
14	1.149	1.319	1.513	1.732	1.980	2.261	2.579	2.937	3.342	3.797
15	1.161	1.346	1.558	1.801	2.079	2.397	2.759	3.172	3.642	4.177
16	1.173	1.373	1.605	1.873	2.183	2.540	2.952	3.426	3.970	4.595
17	1.184	1.400	1.653	1.948	2.292	2.693	3.159	3.700	4.328	5.054
18	1.196	1.428	1.702	2.026	2.407	2.854	3.380	3.996	4.717	5.560
19	1.208	1.457	1.753	2.107	2.527	3.026	3.616	4.316	5.142	6.116
20	1.220	1.486	1.806	2.191	2.653	3.207	3.870	4.661	5.604	6.727
21	1.232	1.516	1.860	2.279	2.786	3.399	4.140	5.034	6.109	7.400
22	1.245	1.546	1.916	2.370	2.925	3.603	4.430	5.436	6.658	8.140
23	1.257	1.577	1.974	2.465	3.071	3.820	4.740	5.871	7.258	8.954
24	1.270	1.608	2.033	2.563	3.225	4.049	5.072	6.341	7.911	9.850
25	1.282	1.641	2.094	2.666	3.386	4.292	5.427	6.848	8.623	10.834
30	1.348	1.811	2.427	3.243	4.322	5.743	7.612	10.062	13.267	17.449
40	1.489	2.208	3.262	4.801	7.040	10.285	14.974	21.724	31.408	45.258
50	1.645	2.691	4.384	7.106	11.467	18.419	29.456	46.900	74.354	117.386

Appendix A COMPOUND SUM OF $1 (cont.)

n	11%	12%	13%	14%	15%	16%	17%	18%	19%	20%
1	1.110	1.120	1.130	1.140	1.150	1.160	1.170	1.180	1.190	1.200
2	1.232	1.254	1.277	1.300	1.322	1.346	1.369	1.392	1.416	1.440
3	1.368	1.405	1.443	1.482	1.521	1.561	1.602	1.643	1.685	1.728
4	1.518	1.574	1.630	1.689	1.749	1.811	1.874	1.939	2.005	2.074
5	1.685	1.762	1.842	1.925	2.011	2.100	2.192	2.288	2.386	2.488
6	1.870	1.974	2.082	2.195	2.313	2.436	2.565	2.700	2.840	2.986
7	2.076	2.211	2.353	2.502	2.660	2.826	3.001	3.185	3.379	3.583
8	2.305	2.476	2.658	2.853	3.059	3.278	3.511	3.759	4.021	4.300
9	2.558	2.773	3.004	3.252	3.518	3.803	4.108	4.435	4.785	5.160
10	2.839	3.106	3.395	3.707	4.046	4.411	4.807	5.234	5.695	6.192
11	3.152	3.479	3.836	4.226	4.652	5.117	5.624	6.176	6.777	7.430
12	3.498	3.896	4.334	4.818	5.350	5.936	6.580	7.288	8.064	8.916
13	3.883	4.363	4.898	5.492	6.153	6.886	7.699	8.599	9.596	10.699
14	4.310	4.887	5.535	6.261	7.076	7.987	9.007	10.147	11.420	12.839
15	4.785	5.474	6.254	7.138	8.137	9.265	10.539	11.974	13.589	15.407
16	5.311	6.130	7.067	8.137	9.358	10.748	12.330	14.129	16.171	18.488
17	5.895	6.866	7.986	9.276	10.761	12.468	14.426	16.672	19.244	22.186
18	6.543	7.690	9.024	10.575	12.375	14.462	16.879	19.673	22.900	26.623
19	7.263	8.613	10.197	12.055	14.232	16.776	19.748	23.214	27.251	31.948
20	8.062	9.646	11.523	13.743	16.366	19.461	23.105	27.393	32.429	38.337
21	8.949	10.804	13.021	15.667	18.821	22.574	27.033	32.323	38.591	46.005
22	9.933	12.100	14.713	17.861	21.644	26.186	31.629	38.141	45.923	55.205
23	11.026	13.552	16.626	20.361	24.891	30.376	37.005	45.007	54.648	66.247
24	12.239	15.178	18.788	23.212	28.625	35.236	43.296	53.108	65.031	79.496
25	13.585	17.000	21.230	26.461	32.918	40.874	50.656	62.667	77.387	95.395
30	22.892	29.960	39.115	50.949	66.210	85.849	111.061	143.367	184.672	237.373
40	64.999	93.049	132.776	188.876	267.856	378.715	533.846	750.353	1051.642	1469.740
50	184.559	288.996	450.711	700.197	1083.619	1670.669	2566.080	3927.189	5988.730	9100.191

Appendix A COMPOUND SUM OF $1 (cont.)

n	21%	22%	23%	24%	25%	26%	27%	28%	29%	30%
1	1.210	1.220	1.230	1.240	1.250	1.260	1.270	1.280	1.290	1.300
2	1.464	1.488	1.513	1.538	1.562	1.588	1.613	1.638	1.664	1.690
3	1.772	1.816	1.861	1.907	1.953	2.000	2.048	2.097	2.147	2.197
4	2.144	2.215	2.289	2.364	2.441	2.520	2.601	2.684	2.769	2.856
5	2.594	2.703	2.815	2.932	3.052	3.176	3.304	3.436	3.572	3.713
6	3.138	3.297	3.463	3.635	3.815	4.001	4.196	4.398	4.608	4.827
7	3.797	4.023	4.259	4.508	4.768	5.042	5.329	5.629	5.945	6.275
8	4.595	4.908	5.239	5.589	5.960	6.353	6.767	7.206	7.669	8.157
9	5.560	5.987	6.444	6.931	7.451	8.004	8.595	9.223	9.893	10.604
10	6.727	7.305	7.926	8.594	9.313	10.086	10.915	11.806	12.761	13.786
11	8.140	8.912	9.749	10.657	11.642	12.708	13.862	15.112	16.462	17.921
12	9.850	10.872	11.991	13.215	14.552	16.012	17.605	19.343	21.236	23.298
13	11.918	13.264	14.749	16.386	18.190	20.175	22.359	24.759	27.395	30.287
14	14.421	16.182	18.141	20.319	22.737	25.420	28.395	31.691	35.339	39.373
15	17.449	19.742	22.314	25.195	28.422	32.030	36.062	40.565	45.587	51.185
16	21.113	24.085	27.446	31.242	35.527	40.357	45.799	51.923	58.808	66.541
17	25.547	29.384	33.758	38.740	44.409	50.850	58.165	66.461	75.862	86.503
18	30.912	35.848	41.523	48.038	55.511	64.071	73.869	85.070	97.862	112.454
19	37.404	43.735	51.073	59.567	69.389	80.730	93.813	108.890	126.242	146.190
20	45.258	53.357	62.820	73.863	86.736	101.720	119.143	139.379	162.852	190.047
21	54.762	65.095	77.268	91.591	108.420	128.167	151.312	178.405	210.079	247.061
22	66.262	79.416	95.040	113.572	135.525	161.490	192.165	228.358	271.002	321.178
23	80.178	96.887	116.899	140.829	169.407	203.477	244.050	292.298	349.592	417.531
24	97.015	118.203	143.786	174.628	211.758	256.381	309.943	374.141	450.974	542.791
25	117.388	144.207	176.857	216.539	264.698	323.040	393.628	478.901	581.756	705.627
30	304.471	389.748	497.904	634.810	807.793	1025.904	1300.477	1645.488	2078.208	2619.936
40	2048.309	2846.941	3946.340	5455.797	7523.156	10346.879	14195.051	19426.418	26520.723	36117.754
50	13779.844	20795.680	31278.301	46889.207	70064.812	104354.562	154942.687	229345.875	338440.000	497910.125

Appendix A COMPOUND SUM OF $1 (cont.)

n	31%	32%	33%	34%	35%	36%	37%	38%	39%	40%
1	1.310	1.320	1.330	1.340	1.350	1.360	1.370	1.380	1.390	1.400
2	1.716	1.742	1.769	1.796	1.822	1.850	1.877	1.904	1.932	1.960
3	2.248	2.300	2.353	2.406	2.460	2.515	2.571	2.628	2.686	2.744
4	2.945	3.036	3.129	3.224	3.321	3.421	3.523	3.627	3.733	3.842
5	3.858	4.007	4.162	4.320	4.484	4.653	4.826	5.005	5.189	5.378
6	5.054	5.290	5.535	5.789	6.053	6.328	6.612	6.907	7.213	7.530
7	6.621	6.983	7.361	7.758	8.172	8.605	9.058	9.531	10.025	10.541
8	8.673	9.217	9.791	10.395	11.032	11.703	12.410	13.153	13.935	14.758
9	11.362	12.166	13.022	13.930	14.894	15.917	17.001	18.151	19.370	20.661
10	14.884	16.060	17.319	18.666	20.106	21.646	23.292	25.049	26.924	28.925
11	19.498	21.199	23.034	25.012	27.144	29.439	31.910	34.567	37.425	40.495
12	25.542	27.982	30.635	33.516	36.644	40.037	43.716	47.703	52.020	56.694
13	33.460	36.937	40.745	44.912	49.469	54.451	59.892	65.830	72.308	79.371
14	43.832	48.756	54.190	60.181	66.784	74.053	82.051	90.845	100.509	111.119
15	57.420	64.358	72.073	80.643	90.158	100.712	112.410	125.366	139.707	155.567
16	75.220	84.953	95.857	108.061	121.713	136.968	154.002	173.005	194.192	217.793
17	98.539	112.138	127.490	144.802	164.312	186.277	210.983	238.747	269.927	304.911
18	129.086	148.022	169.561	194.035	221.822	253.337	289.046	329.471	375.198	426.875
19	169.102	195.389	225.517	260.006	299.459	344.537	395.993	454.669	521.525	597.625
20	221.523	257.913	299.937	348.408	404.270	468.571	542.511	627.443	724.919	836.674
21	290.196	340.446	398.916	466.867	545.764	637.256	743.240	865.871	1007.637	1171.343
22	380.156	449.388	530.558	625.601	736.781	866.668	1018.238	1194.900	1400.615	1639.878
23	498.004	593.192	705.642	838.305	994.653	1178.668	1394.986	1648.961	1946.854	2295.829
24	652.385	783.013	938.504	1123.328	1342.781	1602.988	1911.129	2275.564	2706.125	3214.158
25	854.623	1033.577	1248.210	1505.258	1812.754	2180.063	2618.245	3140.275	3761.511	4499.816
30	3297.081	4142.008	5194.516	6503.285	8128.426	10142.914	12636.086	15716.703	19517.969	24201.043
40	49072.621	66519.313	89962.188	121388.437	163433.875	219558.625	294317.937	393684.687	525508.312	700022.688

Appendix B PRESENT VALUE OF $1

n	1%	2%	3%	4%	5%	6%	7%	8%	9%	10%
1	.990	.980	.971	.962	.952	.943	.935	.926	.917	.909
2	.980	.961	.943	.925	.907	.890	.873	.857	.842	.826
3	.971	.942	.915	.889	.864	.840	.816	.794	.772	.751
4	.961	.924	.888	.855	.823	.792	.763	.735	.708	.683
5	.951	.906	.863	.822	.784	.747	.713	.681	.650	.621
6	.942	.888	.837	.790	.746	.705	.666	.630	.596	.564
7	.933	.871	.813	.760	.711	.665	.623	.583	.547	.513
8	.923	.853	.789	.731	.677	.627	.582	.540	.502	.467
9	.914	.837	.766	.703	.645	.592	.544	.500	.460	.424
10	.905	.820	.744	.676	.614	.558	.508	.463	.422	.386
11	.896	.804	.722	.650	.585	.527	.475	.429	.388	.350
12	.887	.789	.701	.625	.557	.497	.444	.397	.356	.319
13	.879	.773	.681	.601	.530	.469	.415	.368	.326	.290
14	.870	.758	.661	.577	.505	.442	.388	.340	.299	.263
15	.861	.743	.642	.555	.481	.417	.362	.315	.275	.239
16	.853	.728	.623	.534	.458	.394	.339	.292	.252	.218
17	.844	.714	.605	.513	.436	.371	.317	.270	.231	.198
18	.836	.700	.587	.494	.416	.350	.296	.250	.212	.180
19	.828	.686	.570	.475	.396	.331	.277	.232	.194	.164
20	.820	.673	.554	.456	.377	.312	.258	.215	.178	.149
21	.811	.660	.538	.439	.359	.294	.242	.199	.164	.135
22	.803	.647	.522	.422	.342	.278	.226	.184	.150	.123
23	.795	.634	.507	.406	.326	.262	.211	.170	.138	.112
24	.788	.622	.492	.390	.310	.247	.197	.158	.126	.102
25	.780	.610	.478	.375	.295	.233	.184	.146	.116	.102
30	.742	.552	.412	.308	.231	.174	.131	.099	.075	.057
40	.672	.453	.307	.208	.142	.097	.067	.046	.032	.022
50	.608	.372	.228	.141	.087	.054	.034	.021	.013	.009

n	11%	12%	13%	14%	15%	16%	17%	18%	19%	20%
1	.901	.893	.885	.877	.870	.862	.855	.847	.840	.833
2	.812	.797	.783	.769	.756	.743	.731	.718	.706	.694
3	.731	.712	.693	.675	.658	.641	.624	.609	.593	.579
4	.659	.636	.613	.592	.572	.552	.534	.516	.499	.482
5	.593	.567	.543	.519	.497	.476	.456	.437	.419	.402
6	.535	.507	.480	.456	.432	.410	.390	.370	.352	.335
7	.482	.452	.425	.400	.376	.354	.333	.314	.296	.279
8	.434	.404	.376	.351	.327	.305	.285	.266	.249	.233
9	.391	.361	.333	.308	.284	.263	.243	.225	.209	.194
10	.352	.322	.295	.270	.247	.227	.208	.191	.176	.162
11	.317	.287	.261	.237	.215	.195	.178	.162	.148	.135
12	.286	.257	.231	.208	.187	.168	.152	.137	.124	.112
13	.258	.229	.204	.182	.163	.145	.130	.116	.104	.093
14	.232	.205	.181	.160	.141	.125	.111	.099	.088	.078
15	.209	.183	.160	.140	.123	.108	.095	.084	.074	.065
16	.188	.163	.141	.123	.107	.093	.081	.071	.062	.054
17	.170	.146	.125	.108	.093	.080	.069	.060	.052	.045
18	.153	.130	.111	.095	.081	.069	.059	.051	.044	.038
19	.138	.116	.098	.083	.070	.060	.051	.043	.037	.031
20	.124	.104	.087	.073	.061	.051	.043	.037	.031	.026
21	.112	.093	.077	.064	.053	.044	.037	.031	.026	.022
22	.101	.083	.068	.056	.046	.038	.032	.026	.022	.018
23	.091	.074	.060	.049	.040	.033	.027	.022	.018	.015
24	.082	.066	.053	.043	.035	.028	.023	.019	.015	.013
25	.074	.059	.047	.038	.030	.024	.020	.016	.013	.010
30	.044	.033	.026	.020	.015	.012	.009	.007	.005	.004
40	.015	.011	.008	.005	.004	.003	.002	.001	.001	.001
50	.005	.003	.002	.001	.001	.001	.000	.000	.000	.000

Appendix B PRESENT VALUE OF $1 (cont.)

n	21%	22%	23%	24%	25%	26%	27%	28%	29%	30%
1	.826	.820	.813	.806	.800	.794	.787	.781	.775	.769
2	.683	.672	.661	.650	.640	.630	.620	.610	.601	.592
3	.564	.551	.537	.524	.512	.500	.488	.477	.466	.455
4	.467	.451	.437	.423	.410	.397	.384	.373	.361	.350
5	.386	.370	.355	.341	.328	.315	.303	.291	.280	.269
6	.319	.303	.289	.275	.262	.250	.238	.227	.217	.207
7	.263	.249	.235	.222	.210	.198	.188	.178	.168	.159
8	.218	.204	.191	.179	.168	.157	.148	.139	.130	.123
9	.180	.167	.155	.144	.134	.125	.116	.108	.101	.094
10	.149	.137	.126	.116	.107	.099	.092	.085	.078	.073
11	.123	.112	.103	.094	.086	.079	.072	.066	.061	.056
12	.102	.092	.083	.076	.069	.062	.057	.052	.047	.043
13	.084	.075	.068	.061	.055	.050	.045	.040	.037	.033
14	.069	.062	.055	.049	.044	.039	.035	.032	.028	.025
15	.057	.051	.045	.040	.035	.031	.028	.025	.022	.020
16	.047	.042	.036	.032	.028	.025	.022	.019	.017	.015
17	.039	.034	.030	.026	.023	.020	.017	.015	.013	.012
18	.032	.028	.024	.021	.018	.016	.014	.012	.010	.009
19	.027	.023	.020	.017	.014	.012	.011	.009	.008	.007
20	.022	.019	.016	.014	.012	.010	.008	.007	.006	.005
21	.018	.015	.013	.011	.009	.008	.007	.006	.005	.004
22	.015	.013	.011	.009	.007	.006	.005	.004	.004	.003
23	.012	.010	.009	.007	.006	.005	.004	.003	.003	.002
24	.010	.008	.007	.006	.005	.004	.003	.003	.002	.002
25	.009	.007	.006	.005	.004	.003	.003	.002	.002	.001
30	.003	.003	.002	.002	.001	.001	.001	.001	.000	.000
40	.000	.000	.000	.000	.000	.000	.000	.000	.000	.000
50	.000	.000	.000	.000	.000	.000	.000	.000	.000	.000

Appendix B PRESENT VALUE OF $1 (cont.)

n	31%	32%	33%	34%	35%	36%	37%	38%	39%	40%
1	.763	.758	.752	.746	.741	.735	.730	.725	.719	.714
2	.583	.574	.565	.557	.549	.541	.533	.525	.518	.510
3	.445	.435	.425	.416	.406	.398	.389	.381	.372	.364
4	.340	.329	.320	.310	.301	.292	.284	.276	.268	.260
5	.259	.250	.240	.231	.223	.215	.207	.200	.193	.186
6	.198	.189	.181	.173	.165	.158	.151	.145	.139	.133
7	.151	.143	.136	.129	.122	.116	.110	.105	.100	.095
8	.115	.108	.102	.096	.091	.085	.081	.076	.072	.068
9	.088	.082	.077	.072	.067	.063	.059	.055	.052	.048
10	.067	.062	.058	.054	.050	.046	.043	.040	.037	.035
11	.051	.047	.043	.040	.037	.034	.031	.029	.027	.025
12	.039	.036	.033	.030	.027	.025	.023	.021	.019	.018
13	.030	.027	.025	.022	.020	.018	.017	.015	.014	.013
14	.023	.021	.018	.017	.015	.014	.012	.011	.010	.009
15	.017	.016	.014	.012	.011	.010	.009	.008	.007	.006
16	.013	.012	.010	.009	.008	.007	.006	.006	.005	.005
17	.010	.009	.008	.007	.006	.005	.005	.004	.004	.003
18	.008	.007	.006	.005	.005	.004	.003	.003	.003	.002
19	.006	.005	.004	.004	.003	.003	.003	.002	.002	.002
20	.005	.004	.003	.003	.002	.002	.002	.002	.001	.001
21	.003	.003	.003	.002	.002	.002	.001	.001	.001	.001
22	.003	.002	.002	.002	.001	.001	.001	.001	.001	.001
23	.002	.002	.001	.001	.001	.001	.001	.001	.001	.000
24	.002	.001	.001	.001	.001	.001	.001	.000	.000	.000
25	.001	.001	.001	.001	.001	.000	.000	.000	.000	.000
30	.000	.000	.000	.000	.000	.000	.000	.000	.000	.000
40	.000	.000	.000	.000	.000	.000	.000	.000	.000	.000

Appendix C   SUM OF AN ANNUITY OF $1 FOR _n_ PERIODS

n	1%	2%	3%	4%	5%	6%	7%	8%	9%	10%
1	1.000	1.000	1.000	1.000	1.000	1.000	1.000	1.000	1.000	1.000
2	2.010	2.020	2.030	2.040	2.050	2.060	2.070	2.080	2.090	2.100
3	3.030	3.060	3.091	3.122	3.152	3.184	3.215	3.246	3.278	3.310
4	4.060	4.122	4.184	4.246	4.310	4.375	4.440	4.506	4.573	4.641
5	5.101	5.204	5.309	5.416	5.526	5.637	5.751	5.867	5.985	6.105
6	6.152	6.308	6.468	6.633	6.802	6.975	7.153	7.336	7.523	7.716
7	7.214	7.434	7.662	7.898	8.142	8.394	8.654	8.923	9.200	9.487
8	8.286	8.583	8.892	9.214	9.549	9.897	10.260	10.637	11.028	11.436
9	9.368	9.755	10.159	10.583	11.027	11.491	11.978	12.488	13.021	13.579
10	10.462	10.950	11.464	12.006	12.578	13.181	13.816	14.487	15.193	15.937
11	11.567	12.169	12.808	13.486	14.207	14.972	15.784	16.645	17.560	18.531
12	12.682	13.412	14.192	15.026	15.917	16.870	17.888	18.977	20.141	21.384
13	13.809	14.680	15.618	16.627	17.713	18.882	20.141	21.495	22.953	24.523
14	14.947	15.974	17.086	18.292	19.598	21.015	22.550	24.215	26.019	27.975
15	16.097	17.293	18.599	20.023	21.578	23.276	25.129	27.152	29.361	31.772
16	17.258	18.639	20.157	21.824	23.657	25.672	27.888	30.324	33.003	35.949
17	18.430	20.012	21.761	23.697	25.840	28.213	30.840	33.750	36.973	40.544
18	19.614	21.412	23.414	25.645	28.132	30.905	33.999	37.450	41.301	45.599
19	20.811	22.840	25.117	27.671	30.539	33.760	37.379	41.446	46.018	51.158
20	22.019	24.297	26.870	29.778	33.066	36.785	40.995	45.762	51.159	57.274
21	23.239	25.783	28.676	31.969	35.719	39.992	44.865	50.422	56.764	64.002
22	24.471	27.299	30.536	34.248	38.505	43.392	49.005	55.456	62.872	71.402
23	25.716	28.845	32.452	36.618	41.430	46.995	53.435	60.893	69.531	79.542
24	26.973	30.421	34.426	39.082	44.501	50.815	58.176	66.764	76.789	88.496
25	28.243	32.030	36.459	41.645	47.726	54.864	63.248	73.105	84.699	98.346
30	34.784	40.567	47.575	56.084	66.438	79.057	94.459	113.282	136.305	164.491
40	48.885	60.401	75.400	95.024	120.797	154.758	199.630	259.052	337.872	442.580
50	64.461	84.577	112.794	152.664	209.341	290.325	406.516	573.756	815.051	1163.865

Appendix C SUM OF AN ANNUITY OF $1 FOR n PERIODS (cont.)

n	11%	12%	13%	14%	15%	16%	17%	18%	19%	20%
1	1.000	1.000	1.000	1.000	1.000	1.000	1.000	1.000	1.000	1.000
2	2.110	2.120	2.130	2.140	2.150	2.160	2.170	2.180	2.190	2.200
3	3.342	3.374	3.407	3.440	3.472	3.506	3.539	3.572	3.606	3.640
4	4.710	4.779	4.850	4.921	4.993	5.066	5.141	5.215	5.291	5.368
5	6.228	6.353	6.480	6.610	6.742	6.877	7.014	7.154	7.297	7.442
6	7.913	8.115	8.323	8.535	8.754	8.977	9.207	9.442	9.683	9.930
7	9.783	10.089	10.405	10.730	11.067	11.414	11.772	12.141	12.523	12.916
8	11.859	12.300	12.757	13.233	13.727	14.240	14.773	15.327	15.902	16.499
9	14.164	14.776	15.416	16.085	16.786	17.518	18.285	19.086	19.923	20.799
10	16.722	17.549	18.420	19.337	20.304	21.321	22.393	23.521	24.709	25.959
11	19.561	20.655	21.814	23.044	24.349	25.733	27.200	28.755	30.403	32.150
12	22.713	24.133	25.650	27.271	29.001	30.850	32.824	34.931	37.180	39.580
13	26.211	28.029	29.984	32.088	34.352	36.786	39.404	42.218	45.244	48.496
14	30.095	32.392	34.882	37.581	40.504	43.672	47.102	50.818	54.841	59.196
15	34.405	37.280	40.417	43.842	47.580	51.659	56.109	60.965	66.260	72.035
16	39.190	42.753	46.671	50.980	55.717	60.925	66.648	72.938	79.850	87.442
17	44.500	48.883	53.738	59.117	65.075	71.673	78.978	87.067	96.021	105.930
18	50.396	55.749	61.724	68.393	75.836	84.140	93.404	103.739	115.265	128.116
19	56.939	63.439	70.748	78.968	88.211	98.603	110.283	123.412	138.165	154.739
20	64.202	72.052	80.946	91.024	102.443	115.379	130.031	146.626	165.417	186.687
21	72.264	81.698	92.468	104.767	118.809	134.840	153.136	174.019	197.846	225.024
22	81.213	92.502	105.489	120.434	137.630	157.414	180.169	206.342	236.436	271.028
23	91.147	104.602	120.203	138.295	159.274	183.600	211.798	244.483	282.359	326.234
24	102.173	118.154	136.829	158.656	184.166	213.976	248.803	289.490	337.007	392.480
25	114.412	133.333	155.616	181.867	212.790	249.212	292.099	342.598	402.038	471.976
30	199.018	241.330	293.192	356.778	434.738	530.306	647.423	790.932	966.698	1181.865
40	581.812	767.080	1013.667	1341.979	1779.048	2360.724	3134.412	4163.094	5529.711	7343.715
50	1668.723	2399.975	3459.344	4994.301	7217.488	10435.449	15088.805	21812.273	31514.492	45496.094

Appendix C SUM OF AN ANNUITY OF $1 FOR n PERIODS (cont.)

n	21%	22%	23%	24%	25%	26%	27%	28%	29%	30%
1	1.000	1.000	1.000	1.000	1.000	1.000	1.000	1.000	1.000	1.000
2	2.210	2.220	2.230	2.240	2.250	2.260	2.270	2.280	2.290	2.300
3	3.674	3.708	3.743	3.778	3.813	3.848	3.883	3.918	3.954	3.990
4	5.446	5.524	5.604	5.684	5.766	5.848	5.931	6.016	6.101	6.187
5	7.589	7.740	7.893	8.048	8.207	8.368	8.533	8.700	8.870	9.043
6	10.183	10.442	10.708	10.980	11.259	11.544	11.837	12.136	12.442	12.756
7	13.321	13.740	14.171	14.615	15.073	15.546	16.032	16.534	17.051	17.583
8	17.119	17.762	18.430	19.123	19.842	20.588	21.361	22.163	22.995	23.858
9	21.714	22.670	23.669	24.712	25.802	26.940	28.129	29.369	30.664	32.015
10	27.274	28.657	30.113	31.643	33.253	34.945	36.723	38.592	40.556	42.619
11	34.001	35.962	38.039	40.238	42.566	45.030	47.639	50.398	53.318	56.405
12	42.141	44.873	47.787	50.895	54.208	57.738	61.501	65.510	69.780	74.326
13	51.991	55.745	59.778	64.109	68.760	73.750	79.106	84.853	91.016	97.624
14	63.909	69.009	74.528	80.496	86.949	93.925	101.465	109.611	118.411	127.912
15	78.330	85.191	92.669	100.815	109.687	119.346	129.860	141.302	153.750	167.285
16	95.779	104.933	114.983	126.010	138.109	151.375	165.922	181.867	199.337	218.470
17	116.892	129.019	142.428	157.252	173.636	191.733	211.721	233.790	258.145	285.011
18	142.439	158.403	176.187	195.993	218.045	242.583	269.885	300.250	334.006	371.514
19	173.351	194.251	217.710	244.031	273.556	306.654	343.754	385.321	431.868	483.968
20	210.755	237.986	268.783	303.598	342.945	387.384	437.568	494.210	558.110	630.157
21	256.013	291.343	331.603	377.461	429.681	489.104	556.710	633.589	720.962	820.204
22	310.775	356.438	408.871	469.052	538.101	617.270	708.022	811.993	931.040	1067.265
23	377.038	435.854	503.911	582.624	673.626	778.760	900.187	1040.351	1202.042	1388.443
24	457.215	532.741	620.810	723.453	843.032	982.237	1144.237	1332.649	1551.634	1805.975
25	554.230	650.944	764.596	898.082	1054.791	1238.617	1454.180	1706.790	2002.608	2348.765
30	1445.111	1767.044	2160.459	2640.881	3227.172	3941.953	4812.891	5873.172	7162.785	8729.805
40	9749.141	12936.141	17153.691	22728.367	30088.621	39791.957	52570.707	69376.562	91447.375	120389.375

Appendix C SUM OF AN ANNUITY OF $1 FOR n PERIODS (cont.)

n	31%	32%	33%	34%	35%	36%	37%	38%	39%	40%
1	1.000	1.000	1.000	1.000	1.000	1.000	1.000	1.000	1.000	1.000
2	2.310	2.320	2.330	2.340	2.350	2.360	2.370	2.380	2.390	2.400
3	4.026	4.062	4.099	4.136	4.172	4.210	4.247	4.284	4.322	4.360
4	6.274	6.362	6.452	6.542	6.633	6.725	6.818	6.912	7.008	7.104
5	9.219	9.398	9.581	9.766	9.954	10.146	10.341	10.539	10.741	10.946
6	13.077	13.406	13.742	14.086	14.438	14.799	15.167	15.544	15.930	16.324
7	18.131	18.696	19.277	19.876	20.492	21.126	21.779	22.451	23.142	23.853
8	24.752	25.678	26.638	27.633	28.664	29.732	30.837	31.982	33.167	34.395
9	33.425	34.895	36.429	38.028	39.696	41.435	43.247	45.135	47.103	49.152
10	44.786	47.062	49.451	51.958	54.590	57.351	60.248	63.287	66.473	69.813
11	59.670	63.121	66.769	70.624	74.696	78.998	83.540	88.335	93.397	98.739
12	79.167	84.320	89.803	95.636	101.840	108.437	115.450	122.903	130.822	139.234
13	104.709	112.302	120.438	129.152	138.484	148.474	159.166	170.606	182.842	195.928
14	138.169	149.239	161.183	174.063	187.953	202.925	219.058	236.435	255.151	275.299
15	182.001	197.996	215.373	234.245	254.737	276.978	301.109	327.281	355.659	386.418
16	239.421	262.354	287.446	314.888	344.895	377.690	413.520	452.647	495.366	541.985
17	314.642	347.307	383.303	422.949	466.608	514.658	567.521	625.652	689.558	759.778
18	413.180	459.445	510.792	567.751	630.920	700.935	778.504	864.399	959.485	1064.689
19	542.266	607.467	680.354	761.786	852.741	954.271	1067.551	1193.870	1334.683	1491.563
20	711.368	802.856	905.870	1021.792	1152.200	1298.809	1463.544	1648.539	1856.208	2089.188
21	932.891	1060.769	1205.807	1370.201	1556.470	1767.380	2006.055	2275.982	2581.128	2925.862
22	1223.087	1401.215	1604.724	1837.068	2102.234	2404.636	2749.294	3141.852	3588.765	4097.203
23	1603.243	1850.603	2135.282	2462.669	2839.014	3271.304	3767.532	4336.750	4989.379	5737.078
24	2101.247	2443.795	2840.924	3300.974	3833.667	4449.969	5162.516	5985.711	6936.230	8032.906
25	2753.631	3226.808	3779.428	4424.301	5176.445	6052.957	7073.645	8261.273	9642.352	11247.062
30	10632.543	12940.672	15737.945	19124.434	23221.258	28172.016	34148.906	41357.227	50043.625	60500.207

Appendix D PRESENT VALUE OF AN ANNUITY OF $1 FOR *n* PERIODS

n	1%	2%	3%	4%	5%	6%	7%	8%	9%	10%
1	.990	.980	.971	.962	.952	.943	.935	.926	.917	.909
2	1.970	1.942	1.913	1.886	1.859	1.833	1.808	1.783	1.759	1.736
3	2.941	2.884	2.829	2.775	2.723	2.673	2.624	2.577	2.531	2.487
4	3.902	3.808	3.717	3.630	3.546	3.465	3.387	3.312	3.240	3.170
5	4.853	4.713	4.580	4.452	4.329	4.212	4.100	3.993	3.890	3.791
6	5.795	5.601	5.417	5.242	5.076	4.917	4.767	4.623	4.486	4.355
7	6.728	6.472	6.230	6.002	5.786	5.582	5.389	5.206	5.033	4.868
8	7.652	7.326	7.020	6.733	6.463	6.210	5.971	5.747	5.535	5.335
9	8.566	8.162	7.786	7.435	7.108	6.802	6.515	6.247	5.995	5.759
10	9.471	8.983	8.530	8.111	7.722	7.360	7.024	6.710	6.418	6.145
11	10.368	9.787	9.253	8.760	8.306	7.887	7.499	7.139	6.805	6.495
12	11.255	10.575	9.954	9.385	8.863	8.384	7.943	7.536	7.161	6.814
13	12.134	11.348	10.635	9.986	9.394	8.853	8.358	7.904	7.487	7.103
14	13.004	12.106	11.296	10.563	9.899	9.295	8.746	8.244	7.786	7.367
15	13.865	12.849	11.938	11.118	10.380	9.712	9.108	8.560	8.061	7.606
16	14.718	13.578	12.561	11.652	10.838	10.106	9.447	8.851	8.313	7.824
17	15.562	14.292	13.166	12.166	11.274	10.477	9.763	9.122	8.544	8.022
18	16.398	14.992	13.754	12.659	11.690	10.828	10.059	9.372	8.756	8.201
19	17.226	15.679	14.324	13.134	12.085	11.158	10.336	9.604	8.950	8.365
20	18.046	16.352	14.878	13.590	12.462	11.470	10.594	9.818	9.129	8.514
21	18.857	17.011	15.415	14.029	12.821	11.764	10.836	10.017	9.292	8.649
22	19.661	17.658	15.937	14.451	13.163	12.042	11.061	10.201	9.442	8.772
23	20.456	18.292	16.444	14.857	13.489	12.303	11.272	10.371	9.580	8.883
24	21.244	18.914	16.936	15.247	13.799	12.550	11.469	10.529	9.707	8.985
25	22.023	19.524	17.413	15.622	14.094	12.783	11.654	10.675	9.823	9.077
30	25.808	22.397	19.601	17.292	15.373	13.765	12.409	11.258	10.274	9.427
40	32.835	27.356	23.115	19.793	17.159	15.046	13.332	11.925	10.757	9.779
50	39.197	31.424	25.730	21.482	18.256	15.762	13.801	12.234	10.962	9.915

Appendix D PRESENT VALUE OF ANNUITY OF $1 FOR n PERIODS (cont.)

n	11%	12%	13%	14%	15%	16%	17%	18%	19%	20%
1	.901	.893	.885	.877	.870	.862	.855	.847	.840	.833
2	1.713	1.690	1.668	1.647	1.626	1.605	1.585	1.566	1.547	1.528
3	2.444	2.402	2.361	2.322	2.283	2.246	2.210	2.174	2.140	2.106
4	3.102	3.037	2.974	2.914	2.855	2.798	2.743	2.690	2.639	2.589
5	3.696	3.605	3.517	3.433	3.352	3.274	3.199	3.127	3.058	2.991
6	4.231	4.111	3.998	3.889	3.784	3.685	3.589	3.498	3.410	3.326
7	4.712	4.564	4.423	4.288	4.160	4.039	3.922	3.812	3.706	3.605
8	5.146	4.968	4.799	4.639	4.487	4.344	4.207	4.078	3.954	3.837
9	5.537	5.328	5.132	4.946	4.772	4.607	4.451	4.303	4.163	4.031
10	5.889	5.650	5.426	5.216	5.019	4.833	4.659	4.494	4.339	4.192
11	6.207	5.938	5.687	5.453	5.234	5.029	4.836	4.656	4.487	4.327
12	6.492	6.194	5.918	5.660	5.421	5.197	4.988	4.793	4.611	4.439
13	6.750	6.424	6.122	5.842	5.583	5.342	5.118	4.910	4.715	4.533
14	6.982	6.628	6.303	6.002	5.724	5.468	5.229	5.008	4.802	4.611
15	7.191	6.811	6.462	6.142	5.847	5.575	5.324	5.092	4.876	4.675
16	7.379	6.974	6.604	6.265	5.954	5.669	5.405	5.162	4.938	4.730
17	7.549	7.120	6.729	6.373	6.047	5.749	5.475	5.222	4.990	4.775
18	7.702	7.250	6.840	6.467	6.128	5.818	5.534	5.273	5.033	4.812
19	7.839	7.366	6.938	6.550	6.198	5.877	5.585	5.316	5.070	4.843
20	7.963	7.469	7.025	6.623	6.259	5.929	5.628	5.353	5.101	4.870
21	8.075	7.562	7.102	6.687	6.312	5.973	5.665	5.384	5.127	4.891
22	8.176	7.645	7.170	6.743	6.359	6.011	5.696	5.410	5.149	4.909
23	8.266	7.718	7.230	6.792	6.399	6.044	5.723	5.432	5.167	4.925
24	8.348	7.784	7.283	6.835	6.434	6.073	5.747	5.451	5.182	4.937
25	8.442	7.843	7.330	6.873	6.464	6.097	5.766	5.467	5.195	4.948
30	8.694	8.055	7.496	7.003	6.566	6.177	5.829	5.517	5.235	4.979
40	8.951	8.244	7.634	7.105	6.642	6.233	5.871	5.548	5.258	4.997
50	9.042	8.305	7.675	7.133	6.661	6.246	5.880	5.554	5.262	4.999

n	21%	22%	23%	24%	25%	26%	27%	28%	29%	30%
1	.826	.820	.813	.806	.800	.794	.787	.781	.775	.769
2	1.509	1.492	1.474	1.457	1.440	1.424	1.407	1.392	1.376	1.361
3	2.074	2.042	2.011	1.981	1.952	1.923	1.896	1.868	1.842	1.816
4	2.540	2.494	2.448	2.404	2.362	2.320	2.280	2.241	2.203	2.166
5	2.926	2.864	2.803	2.745	2.689	2.635	2.583	2.532	2.483	2.436
6	3.245	3.167	3.092	3.020	2.951	2.885	2.821	2.759	2.700	2.643
7	3.508	3.416	3.327	3.242	3.161	3.083	3.009	2.937	2.868	2.802
8	3.726	3.619	3.518	3.421	3.329	3.241	3.156	3.076	2.999	2.925
9	3.905	3.786	3.673	3.566	3.463	3.366	3.273	3.184	3.100	3.019
10	4.054	3.923	3.799	3.682	3.570	3.465	3.364	3.269	3.178	3.092
11	4.177	4.035	3.902	3.776	3.656	3.544	3.437	3.335	3.239	3.147
12	4.278	4.127	3.985	3.851	3.725	3.606	3.493	3.387	3.286	3.190
13	4.362	4.203	4.053	3.912	3.780	3.656	3.538	3.427	3.322	3.223
14	4.432	4.265	4.108	3.962	3.824	3.695	3.573	3.459	3.351	3.249
15	4.489	4.315	4.153	4.001	3.859	3.726	3.601	3.483	3.373	3.268
16	4.536	4.357	4.189	4.033	3.887	3.751	3.623	3.503	3.390	3.283
17	4.576	4.391	4.219	4.059	3.910	3.771	3.640	3.518	3.403	3.295
18	4.608	4.419	4.243	4.080	3.928	3.786	3.654	3.529	3.413	3.304
19	4.635	4.442	4.263	4.097	3.942	3.799	3.664	3.539	3.421	3.311
20	4.657	4.460	4.279	4.110	3.954	3.808	3.673	3.546	3.427	3.316
21	4.675	4.476	4.292	4.121	3.963	3.816	3.679	3.551	3.432	3.320
22	4.690	4.488	4.302	4.130	3.970	3.822	3.684	3.556	3.436	3.323
23	4.703	4.499	4.311	4.137	3.976	3.827	3.689	3.559	3.438	3.325
24	4.713	4.507	4.318	4.143	3.981	3.831	3.692	3.562	3.441	3.327
25	4.721	4.514	4.323	4.147	3.985	3.834	3.694	3.564	3.442	3.329
30	4.746	4.534	4.339	4.160	3.995	3.842	3.701	3.569	3.447	3.332
40	4.760	4.544	4.347	4.166	3.999	3.846	3.703	3.571	3.448	3.333
50	4.762	4.545	4.348	4.167	4.000	3.846	3.704	3.571	3.448	3.333

Appendix D PRESENT VALUE OF AN ANNUITY OF $1 FOR *n* PERIODS *(cont.)*

n	31%	32%	33%	34%	35%	36%	37%	38%	39%	40%
1	.763	.758	.752	.746	.741	.735	.730	.725	.719	.714
2	1.346	1.331	1.317	1.303	1.289	1.276	1.263	1.250	1.237	1.224
3	1.791	1.766	1.742	1.719	1.696	1.673	1.652	1.630	1.609	1.589
4	2.130	2.096	2.062	2.029	1.997	1.966	1.935	1.906	1.877	1.849
5	2.390	2.345	2.302	2.260	2.220	2.181	2.143	2.106	2.070	2.035
6	2.588	2.534	2.483	2.433	2.385	2.339	2.294	2.251	2.209	2.168
7	2.739	2.677	2.619	2.562	2.508	2.455	2.404	2.355	2.308	2.263
8	2.854	2.786	2.721	2.658	2.598	2.540	2.485	2.432	2.380	2.331
9	2.942	2.868	2.798	2.730	2.665	2.603	2.544	2.487	2.432	2.379
10	3.009	2.930	2.855	2.784	2.715	2.649	2.587	2.527	2.469	2.414
11	3.060	2.978	2.899	2.824	2.752	2.683	2.618	2.555	2.496	2.438
12	3.100	3.013	2.931	2.853	2.779	2.708	2.641	2.576	2.515	2.456
13	3.129	3.040	2.956	2.876	2.799	2.727	2.658	2.592	2.529	2.469
14	3.152	3.061	2.974	2.892	2.814	2.740	2.670	2.603	2.539	2.477
15	3.170	3.076	2.988	2.905	2.825	2.750	2.679	2.611	2.546	2.484
16	3.183	3.088	2.999	2.914	2.834	2.757	2.685	2.616	2.551	2.489
17	3.193	3.097	3.007	2.921	2.840	2.763	2.690	2.621	2.555	2.492
18	3.201	3.104	3.012	2.926	2.844	2.767	2.693	2.624	2.557	2.494
19	3.207	3.109	3.017	2.930	2.848	2.770	2.696	2.626	2.559	2.496
20	3.211	3.113	3.020	2.933	2.850	2.772	2.698	2.627	2.561	2.497
21	3.215	3.116	3.023	2.935	2.852	2.773	2.699	2.629	2.562	2.498
22	3.217	3.118	3.025	2.936	2.853	2.775	2.700	2.629	2.562	2.498
23	3.219	3.120	3.026	2.938	2.854	2.775	2.701	2.630	2.563	2.499
24	3.221	3.121	3.027	2.939	2.855	2.776	2.701	2.630	2.563	2.499
25	3.222	3.122	3.028	2.939	2.856	2.776	2.702	2.631	2.563	2.499
30	3.225	3.124	3.030	2.941	2.857	2.777	2.702	2.631	2.564	2.500
40	3.226	3.125	3.030	2.941	2.857	2.778	2.703	2.632	2.564	2.500
50	3.226	3.125	3.030	2.941	2.857	2.778	2.703	2.632	2.564	2.500

Glossary

accelerated depreciation techniques. Techniques that allow the owner of the asset to take greater amounts of depreciation during the early years of its life, thereby deferring some of the taxes until later years.

accounting rate of return (AROR). A capital budgeting criterion that relates the returns generated by the project, as measured by average accounting profits after tax, to the average dollar size of the investment required.

accrual method. A method of accounting whereby income is recorded when earned, whether or not the income has been received at that time, and expenses are recorded when incurred, whether or not any money has actually been paid out.

accumulated earnings credit. The greater of (1) the profits for the year retained for reasonable business needs, and (2) $150,000 less the retained earnings shown in the balance sheet.

accumulated taxable income. The firm's taxable income less dividends paid and accrued during the year, and less an *accumulated earnings credit.*

acid test ratio: (current assets − inventories)/ current liabilities. This ratio is a more stringent measure of liquidity than the current ratio in that it subtracts inventories (the least liquid current asset) from current assets.

acquisition. A combination of two or more businesses into a single operational entity.

affiliated group. A group of firms related by affiliation, expressed in terms of one firm's owning, either directly or indirectly, 80 percent of the firm paying the dividend.

annuity. A series of equal dollar payments for a specified number of years.

appraisal value. The value of a company as stated by an independent appraisal firm.

arrangement. A reorganizational plan involving a petition to the court requesting that the firm be required to make only partial or a delayed payment to its creditors.

arrearage. An overdue payment, generally referring to omitted preferred stock dividends.

average collection period. Accounts receivable/(annual credit sales/360). A ratio that expresses how rapidly the firm is collecting its credit accounts.

balance sheet. A basic accounting statement that represents the financial position of a firm on a given date.

bankers' acceptances. A draft (order to pay) drawn on a specific bank by a seller of goods in order to obtain payment for goods that have been shipped (sold) to a customer. The customer maintains an account with that specific bank.

bank wire. A private wire service used and supported by approximately 250 banks in the United States for transferring funds, exchanging credit information, or effecting securities transactions.

base-period earn-out. An agreement by which the stockholders of an acquired company receive additional stock in future years provided the firm improves its earnings above those of the base period. Base-period earnings are those in the last year prior to the acquisition.

beta. The relationship between an investment's returns and the market returns. This is a measure of the investment's nondiversifiable risk.

bond. A long-term (ten-year or more) promissory note issued by the borrower, promising to pay the owner of the security a predetermined and fixed amount of interest each year.

bond par value. The face value appearing on the bond, which is to be returned to the bondholder at maturity.

book value. The depreciated value of a company's assets (original cost less accumulated depreciation) less the outstanding liabilities.

book-value weights. The percentage of financing provided by different capital sources as measured by their book values from the company's balance sheet.

break-even analysis. An analytical technique used to determine the quantity of output or sales that results in a zero level of earnings before interest and taxes (EBIT). Relationships among the firm's cost structure, volume of output, and EBIT are studied.

business risk. The relative dispersion or variability in the firm's expected earnings before interest and taxes (EBIT). The nature of the firm's operations causes its business risk. This type of risk is affected by the firm's cost structure, product demand characteristics, and intraindustry competitive position. In capital-structure theory, business risk is distinguished from financial risk. See *financial risk*.

call premium. The difference between the call price and the security's par value.

call provision. A provision that entitles the corporation to repurchase its bonds or preferred stock from their holders at stated prices over specified periods.

capital asset. All property used in conducting a business other than assets held primarily for sale in the ordinary course of business or depreciable and real property used in conducting a business.

capital asset pricing model. An equation stating that the expected rate of return on a project is a function of (1) the risk-free rate, (2) the investment's systematic risk, and (3) the expected risk premium in the market.

capital budgeting. The decision-making process with respect to investment in fixed assets. Specifically it involves measuring the incremental cash flows associated with investment proposals and evaluating those proposed investments.

capital gain or loss. As defined by the revenue code, a gain or loss resulting from the sale or exchange of a capital asset.

capital market. All institutions and procedures that facilitate transactions in long-term financial instruments.

capital rationing. The placing of a limit by the firm on the dollar size of the capital budget.

capital structure. The mix of long-term sources of funds used by the firm. This is also called the firm's *capitalization*. The relative total (percentage) of each type of fund is emphasized.

cash budget. A detailed plan of future cash flows. This budget is composed of four elements: cash receipts, cash disbursements, net change in cash for the period, and new financing needed.

cash flow process. The process of cash generation and disposition in a typical business setting.

certainty equivalents. The amount of cash a person would require with certainty to make him indifferent between this certain sum and a particular risky or uncertain sum.

chattel mortgage agreement. A loan agreement in which the lender can increase his security interest by having specific items of inventory identified in the loan agreement. The borrower retains title to the inventory but cannot sell the items without the lender's consent.

coefficient of variation. A measure of the relative dispersion of a probability distribution—that is, the risk per unit of return. Mathematically it is defined as the standard deviation divided by the expected value.

collateral trust bonds. Bonds secured by common stock and/or bonds.

commercial paper. Short-term, unsecured promissory notes sold by large businesses in order to raise cash. Unlike most other money market instruments, commercial paper has no developed secondary market.

compensating balance. A balance of a given amount that the firm maintains in its demand deposit account. It may be required by either a formal or informal agreement with the firm's commercial bank. Such balances are usually required by the bank (1) on the unused portion of a loan commitment, (2) on the unpaid portion of an outstanding loan, or (3) in exchange for certain services provided by the bank, such as check-clearing or credit information. These balances raise the effective rate of interest paid on borrowed funds.

compounding. The process of determining the future value of a payment or series of payments when applying the concept of compound interest.

compound interest. The situation in which interest paid on the investment during the first period is added to the principal and, during the second period, interest is earned on the original principal plus the interest earned during the first period.

concentration bank. A bank where the firm maintains a major disbursing account.

conglomerate. A multifaceted corporation involved in a variety of products and services.

constant dividend payout ratio. A dividend payment policy in which the percentage of earnings paid out in dividends is held constant. The dollar amount fluctuates from year to year as profits vary.

conversion parity price. The price for which the investor in effect purchases the company's common stock when purchasing a convertible security. Mathematically it is the market price of the convertible security divided by the conversion ratio.

conversion ratio. The number of shares of common stock for which a convertible security can be exchanged.

convertibles. Preferred stock or debentures that can be exchanged for a specified number of shares of common stock at the will of the owner.

corporate bylaws. Regulations that govern the internal affairs of the corporation, designating such items as the time and place of the shareholders' meetings, voting rights, the election process for selecting members of the board of directors, the procedures for issuing and transferring stock certificates, and the policies relating the corporate records.

corporation. An entity that *legally* functions separate and apart from its owners.

cost budgets. Budgets prepared for every major expense category of the firm, such as production cost, selling cost, administrative cost, financing cost, and research and development cost.

cost of capital. The rate that must be earned in order to satisfy the required rate of return of the firm's investors. It may also be defined as the rate of return on investments at which the price of the firm's common stock will remain unchanged.

cost of debt. The rate that has to be received from

an investment in order to achieve the required rate of return for the creditors.

cost of preferred stock. The rate of return that must be earned on the preferred stockholders' investment to satisfy their required rate of return.

cost-volume-profit analysis. Another way of referring to ordinary break-even analysis.

coupon interest rate. The interest to be paid annually on a bond as a percent of par value, which is specified in the contractual agreement.

coverage ratios. A group of ratios that measure a firm's ability to meet its recurring fixed charge obligations, such as interest on long-term debt, lease payments, and/or preferred stock dividends.

cumulative feature. A requirement that all past unpaid preferred stock dividends be paid before any common stock dividends are declared.

current ratio: current assets/current liabilities. A ratio that indicates a firm's degree of liquidity by comparing its current assets to its current liabilities.

date of record. Date at which the stock transfer books are to be closed for determining the investor to receive the next dividend payment. See *ex dividend date.*

debenture. Any unsecured long-term debt.

debt capacity. The maximum proportion of debt that the firm can include in its capital structure and still maintain its lowest composite cost of capital.

debt ratio: total liabilities/total assets. A ratio that measures the extent to which a firm has been financed with debt.

decision tree. A schematic representation of a problem in which all possible outcomes are graphically displayed.

declaration date. The date upon which a dividend is formally declared by the board of directors.

default risk. The uncertainty of expected returns from a security attributable to possible changes in the financial capacity of the security issuer to make future payments to the security owner. Treasury securities are considered to be default-free. Default risk is also referred to as "financial risk" in the context of marketable securities management.

degree of combined leverage. The percentage change in earnings per share caused by a percentage change in sales. It is the product of the degree of operating leverage and the degree of financial leverage.

depository transfer checks. A means for moving funds from local bank accounts to concentration accounts. The depository transfer check itself is an unsigned, nonnegotiable instrument. It is payable only to the bank of deposit for credit to the firm's specific account.

disbursing float. Funds available in the company's bank account until its payment check has cleared through the banking system.

discount rate. The interest rate used in the discounting process.

discounting. The inverse of compounding. This process is used to determine the present value of a cash flow.

dividend payout ratio. The amount of dividends relative to the company's net income or earnings per share.

dividend yield. The dividend per share divided by the price of the security.

EBIT. Common financial notation for *earnings before interest and taxes.*

EBIT-EPS indifference point. The level of earnings before interest and taxes (EBIT) that will equate earnings per share (EPS) between two different financing plans.

EPS. Typical financial notation for *earnings per (common) share.*

earn-out. A deferred payment plan, under which an acquiring firm agrees to make a specified initial payment of cash or stock and additional compensation if the acquired company can maintain or increase earnings. See *base period earn-out.*

economic failure. Situation in which the company's costs exceed its revenues. Stated differently, the internal rates of return on investments are less than the firm's cost of capital.

equipment trust certificates. A cross between lease financing and debt financing used primarily by railroads to finance rolling stock.

ex-dividend date. The date upon which stock brokerage companies have uniformly decided to terminate the right of ownership to the dividend, which is four days prior to the record date.

ex-rights date. The date on or after which the stock sells without rights.

exercise price. The price at which a warrant allows its holder to purchase the firm's common stock.

exercise ratio. The number of shares of stock that can be obtained at the exercise price with one warrant.

expected return. The arithmetic mean or average of all possible outcomes where those outcomes are weighted by the probability that each will occur.

extension. An arrangement requiring that the debtor pay the amount owed in full, but providing an extension in time.

external common equity. A new issue of common stock.

factoring of accounts receivable. The outright sale of a firm's accounts to another party (the factor) without recourse. The factor, in turn, bears the risk of collection.

federal agency securities. Debt obligations of corporations and agencies created to carry out the lending programs of the U. S. government.

federal reserve system. The U. S. central banking system.

field warehouse financing agreement. A security agreement in which inventories are used as collateral, physically separated from the firm's other inventories, and placed under the control of a third-party field warehousing firm.

financial assets. Claims for future payment by one economic unit upon another.

financial intermediaries. Major financial institutions, such as commercial banks, savings and loan associations, credit unions, life insurance companies, and mutual funds, that assist the transfer of savings from economic units with excess savings to those with a shortage of savings.

financial lease. A noncancellable contractual commitment on the part of the firm leasing the asset (the lessee) to make a series of payments to the firm that actually owns the asset (the lessor) for the use of the asset.

financial leverage. The use of securities bearing a fixed (limited) rate of return to finance a portion of the firm's assets. Financial leverage can arise from the use of either debt or preferred stock financing. The use of financial leverage exposes the firm to *financial risk.*

financial markets. Institutions and procedures that facilitate transactions in all types of financial claims (securities).

financial risk. The added variability in earnings available to the firm's common shareholders, and the added chance of insolvency caused by the use of securities bearing a limited rate of return in the firm's financial structure. The use of financial leverage gives rise to financial risk.

financial structure. The mix of *all* funds sources that appear on the right-hand side of the balance sheet.

fixed asset turnover. Sales/fixed assets. A ratio indicating how effectively a firm is using its fixed assets to generate sales.

fixed costs.. Charges that do *not* vary in total amount as sales volume or the quantity of output changes over some relevant range of output.

flotation costs. The underwriter's spread and issuing costs associated with the issuance and marketing of new securities.

formal control. Control vested in the stockholders having the majority of the voting common shares.

functional control. Control executed by the corporate officers in conducting the daily operations.

general partnership. A partnership in which all partners are fully liable for the indebtedness incurred by the partnership.

gross profit margin. Gross profit/net sales. A ratio

denoting the gross profit of the firm as a percentage of net sales.

hurdle rate. The required rate of return used in capital budgeting.

income bond. A bond that requires interest payments only if earned. Failure to meet these interest payments will not result in bankruptcy.

income statement. A basic accounting statement that measures the results of a firm's operations over a specified period, commonly one year. Also known as the profit and loss statement. The bottom line of the income statement shows the firm's profit or loss for the period.

increasing-stream hypothesis of dividend policy. A smoothing of the dividend stream in order to minimize the effect of company reversals. Corporate managers make every effort to avoid a dividend cut, attempting instead to develop a gradually increasing dividend series over the long-term future.

incremental cash flows. The cash flows that result from the acceptance of a capital budgeting project.

indenture. The legal agreement between the firm issuing the bonds and the bond trustee who represents the bondholders, providing the specific terms of the loan agreement.

insolvency. The inability to meet interest payments or to repay debt at maturity.

interest-rate risk. The uncertainty that envelopes the expected returns from a security caused by changes in interest rates. Price changes induced by interest-rate changes are greater for long-term than for short-term financial instruments.

internal common equity. Profits retained within the business for investment purposes.

internal rate of return (IRR). A capital budgeting technique that reflects the rate of return a project earns. Mathematically it is the discount rate that equates the present value of the inflows with the present value of the outflows.

inventory turnover ratio. Cost of goods sold/ inventory. A ratio that measures the number of times a firm's inventories are sold and replaced during the year. This ratio reflects the relative liquidity of inventories.

investment banker. A financial specialist who underwrites and distributes new securities and advises corporate clients about raising new funds.

least-squares regression. A procedure for "fitting" a line through a scatter of observed data points in a way that minimizes the sum of the squared deviations of the points from the fitted line.

leveraged leasing. A leasing arrangement in which the lessor will generally supply equity funds of 20 to 30 percent of the purchase price and borrow the remainder from a third-party lender.

limited partnership. A partnership in which one or more of the partners has limited liability, restricted to the amount of capital he invests in the partnership.

line of credit. Generally an informal agreement or understanding between the borrower and the bank as to the maximum amount of credit the bank will provide the borrower at any one time. Under this type of agreement there is no "legal" commitment on the part of the bank to provide the stated credit. See *revolving credit agreement.*

liquidation by assignment. A proceeding in which the debtor transfers title of the firm's assets to a third party, who has been appointed either by the creditors or by the court. This individual, known as an assignee or trustee, administers the liquidation process and sees that an appropriate distribution is made of the proceeds.

liquidity. A firm's ability to pay its bills on time. Liquidity is related to the ease and quickness with which a firm can convert its noncash assets into cash, as well as the size of the firm's investment in noncash assets vis-à-vis its short-term liabilities.

long-term residual dividend policy. A dividend plan by which the residual capital is distributed smoothly to the investors over the planning period.

mail float. Funds tied up during the time that

elapses from the moment a customer mails his remittance check until the firm begins to process it.

market equilibrium. The situation in which expected returns equal required returns.

market-value weights. The percentage of financing provided by different capital sources, measured by the current market prices of the firm's bonds and preferred and common stock.

marketable securities. Security investments that the firm can quickly convert into cash balances.

maturity date. The date upon which a borrower is to repay a loan.

merger. A combination of two or more businesses into a single operational entity.

money market. All institutions and procedures that facilitate transactions in short-term instruments issued by borrowers with very high credit ratings.

money market mutual funds. Investment companies that purchase a diversified array of short-term, high-grade (money market) debt instruments.

mortgage bonds. Bonds secured by a lien on real property.

mutually exclusive projects. A set of projects that perform essentially the same task, so that acceptance of one will necessarily mean rejection of the others.

negotiable certificates of deposit. Marketable receipts for funds deposited in a bank for a fixed period. The deposited funds earn a fixed rate of interest. More commonly, these are called CD's.

net income. A figure representing the firm's profit or loss for the period. It also represents the earnings available to the firm's common *and* preferred stockholders.

net operating loss carryback and carryforward. A tax provision that permits the taxpayer first to apply the loss against the profits in the three prior years (carryback). If the loss has not been completely absorbed by the profits in these three years, it may be applied to taxable profits in each of the seven following years (carryforward).

net present value (NPV). A capital budgeting concept defined as the present value of the project's annual net cash flows after tax less the project's initial outlay.

net profit margin: net income/sales. A ratio that measures the net income of the firm as a percent of sales.

net working capital. The difference between the firm's current assets and its current liabilities.

normal probability distribution. A special class of bell-shaped distributions with symmetrically decreasing density, where the curve approaches but never reaches the X axis.

operating lease. A contractual commitment on the part of the firm leasing the asset (the lessee) to make a series of payments to the firm that actually owns the asset (the lessor) for use of the asset. An operating lease differs from a financial lease in that it can be canceled at any time after proper notice has been given to the lessor.

operating leverage. The responsiveness·to sales changes of the firm's earnings before interest and taxes. This responsiveness arises from the firm's use of fixed operating costs.

operating profit margin. Net operating income/sales. A firm's earnings before interest and taxes. This ratio serves as an overall measure of operating effectiveness.

opportunity set. The return-risk relationship available for an investor interested in the purchase or sale of securities.

optimal capital structure. The capital structure that minimizes the firm's composite cost of capital (maximizes the common stock price) for raising a given amount of funds.

organized security exchanges. Formal organizations involved in the trading of securities. Such exchanges are tangible entities that conduct auction markets in listed securities.

over-the-counter markets. All security markets *except* the organized exchanges. The money market is an over-the-counter market. Most corporate bonds also are traded in this market.

par value. On the face of a bond, the stated

amount that the firm is to repay upon the maturity date.

partnership. An association of two or more individuals joining together as co-owners to operate a business for profit.

payable-through draft. A legal instrument that has the physical appearance of an ordinary check but is not drawn on a bank. A payable-through draft is drawn on and paid by the issuing firm. The bank serves as a collection point and passes the draft on to the firm.

payback period. A capital budgeting criterion defined as the number of years required to recover the initial cash investment.

payment date. The date on which the company mails a dividend check to each investor.

percent of sales method. A method of financial forecasting that involves estimating the level of an expense, asset, or liability for a future period as a percent of the sales forecast.

perfect markets. Hypothetical markets under the assumptions that (1) information is readily available to all investors at no cost, (2) there are no transaction costs, (3) investment opportunities are readily accessible to all prospective investors, and (4) financial distress and bankruptcy costs are nonexistent.

permanent investment. An investment that the firm expects to hold longer than one year. The firm makes permanent investments in fixed and current assets. Contrast with *temporary investments*.

perpetuity. An annuity with an infinite life.

physical budgets. Budgets for unit sales, personnel or manpower, unit production, inventories, and physical facilities. These budgets are used as the basis for generating cost and profit budgets.

pledging accounts receivable. A loan the firm obtains from a commercial bank or a finance company using its accounts receivable as collateral.

portfolio diversification effect. The fact that variations of the returns from a portfolio or combination of assets may be less than the sum of the variation of the individual assets making up the portfolio.

preauthorized checks (PAC's). A check that re-

sembles the ordinary check but does not contain or require the signature of the person on whose account it is being drawn. A PAC is created only with the individual's legal authorization. The PAC system is advantageous when the firm regularly receives a large volume of payments of a fixed amount from the same customer over a long period.

preemptive right. The right entitling the common shareholder to maintain his proportionate share of ownership in the firm.

present value. The value in today's dollars of a future payment discounted back to present at the required rate of return.

price/earnings ratio (P/E). The ratio of the firm's common stock price to its earnings per share.

price pegging. Buying orders placed by an underwriting syndicate manager for the security being marketed by his selling group. The objective is to stabilize the market price of the new issue.

pro forma income statement. A statement of planned profit or loss for a future period.

processing float. Funds tied up during the time required for the firm to process remittance checks before they can be deposited in the bank.

profit budget. A budget of forecasted profits based on information gleaned from the cost and sales budgets.

profitability index (PI). A capital budgeting criterion defined as the ratio of the present value of the future net cash flows to the initial outlay.

prospectus. A condensed version of the full registration statement filed with the Securities and Exchange Commission that describes a new security issue.

proxy. A means of voting in which a designated party is provided with the temporary power of attorney to vote for the signee at the corporation's annual meeting.

refunding. The process of replacing an old debt issue with the sale of new debt.

registration statement. A lengthy document filed with the Securities and Exchange Commission containing pertinent facts about a firm planning to sell new securities.

remote disbursing. A cash management service specifically designed to extend disbursing float.

reorganization. A procedure, administered by the courts, that attempts to revitalize a firm by changing its operating procedures and capital structure.

repurchase agreements. Legal contracts that involve the sale of short-term securities by a borrower to a lender of funds. The borrower commits to repurchase the securities at a later date at the contract price plus a stated interest charge.

required rate of return. The minimum rate of return necessary to attract an investor to purchase or hold a security. It is also the discount rate that equates the present value of the cash flows with the value of the security.

residual dividend theory. A theory asserting that the dividends to be paid should equal the equity capital *left over* after the financing of profitable investments.

restrictive covenants. Provisions in the loan agreement that place restrictions on the borrower and make the loan immediately payable and due when violated. These restrictive covenants are designed to maintain the borrower's financial condition on a par with that which existed at the time the loan was made.

return on assets. Net income/total assets. This ratio determines the yield on the firm's assets by relating net income to total assets.

return on common equity. Net income available to common/tangible common equity. A ratio relating earned income to the common stockholder's investment.

return-risk line. A specification of the appropriate required rates of return for investments having different amounts of risk.

revolving credit agreement. An understanding between the borrower and the bank as to the amount of credit the bank will be legally obligated to provide the borrower. See *line of credit.*

right. A certificate issued to common stockholders giving them an option to purchase a stated number of new shares at a specified price during a two- to ten-week period.

risk. The possible variation associated with the expected return measured by the standard deviation or coefficient of variation.

risk-adjusted discount rate. A method for incorporating the project's level of risk into the capital budgeting process, in which the discount rate is adjusted upward to compensate for higher-than-normal risk or downward to compensate for lower-than-normal risk.

risk premium. The additional return expected for assuming risk.

riskless rate of return. The rate of return on risk-free investments, such as the interest rate on short-term U. S. government securities.

rule of absolute priority. Rule that the company must completely honor senior claims on assets before settling junior claims.

sale and leaseback arrangement. An arrangement arising when a firm sells land, buildings, or equipment that it already owns and simultaneously enters into an agreement to lease the property back for a specified period, under specific terms.

salvage value. The value of an asset or investment project at the end of its usable life.

scatter diagram method. A method of financial forecasting that involves visually "fitting" a line through a scatter of points so that the distance of points about the line is minimized.

secondary market. Transactions in currently outstanding securities. This is distinguished from the new issues or primary market.

secured credit. Sources of credit that require security in the form of pledged assets. In the event the borrower defaults in payment of principal or interest the lender can seize the pledged assets and sell them to settle the debt.

securities and exchange commission (SEC). The federal agency created by the Securities

Exchange Act of 1934 to enforce federal securities laws.

security market line. The return line that reflects the attitudes of investors regarding the minimal acceptable return for a given level of systematic risk.

selling group. A collection of securities dealers that participate in the distribution of new issues to final investors. A selling group agreement links these dealers to the underwriting syndicate.

semi-variable costs. Charges that behave as variable costs over certain ranges of output and as fixed costs over other ranges of output.

simulation. The process of imitating the performance of an investment project through repeated evaluations, usually using a computer. In the general case, experimentation upon a mathematical model that has been designed to capture the critical realities of the decision-making situation.

sinking fund. A required annual payment that allows for the periodic retirement of debt.

skewed distribution. A distribution that has a longer "tail" to the right or left.

sole proprietorship. A business owned by a single individual.

spontaneous financing. The trade credit and other accounts payable that arise "spontaneously" in the firm's day-to-day operations.

stable dollar dividend per share. A dividend policy that maintains a relatively stable dollar dividend per share over time.

standard deviation. A statistical measure of the spread of a probability distribution calculated by squaring the difference between each outcome and its expected value, weighting each value by its probability, summing over all possible outcomes, and taking the square root of this sum.

statement of changes in financial position. A basic accounting statement, also known as a sources and uses of funds statement, identifying how the firm acquired its funds for the period and what it did with those funds.

stock dividend. A distribution of shares of up to 25 percent of the number of shares currently outstanding, issued on a pro rata basis to the current stockholders.

stock split. A stock dividend exceeding 25 percent of the number of shares currently outstanding.

stretching on trade credit. Failing to pay within the prescribed credit period. For example, under credit terms of 2/10, net 30, a firm would be stretching its trade credit if it failed to pay by the 30th day and paid on the 60th day.

subscription price. The price for which the security may be purchased in a rights offering.

systematic risk (nondiversifiable risk or market related risk). The portion of variations in investment returns that cannot be eliminated through investor diversification. These variations result from factors that affect all stocks.

target debt ratio. A desired proportion of long-term debt in the firm's capital structure. Alternatively, it may be the desired proportion of total debt in the firm's financial structure.

technical insolvency. Situation in which the firm can no longer honor its financial obligations. Although its assets may exceed its total liabilities, thereby indicating a positive net worth, the company simply does not have sufficient liquidity to pay its debts.

temporary financing. Financing (other than spontaneous sources) that will be repaid within a period of one year or less. Included among these sources of short-term debt are secured and unsecured bank loans, commercial paper, loans secured by accounts receivable, and loans secured by inventories.

temporary investments. These investments are comprised of the firm's investment in current assets that will be liquidated and not replaced within a period of one year or less. Examples include seasonal expansions in inventories and accounts receivable.

tender offer. A bid by an interested party, usually a corporation, for controlling interest in another corporation.

term loans. Loans that have maturities of one to ten years and are repaid in periodic installments over the life of the loan. Term loans are usually secured by a chattel mortgage on equipment or a mortgage on real property.

term structure of interest rates. The relationship between interest rates and the term to maturity, where the risk of default is held constant.

terminal warehouse agreement. A security agreement in which the inventories pledged as collateral are transported to a public warehouse that is physically removed from the borrower's premises. This is the safest (and a costly) form of financing secured by inventory.

times interest earned ratio. Earnings before interest and taxes (EBIT)/interest expense. A ratio that measures the firm's ability to meet its interest payments from its annual operating earnings.

total tangible asset turnover. Sales/total tangible assets. An overall measure of the relation between the firm's tangible assets and the sales they generate.

trade credit. Credit made available by a firm's suppliers in conjunction with the acquisition of materials. Trade credit appears on the balance sheet as accounts payable.

transaction loan. A loan where the proceeds are designated for a specific purpose—for example, a bank loan used to finance the acquisition of a piece of equipment.

transit float. Funds tied up during the time necessary for a deposited check to clear through the commercial banking system and become usable funds to the company.

treasury bills. Direct debt obligations of the U. S. government sold on a regular basis by the U. S. Treasury.

trend analysis. An analysis of a firm's financial ratios over time.

uncommitted earnings per share. Earnings per share *minus* sinking-fund payments per share.

underwriting. The purchase and subsequent resale of a new security issue. The risk of selling the new issue at a satisfactory (profitable) price is assumed by the investment banker.

underwriting syndicate. A temporary association of investment bankers formed to purchase a new security issue and quickly resell it at a profit. Formation of the syndicate spreads the risk of loss among several investment bankers, thereby minimizing the risk exposure of any single underwriter.

undiversifiable risk. The portion of the variation in investment returns that cannot be eliminated through investor diversification.

unlisted securities. Securities that are not traded on an organized security exchange.

unsecured credit. All sources of credit that have as their security only the lender's faith in the borrower's ability to repay the funds when due.

unsystematic risk (diversifiable risk or unique risk) The portion of the variation in investment returns that can be eliminated through investor diversification. These variations result from factors that are unique to the particular firm.

value of a bond. The present value of the interest payments, I_t, in period t, plus the present value of the redemption or par value of the indebtedness, M, at the maturity date.

value of a security. The present value of all future cash inflows expected to be received by the investor owning the security.

variable costs. Charges that vary in total as output changes. Variable costs are fixed per unit of output.

voluntary remedy. A voluntary reorganization that is acceptable to the creditors.

warrant. An option to purchase a fixed number of shares of common stock at a predetermined price during a specified time period.

weighted cost of capital. A composite of the individual costs of financing incurred by each capital source. A firm's weighted cost of capital is a function of (1) the individual costs of capital, (2) the capital structure mix, and (3) the level of financing necessary to make the investment.

weighted marginal cost of capital. The composite cost for each additional dollar of financing. The marginal cost of capital represents the appropriate criterion for making investment decisions.

working capital. A concept traditionally defined as a firm's investment in current assets. Net working capital refers to the difference between current assets and current liabilities.

Index

C

D

M

N